Integrated Cisco and UNIX Network Architectures

Gernot Schmied

Cisco Press

800 East 96th Street
Indianapolis, Indiana 46240 USA

Integrated Cisco and UNIX Network Architectures

Gernot Schmied

Copyright© 2005 Cisco Systems, Inc.

Published by:
Cisco Press
800 East 96th Street
Indianapolis, IN 46240 USA

Printed in the United States of America 1 2 3 4 5 6 7 8 9 0

First Printing: September 2004

Library of Congress Cataloging-in-Publication Number: 2002109951

ISBN: 1-58705-121-4

Warning and Disclaimer

This book is designed to provide information about heterogeneous Cisco and UNIX network architectures. Every effort has been made to make this book as complete and as accurate as possible, but no warranty or fitness is implied.

The information is provided on an "as is" basis. The authors, Cisco Press, and Cisco Systems, Inc. shall have neither liability nor responsibility to any person or entity with respect to any loss or damages arising from the information contained in this book or from the use of the discs or programs that may accompany it.

The opinions expressed in this book belong to the author and are not necessarily those of Cisco Systems, Inc.

Trademark Acknowledgments

All terms mentioned in this book that are known to be trademarks or service marks have been appropriately capitalized. Cisco Press or Cisco Systems, Inc. cannot attest to the accuracy of this information. Use of a term in this book should not be regarded as affecting the validity of any trademark or service mark.

BSD Daemon Copyright 1988 by Marshall Kirk McKusick. All rights reserved. ForeRunner is a registered trademark of FORE Systems. All rights reserved. UNIX is a registered trademark of the Open Group. OpenVMS is a trademark of the Hewlett-Packard company. GateD is a registered trademark of NextHop. Linux Penguin logo Copyright Larry Ewing, lewing@isc.tamu.edu, created using GIMP. All rights reserved. NetBSD Copyright 1994–2004 by The NetBSD Foundation, Inc. All rights reserved. OpenBSD logo copyright by OpenBSD and Theo de Raadt, www@openbsd.org. VisualRoute® is a trademark of Visualware, Inc. WANPIPE router is a registered trademark of Sangoma Technologies. ZebOS and IP Infusion are registered trademarks of IP Infusion Inc.

Feedback Information

At Cisco Press, our goal is to create in-depth technical books of the highest quality and value. Each book is crafted with care and precision, undergoing rigorous development that involves the unique expertise of members from the professional technical community.

Readers' feedback is a natural continuation of this process. If you have any comments regarding how we could improve the quality of this book, or otherwise alter it to better suit your needs, you can contact us through e-mail at feedback@ciscopress.com. Please make sure to include the book title and ISBN in your message.

We greatly appreciate your assistance.

Corporate and Government Sales

Cisco Press offers excellent discounts on this book when ordered in quantity for bulk purchases or special sales.

For more information, please contact: **U.S. Corporate and Government Sales**   1-800-382-3419, corpsales@pearsontechgroup.com.

For sales outside the U.S. please contact: **International Sales**   international@pearsoned.com

Publisher	John Wait
Editor-in-Chief	John Kane
Cisco Representative	Anthony Wolfenden
Cisco Press Program Manager	Nannette M. Noble
Executive Editor	Brett Bartow
Acquisitions Editor	Michelle Grandin
Production Manager	Patrick Kanouse
Development Editor	Jill Batistick
Project Editor	Karen A. Gill
Copy Editor	Keith Cline
Technical Editors	Ernest Altbart, Wolfgang Fabics, Paul Jakma
Editorial Assistant	Tammi Barnett
Cover Designer	Louisa Adair
Composition	Interactive Composition Corporation
Indexer	Larry Sweazy

CISCO SYSTEMS

Corporate Headquarters
Cisco Systems, Inc.
170 West Tasman Drive
San Jose, CA 95134-1706
USA
www.cisco.com
Tel: 408 526-4000
      800 553-NETS (6387)
Fax: 408 526-4100

European Headquarters
Cisco Systems International BV
Haarlerbergpark
Haarlerbergweg 13-19
1101 CH Amsterdam
The Netherlands
www-europe.cisco.com
Tel: 31 0 20 357 1000
Fax: 31 0 20 357 1100

Americas Headquarters
Cisco Systems, Inc.
170 West Tasman Drive
San Jose, CA 95134-1706
USA
www.cisco.com
Tel: 408 526-7660
Fax: 408 527-0883

Asia Pacific Headquarters
Cisco Systems, Inc.
Capital Tower
168 Robinson Road
#22-01 to #29-01
Singapore 068912
www.cisco.com
Tel: +65 6317 7777
Fax: +65 6317 7799

Cisco Systems has more than 200 offices in the following countries and regions. Addresses, phone numbers, and fax numbers are listed on the
Cisco.com Web site at www.cisco.com/go/offices.

Argentina • Australia • Austria • Belgium • Brazil • Bulgaria • Canada • Chile • China PRC • Colombia • Costa Rica • Croatia • Czech Republic
Denmark • Dubai, UAE • Finland • France • Germany • Greece • Hong Kong SAR • Hungary • India • Indonesia • Ireland • Israel • Italy
Japan • Korea • Luxembourg • Malaysia • Mexico • The Netherlands • New Zealand • Norway • Peru • Philippines • Poland • Portugal
Puerto Rico • Romania • Russia • Saudi Arabia • Scotland • Singapore • Slovakia • Slovenia • South Africa • Spain • Sweden
Switzerland • Taiwan • Thailand • Turkey • Ukraine • United Kingdom • United States • Venezuela • Vietnam • Zimbabwe

About the Author

Gernot Schmied is an independent consultant, analyst, and researcher located in Vienna, Austria, focusing on systems integration, networking, UNIX, and security. He has worked several years in enterprise and Internet service provider (ISP) environments with a focus on senior engineering and architecture projects, service, and portfolio development. Gernot is interested in the evolution of (G)MPLS, IP over Optical and photonic networking, electrical engineering, and physics in general. In addition to engineering and research, he enjoys martial arts, tennis, outdoor activities, cooking, and eating well. Gernot holds two master degrees in applied physics and information systems and is currently working on his Ph.D. thesis in his "spare" time. Gernot can be contacted at gernot.schmied@iktech.net.

About the Technical Reviewers

Ernest Altbart is currently the head of engineering of Nextra Telekom GmbH, Vienna, Austria. Nextra runs a Cisco-powered, fully MPLS-enabled network, of which Ernest played an integral part in the design. Presently, Ernest specializes in the MPLS-based service area and in solutions such as virtual private networks (VPNs), managed security services, and VPN-integrated mobile access. Ernest has seven years of experience in designing and managing large customer and ISP data networks. Prior to Nextra, Ernest worked at ViaNet, another Austrian-based ISP. In his spare time, Ernest enjoys playing soccer with his son and practicing his jazz piano skills, which he acquired and cultivated during a six-year study at the University of Vienna.

Wolfgang Fabics is a senior networks and telecommunications consultant specializing in carrier and ISP solutions. Having worked with some of the largest Austrian carriers and European service providers in responsible positions from engineering and development to product and key account management, he is not only an expert in network architecture and design, but he also has comprehensive know-how regarding deployment, management, and operations of large-scale heterogeneous networks and services. He holds a degree in communications engineering and electronics from the Technical College (TGM) in Vienna.

Paul Jakma is currently a software engineer with a major UNIX vendor, working on IP protocols. He also maintains the Quagga software routing suite, a fork of GNU Zebra. Paul previously spent several years as a systems administrator with an Irish transactions company, where he designed and implemented its European-wide corporate network infrastructure based mostly around free software, which led to his involvement with GNU Zebra. Paul was sidetracked by a strange and wonderful thing called UNIX, which he discovered while studying electrical and electronic engineering at the University of Strathclyde in Glasgow, Scotland. Outside of computing, he enjoys riding sports motorbikes at track days.

Dedications

I dedicate this work to the loving memory of Dr. Alfred Sagmeister, a dear friend who passed away a few years ago and who taught me a lot about the essence of life—humor and passion.

Acknowledgments

Writing a book represents a challenge impossible to tackle without suggestions, feedback, and inspiration from other sources and people. It also requires the encouragement of those close to you, especially through times of frustration and lack of inspiration. I am particularly grateful for the support of the open-source community and especially the folks of the Zebra/Quagga Project for numerous insights and discussions. Special thanks to Dr. Bill Fenner from Bell Labs for some suggestions on mrouted, Pavlin Radoslavov of ICSI for great insights into PIM and XORP operation, and Gerhard Wieser of Cisco Systems Austria for providing input with regard to the Cisco forwarding architecture. Thanks as well to David Mandelstam and James Scott from Sangoma Technologies and Reinhold Burkhard from Cisco Systems Austria for providing demo equipment. I am especially grateful for the input received from the technical reviewers: Ernest Altbart, Wolfgang Fabics, and Paul Jakma. Finally, thanks to the editorial team of Cisco Press, especially Michelle Grandin, Jill Batistick, Karen Gill, Keith Cline, and Christopher Cleveland, for their willingness to boldly explore new terrain off of traditional Cisco Press roads of engagement.

Contents at a Glance

Table of Contents

Icons Used in This Book

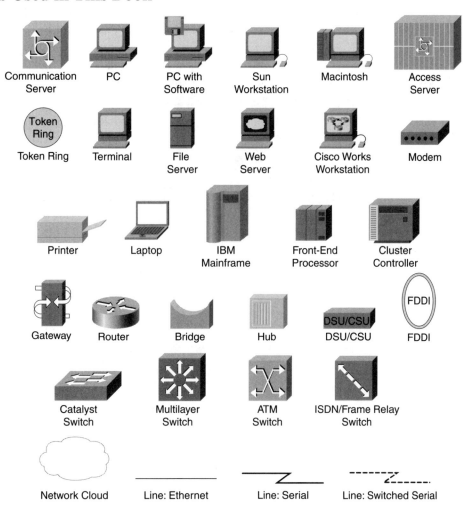

Command Syntax Conventions

The conventions used to present command syntax in this book are the same conventions used in the IOS Command Reference. The Command Reference describes these conventions as follows:

- **Boldface** indicates commands and keywords that are entered literally as shown. In actual configuration examples and output (not general command syntax), boldface indicates commands that are manually input by the user (such as a **show** command).

- *Italics* indicate arguments for which you supply actual values.

- Vertical bars (|) separate alternative, mutually exclusive elements. However, note that on UNIX systems, this represents a pipe as well.

- Square brackets [ ] indicate optional elements.

- Braces { } indicate a required choice.

- Braces within brackets [{ }] indicate a required choice within an optional element.

Introduction

"In the beginning, the routing table was void and without form . . . ."

—Gernot Schmied

The original driving force behind this book was my project experience in the ISP environment. Although technically I am a senior network/telecom engineer, I worked on several projects that involved networking, security, and UNIX systems engineering integration issues and designed integrated gateway solutions for customer premises equipment (CPE) and centralized data-center deployment. This often required cross-department project teams populated with network, systems, and application engineers.

I started to realize several things. First, I noticed a communication problem between network and system engineers resulting from a limited understanding of the other party's working environment and daily business requirements. Second, it became apparent that traditional boundaries of UNIX systems and hardware routers started to change and overlap at certain layers, such as when it came to load balancing, quality of service (QoS), security, and redundancy concepts. Therefore, I started to craft the outline of this book to show the industry the feasibility and potential of integrated Cisco and UNIX routing architectures and synergies beyond routing, based on the maturity and reliability of UNIX TCP/IP stacks.

Of course, what we see now in the industry is a rapid evolution of UNIX-based integrated access devices (IADs)—ranging from small office/home office (SOHO) systems up to carrier-class systems such as Cosine or ImageStream—satisfying needs for intrusion detection, firewalling, cable and DSL access, terminal servers and access concentrators, VPNs, and roaming user support. This is a book about heterogeneous Cisco and UNIX gateways and devices for the benefit of deploying enhanced LAN and WAN services.

Motivation and Rationale

I have thoroughly researched existing books that take a similar approach. Surprisingly, all the related books seem geared toward the beginner and SOHO user/client, not toward the enterprise/ISP arena that requires state-of-the art dynamic routing solutions. These other books appear to have been written by UNIX engineers with a rather weak networking focus. Furthermore, all of them consider only Linux platforms and elaborate particularly on dial-on-demand PPP routing (an aspect of diminishing relevance).

UNIX gateways bring into play different and promising features, with massive performance possibilities at a fraction of the price of dedicated proprietary appliances, and they perform their tasks entirely in software. That said, this book assumes that the reader has taken the Cisco road, so the focus throughout this book is on integration issues, building on the complete Cisco Press treatment of Cisco features and technology in combination with supplementary UNIX literature. The key to successfully building dedicated UNIX gateways is to strip down the kernel and remove unnecessary features and services.

The most important part of this book is the development of heterogeneous lab scenarios and topologies featuring BSD, Linux, Cisco IOS architecture, and several free routing engines such as the public version of GateD, XORP, or Zebra/Quagga.

NOTE	GateD is a registered trademark of NextHop. NextHop Technologies has acquired all the rights to GateD from Merit and the University of Michigan. The GateD Consortium has been dissolved. The last GateD Consortium release was version 3.6 in 1999. In this book, I am referring only to the last publicly available research/educational version GateD 3.6 public when referencing *GateD* (the package) or *gated* (the routing daemon).

Starting with a single workstation or interface, the lab exercises grow in complexity and features. As we advance, platform issues, tips, tricks, caveats, and Cisco IOS integration issues are discussed, analyzed with sniffers, and tested with handcrafted traffic from packet generators and applications. Stress and load testing is essential to successful and representative lab scenarios.

Some lab exercises are designed to explain notoriously difficult or error-prone real-life setups. Necessary technical know-how is presented to the level of detail necessary to get the most out of the lab experiments, without cluttering the flow with fundamentals already covered in other Cisco Press and general TCP/IP books. Finally, the book offers guidance for features better built with Cisco equipment entirely.

The word *integrated* is in the title of this book because of the hooks to the Cisco routing world of products. It is essential to understand coexistence, integration, and migration issues with regard to Cisco routers dominating Internet access and enterprise routing.

Throughout this book, only standard-based nonproprietary protocols are discussed, with one notable exception: the proprietary Cisco Discovery Protocol (CDP). This makes this knowledge useful on virtually every UNIX platform interacting with virtually every standard-compliant vendor routing solution.

The computing industry is in the process of equipping more and more gateways with crypto accelerator cards, ATM adapters, and E1 communication cards with the idea to create integrated access devices (IADs) that combine the features of access routers, firewalls, intrusion detection systems, and more. This development has to a great extent been driven by the availability and maturity of dynamic routing protocols such as Open Shortest Path First (OSPF) and Border Gateway Protocol (BGP). Actually, the forwarding performance of Pentium-class/PCI gateways has never been an issue. Just for historical reasons, people were using only static routing and, eventually, Routing Information Protocol (RIP) on these gateways. For example, the larger Cisco PIX Firewall appliances were equipped with off-the-shelf Peripheral Component Interconnect (PCI) boards with Pentium II processors and standard Ethernet network interface cards (NICs). The only accelerator technology currently used to supplement these designs is hardware crypto accelerator cards for three-stage Data Encryption Standard (3DES) and Advanced Encryption Standard (AES) encryption for IP Security (IPSec) implementations. Multiprocessor systems can live up to these performance requirements easily, and clustering technologies can supplement software-based hot-standby failover mechanisms.

The goal of this book is to bring closer together traditionally separated networking and systems departments. Because of the readiness, availability, and maturity of the operating systems and routing engines, there will definitely be more deployments of UNIX-based routing gateways in the near future, and eventually pure UNIX-powered network realms happily cooperating with Cisco gear.

Audience and Objectives

My target audience consists of UNIX system administrators, network engineers, and network/systems architects who traditionally tackle network assignments with routing appliances such as Cisco enterprise products. After reading this book, the engineers and architects involved can clearly judge the feasibility of pure UNIX or integrated Cisco/UNIX routing with regard to their topology and feature requirements. Open-source software has its strengths and weaknesses, as do integrated appliances. Although this book is certainly beneficial for the SOHO arena, too, I tried to develop scenarios that emphasize enterprise networking requirements; too many authors already focus on (integrated) low-performance SOHO appliances. The scenarios in this book are also applicable to smaller ISPs, communication services providers (CSPs), application service providers (ASPs), and server housing/hosting/data centers.

This book offers UNIX sysadmins the opportunity to enter the world of networking and vice versa. In today's highly competitive IT environments, only engineers who have combined security, sysadmin, and networking skills will prevail. This approach has served me well in both enterprise and ISP environments.

I consider the timing right because of the maturity and stability of the proposed UNIX operating systems and routing software. Both BSD and Linux have proven their value in enterprise and ISP environments and have reached a status of widespread acceptance among system administrators and management decision makers.

From this book, you will learn about the architectural implications of mixed Cisco and UNIX technologies and approaches that will enable you to positively change LAN infrastructures and to satisfy modern data-center needs, such as high availability, fast failover, and clustering.

Chapter Organization

This book consists of three major parts (building blocks). The first two establish the foundation of UNIX systems networking and routing, and the third discusses advanced gateway topics and architectural issues.

- Chapter 1, "Operating System Issues and Features—The Big Picture," introduces the open-source operating systems used heavily throughout this book as well as their position in contrast to Cisco IOS architecture.

- Chapter 2, "User-Space Routing Software," introduces the routing packages discussed in combination with Cisco gear. Installation and setup are covered in great detail.

- Chapter 3, "Kernel Requirements for a Full-Featured Lab," discusses essential features available to all three operating systems. Appendix A contains kernel configuration templates for all of them.

- Chapter 4, "Gateway WAN/Metro Interfaces," discusses WAN interfaces and point-to-point issues that are relevant to the focus of this book.

- Chapter 5, "Ethernet and VLANs," emphasizes the rationale and requirements of the Ethernet and VLAN lab layouts and discusses how to get the most out of them.

- Chapter 6, "The Analyzer Toolbox, DHCP, and CDP," introduces powerful tools such as protocol sniffers and port scanners to investigate protocol behavior and interoperability issues.

- Chapter 7, "The UNIX Routing and ARP Tables," introduces the gateway's view of its connected interfaces.

- Chapter 8, "Static Routing Concepts," extends this view from Chapter 7 to static routes and various metrics.

- Chapter 9, "Dynamic Routing Protocols—Interior Gateway Protocols," starts to inhabit the gateway's routing table with routes learned from or propagated by dynamic routing protocols.

- Chapter 10, "ISP Connectivity with BGP4—An Exterior Gateway Path-Vector Routing Protocol for Interdomain Routing," primarily deals with BGPv4 routing and ISP issues.

- Chapter 11, "VPN Technologies, Tunnel Interfaces, and Architectures," discusses VPN concepts, tunnel designs, and IPSec.

- Chapter 12, "Designing for High Availability," deals with Virtual Router Redundancy Protocol (VRRP) and redundancy features of modern routing protocols.

- Chapter 13, "Policy Routing, Bandwidth Management, and QoS," describes QoS mechanisms and bandwidth management for outbound traffic.

- Chapter 14, "Multicast Architectures," introduces the world of UNIX multicasting from both historical and modern points of view. The UNIX multicast routing daemon, mrouted, and tunnels are discussed in detail.

- Chapter 15, "Network Address Translation," discusses Network Address Translation/Port Address Translation (NAT/PAT) and covers security aspects of NAT. Issues such as static/dynamic NAT and port relaying are discussed.

- Appendix A, "UNIX Kernel Configuration Files," offers relevant parts of the respective UNIX kernel configuration files.

- Appendix B, "The FreeBSD Netgraph Facility," introduces the FreeBSD Netgraph facility.

Reader Requirements and Level of Difficulty

These reader requirements are not carved in stone. They are just to remind you that I have not included introductory material in this book to avoid cluttering the content. I do assume that you have some of the following:

- Basic understanding of the IPv4 protocol stack

- Understanding of UNIX network interfaces and their operation and configuration

- Familiarity with the UNIX command-line interface (shell)

- Ability to compile tools and custom kernels from source

- Understanding of basic networking concepts (cabling, bridges, hubs, NICs, switches, routers, firewalls, proxies)

- Understanding of static routes and dynamic routing protocols

- CCNP-level Cisco IOS experience or intermediate UNIX experience

The level of difficulty varies throughout this book. It is tailored to accommodate the background of intermediate UNIX system administrators and CCNP-level Cisco network engineers.

Rest assured, however; even if you do not fulfill these requirements, you can benefit from the style and information of this book. However, you might be required to use the recommended literature more often to get the most out of working with this book and the concepts within.

How to Read This Book

Although technical in its nature, this book has a clear design and architectural focus. Keep this in mind when proceeding through the content. Some of the example configuration snippets are just proof of concept, whereas others are far developed; adjust them to your needs. My intention is to offer some inspiration as to how these things work together, to go beyond the obvious. Keep Figure I-1 in mind to understand the icons and names used to identify certain operating systems throughout this book. These are in addition to the icons that are more common to all Cisco books.

Figure I-1 *Icon Nomenclature*

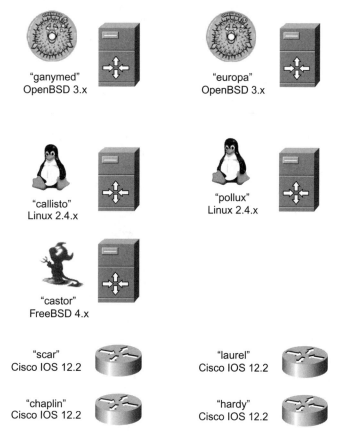

I strongly encourage you to work with the online repository (http://www.iktech.net/unix-routing.html) and the example code provided there. Just visit it once in a while; you might find new additions, errata, links, tricks, and code snippets. I will try to answer requests as soon as possible (to the extent my schedule allows) and update the web page regularly. You can contact me at gernot.schmied@iktech.net.

It was a tremendous challenge and a lot of work to write a publication that covers *five* different operating systems. Keep this in mind before being disappointed about omission of your pet protocol or OS feature or lack of completeness. I tried to fill a demand that is currently covered in neither competitive books nor Internet resources.

UNIX, GNU/Linux, and BSD Operating Systems

My view of the world is that Unices can be assigned to one of three categories depending on their roots: System V related, BSD related, or hybrid approaches such as Linux. The term *UNIX* is a registered trademark of the Open Group (http://www.opengroup.org/) but has been used for decades now as a generic term for all flavors of operating systems from Linux to Sun Solaris and from AIX to FreeBSD. The Open Group's predecessor, the Open Software Foundation (http://www.osf.org/), points to the same entity. *Unices* is the correct plural according to Latin grammar. Throughout this book, UNIX is everything that is not Cisco IOS architecture.

Examples, Labs, and Exercises

This book relies heavily on examples when introducing new or difficult topics. Labs are practical discussions of real-life or academic scenarios that require thorough guidance, elaborate on a particular aspect, or demonstrate a peculiar protocol implementation or behavior. Exercises are designed to experiment with the aspects discussed in the major text, in the examples, and in the labs. The exercises present a less structured approach to a problem that enables you to "tinker" with the fun stuff. Although security is discussed occasionally in this book, the focus is on networking.

Lab Organization

The labs follow the same concept: Via the prompt, the systems are identified by a name running a particular version of an operating system (Example I-1's highlighted text). These setups do not change, but some topologies do. In addition, topological drawings identify operating systems via logos of the popular open-source UNIX operating systems. Therefore, you should be able to identify via the prompt the system and OS that are running. Consider the following example. (Callisto is running Linux 2.4.21.)

Example I-1   *Linux ping Operation*

```
[root@callisto:~#] ping 10.1.1.2
PING 10.1.1.2 (10.1.1.2) from 10.1.1.1 : 56(84) bytes of data.
64 bytes from 10.1.1.2: icmp_seq=1 ttl=64 time=1.15 ms
64 bytes from 10.1.1.2: icmp_seq=2 ttl=64 time=1.15 ms
64 bytes from 10.1.1.2: icmp_seq=3 ttl=64 time=1.15 ms
--- 10.1.1.2 ping statistics ---
3 packets transmitted, 3 received, 0% loss, time 2019ms
rtt min/avg/max/mdev = 1.154/1.156/1.159/0.039 ms
```

Occasionally, you will find remarks and comments inside the code and configuration example boxes marked with either a hash symbol (#), which is the UNIX way of marking comments, or with an exclamation mark (!), the label used for remarks in Cisco IOS configurations.

In the UNIX world, manual pages are referred to in this format: sysctl(8), which refers to section 8 of the manual page for the sysctl utility. You can open this manual page by typing **man 8 sysctl**. It is common practice to refer to manual pages as man pages.

A Few Words on Code Maturity

This book presents tools and packages of varying stability and evolutionary status. Almost all discussed software is production grade and used in production environments in real-life networks and consulting projects. Ultimately, it is up to your thorough evaluation to decide whether a deployment is feasible and under what conditions bleeding-edge features are advisable or justifiable. The label *stable* is as subjective as *scalable* or *robust* and has certainly nothing to do with version numbers. Neither is it possible for me to test all features under all possible conditions. There is only one to blame for lack of evaluation and stress testing.

What This Book Will Not Cover

To prevent the content of this book from getting completely out of control, I made the following decisions:

- This book was not designed as a network encyclopedia that covers everything.

- At the risk of losing beginners, I also reduced the usual clutter, such as the 3567th introduction to IP addressing as well as IOS and UNIX fundamentals.

- This book is meant to put things into perspective and meant to inspire. It is no easy read for the inexperienced, but they might still find it interesting.

- On the other hand, my apologies to stack and kernel gurus for certain simplifications used to present some difficult topics in a digestible way. These simplifications enabled me to focus on content and views that I consider missing from the literature and potentially interesting to the advanced reader. Some aspects might go into a second edition, depending on the feedback I receive.

NOTE   Keep in mind that this is neither a book about security nor about Microsoft integration or interoperability. Security is too vast a field and would require an entire volume of its own. You are welcome to approach me with regard to *related* security questions, however. Because of time constraints and lack of expertise, I cannot respond to requests that relate to Microsoft questions and integration issues.

My approach to this publication was to stop with explanations when further insights would require discussion of stack/kernel internals and source-code implementation. Instead, I took an approach that stems from RFCs and standards. However, learning from the source code is still the best way to understand protocol implementations and network stack internals. This book will explicitly not cover the following topics or foundations:

- IPv6 and the 6BONE
- Firewalls and packet filters
- Channelized T1/E1, PRIs
- Analog/ISDN dial scenarios, including PPP
- Non-IP protocol stacks (IPX/SPX, SNA, AppleTalk, CLNS)
- NetBIOS, NetBEUI
- Operation of CSU/DSUs
- Introduction to dynamic routing protocols
- Introduction to T1/E1/T3/E3, Frame Relay, or ATM
- PPPoA, PPPoE, and DSL bridging mode
- IPSec framework
- IGRP, EIGRP routing protocols
- "Exotic" interfaces (Token Ring, Fibre Channel, FDDI, HSSI)

Topics in Preparation and Under Consideration for a Second Edition

When writing a book, the author is always confronted with the difficult task of deciding which topics to include or exclude (that is, to find the balance of necessary material while avoiding unduly clutter in the discussion). In addition, the evolution of the topics does not stand still to accommodate the editorial process. I also faced the difficult decision of at what point in time to announce a "content freeze." Therefore, the following topics are strong candidates for a second edition, especially XORP and IPv6. Discussions with readers, feedback, and reader wish lists will strongly influence the content of any second edition of this text:

- IPv6
- TACACS+, RADIUS, and Kerberos
- Netflow tools
- SNMP and syslog(ng)
- Linux 2.6 IPSec
- More on XORP/Quagga evolution
- IS-IS evolution
- MPLS
- RSVP/CR-LDP
- Clustering
- More on wireless/cable/DSL architectures

- ATM/Frame Relay X-over Lab + Switch
- OpenBSD native bgpd
- New kernels: NetBSD 2.x, OpenBSD 3.x, FreeBSD 5.x, Linux 2.6.x, IOS 12.3, and eventually MAC OS X and Dragonfly BSD
- Elaboration on MTU and TCP MSS issues
- Linux Netlink facility and BSD divert sockets
- More on multiprotocol/multicast BGP
- RTP (Real Time Protocol) with regard to multicasting

## CHAPTER 1

Operating System Issues and Features—The Big Picture

State-of-the art UNIX operating systems are powerful in performance, robust, rich in features, and come with a lot of ancillary tools and packages out of the box. Due to their performance criteria and robustness, UNIX operating systems are the choice for many critical applications in enterprise and service provider environments, data centers, and machine clusters. GNU packages, especially compilers, form the foundation of most UNIX operating systems, with GNU/Linux being the most prominent open-source representative. Because of high-performance network stacks and a complete set of supported protocols, they are also a good choice for gateways, routers, and firewall systems.

This chapter offers a quick overview of the UNIX flavors used in this book, where they come from, some historical background, and a few words about their strengths and peculiarities. Aspects such as user space, kernel space, and the modular, monolithic, and microkernel approaches are discussed as well; UNIX, UNIX-like, and commercial UNIX derivatives are put into perspective. The embedded Cisco IOS architecture is discussed as a contrasting example of an operating system running on dedicated hardware, optimized and tuned for high-performance packet forwarding and manipulation enabled by specialized application-specific integrated circuits (ASICs) and bus architectures.

Why UNIX Is Viable

When it comes to performance and throughput, a well-tuned combination of low-level software and hardware always has advantages over general-purpose systems. Although modern UNIX platforms employ more powerful CPUs and 64-bit mainboard architectures, ASIC-centered dedicated-purpose hardware still has a slight overall-performance advantage. Nonetheless, the striking advantage of general-purpose UNIX operating systems running on off-the-shelf servers certainly is the price/performance ratio and the intrinsic scripting and customizing capabilities of the UNIX OS and shells.

UNIX gateways successfully started to adopt hardware aspects by incorporating hardware crypto accelerator cards for speeding up Triple Data Encryption Standard (3DES) and Advanced Encryption Standard (AES) crypto processing and network adapters with enhanced I/O buffers and intelligence. Excellent serial WAN cards, Fibre Channel support, and EtherChannel-capable network interface cards (NICs) are available for UNIX as well. Asynchronous cards have been deployed successfully to build cheap terminal servers with high port density.

With regards to port density, UNIX gateways have closed the gap with commercial dedicated appliances by using affordable multiport NICs. In addition, UNIX can now use modern server bus architectures, which are capable of driving Gigabit Ethernet full-duplex NICs and ATM adapters.

UNIX operating systems are not as stripped-down or dedicated as embedded systems software; it is designed for carrying out a lot of tasks besides packet forwarding and processing. Nevertheless, the UNIX IP stacks are mature, perform well, and have been the test bed for a lot of infant technologies long before showing up in commercial hardware appliances. Good examples for this statement are multicasting, quality of service (QoS), and IPv6.

Routing, Forwarding, and Switching Approaches

Before the explosion of routing tables and of forwarded traffic, the classic routing paradigm constituted routing table lookups in increasingly complex routing tables. These tables were populated by more or less scalable and fast-converging dynamic routing protocols together with connected routes and static routes.

This paradigm has changed rapidly with the innovations in switching technology (for example, Cisco Express Forwarding, or CEF, an example of fast switching). This new paradigm tries to switch traffic by tagging it or by facilitating other measures to avoid costly Layer 3 routing table lookups. "Costly" refers to keeping the CPU busy and clogging the bus instead of intra-ASIC or intra-linecard switching/forwarding. As discussed later, the signaling and forwarding is done differently within UNIX IP stacks. Signaling refers to exchanging protocol and reachability information, whereas forwarding actually moves packets, frames, or datagrams between gateway interfaces.

The Evolution of AT&T System V (SVR4) UNIX and 4.4-Lite BSD Derivatives

UNIX was born in the early 1960s at AT&T Research as a robust timesharing operating system to overcome some of the restrictions of Multics (Multiplexed Information and Computing System). Over time, myriad flavors and derivatives have emerged and evolved, while the original MILNET/ARPANET evolved into NFSNET and later into the Internet as we know it today.

With the advent of GNU/Linux, UNIX started to attract unprecedented public attention and widespread acceptance. This also led to more popularity of Berkeley Software Distribution (BSD)-like Unices and finally to Apple Inc.'s decision to shift the Macintosh OS toward an operating system based on FreeBSD. In addition, UNIX started to expand its undisputed reign in the server arena into workstations, notebooks, and even PDAs and cell phones. A new momentum was added to the mix with the introduction of *distributions* as a container for operating systems such as Gentoo, Debian, or RedHat/Fedora in the Linux arena.

I do not have a preference when it comes to UNIX flavors. This book is bias-free and stays away from the religious wars a lot of UNIX aficionados and evangelists engage in nowadays. Open-source as well as commercial and proprietary approaches all have their merits. I see the world as a blend of the AT&T System V (SVR4) UNIX and 4.4-lite BSD derivatives. In a world of POSIX standards, the difference is not such a big deal anymore. Most UNIX or UNIX-like systems offer the same look and feel and directory layout. The differences among these systems are most prevalent when dealing with disk organization and file systems.

Throughout this book, I stick to the three open-source operating systems—OpenBSD, FreeBSD, and Linux—for the discussion of the IP stack and user-space architectures. However, most of the conclusions and concepts are valid on other platforms as well, such as SUN Solaris, Mac OS X/Darwin, and NetBSD.

NOTE   The brand UNIX is, after a long and glorious journey, now a registered trademark of the Open Group (http://www.opengroup.org). Hence, several open-source projects call their architectures *UNIX-like* to avoid copyright issues. I do not make this differentiation throughout this book.

Operating Systems Design Considerations

In the UNIX world, discussions are always going on about the pros and cons of microkernel architectures, modular kernels, embedded systems, real-time operating systems, and monolithic kernel designs. For details, look at the GNU Hurd/Mach web page and the design documents available from the Linux kernel designers. The URL is http://www.gnu.org/software/hurd/hurd.html.

Unfortunately, no single authoritative repository exists for Linux information. However, you can start by reading the classic books from Avi Silberschatz (*Applied Operating System Concepts, Fifth Edition*; Wiley Text Books, 1999) and Andrew S. Tanenbaum (*Modern Operating Systems, Second Edition*; Prentice Hall, 2001) about operating systems design to grasp the concepts and design rationale as well as the Minix foundation of Linux. Knowing the information from these sources will help you go through this book because several examples either facilitate kernel routines or dynamic loadable modules; it will also help you in your career because an understanding of operating concepts will always be an advantage when making difficult choices with regard to future platforms.

Kernel-Space Modules Versus User-Space Applications

Some features such as network drivers, IP Security (IPSec), and IPv6 support are implemented in kernel space, meaning they are an integral part of the kernel sources or are available as dynamically loadable kernel modules. Other features such as httpd or vrrpd are implemented as user-space applications (processes or daemons) and run under special system accounts or (un)privileged users. Because applications can be more easily ported than kernel routines and a lot of stuff such as packet filtering that heavily interacts with the kernel needs to be placed in the kernel, knowing what is implemented in which space will help you as you go through this book.

Cisco IOS Software

Cisco IOS Software has been around for quite some time. The original intention of the developers was to provide a small embedded system for limited-memory and speed-critical packet-switching routing appliances. Speed requirements within embedded systems are usually met by design simplicity and removal of unnecessary features. Cisco IOS Software has a cooperative multitasking kernel architecture featuring several processes and "resembles a loose collection of components and functions linked with the rest of IOS. Everything including the kernel runs in user mode on the CPU and has full access to systems resources."[1]

With the evolution of the Cisco hardware platforms, ASICs designs, and new bus systems, a lot of functionality has been delegated from the CPU to linecards, daughter cards, and custom chips. Cisco has also done a lot of development in the area of fast-switching strategies (Cisco Express Forwarding [CEF], silicon switching, fast switching), whereas almost everything in the IP stack of UNIX operating systems is done on a per-packet or per-frame basis with different per-flow characteristics. Cisco offers a hierarchical command-line interface similar to a UNIX shell, also based on regular expressions to some extent. It resembles an intelligent parser and several modes of operation around a kernel that at least in some aspects seems inspired by UNIX operating system design.

OpenBSD

OpenBSD has the same roots as FreeBSD. It is based on the 4.4-lite BSD UNIX and is designed to run on multiple platforms, and to be small and secure out of the box. This is the reason why it is popular as a gateway or firewall system on less-performing hardware. It is perfectly fine to forward 100-Mbps, full-duplex, wire-speed traffic on a Pentium II PCI system. Additional software is available via packages and ports. OpenBSD offers a mature IPSec and IPv6 implementation, integrated cryptography, and a strong security focus.

FreeBSD

BSD stands for Berkeley Software Distribution, a source-code package from the University of California at Berkeley. The code is based on AT&T's Research's UNIX operating system. The 4.4-lite BSD distribution still represents the foundation of various open-source operating system spin-offs, which evolved into different flavors and led to the incorporation of GNU packages.

NetBSD

NetBSD examples are omitted throughout this book, mainly because of NetBSD's similarity with OpenBSD and FreeBSD. What applies to the latter operating systems usually applies to NetBSD as well, including its heritage from the 4.4-lite BSD operating environment. NetBSD was designed with portability and platform support in mind. It runs on (almost) everything from toasters to Amigas.

Linux

This UNIX-like operating system is based on the work of Linus Torvalds and was inspired to some extent by Andrew Tanenbaum's Minix operating system. However, Torvalds also had in mind to overcome the limitations of Minix and abandon its microkernel concept for the sake of a modular kernel. Over the recent years, it has grown to a huge collaborative effort with thousands of developers.

The recent 2.4 Linux kernel has reached a level of stability and feature-richness that makes it an ideal platform for stability and cutting-edge testing as well. Linux uses a modular kernel design and heavily relies on GNU packages. Therefore, it is more accurate to refer to it as GNU/Linux.

GNU Hurd/Mach

The GNU Hurd is the GNU project's own UNIX kernel. According to their web page, "It is a collection of servers that run on the Mach microkernel to implement file systems, network protocols, file access control, and other features that are implemented by the UNIX kernel or similar kernels (such as Linux)."[2]

GNU Mach itself is the microkernel approach of the GNU system. In other words, a "microkernel provides only a limited functionality, just enough abstraction on top of the hardware to run the rest of the operating system in user space. The GNU Hurd servers and the GNU C library implement the POSIX-compatible base of the GNU system on top of the microkernel architecture provided by Mach."[3]

As time goes by, both the Hurd and GNU Mach probably will be ported to other hardware architectures. Currently it only runs on Intel 32-bit architectures. Nevertheless, its release cycles are much slower than those of Linux or BSD. It is more a proof-of-concept test bed for kernel specialists.

Other Commercial Unices

As mentioned previously, this book focuses on open-source UNIX operating systems, mainly because of transparency reasons and the availability of compilers and tools. I do not include NetBSD in this discussion because it is tailored for portability and does not offer anything remarkable beyond OpenBSD or FreeBSD.

The most dominant commercial operating systems right now are Sun Solaris, Hewlett-Packard HP-UX, and IBM AIX. BSDI is Riverstone's commercial branch of BSD, facilitating Nexthop's GateD code as well as their own extensions. Almost all the big players have additional Linux-centric lines of business.

Summary

This chapter presented a high-level overview of modern operating system concepts and the viability of UNIX-like operating systems, just enough to put Cisco IOS Software into perspective. Concepts such as forwarding, routing, switching, and signaling were introduced. Aspects such as kernel architectures, kernel-space and user-space operation, and real-time and embedded operating systems were discussed as well. In addition, monolithic, micro-kernel, and modular kernel features were discussed, and GNU packages and distributions were put into perspective.

Finally, the dominating open-source UNIX-like operating systems—OpenBSD, FreeBSD, NetBSD, and Linux—were discussed and compared to some specific aspects of Cisco IOS Software.

Recommended Reading

- The OpenBSD website, http://www.openbsd.org
- The FreeBSD website, http://www.freebsd.org
- The NetBSD website, http://www.netbsd.org
- The Linux Documentation Project website, http://www.tldp.com
- The GNU HURD Project website, http://www.gnu.org/software/hurd/hurd.html
- Cisco Systems website, http://www.cisco.com
- The SCO Group website, http://www.sco.com
- Apple OS X website, http://www.apple.com/macosx/
- The Apple Darwin Project website, http://www.apple.com/macosx/features/darwin/
- The IBM AIX operating system website, http://www-1.ibm.com/servers/aix/index.html
- Hewlett-Packard HP-UX website, http://www.hp.com/products1/unix/operating/index.html
- The SUN Solaris 9 operating system website, http://www.sun.com/software/solaris/index.html

- Everything Solaris Repository website, http://www.everythingsolaris.org
- Solaris freeware website, http://www.sunfreeware.com
- *Applied Operating System Concepts*, by Avi Silberschatz et al. (Wiley Text Books, 1999).
- *Distributed Operating Systems*, by Andrew S. Tanenbaum (Prentice Hall, 1994).
- *Distributed Systems: Principles and Paradigms*, by Maarten Van Steen and Andrew S. Tanenbaum (Prentice Hall, 2002).
- *Modern Operating Systems, Second Edition*, by Andrew S. Tanenbaum. (Prentice Hall, 2001).
- *Operating Systems: Design and Implementation, Second Edition*, by Andrew S. Tanenbaum and Albert S. Woodhull (Prentice Hall, 1997).
- *Operating Systems: Internals and Design Principles, Fourth Edition*, by William Stallings (Prentice Hall, 2000).
- *Inside Cisco IOS Software Architecture*, by Vijay Bollapragada et al. (Cisco Press, 2000).

Endnotes

1 *Inside Cisco IOS Software Architecture*, by Vijay Bollapragada et al. (Cisco Press, 2000)

2 http://www.gnu.org

3 http://www.gnu.org

## CHAPTER 2

User-Space Routing Software

As described in Chapter 1, "Operating System Issues and Features — The Big Picture," user-space routing tools run as one single process (monolithic architectures) or as a set of daemons external to the kernel routines, either single-threaded or multithreaded. As long as these daemons are alive, routing information — signaling information to be more precise — can be exchanged or withdrawn and eventually populate the gateway's routing table.

The following sections introduce the most popular and useful among the publicly available routing packages, some of their peculiarities, and how to set things up and run them for the first time. Their functionality and configuration files are discussed in depth in later chapters. As mentioned in the Foreword, some familiarity with TCP/IP, installing rpm packages (Redhat Package Manager), and source-code archives is necessary. Note that rpm archives are now used by many different Linux distributions and are not limited to Redhat/Fedora.

Discussion of the routed daemon operation, of Bird, and of the eXtensible Open Router Platform (XORP) is discussed exhaustively in this chapter and nowhere else, with the exception of a small multicast XORP example in Chapter 14, "Multicast Architectures." The remaining routing engines — GateD, Zebra/Quagga, and MRTd — are used extensively throughout the entire book after their initial introduction in this chapter. In the end, whether these packages are suitable for your definition of *production grade* is up to you to decide; this chapter offers some guidance, though. I am also convinced that a project not being actively maintained anymore (such as the research version of GateD) does not imply that it is not robust, is outdated, or is of questionable benefit. Complex routing protocol implementations are extremely difficult to debug without large-scale deployments, and problems are often caused by wrong topological approaches, poor address planning, or a lack of understanding of the involved protocols.

The GNU Zebra Routing Software

GNU Zebra is a free and mature software package that manages TCP/IP-based routing protocols. Zebra's unique architectural foundation is based on the concept of one single process for each signaling routing protocol. Each module can run, be restarted, or be upgraded independently of the others, which greatly increases the stability of the entire system. In addition, the protocol daemons can be run just to exchange signaling information or populate the system's forwarding table via the Zebra master daemon (zebra). Particularly popular applications that use signaling information are route servers and route reflectors that distribute Border Gateway Protocol (BGP) reachability information. Chapter 10, "ISP Connectivity with BGP4: An Exterior Gateway Path-Vector Routing Protocol for Interdomain Routing," discusses these applications in depth. GNU Zebra does not support or make use of threads yet—it has its own internal cooperative user-space thread model (not really multithreaded). Zebra code constitutes the development foundation for IP Infusion's commercial ZebOS. The following list presents some useful details about the software:

- **Test version**—0.93a + IS-IS patch 0.0.6, free routing software distributed under the GNU General Public License (GPL)

- **Architecture**—Modular, one daemon per routing protocol, one master control daemon (zebra)

- **Resources**—http://www.zebra.org, http://isisd.sourceforge.net, http://www. ipinfusion.com

Feature Description and Architecture of Zebra

The Zebra package is a collection of protocol daemons and supports the following dynamic routing protocols: RIPv1/v2, RIPng, OSPFv2/v3, IS-IS (experimental), and BGP4/4+. In addition, several ancillary protocols such as Internet Group Management Protocol (IGMP) and Simple Network Management Protocol (SNMP) via the SNMP multiplexing facility [SMUX RFC 1227] are implemented. It also supports the Linux and BSD IPv6 stacks as well as interaction with the kernel routing table via updates and routing information redistribution, which occurs between the dynamic routing protocol daemons (such as ospfd or ripd) and the Zebra master process (zebra). Therefore, the zebra daemon acts as a supervisor process (routing manager) to exchange routing information between the kernel routing table and the dynamic routing protocol daemons. It is possible to prohibit injection of routes into the kernel routing table if one only intends to distribute pure signaling information. On the other hand, zebra can be run in a way to retain kernel routes in case of zebra termination, maintenance, or shutdown. The steps in the following section walk you through how to accomplish that.

Installation and Startup of Zebra

Zebra is specialized software that requires a sound understanding of networking and routing protocols. To be sure that the binaries behave as anticipated, I recommend installing from sources whenever possible and comfortable with the procedure. It is not always clear which compile-time options, patches, or configuration details were used to produce binary distributions or rpm packages.

Zebra offers a variety of useful and fine-grained configuration options at compile time; therefore, a detailed installation instruction seems appropriate:

1 Download and extract sources and, optionally, the isisd patch from http://www. zebra.org and http://isisd.sourceforge.net.

Be warned, however, that the IS-IS code is at an early development stage. It is not suitable for production use and does not work with newer Zebra versions greater than 0.93a!

2 Apply the isisd patch (**patch -p1 < isisd-0.0.6-zebra-0.93-pre2.patch**) in the Zebra source directory. This does not work on OpenBSD yet.

3 Type the following:

/.configure --enable-isisd --enable-nssa --enable-ospf-te
--enable-opaque-lsa --enable-multipath=6
--enable-vtysh --enable-tcp-zebra --enable-snmp
--with-libpam --enable-netlink

You can get an overview of the configuration options by typing **/.configure --help**. Mutipath is set to 6 to mimic Cisco multipath default behavior. For SNMP support, the Net-SNMP development package or the UCD-SNMP alternative must be present on the system. Keep in mind that problems still exist with the SMUX support.

4 Type: **make**

5 Type: **make check**

6 Type: **make install**

7 Append these service entries to /etc/services:

zebrasrv	2600/tcp
zebra	2601/tcp
ripd	2602/tcp
ripng	2603/tcp
ospfd	2604/tcp
bgpd	2605/tcp
ospf6d	2606/tcp
isisd	2607/tcp

8 Edit initial config files in /usr/local/etc. Examples are installed there automatically.

9 Fire up daemons by typing the following:

/usr/local/sbin/zebra -d -k -f /usr/local/etc/zebra.conf

/usr/local/sbin/ripd -d -f /usr/local/etc/ripd.conf

/usr/local/sbin/ospfd -d -f /usr/local/etc/ospfd.conf

Note the following interesting options for some daemons:

-k, --keep_kernel	Do not delete old routes that were installed by zebra.
-r, --retain	When the program terminates, retain added routes.
-n, --no_kernel	Do not install a route to the kernel.

10 Check the help menu of the routing daemons. (For example, type **ospfd --help** for further details or consult the manual pages, such as zebra(8).)

11 Check the log files for proper operation. For example, you can type **less -f /var/log/ zebra.log** to check the zebra log. Keep in mind that you have to add the log-file location to the respective daemon configuration file.

The administrator has two options to modify runtime configurations via the command-line interface (CLI):

- **telnet localhost <port> ,e.g. port 2604** connects to the ospfd. Zebra uses ports from 2600 to 2607 for daemon connections. You can also make use of the port aliases specified in Step 7. For example, type **telnet localhost ospfd**.

- Use the integrated Zebra shell vtysh by typing **vtysh**. vtysh expects its configuration to reside in /usr/local/etc/vtysh.conf. This path can be altered at compile time. If you want PAM (Pluggable Authentication Module, primarily used on Linux platforms) support in vtysh, use the configuration option **--with-libpam** at compile time. This requires the PAM development package to be present on the system.

If you encounter strange or esoteric problems during execution, use a sniffer, keep an eye on the logging and debugging output, and keep the following caveats in mind.

CAUTION   Zebra does not (yet) compile on OpenBSD with the isisd patch applied! Although currently Linux is the development platform for the IS-IS extension, this combination works nicely on FreeBSD as well. isisd is a young project with a couple of essential features still missing.

CAUTION   There appears to exist a bug in the way some older BSD Unices deal with default multicasting. The kernel in BSD tries to do a route lookup on the multicast destination 224.0.0.5 (AllSPFRouters), which fails if there is no default route or other route to a general multicast prefix such as 224.0.0.0/4 covering that address. If you encounter this problem, add a static route for that prefix.

NOTE   A great number of problems reported to the newsgroups of the Zebra community are problems essentially caused by a lack of understanding of the BGP, RIP, or OSPF protocols; awkward topologies; screwed address layouts; or just wrong uses for these protocols. This is especially true for OSPF-related questions. These problems cannot be attributed to code instability or lack of standard compliance, although minor bugs still exist.

The Development Roadmap of Zebra

Zebra is rather slowly approaching the 1.0 version. Packaged releases are infrequent, so you are better off retrieving the sources from the Concurrent Versions System (CVS) repository. Due to the maturity, scalability, stability, architecture, and Cisco-like handling, I consider this and its fork Quagga the dominating open-source solution for future software routing. Anyone who can configure Cisco IOS software can configure Zebra, too, almost without ever reading the thorough manual (well, "almost"). This package, together with Quagga and GateD, is used for most of the example labs throughout this book. This is why no example lab is provided here.

The Quagga Project

In 2003, a group of developers decided to pursue a Zebra code fork later named the Quagga Project (http://www.quagga.net). The protagonists of the Quagga Project opted for a fork to provide a more dynamic release cycle, greater community involvement, rapid acceptance of community feedback, and quick incorporation of critical patches. Changes to Zebra will be incorporated into Quagga as well. The Quagga website provides much more documentation and example configurations than the Zebra website. Installation and configuration work exactly as described in the Zebra section. However, Quagga supports additional configuration options that you can display by typing **./configure --help**. I am using the following sequence in my setups:

> **./configure --enable-vtysh --enable-netlink --enable-snmp**
> **--enable-tcp-zebra --enable-nssa --enable-opaque-lsa**
> **--enable-ospf-te --enable-multipath=6 --with-libpam**
> **--enable-vty-group=quagga --enable-rtadv**

This requires that a *quagga* group and *quagga* user are configured on the system (present in /etc/passwd and /etc/groups).

With regard to the configuration examples, it should not make a difference whether you are using Quagga or Zebra. However, many bugs have been fixed in Quagga that are still present in the Zebra code. Some innovations such as route servers are only present in Quagga code. Note that recently another IS-IS daemon was integrated into Quagga that is different from the code available for Zebra (but is actually based on it).

The routed Daemon

routed is a simple RIP-based LAN routing protocol daemon often used to communicate with other RIP hosts and gateways. It supports the Internet Router Discovery Protocol (IRDP) as well. The IRDP is discussed in more detail at the end of Chapter 12, "Designing for High Availability."

In the old days, UNIX administrators did not care about routing beyond the scope of a simple broadcast domain or LAN. RIP was the simple but reliable dynamic routing protocol of choice, supported by virtually any operating system and, combined with static routing entries, did the limited job it was required to do pretty well. routed was the vehicle providing this facility.

Feature Description of routed

routed has been around for a long time and supports RIPv1/v2 and IRDP. All you need to know about routed you can get from the manual page by typing **man routed**. It is a simple and reliable routing tool with the known limitations of RIP routing protocols (scalability and convergence); therefore, it is of arguable use in today's routing environments. According to the man page, it does not always detect unidirectional failures in network interfaces (for example, when the output side fails). Under certain conditions, the routed and kernel routing table might differ when redirects change or add routes. In theory, routed should note any redirects received by reading the related ICMP packets.

Installation of routed

routed comes preinstalled on virtually all UNIX platforms I am aware of. Its configuration file is /etc/gateways. However, the Linux version differs from the BSD versions because of historical reasons. Linux routed exhibits somewhat unanticipated behavior with regard to broadcast and multicast operation as well as summarization. (Lab 2-1 demonstrates this peculiarity.) Because of these implementation differences, I strongly recommend caution with Linux routed setups.

Lab 2-1: routed

This lab creates routing connectivity between the UNIX gateways ganymed, castor, and callisto and the Cisco IOS router scar.

On two gateways, ganymed and castor, routed was started by typing **routed -s -T /var/log/ routed.log**. On callisto, routed was started by typing **routed -s**. The command-line options of routed are slightly different on Linux and BSD Unices. Type **routed -h** or consult the routed man page for details. Figure 2-1 shows the lab topology, and Examples 2-1 and 2-2 show the initial Cisco IOS RIPv2 configuration and UNIX routed configurations, respectively. Note that castor is communicating with scar and ganymed via multicast RIPv2 (224.0.0.9), whereas the Linux routed is only capable of broadcast RIPv1. The callisto /etc/gateways configuration is empty and hence omitted.

Figure 2-1   *The Routed Lab Topology*

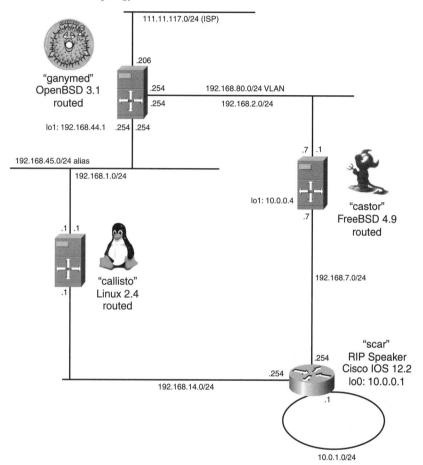

111.11.117.0/24 (ISP)

.206

"ganymed"
OpenBSD 3.1
routed

.254

.254   192.168.80.0/24 VLAN

.254   192.168.2.0/24

lo1: 192.168.44.1   .254 .254

192.168.45.0/24 alias

192.168.1.0/24

.7 .1

lo1: 10.0.0.4

.7

"castor"
FreeBSD 4.9
routed

.1 .1

"callisto"
Linux 2.4
routed

.1

192.168.7.0/24

"scar"
RIP Speaker
Cisco IOS 12.2
lo0: 10.0.0.1

.254

.254

192.168.14.0/24

.1

10.0.1.0/24

Example 2-1   *RIPv2 IOS Router Configuration—Routed Lab 2-1*

```
scar# show running-config
...
!
interface Loopback0
 ip address 10.0.0.1 255.255.255.255
!
interface Ethernet0
 bandwidth 10000
 ip address 192.168.7.254 255.255.255.0
!
interface Ethernet1
 bandwidth 10000
 ip address 192.168.14.254 255.255.255.0
```

continues

Example 2-1 *RIPv2 IOS Router Configuration—Routed Lab 2-1 (Continued)*

```
 ip rip send version 1
 ip rip receive version 1
 !
interface TokenRing0
 ip address 10.0.1.1 255.255.255.0
 early-token-release
 ring-speed 16
 !
router rip
 version 2
 redistribute connected
 network 192.168.7.0
 network 192.168.14.0
 maximum-paths 2
 no auto-summary
 !
ip route 0.0.0.0 0.0.0.0 192.168.14.1
ip route 0.0.0.0 0.0.0.0 192.168.7.7 2
...
```

Example 2-2 *RIP Routed Configurations—Routed Lab 2-1*

```
[root@ganymed:~#] cat /etc/gateways
if=ne4 ripv2 no_rdisc
if=ne5 passive              # Don't send RIP updates to the Internet service provider
if=vlan0 ripv2 no_rdisc

[root@castor:~#] cat /etc/gateways
if=ed0 ripv2 no_rdisc       # Internet Router Discovery Protocol disabled
if=xl0 ripv2 no_rdisc
```

CAUTION   The Linux version of routed offers fewer features than the BSD flavor. Linux routed comes
as part of the NetKit package. According to the accompanying documentation, it was
ported back to Linux from a 1995 version of NetBSD, which explains the differences and
lack of compliance in some aspects of the RIPv2 RFCs. It appears to only support RIPv1
(broadcast). With the parameter **pm_rdisc** in the routed configuration, this router can
be supplied with a route of last resort. Unfortunately, this causes suppression of more
specific routes to castor as well. I have also had troubles with the RIPv2 authentication
parameter; therefore, I strongly recommend the use of RIPv2 under GateD or Zebra/
Quagga instead.

Examples 2-3 through 2-6 show the resulting gateway routing tables.

Example 2-3 *Routing Table Ganymed—Routed Lab 2-1*

```
[root@ganymed:~#] netstat -rn -f inet
Routing tables

Internet:
Destination        Gateway            Flags    Refs     Use    Mtu   Interface
default            111.11.117.1       UGS      4      60443   1500   ne5
10.0.0.1           192.168.80.1       UGH      0          0   1496   vlan0
127/8              127.0.0.1          UGRS     0          0  33224   lo0
127.0.0.1          127.0.0.1          UH       2          8  33224   lo0
192.168.1/24       link#1             UC    -236          0   1500   ne3
192.168.1.1        52:54:5:e3:51:87   UHL      1      45352   1500   ne3
192.168.1.250      8:0:46:64:74:1b    UHL      1      10582   1500   ne3
192.168.1.254      127.0.0.1          UGHS     0         21  33224   lo0
192.168.2/24       link#2             UC       0          0   1500   ne4
192.168.2.7        0:10:5a:c4:2c:4    UHL      1        174   1500   ne4
192.168.2.254      52:54:5:e3:e4:2f   UHL      0          2   1500   lo0
192.168.7/24       192.168.80.1       UG      -1         56   1496   vlan0
192.168.14/24      192.168.2.7        UG       0       1069   1500   ne4
192.168.44.1       192.168.44.1       UH       0          0  33224   lo1
192.168.45/24      link#1             UC       0          0   1500   ne3
192.168.80/24      link#16            UC       0          0   1496   vlan0
192.168.80.1       0:10:5a:c4:2c:4    UHL      2          0   1496   vlan0
111.11.117/24      link#3             UC       0          0   1500   ne5
111.11.117.1       0:5:9a:5a:fb:fc    UHL      1          0   1500   ne5
111.11.117.49      0:e0:7d:9f:9b:dd   UHL      0          0   1500   ne5
```

Example 2-4 *Routing Table Castor—Routed Lab 2-1*

```
[root@castor:~#] netstat -rn -f inet
Routing tables

Internet:
Destination      Gateway            Flags   Refs    Use   Netif Expire
default          192.168.2.254      UGSc    1       3     xl0
10.0.0.1         192.168.7.254      UGH     0       0     ed0
10.0.0.4         10.0.0.4           UH      0      10     lo0
10.0.1/24        192.168.7.254      UGc     0       0     ed0
127.0.0.1        127.0.0.1          UH      1      32     lo0
192.168.1        192.168.80.254     UGc     1     324     vlan8
192.168.2        link#1             UC      2       0     xl0
192.168.2.7      00:10:5a:c4:2c:04  UHLW    3       4     lo0
192.168.2.254    52:54:05:e3:e4:2f  UHLW    2     297     xl0      90
192.168.7        link#2             UCc     1       0     ed0
192.168.14       192.168.7.254      UGc     0       0     ed0
192.168.45       192.168.80.254     UGc     0       0     vlan8
192.168.80       link#15            UC      1       0     vlan8
192.168.80.254   52.54.5.e3.e4.2f   UHLW    3       0     vlan8   1168
111.11.117       192.168.80.254     UGc     0       0     vlan8
```

Also note the highlighted Cisco debug output at the end of Example 2-6. My Cisco IOS Software version refused to send and accept RIPv1 announcements on interface Ethernet1, even though it was explicitly instructed to do so in the configuration. I suspect a RIPv1 implementation bug. This is the reason why callisto and scar do not exchange RIP information.

Example 2-5 *Routing Table Callisto—Routed Lab 2-1*

```
[root@callisto:~#] netstat -rn
Kernel IP routing table
Destination     Gateway         Genmask         Flags MSS Window  irtt Iface
10.0.0.1        192.168.1.254   255.255.255.255 UGH     0 0    ....   0 eth1
192.168.7.0     192.168.1.254   255.255.255.0   UG      0 0           0 eth1
111.11.117.0    192.168.1.254   255.255.255.0   UG      0 0           0 eth1
192.168.2.0     192.168.1.254   255.255.255.0   UG      0 0           0 eth1
192.168.80.0    192.168.1.254   255.255.255.0   UG      0 0           0 eth1
192.168.1.0     0.0.0.0         255.255.255.0   U       0 0           0 eth1
192.168.14.0    192.168.14.1    255.255.255.0   UG      0 0           0 eth0
192.168.14.0    0.0.0.0         255.255.255.0   U       0 0           0 eth0
192.168.45.0    192.168.45.1    255.255.255.0   UG      0 0           0 eth1
192.168.45.0    0.0.0.0         255.255.255.0   U       0 0           0 eth1
127.0.0.0       0.0.0.0         255.0.0.0       U       0 0           0 lo
0.0.0.0         192.168.1.254   0.0.0.0         UG      0 0           0 eth1
```

Example 2-6 *Routing Table Scar—Routed Lab 2-1*

```
scar#show ip route
Codes: C - connected, S - static, I - IGRP, R - RIP, M - mobile, B - BGP
       D - EIGRP, EX - EIGRP external, O - OSPF, IA - OSPF inter area
       N1 - OSPF NSSA external type 1, N2 - OSPF NSSA external type 2
       E1 - OSPF external type 1, E2 - OSPF external type 2, E - EGP
       i - IS-IS, su - IS-IS summary, L1 - IS-IS level-1, L2 - IS-IS level-2
       ia - IS-IS inter area, * - candidate default, U - per-user static route
       o - ODR, P - periodic downloaded static route

Gateway of last resort is 192.168.14.1 to network 0.0.0.0

C    192.168.14.0/24 is directly connected, Ethernet1
R    192.168.45.0/24 [120/2] via 192.168.7.7, 00:00:28, Ethernet0
R    192.168.80.0/24 [120/1] via 192.168.7.7, 00:00:28, Ethernet0
R    111.11.117.0/24 [120/2] via 192.168.7.7, 00:00:28, Ethernet0
     10.0.0.0/8 is variably subnetted, 2 subnets, 2 masks
C       10.0.1.0/24 is directly connected, TokenRing0
C       10.0.0.1/32 is directly connected, Loopback0
C    192.168.7.0/24 is directly connected, Ethernet0
R    192.168.1.0/24 [120/2] via 192.168.7.7, 00:00:28, Ethernet0
R    192.168.2.0/24 [120/1] via 192.168.7.7, 00:00:28, Ethernet0
S*   0.0.0.0/0 [1/0] via 192.168.14.1

scar# show ip rip database
10.0.0.0/8      auto-summary
10.0.0.1/32     directly connected, Loopback0
10.0.1.0/24     directly connected, TokenRing0
192.168.1.0/24    auto-summary
```

Example 2-6 *Routing Table Scar—Routed Lab 2-1 (Continued)*

```
192.168.1.0/24
    [2] via 192.168.7.7, 00:00:05, Ethernet0
192.168.2.0/24    auto-summary
192.168.2.0/24
    [1] via 192.168.7.7, 00:00:05, Ethernet0
192.168.7.0/24    auto-summary
192.168.7.0/24    directly connected, Ethernet0
192.168.14.0/24   auto-summary
192.168.14.0/24   redistributed
    [1] via 0.0.0.0,
192.168.45.0/24    auto-summary
192.168.45.0/24
    [2] via 192.168.7.7, 00:00:05, Ethernet0
192.168.80.0/24    auto-summary
192.168.80.0/24
    [1] via 192.168.7.7, 00:00:05, Ethernet0
111.11.117.0/24    auto-summary
111.11.117.0/24
    [2] via 192.168.7.7, 00:00:05, Ethernet0

scar# debug ip rip
RIP protocol debugging is on
scar# terminal monitor
scar#
00:46:15: RIP: ignored v1 packet from 192.168.14.1 (not enabled on Ethernet1)
00:46:16: RIP: received v2 update from 192.168.7.7 on Ethernet0
00:46:16:     192.168.1.0/24 via 0.0.0.0 in 2 hops
00:46:16:     192.168.2.0/24 via 0.0.0.0 in 1 hops
00:46:16:     192.168.7.0/24 via 0.0.0.0 in 1 hops
00:46:16:     192.168.45.0/24 via 0.0.0.0 in 2 hops
00:46:16:     192.168.80.0/24 via 0.0.0.0 in 1 hops
00:46:16:     111.11.117.0/24 via 0.0.0.0 in 2 hops
00:46:18: RIP: sending v2 update to 224.0.0.9 via Ethernet0 (192.168.7.254)
00:46:18: RIP: build update entries
00:46:18:     10.0.0.1/32 via 0.0.0.0, metric 1, tag 0
00:46:18:     10.0.1.0/24 via 0.0.0.0, metric 1, tag 0
00:46:18:     192.168.14.0/24 via 0.0.0.0, metric 1, tag 0
00:46:45: RIP: ignored v1 packet from 192.168.14.1 (not enabled on Ethernet1)
```

The accompanying tools, rtquery and ripquery, provide useful additional information about RIP speakers; these tools are presented in Example 2-7. Remember that callisto is a RIPv1 speaker (highlighted) and RIP's metric is hop count.

Example 2-7 *Two Useful Tools (rtquery and ripquery)—Routed Lab 2-1*

```
[root@ganymed:~#] rtquery -n 192.168.2.7
192.168.2.7: RIPv2 184 bytes
   10.0.1.0/24        metric  2        nhop=192.168.7.254
   192.168.1.0/24     metric  2        nhop=192.168.80.254
   192.168.2.0/24     metric  1
   192.168.7.0/24     metric  1
   192.168.14.0/24    metric  2        nhop=192.168.7.254
```

continues

Example 2-7   *Two Useful Tools (rtquery and ripquery)—Routed Lab 2-1 (Continued)*

```
     192.168.45.0/24    metric  2          nhop=192.168.80.254
     192.168.80.0/24    metric  1
     10.0.0.1/32        metric  2          nhop=192.168.7.254
   111.11.117.0/24      metric  2          nhop=192.168.80.254

[root@ganymed:~#] rtquery -n 192.168.1.254
192.168.1.254: RIPv2 164 bytes
   192.168.1.0/24       metric  1
   192.168.2.0/24       metric  1
   192.168.7.0/24       metric  2          nhop=192.168.80.1
   192.168.14.0/24      metric  2          nhop=192.168.1.1
   192.168.45.0/24      metric  1
   192.168.80.0/24      metric  1
   10.0.0.1/32          metric  3          nhop=192.168.80.1
 111.11.117.0/24        metric  1

[root@ganymed:~#] rtquery -n 192.168.1.1
192.168.1.1: RIPv1 164 bytes
   10.0.0.1             metric  4
   192.168.1.0          metric  1
   192.168.2.0          metric  2
 111.11.117.0           metric  2
   192.168.7.0          metric  3
   192.168.45.0         metric  1
   192.168.14.0         metric  1
   192.168.80.0         metric  2

[root@ganymed:~#] ripquery 192.168.1.254
164 bytes from ganymed(192.168.1.254) to 192.168.1.254 version 2:
           192.168.1.0/255.255.255.0    router 0.0.0.0          metric  1  tag 0000
           192.168.2.0/255.255.255.0    router 0.0.0.0          metric  1  tag 0000
           192.168.7.0/255.255.255.0    router 192.168.80.1     metric  2  tag 0000
          192.168.14.0/255.255.255.0    router 192.168.1.1      metric  2  tag 0000
          192.168.45.0/255.255.255.0    router 0.0.0.0          metric  1  tag 0000
          192.168.80.0/255.255.255.0    router 0.0.0.0          metric  1  tag 0000
            10.0.0.1/255.255.255.255    router 192.168.80.1     metric  3  tag 0000
         111.11.117.0/255.255.255.0     router 0.0.0.0          metric  1  tag 0000

[root@ganymed:~#] ripquery 192.168.1.1
164 bytes from callisto(192.168.1.1) to 192.168.1.254 version 1:
       10.0.0.1             metric  4
       192.168.1.0          metric  1
       192.168.2.0          metric  2
     111.11.117.0           metric  2
       192.168.7.0          metric  3
       192.168.45.0         metric  1
       192.168.14.0         metric  1
       192.168.80.0         metric  2

[root@ganymed:~#] ripquery 192.168.2.7
184 bytes from castor(192.168.2.7) to 192.168.2.254 version 2:
            10.0.1.0/255.255.255.0       router 192.168.7.254    metric  2  tag 0000
          192.168.1.0/255.255.255.0      router 192.168.80.254   metric  2  tag 0000
```

Example 2-7 *Two Useful Tools (rtquery and ripquery)—Routed Lab 2-1 (Continued)*

```
                      192.168.2.0/255.255.255.0      router 0.0.0.0         metric 1 tag 0000
                      192.168.7.0/255.255.255.0      router 0.0.0.0         metric 1 tag 0000
                     192.168.14.0/255.255.255.0      router 192.168.7.254   metric 2 tag 0000
                     192.168.45.0/255.255.255.0      router 192.168.80.254  metric 2 tag 0000
                     192.168.80.0/255.255.255.0      router 0.0.0.0         metric 1 tag 0000
                         10.0.0.1/255.255.255.255    router 192.168.7.254   metric 2 tag 0000
                     111.11.117.0/255.255.255.0      router 192.168.80.254  metric 2 tag 0000
```

GateD 3.6

For a long time, GateD was the prevalent routing engine of the research community and Internet test beds under the custody of the Merit GateD Consortium (http://www.gated.org).

It was first used to connect the original NFSNET and the emerging regional networks. At that point in time, the source code was basically free. Later, the Merit GateD Consortium changed the licensing and finally handed it over to NextHop. Over time, NextHop Technologies continued the development of the code base and made the product commercially available after adding significant improvements (http://www.nexthop.com). Unfortunately, NextHop removed all traces of the original Merit GateD Consortium 3.6 public release (GateD 3.6), including the manuals from the original http://www.gated.org repository, instead of maintaining the code as an open-research branch. In addition to the 3.6 public release, several 4.0.x development snapshots were made available to the public during the late days of the Consortium. This was alpha software with a lot of IPv6 and multicast stuff and did not compile on my test systems. Give it a try if you are a good and patient programmer. You can also find GateD 3.6.x binaries in most RPM Linux repositories. NextHop is in the business of selling source licenses to big companies such as Riverstone. Some of their customer's command-line interfaces (CLIs) still look a lot like GateD (a hierarchical and structured representation, as you will see) due to their heritage. The following list presents some useful details about the GateD 3.6 public software:

- **Version**—GateD 3.6, Merit GateD Consortium public release, 1999.
- **Architecture**—Modular routing engine, single daemon.
- **Resources**—"Homeless and abandoned." Ask your favourite search engine for GateD 3.6 and retrieve gated-3-6.tar.gz together with the original postscript manual. Some documentation mirrors are still up as well. Due to unclear licensing, I cannot provide these at my repository.

Feature Description

The GateD public release supports RIPv1/v2, EGP, OSPFv2, BGP4, and RDP. There exists a great deal of inaccuracy as to which protocols the public version supports. Its syntax is structured and differs conceptually from what engineers are used to in Cisco IOS Software (several sections and layers of parentheses).

Installation of GateD 3.6

The following installation steps are rather straightforward, but they might assist those of you who are unfamiliar with UNIX installation procedures:

1 Get and extract source archive gated-3-6.tar.gz and the documentation gated.ps.

2 Use **cd** to access the GateD source directory.

3 Check configuration options: **./configure --help**

4 Type: **./configure --enable-gii --disable-ripon --enable-rdisc**

5 Type: **make depend**

6 Type: **make**

7 Type: **make install**

8 Check **gated -h** for options.

9 To fire up the daemon, type **gated -f /etc/gated.cfg** or use the gdc admin utility.

   gated will not start if the config file has a syntax error.

10 Add the following entry to /etc/ services: **gii 616/tcp**

11 Access the GateD Interactive Interface (GII) by typing **telnet localhost gii**

Reliance on Service

gated relies on services of the UNIX kernel for the TCP/IP stack. These services include the following:

- IP forwarding enabled.
- Setting of UDP checksum for RIP on BSD (**sysctl net.inet.udp.checksum = 1**).
- Optional SNMP support (via snmpd/smux).
- Interfaces with the kernel to query interface status, routes, and timers.
- Multicast support (for OSPFv2 and RIPv2).
- On Linux, gated uses the netlink interface. Activate the kernel/user netlink socket under Network Options in the kernel configuration.

TIP   SIGINT causes the current state of all gated tasks, timers, protocols, and tables to be written to /usr/tmp/gated_dump or /var/tmp/gated_dump. GateD comes with several accompanying tools such as ospf_monitor, ripquery, and the gdc user interface.

Maturity, Scalability, and Stability of GateD 3.6

GateD 3.6 is a stable, scalable, and mature system but is no longer maintained. Nevertheless, it is suitable for production deployment, keeping in mind its current state of evolution and feature sets. It has proven its value as an Internet routing platform, especially for BGP, during years of stable operation. If you are looking for state-of-the-art supported code, talk to the folks at NextHop Technologies. Zebra/Quagga and GateD 3.6 are the routing packages used most frequently throughout this book. From now on, GateD will be used as an abbreviation for the "public GateD 3.6 research release."

MRT (Multithreaded Routing Toolkit)

The MRT Project is a monolithic multithreaded routing engine (MRTd) that was developed under a research grant at the University of Michigan. It contains multiprotocol IPv4/IPv6 routing daemons and accompanying analysis and simulation tools. The following list presents some useful details about the software:

- **Version**—MRT 2.2.2a, a partnership between the University of Michigan and Merit Network
- **Architecture**—Monolithic routing engine
- **Resources**—http://www.mrtd.net

Feature Description of MRT

MRT supports BGP4/4+, RIPng, RIPv2, DVMRP, and PIM-DM. The tool uses Cisco IOS Software-like CLI syntax.

Installation of MRT

To get a working MRTd system, follow these steps:

1 Download the binary rpm package for Linux. I was unable to compile it from source on Linux.

2 Install on Linux via **rpm -Uhv mrt-2.2.2a-1.386.rpm**, on BSD systems via the ports tree or from sources (**pkg_add mrtd-2.2.2a.tgz**).

3 Add the following entry to /etc/services:

mrtd   5674/tcp # MRT Routing Daemon

4 Run **mrtd -f /etc/mrtd.conf** or via the start script **/etc/rc.d/init.d/mrtd** (**-n** for no modification of kernel routing table).

5   You can direct log output to a file, which you define in the configuration file (insert **debug all /var/log/mrtd.log**).

6   Configure via Telnet interface (type **telnet 127.0.0.1 mrtd**).

Maturity, Scalability, and Stability of MRT

Although it is no longer actively maintained, the MRT package is mature and scalable. It is used in some labs in combination with GateD and Zebra/Quagga.

The Bird Project

Bird is a routing daemon primarily developed for the Linux operating system. The following list presents some useful details about the software:

- **Version**—Bird 1.0.8 (by Charles University; Prague, Czech Republic; Mathematics and Physics Department)

- **Architecture**—Monolithic routing daemon

- **Resources**—http://bird.network.cz

Feature Description of Bird

The Bird daemon supports IPv4/v6, BGPv4, RIPv2, OSPFv2 (IPv4 only), static routes, and multiple routing tables on Linux. Its configuration syntax is similar to GateD and offers a powerful filter language.

Installation of Bird

The following installation steps are rather straightforward, but they might assist those of you who are unfamiliar with UNIX installation procedures:

1   Get and extract source archive bird-1.0.8.tar.gz and the documentation bird-doc-1.0.8.tar.gz.

2   **cd** to the Bird source directory.

3   Check configuration options: **./configure --help**

4   Type: **./configure -with-protocols='ospf rip pipe static bgp'**

5   Type: **make**

6   Type: **make install**

7   Check **bird -?** for options.

8   To fire up the demon, type: **bird**

The default configuration file is /usr/local/etc/bird.conf.

9   Access bird via the birdc client. Type: **birdc-?**

Maturity, Scalability, and Stability of Bird

I have had only a brief look at the package without interoperability testing. It compiles without a glitch on my Linux platform with IPv6 disabled. IPv6 caused troubles. The architecture itself looks sound.

The XORP Project

XORP is a fairly young but ambitious and promising private research initiative using either traditional UNIX kernel forwarding or the MIT Click Modular Router Project (http://www.pdos.lcs.mit.edu/click/). The first implementation step appears to be focused on edge devices. It is both suitable for research and production environments and is approaching a milestone release 1.0 in summer 2004. The following list presents some useful details about the software:

- **Version**—0.5, alpha developed by The International Computer Science Institute (ICSI) in Berkeley, California
- **Architecture**—eXtensible Open Router Platform software
- **Resources**—http://www.xorp.org

Feature Description of XORP

XORP supports both IPv4 and IPv6. Currently, BGPv4 (IPv4), OSPFv2 (IPv4), PIM-SM/IGMPv1/v2 (IPv4), as well as SNMP support are implemented. The CLI is similar to GateD. The current OSPFv2 implementation is based on John Moy's reference work (http://www.ospf.org).

The MIT Click Modular Router Project

Click is a fast and modular software router developed by MIT consisting of an interconnected collection (a graph) of modules (elements) controlling every aspect of the router's operation. New elements can be added via a C++ interface. Do not confuse these elements with protocol daemons such as in Zebra; this is an entirely different architecture. A router configuration is written in the Click router configuration language providing the glue between logically connected elements. Such a Click router configuration can either be run at the user level, using a driver program, or via a Linux kernel module.

XORP Installation

The following installation steps are rather straightforward, but they might assist those of you who are unfamiliar with UNIX installation procedures:

1   Get and extract source archive xorp-0.5.tar.gz, and **cd** to the XORP source directory.

2   Check configuration options: **./configure --help**

3 Type: **./configure**

4 Type: **make**

5 Type: **make install**

6 Configuration tasks and component administration are done via the xorp_rtrrngr and xorpsh programs.

Maturity, Scalability, and Stability of XORP

The architectural design as well as the rapid evolution process of XORP looks promising. I did not test the package beyond simple compilation, starting and accessing the tools, and reading the architectural design documents—with the exception of the standalone multicast tools, which were tested in Chapter 14. XORP is a strong candidate for elaborate discussion in a second edition of this book.

Multicast Routing Daemons: mrouted and pimd

The mrouted and pimd daemons are discussed in great detail in Chapter 14, an entire chapter dedicated to the UNIX multicast world of standards, protocols, and routing. The multicast examples in Chapter 14 cover the USC pimd, mrouted, and the XORP pimd daemons.

Summary

This chapter offered an introduction to the user-space routing engines used throughout the book (routed, MRT, GateD, Zebra/Quagga) for both the BSD and Linux world of operating systems. In addition, the Bird and XORP projects were briefly discussed, as were topics such as where to get the packages, first-time installation, and caveats. Due to its limitations, the deployment of routed is discouraged in larger networks, especially on Linux systems. As a result of this chapter, the Zebra/Quagga routing engines and XORP are my recommendation for production deployments for the future. Although MRT and GateD public are stable, they are not actively maintained any more. XORP is a project with great potential, but it is still in its infancy.

Chapter 14 discusses mrouted and multicast concepts and architectures, and includes coverage of the mrouted daemon itself, PIM, DVMRP, and IGMP operation.

Recommended Reading

- Linux 2.4 Advanced Routing HOWTO website, http://www.linuxguruz.com/iptables/howto/2.4routing.html

- Linux Advanced Routing & Traffic Control HOWTO website, http://lartc.org/

- The Linux Networking Overview HOWTO website, http://www.tldp.org/HOWTO/Networking-Overview-HOWTO.html
- The GNU Zebra Project website, http://www.zebra.org
- The Quagga Routing Suite website, http://www.quagga.net
- NextHop Technologies GateD website, http://www.gated.org
- Multithreaded Routing Toolkit (MRT) website, http://www.mrtd.net
- The Bird Internet Routing Daemon website, http://bird.network.cz
- The Extensible Open Router Platform (XORP) website, http://www.xorp.org
- The Zebra ISISd project website, http://isisd.sourceforge.net
- IP infusion website, http://www.ipinfusion.com
- MIT's Click Modular Router Project website, http://www.pdos.lcs.mit.edu/click
- The Net-SNMP Home website, http://www.net-snmp.org/
- The Linux-PAM (Pluggable Authentication Modules for Linux) Project website, http://www.kernel.org/pub/linux/libs/pam/

## CHAPTER 3

Kernel Requirements for a Full-Featured Lab

This chapter discusses various important aspects of networking-related kernel configurations on which we will rely heavily as we advance throughout this book. Some of these features need to be enabled at kernel compile time, some utilize loadable kernel modules, and others require user-space configuration tools and utilities such as the firewall or virtual local-area network (VLAN) configuration tasks. In the context of kernel parameters, the sysctl utility is introduced and thoroughly discussed.

This chapter does not cover physical interfaces; Chapter 5, "Ethernet and VLANs," covers them in detail. Essentially, all topics covered here are discussed in greater detail in later chapters. They are presented in this chapter in abbreviated form because you will require this information to prepare your kernel for the labs to come.

The kernel configurations discussed in this chapter represent only some network-relevant parameters and settings. Full configurations for OpenBSD, FreeBSD, NetBSD, and Linux are provided in Appendix A, "UNIX Kernel Configuration Files." I strongly recommend reading this current chapter in parallel with Appendix A.

The sysctl Facility

The sysctl utility retrieves and allows modification of fine-grained kernel parameters on running systems. Parameters can be placed in /etc/sysctl.conf to be set at boot time. Consult the manual page sysctl(8) for further details.

Example 3-1 shows an example output of sysctl and how to alter variables (assign a value). As you can derive from reading the man pages, sysctl works only slightly differently on BSD systems.

Example 3-1 *UNIX sysctl Utility*

```
[root@castor:#] sysctl -a | grep ipsec

net.inet.ipsec.def_policy: 1
net.inet.ipsec.esp_trans_deflev: 1
net.inet.ipsec.esp_net_deflev: 1
net.inet.ipsec.ah_trans_deflev: 1
net.inet.ipsec.ah_net_deflev: 1
net.inet.ipsec.ah_cleartos: 1
```

continues

Example 3-1 *UNIX sysctl Utility (Continued)*

```
net.inet.ipsec.ah_offsetmask: 0
net.inet.ipsec.dfbit: 0
net.inet.ipsec.ecn: 0
net.inet.ipsec.debug: 1
net.inet.ipsec.esp_randpad: -1
net.inet6.ipsec6.def_policy: 1
net.inet6.ipsec6.esp_trans_deflev: 1
net.inet6.ipsec6.esp_net_deflev: 1
net.inet6.ipsec6.ah_trans_deflev: 1
net.inet6.ipsec6.ah_net_deflev: 1
net.inet6.ipsec6.ecn: 0
net.inet6.ipsec6.debug: 1
net.inet6.ipsec6.esp_randpad: -1

[root@castor:~#] sysctl net.inet.ipsec.dfbit=0
net.inet.ipsec.dfbit: 0 -> 0

[root@callisto:~#] sysctl -w net.ipv4.ip_forward=1
```

IP Forwarding Control and Special Interfaces

IP forwarding essentially turns a gateway into a router that is capable of forwarding IP datagrams between directly attached physical or virtual interfaces. In firewall setups, it is often desirable to disable IP forwarding during bootup and firewall initialization for security purposes, not to leave a gateway vulnerable during the booting routine before the firewall inspection engine resumes forwarding control. It is also a good idea to make sure IP forwarding is disabled *before* the firewall terminates at system shutdown. Example 3-2 demonstrates how you can enable/disable IPv4 and multicast forwarding via sysctl parameters. This is possible for IPv6 as well.

Example 3-2 *Linux IP Forwarding-Related sysctl Variables*

```
[root@callisto:~#] sysctl -a | grep forwarding
net.ipv4.conf.pimreg.mc_forwarding = 1
net.ipv4.conf.pimreg.forwarding = 1
net.ipv4.conf.ipsec0.mc_forwarding = 0
net.ipv4.conf.ipsec0.forwarding = 1
net.ipv4.conf.eth1.mc_forwarding = 1
net.ipv4.conf.eth1.forwarding = 1
net.ipv4.conf.eth0.mc_forwarding = 1
net.ipv4.conf.eth0.forwarding = 1
net.ipv4.conf.lo.mc_forwarding = 0
net.ipv4.conf.lo.forwarding = 1
net.ipv4.conf.default.mc_forwarding = 0
net.ipv4.conf.default.forwarding = 1
net.ipv4.conf.all.mc_forwarding = 1
net.ipv4.conf.all.forwarding = 1
```

VLAN Subinterface Support and Trunk Termination (802.1Q)

If you are connecting a UNIX gateway's Ethernet interfaces to a switch or router, you can use this interface to act as an access link or uplink. This interface can also connect multiple VLAN subinterfaces and act as a pipe (trunk) for all these interfaces.

For VLAN tagging, two methods exist: the Cisco System proprietary Inter-Switch Link (ISL) flavor, and the standardized IEEE 802.1Q method. In fact, what we call an uplink is a special case of trunk carrying only one (untagged) VLAN, usually the default VLAN of the switch. Therefore, a UNIX gateway can route between these VLANs ("router on a stick") or form a pipe to a Cisco neighbor using the same subinterface scheme and VLAN tagging. They form logical interfaces on both Cisco and UNIX gateways.

Note that VLANs result in separated broadcast/multicast domains with Media Access Control (MAC) layer isolation. They are a popular way of separating customer access and services in data centers or service provider server segments and are also widely deployed to segment enterprise entities into multiple VLAN realms that can span hundreds of switches.

To support large VLAN switched environments with a lot of trunks, Cisco has developed the proprietary VLAN Trunking Protocol (VTP), which enables switching hierarchies to flood VLAN information on trunk ports. In fact, VLANs are the Ethernet equivalent of a subinterface concept similar to the features Frame Relay provides on serial WAN interfaces or ATM on dedicated ATM interfaces. However, you need to be aware of VLAN security issues, especially if customers are directly connected to the access port of a switch (MAC-level access). In this case, there exists the possibility of VLAN security penetration and denial-of-service (DoS) attacks under certain circumstances, such as heavy load, MAC address spoofing, malicious VLAN labeling from access ports, trunk and spanning-tree manipulation, and so on. This is especially a matter of concern in cable provider access networks and modern metro networks.

All UNIX operating systems under discussion in this chapter support the standardized IEEE 802.1Q VLAN tagging mechanism as long as this option is enabled in the kernel. (See Appendix A for more information.) VTP is not supported under UNIX. The actual configuration of VLAN interfaces usually happens via the **ifconfig** command on BSD and via the **vconfig** command on Linux.

VLAN tagging adds protocol overhead (4 octets in the case of 802.1Q) to the Ethernet frame. This has to be accounted for by manually reducing the maximum frame size via the **ifconfig** command. Otherwise the network interface card (NIC) driver will silently discard the giant frame. In fact, these giants (also called jumbo frames) are a general caveat in Multiprotocol Label Switching (MPLS) and IP Security (IPSec) setups as well. Tagging always adds overhead. You can alter the maximum transmission unit (MTU) by typing **ifconfig {interface} mtu 1496** on Linux or BSD.

NOTE   It is often necessary to alter the MAC address of an Ethernet interface. In particular, cable broadband providers control and provision access via MAC addresses. Whether changing the "burned-in" address is possible or not depends on the hardware and the NIC driver (and therefore the availability of special utilities for this particular purpose). It is not a general feature of the **ifconfig** command you can rely on.

Alias or Secondary Interfaces

Secondary (alias) interfaces can satisfy the requirements to support multiple addresses on one physical interface. This can also be accomplished with VLANs, as discussed in the VLAN section, with the benefit of MAC layer separation. With an alias address configured, the interface essentially listens to relevant traffic on two segments or a second address within the same broadcast domain. This feature has been supported for a long time on almost all operating systems and is popular for virtual web servers. It is referred to as *secondary addresses* on Cisco routers and *virtual interfaces* on Sun Solaris. Examples follow in Chapter 5.

Ethernet Channel Bonding

Ethernet channel bonding describes the physical bundling of multiple full-duplex Fast/Giga Ethernet interfaces (usually two or four) to a virtual pipe of multiplied bandwidth. The resulting channel is transparent to Layer 2 configuration issues and can sustain single- or multiple-link failures of the constituting links.

Experimental channel-bonding drivers for Linux and BSD for selected Fast Ethernet NICs are available. Channel bonding proves particularly useful when using quad Fast Ethernet NICs. In the Cisco context, this feature is referred to as *Fast/Giga EtherChannel*; in the Sun Solaris world, it is known as *Fast/Giga Ethernet trunking*. It offers some scalability and resilience between 100-Mbps and -Gbps interfaces, especially when the platform architecture (system bus) is not capable of driving full-duplex Gigabit Ethernet interfaces. Channel bonding in the UNIX world is often deployed in context with cluster architecture approaches such as Beowulf (http://www.beowulf.org/software/bonding.html). A FreeBSD kernel patch for channel bonding is available as well (http://people.freebsd.org/~wpaul/FEC/) via the NetGraph facility (see Appendix B, "The FreeBSD Netgraph Facility"). It compiled on my system without a glitch. I cannot offer advice and reports beyond this statement because of equipment constraints. On Linux, you have to enable the bonding driver support in the kernel Network Device Support section. It is *essential* to compile this as a module!

Interface Cloning

Usually special interfaces (*pseudo interfaces*) such as tunnels require provisioning at kernel compile-time. However, as a feature of modern UNIX operating systems, these can be added dynamically at runtime when required via, for example, the **ifconfig create** command sequence on BSD or certain dedicated user-space utilities. This has nothing in common with the interface-cloning approaches used by Cisco IOS Software (cloning from a template). Cloned routes are a different concept as well and are discussed in Chapter 8, "Static Routing Concepts."

ECMP (Equal-Cost Multi-Path)

ECMP is an important requirement to enable per-packet/per-destination (per-flow) multipath traffic balancing over multiple equal-cost interfaces. This is of a different nature than the previously discussed interface bonding and is important with regard to load-balancing/ sharing and redundancy architectures. The term *equal cost* refers to an identical metric from the point of view of involved static or dynamic routing schemes.

In contrast to Cisco routers, UNIX IP stacks intrinsically have no perception of per-destination load sharing and *generally* act on a per-packet basis if not configured otherwise (such as in policy routing). Cisco IOS Software defaults to per-destination (per-flow) traffic balancing, as does Cisco Express Forwarding (CEF).

Driver Support for LAN/WAN Interface Cards

The following list offers a quick overview of important interface types supported by popular UNIX operating systems:

- 10/100-Mbps Ethernet and 4/16-Mbps Token Ring adapters have been supported for a long time on all discussed operating systems.

- Although an intriguing concept, 100-Mbps Token Ring has never really generated enough customer interest to penetrate the market.

- Gigabit Ethernet support is sufficiently available as well, but you must take into consideration the performance capabilities of the gateway's bus architecture to feed traffic to these high-performance full-duplex cards. At the time of this writing, 10Gigabit adapters make no sense on these systems and will be more of a feature of 64-bit architectures.

- Fibre Channel adapters are available as well, and they are used primarily to build storage-area networks (SANs).

- Wireless network cards (IEEE 802.11B) are supported for the most prominent chipsets, especially the Cisco Aeronet product line, with the newer 802.11G driver support catching up in Linux 2.6.x and FreeBSD 5.x.

An attractive feature of the discussed UNIX operating systems is the option to use various PCI/ISA WAN interface cards. These flavors include clear-channel or channelized E1 synchronous serial adapters, T3 adapters, PRI cards, and ATM interfaces. These cards come in various flavors with regard to clocking, channelized or clear-channel operation, CSU/DSU integration, duplex transmission, and fractional bandwidths. Well-known producers of these adapters are Sangoma, Cyclades, ImageStream, Stallion, Prosum, and Fore Systems (now Marconi). Usually the vendors provide firmware updates, kernel modules, and utilities for BSD, Linux, and sometimes Sun Solaris. Some of these cards are also gaining popularity for use in software private branch exchange (PBX) systems for enterprise fax and telephony services (FXS/FXO/E1/PRI/BRI interfaces).

Encapsulation Support for WAN Interface Cards

The WAN interfaces I am aware of essentially support the following Layer 2 encapsulations:

- Frame Relay
- X.25
- ATM
- HDLC
- PPP

The supported features with regard to ATM and Frame Relay vary depending on the vendor of these interface cards. I discuss certain aspects in Chapter 4, "Gateway WAN/Metro Interfaces," in a restricted fashion because of limited access to test equipment.

Support for Bridging Interfaces

Running a UNIX workstation in bridging mode offers two interesting possibilities.

The first is the ability to reduce the traffic on the broadcast domain by bridge segmentation. Because of the availability of cheap switches, this is rarely done anymore.

Second, and more interesting, is the ability to add a transparent IP-filtering and traffic-shaping bridge that is nearly impossible to attack from a remote IP address. It is able to inspect all forwarded frames without configured IP addresses on the interfaces; therefore, IP masquerading (Network Address Translation, or NAT) is not possible. It is okay to assign an IP address for administrative purposes, but you must bear in mind that it is the purpose of a bridge to forward *all* traffic, not just IP datagrams. You can either use protocol types for filtering non-IP protocols or use the **blocknonip** option of the OpenBSD brconfig(8) utility. Bridging requires that the interfaces be in promiscuous mode; therefore, the NICs will experience heavier load.

Loop protection in the bridging context is crude. Only Linux supports the 802.1D spanning-tree algorithm, but usually there exists no or only rudimentary Spanning Tree Protocol (STP) support. UNIX gateways were never designed to act as bridges or switches in complicated switch hierarchies/topologies. Therefore, you should prevent loops by design and not rely on the bridging code and its crude loop-protection mechanism to prevent disaster.

Linux and BSD-like operating systems support bridging modes on Ethernet-type interfaces. FreeBSD has expanded the bridging concept to support clustering and VLAN trunks. You will learn more about this feature in Chapter 5. Example 3-3 shows an example of enabling bridging support with a single FreeBSD kernel configuration line.

Example 3-3 *BSD Kernel Bridging Support*

```
options BRIDGE          # for all BSD OSs
```

TCP Tuning

The Transport Control Protocol (TCP) is a far more complicated transport protocol than the User Datagram Protocol (UDP) because of its reliable (connection-oriented) character, more complex header, windowing mechanism, and three-way handshaking. Therefore, most IP stacks allow manipulation of TCP behavior to a large extent. This becomes more and more an issue because, unfortunately, several heavy-load protocols such as HTTP are based on TCP segments for transport. Example 3-4 demonstrates several TCP-related kernel configuration options.

Example 3-4 *TCP sysctl Parameters*

```
[root@callisto:~#] sysctl -a | grep tcp
net.ipv4.tcp_low_latency = 0
net.ipv4.tcp_frto = 0
net.ipv4.tcp_tw_reuse = 0
net.ipv4.tcp_adv_win_scale = 2
net.ipv4.tcp_app_win = 31
net.ipv4.tcp_rmem = 4096        87380       174760
net.ipv4.tcp_wmem = 4096        16384       131072
net.ipv4.tcp_mem = 48128        48640       49152
net.ipv4.tcp_dsack = 1
net.ipv4.tcp_ecn = 0
net.ipv4.tcp_reordering = 3
net.ipv4.tcp_fack = 1
net.ipv4.tcp_orphan_retries = 0
net.ipv4.tcp_max_syn_backlog = 1024
net.ipv4.tcp_rfc1337 = 0
net.ipv4.tcp_stdurg = 0
net.ipv4.tcp_abort_on_overflow = 0
```

continues

Example 3-4   *TCP sysctl Parameters (Continued)*

```
net.ipv4.tcp_tw_recycle = 0
net.ipv4.tcp_syncookies = 0
net.ipv4.tcp_fin_timeout = 60
net.ipv4.tcp_retries2 = 15
net.ipv4.tcp_retries1 = 3
net.ipv4.tcp_keepalive_intvl = 75
net.ipv4.tcp_keepalive_probes = 9
net.ipv4.tcp_keepalive_time = 7200
net.ipv4.tcp_max_tw_buckets = 180000
net.ipv4.tcp_max_orphans = 8192
net.ipv4.tcp_synack_retries = 5
net.ipv4.tcp_syn_retries = 5
net.ipv4.tcp_retrans_collapse = 1
net.ipv4.tcp_sack = 1
net.ipv4.tcp_window_scaling = 1
net.ipv4.tcp_timestamps = 1
```

Tunnel Support

The open-source operating systems under consideration offer a large variety of kernel- and user-space tunnel solutions, with or without protocol transparency, and with or without encryption/compression. The most widely known are as follows:

- IPSec (standard)
- IP-IP (standard)
- GRE/Mobile IP (standard)
- PPTP (standard)
- L2TP (standard)
- CIPE (no standard, kernel and user space)
- VTun (no standard, user space)
- Stunnel (HTTPS) (no standard, user space)

As of this writing, not all of the operating systems support all of these approaches. FreeBSD, for example, only offers early user-space Generic Routing Encapsulation (GRE) support. The safest bet still is to use the same solution for both tunnel endpoints.

What most tunnel solutions have in common is the fact that they reduce the available maximum transmission unit (MTU) size because of encapsulation overhead. You must take this into consideration to prevent fragmentation troubles or breaking path MTU discovery (PMTU).

Multicast Support

Linux and BSD operating systems are easily multicast-enabled with two kernel configuration entries. For a detailed discussion of kernel-space and user-space multicast tools, see Chapter 14, "Multicast Architectures."

Example 3-5 shows related kernel configuration lines for BSD, and Example 3-6 shows the relevant sysctl Linux parameters.

Example 3-5   *Multicast Configuration Options on BSD*

```
options MROUTING # mrouted (DVMRP)
options PIM # PIM-SMv2/PIM-DM
```

Example 3-6   *sysctl Multicast Parameter*

```
[root@callisto:~#] sysctl -a | grep igmp
net.ipv4.igmp_max_memberships = 20

[root@callisto:~#] sysctl -a | grep mc
net.ipv4.conf.pimreg.mc_forwarding = 1
net.ipv4.conf.ipsec0.mc_forwarding = 0
net.ipv4.conf.eth1.mc_forwarding = 1
net.ipv4.conf.eth0.mc_forwarding = 1
net.ipv4.conf.lo.mc_forwarding = 0
net.ipv4.conf.default.mc_forwarding = 0
net.ipv4.conf.all.mc_forwarding = 1
net.ipv4.neigh.pimreg.mcast_solicit = 3
net.ipv4.neigh.ipsec0.mcast_solicit = 0
net.ipv4.neigh.eth1.mcast_solicit = 3
net.ipv4.neigh.eth0.mcast_solicit = 3
net.ipv4.neigh.lo.mcast_solicit = 3
net.ipv4.neigh.default.mcast_solicit = 3

[root@callisto:~#] sysctl -a | grep pim
net.ipv4.conf.pimreg.arp_filter = 0
net.ipv4.conf.pimreg.tag = 0
net.ipv4.conf.pimreg.log_martians = 0
net.ipv4.conf.pimreg.bootp_relay = 0
net.ipv4.conf.pimreg.medium_id = 0
net.ipv4.conf.pimreg.proxy_arp = 0
net.ipv4.conf.pimreg.accept_source_route = 1
net.ipv4.conf.pimreg.send_redirects = 1
net.ipv4.conf.pimreg.rp_filter = 0
net.ipv4.conf.pimreg.shared_media = 1
net.ipv4.conf.pimreg.secure_redirects = 1
net.ipv4.conf.pimreg.accept_redirects = 1
net.ipv4.conf.pimreg.mc_forwarding = 1
net.ipv4.conf.pimreg.forwarding = 1
```

continues

Example 3-6   *sysctl Multicast Parameter (Continued)*

```
net.ipv4.neigh.pimreg.locktime = 100
net.ipv4.neigh.pimreg.proxy_delay = 80
net.ipv4.neigh.pimreg.anycast_delay = 100
net.ipv4.neigh.pimreg.proxy_qlen = 64
net.ipv4.neigh.pimreg.unres_qlen = 3
net.ipv4.neigh.pimreg.gc_stale_time = 60
net.ipv4.neigh.pimreg.delay_first_probe_time = 5
net.ipv4.neigh.pimreg.base_reachable_time = 30
net.ipv4.neigh.pimreg.retrans_time = 100
net.ipv4.neigh.pimreg.app_solicit = 0
net.ipv4.neigh.pimreg.ucast_solicit = 3
net.ipv4.neigh.pimreg.mcast_solicit = 3
```

Firewall and Traffic-Shaping Support

Mature and feature-rich firewalling and masquerading (NAT) support exists for Linux (netfilter/iptables) and BSD (pf, ipf, ipfw). The kernel configuration examples in Appendix A are self-explanatory and commented appropriately. On BSD systems, I do not recommend installing two different firewall systems at the same time unless you have good reasons to do so, such as traffic conditioning. All operating systems under discussion offer sophisticated traffic-shaping and traffic-queuing engines, both in kernel space (ALTQ, dummydev, ipfw) and user space (VTun). These features intrinsically influence traffic *leaving* an interface of the gateway, not entering. In addition, Linux supports advanced quality of service (QoS) mechanisms (TC, DiffServ, RSVP) to make queuing decisions deviating from the default first in, first out (FIFO) behavior. It is also possible to use a routing table-based or firewall-based classifier.

The IPv6 Protocol Stack

All test platforms provide a full IPv6 stack with accompanying tools. However, discussion of IPv6 goes beyond the scope of this book.

Summary

This chapter introduced components of the UNIX kernel configuration files and methods to enable certain networking-relevant features (in combination with the examples presented in Appendix A). In addition, the sysctl utility was introduced; as previously mentioned, sysctl enables you to manipulate certain parameters and aspects of a running system without the need to recompile the kernel image. The examples in this chapter presented features relevant to labs and subsequent discussion in the upcoming chapters.

Recommended Reading

- Manual page of the sysctl(8) utility
- FreeBSD channel bonding kernel patch website, http://people.freebsd.org/~wpaul/FEC/
- The Beowulf Cluster Architecture website, http://www.beowulf.org/software/bonding.html
- Manual page of the brconfig(8) utility

## CHAPTER 4

Gateway WAN/Metro Interfaces

This chapter discusses WAN and metropolitan-access approaches that differ from native switched Ethernet LAN infrastructures. You need to learn about these approaches because the majority of UNIX administrators are aware only of Ethernet network interfaces for connectivity of their beloved systems.

Note that the network access layer delivered to homes and business premises via access/ edge metro architectures is either based (generally) on copper cabling or optical cables. In rural areas, the most commercially feasible solutions are dial/wireless access with rapid deployment of digital subscriber line (DSL) infrastructures operated by smaller regional Internet service providers (ISPs) and occasionally local cable networks. The information in this chapter is presented from the customer's (CPE = Customer Premises Equipment) point of view. This discussion considers CPE gateway functionality and not directly connected isolated clients.

In today's metropolitan areas, the following access solutions can be provided to customers:

- Dial services (analog/ISDN)
- Wireless solutions (laser, microwave, 802.11, GSM, GPRS, UMTS, satellite)
- Plain Ethernet services
- Metro cable access (Ethernet interfaces)
- Synchronous serial digital leased lines (DLLs)
- SDH/SONET links
- ATM or Frame Relay services
- Different flavors of DSL services
- Fiber/UTP/STP to the home (Ethernet offerings up to Gbps or shaped transmission rates)
- Ethernet via existing PSTN cabling with integrated telephony (LRE = Long Reach Ethernet)
- Powerline communications (Internet access via power lines)

Dial-on-Demand Routing: Analog and ISDN Dialup

State-of-the-art digital modems and ISP remote-access platforms support the new ITU V.92 and V.44 standards with features such as better compression, modem-on-hold, quick-connect, and improved upstream performance. However, only time will tell whether ISPs will rush to migrate to these new standards given the development of alternative access technologies with better margin, the risk of introducing instabilities in stable access networks, and the questionable commercial feasibility of upgrading existing equipment, firmware, or software. All modern modems support at least V.90/V.34/V.42bis.

ISDN is available in the form of Basic Rate Interfaces (BRIs) and Primary Rate Interfaces (PRIs) with the capabilities of channel bundling. ISDN is often used for backup scenarios (dial-on-demand routing) and call aggregation, whereas analog modems are often deployed for remote management of network equipment.

In spite of the positive aspects, ISDN backup scenarios are often plagued by the following problems and restrictions:

- Backup for at least 50 percent of business bandwidth is not commercially feasible and essentially means deployment of an access server with one or more PRIs.

- Deployment results in complicated policy routing configurations. For example, what kind of traffic triggers a dial connect? What is the definition of timeouts, of thresholds? What condition triggers teardown of a dial line? Flapping interfaces, Network Address Translation (NAT) scenarios, and IP Security (IPSec) backups further complicate the matter.

- To carriers and service providers, AAA (authentication, authorization and accounting) is a fundamental issue. The effort regarding authentication, IP address allocation, and assignment is considerable for backup scenarios.

- Experience has proven that often carrier DLLs as well as the PSTN use the same trunks originating in the same central office. This defeats the purpose of dial backups and presents a treacherous picture of safety, especially at the edge of these infrastructures, where redundant trunks are rare.

- Businesses tend to favor dual-homed Internet access with their own autonomous system (AS), provider-independent (PI) address block, and flexible Border Gateway Protocol (BGP) routing. This makes ISDN backup scenarios obsolete to a large extent. However, with the maturity of DSL, wireless, and cable networks, these technologies could be used for backup scenarios as well, even in concert with BGP routing. One has to consider slightly different service-level agreements (SLAs) and the issue of availability in the region, though.

Analog modem adapters, ISDN cards, single-chip solutions, and PRI/channelized PCI or ISA adapters are available in many variants. For a small number of PRI adapters, proprietary UNIX drivers are available and complemented by some open-driver initiatives. A discussion of channelized interfaces goes beyond the scope of this book.

Wireless Technologies

Wireless adapter cards and access points for 802.11A/B/G networks are available and have become popular.

Already UNIX kernels support a vast number of different vendor products, with 802.11G drivers catching up. Unfortunately, the Wired Equivalent Privacy (WEP) used for link-layer security is inadequate for modern requirements and can be compromised easily. The successor security architecture (IEEE 802.11I) should be ready by the end of 2004. Several vendors have already started to implement the draft of this standard.

802.11-based networks are plagued by uninvited guests who either connect for free Internet access or for the purpose of sniffing with roaming adapter cards. Therefore, it is highly recommended to add IPSec (3DES/AES) on top of wireless 802.11 networks for transparent encryption, eventually accompanied by measures such as SSH or SSL. Alternative user-space crypto tunnels can be deployed, too. In addition, strong and encrypted authentication is necessary, because MAC-address-based accounting is of limited use, due to the fact that these addresses can be easily changed/spoofed and are tedious to deploy in a vast network of access points. IEEE 802.1X addresses some of these issues.

802.11 is not the only wireless technology available, just the youngest one. Microwave links, satellite links, and laser links will still be available for a long time. The use of GPRS (General Packet Radio Service) and UMTS (Universal Mobile Telecommunications System) is on the rise.

SDH/SONET

Customers can rent Synchronous Digital Hierarchy/Synchronous Optical Network (SDH/SONET) links from carriers and provide their Layer 2 protocol/encapsulation of choice or directly deploy PoS (Packet over SDH/SONET). These links can be acquired either protected (spare port) or unprotected.

For larger enterprise customers, the carriers usually deploy add/drop multiplexers to deliver fractional STM1/OC3 bandwidth. Depending on the linecards of these multiplexers, channels as small as 56/64 kbps could be extracted/injected (*added/dropped* in multiplexer lingo). T1/E1 fractions are the most common when looking at the total number of deployed units, most of them at carrier edge facilities. Due to the increasing bandwidth needs of larger enterprises, such trunks are normally sold as multiples of full T1/E1 rates. In carrier backbones, state-of-the art photonic networks based on optical cross-connects and dense wavelength-division multiplexing (DWDM) technology transport aggregated traffic of multiple 10 to 100 Gbps.

Powerline Communications

Deployment of powerline systems (low-voltage communication) for WAN access requires new equipment at every electrical substation of the energy supplier. The subscriber must be within the rather short and tight distance restrictions of a few hundred meters. Powerline intrinsically is a shared-access technology as well and delivers an Ethernet/USB interface as a demarcation point.

Powerline itself, although initially difficult to deploy, offers the opportunity of new and exciting services: LAN-only powerline in-house cabling, energy management, and remote control of electrical home equipment, just to mention a few.

NOTE   Deployment of T1/E1 symmetrical bandwidth is common. For a technology overview, go to http://www.ipcf.org/powerlineintro.html.

Ethernet to the Home/Premises

With the advances and widespread availability of long- and ultra-long-reach photonic networks, carriers can now provide 10/100/1000-Mbps Ethernet or shaped bandwidths to metropolitan customers, delivering Ethernet demarcation points (optical or copper ports). These services are offered transparently or via virtual LAN (VLAN) or Multiprotocol Label Switching (MPLS) architectures.

Cisco Long-Reach Ethernet (LRE)

Cisco LRE delivers speeds of 5 Mbps to 15 Mbps over legacy category 1/2/3 wiring over several thousand meters. LRE is an extension to the IEEE 802.3 Ethernet standard for single-pair wiring. This requires special switch ports on one end and CPE devices for the office ports on the other end to simultaneously use Plain Old Telephone System (POTS) and Integrated Services Digital Network (ISDN). This is achieved via a sophisticated modulation approach: quadrature amplitude modulation (QAM). Cisco provides a solution that consists of switches, CPE devices, and a POTS splitter for simultaneous use of existing private branch exchange (PBX) equipment.

NOTE   The LRE architecture can coexist with DSL on the same wire bundle facilitating frequency-division multiplexing (FDM).

Synchronous Serial Interface and PRIs

UNIX systems provide excellent support for high-performance T1/E1 and some T3/E3 interface cards, as well as for some High-Speed Serial Interface (HSSI) adapters (up to 52 Mbps) and PRIs. Several vendors provide dedicated drivers and management software for open-source Unices. The NICs integrate nicely into a Cisco WAN network and provide varying telecommunication characteristics:

- Clear-channel/channelized/fractional operation
- Multiple ports
- Physical interfaces: V.35, V.36, X.21, RS-232
- With or without integrated CSU/DSU
- RAS option: with or without integrated digital modems (DSPs)
- PRI signaling
- Internal/external clocking

Almost all synchronous serial NICs support the following Layer 2 encapsulation formats:

- LAPB (X.25 Layer2)
- Frame Relay
- Cisco HDLC
- Synchronous PPP

Frame Relay services are deployed by carriers up to T3 bandwidth in the United States and up to E1 bandwidth in Europe and most other countries in 56/64-kbps or sometimes even smaller increments (subrates/derived channels). Configuration of X.25 or Frame Relay is similar to Cisco configurations with regard to virtual/subinterface concepts and topology (point to point, point to multipoint, and so on).

ATM Interfaces

Some vendors sell PCI ATM interface cards for ATM25 DSL interfaces, 155-Mbps STM-1/OC3, as well as "exotic" 622-Mbps STM-4/OC12 NICs, featuring both optical and electrical RJ-45 interfaces.

OpenBSD, Linux, and FreeBSD provide an ATM stack, but only a limited family of adapters is supported. This family unfortunately includes almost no state-of-the-art models. The best support available for ATM adapters is provided for Marconi ForeRunner and Efficient Networks chipsets. Consult the hardware compatibility list of the respective operating systems for further details.

As far as I have researched the matter, it would be interesting to deploy ATM25 adapter cards for UNIX gateway devices. Unfortunately, few vendors supply PCI models; almost all development effort appears to go into embedded systems for deployment in integrated access devices (IADs). ATM25 supports approximately 10.5-Mbps high-speed, 8-Mbps full-rate, and 4-Mbps or G.Lite downstream speeds and can accommodate ADSL, SDSL, VDSL, and G.SHDSL.

Because I do not own ATM-PCI adapters, no lab is provided in this section. The following sections discuss the Linux and FreeBSD ATM stack and configuration tools in detail. If you own two ATM interfaces cards, you can use an optical crossover cable pair for a nice lab or connect them to an ATM switch for ILMI testing. For RJ-45 crossovers, consult the pin assignments of the vendor's adapter manual.

Linux ATM Support

Unfortunately, there appears to be no further development going on with regard to the Linux ATM Project (http://linux-atm.sourceforge.net), which, of course, does not mean that it is not stable or useful. The drivers are included in up-to-date kernels. In addition, you still need to download the ATM support tools from http://linux-atm.sourceforge.net. Linux ATM implements several ATM-related daemons: atmsigd, ilmid, and atmarpd, as well as several ancillary tools.

Example 4-1 presents configuration of ATM PVC/SVC pairs under Linux. Remember, ATM PVCs are point-to-point abstractions.

To configure the atm0 interface as 10.1.1.1/30 and build a PVC on PHY 0, VPI 0, VCI 51 (emphasized by the shaded text) to the far-end 10.1.1.2/30, type the commands in the order presented in Example 4-1.

Example 4-1   *Simple Linux ATM Interface and PVC Configuration*

```
[root@callisto~#] atmarp -c atm0
[root@callisto~#] ifconfig atm0 10.1.1.1 netmask 255.255.255.252 mtu 4470
[root@callisto~#] atmarp -s 10.1.1.2 0.0.51
```

For an in-depth discussion, consult the Linux ATM-on-Linux HOWTO.

The FreeBSD HARP ATM Subsystem

FreeBSD provides mature ATM support via the Host ATM Research Platform (HARP) software. For configuration details, consult the atm(8) man page and the links in the "Recommended Reading" section.

Cable Access (Ethernet Interfaces)

Cable access can be deployed easily. The vast majority of providers deliver a CPE device (cable modem) that terminates the coax network frequency bands that carry data, TV, and telephony, and provide a standard Ethernet/POTS/ISDN interface as the demarcation point.

To get telephony out of the RF side, an additional termination unit is needed. In contrast to DSL architectures, no additional software or stack components (PPTP, PPPoA, PPPoE) are required on the attached end system or gateway. The cable modem connects via coaxial drop and trunk cables as well as signal repeaters to a carrier's cable head-end. Mixed architectures featuring optical-electrical converters for optical trunk cables are used, too. In contrast to DSL, this is a shared medium; therefore, VLAN architectures and MAC-based access control are commonly deployed and addresses delivered to the customer via Dynamic Host Configuration Protocol (DHCP).

DSL Access

Historically, DSL has been an asymmetric service (ADSL), evolving into a symmetric one (G.SHDSL) designed to replace E1 TDM circuits and provide voice, ATM, raw IP, and ISDN transport.

DSL copper cables are terminated at a central office (CO) DSLAM port (digital subscriber access line multiplexer). The DSLAM serves two purposes:

- One is to physically terminate the subscriber line and separate the voice band from the data bands utilizing an integrated splitter device similar to the one on the customer end; the voice signal is delivered directly to the PSTN network on OSI Layer 1.

- The second purpose is to relay the data traffic to an IP backbone, usually based on ATM or Ethernet. Aggregation and service-selection gateways constitute the distribution layer of modern DSL provider architectures.

Almost all open-source UNIX operating systems provide mature PPTP support required for the PPPoA architectures that are popular in some European countries. Linux, OpenBSD, and FreeBSD support native PPPoE. PPPoA or PPPoE support of your favorite operating system usually requires a modified/patched version of the PPP toolset. Discussion goes beyond the scope of this book, but you can find easily several cookbooks for setup via your favorite search engine or Linux repository. Several DSL NICs are also available (ATM25, splitterless operation). Some of their important characteristics are as follows:

- DSL modes of operation: PPPoA, PPPoE, bridging mode

- DSL flavors: ADSL, HDSL, SDSL, G.SHDSL, G.Lite, VDSL, and so on

- Software requirements of DSL access: PPPoE or PPPoA stack support, PPTP (for example, via Netgraph/mpd daemon under FreeBSD)

Lab 4-1: Synchronous Serial Connection Setup

This lab (as shown in Figure 4-1) facilitates two Sangoma synchronous serial S514/ET1 PCI adapter cards, connected via an RJ-45 crossover cable for point-to-point configuration between a Linux (callisto) and FreeBSD (castor) gateway. This lab deals with Layer 1 and Layer 2 issues; later labs in following chapters add scenarios on top of the data link layer. For the pin layout of the RJ-45 crossover cable as well as the installation of the NIC drivers, consult the Sangoma website.

The NICs used for this lab include a CSU/DSU capable of fractional or clear-channel T1/E1 modes of operation. They can provide clocking or accept external clocking from the network. One side must be configured as a clock master (internal clocking), and the other as a clock slave (line clocking). An erroneous configuration might or might not lead to clock slips and errors over time. In the following lab, the cards are operating as fractional E1, and callisto is providing clocking.

Figure 4-1 *Synchronous Serial Point-to-Point Lab Topology*

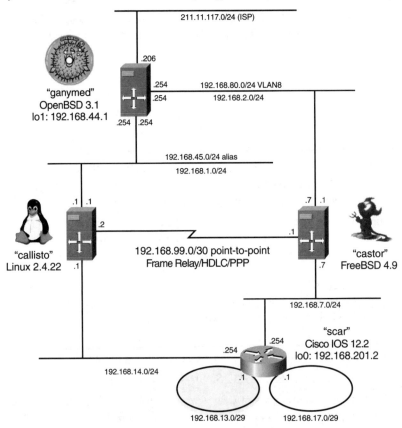

The setup, initialization, and monitoring of these adapter cards is carried out via Sangoma's Wanpipe software, essentially consisting of the wancfg, wanrouter, and wanpipemon tools.

First let us look at Cisco HDLC as a link-layer peer-to-peer protocol (Example 4-2). Logging information goes to /var/log/messages and /var/log/wanrouter. Frame Relay, X.25, and PPP setups pretty much look the same. Example 4-2 presents the result of the NIC setup and concludes with a representation of the NIC configuration as generated by the Sangoma setup tools. The shaded text emphasizes the point-to-point character of the interface.

Example 4-2 *Synchronous-Serial WAN Interface Configuration Featuring CHDLC*

```
[root@callisto:~#] ifconfig -a
...
wp1chdlc  Link encap:Point-to-Point Protocol
          inet addr:192.168.99.2  P-t-P:192.168.99.1  Mask:255.255.255.252
          UP POINTOPOINT RUNNING NOARP  MTU:1500  Metric:1
          RX packets:0 errors:0 dropped:0 overruns:0 frame:0
          TX packets:0 errors:0 dropped:0 overruns:0 carrier:0
          collisions:0 txqueuelen:100
          RX bytes:0 (0.0 b)  TX bytes:0 (0.0 b)
          Interrupt:10 Memory:d0bb6000-d0bb7fff
...

[root@castor:~#] ifconfig -A
...
wpachdlc0: flags=51<UP,POINTOPOINT,RUNNING> mtu 1500
          inet 192.168.99.1 --> 192.168.99.2 netmask 0xfffffffc
...

[root@castor:~#] cat /etc/wanpipe/wanpipe1.conf

#================================================
# WANPIPE1 Configuration File
#================================================
#
# Date: Mon Mar 17 12:33:09 CET 2003
#
# Note: This file was generated automatically
#       by /usr/sbin/wancfg program.
#
#       If you want to edit this file, it is
#       recommended that you use wancfg program
#       to do so.
#================================================
# Sangoma Technologies Inc.
#================================================

[devices]
wanpipe1 = WAN_CHDLC, Comment

[interfaces]
wpachdlc0 = wanpipe1, , WANPIPE, Comment

[wanpipe1]
CARD_TYPE      = S51X
S514CPU        = A
AUTO_PCISLOT   = NO
PCISLOT        = 9
PCIBUS         = 0
MEDIA          = E1
LCODE          = HDB3
FRAME          = NCRC4
```

continues

Example 4-2 *Synchronous-Serial WAN Interface Configuration Featuring CHDLC (Continued)*

```
TE_CLOCK            = NORMAL
ACTIVE_CH           = 10
Firmware            = /etc/wanpipe/firmware/cdual514.sfm
CommPort            = PRI
Receive_Only        = NO
Connection          = Permanent
LineCoding          = NRZ
LineIdle            = FLAG
Interface           = V35
Clocking            = External
BaudRate            = 1540000
MTU                 = 1500
UDPPORT             = 9000
TTL                 = 255
IGNORE_FRONT_END    = NO


[wpachdlc0]
MULTICAST                = NO
IGNORE_DCD               = NO
IGNORE_CTS               = NO
IGNORE_KEEPALIVE         = NO
HDLC_STREAMING           = NO
KEEPALIVE_TX_TIMER       = 10000
KEEPALIVE_RX_TIMER       = 11000
KEEPALIVE_ERR_MARGIN     = 5
SLARP_TIMER              = 0
TRUE_ENCODING_TYPE       = NO
DYN_INTR_CFG      = NO
```

Exercise 4-1: Frame Relay Point-to-Multipoint Setup

Design and implement a point-to-multipoint lab (hub-and-spoke) including two E1 NICs and one Cisco router with an E1 interface connected via crossover cables to a triple-serial-port Cisco router configured for Frame Relay switching. That way, we get a Frame Relay network with a hub and three spokes. Consult Cisco.com for point-to-multipoint and Frame Relay switching details.

Summary

This chapter offered a brief high-level overview of modern WAN access approaches for possible deployment in routing gateways. In addition, this chapter covered some of the WAN technologies that a network might connect to in order to create Internet or VPN access. It also provided some technology comparisons.

Recommended Reading

- FreeBSD PPP & SLIP Handbook, http://www.freebsd.org/doc/en_US.ISO8859-1/books/handbook/ppp-and-slip.html

- A Powerline Introduction website, http://www.ipcf.org/powerlineintro.html

- The Linux ATM Project website, http://linux-atm.sourceforge.net

- DaemonNews Article "Building an ATM Firewall with BSD," http://www.daemonnews.org/200003/atmfirewall.html

- The Host ATM Research Platform (HARP) website, http://www.msci.magic.net/harp/

- Supported FreeBSD ATM interfaces website, http://www.freebsd.org/releases/4.9R/hardware-i386.html#AEN1352

- Sangoma Technologies Corp. website, http://www.sangoma.com

- Prosum website, http://www.prosum.net

- Marconi website, http://www.marconi.com

- Project mpd, which is a FreeBSD PPP daemon based on the Netgraph facility, http://sourceforge.net/projects/mpd/

## CHAPTER 5

Ethernet and VLANs

This chapter deals with all issues and aspects of Ethernet network interface cards (NICs) with regard to the physical and data link layers. It discusses card-specific aspects such as Media Access Control (MAC) address modification, cabling issues, hardware virtual LAN (VLAN) support, as well as aspects of the OS-specific IP stacks such as IP aliases, 802.1Q VLAN support, and bridging modes of operation.

The second half of this chapter investigates the capabilities of these interfaces when connected to switches, routers, or other UNIX gateways. The chapter concludes with a discussion of bridge and VLAN security, Ethernet channel bonding, and some hands-on labs.

Ethernet NICs

Modern Ethernet NICs are cheap and available in many different flavors. I strongly recommend not relying on the cheapest NICs for production applications, because of the limitations of the chipsets used. A sufficient onboard buffer is also essential for TCP performance.

Note that similar to Cisco router interfaces, the adapters need configuration in terms of speed, duplex settings, and maximum transfer unit (MTU). All the necessary parameters can be set with the UNIX **ifconfig** command, available on virtually all UNIX platforms.

On Linux systems, the ifconfig tool has evolved into the ip utility (which is part of the iproute2 package). Consult the ifconfig manual pages and the iproute2-HOWTO for details. We will also use this utility for alias and VLAN configuration. I am well aware that iproute2 has superseded many Linux tools such as ifconfig and route, but these are available on *all* UNIX systems (whereas iproute2 is specific to Linux only).

Autonegotiation of speed and duplex settings has not proven reliable under many circumstances (IEEE 802.3U). The MAC address of some adapters can be changed with a user-space utility provided either by the vendor or the open-source community. This is not possible for all types of NICs. In the worst case, you can use a DOS boot disk with the appropriate utilities. Most vendors also provide firmware upgrades for their products.

NOTE   Exercise care with features such as Wake-On-LAN.

I strongly suggest reading the hardware compatibility notes of your OS releases to ensure proper operation of hardware VLAN support, multicasting, and special features. I also recommend using the same brand of adapters throughout your topology. This makes replacements and driver deployment much easier and does not require kernel recompilation.

Hubs, Bridges, and Multilayer Switches

Because this is not an introductory text, I do not discuss the operation theory of bridges, switches, and hubs. I just want to mention that I am using hubs in my lab setup for the ease of packet sniffing without the need to configure analyzer ports on a switch, which are easily overwhelmed with the traffic of an entire VLAN. This feature is called Switch Port Analyzer (SPAN) on Cisco switches. Besides, I do not own enough switches to build an interesting spanning-tree lab. Therefore, you will find just two limited spanning-tree labs at the end of this chapter so that you can look at the bridge protocol data units (BPDUs) going back and forth between a Linux bridge and a Cisco switch for demonstration purposes.

Of course, I once again warn you about the limited or missing loop-detection mechanisms of some UNIX bridge modes. Take the appropriate topological steps to avoid loops and do not emulate switch functionality with UNIX gateways. Linux, NetBSD, and OpenBSD implement the IEEE 802.1D STP (Spanning-Tree Protocol), which is in charge of loop prevention in switched/bridged topologies in only a crude and limited way.

Instabilities in STP behavior represent the single most severe threat to switched LAN environments with multiple switches and bridges because of the timers involved and the high-performance characteristic of modern switch fabrics. When STP fails, frames might not just circle infinitely; they might multiply (to make the matter even worse). Nevertheless, UNIX bridging modes have their merits in terms of trunk filtering, traffic shaping, and transparent firewalls. Just remember that they are not intended to emulate or replace dedicated switches.

Access Ports, Uplinks, Trunks, and EtherChannel Port Groups

A switch's port can either be a simple access port, an up/downlink to a switch or hub, a trunk port for VLAN transport, or a member of a Fast/Giga EtherChannel port group. A UNIX gateway can be connected to another one via a crossover link, can be connected to a switch, can form a VLAN trunk to another trunking-capable neighbor, or can form high-bandwidth multiport EtherChannel connections.

EtherChannels are often constructed with dedicated dual or quad Fast Ethernet NICs and are able to transport and trunk VLANs. At the time of this writing, they offer an alternative to Gigabit Ethernet NICs, especially with low-end 32-bit servers that might have difficulties feeding Gigabit Ethernet. Nevertheless, it is perfectly feasible to use four isolated NICs of good quality. The only requirement is that the other side of the link is EtherChannel-capable as well. As time passes, we will see a similar feature for Gigabit Ethernet gaining momentum. In general, you will come across one of the following EtherChannel or EtherChannel-like implementations:

- FreeBSD EtherChannel kernel patch, which supports Cisco Fast EtherChannel (via the Netgraph facility). Two or four ports can be combined into a single aggregate interface.

- Linux Ethernet channel bonding.

- Cisco Proprietary Fast EtherChannel (featuring PAgP, or Port Aggregation Protocol).

- The IEEE 802.3AD link aggregation standard (featuring LACP, or Link Aggregate Control Protocol).

- Solaris Ethernet trunking.

- Proprietary drivers for dedicated dual and quad interfaces with configuration utilities.

Useful EtherChannel-related links are presented in the "Recommended Reading" section at the end of this chapter.

Alias Interfaces

As mentioned in Chapter 3, "Kernel Requirements for a Full-Featured Lab," alias interfaces provide a way to assign multiple IP addresses to one physical interface. These addresses can either be from the same network broadcast domain or a different address range. However, they do not provide Layer 2 separation as VLAN tagging does.

You will learn in Chapter 9, "Dynamic Routing Protocols—Interior Gateway Protocols," and Chapter 10, "ISP Connectivity with BGP4: An Exterior Gateway Path-Vector Routing Protocol for Interdomain Routing," how alias information can be transported via dynamic routing protocols and used for virtual servers, redundancy, and Dynamic Name Service (DNS) round-robin configurations. Examples 5-1, 5-2, and 5-3 show the configuration of alias/secondary interfaces on Linux, OpenBSD, and FreeBSD systems; the corresponding statistics; and their representation in the Address Resolution Protocol (ARP) and routing tables. Keep in mind that the "colon" notation (shaded text) of Linux interfaces in general is not exactly equivalent to Cisco IOS subinterfaces.

Example 5-1 *Linux Alias Interface Example*

```
[root@callisto:~#] ifconfig eth1:1 192.168.45.1

[root@callisto:~#] ifconfig eth0:0 192.168.14.14

[root@callisto:~#] ifconfig
eth0      Link encap:Ethernet  HWaddr 00:10:5A:D7:93:60
          inet addr:192.168.14.1  Bcast:192.168.14.255  Mask:255.255.255.0
```

continues

Example 5-1 *Linux Alias Interface Example (Continued)*

```
                UP BROADCAST RUNNING MULTICAST  MTU:1500  Metric:1
                RX packets:0 errors:0 dropped:0 overruns:0 frame:0
                TX packets:1485 errors:0 dropped:0 overruns:0 carrier:0
                collisions:0 txqueuelen:100
                RX bytes:0 (0.0 b)  TX bytes:122180 (119.3 Kb)
                Interrupt:5 Base address:0xd800

eth0:0          Link encap:Ethernet  HWaddr 00:10:5A:D7:93:60
                inet addr:192.168.14.14  Bcast:192.168.14.255  Mask:255.255.255.0
                UP BROADCAST RUNNING MULTICAST  MTU:1500  Metric:1
                Interrupt:5 Base address:0xd800

eth1            Link encap:Ethernet  HWaddr 52:54:05:E3:51:87
                inet addr:192.168.1.1  Bcast:192.168.1.255  Mask:255.255.255.0
                UP BROADCAST RUNNING MULTICAST  MTU:1500  Metric:1
                RX packets:2604 errors:0 dropped:0 overruns:0 frame:0
                TX packets:3166 errors:0 dropped:0 overruns:0 carrier:0
                collisions:7 txqueuelen:100
                RX bytes:691838 (675.6 Kb)  TX bytes:307948 (300.7 Kb)
                Interrupt:9 Base address:0xd400

eth1:1          Link encap:Ethernet  HWaddr 52:54:05:E3:51:87
                inet addr:192.168.45.1  Bcast:192.168.45.255  Mask:255.255.255.0
                UP BROADCAST RUNNING MULTICAST  MTU:1500  Metric:1
                Interrupt:9 Base address:0xd400

lo              Link encap:Local Loopback
                inet addr:127.0.0.1  Mask:255.0.0.0
                UP LOOPBACK RUNNING  MTU:16436  Metric:1
                RX packets:489 errors:0 dropped:0 overruns:0 frame:0
                TX packets:489 errors:0 dropped:0 overruns:0 carrier:0
                collisions:0 txqueuelen:0
                RX bytes:54587 (53.3 Kb)  TX bytes:54587 (53.3 Kb)

[root@callisto:~#] arp -an
? (192.168.1.254) at 48:54:E8:8C:0A:3F [ether] on eth1
? (192.168.14.254) at 00:60:47:1E:AD:B5 [ether] on eth0
? (192.168.45.254) at 48:54:E8:8C:0A:3F [ether] on eth1

[root@callisto:~#] netstat -rn
Kernel IP routing table
Destination     Gateway         Genmask         Flags   MSS Window  irtt Iface
192.168.1.0     0.0.0.0         255.255.255.0   U         0 0         0 eth1
192.168.14.0    0.0.0.0         255.255.255.0   U         0 0         0 eth0
192.168.45.0    0.0.0.0         255.255.255.0   U         0 0         0 eth1
127.0.0.0       0.0.0.0         255.0.0.0       U         0 0         0 lo
0.0.0.0         192.168.1.254   0.0.0.0         UG        0 0         0 eth1

###########################################################################
#     Alternative configuration via the Linux "ip" utility               #
# Note that "ip" differentiates between "secondary" and "alias" addresses #
###########################################################################
```

Example 5-1 *Linux Alias Interface Example (Continued)*

```
[root@callisto:~#] ip address add 192.168.14.14/24 broadcast 255.255.255.0 label
  eth0:0 dev eth0

[root@callisto:~#] ip address show eth0
2: eth0: <BROADCAST,MULTICAST,UP> mtu 1500 qdisc pfifo_fast qlen 100
    link/ether 00:10:5a:d7:93:60 brd ff:ff:ff:ff:ff:ff
    inet 192.168.14.1/24 brd 192.168.14.255 scope global eth0
    inet 192.168.14.14/24 brd 255.255.255.0 scope global secondary eth0:0

[root@callisto:~#] ip address add 192.168.45.1/24 broadcast 255.255.255.0 label
  eth1:1 dev eth1

[root@callisto:~#] ip address show eth1
3: eth1: <BROADCAST,MULTICAST,UP> mtu 1500 qdisc pfifo_fast qlen 100
    link/ether 52:54:05:e3:51:87 brd ff:ff:ff:ff:ff:ff
    inet 192.168.1.1/24 brd 192.168.1.255 scope global eth1
    inet 192.168.45.1/24 brd 192.168.45.255 scope global eth1:1

[root@callisto:~#] ip route show
192.168.1.0/24 dev eth1   scope link
192.168.14.0/24 dev eth0   scope link
192.168.45.0/24 dev eth1   proto kernel   scope link   src 192.168.45.1
127.0.0.0/8 dev lo   scope link
default via 192.168.1.254 dev eth1
```

Example 5-2 *OpenBSD Alias Interface Example*

```
[root@ganymed:~#] ifconfig ne3 alias 192.168.45.254 netmask 255.255.255.0

[root@ganymed:~#] ifconfig -A
lo0: flags=8049<UP,LOOPBACK,RUNNING,MULTICAST> mtu 33224
        inet6 fe80::1%lo0 prefixlen 64 scopeid 0x5
        inet6 ::1 prefixlen 128
        inet 127.0.0.1 netmask 0xff000000
lo1: flags=8049<UP,LOOPBACK,RUNNING,MULTICAST> mtu 33224
        inet 192.168.44.1 netmask 0xffffff00
        inet6 fe80::1%lo1 prefixlen 64 scopeid 0x4
        inet6 ::1 prefixlen 128
ne3: flags=8b63<UP,BROADCAST,NOTRAILERS,RUNNING,PROMISC,ALLMULTI,SIMPLEX,MULTICAST>
        mtu 1500
        media: Ethernet manual
        inet 192.168.1.254 netmask 0xffffff00 broadcast 192.168.1.255
        inet6 fe80::4a54:e8ff:fe8c:a3f%ne3 prefixlen 64 scopeid 0x1
        inet 192.168.45.254 netmask 0xffffff00 broadcast 192.168.45.255
ne4: flags=8863<UP,BROADCAST,NOTRAILERS,RUNNING,SIMPLEX,MULTICAST> mtu 1500
        media: Ethernet 10baseT full-duplex
        inet 192.168.2.254 netmask 0xffffff00 broadcast 192.168.2.255
        inet6 fe80::5054:5ff:fee3:e42f%ne4 prefixlen 64 scopeid 0x2
ne5: flags=8863<UP,BROADCAST,NOTRAILERS,RUNNING,SIMPLEX,MULTICAST> mtu 1500
        media: Ethernet 10baseT full-duplex
        inet 111.11.117.206 netmask 0xffffff00 broadcast 111.11.117.255
        inet6 fe80::5054:5ff:fee3:5187%ne5 prefixlen 64 scopeid 0x3
```

continues

Example 5-2 *OpenBSD Alias Interface Example (Continued)*

```
ppp0: flags=8010<POINTOPOINT,MULTICAST> mtu 1500
ppp1: flags=8010<POINTOPOINT,MULTICAST> mtu 1500
tun0: flags=10<POINTOPOINT> mtu 3000
tun1: flags=10<POINTOPOINT> mtu 3000
enc0: flags=0<> mtu 1536
vlan0: flags=0<> mtu 1500
vlan1: flags=0<> mtu 1500
gre0: flags=8010<POINTOPOINT,MULTICAST> mtu 1450
gif0: flags=8010<POINTOPOINT,MULTICAST> mtu 1280
gif1: flags=8010<POINTOPOINT,MULTICAST> mtu 1280
gif2: flags=8010<POINTOPOINT,MULTICAST> mtu 1280
gif3: flags=8010<POINTOPOINT,MULTICAST> mtu 1280
faith0: flags=8002<BROADCAST,MULTICAST> mtu 1500


[root@ganymed:~#] netstat -rn -f inet
Routing tables

Internet:
Destination         Gateway             Flags    Refs      Use    Mtu    Interface
default             111.11.117.1        UGS         1     3570   1500    ne5
127/8               127.0.0.1           UGRS        0        0   33224   lo0
127.0.0.1           127.0.0.1           UH          2       38   33224   lo0
192.168.1/24        link#1              UC          0        0   1500    ne3
192.168.1.1         52:54:5:e3:51:87    UHL         1     3387   1500    ne3
192.168.1.2         8:0:46:64:74:1b     UHL         1     3049   1500    ne3
192.168.2/24        link#2              UC          0        0   1500    ne4
192.168.2.7         0:10:5a:c4:2c:4     UHL         0     2150   1500    ne4
192.168.44.1        192.168.44.1        UH          0        0   33224   lo1
192.168.45/24       link#1              UC          0        0   1500    ne3
111.11.117/24       link#3              UC          0        0   1500    ne5
111.11.117.1        0:5:9a:5b:23:fc     UHL         1        0   1500    ne5
111.11.117.206      127.0.0.1           UGHS        0        0   33224   lo0
```

Example 5-3 *FreeBSD Alias Interface Example*

```
[root@castor:~#] ifconfig ed0 alias 192.168.7.77 netmask 255.255.255.255

[root@castor:~#] ifconfig
xl0: flags=8b43<UP,BROADCAST,RUNNING,PROMISC,ALLMULTI,SIMPLEX,MULTICAST> mtu 1500
        options=3<rxcsum,txcsum>
        inet 192.168.2.7 netmask 0xffffff00 broadcast 192.168.2.255
        inet6 fe80::210:5aff:fec4:2c04%xl0 prefixlen 64 scopeid 0x1
        ether 00:10:5a:c4:2c:04
        media: Ethernet autoselect (10baseT/UTP)
        status: active
ed0: flags=8a43<UP,BROADCAST,RUNNING,ALLMULTI,SIMPLEX,MULTICAST> mtu 1500
        inet 192.168.7.7 netmask 0xffffff00 broadcast 192.168.7.255
        inet6 fe80::5054:5ff:fee3:e488%ed0 prefixlen 64 scopeid 0x2
        inet 192.168.7.77 netmask 0xffffffff broadcast 192.168.7.77
        ether 52:54:05:e3:e4:88
lp0: flags=8810<POINTOPOINT,SIMPLEX,MULTICAST> mtu 1500
sl0: flags=c010<POINTOPOINT,LINK2,MULTICAST> mtu 552
```

Example 5-3 *FreeBSD Alias Interface Example (Continued)*

```
sl1: flags=c010<POINTOPOINT,LINK2,MULTICAST> mtu 552
ds0: flags=8008<LOOPBACK,MULTICAST> mtu 65532
stf0: flags=0<> mtu 1280
faith0: flags=8002<BROADCAST,MULTICAST> mtu 1500
vlan0: flags=0<> mtu 1500
        ether 00:00:00:00:00:00
        vlan: 0 parent interface: <none>
vlan1: flags=0<> mtu 1500
        ether 00:00:00:00:00:00
        vlan: 0 parent interface: <none>
lo0: flags=8049<UP,LOOPBACK,RUNNING,MULTICAST> mtu 16384
        inet6 ::1 prefixlen 128
        inet6 fe80::1%lo0 prefixlen 64 scopeid 0xb
        inet 127.0.0.1 netmask 0xff000000
ppp0: flags=8010<POINTOPOINT,MULTICAST> mtu 1500
ppp1: flags=8010<POINTOPOINT,MULTICAST> mtu 1500

[root@castor:~#] netstat -rn -f inet
Routing tables

Internet:
Destination        Gateway            Flags    Refs     Use   Netif Expire
default            192.168.2.254      UGSc     4        1836  xl0
127.0.0.1          127.0.0.1          UH       0        0     lo0
192.168.2          link#1             UC       1        0     xl0
192.168.2.254      52:54:05:e3:e4:2f  UHLW     4        0     xl0     592
192.168.7          link#2             UC       0        0     ed0
192.168.7.77/32    link#2             UC       0        0     ed0
```

NOTE   In contrast to "real" physical interfaces (and to BSD aliases), **ifconfig down** does not only shut down the interface, but entirely removes it; it cannot be brought up again with a mere **ifconfig up**, but has to be reassigned the IP address (thus created anew). This is true for several other pseudo-interfaces as well.

Example 5-4 demonstrates a secondary address assignment under Cisco IOS Software as emphasized via the shaded text. Note that Linux differentiates between a secondary address and an interface alias, as demonstrated with the ip tool in Example 5-1 (shaded text).

Example 5-4 *Cisco IOS Secondary Interface Address Example*

```
scar# show running-config
!
...
interface Ethernet1
 bandwidth 10000
 ip address 192.168.14.14 255.255.255.0 secondary
 ip address 192.168.14.254 255.255.255.0
```

continues

Example 5-4 *Cisco IOS Secondary Interface Address Example (Continued)*

```
 no ip proxy-arp
 media-type 10BaseT
!
...

scar# show ip route
Codes: C - connected, S - static, I - IGRP, R - RIP, M - mobile, B - BGP
       D - EIGRP, EX - EIGRP external, O - OSPF, IA - OSPF inter area
       N1 - OSPF NSSA external type 1, N2 - OSPF NSSA external type 2
       E1 - OSPF external type 1, E2 - OSPF external type 2, E - EGP
       i - IS-IS, su - IS-IS summary, L1 - IS-IS level-1, L2 - IS-IS level-2
       ia - IS-IS inter area, * - candidate default, U - per-user static route
       o - ODR, P - periodic downloaded static route

Gateway of last resort is 192.168.14.1 to network 0.0.0.0

C    192.168.14.0/24 is directly connected, Ethernet1
     10.0.0.0/32 is subnetted, 1 subnets
C       10.0.0.1 is directly connected, Loopback0
C    192.168.7.0/24 is directly connected, Ethernet0
S*   0.0.0.0/0 [1/0] via 192.168.14.1

scar# show arp
Protocol  Address          Age (min)  Hardware Addr   Type   Interface
Internet  192.168.14.1          0     0010.5ad7.9360  ARPA   Ethernet1
Internet  192.168.14.14         -     0060.471e.adb5  ARPA   Ethernet1
Internet  192.168.7.7          14     5254.05e3.e488  ARPA   Ethernet0
Internet  192.168.7.254         -     0060.471e.adb2  ARPA   Ethernet0
Internet  192.168.14.254        -     0060.471e.adb5  ARPA   Ethernet1
```

VLAN Configurations

Today, two dominant VLAN tagging methods exist: the Cisco proprietary Inter-Switch Link (ISL) approach and the standardized IEEE 802.1Q method. Note also that VLAN trunks are special ports or interfaces that are capable of delivering multi-VLAN traffic to a directly connected trunk port or interface.

Cisco has developed a proprietary protocol (VTP, or VLAN Trunking Protocol) to distribute VLAN information through a vast switched network without the need to configure VLANs on every switch. The only task left to do for the administrator is to configure a VTP domain and its participants and to assign ports to specific VLANs distributed via VTP. A rather young open standard for that is available as well (see IEEE GVRP - Generic VLAN Registration Protocol).

VLAN setup itself is not difficult to configure, if you adhere to the following:

- To ensure that everything is working, I recommend verifying proper operation with the **arp**, **netstat**, and **ifconfig/ip** commands.

- In addition, check MTU issues with large IP datagrams such as FTP transfers or handcrafted ping packets. 802.1Q VLAN tagging adds 4 overhead octets between the frame header and the payload that need to be accounted for. Therefore, adjust the interface MTU size to 1496 in case that is not done automatically (as is done on BSD systems).

- Keep in mind that the MTU throughout of your subnet should be consistent as well (for example, 1496 octets). Depending on the protocols involved, it might even become necessary to further decrease the MTU. This might be necessary for both the VLAN and parent interfaces.

- Some NICs, such as the Intel FastEtherPro, support large frames and VLAN demultiplexing natively (in firmware) and operate well with the default MTU of 1500. Sometimes patching the drivers also helps.

- Adding alias interfaces to VLAN interfaces works perfectly fine, too, exactly as with physical interfaces.

- All represented platforms have no problem with the Cisco native VLAN1. The alias and VLAN limits of a platform usually can be derived only when investigating the sources.

  Linux imposes a VLAN limit of 4096 VLANs per interface on 2.4.x kernels.

- Remember to restart your firewall when adding/deleting interfaces! Unfortunately, a lot of ill-configured firewall gateways nowadays break two-way-path MTU discovery. Ensure that you allow the proper Internet Control Message Protocol (ICMP) packets through in both directions. (ICMP type 3/code 4 = "fragmentation needed but do not fragment bit set" in combination with the probing IP packets with DF-bit set.)

- Adding frame overhead such as with Multiprotocol Label Switching (MPLS) shim headers or VLAN tagging represents in the view of many switches a so-called giant or jumbo frame, which usually is silently discarded on regular switch ports. If you encounter problems that appear to affect only large frames, check the giant counters of your switch. Most modern switches and IOS/CatOS versions can deal with this issue. As a workaround, you could configure a VLAN trunk.

Figure 5-1 shows the three VLAN topologies discussed in this chapter. Example 5-5 shows the switch VLAN configuration, and Example 5-6 shows the corresponding ARP output. Example 5-7 presents the analogous configuration for the router involved. Example 5-8 provides status information, and Example 5-9 shows the router's ARP table.

Figure 5-1 *VLAN Lab Topologies*

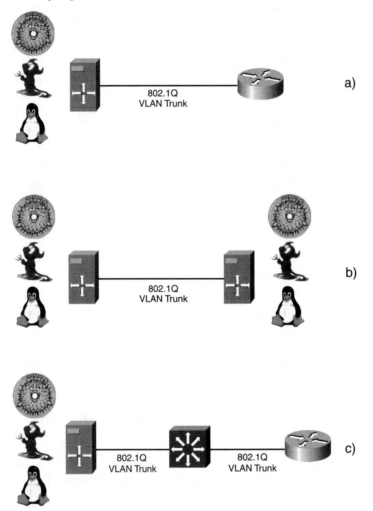

Example 5-5 *Ethernet Switch VLAN Configuration (IOS)*

```
Switch# show running-config
!
ip subnet-zero
!
interface FastEthernet0/1
 switchport mode trunk
!
interface FastEthernet0/2
 switchport mode trunk
!
```

Example 5-5 *Ethernet Switch VLAN Configuration (IOS) (Continued)*

```
interface FastEthernet0/3
 switchport mode trunk
!
interface VLAN1
 ip address 192.168.7.8 255.255.255.0
 no ip directed-broadcast
 no ip route-cache
!
interface VLAN8
 ip address 192.168.80.2 255.255.255.0
 no ip directed-broadcast
 no ip route-cache
!
ip default-gateway 192.168.7.7
!
```

Example 5-6 *VLAN-Related Switch ARP Table*

```
Switch# show arp
Protocol   Address          Age (min)   Hardware Addr   Type    Interface
Internet   192.168.80.1            10   5254.05e3.e488  ARPA    VLAN8
Internet   192.168.80.2             -   0006.5258.5d40  ARPA    VLAN8
Internet   192.168.7.8              -   0006.5258.5d40  ARPA    VLAN1
Internet   192.168.80.254           8   0008.e34d.be81  ARPA    VLAN8
```

Example 5-7 *Router VLAN Configuration*

```
mufasa# show running-config
...
!
interface FastEthernet0/1
 description *** 802.1Q Trunk ***
 no ip address
 no ip mroute-cache
 duplex auto
 speed auto
!
interface FastEthernet0/1.1
 encapsulation dot1Q 1 native
 ip address 192.168.7.254 255.255.255.0
!
interface FastEthernet0/1.8
 encapsulation dot1Q 8
 ip address 192.168.80.254 255.255.255.0
!
...
```

Example 5-8 *Router VLAN Status*

```
mufasa# show vlans

Virtual LAN ID:  1 (IEEE 802.1Q Encapsulation)
   vLAN Trunk Interface:   FastEthernet0/1.1
```

continues

Example 5-8 *Router VLAN Status (Continued)*

```
This is configured as native Vlan for the following interface(s) :
FastEthernet0/1
    Protocols Configured:    Address:              Received:        Transmitted:
        IP               192.168.7.254              0                   19
Virtual LAN ID:  8 (IEEE 802.1Q Encapsulation)
    vLAN Trunk Interface:    FastEthernet0/1.8
    Protocols Configured:    Address:              Received:        Transmitted:
        IP               192.168.80.254            20                   27
```

Example 5-9 *Router VLAN-Related ARP Table*

```
mufasa# show arp
Protocol  Address         Age (min)   Hardware Addr   Type   Interface
Internet  192.168.80.1         7      5254.05e3.e488  ARPA   FastEthernet0/1.8
Internet  192.168.80.2         5      0006.5258.5d40  ARPA   FastEthernet0/1.8
Internet  192.168.7.254        -      0008.e34d.be81  ARPA   FastEthernet0/1.1
Internet  192.168.80.254       -      0008.e34d.be81  ARPA   FastEthernet0/1.8
```

The following two subsections elaborate on VLAN capabilities of FreeBSD, OpenBSD, and Linux and discuss differences and similarities in setup and behavior.

Linux VLAN Capabilities

Late 2.4.x kernels provide 802.1Q VLAN capabilities as a native kernel module. However, one still needs to retrieve the vconfig VLAN administration utility from http://www.candelatech.com/~greear/vlan.html#setup. Most up-to-date Linux distributions already include this utility.

Recently, the capability to define MAC-based VLANs was added via the macvlan_config utility, which is included in the vconfig archive. You still have to apply a kernel patch for that extension, however. Example 5-10 shows the configuration sequence for Linux VLAN interfaces, Example 5-11 shows the resulting status, and Example 5-12 shows additional monitoring information. The shaded text emphasizes the previously mentioned warnings about MTU.

Example 5-10 *Linux VLAN Interface Configuration*

```
[root@callisto:~#] vconfig add eth0 8
[root@callisto:~#] ifconfig vlan8 192.168.80.3/24 mtu 1496
```

Example 5-11 *Linux Interface Status After VLAN Configuration*

```
[root@callisto:~#] ifconfig
eth0     Link encap:Ethernet  HWaddr 00:10:5A:D7:93:60
         inet addr:192.168.14.1  Bcast:192.168.14.255  Mask:255.255.255.0
         UP BROADCAST RUNNING MULTICAST  MTU:1500  Metric:1
         RX packets:124 errors:0 dropped:0 overruns:0 frame:0
```

Example 5-11 *Linux Interface Status After VLAN Configuration (Continued)*

```
             TX packets:28 errors:0 dropped:0 overruns:0 carrier:0
             collisions:0 txqueuelen:100
             RX bytes:9246 (9.0 Kb)  TX bytes:2478 (2.4 Kb)
             Interrupt:5 Base address:0xd800

eth1         Link encap:Ethernet  HWaddr 52:54:05:E3:51:87
             inet addr:192.168.1.1  Bcast:192.168.1.255  Mask:255.255.255.0
             UP BROADCAST RUNNING MULTICAST  MTU:1500  Metric:1
             RX packets:9007 errors:0 dropped:0 overruns:0 frame:0
             TX packets:5240 errors:0 dropped:0 overruns:0 carrier:0
             collisions:37 txqueuelen:100
             RX bytes:1891927 (1.8 Mb)  TX bytes:497578 (485.9 Kb)
             Interrupt:9 Base address:0xd400

lo           Link encap:Local Loopback
             inet addr:127.0.0.1  Mask:255.0.0.0
             UP LOOPBACK RUNNING  MTU:16436  Metric:1
             RX packets:84 errors:0 dropped:0 overruns:0 frame:0
             TX packets:84 errors:0 dropped:0 overruns:0 carrier:0
             collisions:0 txqueuelen:0
             RX bytes:6308 (6.1 Kb)  TX bytes:6308 (6.1 Kb)

vlan1        Link encap:Ethernet  HWaddr 00:10:5A:D7:93:60
             inet addr:192.168.7.10  Bcast:192.168.7.255  Mask:255.255.255.0
             UP BROADCAST RUNNING MULTICAST  MTU:1496  Metric:1
             RX packets:0 errors:0 dropped:0 overruns:0 frame:0
             TX packets:0 errors:0 dropped:0 overruns:0 carrier:0
             collisions:0 txqueuelen:0
             RX bytes:0 (0.0 b)  TX bytes:0 (0.0 b)

vlan8        Link encap:Ethernet  HWaddr 00:10:5A:D7:93:60
             inet addr:192.168.80.3  Bcast:192.168.80.255  Mask:255.255.255.0
             UP BROADCAST RUNNING MULTICAST  MTU:1496  Metric:1
             RX packets:21 errors:0 dropped:0 overruns:0 frame:0
             TX packets:24 errors:0 dropped:0 overruns:0 carrier:0
             collisions:0 txqueuelen:0
             RX bytes:1764 (1.7 Kb)  TX bytes:2168 (2.1 Kb)
```

Example 5-12 *Linux VLAN-Related Status Information*

```
[root@callisto:~#] netstat -rn
Kernel IP routing table
Destination     Gateway         Genmask         Flags  MSS Window  irtt Iface
192.168.7.0     0.0.0.0         255.255.255.0   U      40 0           0 vlan1
192.168.80.0    0.0.0.0         255.255.255.0   U      40 0           0 vlan8
192.168.1.0     0.0.0.0         255.255.255.0   U      40 0           0 eth1
192.168.14.0    0.0.0.0         255.255.255.0   U      40 0           0 eth0
127.0.0.0       0.0.0.0         255.0.0.0       U      40 0           0 lo
0.0.0.0         192.168.1.254   0.0.0.0         UG     40 0           0 eth1
```

continues

Example 5-12 *Linux VLAN-Related Status Information (Continued)*

```
[root@callisto:~#] arp -an
? (192.168.1.2) at 08:00:46:64:74:1B [ether] on eth1
? (192.168.1.254) at 48:54:E8:8C:0A:3F [ether] on eth1
? (192.168.80.1) at 52:54:05:E3:E4:88 [ether] on vlan8

[root@callisto:~#] less /proc/net/vlan/config
VLAN Dev name    | VLAN ID
Name-Type: VLAN_NAME_TYPE_PLUS_VID_NO_PAD
vlan1            | 1  | eth0
vlan8            | 8  | eth0

[root@callisto:~#] less /proc/net/vlan/vlan8
vlan8  VID: 8    REORDER_HDR: 1  dev->priv_flags: 1
          total frames received:         21
          total bytes received:         1764
       Broadcast/Multicast Rcvd:         0

          total frames transmitted:      24
          total bytes transmitted:       2168
              total headroom inc:        0
              total encap on xmit:       24
Device: eth0
INGRESS priority mappings: 0:0  1:0  2:0  3:0  4:0  5:0  6:0 7:0
EGRESSS priority Mappings:

[root@callisto:~#] less /proc/net/vlan/vlan1
vlan1  VID: 1    REORDER_HDR: 1  dev->priv_flags: 1
          total frames received:          0
          total bytes received:           0
       Broadcast/Multicast Rcvd:          0

          total frames transmitted:       0
          total bytes transmitted:        0
              total headroom inc:         0
              total encap on xmit:        0
Device: eth0
INGRESS priority mappings: 0:0  1:0  2:0  3:0  4:0  5:0  6:0 7:0
EGRESSS priority Mappings:
```

FreeBSD/OpenBSD VLAN Capabilities

FreeBSD/OpenBSD setup is straightforward and works the same way for both operating systems. The MTU size is adjusted automatically during setup of the VLAN interfaces.

Consult the BSD vlan(4) and ifconfig(8) man pages for further details about these platforms. Example 5-13 shows the configuration steps for FreeBSD VLAN setup, Example 5-14 shows the resulting interface status, and Example 5-15 provides additional status information.

Example 5-13 *BSD VLAN Configuration*

```
[root@castor:~#] ifconfig vlan8 create
[root@castor:~#] ifconfig vlan8 vlan 8 vlandev ed0
[root@castor:~#] ifconfig vlan8 192.168.80.1/24
```

Example 5-14 *FreeBSD Interface Status After VLAN Configuration*

```
[root@castor:~#] ifconfig -a
xl0: flags=8b43<UP,BROADCAST,RUNNING,PROMISC,ALLMULTI,SIMPLEX,MULTICAST> mtu 1500
        options=3<rxcsum,txcsum>
        inet 192.168.2.7 netmask 0xffffff00 broadcast 192.168.2.255
        inet6 fe80::210:5aff:fec4:2c04%xl0 prefixlen 64 scopeid 0x1
        ether 00:10:5a:c4:2c:04
        media: Ethernet autoselect (10baseT/UTP)
        status: active
ed0: flags=8a43<UP,BROADCAST,RUNNING,ALLMULTI,SIMPLEX,MULTICAST> mtu 1500
        inet 192.168.7.7 netmask 0xffffff00 broadcast 192.168.7.255
        inet6 fe80::5054:5ff:fee3:e488%ed0 prefixlen 64 scopeid 0x2
        ether 52:54:05:e3:e4:88
lo0: flags=8049<UP,LOOPBACK,RUNNING,MULTICAST> mtu 16384
        inet6 ::1 prefixlen 128
        inet6 fe80::1%lo0 prefixlen 64 scopeid 0xb
        inet 127.0.0.1 netmask 0xff000000
vlan8: flags=8843<UP,BROADCAST,RUNNING,SIMPLEX,MULTICAST> mtu 1496
        inet6 fe80::210:5aff:fec4:2c04%vlan8 prefixlen 64 scopeid 0xe
        inet 192.168.80.1 netmask 0xffffff00 broadcast 255.255.255.0
        ether 52:54:05:e3:e4:88
        vlan: 8 parent interface: ed0
...
```

Example 5-15 *FreeBSD VLAN Status Information*

```
[root@castor:~#] netstat -rn -f inet
Routing tables

Internet:
Destination        Gateway            Flags    Refs      Use   Netif Expire
default            192.168.2.254      UGSc       5      3826    xl0
127.0.0.1          127.0.0.1          UH         0         0    lo0
192.168.2          link#1             UC         1         0    xl0
192.168.2.254      52:54:05:e3:e4:2f  UHLW       5         0    xl0      694
192.168.7          link#2             UC         1         0    ed0
192.168.7.7        52:54:05:e3:e4:88  UHLW       0         4    lo0
192.168.80         link#14            UC         1         0    vlan8
192.168.80.1       52.54.5.e3.e4.88   UHLW       0         4    lo0

[root@castor:~#] arp -an
? (192.168.2.254) at 52:54:05:e3:e4:2f on xl0 [ethernet]
? (192.168.7.7) at 52:54:05:e3:e4:88 on ed0 permanent [ethernet]
? (192.168.80.1) at 52:54:05:e3:e4:88 on vlan8 permanent [vlan]
? (192.168.80.2) at (incomplete) on vlan8 [vlan]
? (192.168.80.3) at 00:10:5a:d7:93:60 on vlan8 [vlan]
```

A Few Words on Cabling

In our lab setups, we typically require several kinds of RJ-45 connections: rollover (Console), Ethernet crossover (X-over), and standard Ethernet straight-through cabling. For a reminder of the pin assignments, check Cisco.com (http://www.cisco.com/univercd/cc/td/doc/product/access/acs_mod/cis3600/hw_inst/cabling/marcabl.htm).

Serial X-over cables are an entirely different matter due to the variety of interfaces. Again, refer to Cisco.com for details. Optical PCI ATM adapters can be connected back to back via a simple optical X-over cable pair without the need for an ATM switch. However, you will not be able to test network-to-network interface (NNI), switched virtual circuit (SVC), or interim local management interface (ILMI) features without an intermediary switch.

Lab 5-1: FreeBSD Bridge Cluster Lab

This lab introduces the FreeBSD approach to bridging. Bridging is available on OpenBSD and Linux as well; however, FreeBSD offers a unique feature named *bridge-clusters*. A cluster is an independent set of connected Ethernet or VLAN interfaces uniquely identified by a cluster ID. Consult the manual pages bridge(4), ng_bridge(4), vlan(4), and netgraph(4) for further details.

Example 5-16 shows the configuration sequence for bridging between two gateway interfaces (xl0 and ed0) via (default) cluster ID 1. Before we start, we have to turn bridging on via sysctl, however. The result of this configuration is presented in Example 5-17, the general concept in Figure 5-2.

Example 5-16 *Plain Bridging Between Two Interfaces*

```
[root@castor:~#] sysctl net.link.ether.bridge=1
 net.link.ether.bridge: 1 -> 1

[root@castor:~#] sysctl net.link.ether.bridge_cfg=xl0:1,ed0:1
 net.link.ether.bridge_cfg: xl0:1 -> xl0:1,ed0:1
```

Figure 5-2 *VLAN and Trunk Bridging*

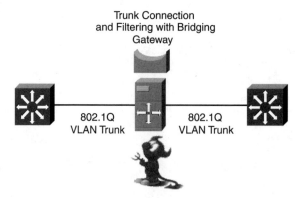

Example 5-17 *FreeBSD Bridging-Related Status Information*

```
[root@castor:~#] sysctl -a | grep bridge
net.link.ether.bridge_cfg: xl0:1,ed0:1
net.link.ether.bridge: 1
net.link.ether.bridge_ipfw: 0
net.link.ether.bridge_ipfw_drop: 0
net.link.ether.bridge_ipfw_collisions: 0
```

The configuration in Figure 5-3 and Example 5-18 is derived from the bridge(4) man page and presents a bridge-cluster setup example involving VLANs and parent interfaces. Interface ed0 acts as a VLAN trunk interface transporting VLANs 8 and 9. The sysctl configuration statement directs packets for VLAN 8 to physical interface xl0, and packets for VLAN 9 to xl1. The logical relationship is established by the two cluster identifiers that tie VLAN 8 to xl0 (cluster ID 34) and VLAN 9 to xl1 (cluster ID 35).

Figure 5-3   *VLAN Access Port and Trunk Bridging*

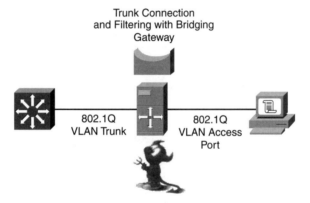

Example 5-18 *FreeBSD Bridge-Cluster Setup*

```
[root@castor:~#] sysctl net.link.ether.bridge_cfg=vlan8:34,xl0:34,vlan9:35,xl1:35
[root@castor:~#] ifconfig vlan8 create
[root@castor:~#] ifconfig vlan9 create
[root@castor:~#] ifconfig vlan8 vlan 8 vlandev ed0
[root@castor:~#] ifconfig vlan9 vlan 9 vlandev ed0
```

You can certainly use advanced features such as filtering and traffic shaping on bridged interfaces, VLANs, and trunks as well.

Lab 5-2: Linux Bridging and the Spanning Tree

The Linux bridge administration is done via the brctl tool. Consult the man page for details and look at the Linux Bridge-STP-HOWTO (http://www.tldp.org/HOWTO/BRIDGE-STP-HOWTO/index.html) and http://bridge.sourceforge.net.

The following setup (Example 5-19) bridges between the two interfaces eth0 and eth1 of the callisto Linux gateway (setup and removal). Example 5-20 provides interface status information of the bridge setup, and Example 5-21 shows a more detailed experience with the brctl tool. Finally, Example 5-22 presents a short sniffer session to capture STP packets.

Example 5-19 *Linux Bridge Configuration*

```
[root@callisto:~#] brctl addbr mybridge
[root@callisto:~#] brctl addif mybridge eth0
[root@callisto:~#] brctl addif mybridge eth1
[root@callisto:~#] ifconfig mybridge up

[root@callisto:~#] ifconfig mybridge down
[root@callisto:~#] brctl delbr mybridge
```

Example 5-20 *Linux Bridge Configuration Interface Status*

```
[root@callisto:~#] ifconfig
eth0      Link encap:Ethernet  HWaddr 00:10:5A:D7:93:60
          inet addr:192.168.14.1  Bcast:192.168.14.255  Mask:255.255.255.0
          UP BROADCAST RUNNING MULTICAST  MTU:1500  Metric:1
          RX packets:0 errors:0 dropped:0 overruns:0 frame:0
          TX packets:6 errors:0 dropped:0 overruns:0 carrier:0
          collisions:0 txqueuelen:100
          RX bytes:0 (0.0 b)  TX bytes:360 (360.0 b)
          Interrupt:5 Base address:0xd800

eth1      Link encap:Ethernet  HWaddr 52:54:05:E3:51:87
          inet addr:192.168.1.1  Bcast:192.168.1.255  Mask:255.255.255.0
          UP BROADCAST RUNNING MULTICAST  MTU:1500  Metric:1
          RX packets:58 errors:0 dropped:0 overruns:0 frame:0
          TX packets:48 errors:0 dropped:0 overruns:0 carrier:0
          collisions:0 txqueuelen:100
          RX bytes:4325 (4.2 Kb)  TX bytes:3625 (3.5 Kb)
          Interrupt:9 Base address:0xd400

mybridge  Link encap:Ethernet  HWaddr 00:10:5A:D7:93:60
          UP BROADCAST RUNNING MULTICAST  MTU:1500  Metric:1
          RX packets:0 errors:0 dropped:0 overruns:0 frame:0
          TX packets:0 errors:0 dropped:0 overruns:0 carrier:0
          collisions:0 txqueuelen:0
          RX bytes:0 (0.0 b)  TX bytes:0 (0.0 b)
```

Example 5-21 *Linux brctl Tool*

```
[root@callisto:~#] brctl
commands:
        addbr           <bridge>                        add bridge
        addif           <bridge> <device>               add interface to bridge
        delbr           <bridge>                        delete bridge
        delif           <bridge> <device>               delete interface from bridge
        show                                            show a list of bridges
        showmacs        <bridge>                        show a list of mac addrs
        showstp         <bridge>                        show bridge stp info
```

Example 5-21 *Linux brctl Tool (Continued)*

```
                  setageing       <bridge> <time>        set ageing time
                  setbridgeprio   <bridge> <prio>        set bridge priority
                  setfd           <bridge> <time>        set bridge forward delay
                  setgcint        <bridge> <time>        set garbage collection interval
                  sethello        <bridge> <time>        set hello time
                  setmaxage       <bridge> <time>        set max message age
                  setpathcost     <bridge> <port> <cost> set path cost
                  setportprio     <bridge> <port> <prio> set port priority
                  stp             <bridge> <state>       turn stp on/off

[root@callisto:~#] brctl show
bridge name     bridge id                 STP enabled    interfaces
mybridge                8000.00105ad79360      yes     eth0
                                                        eth1
[root@callisto:~#] brctl showmacs mybridge
port no mac addr                 is local?       ageing timer
   1    00:06:52:58:5d:44        no              0.93
   1    00:10:5a:d7:93:60        yes             0.00
   2    48:54:e8:8c:0a:3f        no              9.62
   2    52:54:05:e3:51:87        yes             0.00
   1    52:54:05:e3:e4:88        no              9.62

[root@callisto:~#] brctl showstp mybridge
mybridge
  bridge id            8000.00105ad79360
  designated root      8000.000652585d40
  root port            1                    path cost                 100
  max age              20.00                bridge max age            20.00
  hello time           2.00                 bridge hello time         2.00
  forward delay        15.00                bridge forward delay      15.00
  ageing time          300.00               gc interval               4.00
  hello timer          0.00                 tcn timer                 0.00
  topology change timer 0.00                gc timer                  3.24
  flags                TOPOLOGY_CHANGE

eth0 (1)
  port id              8001                 state                forwarding
  designated root      8000.000652585d40    path cost                 100
  designated bridge    8000.000652585d40    message age timer         1.20
  designated port      800a                 forward delay timer       0.00
  designated cost      0                    hold timer                0.00
  flags

eth1 (2)
  port id              8002                 state                forwarding
  designated root      8000.000652585d40    path cost                 100
  designated bridge    8000.00105ad79360    message age timer         0.00
  designated port      8002                 forward delay timer       0.00
  designated cost      100                  hold timer                0.00
  flags
```

Example 5-22 *STP Operation on a Linux Bridge*

```
[root@callisto:~#] tethereal -i eth1
Capturing on eth1
  8.001048     callisto -> 01:80:c2:00:00:00 STP Conf. Root =
32768/00:06:52:58:5d:40  Cost = 100  Port = 0x8002
```

Lab 5-3: OpenBSD Bridging and Spanning Tree

The OpenBSD brconfig utility is used for user-space bridge administration. Consult the man page for details.

Example 5-23 shows the interface status before bridge initialization, Example 5-24 shows the bridge configuration commands, and Examples 5-25 through 5-27 show the resulting status information.

Example 5-23 *OpenBSD Bridge Interfaces Before Initialization*

```
[root@ganymed:~#] ifconfig -A
...
bridge0: flags=0<> mtu 1500
bridge1: flags=0<> mtu 1500
...
```

Example 5-24 *OpenBSD Bridge Configuration*

```
[root@ganymed:~#] brconfig bridge0 add ne5
[root@ganymed:~#] brconfig bridge0 add ne4
[root@ganymed:~#] brconfig bridge0 up
```

Example 5-25 *OpenBSD Bridge Interfaces After Initialization*

```
[root@ganymed:~#] ifconfig -A
...
bridge0: flags=41<UP,RUNNING> mtu 1500
bridge1: flags=0<> mtu 1500
...
```

Example 5-26 *OpenBSD Bridge Group Members*

```
[root@ganymed:~#] brconfig bridge0 addr
00:05:9a:5b:23:fc ne5 1 flags=0<>
00:10:5a:c4:2c:04 ne4 1 flags=0<>
```

Example 5-27 *OpenBSD Bridge Detail Information*

```
[root@ganymed:~#] brconfig -a
bridge0: flags=41<UP,RUNNING>
        Configuration:
                priority 32768 hellotime 2 fwddelay 15 maxage 15
        Interfaces:
                ne4 flags=3<LEARNING,DISCOVER>
                        port 2 priority 128
                ne5 flags=3<LEARNING,DISCOVER>
                        port 3 priority 128
        Addresses (max cache: 100, timeout: 240):
                00:05:9a:5b:23:fc ne5 1 flags=0<>
                00:10:5a:c4:2c:04 ne4 1 flags=0<>
```

A Few Words on Layer 2 Security

Although security considerations are explicitly not part of this book, the following brief discussion of Layer 2 security is the famous exception to the rule. To put things into perspective, just consider the following statements and suggestions when dealing with Layer 2 security:

- In essence, VLANs are not impenetrable, and neither are VLAN trunks.
- STP is slowly converging. If failing, it effectively brings down entire switched networks.
- The more performing a device is, the more it is vulnerable to denial of service (DoS) attacks, and the more disastrous the effects get. If you do not believe this statement, try a **debug all** on a Cisco 12000 backbone router.
- Always configure passwords when using VTP.
- Protect important devices (gateways) with permanent (static) MAC entries.
- Spoofing attacks work using three hooks on several layers:
  — ARP protocol/caches
  — IP source address spoofing
  — DNS resolution

Possible attack patterns include the following:

- Switch saturation might lead to VLAN leaking
- Broadcast and multicast issues
- ARP cache poisoning
- VLAN hopping (forged VLAN identifiers)
- VTP attacks
- STP attacks (BPDUs)

Exercise 5-1: Linux/FreeBSD Ethernet Channel Bonding

Because I do not own enough equipment to build a useful lab, I leave this lab as an exercise to those who want to try. It is not difficult; just follow the instructions in the excellent Linux kernel documentation bonding.txt that comes with the kernel sources and look at the remarks in the ifenslave.c code. This is a truly versatile feature. As guidance, consider the following course of action:

1 I suggest trying Linux-to-Linux bonding via crossover cables as a warm-up exercise. And here comes the good news: This also works with Gigabit Ethernet interfaces!

2   If this works, try to bring up a Fast EtherChannel setup with a Cisco switch. I strongly suggest reading the Cisco.com white papers listed in the "Recommended Reading" section about the Cisco EtherChannel implementation, features, and caveats. Try a channel with two or four interfaces to avoid troubles. Do not expect this setup to work with either PAgP or LACP protocols!

3   If you are blessed with a dual- or quad-port NIC that is recognized by your Linux system, try to configure bonding.

4   If this works as well, observe the load balancing, play with parameters passed to the bonding kernel module, try different transmit policies, and pull one connection to see how the channel behaves.

5   If this works to your satisfaction, try to configure VLAN trunks over your channel and repeat the testing procedure.

6   If you are adventurous and familiar with Sun Solaris trunking configuration, you can try to form a Linux-to-Solaris channel. (Let me know how this behaves.)

7   Try to configure a FreeBSD-to-FreeBSD and Linux-to-FreeBSD channel with the configuration and patch provided below.

If you are interested in the Beowulf cluster package, you can look at how this feature is used for scalable network I/O operation at http://www.beowulf.org/software/bonding.html.

As a little help, Example 5-28 offers a short description of how to configure Cisco-compliant Fast EtherChannel on FreeBSD with two interfaces (ed0, ed1) via the netgraph(3) library after applying the patch from http://people.freebsd.org/~wpaul/FEC/. Example 5-29 shows the resulting status.

Example 5-28 *FreeBSD FastEtherChannel Setup*

```
[root@castor:~#] kldload ng_fec.ko
[root@castor:~#] ngctl mkpeer fec dummy fec
[root@castor:~#] ngctl msg fec0: add_iface '"ed0"'
[root@castor:~#] ngctl msg fec0: add_iface '"ed1"'
[root@castor:~#] ngctl msg fec0: set_mode_inet
```

Example 5-29 *FreeBSD FastEtherChannel Status Information*

```
[root@castor:~#] ifconfig -a
fec0: flags=8802<BROADCAST,SIMPLEX,MULTICAST> mtu 1500
        ether 52:54:05:e3:e4:88
        media: Ethernet none
        status: active
```

Exercise 5-2: STP Operation

Design a switching lab with topology loops featuring VLAN trunks (802.1Q) and one STP-capable UNIX gateway that bridges two VLAN trunks. Observe the STP behavior with monitoring commands (blocking/forwarding) and the BPDUs with a packet analyzer. Then redesign your topology toward a ring-free tree structure by pulling a cable and alter STP default parameters. Try to simulate a hacker attack from one of your switch access ports that belongs to a VLAN. Try to inject fake STP, VTP (if applicable), and VLAN frames with the purpose of manipulating ARP caches, compromising VLAN security, and causing havoc by injecting fake STP information. If you succeed, think about strategies to deal with these attempts, and, while you are at it, derive a Layer 2 security policy for your environment.

Summary

This chapter introduced the important concepts of alias interfaces (secondary addresses), VLAN tagging and trunking, and UNIX bridge and STP operation. It also provided introductory information about the UNIX channel bonding (FastEtherChannel) facilities and advanced bridging capabilities of the FreeBSD operating system. Nevertheless, it also concluded that UNIX gateways are not designed for integration into a large switching/ bridging hierarchy due to the nature and some limitations of their STP implementation.

Recommended Reading

- *Interconnections, Second Edition*, by Radia Perlman. (Addison-Wesley, 1999).
- *Cisco LAN Switching*, by Kennedy Clark and Kevin Hamilton. (Pearson Higher Education, 1999).
- *Building Cisco Multilayer Switched Networks*, by Karen Webb. (Cisco Press, 2000).
- The ifconfig manual page, ifconfig(8)
- The iproute Utility Suite HOWTO, http://www.linuxgrill.com/iproute2.doc.html
- The vlan manual page, vlan(4)
- The bridge manual page, bridge(4)
- IEEE 802.3AD, http://standards.ieee.org/getieee802
- FreeBSD EtherChannel kernel patch, http://people.freebsd.org/~wpaul/FEC/
- Linux bonding driver, http://www.sourceforge.net/projects/bonding
- Cisco white papers about Fast EtherChannel http://www.cisco.com/en/US/tech/ tk389/tk213/tech_protocol_family_home.html
- vconfig Linux VLAN administration utility http://www.candelatech.com/~greear/ vlan.html#setup
- Cisco CCO cabling information, http://www.cisco.com/univercd/cc/td/doc/product/ access/acs_mod/cis3600/hw_inst/cabling/marcabl.htm
- Linux Bridge-STP HOWTO, http://www.tldp.org/HOWTO/BRIDGE-STP-HOWTO/ index.html
- Linux Ethernet bridging, http://bridge.sourceforge.net

## CHAPTER 6

The Analyzer Toolbox, DHCP, and CDP

One of the great advantages of UNIX gateways is the availability of literally thousands of open-source tools and user space utilities. This chapter covers some of them that have proven very useful.

NOTE This chapter intentionally does not cover security-related tools, a subject area far too vast for this book.

The tools covered in this chapter are just a selection from a personal point of view. While on the subject of sniffers, this chapter takes a thorough look at Dynamic Host Configuration Protocol (DHCP) and the Cisco Discovery Protocol (CDP). This is done in the labs that close out the chapter.

Terminal Emulation Software

Terminal emulation packages are used to connect to various external communication program interfaces, such as tn3270 and vt100, and most commonly to directly attached serial interfaces (modems, console ports). The most popular tools are as follows:

- minicom (UNIX)
- C-Kermit (UNIX, VMS), Kermit 95 (Windows)
- TeraTerm Pro (Windows)
- Hyperterm (Windows)

Figure 6-1 shows the main functions of the minicom utility.

Most of the console ports use the connection settings 9600-8-N-1 (9600 bps, 8 data bits, no parity, 1 stop bit). Some require rollover, crossover, or straight-through cabling. They can run at speeds up to 115,200 bps. Older equipment might not have the Universal

Asynchronous Receivers/Transmitters (UARTs) to support that speed and hit the ceiling at 38,400 bps. Figure 6-2 shows the communications settings for TeraTerm as an example.

Figure 6-1 *minicom Main Menu*

Figure 6-2 *TeraTerm Pro Communication Settings*

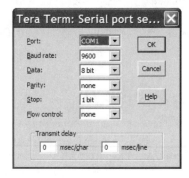

Secure Shell Tools

The Secure Shell protocol (SSH) is a secure replacement for **telnet** and **rlogin**. Consult http://www.openssh.org and http://www.ietf.org for everything related to SSH. The SSH protocol should not require an introduction. Three graphical tools have proven useful:

- Putty (Windows and UNIX graphical user interfaces [GUIs] for SSH, see Figures 6-3 and 6-4)

- WinSCP (Windows GUIs for Secure Copy [SCP], see Figure 6-5)
- SecPanel (UNIX GUI for SSH, see Figure 6-6)

These tools come with an ancillary agent that can assist you with administering automated connection-establishment based on key pairs (*agent forwarding*). With such, you are required to enter key passphrases only once when the agent initializes. The agent needs to remain active, though.

Figure 6-3   *Putty SSH Manager*

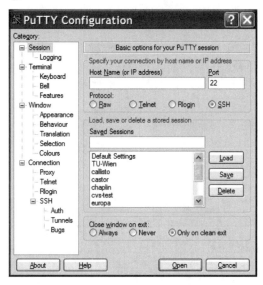

Figure 6-4   *Pageant—Putty's SSH Agent*

Figure 6-5 *WinSCP—A GUI for SCP*

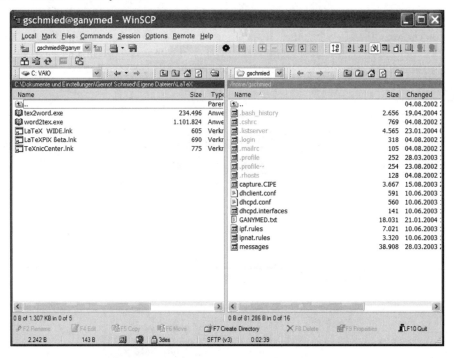

Figure 6-6 *UNIX SecPanel SSH Manager*

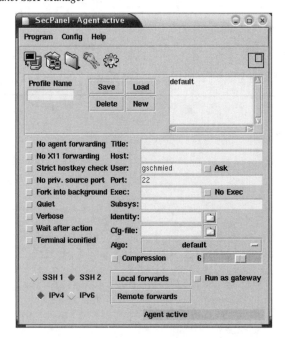

Protocol Analyzer

Protocol analyzers (also called sniffers) are versatile tools for a variety of tasks:

- Debugging network problems
- Verifying proper operation of cryptographic protocols
- Diagnosing flawed protocol implementations
- Identifying unwanted traffic
- Replaying of stored traffic for testing purposes
- Reverse-engineering protocol implementations
- Performing security checks
- Identifying network background noise (broadcast protocols, NetBIOS, Appletalk)

If you ever find yourself confronted with learning or reverse-engineering an unknown or unfamiliar protocol, equip yourself with a sniffer, a hex editor, test gear, and any RFCs or standard documents you can find and start investigating the behavior of the protocol, the types of headers involved, the state transitions, and so on. This is really the best way of understanding the internals of protocols, and probably the most efficient as well. If available, you can also compare your observations with open source implementations and derive additional clues from the sources. When debugging a real-life problem, it is always a good approach to start from the bottom and work your way to the top of the stack in a structured manner.

Most UNIX systems come with tcpdump installed, which is a standard text-based protocol analyzer. Several graphical front ends and ancillary tools exist for tcpdump. By the way, Solaris provides the snoop utility for sniffing. Most people's tool of choice is the ethereal graphical protocol analyzer, which also provides a text-only version called tethereal (see Figure 6-7). The ngrep tool enables you to apply the functionality of the well-known UNIX grep utility to the network layer. It is a practical tool as well.

Figure 6-7 *GUI of the Ethereal Sniffer*

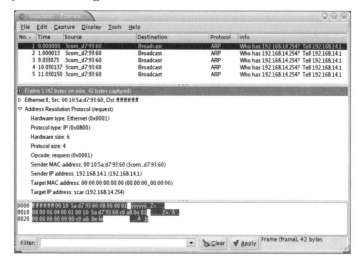

Statistical Tools

ntop, designed by Dr. Luca Deri, is an advanced graphical tool to dissect network traffic, derive statistics, and produce traffic distributions (see Figure 6-8). It is also capable of operating as a NetFlow collector/probe and runs on an embedded web server. You can download it from http://www.ntop.org.

Figure 6-8 *ntop User Interface*

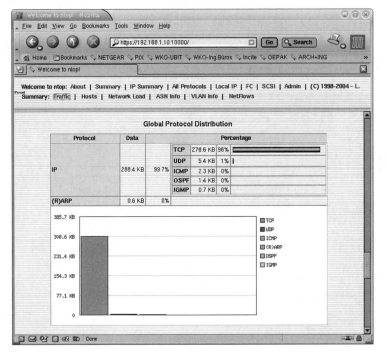

Port Scanners

Modern port scanners can probe in stealthy, patient, and subtle ways, in combination with operating system fingerprinting, which refers to the art of guessing the operating system from stack peculiarities and additional hints derived from intelligent probing. Two of the most popular tools are the nmap and strobe programs. Example 6-1 provides two examples of these tools in action. The /etc/services file on UNIX systems provides a mapping between TCD/UDP port numbers and their textual names. This list is maintained by Internet Assigned Numbers Authority (IANA, http://www.iana.org/assignments/port-numbers) and consists of three port groups:

- Well-known ports (0–1023)
- Registered ports (1024–49151)
- Dynamic ports (49152–65535)

Example 6-1   nmap *and* strobe *Port-Scan Examples*

```
[root@castor:~#] nmap -p 1-4000 localhost

Starting nmap V. 2.54BETA34 ( www.insecure.org/nmap/ )
Interesting ports on localhost.nerdzone.org (127.0.0.1):
(The 3994 ports scanned but not shown below are in state: closed)
Port       State       Service
22/tcp     open        ssh
1899/tcp   open        unknown
2070/tcp   open        unknown
2410/tcp   open        unknown
2560/tcp   open        unknown
3046/tcp   open        unknown

Nmap run completed -- 1 IP address (1 host up) scanned in 23 seconds

[root@ganymed:~#] strobe -b 1 -e 4000 localhost
strobe 1.05 (c) 1995-1999 Julian Assange <proff@iq.org>.
localhost    22 ssh            Secure Shell - RSA encrypted rsh
                -> SSH-2.0-OpenSSH_3.4\n
localhost    80 http           www www-http World Wide Web HTTP
             www               World Wide Web HTTP [TXL]
```

socklist and netstat

socklist(8) is a useful tool for displaying open TCP/UDP sockets in an overview fashion
(see Example 6-2).

Example 6-2   socklist *Output*

```
[root@callisto:~#] socklist
type  port    inode    uid    pid    fd   name
tcp   32768      986     29    681     6   rpc.statd
tcp   32769     1058      0    754     4   rpc.mountd
tcp     929     1042      0    749     4   rpc.rquotad
tcp   32770     1632      0   1157     6   xinetd
tcp     963     1631      0   1157     5   xinetd
tcp     139     1183      0    844     9   smbd
tcp     111      913      0    653     4   portmap
tcp    6000     1986      0   1449     1   X
tcp   10000     1924      0   1385     4   miniserv.pl
tcp      21     1636      0   1157     9   xinetd
tcp      22     1520      0   1066     3   sshd
tcp     505     2968      0   1343     4   rcd
tcp   33424    28161    500   3704    47   mozilla-bin
tcp      22    27806      0   3776     4   sshd
udp   32768      983     29    681     4   rpc.statd
udp    2049     1082      0      0     0
udp   32769     1055      0    754     3   rpc.mountd
udp   32770     1088      0      0     0
udp     137     3257      0    849    15   nmbd
udp     137     1194      0    849    10   nmbd
udp     137     1192      0    849     8   nmbd
```

continues

Example 6-2 socklist *Output (Continued)*

```
udp    137      1189      0    849    6  nmbd
udp    138      3258      0    849   16  nmbd
udp    138      1195      0    849   11  nmbd
udp    138      1193      0    849    9  nmbd
udp    138      1190      0    849    7  nmbd
udp  10000      1925      0   1385    5  miniserv.pl
udp    926      1037      0    749    3  rpc.rquotad
udp     69      1635      0   1157    8  xinetd
udp    111       910      0    653    3  portmap
udp    500      1515      0    939   10  pluto
udp    123      1704      0   1175    7  ntpd
udp    123      1703      0   1175    6  ntpd
udp    123      1702      0   1175    5  ntpd
udp    123      1701      0   1175    4  ntpd
```

netstat(8) provides additional details about the UNIX network subsystem, such as network connections, routing tables, interface statistics, and multicast memberships (see Example 6-3).

Example 6-3 netstat *Output*

```
[root@callisto:~#] netstat -i
Kernel Interface table
Iface   MTU Met    RX-OK RX-ERR RX-DRP RX-OVR   TX-OK TX-ERR TX-DRP TX-OVR Flg
eth0   1500   0       0      0      0      0     439      0      0      0 BMRU
eth1   1500   0   10098      0      0      0    8208      0      0      0 BMRU
eth1:  1500   0    - no statistics available -                          BMRU
ipsec 16260   0       0      0      0      0    7096      0    129      0 ORU
lo    16436   0      64      0      0      0      64      0      0      0 LRU


[root@callisto:~#] netstat -l
Active Internet connections (only servers)
Proto Recv-Q Send-Q Local Address           Foreign Address         State
tcp        0      0 *:32768                 *:*                     LISTEN
tcp        0      0 *:32769                 *:*                     LISTEN
tcp        0      0 *:929                   *:*                     LISTEN
tcp        0      0 localhost:32770         *:*                     LISTEN
tcp        0      0 *:pkcipe                *:*                     LISTEN
tcp        0      0 *:netbios-ssn           *:*                     LISTEN
tcp        0      0 *:sunrpc                *:*                     LISTEN
tcp        0      0 *:x11                   *:*                     LISTEN
tcp        0      0 callisto:10000          *:*                     LISTEN
tcp        0      0 *:ftp                   *:*                     LISTEN
tcp        0      0 *:ssh                   *:*                     LISTEN
tcp        0      0 *:505                   *:*                     LISTEN
udp        0      0 *:32768                 *:*
udp        0      0 *:nfs                   *:*
udp        0      0 *:32769                 *:*
udp        0      0 *:32770                 *:*
udp        0      0 192.168.45.2:netbios-ns *:*
udp        0      0 192.168.14.1:netbios-ns *:*
udp        0      0 callisto:netbios-ns     *:*
udp        0      0 *:netbios-ns            *:*
udp        0      0 192.168.45.:netbios-dgm *:*
udp        0      0 192.168.14.:netbios-dgm *:*
```

Example 6-3 netstat *Output (Continued)*

```
udp        0        0 callisto:netbios-dgm    *:*
udp        0        0 *:netbios-dgm           *:*
udp        0        0 *:10000                 *:*
udp        0        0 *:926                   *:*
udp        0        0 *:tftp                  *:*
udp        0        0 *:sunrpc                *:*
udp        0        0 callisto:isakmp         *:*
udp        0        0 callisto:ntp            *:*
udp        0        0 192.168.14.1:ntp        *:*
udp        0        0 localhost:ntp           *:*
udp        0        0 *:ntp                   *:*
Active UNIX domain sockets (only servers)
Proto RefCnt Flags       Type     State       I-Node Path
unix  2      [ ACC ]     STREAM   LISTENING   2969   /var/run/rcd/rcd
unix  2      [ ACC ]     STREAM   LISTENING   2564   /tmp/ksocket-gschmied/
kdeinit-:0
unix  2      [ ACC ]     STREAM   LISTENING   2569   /tmp/.ICE-unix/dcop1571-
1062316048
unix  2      [ ACC ]     STREAM   LISTENING   2704   /tmp/.ICE-unix/1598
unix  2      [ ACC ]     STREAM   LISTENING   2592   /tmp/ksocket-gschmied/
klauncherKIy0fa.slave-socket
unix  2      [ ACC ]     STREAM   LISTENING   1404   /var/run/pluto.ctl
unix  2      [ ACC ]     STREAM   LISTENING   2675   /tmp/mcop-gschmied/
callisto-0631-3f51a81c
unix  2      [ ACC ]     STREAM   LISTENING   1987   /tmp/.X11-unix/X0
unix  2      [ ACC ]     STREAM   LISTENING   1712   /dev/gpmctl
unix  2      [ ACC ]     STREAM   LISTENING   1766   /tmp/.font-unix/fs7100


[root@callisto:~#] netstat -s
Ip:
    11160 total packets received
    0 forwarded
    0 incoming packets discarded
    11143 incoming packets delivered
    10339 requests sent out
Icmp:
    0 ICMP messages received
    0 input ICMP messages failed.
    ICMP input histogram:
    4 ICMP messages sent
    0 ICMP messages failed
    ICMP output histogram:
        destination unreachable: 4
Tcp:
    703 active connections openings
    2 passive connection openings
    0 failed connection attempts
    2 connection resets received
    2 connections established
    10272 segments received
    9535 segments sent out
    37 segments retransmitted
    0 bad segments received.
    2 resets sent
```

continues

Example 6-3 netstat *Output (Continued)*

```
Udp:
    875 packets received
    4 packets to unknown port received.
    0 packet receive errors
    800 packets sent
TcpExt:
    ArpFilter: 0
    21 TCP sockets finished time wait in fast timer
    597 delayed acks sent
    2 delayed acks further delayed because of locked socket
    Quick ack mode was activated 30 times
    3 packets directly queued to recvmsg prequeue.
    1 packets directly received from prequeue.
    4825 packets header predicted
    TCPPureAcks: 1549
    TCPHPAcks: 2674
    TCPRenoRecovery: 0
    TCPSackRecovery: 0
    TCPSACKReneging: 0
    TCPFACKReorder: 0
    TCPSACKReorder: 0
    TCPRenoReorder: 0
    TCPTSReorder: 0
    TCPFullUndo: 0
    TCPPartialUndo: 0
    TCPDSACKUndo: 0
    TCPLossUndo: 9
    TCPLoss: 0
    TCPLostRetransmit: 0
    TCPRenoFailures: 0
    TCPSackFailures: 0
    TCPLossFailures: 0
    TCPFastRetrans: 0
    TCPForwardRetrans: 0
    TCPSlowStartRetrans: 0
    TCPTimeouts: 22
    TCPRenoRecoveryFail: 0
    TCPSackRecoveryFail: 0
    TCPSchedulerFailed: 0
    TCPRcvCollapsed: 0
    TCPDSACKOldSent: 10
    TCPDSACKOfoSent: 0
    TCPDSACKRecv: 1
    TCPDSACKOfoRecv: 0
    TCPAbortOnSyn: 0
    TCPAbortOnData: 0
    TCPAbortOnClose: 1
    TCPAbortOnMemory: 0
    TCPAbortOnTimeout: 0
    TCPAbortOnLinger: 0
    TCPAbortFailed: 0
    TCPMemoryPressures: 0
```

The Linux **netstat -M** command sequence additionally displays masqueraded connections. **netstat** options can be combined with the **-ev** switch for extended and even more verbose output (type **netstat -ev**). We will extensively rely on **netstat -rn** (the routing table) and **netstat -i**. **netstat -i** presents interface counter statistics such as transmitted and received frames, frame errors, and dropped frames. The **netstat -g** multicast command sequence is discussed in detail in Chapter 14, "Multicast Architectures."

Note that **netstat** displays various types of sockets:

- TCP
- UDP
- Raw
- UNIX domain sockets

Ping and Traceroute Combinations

Among the most useful tools for a network engineer's toolbox are those that combine ping, DNS lookup, and traceroute capabilities. This section introduces three of them (mtr, PingPlotter, and VisualRoute).

mtr is a command-line tool for real-time path surveillance and statistics. PingPlotter and VisualRoute are commercial graphical tools available as trial downloads that add a great deal of statistics and correlation analysis to the ping and traceroute tools and allow probing over an extended period of time. Figures 6-9 through 6-11 provide example screenshots of these tools. VisualRoute is a product of Visualware Inc. (http://www.visualware.com), and PingPlotter is a product of Nessoft, LLC (http://www.nessoft.com).

Figure 6-9   *mtr Utility*

Figure 6-10   *PingPlotter*

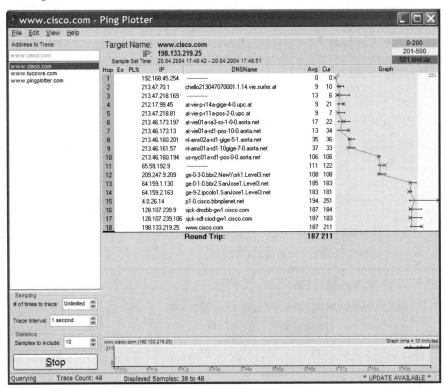

NOTE   Just a reminder when filtering IP traffic: The UNIX traceroute implementations use Internet
Control Message Protocol (ICMP) *and* User Datagram Protocol (UDP), whereas the
Windows implementation relies solely on ICMP. However, some UNIX traceroutes can be
forced to use ICMP probe packets as well.

UNIX gateways are capable of resembling what is referred to as an *extended ping* in the
Cisco world. This can be accomplished with the command-line switch **ping -I [ifaddr]** on
OpenBSD and Linux, and **ping -S [ifaddr]** on FreeBSD. There is also an equivalent for an
extended trace on UNIX. This is done via the **traceroute -s [ifaddr]** command sequence
on OpenBSD and FreeBSD. Both the ping and traceroute commands under UNIX have
interesting and nontrivial features. Look at the man pages for further details.

If you require pings or traces from distant sources, you can find a variety of looking glasses
and Domain Name System (DNS)/whois front ends all over the Internet (http://www.
traceroute.org). You will read more about this in Chapter 10, "ISP Connectivity with
BGPv4: An Exterior Gateway Path-Vector Routing Protocol for Interdomain Routing."
Figure 6-12 shows an example looking-glass web interface of the Vienna Internet exchange
(VIX), a public noncommercial peering point in Austria (http://www.vix.at).

Figure 6-11 *VisualRoute*

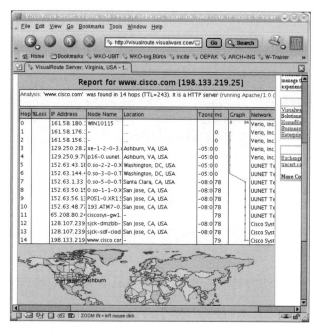

Figure 6-12 *Looking Glass of the Vienna Internet Exchange (VIX)*

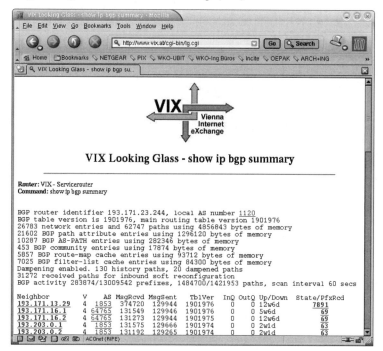

DNS Auditing Tools

DNS consists of two parts: a resolver (the client part) and Internet name server hierarchies. Consult the manual pages for operation details as well as the man page for resolver(3) or resolv.conf(5). The most widespread package is the Berkeley Internet Name Domain (BIND) toolset; however, there are alternatives and new approaches for securing name server communications and signing/hashing information exchange (DNSsec). Discussion of these tools goes beyond the scope of this book. We will use them in a limited way when discussing DNS round-robin (DNS RR) as a load-balancing approach. The standard query tools are nslookup, dig, and host (see Example 6-4).

Example 6-4 *DNS Toolbox*—dig, nslookup, *and* host

```
[root@callisto:~#] dig www.cisco.com

; <<>> DiG 9.2.2 <<>> www.cisco.com
;; global options:  printcmd
;; Got answer:
;; ->>HEADER<<- opcode: QUERY, status: NOERROR, id: 61084
;; flags: qr rd ra; QUERY: 1, ANSWER: 1, AUTHORITY: 2, ADDITIONAL: 0

;; QUESTION SECTION:
;www.cisco.com.                  IN      A

;; ANSWER SECTION:
www.cisco.com.          36356   IN      A       198.133.219.25

;; AUTHORITY SECTION:
cisco.com.              38430   IN      NS      ns1.cisco.com.
cisco.com.              38430   IN      NS      ns2.cisco.com.

;; Query time: 9 msec
;; SERVER: 195.34.133.10#53(195.34.133.10)
;; WHEN: Sat Jan 31 10:31:42 2004
;; MSG SIZE  rcvd: 83

[root@callisto:~#] nslookup www.cisco.com
Note:  nslookup is deprecated and may be removed from future releases.
Consider using the `dig' or `host' programs instead.  Run nslookup with
the `-sil[ent]' option to prevent this message from appearing.
Server:         195.34.133.10
Address:        195.34.133.10#53

Non-authoritative answer:
Name:   www.cisco.com
Address: 198.133.219.25

[root@callisto:~#] host www.cisco.com
www.cisco.com has address 198.133.219.25
```

In addition, it is worth mentioning another useful tool, dnstracer; Example 6-5 shows it in use.

Example 6-5 *dnstracer Example Output*

```
[root@callisto:~#] dnstracer -s . www.cisco.com -o
Tracing to www.cisco.com via A.ROOT-SERVERS.NET, timeout 15 seconds
A.ROOT-SERVERS.NET [.] (198.41.0.4)
 |\___ M.GTLD-SERVERS.NET [com] (192.55.83.30)
 |     |\___ NS2.cisco.com [cisco.com] (192.135.250.69) Got authoritative answer
 |     \___ NS1.cisco.com [cisco.com] (128.107.241.185) Got authoritative answer
 |\___ E.GTLD-SERVERS.NET [com] (192.12.94.30)
 |     |\___ NS2.cisco.com [cisco.com] (192.135.250.69) (cached)
 |     \___ NS1.cisco.com [cisco.com] (128.107.241.185) (cached)
 |\___ K.GTLD-SERVERS.NET [com] (192.52.178.30)
 |     |\___ NS2.cisco.com [cisco.com] (192.135.250.69) (cached)
 |     \___ NS1.cisco.com [cisco.com] (128.107.241.185) (cached)
 |\___ J.GTLD-SERVERS.NET [com] (192.48.79.30)
 |     |\___ NS2.cisco.com [cisco.com] (192.135.250.69) (cached)
 |     \___ NS1.cisco.com [cisco.com] (128.107.241.185) (cached)
 |\___ F.GTLD-SERVERS.NET [com] (192.35.51.30)
 |     |\___ NS2.cisco.com [cisco.com] (192.135.250.69) (cached)
 |     \___ NS1.cisco.com [cisco.com] (128.107.241.185) (cached)
 |\___ L.GTLD-SERVERS.NET [com] (192.41.162.30)
 |     |\___ NS2.cisco.com [cisco.com] (192.135.250.69) (cached)
 |     \___ NS1.cisco.com [cisco.com] (128.107.241.185) (cached)
 |\___ D.GTLD-SERVERS.NET [com] (192.31.80.30)
 |     |\___ NS2.cisco.com [cisco.com] (192.135.250.69) (cached)
 |     \___ NS1.cisco.com [cisco.com] (128.107.241.185) (cached)
 |\___ B.GTLD-SERVERS.NET [com] (192.33.14.30)
 |     |\___ NS2.cisco.com [cisco.com] (192.135.250.69) (cached)
 |     \___ NS1.cisco.com [cisco.com] (128.107.241.185) (cached)
 |\___ I.GTLD-SERVERS.NET [com] (192.43.172.30)
 |     |\___ NS2.cisco.com [cisco.com] (192.135.250.69) (cached)
 |     \___ NS1.cisco.com [cisco.com] (128.107.241.185) (cached)
 |\___ C.GTLD-SERVERS.NET [com] (192.26.92.30)
 |     |\___ NS2.cisco.com [cisco.com] (192.135.250.69) (cached)
 |     \___ NS1.cisco.com [cisco.com] (128.107.241.185) (cached)
 |\___ H.GTLD-SERVERS.NET [com] (192.54.112.30)
 |     |\___ NS2.cisco.com [cisco.com] (192.135.250.69) (cached)
 |     \___ NS1.cisco.com [cisco.com] (128.107.241.185) (cached)
 |\___ G.GTLD-SERVERS.NET [com] (192.42.93.30)
 |     |\___ ns2.cisco.com [cisco.com] (192.135.250.69) (cached)
 |     \___ ns1.cisco.com [cisco.com] (128.107.241.185) (cached)
  \___ A.GTLD-SERVERS.NET [com] (192.5.6.30)
        |\___ ns2.cisco.com [cisco.com] (192.135.250.69) (cached)
        \___ ns1.cisco.com [cisco.com] (128.107.241.185) (cached)

NS1.cisco.com (128.107.241.185)        www.cisco.com -> 198.133.219.25
NS2.cisco.com (192.135.250.69)         www.cisco.com -> 198.133.219.25
```

The Windows Sam Spade freeware toolbox contains all of these tools and more, as shown in Figure 6-13.

Figure 6-13 *Windows Sam Spade Toolbox*

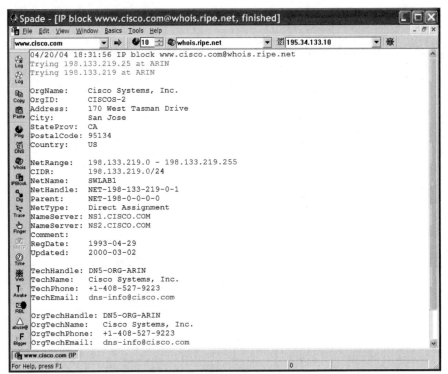

Traffic and Packet Generators

This section discusses the packet-generation capabilities of the BSD ipfilter firewall package, the Linux kernel module packet generator, and some additional tools for heavy load testing and simulated denial-of-service (DoS) patterns. This arsenal is useful to test traffic shapers, forwarding, filtering performance, network quality of service (QoS), stateful inspection, and Network Address Translation (NAT), just to name a few. Traffic generators generally are concerned with a huge amount of output, whereas packet generators typically are used as a "scalpel" to test firewalls and protocol implementations/ compliance.

CAUTION   Exercise extreme care when using these facilities in real-life networks; they are extremely powerful. Check the traffic with a sniffer; you will find what is going on pretty impressive.

What You Need in a Small Toolbox

The following tools have proven useful for packet and traffic creation as well as network testing. They are quite similar in nature, and it is really up to you to decide on a favorite:

- Aicmpsend
- Sendip
- IP Sorcery (ipmagic/magic tools)
- Excalibur
- Hping2
- Traffic (client/server)
- Scapy

Example 6-6 presents aicmpsend, sendip, and ipmagic in action. You can deploy them to test security installations and protocol behavior. See the "Recommended Reading" section at the end of this chapter for download locations of these tools.

Example 6-6 *Selection of Packet-Generator Tools*

```
[root@callisto:~#] aicmpsend -d 192.168.1.1 -E
ICMP packet:  1    TTL=64
Sending ICMP error from 127.0.0.1 to 192.168.1.1.
Data:
ICMP error:  Echo

[root@callisto:~#] sendip -p ipv4 192.168.1.254

[root@callisto:~#] ipmagic -h
Usage: ipmagic [options]
IP: [-is|-id|-ih|-iv|-il|-it|-io|-id|-ip]
-is: source host or address def. 127.0.0.1
-id: source destination or address def. 127.0.0.1
-ih: IP header length def. 5
-iv: IP version def. 4
-il: Time-to-Live def. 64
-it: Type-of-Service def. 0
-io: IP frag offset [(D)on't Fragment|(M)ore Fragments|(F)ragment|(N)one]
-i:  IP packet ID for fragmentation def. 0
-ip: IP protocol [TCP|UDP|ICMP|IP] def. TCP
-iO: IP options
TCP: [-ts|-td|-to|-tq|-ta|-tf|-tw|-tu]
-ts: TCP source port, def. rand()
-td: TCP destination port def. 80
-to: TCP data offset of header def. 5
-tq: TCP sequence number def. rand()
-ta: TCP ack sequence number def. 0
-tf: TCP flags [(S)yn|(A)ck|(F)in|(P)ush|(R)st|(U)rg|(N)one] def. S
-tw: TCP Window Size def. rand()
-tu: TCP urg pointer def. 0
UDP: [-us|-ud|-ul]
```

continues

Example 6-6   *Selection of Packet-Generator Tools (Continued)*

```
-us: UDP source port def. rand()
-ud: UDP destination port def. 161
-ul: UDP length
      RIP: [-uR|-uRc|-uRv]
      -uR: Send default RIP packet to port 520
      -uRc: RIP command [RQ|RS|TN|TF|SR|TQ|TS|TA|UQ|US|UA] def. RQ
      For a list of RIP commands run program with -h rip
      -uRv: RIP version [1|2] def. 2
Note: Entry Tables should be used with response packets[RS|TS|US]
      -uRa(1|2|etc.): RIP Entry table Address exmp. -uRa1
      -uRn(1|2|etc.): RIP Entry table Netmask, exmp. -uRn2
      -uRh(1|2|etc.): RIP Entry table Next Hop, exmp. -uRn(num)
      -uRm(1|2|etc.): RIP Entry table Metric
      -uRr(1|2|etc.): RIP Entry table Route Tag
      -uRe: Add default RIP entry table to packet
ICMP: [-ct|-cs]
-ct: ICMP type def. ECHO REQUEST
-cs: ICMP sub code def. 0
-ci: ICMP sequence ID def. 0
For list of ICMP Types and Subcodes run program with -h icmp.
IGMP:[-gt|-gc|-ga|-gn]
-gt: IGMP type [D|L|M|MT|MR|P|R1|R2|R3] def. M
-gc: IGMP sub code for types P and D def. 0
-gm: IGMP Max. resp. Time for Queries ie. MR
-ga: IGMP group address def. 0
-gn: IGMP no router alert or no internetwork Type-Of-Service [r|i|l]
For list of IGMP Types and Subcodes run program with -h igmp.
OSPF:[-ov|-ot|-or|-oe|-oa|-ou]
-ov: OSPF Version
-ot: OSPF Type[(H)ello|(D)b Desc.|(R)equest|(U)pdate|(A)ck]
-or: OSPF Router ID
-oe: OSPF Area ID
-oa: OSPF Auth Type[(N)one|(P)ass|(C)rypto]
-ou <data>: OSPF Authentication Data
-D "<data>": for datapayload
-N <num packets>: send <num packets> number packets
-S <verbosity>: (v)erbose, (s)hort, (t)urn off packet snoop
-v: print version
```

The BSD ipfilter Traffic Generator

The BSD ipfilter stateful firewall package comes equipped with the following tools primarily designed for firewall testing:

- ipsend
- ipresend
- iptest

Consult the manual pages for further information. Example 6-7 and Example 6-8 present demonstrations of the BSD iptest, ipsend, and ipresend tools.

Example 6-7 *BSD ipfilter Ancillary Tools in Action*

```
[root@castor:~#] iptest
Usage: iptest [options] dest
        options:
                    -d device      Send out on this device
                    -g gateway     IP gateway to use if non-local dest.
                    -m mtu         fake MTU to use when sending out
                    -p pointtest
                    -s src         source address for IP packet
                    -1             Perform test 1 (IP header)
                    -2             Perform test 2 (IP options)
                    -3             Perform test 3 (ICMP)
                    -4             Perform test 4 (UDP)
                    -5             Perform test 5 (TCP)
                    -6             Perform test 6 (overlapping fragments)
                    -7             Perform test 7 (random packets)

[root@castor:~#] iptest -d ed0 -g 192.168.7.254 -1 192.168.14.1
Device:  ed0
Source:  192.168.7.7
Dest:    192.168.14.1
Gateway: 192.168.7.254
mtu:     1500
1.1. sending packets with ip_hl < ip_len
7
1.2. sending packets with ip_hl > ip_len
12
1.3. ip_v < 4
3
1.4. ip_v > 4
15
1.5.0 ip_len < packet size (size++, long packets)
63
1.5.1 ip_len < packet size (ip_len-, short packets)
10
1.6.0 ip_len > packet size (increase ip_len)
63
1.6.1 ip_len > packet size (size--, short packets)
10
1.7.0 Zero length fragments (ip_off = 0x2000)
1.7.1 Zero length fragments (ip_off = 0x3000)
1.7.2 Zero length fragments (ip_off = 0xa000)
1.7.3 Zero length fragments (ip_off = 0x0100)
1.8.1 63k packet + 1k fragment at offset 0x1ffe
65792
1.8.2 63k packet + 1k fragment at offset 0x1ffe
skip 12800
skip 37376
skip 61952
65792
1.8.3 33k packet
33536
```

continues

Example 6-7 *BSD ipfilter Ancillary Tools in Action (Continued)*

```
1.9. ip_off & 0x8000 == 0x8000
1.10.0 ip_ttl = 255
1.10.1 ip_ttl = 128
1.10.2 ip_ttl = 0
```

Example 6-8 *Example Use of the* **ipsend** *Utility*

```
[root@castor:~#] ipsend
Usage: ipsend [options] dest [flags]
        options:
                -d      debug mode
                -i device       Send out on this device
                -f fragflags    can set IP_MF or IP_DF
                -g gateway      IP gateway to use if non-local dest.
                -I code,type[,gw[,dst[,src]]]   Set ICMP protocol
                -m mtu          fake MTU to use when sending out
                -P protocol     Set protocol by name
                -s src          source address for IP packet
                -T              Set TCP protocol
                -t port         destination port
                -U              Set UDP protocol
                -v      verbose mode
                -w <window>     Set the TCP window size
Usage: ipsend [-dv] -L <filename>
        options:
                -d      debug mode
                -L filename     Use IP language for sending packets
                -v      verbose mode

[root@castor:~#] ipsend -i ed0 -P tcp -g 192.168.7.254 192.168.14.1
Device:  ed0
Source:  192.168.7.7
Dest:    192.168.14.1
Gateway: 192.168.7.254
mtu:     1500

[root@castor:~#] ipresend
Usage: ipresend [options] <-r filename|-R filename>
                -r filename     snoop data file to resend
                -R filename     libpcap data file to resend
        options:
                -d device       Send out on this device
                -g gateway      IP gateway to use if non-local dest.
                -m mtu          fake MTU to use when sending out
```

The Linux Kernel Packet Generator

The Linux packet generator requires compiled-in support as a kernel module (pktgen.o); it is used via a script derived from its documentation (pktgen.txt in the Linux 2.4.x kernel documentation folder). The source code of this script is also provided in Example 6-9.

Example 6-9 *Script That Interacts with the Linux Kernel Packet-Generator Module*

```
#! /bin/sh

modprobe pktgen

function pgset() {
    local result

    echo $1 > /proc/net/pg

    result=`cat /proc/net/pg | fgrep "Result: OK:"`
    if [ "$result" = "" ]; then
        cat /proc/net/pg | fgrep Result:
    fi
}

function pg() {
    echo inject > /proc/net/pg
    cat /proc/net/pg
}

pgset "odev eth0"        # set output interface
pgset "dst 192.168.7.7"  # set IP destination address
pgset "count 40000"      # set numbers of packets to send

#pgset "multiskb 1"       use multiple SKBs for packet generation
#pgset "multiskb 0"       use single SKB for all transmits
#pgset "pkt_size 9014"    sets packet size to 9014
#pgset "frags 5"          packet will consist of 5 fragments
#pgset "ipg 5000"         sets artificial gap inserted between packets
#                         to 5000 nanoseconds
#pgset "dstmac 00:00:00:00:00:00"    sets MAC destination address
#pgset stop               aborts injection
```

Performance-Testing and Network-Benchmarking Tools

This family of tools provides network performance information and benchmarking by usually taking a client/server approach that allows collecting very accurate end-to-end information and statistics. These tools are powerful and complex; refer to the repository documentation for further details. Some interesting representatives of this family of tools are as follows:

- Netperf (Network Performance Benchmarking)
- NetPIPE (Network Protocol Independent Performance Evaluator)
- ttcp/wsttcp (Test TCP [TTCP]; a benchmarking tool for measuring TCP and UDP performance)

NOTE   A thorough discussion of network performance measurement would dive too much into stack internals and go far beyond the scope of this book.

Lab 6-1: Using Sniffers—DHCP Example

Most UNIX systems use the Internet Standards Consortium (ISC) DHCP package, which includes these tools:

- A DHCP server (dhcpd)
- A DHCP client (dhclient)
- A DHCP relay agent (dhcrelay)
- The dhcping and dhcdump utilities

DHCP relays are necessary when the DHCP server does not reside on the same subnet as the DHCP client. The package can be retrieved from http://www.isc.org/products/DHCP/.

In this lab, we will observe a typical client/server session to practice with the protocol analyzers described in this chapter. Figure 6-14 shows the lab setup for the DHCP scenario.

Figure 6-14 *DHCP Lab Scenario*

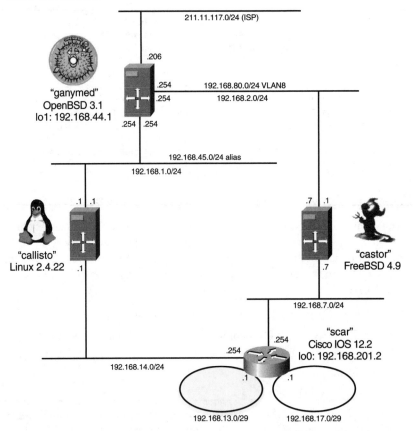

The ISC DHCP package keeps track of leases in /var/db/dhcpd.leases and consists of two configuration files:

- /etc/dhcpd.conf
- /etc/dhclient.conf

This package offers a variety of options and features, much more than can be covered in this lab. The example configurations in this chapter are provided without comments; consult the manual pages and package documentation for further details. The package sources contain all relevant RFCs and draft proposals.

Example 6-10 shows an example of the UNIX dhcpd configuration; Example 6-11 shows the start procedure for a particular interface.

Example 6-10 *Castor /etc/dhcpd.conf*

```
[root@castor:~#] cat /etc/dhcpd.conf

authoritative;
ddns-update-style ad-hoc;

subnet 192.168.7.0 netmask 255.255.255.0 {
  range 192.168.7.10 192.168.7.250;
  option routers 192.168.7.7;
  default-lease-time 600;
  max-lease-time 7200;
  option domain-name-servers 195.34.133.10,195.34.133.11;
}
```

Example 6-11 *Starting the DHCP Daemon*

```
[root@castor:~#] dhcpd -cf /etc/dhcpd.conf -lf /var/db/dhcpd.leases ed0
```

This setup was tested with a Windows XP notebook. Example 6-12 shows the resulting sniffer output on castor, and Example 6-13 shows the corresponding log entries. In Example 6-13, you can also observe the initial lease and the result of the Windows command sequences **ipconfig /release** and **ipconfig /renew**.

Example 6-12 *Sniffing the DHCP Dialogue*

```
[root@castor:~#] tethereal -i ed0
0.000000 192.168.7.250 -> castor DHCP DHCP Request  - Transaction ID 0xe9603354
0.015647 castor -> 192.168.7.250 DHCP DHCP ACK      - Transaction ID 0xe9603354
6.196025 192.168.7.250 -> castor DHCP DHCP Release  - Transaction ID 0xdc19cc67
```

Example 6-13 *DHCP Daemon Operation Logs in the /var/db/dhcpd.leases File*

```
[root@castor:~#] cat /var/db/dhcpd.leases

lease 192.168.7.250 {
  starts 1 2002/11/25 10:44:45;
  ends 1 2002/11/25 10:54:45;
  binding state active;
```

continues

Example 6-13 *DHCP Daemon Operation Logs in the /var/db/dhcpd.leases File (Continued)*

```
      next binding state free;
      hardware ethernet 08:00:46:64:74:1b;                # initial lease
      uid "\001\010\000Fdt\033";
      client-hostname "pollux";
    }
    lease 192.168.7.250 {
      starts 1 2002/11/25 10:44:45;
      ends 1 2002/11/25 10:44:52;                         # release
      tstp 1 2002/11/25 10:44:52;
      binding state free;
      hardware ethernet 08:00:46:64:74:1b;
      uid "\001\010\000Fdt\033";
    }
    lease 192.168.7.250 {
      starts 1 2002/11/25 10:45:06;
      ends 1 2002/11/25 10:55:06;
      binding state active;                               # renew
      next binding state free;
      hardware ethernet 08:00:46:64:74:1b;
      uid "\001\010\000Fdt\033";
      client-hostname "pollux";
    }
```

Now we will configure a DHCP server on a Cisco router (scar) and request and release a DHCP address from a UNIX client workstation (castor). The corresponding client configuration is shown in Example 6-14, the corresponding server configuration in Example 6-15. Examples 6-16 and 6-17 show the resulting protocol dialogue and statistics, including a release request and completion.

Example 6-14 */etc/dhclient.conf on Castor*

```
[root@castor:~#] cat /etc/dhclient.conf

request subnet-mask, broadcast-address, time-offset, routers,
        domain-name, domain-name-servers, host-name;
require subnet-mask, domain-name-servers;
timeout 60;
retry 60;
reboot 10;
select-timeout 5;
initial-interval 2;
script "/etc/dhclient-script";
media "-link0 -link1 -link2", "link0 link1";
reject 192.168.7.253;
```

Example 6-15 *Cisco DHCP Server Configuration*

```
scar# show running-config
...
!
ip dhcp excluded-address 192.168.7.254
ip dhcp excluded-address 192.168.7.7
```

Example 6-15 *Cisco DHCP Server Configuration (Continued)*

```
!
ip dhcp pool LAN
   network 192.168.7.0 255.255.255.0
   default-router 192.168.7.254
   dns-server 195.34.133.10
!
...
```

Example 6-16 *DHCP Client Request*

```
[root@castor:~#] tethereal -i ed0
 15.654523   0.0.0.0 -> 255.255.255.255 DHCP DHCP Discover - Transaction ID 0xaf358d15
 17.657345 192.168.7.254 -> 192.168.7.2  DHCP DHCP Offer    - Transaction ID 0xaf358d15
 18.837461   0.0.0.0 -> 255.255.255.255 DHCP DHCP Request  - Transaction ID 0xaf358d15
 18.845023 192.168.7.254 -> 192.168.7.2  DHCP DHCP ACK      - Transaction ID 0xaf358d15


[root@castor:~#] dhclient ed0

[root@castor:~#] dhclient -r

[root@castor:~#] cat /var/db/dhclient.leases

lease {
  interface "ed0";
  fixed-address 192.168.7.2;
  medium "-link0 -link1 -link2";
  option subnet-mask 255.255.255.0;
  option routers 192.168.7.254;
  option dhcp-lease-time 86400;
  option dhcp-message-type 5;
  option domain-name-servers 195.34.133.10;
  option dhcp-server-identifier 192.168.7.254;
  option dhcp-renewal-time 43200;
  option dhcp-rebinding-time 75600;
  renew 2 2002/11/26 22:59:31;
  rebind 2 2002/11/26 22:59:31;
  expire 2 2002/11/26 22:59:31;
}
```

Example 6-17 *Cisco DHCP Server-Side Statistics*

```
scar# show ip dhcp binding
IP address        Hardware address        Lease expiration        Type
192.168.7.2       5254.05e3.e488          Mar 02 1993 01:28 AM    Automatic


scar# show ip dhcp server statistics
Memory usage        13270
Address pools       1
Database agents     0
Automatic bindings  1
Manual bindings     0
Expired bindings    0
Malformed messages  0
```

continues

Example 6-17 *Cisco DHCP Server-Side Statistics (Continued)*

```
Message             Received
BOOTREQUEST         0
DHCPDISCOVER        1
DHCPREQUEST         1
DHCPDECLINE         0
DHCPRELEASE         1
DHCPINFORM          4

Message             Sent
BOOTREPLY           0
DHCPOFFER           1
DHCPACK             1
DHCPNAK             0
```

NOTE   dhcping is a DHCP client tool that can be deployed to monitor a DHCP server. It is based on DHCP_INFORM, DHCP_REQUEST, and DHCP_RELEASE packets. Consult the man page dhcping(8) for further details.

Lab 6-2: UNIX CDP Configuration

Sometimes it is convenient to use the Cisco Discovery Protocol (CDP) to get an overview over a Cisco topology, especially when familiarizing yourself with an unknown network. CDP is also helpful when dealing with integration of UNIX gateways into an existing Cisco Works network management infrastructure. Cisco Works, for example, heavily relies on CDP. UNIX workstations can send CDP packets to Cisco neighbors.

Depending on the tool, these packets are either CDPv1 or CDPv2. Four UNIX CDP implementations pretty much achieve the same:

- cdpd
- cdpr
- scdp
- lcdpd (Linux kernel patch)

Because UNIX workstations usually do not care about CDP neighbors, they transmit only CDP packets; they do not digest received protocol information. Example 6-18 shows the CDP configurations of the lab gateways. The callisto scdp crontab entry is activated every 60 seconds to match the Cisco default timers.

Example 6-18 *CDP Configuration*

```
Castor: /usr/local/libexec/cdpd -a
Callisto crontab entry: * * * * * /usr/local/bin/scdp -i eth0 -v2
Scar: Cisco CDP can be enabled per-interface via the cdp enable command
```

The result of this setup is shown in Example 6-19, and Example 6-20 shows a sniffer trace of the CDP protocol traffic.

Example 6-19 *CDP Lab Operation*

```
scar# show cdp neighbors
Capability Codes: R - Router, T - Trans Bridge, B - Source Route Bridge
                  S - Switch, H - Host, I - IGMP, r - Repeater

Device ID        Local Intrfce     Holdtme    Capability  Platform  Port ID
callisto         Eth 1             124        H           Linux     eth0
castor           Eth 0             147        H           i386      ed0

scar# show cdp neighbors detail
-------------------------
Device ID: callisto
Entry address(es):
  IP address: 192.168.14.1
Platform: Linux,  Capabilities: Host
Interface: Ethernet1,  Port ID (outgoing port): eth0
Holdtime : 178 sec
Version : 2
advertisement version: 1
-------------------------
Device ID: castor
Entry address(es):
 .IP address: 192.168.7.7
Platform: i386,  Capabilities: Host
Interface: Ethernet0,  Port ID (outgoing port): ed0
Holdtime : 142 sec
Version :
FreeBSD 4.9-RELEASE FreeBSD 4.9-RELEASE #0: Tue Nov
advertisement version: 1
```

Example 6-20 *CDP Protocol Behavior—Sniffer Output*

```
[root@callisto:~#] tcpdump -i eth0 ether dst 01:00:0c:cc:cc:cc
tcpdump: listening on eth0
14:41:00.784334 CDP v1, ttl=180s
        DevID 'callisto'
        Addr (1): IPv4 192.168.14.1
        PortID 'eth0'
        CAP 0x10
        Version: (suppressed)
        Platform: 'Linux'
14:41:04.922217 CDP v2, ttl=180s
        DevID 'scar'
        Addr (1): IPv4 192.168.14.254
        PortID 'Ethernet1'
        CAP 0x01
        [!cdp]
```

continues

Example 6-20 *CDP Protocol Behavior—Sniffer Output (Continued)*

```
14:41:04.923162 CDP v1, ttl=180s
        DevID 'scar'
        Addr (1): IPv4 192.168.14.254
        PortID 'Ethernet1'
        CAP 0x01
        [!cdp]

[root@castor~#] tcpdump -i ed0 ether dst 01:00:0c:cc:cc:cc
tcpdump: listening on ed0
14:09:04.837219 CDP v2, ttl=180s
        DevID 'scar'
        Addr (1): IPv4 192.168.7.254
        PortID 'Ethernet0'
        CAP 0x01
        [!cdp]
14:09:04.838186 CDP v1, ttl=180s
        DevID 'scar'
        Addr (1): IPv4 192.168.7.254
        PortID 'Ethernet0'
        CAP 0x01
        [!cdp]
14:11:24.686029 CDP v1, ttl=180s
        DevID 'castor'
        Addr (1): IPv4 192.168.7.7
        PortID 'ed0'
        CAP 0x10
        [!cdp]
```

Summary

This chapter introduced several families of tools that have proven useful in the context of network testing and monitoring. Packet analyzer, port scanner, ping, and traceroute tools were discussed. If you are looking for a particular tool, see the http://www. freshmeat.net repository. In addition, the generation of special-purpose packets and volume traffic was discussed. This chapter also briefly introduced available UNIX DHCP implementations.

The chapter's two labs featured packet-analyzer investigations of the DHCP and CDP protocols. The "Recommended Reading" section provides links to the tool repositories.

Chapter 7, "The UNIX Routing and ARP Tables," covers Media Access Control (MAC) and Address Resolution Protocol (ARP) tools.

Recommended Reading

- The Freshmeat Open Source Repository, http://www.freshmeat.net
- minicom, http://www.netsonic.fi/~walker/minicom.html

- C-Kermit, (UNIX, VMS)/Kermit 95 (Windows), http://www.columbia.edu/kermit/ckermit.html
- TeraTerm Pro (Windows), http://hp.vector.co.jp/authors/VA002416/teraterm.html, http://www.zip.com.au/~roca/ttssh.html
- Ethereal, http://www.ethereal.com
- ngrep, http://ngrep.sourceforge.net
- tcpdump, www.tcpdump.org
- nmap, www.nmap.org
- strobe, http://www.luyer.net/software/strobe-classb/
- mtr, http://www.bitwizard.nl/mtr/
- BIND, http://www.isc.org
- dnstracer, http://www.mavetju.org/unix/general.php
- aicmpsend, http://www.elxsi.de
- sendip, http://www.earth.li/projectpurple/progs/sendip.html
- IP Sorcery, http://www.informony.com/ipsorcery.html
- Packet Excalibur, http://www.securitybugware.org/excalibur/
- hping2, http://www.hping.org
- Traffic, http://galileo.spaceports.com/~rsandila/traffic.html
- cdpd, http://netcert.tripod.com/ccna/switches/cdp.html
- cdpr, http://www.monkeymental.com/nuke/index.php
- lcdpd, http://lcdpd.sourceforge.net/
- Netperf, http://www.netperf.org/netperf/NetperfPage.html
- NetPIPE, http://www.scl.ameslab.gov/netpipe/
- ttcp/wsttcp, http://www.pcausa.com/Utilities/pcattcp.htm, http://www.cisco.com/warp/public/471/ttcp.html
- Sam Spade, http://www.samspade.org/ssw/
- Scapy, http://www.cartel-securite.fr/pbiondi//projects/scapy.html
- ISC-DHCP ancillary tools, http://www.mavetju.org/unix/general.php

The UNIX Routing and ARP Tables

The interfaces of a UNIX gateway can be divided into two groups: logical (virtual) and physical interfaces.

Chapter 5, "Ethernet and VLANs," already introduced the concept of virtual LAN (VLAN) interfaces as an example for a logical interface, as well as alias (secondary) interface configuration. Data link layer address resolution works differently on WAN links. You must consider special Address Resolution Protocol (ARP) issues that are related to point-to-point or point-to-multipoint (Frame Relay) setups.

This chapter introduces the ARP operation as well as the gateway's view of its directly connected physical and logical interfaces. You have already learned in Chapter 5 how they become represented in the kernel routing and ARP tables, and how their deletion or disappearance affects these tables. As you will see, ARP operation can take on different manifestations, such as proxy ARP or gratuitous ARP, regular ARP and reverse/inverse ARP. A discussion of routing table tools (netstat, route, iproute2) concludes the chapter.

Address Resolution: ARP and RARP

ARP, due to its apparent simplicity, is a rather overlooked concept, and sometimes its effect on the well being of network infrastructures is underestimated. ARP-related issues are fairly common in complex scenarios and often poorly understood by non-networking folks. Therefore, this section offers an overview of several manifestations of the ARP protocol itself and related aspects.

For a good understanding of network dynamics, it is also mandatory to understand the timers involved with regard to ARP and switch table entries and their lifetime. ARP table entries have a lifetime in the range of minutes up to tens of minutes, depending on the operating system under discussion.

Politely behaving implementations such as Cisco IOS Software display ARP cache timers within the ARP output. This information will hopefully assist in tracking and resolving problems such as incomplete ARP entries, duplicate IP addresses, and security issues such as spoofing and sniffing. Ethernet MAC addresses can be spoofed easily given physical access to the network segment or VLAN under consideration. Example 7-1 presents an overview of the capabilities of the Linux and BSD **arp** commands (essentially **show**, **add**, and **delete**). Static ARP entries can as well be deployed via a configuration file. You will read more about the **temp/pub** flags of the **arp** command in the following sections.

Example 7-1   *Linux and BSD ARP Utility Features*

```
[root@callisto:~#] arp -?
Usage:
  arp [-vn]   [<HW>] [-i <if>] [-a] [<hostname>]            <-Display ARP cache
  arp [-v]          [-i <if>] -d  <hostname> [pub][nopub]   <-Delete ARP entry
  arp [-vnD] [<HW>] [-i <if>] -f  [<filename>]              <-Add entry from file
  arp [-v]   [<HW>] [-i <if>] -s  <hostname> <hwaddr> [temp][nopub] <-Add entry
  arp [-v]   [<HW>] [-i <if>] -s  <hostname> <hwaddr> [netmask <nm>] pub  <-''-
  arp [-v]   [<HW>] [-i <if>] -Ds <hostname> <if> [netmask <nm>] pub      <-''-

          -a                      display (all) hosts in alternative (BSD) style
          -e                      display (all) hosts in default (Linux) style
          -s, --set               set a new ARP entry
          -d, --delete            delete a specified entry
          -v, --verbose           be verbose
          -n, --numeric           don't resolve names
          -i, --device            specify network interface (e.g. eth0)
          -D, --use-device        read <hwaddr> from given device
          -A, -p, --protocol      specify protocol family
          -f, --file              read new entries from file or from /etc/ethers

    <HW>=Use '-H <hw>' to specify hardware address type. Default: ether
    List of possible hardware types (which support ARP):
      strip (Metricom Starmode IP) ash (Ash) ether (Ethernet)
      tr (16/4 Mbps Token Ring) tr (16/4 Mbps Token Ring (New)) ax25 (AMPR AX.25)
      netrom (AMPR NET/ROM) rose (AMPR ROSE) arcnet (ARCnet)
      dlci (Frame Relay DLCI) fddi (Fiber Distributed Data Interface) hippi (HIPPI)
      irda (IrLAP) x25 (generic X.25)

[root@castor:~#] arp
usage: arp [-n] hostname
       arp [-n] -a
       arp -d hostname [pub]
       arp -d -a
       arp -s hostname ether_addr [temp] [pub]
       arp -S hostname ether_addr [temp] [pub]
       arp -f filename

[root@callisto:~#] rarp -?
rarp: invalid option -- ?
Usage: rarp -a                              list entries in cache.
       rarp -d <hostname>                   delete entry from cache.
       rarp [<HW>] -s <hostname> <hwaddr>   add entry to cache.
       rarp -f                              add entries from /etc/ethers.
       rarp -V                              display program version.

    <HW>=Use '-H <hw>' to specify hardware address type. Default: ether
    List of possible hardware types (which support ARP):
      strip (Metricom Starmode IP) ash (Ash) ether (Ethernet)
      tr (16/4 Mbps Token Ring) tr (16/4 Mbps Token Ring (New)) ax25 (AMPR AX.25)
      netrom (AMPR NET/ROM) rose (AMPR ROSE) arcnet (ARCnet)
```

Example 7-1   *Linux and BSD ARP Utility Features (Continued)*

```
        dlci (Frame Relay DLCI) fddi (Fiber Distributed Data Interface) hippi (HIPPI)
        irda (IrLAP) x25 (generic X.25)

[root@callisto:~#] rarp -a
This kernel does not support RARP.

##### My LAB kernel does not support netboot such as RARP/BOOTP ######
##### This has to be configured at compile time ######################
```

Proxy ARP

Proxy almost always means "to act on someone's behalf"; this is exactly what happens when a manual ARP entry is configured with the publish tag on BSD. This is explained perfectly in the BSD arp(8) manual page.

In the particular case of proxy ARP, the system responds to ARP requests for that entry as if it were the target of the request with its own MAC address, thereby impersonating an ARP server. This is essentially relevant only for hosts without a default gateway or routing table configured or certain boot or transitional situations. The use of proxy ARP in modern routed and subnet-aware networks is discouraged but occasionally found in context with failover protocols. Regarding this issue, I found an interesting quote from the Linux arp(7) man page:

Linux will automatically add a non-permanent proxy arp entry when it receives a request for an address it forwards to and proxy arp is enabled on the receiving interface. When there is a reject route for the target no proxy arp entry is added . . . Support for proxy arp entries for networks (netmask not equal 0xffffffff) was dropped in Linux 2.2. It is replaced by automatic proxy arp setup by the kernel for all reachable hosts on other interfaces (when forwarding and proxy arp is enabled for the interface).[1]

Example 7-2 shows the sysctl parameters that affect proxy ARP behavior and ARP filtering on Linux systems.

ARP_filter

For a better understanding of the ARP_filter, consider this quote from the Linux kernel documentation (ip-sysctl.txt):

arp_filter - BOOLEAN

1 - Allows you to have multiple network interfaces on the same subnet, and have the ARPs for each interface be answered based on whether or not the kernel would route a packet from the ARP'd IP out that interface (therefore you must use source based routing for this to work). In other words it allows control of which cards (usually 1) will respond to an arp request.

0 - (default) The kernel can respond to arp requests with addresses from other interfaces. This may seem wrong but it usually makes sense, because it increases the chance of successful communication. IP addresses are owned by the complete host on Linux, not by particular interfaces. Only for more complex setups like load-balancing does this behaviour cause problems.

Example 7-2 *Proxy ARP Parameters for Linux Interfaces*

```
[root@callisto:~#] sysctl -a | grep arp
net.ipv4.conf.eth1.arp_ignore = 0
net.ipv4.conf.eth1.arp_announce = 0
net.ipv4.conf.eth1.arp_filter = 0
net.ipv4.conf.eth1.proxy_arp = 0
net.ipv4.conf.eth0.arp_ignore = 0
net.ipv4.conf.eth0.arp_announce = 0
net.ipv4.conf.eth0.arp_filter = 0
net.ipv4.conf.eth0.proxy_arp = 0
net.ipv4.conf.lo.arp_ignore = 0
net.ipv4.conf.lo.arp_announce = 0
net.ipv4.conf.lo.arp_filter = 0
net.ipv4.conf.lo.proxy_arp = 0
net.ipv4.conf.default.arp_ignore = 0
net.ipv4.conf.default.arp_announce = 0
net.ipv4.conf.default.arp_filter = 0
net.ipv4.conf.default.proxy_arp = 0
net.ipv4.conf.all.arp_ignore = 0
net.ipv4.conf.all.arp_announce = 0
net.ipv4.conf.all.arp_filter = 0
net.ipv4.conf.all.proxy_arp = 0
```

ARP Cache

The route and ARP cache are intimately related via MAC resolution or data-link identifiers, or, to be more general, by "next-hop" addresses and directly attached physical and logical interfaces. Example 7-3 shows an example of the Linux ARP table. "Incomplete" entries (shaded text) would mean that no ARP replies were received for that particular MAC address resolution attempt.

Example 7-3 *Linux ARP Table*

```
[root@callisto:~#] arp
Address                HWtype  HWaddress          Flags Mask       Iface
pollux                 ether   08:00:46:64:74:1B  C                eth1
ganymed                ether   48:54:E8:8C:0A:3F  C                eth1
192.168.14.254         ether   00:00:0C:1A:A9:AB  C                eth0

[root@callisto:~#] arp -a
pollux (192.168.1.250) at 08:00:46:64:74:1B [ether] on eth1
europa (192.168.1.254) at 48:54:E8:8C:0A:3F [ether] on eth1
scar (192.168.14.254) at <incomplete> on eth0
```

Static ARP Entries

Static ARP entries serve different purposes: They make smaller network setups more predictable, enhance security, and can be required in context with static Network Address Translation (NAT) entries of firewall gateways. Example 7-4 shows two examples for static

ARP entries on Linux and BSD systems. Note that these are examples for *temporary* manual entries (in contrast to permanent). The OpenBSD example **temp** flag results in proxy ARP behavior (as demonstrated in the highlighted text).

Example 7-4 *Two Examples of Static ARP Entries*

```
[root@callisto:~#] arp -s 192.168.1.55 A3:A3:A3:A3:A3:A3 temp
[root@callisto:~#] arp
Address                 HWtype  HWaddress          Flags Mask          Iface
pollux                  ether   08:00:46:64:74:1B  C                   eth1
ganymed                 ether   48:54:E8:8C:0A:3F  C                   eth1
192.168.14.254          ether   00:00:0C:1A:A9:AB  C                   eth0
192.168.1.55            ether   A3:A3:A3:A3:A3:A3  C                   eth1

[root@ganymed:~#] arp -s 192.168.1.55 A3:A3:A3:A3:A3:A3 pub temp
[root@ganymed:~#] arp -an
? (192.168.1.1) at 52:54:05:e3:51:87
? (192.168.1.2) at 08:00:46:64:74:1b
? (192.168.1.55) at a3:a3:a3:a3:a3:a3 published
? (192.168.2.7) at 00:10:5a:c4:2c:04
? (111.11.117.1) at 00:05:9a:5b:23:fc
```

Gratuitous ARP

Gratuitous ARP resembles emission of an unsolicited ARP reply to which no request was sent or received. This is quite common behavior during bootstrap or boot procedures of several operating systems when they initialize their IP stacks. When a computer receives a new interface or another change occurs, it can update all neighboring ARP caches with one gratuitous ARP packet to FF:FF:FF:FF:FF:FF.

A second important application is checking for duplicate IP addresses. The initializing IP stack would not complete its initialization sequence upon detection of such a situation. There exist security and performance implications when accepting gratuitous ARP packets; therefore, routers and switches can be configured to ignore them. This feature can be used to maliciously take over IP addresses.

Gratuitous ARP plays an important role in modern Hot Standby Routing Protocol (HSRP) and heartbeat failover configurations, and sometimes in context of static NAT. Example 7-5 shows a sniffing example of a booting operating system, and Example 7-6 shows relevant Cisco IOS commands to influence proxy ARP and gratuitous ARP behavior. I would not recommend touching the default settings unless you know well what you want to accomplish.

Example 7-5 *Gratuitous ARP at BSD IP Stack Initialization*

```
[root@ganymed:~#] tethereal -i ne4
Capturing on ne4
  0.000000 castor.nerdzone.org -> ff:ff:ff:ff:ff:ff ARP Who has 192.168.2.7?
    Tell 192.168.2.7
```

Example 7-6 *Improving Cisco Security and Performance*

```
scar(config-if)# no ip proxy-arp

scar(config)# no ip gratuitous-arps

scar# show arp
Protocol  Address         Age (min)  Hardware Addr   Type   Interface
Internet  192.168.13.1        -      0000.3058.9555  SNAP   TokenRing0
Internet  192.168.14.1        0      0010.5ad7.9360  ARPA   Ethernet1
Internet  192.168.7.7        11      5254.05e3.e488  ARPA   Ethernet0
Internet  192.168.17.1        -      0000.3058.95b5  SNAP   TokenRing1
Internet  192.168.7.254       -      0000.0c1a.a9a8  ARPA   Ethernet0
Internet  192.168.14.254      -      0000.0c1a.a9ab  ARPA   Ethernet1
```

NOTE   UNIX workstations also send out gratuitous ARP when initializing alias or VLAN interfaces.

Reverse ARP (RARP), the Bootstrap Protocol (BOOTP), and Dynamic Host Configuration Protocol (DHCP)

UNIX workstations can run a rarpd to respond to RARP requests of diskless or client workstations. It can return an IP address for a requesting MAC address as well as a bootable image via Trivial File Transfer Protocol (TFTP). There also exists a bootpd in the BSD world.

BOOTP, Preboot Execution Environment (PXE), and DHCP approaches have largely superseded RARP. Because network-bootable client issues go beyond the scope of this book, no examples are provided. Consult the man pages for rarpd, bootpd, and the links provided in the "Recommended Reading" section for further information. Example 7-7 shows the relevant sysctl parameters to influence BOOTP behavior on Linux systems.

NOTE   The ISC-DHCP server discussed in Chapter 6, "The Analyzer Toolbox, DHCP, and CDP," can answer both DHCP and BOOTP requests.

Example 7-7 *Linux Can Relay BOOTP Requests*

```
[root@callisto:~#] sysctl -a | grep bootp
net.ipv4.conf.eth1.bootp_relay = 0
net.ipv4.conf.eth0.bootp_relay = 0
net.ipv4.conf.lo.bootp_relay = 0
net.ipv4.conf.default.bootp_relay = 0
net.ipv4.conf.all.bootp_relay = 0
```

TFTP

TFTP is a lightweight protocol without any security that allows storage, retrieval, and creation of files in a particular directory. On UNIX systems, it is usually started via the (x)inetd super server. UNIX operating systems usually provide a native TFTP service out of the box. It is a broadcast protocol commonly used in network-boot environments together with DHCP, BOOTP, PXE, and RARP. In addition, it is often used to store and retrieve configurations for network elements. Recently there was interest in multicast TFTP servers to efficiently and simultaneously boot multiple clients.

There essentially exist several improved versions of TFTP server implementations:

- **utftpd**—Represents my TFTP UNIX implementation of choice. It consists of a client and a server. According to its creator, it offers "fine-grained access control, support for blksize (RFC 2348) and timeout options, and support for revision control" (http://www.ohse.de/uwe/software/utftpd.html).

- **tftpd-hpa**—An enhanced version of the BSD tftpd called tftp-hpa that has TCP wrapper support as well (http://www.kernel.org/pub/software/network/tftp/).

- **atftp**—Advanced TFTP client and server is multithreaded, supports libwrap (the TCP wrapper library), and is fully compliant with all relevant standards. You can downloaded it from ftp://ftp.mamalinux.com/pub/atftp/.

- **The Solarwinds TFTP server**—If you require a TFTP server for Windows, you can use the free tool from Solarwinds (http://www.solarwinds.net).

NOTE   TFTP is an inherently insecure protocol without a password facility. Therefore, it is strongly advised to compile your TFTP server of choice with TCP wrapper support to protect the server or place it behind a packet filter or firewall. utftp and Solarwinds TFTP provide an internal security mechanism that can filter based on source IP address.

Inverse ARP (InARP), UNARP, and DirectedARP

Inverse ARP is a feature used in ATM and Frame Relay dynamic address mapping. It is used to request the next-hop protocol address given a data-link connection identifier (DLCI) or ATM virtual path identifier/virtual circuit identifier (VPI/VCI) pair. The result is an address-to-DLCI or -VPI/VCI mapping table. In addition, static mappings can be configured. Inverse ARP is a multiprotocol mechanism on Cisco routers and turned on per default for Frame Relay (all protocols). Go to Cisco.com for example configurations.

Examples 7-8 and 7-9 show a brief hub-and-spoke Frame Relay configuration example to emphasize this point. Keep in mind that this setup requires an intermediate Frame Relay switch; hence the name "Frame Relay" or "cell relay" for ATM networks. This will not work in a crossover fashion. Every Layer 2 WAN protocol deals with ARP issues in its own way.

Example 7-8   *Cisco Frame Relay Point-to-Multipoint Example (Hub Configuration Fragment)*

```
scar# show running-config
...
!
interface Serial1
 no ip address
 encapsulation frame-relay
!
interface Serial1.1 multipoint
 ip address 10.1.1.3 255.255.255.0
 frame-relay map ip 10.1.1.1 160 broadcast
!
...
```

Example 7-9   *Cisco Frame Relay Point-to-Multipoint Example (Spoke Configuration Fragment)*

```
simba# show running-config
...
!
interface Serial0
 ip address 4.0.1.1 255.255.255.0
 encapsulation frame-relay
 frame-relay map ip 10.1.1.2 140 broadcast
!
...
```

Interesting future developments (quoted from the RFCs) include the following:

UNARP (RFC 1868):

The Address Resolution Protocol allows an IP node to determine the hardware (datalink) address of a neighboring node on a broadcast network. The protocol depends on timers to age away old ARP entries. This document specifies a trivial modification to the ARP mechanism, not the packet format, which allows a node to announce that it is leaving the network and that all other nodes should modify their ARP tables accordingly.

DirectedARP (RFC 1433):

Directed ARP is a dynamic address resolution procedure that enables hosts and routers to resolve advertised potential next-hop IP addresses on foreign IP networks to their associated link level addresses.

Power of the Linux ip, netstat, and route Utilities

These tools form the heart of UNIX routing configuration and observation. However, they provide far more features than can be discussed in this text. For details and operating system variations beyond the most important facilities, consult the manual pages. We will heavily rely on these tools and introduce features as we proceed.

Linux provides a new approach to unified administration via the iproute2 facility (see Example 7-10). The command itself is called **ip**. You can get help for the ip tool by typing **ip help**. This also works at sublevels. Example 7-10 prints the interface statistics equivalent to ifconfig, the link status, the routing table, and its neighbors from a MAC point of view.

Example 7-10 *Linux ip Facility*

```
[root@callisto:~#] ip
Usage: ip [ OPTIONS ] OBJECT { COMMAND | help }
where  OBJECT := { link | addr | route | rule | neigh | tunnel |
                   maddr | mroute | monitor }
       OPTIONS := { -V[ersion] | -s[tatistics] | -r[esolve] |
                   -f[amily] { inet | inet6 | ipx | dnet | link } | -o[neline] }

[root@callisto:~#] ip -s addr
1: lo: <LOOPBACK,UP> mtu 16436 qdisc noqueue
    link/loopback 00:00:00:00:00:00 brd 00:00:00:00:00:00
    inet 127.0.0.1/8 brd 127.255.255.255 scope host lo
2: eth0: <BROADCAST,MULTICAST,PROMISC,UP> mtu 1500 qdisc pfifo_fast qlen 100
    link/ether 00:10:5a:d7:93:60 brd ff:ff:ff:ff:ff:ff
    inet 192.168.14.1/24 brd 192.168.14.255 scope global eth0
3: eth1: <BROADCAST,MULTICAST,UP> mtu 1500 qdisc pfifo_fast qlen 100
    link/ether 52:54:05:e3:51:87 brd ff:ff:ff:ff:ff:ff
    inet 192.168.1.1/24 brd 192.168.1.255 scope global eth1

[root@callisto:~#] ip -s link
1: lo: <LOOPBACK,UP> mtu 16436 qdisc noqueue
    link/loopback 00:00:00:00:00:00 brd 00:00:00:00:00:00
    RX: bytes  packets  errors  dropped overrun mcast
    4834       66       0       0       0       0
    TX: bytes  packets  errors  dropped carrier collsns
    4834       66       0       0       0       0
2: eth0: <BROADCAST,MULTICAST,PROMISC,UP> mtu 1500 qdisc pfifo_fast qlen 100
    link/ether 00:10:5a:d7:93:60 brd ff:ff:ff:ff:ff:ff
    RX: bytes  packets  errors  dropped overrun mcast
    0          0        0       0       0       0
    TX: bytes  packets  errors  dropped carrier collsns
    21850      265      0       0       0       0
3: eth1: <BROADCAST,MULTICAST,UP> mtu 1500 qdisc pfifo_fast qlen 100
    link/ether 52:54:05:e3:51:87 brd ff:ff:ff:ff:ff:ff
    RX: bytes  packets  errors  dropped overrun mcast
    3246131    5550     0       0       0       151
    TX: bytes  packets  errors  dropped carrier collsns
    609700     5029     0       0       0       78

[root@callisto:~#] ip -s route
192.168.1.0/24 dev eth1  scope link
192.168.14.0/24 dev eth0  scope link
```

continues

Example 7-10 *Linux ip Facility (Continued)*

```
127.0.0.0/8 dev lo  scope link
default via 192.168.1.254 dev eth1

[root@callisto:~#] ip -s neigh
192.168.1.2 dev eth1 lladdr 08:00:46:64:74:1b ref 1 used 19/0/18 nud reachable
192.168.1.254 dev eth1 lladdr 48:54:e8:8c:0a:3f ref 13 used 193/220/325 nud stale
```

Example 7-11 demonstrates several different approaches to print the routing table. Examples 7-11 through 7-18 present various examples of the netstat and route utilities and explain the abbreviations used in the UNIX routing tables (collected from different man pages). As usual, consult the command's manual pages for further details.

Example 7-11 *Linux netstat and route in Action*

```
[root@callisto:~#] netstat -rn
Kernel IP routing table
Destination     Gateway         Genmask          Flags   MSS Window  irtt Iface
192.168.1.0     0.0.0.0         255.255.255.0    U        40 0           0 eth1
192.168.14.0    0.0.0.0         255.255.255.0    U        40 0           0 eth0
127.0.0.0       0.0.0.0         255.0.0.0        U        40 0           0 lo
0.0.0.0         192.168.1.254   0.0.0.0          UG       40 0           0 eth1

[root@callisto:~#] route -n
Kernel IP routing table
Destination     Gateway         Genmask          Flags Metric Ref    Use Iface
192.168.1.0     0.0.0.0         255.255.255.0    U     0      0        0 eth1
192.168.14.0    0.0.0.0         255.255.255.0    U     0      0        0 eth0
127.0.0.0       0.0.0.0         255.0.0.0        U     0      0        0 lo
0.0.0.0         192.168.1.254   0.0.0.0          UG    0      0        0 eth1

[root@callisto:~#] route -een
Kernel IP routing table
Destination  Gateway        Genmask        Flags Metric Ref Use Iface MSS Window  irtt
192.168.1.0  0.0.0.0        255.255.255.0  U     0      0   0   eth1   40  0       0
192.168.14.0 0.0.0.0        255.255.255.0  U     0      0   0   eth0   40  0       0
127.0.0.0    0.0.0.0        255.0.0.0      U     0      0   0   lo     40  0       0
0.0.0.0      192.168.1.254 0.0.0.0         UG    0      0   0   eth1   40  0       0
```

Example 7-12 *Possible Routing Table Flags (Linux)*

```
U (route is up)
H (target is a host)
G (use gateway)
R (reinstate route for dynamic routing)
D (dynamically installed by daemon or redirect)
M (modified from routing daemon or redirect)
A (installed by addrconf)
C (cache entry)
! (reject route)
```

Example 7-13 *Possible Routing Table Flags (FreeBSD)*

```
1    RTF_PROTO1      Protocol specific routing flag #1
2    RTF_PROTO2      Protocol specific routing flag #2
3    RTF_PROTO3      Protocol specific routing flag #3
B    RTF_BLACKHOLE   Just discard pkts (during updates)
b    RTF_BROADCAST   The route represents a broadcast address
C    RTF_CLONING     Generate new routes on use
c    RTF_PRCLONING   Protocol-specified generate new routes on use
D    RTF_DYNAMIC     Created dynamically (by redirect)
G    RTF_GATEWAY     Destination requires forwarding by intermediary
H    RTF_HOST        Host entry (net otherwise)
L    RTF_LLINFO      Valid protocol to link address translation
M    RTF_MODIFIED    Modified dynamically (by redirect)
R    RTF_REJECT      Host or net unreachable
S    RTF_STATIC      Manually added
U    RTF_UP          Route usable
W    RTF_WASCLONED   Route was generated as a result of cloning
X    RTF_XRESOLVE    External daemon translates proto to link address
```

Example 7-14 *Possible Routing Table Flags (OpenBSD)*

```
1    RTF_PROTO1      Protocol specific routing flag #1.
2    RTF_PROTO2      Protocol specific routing flag #2.
3    RTF_PROTO3      Protocol specific routing flag #3.
B    RTF_BLACKHOLE   Just discard pkts (during updates).
C    RTF_CLONING     Generate new routes on use.
D    RTF_DYNAMIC     Created dynamically (by redirect).
G    RTF_GATEWAY     Destination requires forwarding by intermediary.
H    RTF_HOST        Host entry (net otherwise).
L    RTF_LLINFO      Valid protocol to link address translation.
M    RTF_MODIFIED    Modified dynamically (by redirect).
R    RTF_REJECT      Host or net unreachable.
S    RTF_STATIC      Manually added.
U    RTF_UP          Route usable.
X    RTF_XRESOLVE    External daemon translates proto to link address.
```

Example 7-15 *OpenBSD route in Action*

```
[root@ganymed:~#] route -nv show
Routing tables

Internet:
Destination       Gateway           Flags
default           111.11.117.1      UG
127.0.0.0         127.0.0.1         UG
127.0.0.1         127.0.0.1         UH
192.168.1.0       link#1            U
192.168.1.1       52:54:5:e3:51:87  UH
192.168.1.2       8:0:46:64:74:1b   UH
192.168.2.0       link#2            U
192.168.2.7       0:10:5a:c4:2c:4   UH
```

continues

Example 7-15 *OpenBSD route in Action (Continued)*

```
192.168.44.1      192.168.44.1      UH
192.168.45.0      link#1            U
111.11.117.0      link#3            U
111.11.117.1      0:5:9a:5b:23:fc   UH
111.11.117.206    127.0.0.1         UGH
```

Example 7-16 *OpenBSD netstat*

```
[root@ganymed:~#] netstat -rn -f inet
Routing tables

Internet:
Destination      Gateway           Flags   Refs   Use    Mtu    Interface
default          111.11.117.1      UGS     3      7564   1500   ne5
127/8            127.0.0.1         UGRS    0      0      33224  lo0
127.0.0.1        127.0.0.1         UH      2      0      33224  lo0
192.168.1/24     link#1            UC      0      0      1500   ne3
192.168.1.1      52:54:5:e3:51:87  UHL     0      5450   1500   ne3
192.168.1.2      8:0:46:64:74:1b   UHL     1      2840   1500   ne3
192.168.2/24     link#2            UC      0      0      1500   ne4
192.168.2.7      0:10:5a:c4:2c:4   UHL     0      652    1500   ne4
192.168.44.1     192.168.44.1      UH      0      0      33224  lo1
192.168.45/24    link#1            UC      0      0      1500   ne3
111.11.117/24    link#3            UC      0      0      1500   ne5
111.11.117.1     0:5:9a:5b:23:fc   UHL     1      0      1500   ne5
111.11.117.206   127.0.0.1         UGHS    0      0      33224  lo0
```

Example 7-17 *FreeBSD netstat*

```
[root@castor:~#] netstat -rn -f inet
Routing tables

Internet:
Destination      Gateway           Flags   Refs   Use    Netif Expire
default          192.168.2.254     UGSc    4      1064   xl0
127.0.0.1        127.0.0.1         UH      0      0      lo0
192.168.2        link#1            UC      1      0      xl0
192.168.2.254    52:54:05:e3:e4:2f UHLW    5      27     xl0    603
192.168.7        link#2            UC      1      0      ed0
192.168.7.254    00:00:0c:1a:a9:a8 UHLW    1      28     ed0    396
```

Example 7-18 *Effect of Interfaces/Line Protocols Going Down*

```
[root@callisto:~#] ifconfig eth0 down
[root@callisto:~#] route -n
Kernel IP routing table
```

Example 7-18 *Effect of Interfaces/Line Protocols Going Down (Continued)*

```
Destination     Gateway       Genmask         Flags Metric Ref   Use Iface
192.168.1.0     0.0.0.0       255.255.255.0   U     0      0       0 eth1
127.0.0.0       0.0.0.0       255.0.0.0       U     0      0       0 lo
0.0.0.0         192.168.1.254 0.0.0.0         UG    0      0       0 eth1
```

ARP-Related Tools

ARP is an important protocol both from a networking and a security point of view. From a practical point of view, it often becomes an issue when changing network adapters, dealing with HSRP/VRRP (Virtual Router Redundancy Protocol), and dealing with static NAT entries of firewalls. Modern ARP sniffers and spoofing utilities can cause havoc even in switched environments. Note that due to the lack of security within the ARP protocol, ARP replies are generally accepted without hesitation.

Among the most interesting tools are iptraf (see Figure 7-1) and ettercap (Figure 7-2). iptraf includes a LAN station (MAC) monitor, traffic statistics, and helpful statistics about protocol families (TCP/UDP/IP/ICMP) and packet sizes. ettercap is a versatile tool in switched and nonswitched environments. You can use it for ARP poisoning, man-in-the-middle attacks, OS fingerprinting, sniffing, and other tasks.

Figure 7-1   *IPTraf MAC Accounting*

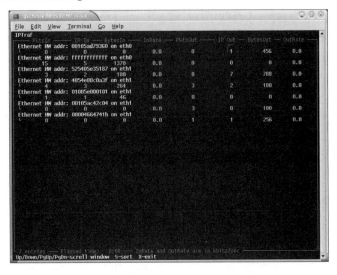

Figure 7-2 *ettercap Toolbox*

Other interesting standard command-line utilities are discussed in the following list and demonstrated in Example 7-19.

- arpwatch/arpmonitor
- arpoison
- arpspoof (part of the dsniff package)
- arping
- arp-sk

For details, consult the man pages. Example 7-19 presents the arping tool, which combines the well-known ping behavior with ARP information. arp-sk is a flexible and versatile tool to dig deep into ARP statistics and ARP simulation. Finally, arpwatch and arpmonitor turn your workstation into a monitoring station for ARP traffic.

Example 7-19 *Some Examples of ARP Monitoring*

```
[root@callisto:~#] arping
Usage: arping [-fqbDUAV] [-c count] [-w timeout] [-I device] [-s source]
  destination
  -f : quit on first reply
  -q : be quiet
  -b : keep broadcasting, don't go unicast
  -D : duplicate address detection mode
  -U : Unsolicited ARP mode, update your neighbours
  -A : ARP answer mode, update your neighbours
  -V : print version and exit
```

Example 7-19 *Some Examples of ARP Monitoring (Continued)*

```
 -c count : how many packets to send
 -w timeout : how long to wait for a reply
 -I device : which ethernet device to use (eth0)
 -s source : source ip address
 destination : ask for what ip address

[root@callisto:~#] arping -I eth1 192.168.1.254
ARPING 192.168.1.254 from 192.168.1.1 eth1
Unicast reply from 192.168.1.254 [48:54:E8:8C:0A:3F]  0.941ms
Unicast reply from 192.168.1.254 [48:54:E8:8C:0A:3F]  0.871ms
Unicast reply from 192.168.1.254 [48:54:E8:8C:0A:3F]  0.882ms
Unicast reply from 192.168.1.254 [48:54:E8:8C:0A:3F]  0.889ms
Unicast reply from 192.168.1.254 [48:54:E8:8C:0A:3F]  0.877ms
Sent 5 probes (1 broadcast(s))
Received 5 response(s)

[root@callisto:~#] arp-sk
arp-sk version 0.0.15 (Sun Dec  1 18:35:24 CET 2002)
Author: Frederic Raynal <pappy@security-labs.org>

Usage: arp-sk
-w --who-has        send a ARP Who-has
-r --reply          send a ARP Reply
-p --arping         (bad) RARP emulation (NOT YET IMPLEMANTED)
-m --arpmim         Man in the Middle (NOT YET IMPLEMANTED)

-d --dst            dst in link layer (<hotname|hostip|MAC>)
-s --src            dst in link layer (<hotname|hostip|MAC>)
--rand-hwa          set random addresses in link header
--rand-hwa-dst      set random dst in link header
--rand-hwa-src      set random src in link header

-D --arp-dst        dst in ARP message ([hostname|hostip][:MAC])
-S --arp-src        dst in ARP message ([hostname|hostip][:MAC])
--rand-arp          set random addresses in ARP message
--rand-arp-dst      set random dst addresses in ARP message
--rand-arp-src      set random src addresses in ARP message
--rand-arp-hwa-dst set random dst MAC address in ARP message
--rand-arp-log-dst set random dst IP address in ARP message
--rand-arp-hwa-src set random src MAC address in ARP message
--rand-arp-log-src set random src IP address in ARP message

-i --interface      specify interface (eth0)
-c --count          # of packets to send (infinity)
-t --time           wait the specified number of seconds between sending \
                    each packet (or X micro seconds with -t uX)
--rand-time         randomize the sending period of the packets
```

continues

Example 7-19 *Some Examples of ARP Monitoring (Continued)*

```
--beep                beeps for each packet sent
-a --addr-spaces      addresses to use in the ARP packet (eth/ip)
-n --network          broadcast address to use for icmp-timestamp
--use-ts              an icmp-timestamp is sent to resolve MAC to IP
-N --call-dns         force address resolution in outputs (default is off)
-V --version          print version and exit
-h --help             this help :)

[root@callisto:~#] arp-sk -i eth1 192.168.1.254
- Warning: no mode given, using default.
+ Running mode "reply"
+ Ifname: eth1
+ Source MAC: 52:54:05:e3:51:87
+ Source ARP MAC: 52:54:05:e3:51:87
+ Source ARP IP : 192.168.1.1
+ Target MAC: ff:ff:ff:ff:ff:ff
+ Target ARP MAC: ff:ff:ff:ff:ff:ff
+ Target ARP IP : 255.255.255.255

--- Start classical sending ---
TS: 18:48:45.447550
To: ff:ff:ff:ff:ff:ff From: 52:54:05:e3:51:87 0x0806
    ARP For 255.255.255.255 (ff:ff:ff:ff:ff:ff):
        192.168.1.1 is at 52:54:05:e3:51:87

TS: 18:48:50.445497
To: ff:ff:ff:ff:ff:ff From: 52:54:05:e3:51:87 0x0806
    ARP For 255.255.255.255 (ff:ff:ff:ff:ff:ff):
        192.168.1.1 is at 52:54:05:e3:51:87

--- 255.255.255.255 (ff:ff:ff:ff:ff:ff) statistic ---
To: ff:ff:ff:ff:ff:ff From: 52:54:05:e3:51:87 0x0806
    ARP For 255.255.255.255 (ff:ff:ff:ff:ff:ff):
        192.168.1.1 is at 52:54:05:e3:51:87
Total time: 10 sec

[root@callisto:~#] arpwatch -?
Version 2.1a11
usage: arpwatch [-dN] [-f datafile] [-i interface] [-n net[/width]] [-r file]

###### arpwatch running in debug mode without detaching from terminal ######

[root@callisto:~#] arpwatch -i eth1 -d

From: arpwatch (Arpwatch)
To: root
Subject: new station (callisto)
```

Example 7-19 *Some Examples of ARP Monitoring (Continued)*

```
                  hostname: callisto
                ip address: 192.168.1.1
          ethernet address: 52:54:5:e3:51:87
           ethernet vendor: <unknown>
                 timestamp: Saturday, January 31, 2004 19:02:40 +0100

[root@callisto:~#] arpmonitor
 -i ????
Usage mode:
./arpmonitor -i <interface> -s|e -p
-i <interface> , interface to check
-s or -e , output: <s>yslog or std<e>rr - default: syslog
-p setup promisc mode (auto clean on ctrl-C) - default: no promisc mode

[root@callisto:~#] arpmonitor -i eth1 -e
eth1ArpMonitor: Initializing...
ArpMonitor: HW address: 52:54:05:E3:51:87
ArpMonitor: IP address: 192.168.1.1
ArpMonitor: Netmask : 255.255.255.0
ArpMonitor: Broadcast : 192.168.1.255
ArpMonitor: received SIGINT, giving up
```

Lab 7-1: ARP Security Issues

This lab's task is to experiment with networking and security issues of the various
manifestations of the ARP protocol. As already mentioned, this book pretty much excludes
security discussions and has a different focus. However, every aspect of networking and
systems administration has related security aspects as well. Equipped with tools such as
ettercap, arping, arp-sk, and the toolbox of Chapter 6, try to get a feeling of how easy or
difficult it is to do the following:

- MAC spoofing
- ARP spoofing
- ARP cache poisoning
- MAC-based DoS (denial of service)
- Man-in-the-middle attacks
- Proxying and hijacking

Study networking aspects such as proxy ARP behavior of your operating system and
derive a security policy to cope with threads and weaknesses originating from the ARP
suite of protocols. For hints, inspiration, and guidance, look at the sources mentioned in the
"Recommended Reading" section at the end of this chapter.

Summary

This chapter introduced the way UNIX gateways deal with several aspects of the ARP protocol. It offered a first, more intimate look at the UNIX routing table and its view of connected physical and existing logical interfaces.

In the following chapters, we will populate this routing table with static routes and routes learned via dynamic routing protocols and shift the focus more and more toward dynamic setups.

Recommended Reading

- The arp(8) manual pages
- The route(8) manual page
- The netstat(8) manual page
- The iproute2 Utility Suite HOWTO, http://www.linuxgrill.com/iproute2-toc.html
- sysctl Linux Kernel documentation (ip-sysctl.txt)
- A Linux Proxy-ARP HOWTO, http://www.ibiblio.org/pub/Linux/docs/HOWTO/ unmaintained/mini/Proxy-ARP
- The ProxyARP Subnetting HOWTO, http://www.tldp.org/HOWTO/mini/ Proxy-ARP-Subnet/index.html
- UNARP (RFC 1868)
- DirectedARP (RFC 1433)
- Address Takeover, http://www.vergenet.net/linux/fake
- FreeBSD Diskless operation manual, http://www.freebsd.org/doc/en_US.ISO8859-1/ books/handbook/network-diskless.html
- HOWTO Clone Disk Images on Linux Booted from a Network, http://www.tldp.org/ HOWTO/Clone-HOWTO/index.html
- Spoofing manual, http://rr.sans.org/threats/spoofing.php
- The six ARP types, http://www.wildpackets.com/resources/tips/2000_11
- Altering ARP Tables, http://packetstorm.decepticons.org/papers/general/ Altering_ARP_Tables_v_1.00.htm
- arp-sk, http://www.arp-sk.org/
- Protecting Your IP Network Infrastructure, http://www.arp-sk.org/doc/ BHAMS2001-SecIP-v105-full.pdf
- ettercap, http://ettercap.sourceforge.net/
- arpsend, http://www.net.princeton.edu/software/arpsend/
- arpmonitor, http://planeta.terra.com.br/informatica/gleicon/code/index.html

- arpoison, http://web.syr.edu/~sabuer/arpoison/
- arpspoof, http://monkey.org/~dugsong/dsniff/
- arping, http://www.habets.pp.se/synscan/programs.php
- arp-sk, http://www.arp-sk.org/
- iptraf, http://iptraf.seul.org/
- ettercap, http://ettercap.sourceforge.net
- The utftpd TFTP implementation, http://www.ohse.de/uwe/software/utftpd.html

Endnote

1 Linux arp(7) man page

## CHAPTER 8

Static Routing Concepts

The purpose of this chapter is a last close look into the UNIX routing table and forwarding information base populated with connected interface routes and static routes. Some aspects are fundamental to understand how this view changes when dynamic routing protocols take over control of the routing table. This chapter also discusses certain aspects that UNIX does differently from Cisco IOS Software. Finally, the chapter deals with two special issues: floating static routes and the unique Equal-Cost Multi-Path (ECMP) feature of Linux.

NOTE   We start populating the forwarding table via powerful dynamic routing protocols in Chapter 9, "Dynamic Routing Protocols—Interior Gateway Protocols."

Administrative Distance and Metric

Cisco IOS Software uses the concept of administrative distance to decide which routes to place in the routing table when learned via different dynamic routing protocol sources. In other words, the administrative distance is used to compare routes originating from different routing protocols (including static and connected), whereas the metric is used to compare routes within one single source of origin or family. The default administrative distance value itself is a proprietary concept and derived from quality aspects of old or modern routing protocols. What matters more is its value for relative comparison. Several other vendors have implemented the Cisco numeric values for administrative distances. However, this is merely common practice and not based on standards.

NOTE   For the discussion in this chapter, the terms *routing table* and *forwarding table* are used interchangeably, because this is common practice in the literature as well. However, understanding of the difference between those terms and the *Forwarding Information Base* (FIB) and *Routing Information Base* (RIB) is of paramount importance for a thorough grasp of the structures where dynamic routing protocols store their information and how it is ultimately used for forwarding decisions by the stack.

UNIX routing tables and forwarding information bases do not employ the concept of administrative distance per se. Directly connected interfaces, static routes to gateways or interfaces, as well as routes learned via dynamic routing protocols are expressed in terms of metrics/hop count. However, some routing engines such as MRTd, Zebra, or GateD use an administrative distance or equivalent for *internal* comparison and FIB population. UNIX routing tables employ the fundamental concept of "most specific route/prefix first" as well.

Because Cisco IOS Software employs administrative distances, it uses them to differentiate connected routes (0 or 1) from static routes (usually 1). The subtle reason why connected routes can appear with an administrative distance of both 0 and 1 is explained in the section "The Near and Far End of a Link" later in this chapter. As one notable difference to UNIX forwarding tables, Cisco IOS Software static routes differ from each other in terms of administrative distance. In the UNIX world, they solely differ in terms of metric and nothing else. In the view of the Cisco IOS designers, the view of metrics for connected and static routes is not applicable and reserved for dynamic routes to express the preference of a route.

There is one notable difference between Linux and the BSD world of operating systems: BSD Unices do not provide a metric when adding routes via the **route** command. In contrast, all BSD **ifconfig** implementations are capable of metric assignments to an interface.

Classful Routing, VLSM, and CIDR

In this book, I religiously stick to a classless point of view. Classful behavior and archaic routing protocols supporting only classful routing have disappeared almost entirely.

Variable length subnet mask (VLSM) enables us to think and route beyond the limited view of address octets, and classless interdomain routing (CIDR) enables us to form aggregates and summarize prefixes. A prefix is a network/bitmask representation of a classless network, such as 172.16.0.0/12.

Default Gateways, Default Routes, and Route(s) of Last Resort

The UNIX routing table is intimately connected to the Address Resolution Protocol (ARP) cache for next-hop Layer 2 address resolution. This becomes obvious when looking at the timer (expire) column of BSD routing table output. In contrast to Cisco IOS Software, UNIX does not employ the concept of a *default network*. There is no notable difference between the terms *default route* and *route of last resort*. The naming difference has historical reasons. The Cisco IOS **ip default-gateway** command is used when IP routing is disabled and should not be confused with **ip route default**, which actually adds an explicit default routing entry.

Route Caches, Routing Tables, Forwarding Tables, and the ISO Context

UNIX gateways provide a forwarding table (forwarding information base, or FIB in ISO-speak) and generally a derived route cache that contains the best available next hop for a particular destination prefix/aggregate. The implementation of route caches is platform-specific. When a routing lookup occurs, the cache table is consulted first and as a fallback mechanism, the FIB is then consulted (see Figure 8-1). This triggers the lookup result to be placed in the cache and speed up future lookups. You can also see the FIB as an internal data structure representing the commonly known routing or forwarding table.

Figure 8-1   *UNIX FIB (Forwarding Information Base)*

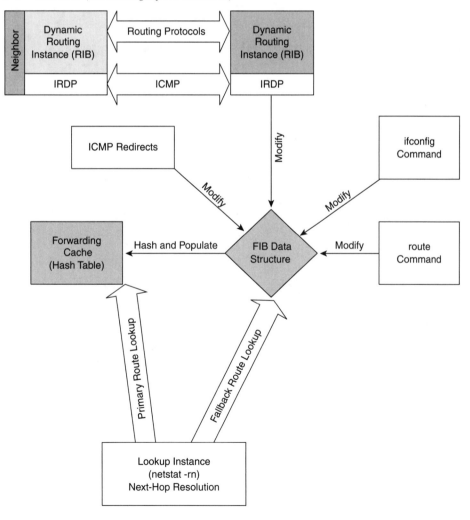

Very well, but how is the FIB populated?

Dynamic routing protocols internally operate based on a Routing Information Base (RIB) that has awareness of preference/administrative distance. The "essence" (a single best prefix entry among several possible candidates) of these protocol daemon RIBs is presented to the operating system via a protocol master daemon such as zebra or gated in a consolidated metric-only fashion (see Figure 8-2). This prefix is often referred to as *active route*. Under the hood, these controller daemons interact with forwarding information base data structures via the routing socket interface or the ioctl() interface. Therefore, the forwarding table is a collection of *active routes*. Once again, as a tribute to established practice (or sloppiness), I use *forwarding table* and *routing table* interchangeable, although it would be more accurate to relate the forwarding table with the FIB and the routing table with the RIB.

Figure 8-2   *UNIX FIB (Forwarding Information Base) and Dynamic Signaling Daemons*

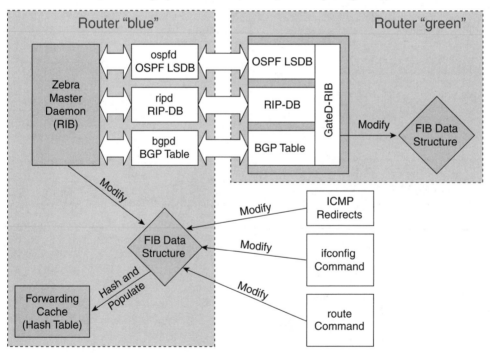

Figure 8-2 shows a schematic representation of the connection of two routing engines (GateD and Zebra) via unicast or multicast mechanisms such as Open Shortest Path First (OSPF), Routing Information Protocol (RIP), or Border Gateway Protocol (BGP). OSPF facilitates its own link-state database (LSDB), RIP maintains the RIP database, and BGP feeds network layer reachability information (NLRI) into its own table structure (the BGP table). These protocol daemons directly exchange signaling information over IP networks. Finally, Internet Control Message Protocol (ICMP) redirects, as well as manual route instructions via **route** and **ifconfig** commands, alter the FIB structures (metric-aware only), too.

IP router implementations sometimes vary in terms of how they deal with equal-cost routes in the FIB and how they present these entries in the forwarding table. Linux provides a unique implementation of ECMP—actually the only one among the open-source UNIX operating systems. The BSD designers followed the philosophy that ifconfig and static routes should be sufficient to bring systems up in a network; everything beyond that core functionality is left to dynamic routing protocols on purpose. Last but not least, the Internet Router Discovery Protocol (IRDP) operation as sketched in Figure 8-1 is based on router advertisement and router solicitation ICMP type 9/10 code 0 query messages (RFC 1256) and can place default routes in the FIB as well.

In Cisco IOS Software, the view changes in that the forwarding/routing table is the output of the **show ip route** command, including the lowest-cost paths or duplicate equal-cost paths. The dynamic routing protocol instances have their own database structures on UNIX *and* Cisco IOS Software that feed the forwarding table, such as the OSPF LSDB or BGP table as previously mentioned (see Figure 8-2). Figure 8-3 differentiates between a "pre-Cisco Express Forwarding (CEF) scenario" and a CEF scenario (state of the art). CEF is recommended for all modern deployments. For an in-depth look at CEF operation and the CEF-MPLS (Multiprotocol Label Switching) relationship, consult Cisco.com.

Linux differs in the way that it supports multiple simultaneous routing tables, essentially offering differentiated policy routing (**ip route list table #**). This is also the reason why the zebra master daemon on Linux offers a **show table** and a **table** config mode command. At the time of this writing, the zebra master daemon is able only to assign zebra static routes to designated routing tables. Unfortunately, this is not the case for the dynamic protocol daemons (a nice-to-have feature for policy routing on Linux).

Figure 8-3   *Cisco IOS FIB (Forwarding Information Base)*

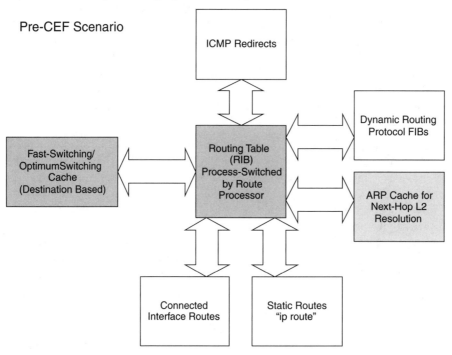

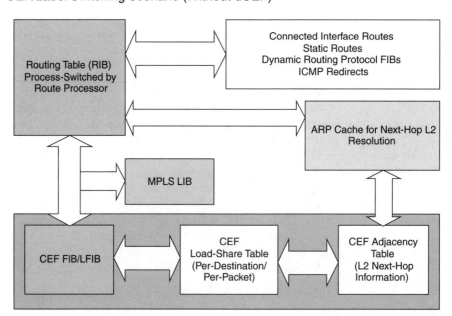

The Near and Far End of a Link

Cisco IOS Software differentiates in terms of administrative-distance static routes pointing to a directly connected interface and routes pointing toward the far end of an attached link. The administrative distance is 0 for the former and 1 for the latter. Although UNIX gateways do have the notion of static routes pointing to directly connected interfaces, they do not share this view of far ends in general, but rather from a hop-count point of view.

The route Command—Adding and Removing Routes

The UNIX **route** command is the generic interface to manipulate the kernel's IP routing table or cache. It essentially can add, delete, and monitor entries and can flush the entire forwarding table. The tool works a little bit differently on Linux systems. In addition, Linux provides the alternative ip utility from the iproute2 package with everything under one hood.

NOTE   You can retrieve everything there is to know about adding and deleting routes from the following man pages on BSD and Linux systems: route(4), route(8), rtentry(9), rtalloc(9), arp(4), arp(8), ifconfig(8). For Linux systems, you can access further information from the structures of the proc system and the manual page proc(5).

Example 8-1 shows the commands necessary to access routing-relevant proc information on Linux systems; Example 8-2 is a reminder of the routing table flags on Linux and FreeBSD as described by the route and netstat manual pages. These flags are implementation-specific, as is the representation of the routing table on NetBSD, FreeBSD, OpenBSD, and Linux. Specific details can be derived only from inspecting the kernel code.

Example 8-1 *Retrieving Linux proc System Information*

```
[root@callisto:~#] cat /proc/net/route
[root@callisto:~#] cat /proc/net/rt_cache
[root@callisto:~#] cat /proc/net/rt_cache_stat
```

Example 8-2 *Linux and FreeBSD Routing Table Flags*

```
### Linux ###
                U (route is up)
                H (target is a host)
                G (use gateway)
                R (reinstate route for dynamic routing)
                D (dynamically installed by daemon or redirect)
                M (modified from routing daemon or redirect)
```

                                                                    continues

Example 8-2 *Linux and FreeBSD Routing Table Flags (Continued)*

```
                       A (installed by addrconf)
                       C (cache entry)
                       ! (reject route)

### FreeBSD ###
1     RTF_PROTO1       Protocol specific routing flag #1
2     RTF_PROTO2       Protocol specific routing flag #2
3     RTF_PROTO3       Protocol specific routing flag #3
B     RTF_BLACKHOLE    Just discard pkts (during updates)
b     RTF_BROADCAST    The route represents a broadcast address
C     RTF_CLONING      Generate new routes on use
c     RTF_PRCLONING    Protocol-specified generate new routes on use
D     RTF_DYNAMIC      Created dynamically (by redirect)
G     RTF_GATEWAY      Destination requires forwarding by intermediary
H     RTF_HOST         Host entry (net otherwise)
L     RTF_LLINFO       Valid protocol to link address translation
M     RTF_MODIFIED     Modified dynamically (by redirect)
R     RTF_REJECT       Host or net unreachable
S     RTF_STATIC       Manually added
U     RTF_UP           Route usable
W     RTF_WASCLONED    Route was generated as a result of cloning
X     RTF_XRESOLVE     External daemon translates proto to link address
```

Route Cloning

Cloned routes are a concept unique to BSD networks stacks. The concept refers to on-demand generation (cloning) of host routes (/32). In other words (quoted from the FreeBSD arp(4) manual page), "The ARP cache is stored in the system routing table as dynamically created host routes. The route to a directly attached Ethernet network is installed as a 'cloning' route (one with the RTF_CLONING flag set), causing routes to individual hosts on that network to be created on demand."[1] The actual cloning template (or parent) is marked with (C = generate new routes on use), the instantiated cloned host route (child) with (W = was cloned) in the system routing table. The associated ref_counter indicates how many existing connections use that particular entry, which is also correlated with an expire_timer (usually 3600 seconds). Cloned routes time out periodically after initial validation as long as they are not used.

Examples 8-3 through 8-5 show the differences in **arp** and **netstat** command output on OpenBSD, Linux, and FreeBSD operating systems to demonstrate the connection between next-hop/interface Media Access Control (MAC) resolution and similarities between **route** and **netstat** commands. In addition, interface statistics with netstat are presented, as are usage statistics of routing table entries. All routing tables present prefix entries, flags, a reference counter for the number of uses of a prefix, and a usage counter for the number of packets that were forwarded along that route out of the associated physical interface. Additional parameters of netstat output are system-specific.

Example 8-3 *OpenBSD* **arp** *and* **netstat** *Output*

```
[root@ganymed:~#] arp -an
? (192.168.1.1) at 52:54:05:e3:51:87
? (192.168.1.2) at 08:00:46:64:74:1b
? (192.168.2.7) at 00:10:5a:c4:2c:04
? (111.11.117.1) at 00:05:9a:5b:23:fc

[root@ganymed:~#] netstat -rna -f inet
Routing tables
Internet:
Destination        Gateway            Flags   Refs    Use   Mtu  Interface
default            111.11.117.1       UGS       3   11991  1500  ne5
127/8              127.0.0.1          UGRS      0       0 33224  lo0
127.0.0.1          127.0.0.1          UH        2       0 33224  lo0
192.168.1/24       link#1             UC        0       0  1500  ne3
192.168.1.1        52:54:5:e3:51:87   UHL       0    8801  1500  ne3
192.168.1.2        8:0:46:64:74:1b    UHL       1    4451  1500  ne3
192.168.1.254      127.0.0.1          UGHS      0       0 33224  lo0
192.168.2/24       link#2             UC        0       0  1500  ne4
192.168.2.7        0:10:5a:c4:2c:4    UHL       0    2111  1500  ne4
192.168.44.1       192.168.44.1       UH        0       0 33224  lo1
192.168.45/24      link#1             UC        0       0  1500  ne3
111.11.117/24      link#3             UC        0       0  1500  ne5
111.11.117.1       0:5:9a:5b:23:fc    UHL       1       0  1500  ne5

[root@ganymed:~#] netstat -in -f inet
Name  Mtu    Network    Address          Ipkts Ierrs  Opkts Oerrs Colls
lo0   33224  <Link>                          0     0      0     0     0
lo0   33224  fe80::/64  fe80::1             0     0      0     0     0
lo0   33224  ::1/128    ::1                 0     0      0     0     0
lo0   33224  127/8      127.0.0.1           0     0      0     0     0
lo1   33224  <Link>                          0     0      0     0     0
lo1   33224  192.168.44/ 192.168.44.1        0     0      0     0     0
lo1   33224  fe80::/64  fe80::1             0     0      0     0     0
lo1   33224  ::1/128    ::1                 0     0      0     0     0
ne3   1500   <Link>     48:54:e8:8c:0a:3f  17263     0  13427     0   329
ne3   1500   192.168.1/2 192.168.1.254     17263     0  13427     0   329
ne3   1500   fe80::/64  fe80::4a54:e8ff:f  17263     0  13427     0   329
ne3   1500   192.168.45/ 192.168.45.254    17263     0  13427     0   329
ne4   1500   <Link>     52:54:05:e3:e4:2f   2503   234   2247     0     0
ne4   1500   192.168.2/2 192.168.2.254      2503   234   2247     0     0
ne4   1500   fe80::/64  fe80::5054:5ff:fe   2503   234   2247     0     0
ne5   1500   <Link>     52:54:05:e3:51:87  11531  1253  12040     0     0
ne5   1500   111.11.117/ 111.11.117.206    11531  1253  12040     0     0
ne5   1500   fe80::/64  fe80::5054:5ff:fe  11531  1253  12040     0     0

[root@ganymed:~#] netstat -rs
routing:
        0 bad routing redirects
        0 dynamically created routes
        0 new gateways due to redirects
        10 destinations found unreachable
        0 uses of a wildcard route
```

Example 8-4 also demonstrates an advanced feature of Linux: TCP parameters such as the TCP Maximum Segment Size (MSS) and the TCP Window Size, which can be altered on a per-prefix basis (shaded text). For a better understanding, consider the following technical details quoted from the Linux route(8) manual page:

mss M:

set the TCP Maximum Segment Size (MSS) for connections over this route to M bytes. The default is the device MTU minus headers, or a lower MTU when path mtu discovery occurred [sic]. This setting can be used to force smaller TCP packets on the other end when path mtu discovery does not work (usually because of misconfigured firewalls that block ICMP Fragmentation Needed)

window W:

set the TCP window size for connections over this route to W bytes. This is typically only used on AX.25 networks and with drivers unable to handle back to back frames.[2]

Example 8-4 *Linux **arp** and **netstat** Output*

```
[root@callisto:~#] arp -an
? (192.168.1.2) at 08:00:46:64:74:1B [ether] on eth1
? (192.168.1.254) at 48:54:E8:8C:0A:3F [ether] on eth1

[root@callisto:~#] netstat -rnva
Kernel IP routing table
Destination     Gateway         Genmask         Flags   MSS Window  irtt Iface
192.168.1.0     0.0.0.0         255.255.255.0   U       40 0           0 eth1
192.168.1.0     0.0.0.0         255.255.255.0   U       40 0           0 ipsec0
192.168.14.0    0.0.0.0         255.255.255.0   U       40 0           0 eth0
127.0.0.0       0.0.0.0         255.0.0.0       U       40 0           0 lo
0.0.0.0         192.168.1.254   0.0.0.0         UG      40 0           0 eth1

[root@callisto:~#] netstat -i
Kernel Interface table
Iface   MTU Met   RX-OK RX-ERR RX-DRP RX-OVR   TX-OK TX-ERR TX-DRP TX-OVR Flg
eth0    1500  0     276      0      0      0     166      0      0      0 BMRU
eth1    1500  0   14889      0      0      0    9260      0      0      0 BMRU
ipsec  16260  0       0      0      0      0       0      0      0      0 ORU
lo     16436  0      64      0      0      0      64      0      0      0 LRU

[root@callisto:~#] route -nee
Kernel IP routing table
Destination     Gateway         Genmask         Flags Metric Ref Use Iface  MSS Window irtt
192.168.1.0     0.0.0.0         255.255.255.0   U     0      0   0   eth1   40  0      0
192.168.1.0     0.0.0.0         255.255.255.0   U     0      0   0   ipsec0 40  0      0
192.168.14.0    0.0.0.0         255.255.255.0   U     0      0   0   eth0   40  0      0
127.0.0.0       0.0.0.0         255.0.0.0       U     0      0   0   lo     40  0      0
0.0.0.0         192.168.1.254 0.0.0.0           UG    0      0   0   eth1   40  0      0
```

The highlighted text in Example 8-5 emphasizes the timer correlation of ARP cache entries and the forwarding table on FreeBSD for cloned routes (ARP neighbors). On BSD systems, you can manually adjust the route_expire sysctl parameter **net.inet.ip.rtexpire**, which defaults to 3600 seconds. Connected routes are created for each interface attached to the local host. Examples of the ip Linux facility are left to the lab because it is specific only to Linux, whereas **netstat** and **route** are generic tools of all Unices.

Example 8-5 *FreeBSD* **arp** *and* **netstat** *Output*

```
[root@castor:~#] arp -an
? (192.168.2.254) at 52:54:05:e3:e4:2f on xl0 [ethernet]
? (192.168.7.254) at 00:00:0c:1a:a9:a8 on ed0 [ethernet]

[root@castor:~#] netstat -rnaW -f inet
Routing tables
Internet:
Destination        Gateway            Flags   Refs    Use    Mtu   Netif Expire
default            192.168.2.254      UGSc    4       6      1500  xl0
127.0.0.1          127.0.0.1          UH      0       0      16384 lo0
192.53.103.103     192.168.2.254      UGHW3   0       63     1500  xl0   3314
192.53.103.104     192.168.2.254      UGHW    1       64     1500  xl0
192.168.1.2        192.168.2.254      UGHW    1       1207   1500  xl0
192.168.2          link#1             UC      2       0      1500  xl0
192.168.2.254      52:54:05:e3:e4:2f  UHLW    3       3      1500  xl0   1028
192.168.7          link#2             UC      1       0      1500  ed0
192.168.7.254      00:00:0c:1a:a9:a8  UHLW    1       5      1500  ed0   1038
195.34.133.10      192.168.2.254      UGHW3   0       14     1500  xl0   3440

[root@castor:~#] netstat -i -f inet
Name  Mtu    Network    Address         Ipkts Ierrs   Opkts Oerrs  Coll
xl0   1500   192.168.2  192.168.2.7     2260  -       3303  -      -
ed0   1500   192.168.7  castor          260   -       1214  -      -
lo0   16384  your-net   localhost       0     -       0     -      -

[root@castor:~#] netstat -rs
routing:
        0 bad routing redirects
        0 dynamically created routes
        0 new gateways due to redirects
        3 destinations found unreachable
        0 uses of a wildcard route
        1 route not in table but not freed
```

Blackholes and Reject/Prohibit Routes

These special routes can be deployed to install blocking routes that result in route lookup failure. BSD Unices differentiate between **-reject** (emit an ICMP unreachable when matched) and **-blackhole** (silently discard). An example is presented in Example 8-6. This is similar to deny/reject settings of modern firewalls.

Example 8-6 *FreeBSD* **reject/blackhole** *Static Routing Entries*

```
[root@castor:~#] route add -net 10.0.0.0/8 192.168.2.254 -reject
[root@castor:~#] route add -net 10.0.0.0/8 192.168.2.254 -blackhole
```

Similar flags exist for the Linux **ip route** command (**prohibit/blackhole/unreachable**), as demonstrated in Example 8-7. If you requires an interface packet sink, you can use the BSD ds0 interface (**pseudo-device disc**) or the Linux dummy0 interface (**ifconfig dummy0**).

Example 8-7 *Linux* **prohibit/blackhole/unreachable** *Static Routing Entries*

```
[root@callisto:~#] route add -net 10.0.0.0 netmask 255.0.0.0 reject
[root@callisto:~#] ip route add prohibit 172.16.1.0/24
[root@callisto:~#] ip route add blackhole 172.16.2.0/24
[root@callisto:~#] ip route add unreachable 172.16.3.0/24

[root@callisto:~#] netstat -rn
Kernel IP routing table
Destination     Gateway         Genmask         Flags   MSS Window  irtt Iface
172.16.2.0      0.0.0.0         255.255.255.0   U       40 0         0 *
192.168.1.0     0.0.0.0         255.255.255.0   U       40 0         0 eth1
192.168.1.0     0.0.0.0         255.255.255.0   U       40 0         0 ipsec0
172.16.1.0      -               255.255.255.0   !       - -         - -
172.16.3.0      -               255.255.255.0   !       - -         - -
192.168.14.0    0.0.0.0         255.255.255.0   U       40 0         0 eth0
10.0.0.0        -               255.0.0.0       !       - -         - -
127.0.0.0       0.0.0.0         255.0.0.0       U       40 0         0 lo
0.0.0.0         192.168.1.254   0.0.0.0         UG      40 0         0 eth1
```

Floating Static Routes

Floating static routes are a useful and simple measure to provide backup routes via another hop or link. However, a floating static route just "lurks" there and does not provide load balancing! This can be as simple as two default routes that just differ in terms of metric or cost. As long as the preferred route with the better metric is available, the floating static route with the less attractive metric floats unused but suddenly takes over if the preferred route disappears. A requirement is an operating system that supports metrics for static routes. Lab 8-1 shows an example of this setup.

Equal-Cost Multi-Path (ECMP) Routing

Equal-Cost Multi-Path (ECMP) is a forwarding mechanism for routing packets along multiple paths of equal cost with the goal to achieve almost equally distributed link load sharing. This, of course, significantly impacts a router's next-hop (path) decision.

For further details, look at RFC 2991, "Multipath Issues in Unicast and Multicast Next-Hop Selection," and RFC 2992, "Analysis of an Equal-Cost Multi-Path Algorithm."

ECMP is available only for Linux in the open-source UNIX world; it solely is a feature of the underlying network stack. The terminology stems from the world of link-state routing protocols, which facilitate a cost-based metric; OSPF and Intermediate System-to-Intermediate System (IS-IS) explicitly allow ECMP routing. Load balancing can be carried out based on equal cost or unequal cost, per packet or per destination.

Because of the absence of a metric (weight), static routes under Cisco IOS Software support only equal-cost load sharing. To disable destination-based fast switching, you can force Cisco IOS Software to process switch on a per-packet basis with the interface command **no ip route-cache**. However, this does not affect CEF. Use **ip load-sharing per-packet** in that case.

As previously mentioned, UNIX stacks in general have a per-packet-based view of the world, in contrast to the Cisco default per-connection view (CEF, fast-switching cache). This behavior changes when enabling ECMP in the Linux kernel or deploying a route cache. In that case, the Linux OS performs per-flow balancing that can be changed to per-packet behavior with the **equalize** flag of the **ip route** command. Besides its merits, it can introduce performance issues because of stream rearrangement, in particular when dealing with real-time Voice over IP (VoIP) traffic. This has to be taken into consideration as well when changing Cisco forwarding settings from per destination to per packet. Figure 8-4 shows a possible scenario for ECMP where load balancing is desirable.

Figure 8-4   *ECMP Example Architecture*

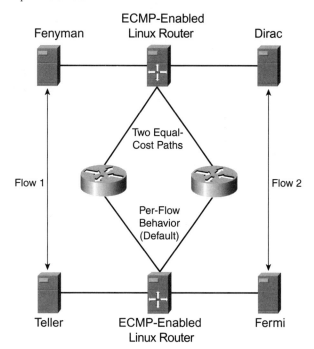

Lab 8-1: Interface Metrics, Floating Static Routes, and Multiple Equal-Cost Routes (ECMP)

Example 8-8 demonstrates the use of different metrics (the least preferable is referred to as a floating static route) for the same prefix as well as equal metrics for load balancing. The BSD world only supplies metrics in context with interfaces (see Example 8-9). This is not a deficiency, but is instead a design choice to leave these issues to dynamic routing protocols.

If you use two routes with an equal metric value, load balancing is done on a per-connection basis; if you specify the Linux **equalize** keyword on two routes, load balancing is done on a per-packet basis. In this case, the route is just recomputed for every packet. Without it, the route stays cached and bound to a specific next hop as long as it is up and alive.

Example 8-8 starts with adding two unequal-cost routes to the same destination prefix via the **route** and different prefixes via the **ip route** command sequence to demonstrate a floating static route setup. This is different on a Cisco router: The floating static route is added only to the routing table "on demand," when the preferable prefix route fails, hence the name *floating*. The second command sequence of Example 8-8 establishes a mix of per-destination and per-packet (**equalize**) load-balanced ECMP. As you can see from the following output in Example 8-9, both unequal metric routes are placed in the routing table. The ECMP routes have the same weight, 1, and the two per-packet load-balanced ECMP routes are labeled with the **equalize** flag (shaded text).

Example 8-8 *Linux ECMP Setup Example*

```
[root@callisto:~#] route add -net 11.1.1.0/24 metric 2 gw 192.168.1.254
[root@callisto:~#] route add -net 11.1.1.0/24 metric 1 gw 192.168.14.254
[root@callisto:~#] ip route add 11.1.2.0/24 via 192.168.1.254 metric 2
[root@callisto:~#] ip route add 11.1.2.0/24 via 192.168.14.254 metric 1
[root@callisto:~#] ip route add 10.1.1.0/24 equalize nexthop via 192.168.1.254 dev eth1
                   nexthop via 192.168.14.254 dev eth0
[root@callisto:~#] ip route add 10.1.5.0/24 nexthop via 192.168.1.254 nexthop via
                   192.168.14.254
```

Example 8-9 *Linux ECMP Setup Result*

```
[root@callisto:~#] ip route help
Usage: ip route { list | flush } SELECTOR
       ip route get ADDRESS [ from ADDRESS iif STRING ]
                           [ oif STRING ] [ tos TOS ]
       ip route { add | del | change | append | replace | monitor } ROUTE
SELECTOR := [ root PREFIX ] [ match PREFIX ] [ exact PREFIX ]
            [ table TABLE_ID ] [ proto RTPROTO ]
            [ type TYPE ] [ scope SCOPE ]
ROUTE := NODE_SPEC [ INFO_SPEC ]
```

Example 8-9   *Linux ECMP Setup Result (Continued)*

```
NODE_SPEC := [ TYPE ] PREFIX [ tos TOS ]
              [ table TABLE_ID ] [ proto RTPROTO ]
              [ scope SCOPE ] [ metric METRIC ]
INFO_SPEC := NH OPTIONS FLAGS [ nexthop NH ]...
NH := [ via ADDRESS ] [ dev STRING ] [ weight NUMBER ] NHFLAGS
OPTIONS := FLAGS [ mtu NUMBER ] [ advmss NUMBER ]
            [ rtt NUMBER ] [ rttvar NUMBER ]
            [ window NUMBER] [ cwnd NUMBER ] [ ssthresh REALM ]
            [ realms REALM ]
TYPE := [ unicast | local | broadcast | multicast | throw |
          unreachable | prohibit | blackhole | nat ]
TABLE_ID := [ local | main | default | all | NUMBER ]
SCOPE := [ host | link | global | NUMBER ]
FLAGS := [ equalize ]
NHFLAGS := [ onlink | pervasive ]
RTPROTO := [ kernel | boot | static | NUMBER ]


[root@callisto:~#] ip route show
192.168.1.0/24 dev eth1  scope link
192.168.1.0/24 dev ipsec0  proto kernel  scope link  src 192.168.1.1
10.1.5.0/24
        nexthop via 192.168.1.254  dev eth1 weight 1
        nexthop via 192.168.14.254  dev eth0 weight 1
192.168.14.0/24 dev eth0  scope link
11.1.2.0/24 via 192.168.14.254 dev eth0  metric 1
11.1.2.0/24 via 192.168.1.254 dev eth1  metric 2
10.1.1.0/24 equalize
        nexthop via 192.168.1.254  dev eth1 weight 1
        nexthop via 192.168.14.254  dev eth0 weight 1
11.1.1.0/24 via 192.168.14.254 dev eth0  metric 1
11.1.1.0/24 via 192.168.1.254 dev eth1  metric 2
127.0.0.0/8 dev lo  scope link
default via 192.168.1.254 dev eth1

[root@callisto:~#] route -n
Kernel IP routing table
Destination     Gateway         Genmask         Flags Metric Ref    Use Iface
192.168.1.0     0.0.0.0         255.255.255.0   U     0      0        0 eth1
192.168.1.0     0.0.0.0         255.255.255.0   U     0      0        0 ipsec0
10.1.5.0        192.168.1.254   255.255.255.0   UG    0      0        0 eth1
192.168.14.0    0.0.0.0         255.255.255.0   U     0      0        0 eth0
11.1.2.0        192.168.14.254  255.255.255.0   UG    1      0        0 eth0
11.1.2.0        192.168.1.254   255.255.255.0   UG    2      0        0 eth1
10.1.1.0        192.168.1.254   255.255.255.0   UG    0      0        0 eth1
11.1.1.0        192.168.14.254  255.255.255.0   UG    1      0        0 eth0
11.1.1.0        192.168.1.254   255.255.255.0   UG    2      0        0 eth1
127.0.0.0       0.0.0.0         255.0.0.0       U     0      0        0 lo
0.0.0.0         192.168.1.254   0.0.0.0         UG    0      0        0 eth1
```

As previously mentioned, BSD Unices do not provide metrics in context with the **route** command. However, you can assign metrics to interfaces, as demonstrated in Example 8-10 (shaded text).

Example 8-10 *Example for OpenBSD Interface Metrics*

```
[root@ganymed:~#] ifconfig ne4 metric 5
[root@ganymed:~#] ifconfig -A
...
ne4: flags=8863<UP,BROADCAST,NOTRAILERS,RUNNING,SIMPLEX,MULTICAST> metric 5 mtu 1500
        media: Ethernet 10baseT full-duplex
        inet 192.168.2.254 netmask 0xffffff00 broadcast 192.168.2.255
        inet6 fe80::5054:5ff:fee3:e42f%ne4 prefixlen 64 scopeid 0x2
...
```

Linux TEQL (True Link Equalizer)

Several approaches exist to accomplish traffic flows over equal- or unequal-cost paths or interfaces. We have investigated Ethernet channel bonding (Layer 1) and ECMP so far. Other approaches are as follows:

- PPP Multilink (/usr/src/linux/Documentation/networking/ppp_generic.txt), which is still an experimental feature of the Linux kernel but is available on BSD Unices via mpd (Netgraph Multilink PPP daemon).

- TEQL, the "true" (or "trivial") link equalizer, which is unique to the Linux kernel. TEQL facilitates a queuing approach via the tc (traffic control) tool, which is an integral part of the Linux iproute2 suite of tools.

As always with link equalizing or ECMP, consider the negative implications of packet reordering, especially with heavily unbalanced links. (Note the following caveat.) TEQL support has to be compiled as a kernel module. Example 8-11 shows an example setup equalizing over two Ethernet network interface cards (NICs). TEQL uses its own virtual device, teql0.

Example 8-11 *Joining Slaves to a Linux Equalizer Interface*

```
[root@ganymed:~#] insmod sch_teql

[root@ganymed:~#] tc qdisc add dev eth0 root teql0
[root@ganymed:~#] tc qdisc add dev eth1 root teql0

[root@callisto:~#] ifconfig -a
teql0     Link encap:UNSPEC  HWaddr 00-00-00-00-00-00-00-00-00-00-00-00-00-00-00-00
          NOARP  MTU:1500  Metric:1
          RX packets:0 errors:0 dropped:0 overruns:0 frame:0
          TX packets:0 errors:0 dropped:0 overruns:0 carrier:0
          collisions:0 txqueuelen:100
          RX bytes:0 (0.0 b)  TX bytes:0 (0.0 b)
```

Example 8-11 *Joining Slaves to a Linux Equalizer Interface (Continued)*

```
[root@callisto:~#] tc -s qdisc
qdisc teql0 8001: dev eth0
Sent 0 bytes 0 pkts (dropped 0, overlimits 0)
qdisc teql0 8002: dev eth1
Sent 0 bytes 0 pkts (dropped 0, overlimits 0)
```

CAUTION   As Alexej Kuznetsov's said, "This device (teql0) puts no limitations on physical slave characteristics; [for example,] it will equalize 9600-baud line and 100-Mb Ethernet perfectly. Certainly, [a] large difference in link speeds will make the resulting equalized link unusable because of huge packet reordering. I estimate an upper useful difference as ~10 times."[3]

Adding Static Routes via Routing Daemons

Based on this chapter, you should now understand why adding static routes from the UNIX command line differs from adding static routes to the configuration of routing protocol daemons. The former acts directly on the FIB, whereas the latter acts on the RIB.

You should also note that because of this design paradigm, the routing engines differentiate between redistributing static routes added via routing protocol daemons and kernel routes added via the shell. For a complete treatise, three example configuration fragments for MRTd, GateD, and Zebra are offered (Examples 8-12 through 8-14). You can configure a preference value (administrative distance in Cisco notation) for comparison with other internal routing feeds, whereas from the UNIX shell only metrics are possible.

Example 8-12 *MRTd Static Routes*

```
[root@callisto:~#] cat /etc/mrtd.conf
...
router rip
  network 192.168.1.0/24
  network 192.168.14.0/24
  redistribute connected
  redistribute static
  redistribute kernel
!
route 0.0.0.0/0  192.168.1.254 1
...
```

Example 8-13 *GateD Static Routes*

```
[root@callisto:~#] cat /etc/gated.conf
...
static{
        host 172.16.5.5 gateway 192.168.1.254 reject;
        host 172.16.5.6 gateway 192.168.1.254 retain;
```

continues

Example 8-13 *GateD Static Routes (Continued)*

```
host 172.16.5.7 gateway 192.168.1.254 noinstall;
        172.16.1.0 mask 255.255.255.0 gateway 192.168.1.254 preference 1
        interface eth1;
        172.16.2.0 masklen 24 gateway 192.168.1.254 blackhole;
        default gateway 192.168.1.254;
};
export proto rip{
        proto static;
        proto direct;
        proto kernel;
};
...
```

Example 8-14 *Zebra Static Routes*

```
[root@callisto:~#] cat /usr/local/etc/zebra.conf
...
ip route 172.16.7.0/24 eth1 1
ip route 172.16.44.0/24 Null0
...
```

Summary

This chapter went into great length to explain the UNIX routing architecture with regard to the FIB and route caches, the way they are populated with entries, and their similarities and differences compared to the Cisco IOS architecture. This is important to understand how the view changes when dynamic routing protocols take over control in the following chapters. Therefore, this chapter elaborated on the representation of connected and static routes, issues such as metric and blackhole routes, and configuration via the Linux ip route and platform-independent route utilities. Special setups such as floating static routes, ECMP, and TEQL were discussed and demonstrated in a lab scenario, concluding with a short preview of how you can use static routes from within routing protocol engines.

Recommended Reading

- The route manual page

- The netstat manual page

- The arp manual page

- The ifconfig manual page

- Alexej Kuznetsov's TEQL Linux source file sch_teql.c (included in the Linux sources)

- RFC 2991, "Multipath Issues in Unicast and Multicast Next-Hop Selection"

- RFC 2992, "Analysis of an Equal-Cost Multi-Path Algorithm"
- PPP Multilink /usr/src/linux/Documentation/networking/ppp_generic.txt
- RFC 1990, "PPP Multilink Protocol (MP)"
- RFC 2125, "PPP Bandwidth Allocation Protocol—Supports unlimited Number of ML-PPP Bundles"

Endnotes

1 FreeBSD arp(4) manual page

2 Linux route(8) manual page

3 Alexej Kuznetsov's TEQL Linux source file sch_teql.c

## CHAPTER 9

Dynamic Routing Protocols— Interior Gateway Protocols

This chapter forms the heart of this book and represents my original impulse to write about UNIX routing.

It is almost impossible to tame and reliably operate rapidly changing environments and topologies solely with the use of static routes. This especially is an issue in Internet service provider (ISP) networks with large numbers of dynamically created routes via PPP-connections from dial or Digital Subscriber Line (DSL) customers. However, the main purpose of dynamic routing is providing high availability in case of node or link failures. Dynamic routing protocols were designed to adapt to topology changes and distribute routing information within an autonomous system, based on an underlying algorithm.

This chapter discusses the two families of Interior Gateway Routing Protocols (IGRPs) and provides extensive lab scenarios using Routing Information Protocol (RIP), Open Shortest Path First (OSPF), and a quick introduction to Intermediate System-to-Intermediate System (IS-IS), which most likely is rather exotic or even alien to UNIX and even some network folks. Based on the insight of the previous chapter, this chapter extends the view to how dynamic routing protocols populate the kernel routing table and takes a closer look at making proper choices for deployment based on essential characteristics of these protocols as well as service and topology requirements. This chapter also introduces the concept of *areas*—virtual segmentations of network realms—a specialty of link-state routing protocols. Special topics such as route exports and redistribution, Equal-Cost Multi-Path (ECMP) issues, and traffic-engineering extensions conclude the chapter.

Interaction with the UNIX Routing Table

As mentioned in Chapter 8, "Static Routing Concepts," dynamic routing protocol implementations use *administrative distance* (preference) for internal comparison and weighting. Based on these criteria, the UNIX Forwarding Information Base (FIB) is populated with the result of the internal comparison. The UNIX FIB has no knowledge of administrative distances; only *metrics* are relevant for forwarding table lookups. Depending on the configuration, these routes are removed or retained after shutdown of the routing daemon(s). From this point of view, the kernel interface resembles a routing protocol by itself and is treated similarly, especially during system startup and redistribution of kernel routes.

Classification of Dynamic Routing Protocols

Dynamic routing protocols are based on an algorithm, such as Bellman-Ford-Fulkerson, Dijkstra SPF (Shortest Path First), or the Enhanced Interior Gateway Routing Protocol (EIGRP) DUAL (Diffuse Update Algorithm). Based on these algorithms, dynamic IGPs can be classified in link-state and distance-vector protocols.

NOTE   The Border Gateway Protocol (BGP) discussed in the next chapter represents a path-vector protocol essentially based on a distance-vector approach as well.

The main task of these protocols is path determination and calculation. With multiple paths to a destination prefix, the protocol makes intrinsic decisions based on metrics/cost/preference assigned to routes. Such a label is a measure of preference *within* a particular routing protocol. It can be simple, such as hop count for RIP, or a composite metric such as with EIGRP based on load, reliability, delay, and bandwidth, or cost based in a generic way such as with OSPF.

Link-State Protocols

Link-state protocols such as OSPF are cost-based, and the cost is usually derived from the link bandwidth. When a protocol has a stable view of the topology, it is referred to as having *converged* or achieved equilibrium. Do not confuse this view with the notion of converged networks meaning voice, video, data, and storage over one consolidated IP infrastructure.

The task of computing shortest paths in a network is a mathematical problem tackled with graph theory. You will read more about that in the section "Introduction to Link-State Routing Protocols" later in this chapter. Nevertheless, one cannot argue that link-state protocols are superior in every aspect per se.

Distance-Vector Protocols

Distance-vector protocols usually broadcast full table updates. Deviation from this case is referred to as an asynchronous, triggered, flash, or incremental update.

Note the following:

The name distance vector is derived from the fact that routes are advertised as vectors of (distance, direction), where distance is defined in terms of a metric and direction is defined in terms of the next-hop router.[1]

For loop prevention, *simple split horizon* or *split horizon with poisoned reverse* is used in distance-vector protocols. A thorough discussion of loop detection, prevention, and termination goes beyond the scope of this book. I recommend Jeff Doyle's two volumes of *Routing TCP/IP* (Cisco Press; 1998 and 2001, respectively) for further information.

From RIP to EIGRP

The following subsections briefly introduce the RIP, IGRP, and EIGRP routing protocols. IGRP and EIGRP were developed to overcome the limitations of the original RIP design.

RIP—A Distance-Vector Routing Protocol (Bellman-Ford-Fulkerson)

RIP had been around for quite a while. As Jeff Doyle put it, "RIP is either unjustly maligned or undeservedly popular."[2] RIP comes in two flavors: RIPv1, which is classful, and RIPv2, which is classless. It supports multicast, broadcast, and (under certain conditions) unicast behavior. The most dominant constraint of both RIP versions is the hop-count limit of 15, which limits the network diameter of deployments.

RIP is a distance-vector protocol, designed for rather small networks, contiguous address blocks, and homogeneous data links. From the protocol point of view, RIPv1 and RIPv2 speakers and listeners can happily coexist; the necessary compatibility mechanisms work well. However, this usually introduces undesirable effects with regard to classful behavior and summarization. Therefore, the recommendation is not to use RIPv1 whenever possible or at least not mix RIPv1 and RIPv2. In addition, RIPv2 introduces authentication and prefix tagging and is based on multicast transmission facilitating 224.0.0.9 and 520/udp as a transport vehicle.

Contrasting common beliefs that it is archaic and obsolete, RIP still plays an important role in system-integration scenarios. It is the least common denominator for Microsoft gateways and cheap appliance routers that lack support of more sophisticated dynamic routing protocols. Besides, in small LAN topologies, RIP certainly is up to the job, and system administrators can easily grasp its concepts and feel comfortable. Service providers can as well easily control RIP routes within customer virtual private networks (VPNs), while allowing customer premises equipment (CPE) to inject routes themselves.

(E)IGRP

The proprietary Cisco protocols IGRP and EIGRP were originally developed to overcome some of the limitations of RIP. IGRP has almost entirely disappeared and is not deployed anymore, although it is still supported.

EIGRP has evolved into quite a powerful and useful routing protocol including advanced features, the DUAL algorithm (Diffuse Update Algorithm), and a composite metric. EIGRP is the only routing protocol that supports non-IP network layer protocols such as AppleTalk and Internetwork Packet Exchange (IPX), with the notable exception of IS-IS, which natively supports IP and ISO CLNP (Connectionless Network Protocol).

Discussion of (E)IGRP goes beyond the scope of this book. Once again, I recommend Jeff Doyle's excellent two volumes of *Routing TCP/IP* for an in-depth introduction as well Ivan Pepelnjak's classic textbook *EIGRP Network Design Solutions* (Cisco Press, 2000).

Lab 9-1: RIPv2 Scenario

For this lab, GateD is running on ganymed, MRTd is running on castor and callisto, and Cisco IOS Software is running on scar. Figure 9-1 shows the topology.

Figure 9-1 *RIPv2 Lab Topology*

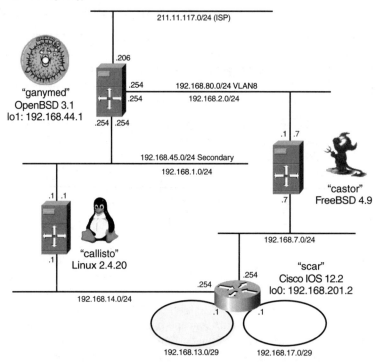

For a detailed log output of gated, send a **kill –SIGINT** to the running gated process. You can also access the gated interactive interface via **telnet localhost 616** or use the **ripquery** utility for RIP status information. A possible expansion of this setup would be to include routed, which was discussed thoroughly in Chapter 1, "Operating System Issues and Features—The Big Picture."

The lab uses regular interfaces, VLAN interfaces, alias addresses, and loopback addresses to demonstrate the independence of the routing engines from Layer 2 and virtual interfaces. This is also valid for WAN subinterfaces and tunnels of various kinds as long as the operating system is capable of providing a proper interface abstraction (virtual interface).

As you can see from the routing table outputs, the dynamic daemons internally use the concept of administrative distance (preference), but externally only the notion of metrics has relevance. Throughout this lab, we use RIPv2 multicast only. Example 9-1 shows the 224.0.0.9 multicast address in the netstat output (highlighted line); it is automatically added by the kernel.

NOTE   Per default, GateD turns RIP on. If you do not want to run the RIP module, you have to explicitly turn it off in the GateD configuration file with the command **rip off** (as presented in the GateD configuration in Example 9-1) or disable this behavior at compile time, as demonstrated in the GateD setup in Chapter 1.

Example 9-1 *GateD RIPv2 Configuration and Output on Ganymed*

```
[root@ganymed:~#] cat /etc/gated.cfg
#rip off;
rip on{
        interface ne4 ne3 vlan0
                ripin
                ripout
                version 2 multicast;
};

[root@ganymed:~#] netstat -rn -f inet
Routing tables
Internet:
Destination        Gateway            Flags   Refs    Use    Mtu   Interface
default            111.11.117.1       UGS      1     3831   1500   ne5
127/8              127.0.0.1          UR       0        0  33224   lo0
127.0.0.1          127.0.0.1          UH       1        0  33224   lo0
192.168.1/24       link#1             UC    -210        0   1500   ne3
192.168.1.1        52:54:5:e3:51:87   UHL      1     1916   1500   ne3
192.168.1.2        8:0:46:64:74:1b    UHL      1     4615   1500   ne3
192.168.1.254      127.0.0.1          UGHS     0        0  33224   lo0
192.168.2/24       link#2             UC       0        0   1500   ne4
192.168.2.7        0:10:5a:c4:2c:4    UHL      5     2505   1500   ne4
192.168.7/24       192.168.2.7        UG       2      821   1500   ne4
192.168.13.0/29    192.168.2.7        UG       0        0   1500   ne4
192.168.14/24      192.168.1.1        UG       0        0   1500   ne3
192.168.17.0/29    192.168.2.7        UG       0        0   1500   ne4
192.168.44.1       192.168.44.1       UH       0        0  33224   lo1
192.168.45/24      192.168.2.7        UG       0        0   1500   ne4
192.168.80/24      link#16            UC       0        0   1496   vlan0
192.168.201.2      192.168.2.7        UGH      0        0   1500   ne4
111.11.117/24      link#3             UC       0        0   1500   ne5
111.11.117.1       0:5:9a:5b:23:fc    UHL      1        0   1500   ne5
224.0.0.9          127.0.0.1          UH       1     1315  33224   lo0
```

Example 9-2 shows the advanced capabilities of the Linux ip tool. It presents the dynamic source that the routes were learned from via identifiers (Zebra, MRT, GateD), as well as the callisto MRTd configuration. The MRTd intrinsic routing table shows how cost (preference) is used internally with regard to the RIB (highlighted text). Note that connected and static routes are explicitly marked as *Kernel* in the MRTd global routing table (highlighted text). Example 9-3 presents the topology from castor's point of view.

Example 9-2 *MRTd RIPv2 Configuration and Output on Callisto*

```
[root@callisto:~#] ip route
192.168.201.2 via 192.168.14.254 dev eth0  proto mrt
192.168.44.1 via 192.168.45.254 dev eth1  proto mrt
192.168.17.0/29 via 192.168.14.254 dev eth0  proto mrt
192.168.13.0/29 via 192.168.14.254 dev eth0  proto mrt
192.168.7.0/24 via 192.168.14.254 dev eth0  proto mrt
111.11.117.0/24 via 192.168.45.254 dev eth1  proto mrt
192.168.2.0/24 via 192.168.45.254 dev eth1  proto mrt
192.168.80.0/24 via 192.168.45.254 dev eth1  proto mrt
192.168.1.0/24 dev eth1  scope link
192.168.1.0/24 dev ipsec0  proto kernel  scope link  src 192.168.1.1
192.168.14.0/24 dev eth0  scope link
192.168.45.0/24 dev eth1  proto kernel  scope link  src 192.168.45.1
127.0.0.0/8 dev lo  scope link
default via 192.168.1.254 dev eth1

[root@callisto:~#] netstat -rne
Kernel IP routing table
Destination     Gateway         Genmask         Flags Metric Ref    Use Iface
192.168.201.2   192.168.14.254  255.255.255.255 UGH   0      0        0 eth0
192.168.44.1    192.168.45.254  255.255.255.255 UGH   0      0        0 eth1
192.168.17.0    192.168.14.254  255.255.255.248 UG    0      0        0 eth0
192.168.13.0    192.168.14.254  255.255.255.248 UG    0      0        0 eth0
192.168.7.0     192.168.14.254  255.255.255.0   UG    0      0        0 eth0
111.11.117.0    192.168.45.254  255.255.255.0   UG    0      0        0 eth1
192.168.2.0     192.168.45.254  255.255.255.0   UG    0      0        0 eth1
192.168.80.0    192.168.45.254  255.255.255.0   UG    0      0        0 eth1
192.168.1.0     0.0.0.0         255.255.255.0   U     0      0        0 eth1
192.168.1.0     0.0.0.0         255.255.255.0   U     0      0        0 ipsec0
192.168.14.0    0.0.0.0         255.255.255.0   U     0      0        0 eth0
192.168.45.0    0.0.0.0         255.255.255.0   U     0      0        0 eth1
127.0.0.0       0.0.0.0         255.0.0.0       U     0      0        0 lo
0.0.0.0         192.168.1.254   0.0.0.0         UG    0      0        0 eth1

callisto-MRTd# sh config
!
enable password ********
router rip
  network 192.168.1.0/24
  network 192.168.14.0/24
  redistribute connected
  redistribute static
  redistribute kernel
!
route 0.0.0.0/0  192.168.1.254
debug all /var/log/mrtd.log 0

callisto-MRTd# sh rib
38 active prefixes
17 active generic attributes
13 active route heads
17 active route nodes
```

Example 9-2 *MRTd RIPv2 Configuration and Output on Callisto (Continued)*

```
7 inet gateway(s)/nexthop(s) registered
    0.0.0.0       on lo flags 0x8 (count 3)
    0.0.0.0       on eth0 flags 0x8 (count 4)
    0.0.0.0       on eth1 flags 0x8 (count 7)
    0.0.0.0       on ipsec0 flags 0x8 (count 3)
    192.168.1.254        on eth1 flags 0x2 (count 1264)
    192.168.14.254       on eth0 flags 0x2 (count 668)
    192.168.45.254       on eth1 flags 0x2 (count 19)

callisto-MRTd# sh ip rip
Routing Protocol is "rip"
Listening on port 520 (socket 13)
Sending updates every 30 seconds jitter [-50..50], next due in 20 seconds
Triggered update and split horizon (no poisoned reverse) implemented
Invalid after 180, hold down 120, flushed after 300 seconds
Interface enabled: eth1 eth0
Number of routes in routing table: 12

Callisto-MRTd# sh ip rip routes
  P Pref Time      Destination           Next Hop          If     Cost Time
* R 120 04:57:04 0.0.0.0/0              192.168.14.254    eth0      2   20
> S   1 05:04:39 0.0.0.0/0              192.168.1.254     eth1      1  ----
* R 120 05:04:30 192.168.1.0/24         192.168.45.254    eth1      2    2
> C   0 05:04:39 192.168.1.0/24         0.0.0.0           ipsec0    1  ----
  R 120 00:00:20 192.168.2.0/24         192.168.14.254    eth0      3   20
> R 120 00:00:02 192.168.2.0/24         192.168.45.254    eth1      2    2
  R 120 00:00:02 192.168.7.0/24         192.168.45.254    eth1      3    2
> R 120 04:57:06 192.168.7.0/24         192.168.14.254    eth0      2   20
  R 120 00:00:02 192.168.13.0/29        192.168.45.254    eth1      4    2
> R 120 04:56:44 192.168.13.0/29        192.168.14.254    eth0      2   20
* R 120 05:02:39 192.168.14.0/24        192.168.45.254    eth1      3    2
> C   0 05:04:39 192.168.14.0/24        0.0.0.0           eth0      1  ----
  R 120 00:00:02 192.168.17.0/29        192.168.45.254    eth1      4    2
> R 120 04:56:23 192.168.17.0/29        192.168.14.254    eth0      2   20
> R 120 00:00:02 192.168.44.1/32        192.168.45.254    eth1      2    2
* R 120 00:00:02 192.168.45.0/24        192.168.45.254    eth1      5    2
> C   0 00:47:47 192.168.45.0/24        0.0.0.0           eth1      1  ----
  R 120 00:00:20 192.168.80.0/24        192.168.14.254    eth0      3   20
> R 120 00:00:02 192.168.80.0/24        192.168.45.254    eth1      2    2
  R 120 00:00:02 192.168.201.2/32       192.168.45.254    eth1      4    2
> R 120 04:57:06 192.168.201.2/32       192.168.14.254    eth0      2   20
> R 120 00:00:02 111.11.117.0/24        192.168.45.254    eth1      2    2

callisto-MRTd# sh ip routes
Number of Unique Destinations: 13, Number of Entries: 17
Status code: > best, * valid, i - internal, x - no next-hop, X - no install
  P Pref Time      Destination           Next Hop          If     Kernel
> S   1 05:04:57 0.0.0.0/0              192.168.1.254     eth1     K
  R 120 04:57:22 0.0.0.0/0              192.168.14.254    eth0
>iC   0 05:04:57 127.0.0.0/8            0.0.0.0           lo       K
> C   0 05:04:57 192.168.1.0/24         0.0.0.0           ipsec0   K
  R 120 05:04:48 192.168.1.0/24         192.168.45.254    eth1
> R 120 00:00:20 192.168.2.0/24         192.168.45.254    eth1
```

continues

Example 9-2 *MRTd RIPv2 Configuration and Output on Callisto (Continued)*

```
> R   120 04:57:24 192.168.7.0/24          192.168.14.254      eth0
> R   120 04:57:02 192.168.13.0/29         192.168.14.254      eth0
> C     0 05:04:57 192.168.14.0/24         0.0.0.0             eth0    K
  R   120 05:02:57 192.168.14.0/24         192.168.45.254      eth1
> R   120 04:56:41 192.168.17.0/29         192.168.14.254      eth0
> R   120 00:00:20 192.168.44.1/32         192.168.45.254      eth1
> C     0 00:48:05 192.168.45.0/24         0.0.0.0             eth1
  R   120 00:00:20 192.168.45.0/24         192.168.45.254      eth1
> R   120 00:00:20 192.168.80.0/24         192.168.45.254      eth1
> R   120 04:57:24 192.168.201.2/32        192.168.14.254      eth0
> R   120 00:00:20 111.11.117.0/24         192.168.45.254      eth1
```

Example 9-3 *MRTd RIPv2 Configuration and Output on Castor*

```
castor-MRTd# sh config
!
enable password ********
router rip
  network 192.168.2.0/24
  network 192.168.7.0/24
  network 192.168.80.0/24
  redistribute connected
  redistribute static
  redistribute kernel
!
route 0.0.0.0/0  192.168.2.254
debug all /var/log/mrtd.log 0

castor-MRTd# show timers
Timer Master: Interval=(37), NextFire=(5)
Timer RIP update timer: Interval 37 Base 30 Exponent 0 Jitter 0 [-50..50] Flags 0x20
  Timeleft 5
Timer kernel routes timeout timer: Interval 120 Base 120 Exponent 0 Jitter 0 [0..0]
  Flags 0x9 Timeleft 88
Timer RIP aging timer: Interval 180 Base 180 Exponent 0 Jitter 0 [0..0] Flags 0x1
  Timeleft 148
Timer UII timeout timer: Interval 300 Base 300 Exponent 0 Jitter 0 [0..0] Flags 0x1
  Timeleft 300
Timer RIP flash timer: Interval 0 Base 0 Exponent 0 Jitter 0 [0..0] Flags 0x1 OFF
Timer igmp aging timer: Interval 0 Base 260 Exponent 0 Jitter 0 [0..0] Flags 0x1 OFF
Timer igmp aging timer: Interval 0 Base 260 Exponent 0 Jitter 0 [0..0] Flags 0x1 OFF
Timer RIP update timer: Interval 0 Base 30 Exponent 0 Jitter 0 [-50..50] Flags 0x20
  OFF
Timer RIP aging timer: Interval 0 Base 180 Exponent 0 Jitter 0 [0..0] Flags 0x1 OFF
Timer RIP flash timer: Interval 0 Base 0 Exponent 0 Jitter 0 [0..0] Flags 0x1 OFF
Timer PIM prune timer: Interval 0 Base 0 Exponent 0 Jitter 0 [0..0] Flags 0x1 OFF
Timer PIM join timer: Interval 0 Base 0 Exponent 0 Jitter 0 [0..0] Flags 0x1 OFF
Timer PIM graft timer: Interval 0 Base 0 Exponent 0 Jitter 0 [0..0] Flags 0x1 OFF
Timer PIM route timer: Interval 0 Base 15 Exponent 0 Jitter 0 [0..0] Flags 0x0 OFF
Timer BGP house keeping timer: Interval 0 Base 15 Exponent 0 Jitter 0 [0..0] Flags
  0x0 OFF

castor-MRTd# sh rib
55 active prefixes
```

Example 9-3 *MRTd RIPv2 Configuration and Output on Castor (Continued)*

```
20 active generic attributes
18 active route heads
21 active route nodes
8 inet gateway(s)/nexthop(s) registered
    0.0.0.0      on xl0 flags 0x8 (count 4)
    0.0.0.0      on ed0 flags 0x8 (count 4)
    0.0.0.0      on lo0 flags 0x8 (count 2)
    0.0.0.0      on vlan8 flags 0x8 (count 4)
    127.0.0.1    on lo0 flags 0x1 (count 2)
    192.168.2.254      on xl0 flags 0x2 (count 170)
    192.168.7.254      on ed0 flags 0x2 (count 172)
    192.168.80.254     on vlan8 flags 0x2 (count 154)
2 inet6 gateway(s)/nexthop(s) registered
    ::  on lo0 flags 0x8 (count 2)
    ::1 on lo0 flags 0x1 (count 5)

castor-MRTd# sh ip rip
Routing Protocol is "rip"
Listening on port 520 (socket 12)
Sending updates every 30 seconds jitter [-50..50], next due in 22 seconds
Triggered update and split horizon (no poisoned reverse) implemented
Invalid after 180, hold down 120, flushed after 300 seconds
Interface enabled: xl0 ed0 vlan8
Number of routes in routing table: 12

Castor-MRTd# sh ip rip routes
  P Pref Time     Destination        Next Hop         If     Cost Time
> S   1 01:10:55 0.0.0.0/0          192.168.2.254    xl0     1 ----
  R 120 00:00:04 192.168.1.0/24     192.168.80.254   vlan8   2    4
  R 120 00:00:23 192.168.1.0/24     192.168.7.254    ed0     3   23
> R 120 01:10:55 192.168.1.0/24     192.168.2.254    xl0     2    4
* R 120 01:10:20 192.168.2.0/24     192.168.80.254   vlan8   2    4
> C   0 01:10:55 192.168.2.0/24     0.0.0.0          xl0     1 ----
* R 120 01:10:20 192.168.7.0/24     192.168.80.254   vlan8   3    4
> C   0 01:10:55 192.168.7.0/24     0.0.0.0          ed0     1 ----
  R 120 00:00:04 192.168.13.0/29    192.168.2.254    xl0     4    4
  R 120 00:00:04 192.168.13.0/29    192.168.80.254   vlan8   4    4
> R 120 01:10:55 192.168.13.0/29    192.168.7.254    ed0     2   23
  R 120 00:00:04 192.168.14.0/24    192.168.2.254    xl0     3    4
  R 120 00:00:04 192.168.14.0/24    192.168.80.254   vlan8   3    4
> R 120 01:10:55 192.168.14.0/24    192.168.7.254    ed0     2   23
  R 120 00:00:04 192.168.17.0/29    192.168.2.254    xl0     4    4
  R 120 00:00:04 192.168.17.0/29    192.168.80.254   vlan8   4    4
> R 120 01:10:55 192.168.17.0/29    192.168.7.254    ed0     2   23
  R 120 00:00:04 192.168.44.1/32    192.168.80.254   vlan8   2    4
> R 120 01:10:55 192.168.44.1/32    192.168.2.254    xl0     2    4
  R 120 00:00:04 192.168.45.0/24    192.168.2.254    xl0     5    4
> R 120 01:07:01 192.168.45.0/24    192.168.7.254    ed0     3   23
* R 120 01:10:55 192.168.80.0/24    192.168.2.254    xl0     2    4
> C   0 01:10:55 192.168.80.0/24    0.0.0.0          vlan8   1 ----
  R 120 00:00:04 192.168.201.2/32   192.168.2.254    xl0     4    4
  R 120 00:00:04 192.168.201.2/32   192.168.80.254   vlan8   4    4
```

continues

Example 9-3 *MRTd RIPv2 Configuration and Output on Castor (Continued)*

```
> R  120 01:10:55 192.168.201.2/32        192.168.7.254        ed0      2   23
  R  120 00:00:04 111.11.117.0/24         192.168.80.254       vlan8    2    4
> R  120 01:10:55 111.11.117.0/24         192.168.2.254        xl0      2    4

castor-MRTd# sh ip routes
Number of Unique Destinations: 14, Number of Entries: 17
Status code: > best, * valid, i - internal, x - no next-hop, X - no install
   P Pref Time     Destination            Next Hop             If    Kernel
> S    1 01:10:59 0.0.0.0/0              192.168.2.254         xl0     K
>iC    0 01:10:59 127.0.0.0/8            0.0.0.0               lo0
>iC  250 01:10:59 127.0.0.1/32           127.0.0.1             lo0     K
> R  120 01:10:59 192.168.1.0/24         192.168.2.254         xl0     K
> C    0 01:10:59 192.168.2.0/24         0.0.0.0               xl0     K
  R  120 01:10:24 192.168.2.0/24         192.168.80.254        vlan8
> C    0 01:10:59 192.168.7.0/24         0.0.0.0               ed0     K
  R  120 01:10:24 192.168.7.0/24         192.168.80.254        vlan8
> R  120 01:10:59 192.168.13.0/29        192.168.7.254         ed0
> R  120 01:10:59 192.168.14.0/24        192.168.7.254         ed0
> R  120 01:10:59 192.168.17.0/29        192.168.7.254         ed0
> R  120 01:10:59 192.168.44.1/32        192.168.2.254         xl0     K
> R  120 01:07:05 192.168.45.0/24        192.168.7.254         ed0     K
> C    0 01:10:59 192.168.80.0/24        0.0.0.0               vlan8   K
  R  120 01:10:59 192.168.80.0/24        192.168.2.254         xl0
> R  120 01:10:59 192.168.201.2/32       192.168.7.254         ed0
> R  120 01:10:59 111.11.117.0/24        192.168.2.254         xl0     K

[root@castor:~#]netstat -rn -f inet
Routing tables

Internet:
Destination        Gateway           Flags   Refs    Use  Netif Expire
default            192.168.2.254     UGSc      2      14   xl0
127.0.0.1          127.0.0.1         UH        1    4193   lo0
192.168.1          192.168.2.254     UGc       1       0   xl0
192.168.2          link#1            UC        2       0   xl0
192.168.2.254      52:54:05:e3:e4:2f UHLW      5     130   xl0   1073
192.168.7          link#2            UC        1       0   ed0
192.168.7.254      00:00:0c:1a:a9:a8 UHLW      6     142   ed0    116
192.168.13/29      192.168.7.254     UGc       0       0   ed0
192.168.14         192.168.7.254     UGc       0       0   ed0
192.168.17/29      192.168.7.254     UGc       0       0   ed0
192.168.44.1/32    192.168.2.254     UGc       0       0   xl0
192.168.45         192.168.7.254     UGc       0      20   ed0
192.168.80         link#14           UC        1       0   vlan8
192.168.80.1       0.10.5a.c4.2c.4   UHLW      0      34   lo0
192.168.201.2/32   192.168.7.254     UGc       0       0   ed0
111.11.117         192.168.2.254     UGc       0       0   xl0
```

Example 9-4 shows a standard Cisco RIPv2 configuration, and Example 9-5 shows the corresponding Cisco Express Forwarding (CEF) output to demonstrate CEF's view of two equal-cost paths with *per-packet load sharing* configured (highlighted text). This CEF example should also be seen as a demonstration of the forwarding discussion in Chapter 8.

NOTE   This book does not contain a detailed CEF introduction. Consult Cisco.com for a better understanding of Example 9-5, which is presented only to show the correlation of the CEF and routing table.

Example 9-4   *Cisco IOS RIPv2 Configuration and Output on Scar*

```
scar# sh running-config
...
router rip
 version 2
 traffic-share min across-interfaces
 redistribute connected
 redistribute static
 passive-interface Serial0
 passive-interface Serial1
 passive-interface Serial2
 passive-interface Serial3
 network 192.168.7.0
 network 192.168.14.0
 maximum-paths 2
 no auto-summary
...

scar# sh ip rip database
0.0.0.0/0      auto-summary
0.0.0.0/0      redistributed
    [1] via 0.0.0.0,
192.168.1.0/24    auto-summary
192.168.1.0/24
    [1] via 192.168.14.1, 00:00:04, Ethernet1
192.168.2.0/24    auto-summary
192.168.2.0/24
    [1] via 192.168.7.7, 00:00:14, Ethernet0
192.168.7.0/24    auto-summary
192.168.7.0/24    directly connected, Ethernet0
192.168.13.0/24    auto-summary
192.168.13.0/29    redistributed
    [1] via 0.0.0.0,
192.168.14.0/24    auto-summary
192.168.14.0/24    directly connected, Ethernet1
192.168.17.0/24    auto-summary
192.168.17.0/29    redistributed
    [1] via 0.0.0.0,
192.168.44.0/24    auto-summary
192.168.44.1/32
    [2] via 192.168.7.7, 00:00:14, Ethernet0
    [2] via 192.168.14.1, 00:00:04, Ethernet1
192.168.45.0/24    auto-summary
192.168.45.0/24
    [1] via 192.168.14.1, 00:00:04, Ethernet1
192.168.80.0/24    auto-summary
192.168.80.0/24
    [1] via 192.168.7.7, 00:00:14, Ethernet0
```

continues

Example 9-4 *Cisco IOS RIPv2 Configuration and Output on Scar (Continued)*

```
192.168.201.0/24    auto-summary
192.168.201.2/32    redistributed
    [1] via 0.0.0.0,
111.11.117.0/24     auto-summary
111.11.117.0/24
    [2] via 192.168.7.7, 00:00:14, Ethernet0
    [2] via 192.168.14.1, 00:00:04, Ethernet1

scar# sh ip route
Codes: C - connected, S - static, I - IGRP, R - RIP, M - mobile, B - BGP
       D - EIGRP, EX - EIGRP external, O - OSPF, IA - OSPF inter area
       N1 - OSPF NSSA external type 1, N2 - OSPF NSSA external type 2
       E1 - OSPF external type 1, E2 - OSPF external type 2, E - EGP
       i - IS-IS, L1 - IS-IS level-1, L2 - IS-IS level-2, ia - IS-IS inter area
       * - candidate default, U - per-user static route, o - ODR
       P - periodic downloaded static route

Gateway of last resort is 192.168.7.7 to network 0.0.0.0

     192.168.13.0/29 is subnetted, 1 subnets
C       192.168.13.0 is directly connected, TokenRing0
C    192.168.14.0/24 is directly connected, Ethernet1
     192.168.44.0/32 is subnetted, 1 subnets
R       192.168.44.1 [120/2] via 192.168.14.1, 00:00:12, Ethernet1
                     [120/2] via 192.168.7.7, 00:00:06, Ethernet0
R    192.168.45.0/24 [120/1] via 192.168.14.1, 00:00:12, Ethernet1
     192.168.201.0/32 is subnetted, 1 subnets
C       192.168.201.2 is directly connected, Loopback0
R    192.168.80.0/24 [120/1] via 192.168.7.7, 00:00:06, Ethernet0
R    111.11.117.0/24 [120/2] via 192.168.14.1, 00:00:12, Ethernet1
                     [120/2] via 192.168.7.7, 00:00:06, Ethernet0
C    192.168.7.0/24 is directly connected, Ethernet0
     192.168.17.0/29 is subnetted, 1 subnets
C       192.168.17.0 is directly connected, TokenRing1
R    192.168.1.0/24 [120/1] via 192.168.14.1, 00:00:12, Ethernet1
R    192.168.2.0/24 [120/1] via 192.168.7.7, 00:00:06, Ethernet0
S*   0.0.0.0/0 [1/0] via 192.168.7.7

scar# sh ip route 192.168.44.1
Routing entry for 192.168.44.1/32
  Known via "rip", distance 120, metric 2
  Redistributing via rip
  Last update from 192.168.7.7 on Ethernet0, 00:00:01 ago
  Routing Descriptor Blocks:
    192.168.14.1, from 192.168.14.1, 00:00:16 ago, via Ethernet1
      Route metric is 2, traffic share count is 1
  * 192.168.7.7, from 192.168.7.7, 00:00:01 ago, via Ethernet0
      Route metric is 2, traffic share count is 1

scar# traceroute 192.168.44.1
Type escape sequence to abort.
Tracing the route to 192.168.44.1
```

Example 9-4 *Cisco IOS RIPv2 Configuration and Output on Scar (Continued)*

```
  1 192.168.7.7 0 msec
    192.168.14.1 4 msec
    192.168.7.7 0 msec
  2 192.168.44.1 4 msec 0 msec 0 msec
```

Example 9-5 *Cisco IOS CEF Configuration and Output on Scar*

```
scar# sh ip cef summary
IP CEF with switching (Table Version 43), flags=0x0
  30 routes, 0 reresolve, 0 unresolved (0 old, 0 new), peak 1
  30 leaves, 18 nodes, 22496 bytes, 52 inserts, 22 invalidations
  2 load sharing elements, 632 bytes, 2 references
  universal per-destination load sharing algorithm, id C5B17D30
  3(0) CEF resets, 4 revisions of existing leaves
  Resolution Timer: Exponential (currently 1s, peak 1s)
  2 in-place/0 aborted modifications
  refcounts:  4905 leaf, 4864 node
Adjacency Table has 2 adjacencies

scar# sh ip cef
Prefix             Next Hop          Interface
0.0.0.0/0          192.168.7.7       Ethernet0
0.0.0.0/32         receive
192.168.1.0/24     192.168.14.1      Ethernet1
192.168.2.0/24     192.168.7.7       Ethernet0
192.168.7.0/24     attached          Ethernet0
192.168.7.0/32     receive
192.168.7.7/32     192.168.7.7       Ethernet0
192.168.7.254/32   receive
192.168.7.255/32   receive
192.168.13.0/29    attached          TokenRing0
192.168.13.0/32    receive
192.168.13.1/32    receive
192.168.13.7/32    receive
192.168.14.0/24    attached          Ethernet1
192.168.14.0/32    receive
192.168.14.1/32    192.168.14.1      Ethernet1
192.168.14.254/32  receive
192.168.14.255/32  receive
192.168.17.0/29    attached          TokenRing1
192.168.17.0/32    receive
192.168.17.1/32    receive
192.168.17.7/32    receive
192.168.44.1/32    192.168.14.1      Ethernet1
                   192.168.7.7       Ethernet0
192.168.45.0/24    192.168.14.1      Ethernet1
192.168.80.0/24    192.168.7.7       Ethernet0
192.168.201.2/32   receive
111.11.117.0/24    192.168.14.1      Ethernet1
                   192.168.7.7       Ethernet0
224.0.0.0/4        0.0.0.0
224.0.0.0/24       receive
255.255.255.255/32 receive
```

continues

Example 9-5 *Cisco IOS CEF Configuration and Output on Scar (Continued)*

```
scar# sh ip cef 192.168.44.1
192.168.44.1/32, version 40, per-packet sharing
0 packets, 0 bytes
  via 192.168.14.1, Ethernet1, 0 dependencies
    traffic share 1, current path
    next hop 192.168.14.1, Ethernet1
    valid adjacency
  via 192.168.7.7, Ethernet0, 0 dependencies
    traffic share 1
    next hop 192.168.7.7, Ethernet0
    valid adjacency
  0 packets, 0 bytes switched through the prefix

scar# sh cef not-cef-switched
CEF Packets passed on to next switching layer
Slot  No_adj No_encap Unsupp'ted Redirect  Receive  Options   Access     Frag
RP        0       0         0        0       2987       0        0         0

scar#sh cef drop
CEF Drop Statistics
Slot  Encap_fail  Unresolved Unsupported    No_route    No_adj  ChkSum_Err
RP          0          0          0             4          0         0
```

Now you can replace the castor mrtd with the Zebra zebra and ripd (as shown in Example 9-6).

Example 9-6 *Zebra RIPv2 Configuration and Output on Castor*

```
[root@castor:~#] telnet localhost 2602
Trying 127.0.0.1...
Connected to localhost (127.0.0.1)
Escape character is '^]'.
Hello, this is zebra (version 0.94).
Copyright 1996-2002 Kunihiro Ishiguro.
User Access Verification
Password:

castor-ripd# sh running-config
Current configuration:
!
hostname castor-ripd
password zebra
log file /var/log/ripd.log
!
interface xl0
 ip rip send version 2
 ip rip receive version 2
!
interface ed0
 ip rip send version 2
 ip rip receive version 2
!
interface lo0

interface vlan8
```

Example 9-6 *Zebra RIPv2 Configuration and Output on Castor (Continued)*

```
router rip
 redistribute kernel
 redistribute connected
 redistribute static
 network 192.168.2.0/24
 network 192.168.7.0/24
 network 192.168.80.0/24
!
line vty
!
end

castor-ripd# sh ip protocols
Routing Protocol is "rip"
  Sending updates every 30 seconds with +/-50%, next due in 8 seconds
  Timeout after 180 seconds, garbage collect after 120 seconds
  Outgoing update filter list for all interface is not set
  Incoming update filter list for all interface is not set
  Default redistribution metric is 1
  Redistributing: kernel connected static
  Default version control: send version 2, receive version 2
    Interface       Send  Recv   Key-chain
    xl0              2     2
    ed0              2     2
    vlan8            2     2
  Routing for Networks:
    192.168.2.0/24
    192.168.7.0/24
    192.168.80.0/24
  Routing Information Sources:
    Gateway          BadPackets BadRoutes  Distance Last Update
    192.168.2.254            0         0      120   00:00:21
    192.168.7.254            0         0      120   00:00:25
    192.168.80.254          0         0      120   00:00:21
  Distance: (default is 120)

castor-ripd# sh ip rip
Codes: R - RIP, C - connected, O - OSPF, B - BGP
       (n) - normal, (s) - static, (d) - default, (r) - redistribute,
       (i) - interface

      Network           Next Hop        Metric From        Time
K(r) 0.0.0.0/0          192.168.2.254        1 self
K(r) 192.168.1.0/24     192.168.2.254        1 self
C(i) 192.168.2.0/24     0.0.0.0              1 self
C(i) 192.168.7.0/24     0.0.0.0              1 self
K(r) 192.168.13.0/29    192.168.7.254        1 self
K(r) 192.168.14.0/24    192.168.7.254        1 self
K(r) 192.168.17.0/29    192.168.7.254        1 self
K(r) 192.168.44.1/32    192.168.2.254        1 self
K(r) 192.168.45.0/24    192.168.7.254        1 self
C(i) 192.168.80.0/24    0.0.0.0              1 self
K(r) 192.168.201.2/32   192.168.7.254        1 self
K(r) 111.11.117.0/24    192.168.2.254        1 self
```

Lab 9-2: RIP Neighbor Granularity

For this lab, we look at the communication between scar (running Cisco IOS RIPv2 as well in Example 9-7) and callisto (running Zebra RIPv2 in Example 9-8). A combination of the **passive-interface** and **neighbor** commands offers granularity in the choice of RIP neighbors that cannot be achieved with the **network** command alone.

This lab results in unicast RIPv2 communication between the two neighbors, while suppressing multicast messages on 192.168.14.0/24 via the **passive-interface** command. An additional benefit of the unicast **neighbor** command is its use for nonbroadcast media such as Frame Relay. The same effect (unicast behavior) can be accomplished with GateD via the **sourcegateways <gateway_list>** clause in the RIP configuration section.

For even more granularity, Zebra, GateD, and to some extent MRTd offer offset- lists, route maps, distribute lists, access lists, and metric and distance/preference manipulation.

Example 9-7 *Cisco IOS RIPv2 Neighbor Configuration on Scar*

```
scar# sh running-config
...
router rip
 version 2
 traffic-share min across-interfaces
 redistribute connected
 redistribute static
 passive-interface Ethernet1
 passive-interface Serial0
 passive-interface Serial1
 passive-interface Serial2
 passive-interface Serial3
 network 192.168.7.0
 network 192.168.14.0
 neighbor 192.168.14.1
 maximum-paths 2
 no auto-summary
...
```

Example 9-8 *Zebra RIPv2 Neighbor Configuration on Callisto*

```
[root@callisto:~#] cat /usr/local/etc/ripd.conf
...
router rip
 redistribute connected
 redistribute static
 network 192.168.1.0/24
 network 192.168.14.0/24
 neighbor 192.168.14.254
 passive-interface eth0
...
```

Lab 9-3: RIPv2 via GateD

All UNIX gateways are running GateD now to demonstrate its RIP capabilities. The GateD Interactive Interface (GII), as shown in Example 9-9, provides the RIP information on callisto.

Example 9-9 *GateD RIPv2 Configuration and Output on Callisto*

```
[root@callisto:~#] cat /etc/gated.cfg
rip on{
        interface eth0 eth1
                ripin
                ripout
                version 2 multicast;
};

[root@callisto:~#] telnet localhost 616
Trying 127.0.0.1...
Connected to localhost (127.0.0.1).
Escape character is '^]'.
Password?
100 Gated Interactive Interface. Version gated-public-3_6

GateD-callisto> show interface
100 #ind name     address        mtu        flags
100 #1   lo       127.0.0.1      16436/16372 Up Loopback
100 #2   eth0     192.168.14.1   1500/1436 Up Broadcast Multicast
100 #3   eth1     192.168.1.1    1500/1436 Up Broadcast Multicast
100 #3   eth1     192.168.45.253 1500/1436 Up Broadcast Multicast

GateD-callisto> show timer
100 Name                     Task    Last   Next   Intrvl Jitter flags
100 AGE                      IF      00:00s 00:57s 00:00s 00:00s <OneShot>
100 Flash                    RIP     00:01s 00:00s 00:00s 00:00s <Inactive>
100 Update                   RIP     00:03s 00:27s 00:30s 00:00s <>
100 Age                      RIP     00:00s 00:35s 00:00s 00:00s <OneShot>
100 IfCheck                  KRT     00:08s 00:07s 00:15s 00:00s <>
100 Timeout                  KRT     00:00s 00:00s 00:00s 00:00s <OneShot Inactive>
100 Age                      Redirect 00:00s 00:52s 00:00s 00:00s <OneShot>
100 Startup                  SMUX    01:00s 00:00s 01:00s 00:00s <>

GateD-callisto> show rip summary
100 Gateway       LastHeard    Flags
100 192.168.14.1        0
100 192.168.1.1         0
100 192.168.45.253      0
100 192.168.1.254     1334       A
100 192.168.45.254     909       A
100 192.168.14.254    1339       A
100 RIP summary, 6 gateways.
100 Flags:
100 S   This is a source gateway
100 T   This is a trusted gateway
100 A   We have accepted a packet from this gateway
```

continues

Example 9-9　*GateD RIPv2 Configuration and Output on Callisto (Continued)*

```
100 R    We have rejected a packet from this gateway
100 Q    We have received a RIP query packet from this gateway
100 F    This gateway failed authentication

GateD-callisto> show rip routes 0/0
100 Proto       Route/Mask NextHop        Tag
100 RIP           0.0.0.0/0  192.168.14.254    0
100 RIP         192.168.2/24 192.168.1.254     0
100 RIP         192.168.7/24 192.168.14.254    0
100 RIP        192.168.13/29 192.168.14.254    0
100 RIP        192.168.17/29 192.168.14.254    0
100 RIP      192.168.44.1/32 192.168.1.254     0
100 RIP        192.168.80/24 192.168.1.254     0
100 RIP     192.168.201.2/32 192.168.14.254    0
100 RIP        111.11.117/24 192.168.1.254     0

GateD-callisto> show ip walkdown 0/0
100 RIP           0.0.0.0/0  192.168.14.254  IGP (Id 1)
100 Sta               127/8  127.0.0.1       IGP (Id 1)
100 Dir         127.0.0.1/32 127.0.0.1       IGP (Id 1)
100 Dir         192.168.1/24 192.168.1.1     IGP (Id 1)
100 RIP         192.168.2/24 192.168.1.254   IGP (Id 1)
100 RIP         192.168.7/24 192.168.14.254  IGP (Id 1)
100 RIP        192.168.13/29 192.168.14.254  IGP (Id 1)
100 Dir        192.168.14/24 192.168.14.1    IGP (Id 1)
100 RIP        192.168.17/29 192.168.14.254  IGP (Id 1)
100 RIP      192.168.44.1/32 192.168.1.254   IGP (Id 1)
100 Dir        192.168.45/24 192.168.45.253  IGP (Id 1)
100 RIP        192.168.80/24 192.168.1.254   IGP (Id 1)
100 RIP     192.168.201.2/32 192.168.14.254  IGP (Id 1)
100 RIP        111.11.117/24 192.168.1.254   IGP (Id 1)

GateD-callisto> show ip route 192.168.7.0/24
100 Route 192.168.7 - 255.255.255 entries 1 Announced 1 Depth 0 <>
100    Proto Next Hop       Source Gwt      Preference/2 Metric/2
100 * RIP    192.168.14.254  192.168.14.254  100/0          2/0
```

Exercise 9-1: RIPv2 over Frame Relay Topologies

If you are blessed with a WAN network interface card (NIC) that supports Frame Relay, try
to configure RIPv2 for a Frame Relay WAN network using the **neighbor** feature discussed
in Lab 9-2.

Exercise 9-2: RIPv2 Metric Manipulation and Redistribution Control

Use the **offset-list** command in the RIP router section to manipulate the metric for
incoming/outgoing updates. In addition, use the **distribute-list** command in combination
with the **default-metric** command to add granularity to the redistribution of routing

updates, and **default-information originate** to inject default routes. Remember that the **passive-interface** command results in the respective interface not sending any updates except to RIP neighbors specified with the **neighbor** command. This does not affect the processing of received updates.

Introduction to Link-State Routing Protocols

Link-state routing protocols are based on Edsger W. Dijkstra's Shortest Path First (SPF) algorithm, a result of applied graph theory. Link-state protocols establish and maintain adjacencies via hello packets (connection-oriented) with their neighbors (peers), speaking the same routing protocol. The name *link-state* stems from the underlying concept that every participant distributes (floods) all the information states and conditions of its directly attached links.

The routers communicate via link-state advertisements (LSAs) with all their established neighbors. This behavior is referred to as *flooding*. The receiving routers never alter the LSA information, but add a copy to their link-state databases. After some convergence time, all the participants have a full, identical, and complete view (graph) of the area topology stored in their topology databases. Every router now calculates its own best paths (SPF) for all prefixes from its individual point of view and position in this topology. Hellos are also used as a keepalive mechanism between adjacent neighbors.

NOTE   A new approach referred to as *incremental SPF (iSPF)* or *incremental Dijkstra* allows SPF protocols to converge faster under certain conditions by recomputing only the part of the shortest path tree (SPT) that has changed. This calculation is considerably faster only under special circumstances. For more information, search Cisco.com for "incremental SPF" or "incremental Dijkstra." At the time of this writing, the implementation solely is a proprietary vendor playground.

The following discussion introduces two fundamental concepts of organizing routing realms: areas and autonomous systems.

Area Concepts

Areas are smaller realms (subsets) of a routing domain (autonomous system). It became obvious during the design of link-state protocols that the intrinsic mechanisms become problematic in large flat topologies with several hundreds to thousands of nodes. This involved convergence time, link bandwidth, node memory, and CPU consumption. The designers' response was a subdivision-area concept and, recently, incremental approaches to SPF.

Area separation in terms of a contiguous backbone area and attached leaf areas via area border routers (ABRs) considerably improved the matter by restricting LSA flooding to the area boundaries. This resulted in smaller topology databases, faster SPF computation with less memory/CPU consumption, and ultimately improved convergence behavior.

ABRs maintain several databases and need to be consulted for interarea routing. In general, ABRs inject default routes into the leaf area. OSPF has a "rich" repertoire of leaf-area flavors: stub areas, total stub areas, not so stubby areas (NSSAs), and NSSA total stub. For a concise discussion of the differences, see the "Recommended Reading" section at the end of this chapter.

All leaf areas need to have at least one connection to the backbone area. If this is not possible because of migration constraints or topology limitations, OSPF virtual links are used to establish backbone connectivity via a *transit area*. This concept is not implemented (or necessary) in IS-IS. Both protocols use a contiguous backbone.

Table 9-1 shows the four different area specifiers used within Cisco IOS Software and their GateD and Zebra counterparts if applicable.

Table 9-1   *OSPF Area Flavors*

Area Specifier	GateD Notation	Zebra Notation
Stub	Stub	Stub
Total stub	Stub + restrict clause	Stub, no summary
NSSA	Not implemented	NSSA
NSSA total stub	Not implemented	NSSA, no summary

NOTE   One short bit of advice: Do not expect OSPF to compensate for poorly designed topologies or address planning!

The Full Picture—Autonomous Systems and Areas

Figure 9-2 shows a complete view of the macroscopic world. Autonomous systems can be organized into areas—either a flat backbone area or a backbone area with multiple connected leaf areas. Autonomous systems are not isolated; they communicate via Exterior Gateway Protocols (EGPs) with other autonomous systems, upstream carriers, or public peering points. BGPv4 is the dominant EGP used in today's Internet.

NOTE   Chapter 10, "ISP Connectivity with BGPv4: An Exterior Gateway Path-Vector Routing Protocol for Interdomain Routing," is dedicated to BGPv4 and interdomain issues.

Figure 9-2   *Autonomous Systems and Areas*

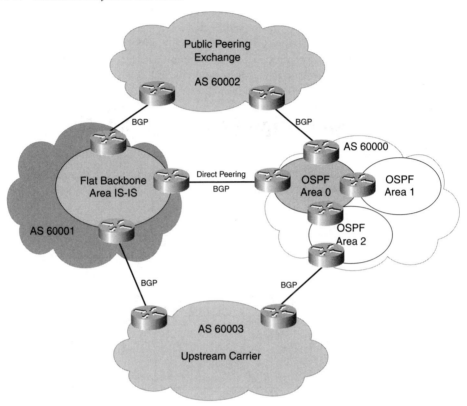

OSPFv2

OSPF (Open Shortest Path First) is the most popular among the link-state routing protocols. The current IPv4 version, OSPFv2, is widely deployed throughout carrier, ISP, and enterprise networks. OSPFv3 essentially is an IPv6-enabled OSPF. It is a well documented protocol in terms of standards, books, guides, and white paper density.

The knowledge level is high among those who deploy and operate OSPFv2. Integrated IS-IS, however, is catching up in popularity, although those familiar with its addressing already appreciate its simplicity. OSPF is multicast-based (224.0.0.5 = AllSPFRouters, 224.0.0.6 = AllDRouters).

OSPF facilitates 11 different LSA types. This is the biggest obstacle and source for confusion that OSPF apprentices face. OSPF and IS-IS both support Equal-Cost Multi-Path (ECMP), an important feature for optimal link utilization. OSPF uses an arbitrary metric (cost) that is based on link bandwidth in the Cisco implementation.

The Cisco IOS implementation will do equal-cost load balancing for up to six equal-cost routes for OSPF and IS-IS. This condition is characterized by including all routes in the forwarding table. Route tagging and authentication are additional features of modern implementations. Traffic-engineering extensions to OSPF (OSPF-TE) via TE-LSAs are available as well. Traffic engineering in combination with leaf-area concepts is particularly difficult to implement, given the intrinsic behavior of link-state routing protocols.

Lab 9-4: Leaf-Area Design Featuring GateD and Cisco IOS

The topology used in this lab is presented in Figure 9-3. Although this is a rather complex lab, do not get intimidated beforehand.

Figure 9-3   *OSPF Area Lab*

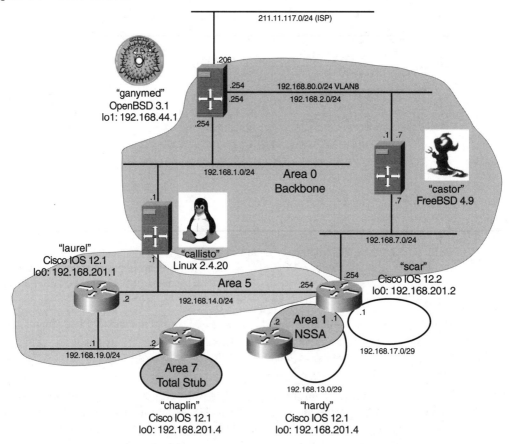

Three additional Cisco Routers—laurel, hardy and chaplin—are introduced. Each of them has a loopback address configured that is used as the router ID for the OSPF router process configurations as well.

All three UNIX gateways are running GateD. For demonstration of the area concept, four distinct areas have been introduced:

- A backbone area 0
- A regular leaf area 5
- A total stub leaf area 7
- An NSSA leaf area 1 (This area also uses a network range statement for a summary ABR advertisement into the backbone area.)

Examples 9-10 through 9-18 present the Cisco IOS Software and GateD configurations, the kernel routing table, as well as ospf_monitor output and output from the GateD interactive user interface (GII). The ospf_monitor utility requires a start file in the examples named /etc/ospf.mon.

I am aware of the fact that these example listings are somewhat lengthy. Keep in mind that they mostly present status output and serve the purpose that you do not have to rebuild every lab to get the most out of it.

CAUTION   GateD's OSPF operation did not like Linux alias interfaces (eth1:1) in the config file. This appears to be rather a parser (the colon) than an implementation problem. This is the reason why it was removed from Figure 9-3. It will be reintroduced when configuring the same lab with Zebra instances. The use of this notation is deprecated anyway on Linux and will most likely disappear pretty soon.

Example 9-10 shows castor's GateD configuration and accompanying output. The **export proto ospfase{}** clause is required for route export (*redistribution* in Cisco terminology). The export of connected interface routes (=direct) and static routes is equivalent to the Cisco IOS experience. The redistribution of kernel routes exports prefixes added via the kernel interface (usually added manually). Remember that these are separate entities on a UNIX gateway.

What are ASE routes exactly? They are autonomous system external routes. This is consistent with Cisco IOS notation. According to Cisco IOS notation, a router that redistributes routes into OSPF is referred to as an autonomous system boundary router (ASBR); the same applies to redistributed routes.

The GateD interactive interface command **show ip walkdown 0/0** shows GateD's view of direct, static, connected, kernel, and OSPF routes. The **show kernel** capabilities are especially important when adding static routes to the gated.cfg file, because not all options (**blackhole**, **reject**, **hide**, and so on) are supported by all operating systems. GateD also communicates this via syslog statements to /var/log/messages.

<table>
<tr><td>**NOTE**</td><td>Example 9-10 also presents an overview of OSPF-related timers, which might prove useful to track down adjacency problems. If you have difficulties understanding general OSPF concepts, turn to the "Recommended Reading" section; this book does not offer an in-depth introduction to OSPF or IS-IS.</td></tr>
</table>

Example 9-10 *Castor GateD Configuration and Output*

```
[root@castor:~#] cat /etc/gated.cfg
routerid 192.168.2.7;
rip off;
ospf yes{
        backbone{
                networks{
                        192.168.2.0  mask 255.255.255.0;
                        192.168.7.0  mask 255.255.255.0;
                        192.168.80.0 mask 255.255.255.0;
                };
                interface xl0 ed0 vlan8;
        };
};
export proto ospfase{
        proto static;
        proto direct;
        proto kernel;
};

[root@castor:~#] netstat -rn -f inet
Routing tables

Internet:
Destination       Gateway            Flags   Refs    Use  Netif Expire
default           192.168.2.254      UGSc       2     15    xl0
127               127.0.0.1          URc        0      0    lo0
127.0.0.1         127.0.0.1          UH         0     38    lo0
192.168.1         192.168.2.254      UGc        1     45    xl0
192.168.1.254     192.168.2.254      UGH        0     34    xl0
192.168.2         link#1             UC         1      0    xl0
192.168.2.254     52:54:05:e3:e4:2f  UHLW       9     19    xl0    398
192.168.7         link#2             UC         1      0    ed0
192.168.7.254     00:00:0c:1a:a9:a8  UHLW       5     68    ed0    490
192.168.13/29     192.168.7.254      UGc        0     11    ed0
192.168.14        192.168.2.254      UGc        0      0    xl0
192.168.16/23     192.168.7.254      UGc        0      0    ed0
192.168.19        192.168.2.254      UGc        0      0    xl0
192.168.80        link#14            UC         1      0    vlan8
192.168.80.254    52.54.5.e3.e4.2f   UHLW       0      0    vlan8   120
192.168.201.1     192.168.2.254      UGH        0      0    xl0
```

Example 9-10 *Castor GateD Configuration and Output (Continued)*

```
192.168.201.2      192.168.7.254     UGH      0        0    ed0
192.168.201.3      192.168.7.254     UGH      1       14    ed0
192.168.201.4      192.168.2.254     UGH      0        0    x10
111.11.117         192.168.2.254     UGc      0        0    x10
224.0.0.5          127.0.0.1         UH       0        0    lo0
224.0.0.6          127.0.0.1         UH       0        0    lo0


[root@castor:~#] telnet localhost 616
Trying 127.0.0.1...
Connected to localhost (127.0.0.1).
Escape character is '^]'.
Password?
100 Gated Interactive Interface. Version gated-public-3_6


GateD-castor> show interface
100 #ind name     address       mtu       flags
100 #1   x10      192.168.2.7   1500/1436 Up Broadcast Multicast Simplex Allmulti
100 #2   ed0      192.168.7.7   1500/1436 Up Broadcast Multicast Simplex Allmulti
100 #13  lo0      127.0.0.1     16384/16320 Up Loopback Multicast
100 #14  vlan8    192.168.80.1  1496/1432 Up Broadcast Multicast Simplex


GateD-castor> show ip walkdown 0/0
100 Ker          0.0.0.0/0  192.168.2.254   IGP (Id 1)
100 Sta             127/8   127.0.0.1       IGP (Id 1)
100 Dir       127.0.0.1/32  127.0.0.1       IGP (Id 1)
100 OSP      192.168.1/24   192.168.2.254   IGP (Id 1)
100 Ker    192.168.1.2/32   192.168.2.254   IGP (Id 1)
100 OSP  192.168.1.254/32   192.168.2.254   IGP (Id 1)
100 Dir       192.168.2/24  192.168.2.7     IGP (Id 1)
100 Dir       192.168.7/24  192.168.7.7     IGP (Id 1)
100 OSP      192.168.13/29  192.168.7.254   IGP (Id 1)
100 OSP      192.168.14/24  192.168.2.254   IGP (Id 1)
100 OSP      192.168.16/23  192.168.7.254   IGP (Id 1)
100 OSP      192.168.19/24  192.168.2.254   IGP (Id 1)
100 Dir      192.168.80/24  192.168.80.1    IGP (Id 1)
100 OSP  192.168.201.1/32   192.168.2.254   IGP (Id 1)
100 OSP  192.168.201.2/32   192.168.7.254   IGP (Id 1)
100 OSP  192.168.201.3/32   192.168.7.254   IGP (Id 1)
100 OSP  192.168.201.4/32   192.168.2.254   IGP (Id 1)
100 OSP     111.11.117/24   192.168.2.254   IGP (Id 1)


GateD-castor> show ip route 192.168.16.0/23
100 Route 192.168.16 - 255.255.254 entries 1 Announced 1 Depth 0 <>
100    Proto Next Hop      Source Gwt    Preference/2 Metric/2 etc...
100 * OSPF  192.168.7.254   ---           10/0    7/-1         0        22:16:49
IGP (Id 1) <Int Gateway ActiveU Unicast>


GateD-castor> show timer
100 Name                    Task   Last   Next   Intrvl Jitter flags
100 AGE                 IF     00:00s 00:05s 00:00s 00:00s <OneShot>
100 Retransmit          OSPF   00:04s 00:01s 00:05s 00:00s <>
100 Adjacency           OSPF   00:00s 00:15s 00:00s 00:00s <OneShot>
```

continues

Example 9-10 *Castor GateD Configuration and Output (Continued)*

```
100 Hello          OSPF     00:09s 00:01s 00:10s 00:00s <HiPrio>
100 Retransmit     OSPF     00:00s 00:05s 00:05s 00:00s <>
100 Adjacency      OSPF     00:00s 00:09s 00:00s 00:00s <OneShot>
100 Hello          OSPF     00:00s 00:10s 00:10s 00:00s <HiPrio>
100 Retransmit     OSPF     00:01s 00:04s 00:05s 00:00s <>
100 Adjacency      OSPF     00:00s 00:14s 00:00s 00:00s <OneShot>
100 Hello          OSPF     00:01s 00:09s 00:10s 00:00s <HiPrio>
100 Lock           OSPF     00:01s 00:04s 00:05s 00:00s <>
100 Ack            OSPF     00:06s 00:00s 00:00s 00:00s <HiPrio Inactive>
100 LSDBAseAge     OSPF     00:24s 00:37s 01:01s 00:00s <>
100 LSDBSumAge     OSPF     02:44s 12:16s 15:00s 00:00s <>
100 LSDBIntAge     OSPF     03:48s 11:12s 15:00s 00:00s <>
100 LSAGenInt      OSPF     22:34s 07:26s 30:00s 00:00s <>
100 LSAGenAse      OSPF     00:05s 00:02s 00:07s 00:00s <>
100 AseQueue       OSPF     19:33s 00:00s 00:00s 00:00s <Inactive>
100 IfCheck        KRT      00:11s 00:49s 01:00s 00:00s <>
100 Timeout        KRT      00:00s 00:00s 00:00s 00:00s <OneShot Inactive>
100 Age            Redirect 00:00s 00:49s 00:00s 00:00s <OneShot>
100 Startup        SMUX     00:11s 00:49s 01:00s 00:00s <>

GateD-castor> show kernel
100 Kernel options: <> Support: <Reject Blackhole VarMask Host>
100 IP forwarding: 1 UDP checksums 1
100 The time is 22:18:47
```

Example 9-11 introduces the powerful ospf_monitor utility with its accompanying
configuration file and the resulting monitoring output. It is part of the GateD binaries.
The configuration file just includes remote hosts, which should be monitored. The
especially helpful thing about ospf_monitor is that it offers a rich set of queries for local
and remote hosts running GateD. At the beginning of Example 9-11, the **ospf_monitor
help** facility explains the abbreviated queries used.

Example 9-11 *Callisto ospf_monitor Output for Remote Host Castor*

```
[root@callisto:~#] cat /etc/ospf.mon
192.168.1.254    ganymed
192.168.1.1      callisto
192.168.2.7      castor
192.168.1.2      pollux

[root@callisto:~#] ospf_monitor /etc/ospf.mon

[ 1 ] dest command params > ?
Local commands:
    ?: help
    ?R: remote command information
    d: show configured destinations
    h: show history
    x: exit
    @ <remote command>: use last destination
    @<dest index> <remote command>: use configured destination
```

Example 9-11 *Callisto ospf_monitor Output for Remote Host Castor (Continued)*

```
    F <filename>: write monitor information to filename
    S: write monitor information to stdout (default)

[ 2 ] dest command params > ?R
Remote-commands:
  a <area id> <type> <ls id> <adv rtr>: show link state advertisement
  c: show cumulative log
  e: show cumulative errors
  l: <retrans> dump lsdb (except for ASEs)
  A: <retrans> dump ASEs
  W: <retrans> dump ASEs with LSIDs
  o: print ospf routing table
  I: show interfaces
  h: show next hops
  N <r>: show neighbors - if r is set will print retrans lst

[ 3 ] dest command params > d
1: 192.168.1.254    ganymed
2: 192.168.1.1      callisto
3: 192.168.2.7      castor
4: 192.168.1.2      pollux

[ 4 ] dest command params > @3 N
   remote-command <N> sent to 192.168.2.7

        Source <<192.168.2.7      castor>>

Interface: 192.168.2.7    Area: 0.0.0.0
Router Id        Nbr IP Addr    State      Mode    Prio
--------------------------------------------------------
192.168.44.1     192.168.2.254  Full       Slave   1

Interface: 192.168.7.7    Area: 0.0.0.0
Router Id        Nbr IP Addr    State      Mode    Prio
--------------------------------------------------------
192.168.201.2    192.168.7.254  Full       Slave   1

Interface: 192.168.80.1   Area: 0.0.0.0
Router Id        Nbr IP Addr    State      Mode    Prio
--------------------------------------------------------
192.168.44.1     192.168.80.254 Full       Slave   1
done

[ 5 ] dest command params > @3 I
   remote-command <I> sent to 192.168.2.7

        Source <<192.168.2.7      castor>>

Area: 0.0.0.0
IP Address      Type  State    Cost Pri DR              BDR
----------------------------------------------------------------
192.168.2.7     Bcast DR Other 1    0   192.168.2.254   None
```

continues

Example 9-11 *Callisto ospf_monitor Output for Remote Host Castor (Continued)*

```
192.168.7.7    Bcast DR Other 1    0    192.168.7.254    None
192.168.80.1   Bcast DR Other 1    0    192.168.80.254   None
done
[ 7 ] dest command params > @3 h
   remote-command <h> sent to 192.168.2.7

           Source <<192.168.2.7      castor>>
Next hops:

Address          Type       Refcount  Interface
-----------------------------------------------------------
192.168.2.7      Direct           3  192.168.2.7    xl0
192.168.2.254    Neighbor        30  192.168.2.7    xl0
192.168.7.7      Direct           3  192.168.7.7    ed0
192.168.7.254    Neighbor        16  192.168.7.7    ed0
192.168.80.1     Direct           3  192.168.80.1   vlan8
192.168.80.254   Neighbor         1  192.168.80.1   vlan8
done

[ 8 ] dest command params > @3 o
   remote-command <o> sent to 192.168.2.7

           Source <<192.168.2.7      castor>>
AS Border Routes:
Router          Cost AdvRouter       NextHop(s)
-------------------------------------------------
Area 0.0.0.0:
192.168.2.7        0 192.168.2.7
192.168.201.2      1 192.168.201.2    192.168.7.254
192.168.44.1       1 192.168.44.1     192.168.2.254
192.168.1.1        2 192.168.1.1      192.168.2.254

Total AS Border routes: 4

Area Border Routes:
Router          Cost AdvRouter       NextHop(s)
-------------------------------------------------
Area 0.0.0.0:
192.168.201.4     13 192.168.201.4    192.168.2.254
192.168.201.2      1 192.168.201.2    192.168.7.254
192.168.1.1        2 192.168.1.1      192.168.2.254

Total Area Border Routes: 3

Summary AS Border Routes:
Router          Cost AdvRouter       NextHop(s)
-------------------------------------------------
192.168.201.1      3 192.168.1.1      192.168.2.254
Total Summary AS Border Routes: 1

Networks:
Destination     Area            Cost Type NextHop        AdvRouter
------------------------------------------------------------------------
192.168.7       0.0.0.0            1 Net  192.168.7.7    192.168.201.2
```

Example 9-11 *Callisto ospf_monitor Output for Remote Host Castor (Continued)*

```
192.168.201.2      0.0.0.0            2 Stub 192.168.7.254   192.168.201.2
192.168.16/23      0.0.0.0            7 SNet 192.168.7.254   192.168.201.2
192.168.13.0/29    0.0.0.0            7 SNet 192.168.7.254   192.168.201.2
192.168.201.3      0.0.0.0            8 SNet 192.168.7.254   192.168.201.2
192.168.2          0.0.0.0            1 Net  192.168.2.7     192.168.44.1
192.168.80         0.0.0.0            1 Net  192.168.80.1    192.168.44.1
192.168.1          0.0.0.0            2 Net  192.168.2.254   192.168.44.1
192.168.19         0.0.0.0           13 SNet 192.168.2.254   192.168.1.1
192.168.14         0.0.0.0            3 SNet 192.168.2.254   192.168.1.1
192.168.201.1      0.0.0.0            4 SNet 192.168.2.254   192.168.1.1
192.168.201.4      0.0.0.0           14 SNet 192.168.2.254   192.168.201.4
ASEs:
Destination        Cost E    Tag NextHop         AdvRouter
-----------------------------------------------------------------------------
0.0.0.0               1    1 c0000000 192.168.2.254   192.168.44.1
111.11.117            1    1 c0000000 192.168.2.254   192.168.44.1
192.168.1.254         1    1 c0000000 192.168.2.254   192.168.44.1
Total nets: 12
       Intra Area: 4   Inter Area: 8   ASE: 3
done


[ 10 ] dest command params > @3 e
   remote-command <e> sent to 192.168.2.7


         Source <<192.168.2.7      castor>>
Packets Received:
  5: Monitor request              549: Hello
 13: DB Description                 0: Link-State Req
 86: Link-State Update             20: Link-State Ack

Packets Sent:
  0: Monitor response             551: Hello
 14: DB Description                 3: Link-State Req
 96: Link-State Update             28: Link-State Ack

Errors:
  0: IP: bad destination           0: IP: bad protocol
  0: IP: received my own packet    0: OSPF: bad packet type
  0: OSPF: bad version             0: OSPF: bad checksum
  0: OSPF: bad area id             0: OSPF: area mismatch
  0: OSPF: bad virtual link        0: OSPF: bad authentication type
  0: OSPF: bad authentication key  0: OSPF: packet too small
  0: OSPF: packet size > ip length 0: OSPF: transmit error
  0: OSPF: interface down          0: OSPF: unknown neighbor
  0: HELLO: netmask mismatch       0: HELLO: hello timer mismatch
  0: HELLO: dead timer mismatch    0: HELLO: extern option mismatch
  0: HELLO: router id confusion    0: HELLO: virtual neighbor unknown
  0: HELLO: NBMA neighbor unknown  0: DD: neighbor state low
  0: DD: router id confusion       0: DD: extern option mismatch
  0: DD: unknown LSA type          0: LS ACK: neighbor state low
  0: LS ACK: bad ack               0: LS ACK: duplicate ack
  0: LS ACK: Unknown LSA type      0: LS REQ: neighbor state low
```

continues

Example 9-11 *Callisto ospf_monitor Output for Remote Host Castor (Continued)*

```
0: LS REQ: empty request          0: LS REQ: bad request
0: LS UPD: neighbor state low      0: LS UPD: newer self-gen LSA
0: LS UPD: LSA checksum bad        3: LS UPD: received less recent LSA
0: LS UPD: unknown LSA type
done

[ 11 ] dest command params > @3 c
  remote-command <c> sent to 192.168.2.7

        Source <<192.168.2.7      castor>>
IO stats
      Input  Output  Type
          6       0  Monitor request
        561     566  Hello
         13      14  DB Description
          0       3  Link-State Req
         88     100  Link-State Update
         21      28  Link-State Ack
      ASE: 7 checksum sum 387C5

      LSAs originated: 10     received: 73
              Router: 5  ASE: 5

      Area 0.0.0.0:
              Neighbors: 3     Interfaces: 3
              Spf: 11 Checksum sum EE7DB
              DB: rtr: 5 net: 4 sumasb: 6 sumnet: 13

Routing Table:
        Intra Area: 4   Inter Area: 8   ASE: 3
done
```

Examples 9-12 and 9-13 show the configuration of two virtual links to connect the isolated total stub area 7 to the backbone area via a transit area 5. Virtual links always connect two ABRs; in our example, the two virtual links connect scar/callisto and chaplin. GateD uses different default timer settings than Cisco IOS Software; this explains the additional configuration lines in the callisto gated.conf file to bring the tunnels up. Callisto and scar act as ABRs.

Example 9-12 *Callisto GateD Configuration and Output*

```
[root@callisto:~#] cat /etc/gated.conf
routerid 192.168.1.1;
rip off;
ospf yes{
        backbone{
                networks{
                        192.168.1.0  mask 255.255.255.0;
                };
                interface eth1;
                virtuallink neighborid 192.168.201.4 transitarea 5 {
                        hellointerval 10;
```

Example 9-12 *Callisto GateD Configuration and Output (Continued)*

```
                              routerdeadinterval 40;
                              retransmitinterval 5;
                              transitdelay 40;
                    };
          };
          area 5{
                    networks{
                              192.168.14.0  mask 255.255.255.0;
                    };
                    interface eth0;
          };
};
static{
          default gateway 192.168.1.254;
};
export proto ospfase{
          proto static{all; };
          proto direct{all; };
          proto kernel{all; };
};

[root@callisto:~#] ip route
192.168.201.2 via 192.168.1.254 dev eth1  proto gated
192.168.201.3 via 192.168.1.254 dev eth1  proto gated
192.168.201.1 via 192.168.14.2 dev eth0  proto gated
192.168.1.2 via 192.168.1.254 dev eth1  proto gated
224.0.0.6 via 127.0.0.1 dev lo  proto gated  scope link
192.168.201.4 via 192.168.14.2 dev eth0  proto gated
224.0.0.5 via 127.0.0.1 dev lo  proto gated  scope link
192.168.1.254 via 192.168.1.254 dev eth1  proto gated
127.0.0.1 dev lo  proto gated  scope link
192.168.13.0/29 via 192.168.1.254 dev eth1  proto gated
192.168.7.0/24 via 192.168.1.254 dev eth1  proto gated
111.11.117.0/24 via 192.168.1.254 dev eth1  proto gated
192.168.19.0/24 via 192.168.14.2 dev eth0  proto gated
192.168.2.0/24 via 192.168.1.254 dev eth1  proto gated
192.168.80.0/24 via 192.168.1.254 dev eth1  proto gated
192.168.1.0/24 dev eth1  proto gated  scope link
192.168.14.0/24 dev eth0  scope link
192.168.16.0/23 via 192.168.1.254 dev eth1  proto gated
unreachable 127.0.0.0/8  proto gated  scope link
default via 192.168.1.254 dev eth1

[root@callisto:~#] netstat -rne
Kernel IP routing table
Destination     Gateway         Genmask         Flags Metric Ref    Use Iface
192.168.201.2   192.168.1.254   255.255.255.255 UGH   0      0        0 eth1
192.168.201.3   192.168.1.254   255.255.255.255 UGH   0      0        0 eth1
192.168.201.1   192.168.14.2    255.255.255.255 UGH   0      0        0 eth0
192.168.1.2     192.168.1.254   255.255.255.255 UGH   0      0        0 eth1
```

continues

Example 9-12 *Callisto GateD Configuration and Output (Continued)*

```
224.0.0.6       127.0.0.1       255.255.255.255 UGH   0       0       0 lo
192.168.201.4   192.168.14.2    255.255.255.255 UGH   0       0       0 eth0
224.0.0.5       127.0.0.1       255.255.255.255 UGH   0       0       0 lo
192.168.1.254   192.168.1.254   255.255.255.255 UGH   0       0       0 eth1
127.0.0.1       0.0.0.0         255.255.255.255 UH    0       0       0 lo
192.168.13.0    192.168.1.254   255.255.255.248 UG    0       0       0 eth1
192.168.7.0     192.168.1.254   255.255.255.0   UG    0       0       0 eth1
111.11.117.0    192.168.1.254   255.255.255.0   UG    0       0       0 eth1
192.168.19.0    192.168.14.2    255.255.255.0   UG    0       0       0 eth0
192.168.2.0     192.168.1.254   255.255.255.0   UG    0       0       0 eth1
192.168.80.0    192.168.1.254   255.255.255.0   UG    0       0       0 eth1
192.168.1.0     0.0.0.0         255.255.255.0   U     0       0       0 eth1
192.168.14.0    0.0.0.0         255.255.255.0   U     0       0       0 eth0
192.168.16.0    192.168.1.254   255.255.254.0   UG    0       0       0 eth1
127.0.0.0       -               255.0.0.0       !     0       -       0 -
0.0.0.0         192.168.1.254   0.0.0.0         UG    0       0       0 eth1


[root@callisto:~#] ospf_monitor /etc/ospf.mon
listening on 0.0.0.0.33862
[ 1 ] dest command params > @2 N
    remote-command <N> sent to 192.168.1.1


            Source <<192.168.1.1      callisto>>


Interface: 192.168.1.1    Area: 0.0.0.0
Router Id       Nbr IP Addr     State       Mode    Prio
---------------------------------------------------
192.168.44.1    192.168.1.254   Full        Slave   1


Interface: 192.168.14.1   Area: 0.0.0.5
Router Id       Nbr IP Addr     State       Mode    Prio
---------------------------------------------------
192.168.201.1   192.168.14.2    Full        Slave   1
192.168.201.2   192.168.14.254  Full        Slave   1


Virtual links:
Interface       Router Id       Nbr IP Addr     State       Mode    Prio
------------------------------------------------------------------
192.168.14.1    192.168.201.4   192.168.19.2    Full        Slave   0
done


[ 5 ] dest command params > @2 I
    remote-command <I> sent to 192.168.1.1


            Source <<192.168.1.1      callisto>>


Area: 0.0.0.0
IP Address      Type  State     Cost Pri DR              BDR
------------------------------------------------------------------
192.168.1.1     Bcast DR Other 1    0   192.168.1.254   None
```

Example 9-12 *Callisto GateD Configuration and Output (Continued)*

```
Area: 0.0.0.5
IP Address     Type  State   Cost Pri DR            BDR
-------------------------------------------------------------------
192.168.14.1   Bcast DR Other 1    0   192.168.14.254 192.168.14.2

Virtual Links:
Transit Area    Router ID     Remote IP      Local IP       Type State  Cost
--------------------------------------------------------------------------
-
0.0.0.5         192.168.201.4 192.168.19.2   192.168.14.1   Virt P To P  11
done

[ 7 ] dest command params > @2 h
   remote-command <h> sent to 192.168.1.1

        Source <<192.168.1.1     callisto>>
Next hops:

Address         Type    Refcount  Interface
----------------------------------------------------------
192.168.1.1     Direct      3  192.168.1.1    eth1
192.168.1.254   Neighbor   33  192.168.1.1    eth1
192.168.14.1    Direct      3  192.168.14.1   eth0
192.168.14.2    Neighbor   15  192.168.14.1   eth0
192.168.14.254  Neighbor    4  192.168.14.1   eth0
192.168.19.2    Neighbor    1  192.168.14.1   eth0
done

[ 10 ] dest command params > @2 c
   remote-command <c> sent to 192.168.1.1

        Source <<192.168.1.1     callisto>>
IO stats
     Input  Output  Type
        13      0  Monitor request
      8720   8225  Hello
        75    129  DB Description
        27     34  Link-State Req
       568    479  Link-State Update
       221    315  Link-State Ack
     ASE: 7 checksum sum 381C8

     LSAs originated: 159    received: 359
            Router: 20  SumNet: 104  SumASB: 29  ASE: 6

     Area 0.0.0.0:
            Neighbors: 2    Interfaces: 1
            Spf: 28 Checksum sum 10C3EC
            DB: rtr: 5 net: 4 sumasb: 6 sumnet: 13

     Area 0.0.0.5:
            Neighbors: 2    Interfaces: 1
```

continues

Example 9-12 *Callisto GateD Configuration and Output (Continued)*

```
                       Spf: 18 Checksum sum 14C6DE
                       DB: rtr: 4 net: 2 sumasb: 9 sumnet: 27

Routing Table:
       Intra Area: 6   Inter Area: 6   ASE: 5
Done

[ 12 ] dest command params > @2 o
   remote-command <o> sent to 192.168.1.1

          Source <<192.168.1.1      callisto>>
AS Border Routes:
Router          Cost AdvRouter       NextHop(s)
-------------------------------------------------

Area 0.0.0.0:
192.168.2.7        2 192.168.2.7     192.168.1.254
192.168.201.2      3 192.168.201.2   192.168.1.254
192.168.44.1       1 192.168.44.1    192.168.1.254
192.168.1.1        0 192.168.1.1

Area 0.0.0.5:
192.168.201.2      1 192.168.201.2   192.168.14.254
192.168.201.1      1 192.168.201.1   192.168.14.2
192.168.1.1        0 192.168.1.1

Total AS Border routes: 7

Area Border Routes:
Router          Cost AdvRouter       NextHop(s)
-------------------------------------------------

Area 0.0.0.0:
192.168.201.4     11 192.168.201.4   192.168.14.2
192.168.201.2      3 192.168.201.2   192.168.1.254
192.168.1.1        0 192.168.1.1

Area 0.0.0.5:
192.168.201.4     11 192.168.201.4   192.168.14.2
192.168.201.2      1 192.168.201.2   192.168.14.254
192.168.1.1        0 192.168.1.1

Total Area Border Routes: 6

Summary AS Border Routes:
Router          Cost AdvRouter       NextHop(s)
-------------------------------------------------

Networks:
Destination     Area           Cost Type NextHop        AdvRouter
-----------------------------------------------------------------------
192.168.1        0.0.0.0          1 Net  192.168.1.1    192.168.44.1
192.168.14       0.0.0.5          1 Net  192.168.14.1   192.168.201.2
192.168.19       0.0.0.5         11 Net  192.168.14.2   192.168.201.4
```

Example 9-12 *Callisto GateD Configuration and Output (Continued)*

```
192.168.201.1    0.0.0.5        2 Stub 192.168.14.2   192.168.201.1
192.168.2        0.0.0.0        2 Net  192.168.1.254   192.168.44.1
192.168.80       0.0.0.0        2 Net  192.168.1.254   192.168.44.1
192.168.201.2    0.0.0.0        4 Stub 192.168.1.254   192.168.201.2
192.168.16/23    0.0.0.0        9 SNet 192.168.1.254   192.168.201.2
192.168.7        0.0.0.0        3 Net  192.168.1.254   192.168.201.2
192.168.201.3    0.0.0.0       10 SNet 192.168.1.254   192.168.201.2
192.168.13.0/29  0.0.0.0        9 SNet 192.168.1.254   192.168.201.2
192.168.201.4    0.0.0.0       12 SNet 192.168.14.2    192.168.201.4
ASEs:
Destination      Cost E    Tag NextHop        AdvRouter
--------------------------------------------------------------------
0.0.0.0            1    1 c0000000 192.168.1.254    192.168.44.1
111.11.117         1    1 c0000000 192.168.1.254    192.168.44.1
192.168.1.254      1    1 c0000000 192.168.1.254    192.168.44.1
192.168.1.2        2    1 c0000000 192.168.1.254    192.168.2.7
192.168.1.1        2    1 c0000000 192.168.1.254    192.168.2.7
Total nets: 12
        Intra Area: 6   Inter Area: 6   ASE: 5
done
```

Example 9-13 *Callisto GateD Diagnostic Output*

```
[root@callisto:~#] telnet localhost 616
Trying 127.0.0.1...
Connected to localhost (127.0.0.1).
Escape character is '^]'.
Password?
100 Gated Interactive Interface. Version gated-public-3_6

GateD-callisto> show kernel
100 Kernel options: <> Support: <Reject VarMask Host Multipath>
100 IP forwarding: 1 UDP checksums 1
100 The time is 22:43:18

GateD-callisto> show timer
100 Name                    Task    Last    Next   Intrvl Jitter Flags
100 AGE            IF       00:00s 02:30s 00:00s 00:00s <OneShot>
100 Retransmit     OSPF     00:00s 00:05s 00:05s 00:00s <>
100 Adjacency      OSPF     00:00s 00:00s 00:00s 00:00s <OneShot>
100 Hello          OSPF     00:05s 00:05s 00:10s 00:00s <HiPrio>
100 Retransmit     OSPF     00:01s 00:04s 00:05s 00:00s <>
100 Adjacency      OSPF     00:00s 00:15s 00:00s 00:00s <OneShot>
100 Hello          OSPF     00:06s 00:04s 00:10s 00:00s <HiPrio>
100 Retransmit     OSPF     00:01s 00:04s 00:05s 00:00s <>
100 Adjacency      OSPF     00:00s 00:22s 00:00s 00:00s <OneShot>
100 Hello          OSPF     00:06s 00:04s 00:10s 00:00s <HiPrio>
100 Lock           OSPF     00:00s 00:05s 00:05s 00:00s <>
100 Lock           OSPF     00:01s 00:04s 00:05s 00:00s <>
100 Ack            OSPF     06:14s 00:00s 00:00s 00:00s <HiPrio Inactive>
100 LSDBAseAge     OSPF     00:56s 00:05s 01:01s 00:00s <>
```

continues

Example 9-13 *Callisto GateD Diagnostic Output (Continued)*

```
100 LSDBSumAge        OSPF      02:59s 12:01s 15:00s 00:00s <>
100 LSDBIntAge        OSPF      04:03s 10:57s 15:00s 00:00s <>
100 LSAGenSum         OSPF      06:15s 23:45s 30:00s 00:00s <>
100 LSAGenInt         OSPF      07:49s 22:11s 30:00s 00:00s <>
100 LSAGenAse         OSPF      00:06s 00:01s 00:07s 00:00s <>
100 AseQueue          OSPF      128:25s 00:00s 00:00s 00:00s <Inactive>
100 IfCheck           KRT       00:02s 00:13s 00:15s 00:00s <>
100 Timeout           KRT       00:00s 00:00s 00:00s 00:00s <OneShot Inactive>
100 Age               Redirect  00:00s 02:58s 00:00s 00:00s <OneShot>
100 Startup           SMUX      00:26s 00:34s 01:00s 00:00s <>

GateD-callisto> show interface
100 #ind Name    Address         Mtu         Flags
100 #1   lo      127.0.0.1       16436/16372 Up Loopback
100 #2   eth0    192.168.14.1    1500/1436 Up Broadcast Multicast
100 #3   eth1    192.168.1.1     1500/1436 Up Broadcast Multicast
100 #3   eth1    192.168.45.253  1500/1436 Up Broadcast Multicast

GateD-callisto> show ip walkdown 0/0
100 Sta        0.0.0.0/0  192.168.1.254   IGP (Id 1)
100 Sta            127/8  127.0.0.1       IGP (Id 1)
100 Dir    127.0.0.1/32  127.0.0.1       IGP (Id 1)
100 Dir    192.168.1/24  192.168.1.1     IGP (Id 1)
100 ---    192.168.1.1/32  ---
100 OSP    192.168.1.2/32  192.168.1.254   IGP (Id 1)
100 OSP  192.168.1.254/32  192.168.1.254   IGP (Id 1)
100 OSP    192.168.2/24  192.168.1.254   IGP (Id 1)
100 OSP    192.168.7/24  192.168.1.254   IGP (Id 1)
100 OSP   192.168.13/29  192.168.1.254   IGP (Id 1)
100 Dir   192.168.14/24  192.168.14.1    IGP (Id 1)
100 OSP   192.168.16/23  192.168.1.254   IGP (Id 1)
100 OSP   192.168.19/24  192.168.14.2    IGP (Id 1)
100 OSP   192.168.80/24  192.168.1.254   IGP (Id 1)
100 OSP  192.168.201.1/32  192.168.14.2    IGP (Id 1)
100 OSP  192.168.201.2/32  192.168.1.254   IGP (Id 1)
100 OSP  192.168.201.3/32  192.168.1.254   IGP (Id 1)
100 OSP  192.168.201.4/32  192.168.14.2    IGP (Id 1)
100 OSP   111.11.117/24  192.168.1.254   IGP (Id 1)
```

NOTE Problems with adjacency establishment (gateways stuck in the *two-way* state) are often because of a problem of Designated Router/Backup Designated Router (DR/BDR) election. Defining different priority values can resolve this matter.

Example 9-14 presents the GateD configuration and output of the backbone area gateway ganymed with an example for priority statements to influence DR/BDR election.

Example 9-14 *Ganymed GateD Configuration and Routing Table*

```
[root@ganymed:~#] cat /etc/gated.cfg
routerid 192.168.44.1;
rip off;
ospf yes{
        backbone{
                networks{
                        192.168.1.0  mask 255.255.255.0;
                        192.168.2.0  mask 255.255.255.0;
                        192.168.80.0 mask 255.255.255.0;
                };
                interface ne3{
                        priority 1;
                };
                interface ne4{
                        priority 1;
                };
                interface vlan0{
                        priority 1;
                };
        };
};
export proto ospfase{
        proto static{all; };
        proto direct{all; };
        proto kernel{all; };
};

[root@ganymed:~#] netstat -rn -f inet
Routing tables

Internet:
Destination         Gateway             Flags     Refs     Use     Mtu   Interface
default             111.11.117.1        UGS          3    26477    1500   ne5
127/8               127.0.0.1           UR           0        0   33224   lo0
127.0.0.1           127.0.0.1           UH           1        2   33224   lo0
192.168.1/24        link#1              UC       -1850        0    1500   ne3
192.168.1.1         52:54:5:e3:51:87    UHL          4    19241    1500   ne3
192.168.1.2         8:0:46:64:74:1b     UHL          1    16446    1500   ne3
192.168.1.254       127.0.0.1           UGHS         0        0   33224   lo0
192.168.2/24        link#2              UC           0        0    1500   ne4
192.168.2.7         0:10:5a:c4:2c:4     UHL          5     4101    1500   ne4
192.168.7/24        192.168.2.7         UG           0       68    1496   ne4
192.168.13.0/29     192.168.2.7         UG           0       11    1500   ne4
192.168.14/24       192.168.1.1         UG          -2        2    1500   ne3
192.168.16/23       192.168.2.7         UG           0        0    1496   ne4
192.168.19/24       192.168.1.1         UG           0        0    1500   ne3
192.168.44.1        192.168.44.1        UH           0        0   33224   lo1
192.168.80/24       link#16             UC           0        0    1496   vlan0
192.168.201.1       192.168.1.1         UGH          0        0    1500   ne3
192.168.201.2       192.168.2.7         UGH          0        0    1496   ne4
192.168.201.3       192.168.2.7         UGH          1       53    1500   ne4
192.168.201.4       192.168.1.1         UGH          0        0    1500   ne3
```

continues

Example 9-14 *Ganymed GateD Configuration and Routing Table (Continued)*

```
111.11.117/24      link#3            UC     0        0    1500   ne5
111.11.117.1       0:5:9a:5b:23:fc   UHL    1        0    1500   ne5
224.0.0.5          127.0.0.1         UH     1     3082   33224   lo0
224.0.0.6          127.0.0.1         UH     0        0   33224   lo0
```

Example 9-15 shows the ABR router configuration of scar featuring a **summary-address** statement for testing purposes. The **area 1 range 192.168.16.0 255.255.254.0** statement in Example 9-15 enables the ABR scar to consolidate contiguous address ranges into one summary advertisement (at bit-boundaries only, of course). Do not confuse it with the **summary-address** statement, which has a similar effect when redistribution of foreign protocols into OSPF comes into play.

Example 9-15 *Scar Configuration and Diagnostic Output*

```
scar# show running-config
...
router ospf 1
 router-id 192.168.201.2
 log-adjacency-changes
 area 1 nssa default-information-originate
 area 1 range 192.168.16.0 255.255.254.0
 area 5 virtual-link 192.168.201.4
 summary-address 172.16.0.0 255.240.0.0
 redistribute connected subnets
 redistribute static subnets
 passive-interface Serial0
 passive-interface Serial1
 passive-interface Serial2
 passive-interface Serial3
 network 192.168.7.0 0.0.0.255 area 0
 network 192.168.13.0 0.0.0.7 area 1
 network 192.168.14.0 0.0.0.255 area 5
 network 192.168.17.0 0.0.0.7 area 1
 network 192.168.201.2 0.0.0.0 area 0
 maximum-paths 2
...
ip route 0.0.0.0 0.0.0.0 192.168.7.7
ip route 0.0.0.0 0.0.0.0 192.168.14.1 200
...

scar# sh ip ospf neighbor
Neighbor ID     Pri   State          Dead Time   Address        Interface
192.168.2.7       0   FULL/DROTHER   00:00:33    192.168.7.7    Ethernet0
192.168.201.1     1   FULL/BDR       00:00:38    192.168.14.2   Ethernet1
192.168.1.1       0   FULL/DROTHER   00:00:30    192.168.14.1   Ethernet1
192.168.201.3     1   FULL/DR        00:00:30    192.168.13.2   TokenRing0

scar# sh ip ospf border-routers
OSPF Process 1 internal Routing Table
Codes: i - Intra-area route, I - Inter-area route
```

Example 9-15 *Scar Configuration and Diagnostic Output (Continued)*

```
i 192.168.44.1 [11] via 192.168.7.7, Ethernet0, ASBR, Area 0, SPF 40
i 192.168.1.1 [12] via 192.168.7.7, Ethernet0, ABR/ASBR, Area 0, SPF 40
i 192.168.1.1 [10] via 192.168.14.1, Ethernet1, ABR/ASBR, Area 5, SPF 24
i 192.168.201.3 [6] via 192.168.13.2, TokenRing0, ASBR, Area 1, SPF 11
i 192.168.201.1 [10] via 192.168.14.2, Ethernet1, ASBR, Area 5, SPF 24
i 192.168.201.4 [20] via 192.168.14.2, Ethernet1, ABR, Area 0, SPF 40
i 192.168.201.4 [20] via 192.168.14.2, Ethernet1, ABR, Area 5, SPF 24
i 192.168.2.7 [10] via 192.168.7.7, Ethernet0, ASBR, Area 0, SPF 40

scar# sh ip ospf virtual-links
Virtual Link OSPF_VL0 to router 192.168.201.4 is up
  Run as demand circuit
  DoNotAge LSA not allowed (Number of DCbitless LSA is 10).
  Transit area 5, via interface Ethernet1, Cost of using 20
  Transmit Delay is 1 sec, State POINT_TO_POINT,
  Timer intervals configured, Hello 10, Dead 40, Wait 40, Retransmit 5
    Hello due in 00:00:00
    Adjacency State FULL (Hello suppressed)
    Index 2/4, retransmission queue length 0, number of retransmission 2
    First 0x0(0)/0x0(0) Next 0x0(0)/0x0(0)
    Last retransmission scan length is 2, maximum is 2
    Last retransmission scan time is 0 msec, maximum is 0 msec

scar# sh ip ospf summary-address
OSPF Process 1, Summary-address
172.16.0.0/255.240.0.0 Metric 16777215, Type 0, Tag 0

scar# sh ip route
Codes: C - connected, S - static, I - IGRP, R - RIP, M - mobile, B - BGP
       D - EIGRP, EX - EIGRP external, O - OSPF, IA - OSPF inter area
       N1 - OSPF NSSA external type 1, N2 - OSPF NSSA external type 2
       E1 - OSPF external type 1, E2 - OSPF external type 2, E - EGP
       i - IS-IS, L1 - IS-IS level-1, L2 - IS-IS level-2, ia - IS-IS inter area
       * - candidate default, U - per-user static route, o - ODR
       P - periodic downloaded static route

Gateway of last resort is 192.168.7.7 to network 0.0.0.0

     192.168.13.0/29 is subnetted, 1 subnets
C       192.168.13.0 is directly connected, TokenRing0
C    192.168.14.0/24 is directly connected, Ethernet1
     192.168.201.0/32 is subnetted, 4 subnets
O       192.168.201.1 [110/11] via 192.168.14.2, 00:56:24, Ethernet1
O       192.168.201.3 [110/7] via 192.168.13.2, 01:01:52, TokenRing0
C       192.168.201.2 is directly connected, Loopback0
O IA    192.168.201.4 [110/21] via 192.168.14.2, 00:56:24, Ethernet1
O    192.168.80.0/24 [110/11] via 192.168.7.7, 00:56:24, Ethernet0
O E2 111.11.117.0/24 [110/1] via 192.168.7.7, 00:56:14, Ethernet0
C    192.168.7.0/24 is directly connected, Ethernet0
     192.168.17.0/29 is subnetted, 1 subnets
C       192.168.17.0 is directly connected, TokenRing1
     192.168.1.0/24 is variably subnetted, 4 subnets, 2 masks
```

continues

Example 9-15 *Scar Configuration and Diagnostic Output (Continued)*

```
O E2    192.168.1.1/32 [110/1] via 192.168.7.7, 00:40:20, Ethernet0
O       192.168.1.0/24 [110/12] via 192.168.7.7, 00:56:24, Ethernet0
O E2    192.168.1.2/32 [110/1] via 192.168.7.7, 00:56:14, Ethernet0
O E2    192.168.1.254/32 [110/1] via 192.168.7.7, 00:56:14, Ethernet0
O      192.168.2.0/24 [110/11] via 192.168.7.7, 00:56:24, Ethernet0
O      192.168.19.0/24 [110/20] via 192.168.14.2, 00:56:24, Ethernet1
S*     0.0.0.0/0 [1/0] via 192.168.7.7
O      192.168.16.0/23 is a summary, 01:01:52, Null0

scar# sh ip ospf
 Routing Process "ospf 1" with ID 192.168.201.2
 Supports only single TOS(TOS0) routes
 Supports opaque LSA
 It is an area border and autonomous system boundary router
 Redistributing External Routes from,
     connected, includes subnets in redistribution
     static, includes subnets in redistribution
 SPF schedule delay 5 secs, Hold time between two SPFs 10 secs
 Minimum LSA interval 5 secs. Minimum LSA arrival 1 secs
 Number of external LSA 7. Checksum Sum 0x375CE
 Number of opaque AS LSA 0. Checksum Sum 0x0
 Number of DCbitless external and opaque AS LSA 7
 Number of DoNotAge external and opaque AS LSA 0
 Number of areas in this router is 3. 2 normal 0 stub 1 nssa
 External flood list length 0
    Area BACKBONE(0)
        Number of interfaces in this area is 3
        Area has no authentication
        SPF algorithm executed 40 times
        Area ranges are
        Number of LSA 28. Checksum Sum 0x109802
        Number of opaque link LSA 0. Checksum Sum 0x0
        Number of DCbitless LSA 10
        Number of indication LSA 0
        Number of DoNotAge LSA 0
        Flood list length 0
    Area 1
        Number of interfaces in this area is 2
        It is a NSSA area
        Perform type-7/type-5 LSA translation
        generates NSSA default route with cost 1
        Area has no authentication
        SPF algorithm executed 11 times
        Area ranges are
           192.168.16.0/23 Active(6) Advertise
        Number of LSA 13. Checksum Sum 0x72D48
        Number of opaque link LSA 0. Checksum Sum 0x0
        Number of DCbitless LSA 0
        Number of indication LSA 0
        Number of DoNotAge LSA 0
        Flood list length 0
```

Example 9-15 *Scar Configuration and Diagnostic Output (Continued)*

```
    Area 5
        Number of interfaces in this area is 1
        Area has no authentication
        SPF algorithm executed 24 times
        Area ranges are
        Number of LSA 42. Checksum Sum 0x149EF2
        Number of opaque link LSA 0. Checksum Sum 0x0
        Number of DCbitless LSA 12
        Number of indication LSA 0
        Number of DoNotAge LSA 0
        Flood list length 0
```

Examples 9-16, 9-17, and 9-18 present the Cisco IOS configurations of the hardy, laurel, and chaplin routers. These are straightforward standard OSPF configurations featuring a virtual link and different leaf-area types.

Example 9-16 *Hardy Configuration and Diagnostic Output*

```
hardy# sh running-config
...
router ospf 1
 router-id 192.168.201.3
 log-adjacency-changes
 area 1 nssa
 redistribute connected subnets tag 1
 redistribute static subnets tag 1
 network 192.168.13.0 0.0.0.255 area 1
 network 192.168.201.3 0.0.0.0 area 1
 maximum-paths 2
...

hardy# sh ip ospf
 Routing Process "ospf 1" with ID 192.168.201.3
 Supports only single TOS(TOS0) routes
 Supports opaque LSA
 It is an autonomous system boundary router
 Redistributing External Routes from,
    connected, includes subnets in redistribution
    static, includes subnets in redistribution
 SPF schedule delay 5 secs, Hold time between two SPFs 10 secs
 Minimum LSA interval 5 secs. Minimum LSA arrival 1 secs
 Number of external LSA 0. Checksum Sum 0x0
 Number of opaque AS LSA 0. Checksum Sum 0x0
 Number of DCbitless external and opaque AS LSA 0
 Number of DoNotAge external and opaque AS LSA 0
 Number of areas in this router is 1. 0 normal 0 stub 1 nssa
 External flood list length 0
    Area 1
        Number of interfaces in this area is 2
        It is a NSSA area
        Area has no authentication
        SPF algorithm executed 9 times
```

continues

Example 9-16 *Hardy Configuration and Diagnostic Output (Continued)*

```
        Area ranges are
        Number of LSA 13. Checksum Sum 0x7274B
        Number of opaque link LSA 0. Checksum Sum 0x0
        Number of DCbitless LSA 0
        Number of indication LSA 0
        Number of DoNotAge LSA 0
        Flood list length 0

hardy# sh ip ospf interface
Loopback0 is up, line protocol is up
  Internet Address 192.168.201.3/32, Area 1
  Process ID 1, Router ID 192.168.201.3, Network Type LOOPBACK, Cost: 1
  Loopback interface is treated as a stub Host
TokenRing0 is up, line protocol is up
  Internet Address 192.168.13.2/29, Area 1
  Process ID 1, Router ID 192.168.201.3, Network Type BROADCAST, Cost: 6
  Transmit Delay is 1 sec, State DR, Priority 1
  Designated Router (ID) 192.168.201.3, Interface address 192.168.13.2
  Backup Designated router (ID) 192.168.201.2, Interface address 192.168.13.1
  Timer intervals configured, Hello 10, Dead 40, Wait 40, Retransmit 5
    Hello due in 00:00:08
  Index 1/1, flood queue length 0
  Next 0x0(0)/0x0(0)
  Last flood scan length is 2, maximum is 2
  Last flood scan time is 0 msec, maximum is 0 msec
  Neighbor Count is 1, Adjacent neighbor count is 1
    Adjacent with neighbor 192.168.201.2  (Backup Designated Router)
  Suppress hello for 0 neighbor(s)

hardy# sh ip ospf database

        OSPF Router with ID (192.168.201.3) (Process ID 1)


                Router Link States (Area 1)

Link ID          ADV Router       Age         Seq#        Checksum Link count
192.168.201.2    192.168.201.2    516         0x80000019 0xCB5D    2
192.168.201.3    192.168.201.3    688         0x80000009 0x97E1    2

                Net Link States (Area 1)

Link ID          ADV Router       Age         Seq#        Checksum
192.168.13.2     192.168.201.3    688         0x80000005 0x67B5

                Summary Net Link States (Area 1)

Link ID          ADV Router       Age         Seq#        Checksum
192.168.1.0      192.168.201.2    262         0x80000008 0x4044
192.168.2.0      192.168.201.2    262         0x80000003 0x3554
192.168.7.0      192.168.201.2    778         0x80000018 0xC9A6
192.168.14.0     192.168.201.2    1541        0x8000001D 0x72F1
```

Example 9-16 *Hardy Configuration and Diagnostic Output (Continued)*

```
192.168.19.0    192.168.201.2    778    0x80000004 0xD19C
192.168.80.0    192.168.201.2    262    0x80000003 0xD763
192.168.201.1   192.168.201.2    778    0x80000004 0x932C
192.168.201.2   192.168.201.2    1541   0x80000011 0xBB0
192.168.201.4   192.168.201.2    778    0x80000004 0xD9D8


                Type-7 AS External Link States (Area 1)


Link ID         ADV Router       Age    Seq#        Checksum Tag
0.0.0.0         192.168.201.2    516    0x80000003 0x8876   0
```

Example 9-17 *Chaplin Configuration and Diagnostic Output*

```
chaplin# sh running-config
...
router ospf 1
 router-id 192.168.201.4
 log-adjacency-changes
 area 5 virtual-link 192.168.1.1
 area 5 virtual-link 192.168.201.2
 area 7 stub no-summary
 passive-interface Serial0
 passive-interface Serial1
 network 192.168.19.0 0.0.0.255 area 5
 network 192.168.201.4 0.0.0.0 area 7
 maximum-paths 2
...

chaplin# sh ip ospf virtual-links
Virtual Link OSPF_VL1 to router 192.168.1.1 is up
  Run as demand circuit
  DoNotAge LSA not allowed (Number of DCbitless LSA is 10).
  Transit area 5, via interface Ethernet0, Cost of using 20
  Transmit Delay is 1 sec, State POINT_TO_POINT,
  Timer intervals configured, Hello 10, Dead 40, Wait 40, Retransmit 5
    Hello due in 00:00:05
    Adjacency State FULL
    Index 2/3, retransmission queue length 0, number of retransmission 2
    First 0x0(0)/0x0(0) Next 0x0(0)/0x0(0)
    Last retransmission scan length is 2, maximum is 2
    Last retransmission scan time is 0 msec, maximum is 0 msec
Virtual Link OSPF_VL0 to router 192.168.201.2 is up
  Run as demand circuit
  DoNotAge LSA not allowed (Number of DCbitless LSA is 10).
  Transit area 5, via interface Ethernet0, Cost of using 20
  Transmit Delay is 1 sec, State POINT_TO_POINT,
  Timer intervals configured, Hello 10, Dead 40, Wait 40, Retransmit 5
    Hello due in 00:00:05
    Adjacency State FULL (Hello suppressed)
```

continues

Example 9-17 *Chaplin Configuration and Diagnostic Output (Continued)*

```
        Index 1/2, retransmission queue length 0, number of retransmission 3
        First 0x0(0)/0x0(0) Next 0x0(0)/0x0(0)
        Last retransmission scan length is 2, maximum is 2
        Last retransmission scan time is 4 msec, maximum is 4 msec

chaplin# sh ip ospf border-routers

OSPF Process 1 internal Routing Table

Codes: i - Intra-area route, I - Inter-area route

i 192.168.44.1 [21] via 192.168.19.1, Ethernet0, ASBR, Area 0, SPF 14
i 192.168.1.1 [20] via 192.168.19.1, Ethernet0, ABR/ASBR, Area 0, SPF 14
i 192.168.1.1 [20] via 192.168.19.1, Ethernet0, ABR/ASBR, Area 5, SPF 5
i 192.168.201.2 [20] via 192.168.19.1, Ethernet0, ABR/ASBR, Area 0, SPF 14
i 192.168.201.2 [20] via 192.168.19.1, Ethernet0, ABR/ASBR, Area 5, SPF 5
i 192.168.201.1 [10] via 192.168.19.1, Ethernet0, ASBR, Area 5, SPF 5
i 192.168.2.7 [22] via 192.168.19.1, Ethernet0, ASBR, Area 0, SPF 14

chaplin# sh ip route
Codes: C - connected, S - static, I - IGRP, R - RIP, M - mobile, B - BGP
       D - EIGRP, EX - EIGRP external, O - OSPF, IA - OSPF inter area
       N1 - OSPF NSSA external type 1, N2 - OSPF NSSA external type 2
       E1 - OSPF external type 1, E2 - OSPF external type 2, E - EGP
       i - IS-IS, L1 - IS-IS level-1, L2 - IS-IS level-2, ia - IS-IS inter area
       * - candidate default, U - per-user static route, o - ODR
       P - periodic downloaded static route

Gateway of last resort is 192.168.19.1 to network 0.0.0.0

      192.168.13.0/29 is subnetted, 1 subnets
O IA    192.168.13.0 [110/26] via 192.168.19.1, 01:12:23, Ethernet0
O       192.168.14.0/24 [110/20] via 192.168.19.1, 01:12:23, Ethernet0
      192.168.201.0/32 is subnetted, 4 subnets
O       192.168.201.1 [110/11] via 192.168.19.1, 01:12:23, Ethernet0
O IA    192.168.201.3 [110/27] via 192.168.19.1, 01:12:23, Ethernet0
O       192.168.201.2 [110/21] via 192.168.19.1, 01:12:23, Ethernet0
C       192.168.201.4 is directly connected, Loopback0
O       192.168.80.0/24 [110/22] via 192.168.19.1, 01:12:23, Ethernet0
O E2 111.11.117.0/24 [110/1] via 192.168.19.1, 01:12:13, Ethernet0
O       192.168.7.0/24 [110/23] via 192.168.19.1, 01:12:23, Ethernet0
      192.168.1.0/24 is variably subnetted, 4 subnets, 2 masks
O E2    192.168.1.1/32 [110/1] via 192.168.19.1, 00:56:19, Ethernet0
O       192.168.1.0/24 [110/21] via 192.168.19.1, 01:12:23, Ethernet0
O E2    192.168.1.2/32 [110/1] via 192.168.19.1, 01:12:13, Ethernet0
O E2    192.168.1.254/32 [110/1] via 192.168.19.1, 01:12:13, Ethernet0
O       192.168.2.0/24 [110/22] via 192.168.19.1, 01:12:23, Ethernet0
C       192.168.19.0/24 is directly connected, Ethernet0
O*E2 0.0.0.0/0 [110/1] via 192.168.19.1, 01:12:13, Ethernet0
O IA 192.168.16.0/23 [110/26] via 192.168.19.1, 01:12:23, Ethernet0
```

Example 9-18 *Laurel Configuration and Diagnostic Output*

```
laurel# sh running-config
...
router ospf 1
 router-id 192.168.201.1
 log-adjacency-changes
 redistribute connected subnets
 redistribute static subnets
 passive-interface Serial0
 passive-interface Serial1
 network 192.168.14.0 0.0.0.255 area 5
 network 192.168.19.0 0.0.0.255 area 5
 network 192.168.201.1 0.0.0.0 area 5
...

laurel# sh ip ospf
 Routing Process "ospf 1" with ID 192.168.201.1 and Domain ID 0.0.0.1
 Supports only single TOS(TOS0) routes
 Supports opaque LSA
 It is an autonomous system boundary router
 Redistributing External Routes from,
    connected, includes subnets in redistribution
    static, includes subnets in redistribution
 SPF schedule delay 5 secs, Hold time between two SPFs 10 secs
 Minimum LSA interval 5 secs. Minimum LSA arrival 1 secs
 Number of external LSA 7. Checksum Sum 0x36FD1
 Number of opaque AS LSA 0. Checksum Sum 0x0
 Number of DCbitless external and opaque AS LSA 7
 Number of DoNotAge external and opaque AS LSA 0
 Number of areas in this router is 1. 1 normal 0 stub 0 nssa
 External flood list length 0
    Area 5
        Number of interfaces in this area is 3
        Area has no authentication
        SPF algorithm executed 4 times
        Area ranges are
        Number of LSA 42. Checksum Sum 0x146F0A
        Number of opaque link LSA 0. Checksum Sum 0x0
        Number of DCbitless LSA 12
        Number of indication LSA 0
        Number of DoNotAge LSA 0
        Flood list length 0

laurel# sh ip ospf neighbor

Neighbor ID     Pri   State         Dead Time   Address          Interface
192.168.201.4     1   FULL/DR       00:00:38    192.168.19.2     Ethernet1
192.168.201.2     1   FULL/DR       00:00:30    192.168.14.254   Ethernet0
192.168.1.1       0   FULL/DROTHER  00:00:38    192.168.14.1     Ethernet0
```

Exercise 9-3: Exporting Loopback Addresses

Why does GateD not export/redistribute ganymed's lo1 interface address 192.168.44.1? If you figure it out, let me know.

Lab 9-5: Leaf-Area Design Featuring Zebra and Cisco IOS Software

This lab features the same topology as Lab 9-4 (Figure 9-3) with the difference that all UNIX gateways are running the Zebra zebra/ospfd now instead of GateD. However, they are implementing the same functionality.

NOTE   The configurations of the Cisco IOS routers are exactly as in Lab 9-4; therefore, they are omitted here.

Examples 9-19 to 9-21 present the Zebra ospfd configurations and relevant **show** commands for the three UNIX gateways callisto, castor, and ganymed. These examples also show the routing situation from the gateway's routing table point of view. Therefore, we can compare the OSPF RIB link-state database (LSDB) and the UNIX forwarding table.

Example 9-19 *Zebra OSPF Configuration and Output on Callisto*

```
[root@callisto:~#] telnet localhost 2604
Trying 127.0.0.1...
Connected to localhost (127.0.0.1).
Escape character is '^]'.
Hello, this is zebra (version 0.94).
Copyright 1996-2002 Kunihiro Ishiguro.
User Access Verification
Password:

callisto-ospfd# show running-config

Current configuration:
!
hostname callisto-ospfd
password 8 m6eyKycFMHniQ
enable password 8 bjYlnA9YLBWyM
log file /var/log/ospfd.log
service advanced-vty
service password-encryption
!
interface lo
!
interface eth0
```

Example 9-19 *Zebra OSPF Configuration and Output on Callisto (Continued)*

```
!
interface eth1
!
interface ipsec0
!
interface ipsec1
!
interface ipsec2
!
interface ipsec3
!
interface eth1:1
!
interface lo1
!
router ospf
 ospf router-id 192.168.1.1
 compatible rfc1583
 redistribute connected
 redistribute static
 network 192.168.1.0/24 area 0
 network 192.168.14.0/24 area 5
 network 192.168.45.0/24 area 0
 area 5 virtual-link 192.168.201.4
 capability opaque
!
access-list 1 remark vty-protection
access-list 1 permit 127.0.0.1
access-list 1 permit 192.168.1.0 0.0.0.255
!
line vty
 access-class 1
 exec-timeout 15 0
!
end

callisto-ospfd# show ip ospf
 OSPF Routing Process, Router ID: 192.168.1.1
 Supports only single TOS (TOS0) routes
 This implementation conforms to RFC2328
 RFC1583Compatibility flag is enabled
 OpaqueCapability flag is enabled
 SPF schedule delay 5 secs, Hold time between two SPFs 10 secs
 Refresh timer 10 secs
 This router is an ABR, ABR type is: Standard (RFC2328)
 This router is an ASBR (injecting external routing information)
 Number of external LSA 3
 Number of areas attached to this router: 2

 Area ID: 0.0.0.0 (Backbone)
   Number of interfaces in this area: Total: 2, Active: 3
   Number of fully adjacent neighbors in this area: 2
```

continues

Example 9-19 *Zebra OSPF Configuration and Output on Callisto (Continued)*

```
      Area has no authentication
      SPF algorithm executed 12 times
      Number of LSA 29

 Area ID: 0.0.0.5
    Shortcutting mode: Default, S-bit consensus: no
    Number of interfaces in this area: Total: 1, Active: 2
    Number of fully adjacent neighbors in this area: 2
    Area has no authentication
    Number of full virtual adjacencies going through this area: 1
    SPF algorithm executed 12 times
    Number of LSA 35

callisto-ospfd# show ip ospf interface
lo is up, line protocol is up
  OSPF not enabled on this interface
eth0 is up, line protocol is up
  Internet Address 192.168.14.1/24, Area 0.0.0.5
  Router ID 192.168.1.1, Network Type BROADCAST, Cost: 10
  Transmit Delay is 1 sec, State DR, Priority 1
  Designated Router (ID) 192.168.1.1, Interface Address 192.168.14.1
  Backup Designated Router (ID) 192.168.201.2, Interface Address 192.168.14.254
  Timer intervals configured, Hello 10, Dead 40, Wait 40, Retransmit 5
    Hello due in 00:00:04
  Neighbor Count is 2, Adjacent neighbor count is 2
eth1 is up, line protocol is up
  Internet Address 192.168.1.1/24, Area 0.0.0.0
  Router ID 192.168.1.1, Network Type BROADCAST, Cost: 10
  Transmit Delay is 1 sec, State Backup, Priority 1
  Designated Router (ID) 192.168.1.254, Interface Address 192.168.1.254
  Backup Designated Router (ID) 192.168.1.1, Interface Address 192.168.1.1
  Timer intervals configured, Hello 10, Dead 40, Wait 40, Retransmit 5
    Hello due in 00:00:09
  Neighbor Count is 1, Adjacent neighbor count is 1
ipsec0 is up, line protocol is up
  OSPF not enabled on this interface
ipsec1 is down, line protocol is down
  OSPF not enabled on this interface
ipsec2 is down, line protocol is down
  OSPF not enabled on this interface
ipsec3 is down, line protocol is down
  OSPF not enabled on this interface
eth1:1 is down, line protocol is down
  OSPF not enabled on this interface
lo1 is down, line protocol is down
  OSPF not enabled on this interface
VLINK0 is up, line protocol is up
  Internet Address 192.168.14.1/24, Area 0.0.0.0
  Router ID 192.168.1.1, Network Type VIRTUALLINK, Cost: 20
  Transmit Delay is 1 sec, State Point-To-Point, Priority 1
  No designated router on this network
  No backup designated router on this network
```

Example 9-19 *Zebra OSPF Configuration and Output on Callisto (Continued)*

```
  Timer intervals configured, Hello 10, Dead 40, Wait 40, Retransmit 5
    Hello due in 00:00:09
  Neighbor Count is 1, Adjacent neighbor count is 1

callisto-ospfd# show ip ospf neighbor

Neighbor ID    Pri  State        Dead Time   Address         Interface        RXmtL
RqstL DBsmL
192.168.201.4   1   Full/DROther  00:00:34   192.168.19.2    VLINK0              0
0    0
192.168.201.1   1   Full/DROther  00:00:36   192.168.14.2    eth0:192.168.14.1   0
0    0
192.168.201.2   1   Full/Backup   00:00:36   192.168.14.254  eth0:192.168.14.1   0
0    0
192.168.1.254   1   Full/DR       00:00:38   192.168.1.254   eth1:192.168.1.1    0
0    0

callisto-ospfd# show ip ospf neighbor detail
 Neighbor 192.168.201.4, interface address 192.168.19.2
    In the area 0.0.0.0 via interface VLINK0
    Neighbor priority is 1, State is Full, 4 state changes
    DR is 0.0.0.0, BDR is 0.0.0.0
    Options 98 *|O|DC|-|-|-|E|*
    Dead timer due in 00:00:31
    Database Summary List 0
    Link State Request List 0
    Link State Retransmission List 0
    Thread Inactivity Timer on
    Thread Database Description Retransmision off
    Thread Link State Request Retransmission off
    Thread Link State Update Retransmission on

 Neighbor 192.168.201.1, interface address 192.168.14.2
    In the area 0.0.0.5 via interface eth0
    Neighbor priority is 1, State is Full, 5 state changes
    DR is 192.168.14.1, BDR is 192.168.14.254
    Options 66 *|O|-|-|-|-|E|*
    Dead timer due in 00:00:33
    Database Summary List 0
    Link State Request List 0
    Link State Retransmission List 0
    Thread Inactivity Timer on
    Thread Database Description Retransmision off
    Thread Link State Request Retransmission on
    Thread Link State Update Retransmission on

 Neighbor 192.168.201.2, interface address 192.168.14.254
    In the area 0.0.0.5 via interface eth0
    Neighbor priority is 1, State is Full, 5 state changes
    DR is 192.168.14.1, BDR is 192.168.14.254
    Options 66 *|O|-|-|-|-|E|*
    Dead timer due in 00:00:33
```

continues

Example 9-19 *Zebra OSPF Configuration and Output on Callisto (Continued)*

```
            Database Summary List 0
            Link State Request List 0
            Link State Retransmission List 0
            Thread Inactivity Timer on
            Thread Database Description Retransmision off
            Thread Link State Request Retransmission on
            Thread Link State Update Retransmission on

   Neighbor 192.168.1.254, interface address 192.168.1.254
      In the area 0.0.0.0 via interface eth1
      Neighbor priority is 1, State is Full, 6 state changes
      DR is 192.168.1.254, BDR is 192.168.1.1
      Options 66 *|O|-|-|-|-|E|*
      Dead timer due in 00:00:35
      Database Summary List 0
      Link State Request List 0
      Link State Retransmission List 0
      Thread Inactivity Timer on
      Thread Database Description Retransmision off
      Thread Link State Request Retransmission on
      Thread Link State Update Retransmission on


callisto-ospfd# show ip ospf border-routers
============ OSPF router routing table =============
R     192.168.1.1       IA [40] area: 0.0.0.0, ASBR
                            via 192.168.1.254, eth1
                            via 192.168.14.254, eth0
                            via 192.168.14.2, eth0
R     192.168.1.254        [10] area: 0.0.0.0, ASBR
                            via 192.168.1.254, eth1
R     192.168.2.7          [20] area: 0.0.0.0, ASBR
                            via 192.168.1.254, eth1
                            via 192.168.14.254, eth0
R     192.168.201.1        [10] area: 0.0.0.5, ASBR
                            via 192.168.14.2, eth0
R     192.168.201.2        [30] area: 0.0.0.0, ABR, ASBR
                            via 192.168.1.254, eth1
                            [10] area: 0.0.0.5, ABR, ASBR
                            via 192.168.14.254, eth0
R     192.168.201.4        [20] area: 0.0.0.5, ABR
                            via 192.168.14.2, eth0


callisto-ospfd# show ip ospf database

        OSPF Router with ID (192.168.1.1)

            Router Link States (Area 0.0.0.0)

Link ID           ADV Router        Age  Seq#       CkSum  Link count
192.168.1.1       192.168.1.1       170  0x80000006 0x724f 2
192.168.1.254     192.168.1.254     301  0x80000007 0xeb38 3
192.168.2.7       192.168.2.7       262  0x8000000a 0x8e5a 3
```

Example 9-19 *Zebra OSPF Configuration and Output on Callisto (Continued)*

```
192.168.201.2    192.168.201.2    1887 0x80000004 0x7a3f 3
192.168.201.4    192.168.201.4    1912 0x80000003 0xeafe 2

                 Net Link States (Area 0.0.0.0)

Link ID          ADV Router       Age  Seq#       CkSum
192.168.1.254    192.168.1.254    592 0x80000003 0x8a26
192.168.2.254    192.168.1.254    305 0x80000003 0xc4e3
192.168.7.7      192.168.2.7      267 0x80000003 0x6264
192.168.80.254   192.168.1.254    305 0x80000003 0x67f2

                 Summary Link States (Area 0.0.0.0)

Link ID          ADV Router       Age  Seq#       CkSum  Route
192.168.13.0     192.168.201.2    1887 0x80000002 0xbbd5 192.168.13.0/29
192.168.14.0     192.168.1.1       683 0x80000003 0x6608 192.168.14.0/24
192.168.14.0     192.168.201.2    1887 0x80000004 0xfe84 192.168.14.0/24
192.168.14.0     192.168.201.4    1912 0x80000002 0x5b1e 192.168.14.0/24
192.168.16.0     192.168.201.2    1887 0x80000002 0xbfc8 192.168.16.0/23
192.168.19.0     192.168.1.1       813 0x80000003 0x93cb 192.168.19.0/24
192.168.19.0     192.168.201.2    1887 0x80000002 0x3046 192.168.19.0/24
192.168.19.0     192.168.201.4    1912 0x80000002 0xbfbe 192.168.19.0/24
192.168.201.1    192.168.1.1      1513 0x80000002 0x575a 192.168.201.1/32
192.168.201.1    192.168.201.2    1887 0x80000002 0xf1d5 192.168.201.1/32
192.168.201.1    192.168.201.4    1912 0x80000002 0xe5df 192.168.201.1/32
192.168.201.3    192.168.201.2    1887 0x80000002 0xb514 192.168.201.3/32
192.168.201.4    192.168.201.4    1912 0x80000002 0x6369 192.168.201.4/32

                 ASBR-Summary Link States (Area 0.0.0.0)

Link ID          ADV Router       Age  Seq#       CkSum
192.168.1.1      192.168.201.2    1887 0x80000002 0x7a16
192.168.1.1      192.168.201.4    1912 0x80000002 0xd2b1
192.168.201.1    192.168.1.1       253 0x80000003 0x3d73
192.168.201.1    192.168.201.2    1887 0x80000002 0xd9ed
192.168.201.1    192.168.201.4    1912 0x80000002 0xcdf7
192.168.201.2    192.168.1.1       843 0x80000003 0x337c
192.168.201.2    192.168.201.4    1912 0x80000002 0x2892

                 Router Link States (Area 0.0.0.5)

Link ID          ADV Router       Age  Seq#       CkSum  Link count
192.168.1.1      192.168.1.1       171 0x80000007 0xa1d3 1
192.168.201.1    192.168.201.1    1789 0x80000004 0x521e 3
192.168.201.2    192.168.201.2    1885 0x80000003 0x715a 1
192.168.201.4    192.168.201.4    1913 0x80000004 0xebce 1

                 Net Link States (Area 0.0.0.5)

Link ID          ADV Router       Age  Seq#       CkSum
192.168.14.1     192.168.1.1       191 0x80000004 0x8f0b
192.168.19.2     192.168.201.4    1913 0x80000002 0xa572
```

continues

Example 9-19 *Zebra OSPF Configuration and Output on Callisto (Continued)*

```
                        Summary Link States (Area 0.0.0.5)

   Link ID          ADV Router       Age  Seq#        CkSum  Route
   192.168.1.0      192.168.1.1      833  0x80000003  0xf585 192.168.1.0/24
   192.168.1.0      192.168.201.2    1885 0x80000002  0x5b23 192.168.1.0/24
   192.168.1.0      192.168.201.4    1913 0x80000002  0x4f2d 192.168.1.0/24
   192.168.2.0      192.168.1.1      1393 0x80000003  0x4f21 192.168.2.0/24
   192.168.2.0      192.168.201.2    1885 0x80000002  0xeb9b 192.168.2.0/24
   192.168.2.0      192.168.201.4    1913 0x80000002  0xa8c8 192.168.2.0/24
   192.168.7.0      192.168.201.2    1885 0x80000004  0x4c3e 192.168.7.0/24
   192.168.7.0      192.168.201.4    1913 0x80000002  0x0d69 192.168.7.0/24
   192.168.13.0     192.168.201.2    1885 0x80000002  0xbbd5 192.168.13.0/29
   192.168.13.0     192.168.201.4    1913 0x80000002  0x7803 192.168.13.0/29
   192.168.16.0     192.168.201.2    1885 0x80000002  0xbfc8 192.168.16.0/23
   192.168.16.0     192.168.201.4    1913 0x80000002  0x7cf5 192.168.16.0/23
   192.168.80.0     192.168.1.1      1653 0x80000002  0xf32f 192.168.80.0/24
   192.168.80.0     192.168.201.2    1885 0x80000002  0x8eaa 192.168.80.0/24
   192.168.80.0     192.168.201.4    1913 0x80000002  0x4bd7 192.168.80.0/24
   192.168.201.2    192.168.201.2    1885 0x80000002  0x834d 192.168.201.2/32
   192.168.201.2    192.168.201.4    1913 0x80000002  0x407a 192.168.201.2/32
   192.168.201.3    192.168.201.2    1885 0x80000002  0xb514 192.168.201.3/32
   192.168.201.3    192.168.201.4    1913 0x80000002  0x7241 192.168.201.3/32
   192.168.201.4    192.168.201.2    1885 0x80000002  0x3882 192.168.201.4/32
   192.168.201.4    192.168.201.4    1913 0x80000002  0x6369 192.168.201.4/32


                     ASBR-Summary Link States (Area 0.0.0.5)

   Link ID          ADV Router       Age  Seq#        CkSum
   192.168.1.1      192.168.201.2    1885 0x80000002  0x4339
   192.168.1.1      192.168.201.4    1913 0x80000002  0xd2b1
   192.168.1.254    192.168.1.1      763  0x80000003  0xf189
   192.168.1.254    192.168.201.2    1885 0x80000002  0xf295
   192.168.1.254    192.168.201.4    1913 0x80000002  0x4b31
   192.168.2.7      192.168.201.2    1885 0x80000002  0x3356
   192.168.2.7      192.168.201.4    1913 0x80000002  0xef83
   192.168.201.2    192.168.201.4    1913 0x80000002  0x2892


                        AS External Link States

   Link ID          ADV Router       Age  Seq#        CkSum  Route
   172.16.7.0       192.168.2.7      1218 0x80000002  0x92f4 E2 172.16.7.0/24 [0x0]
   192.168.44.0     192.168.1.254    1726 0x80000003  0x03ba E2 192.168.44.0/24 [0x0]
   111.11.117.0     192.168.1.254    694  0x80000003  0x7c5c E2 111.11.117.0/24 [0x0]

callisto-ospfd# show ip ospf route
============ OSPF network routing table ============
N    192.168.1.0/24        [10] area: 0.0.0.0
                           directly attached to eth1
N    192.168.2.0/24        [20] area: 0.0.0.0
                           via 192.168.1.254, eth1
N    192.168.7.0/24        [20] area: 0.0.0.0
                           via 192.168.14.254, eth0
```

Example 9-19 *Zebra OSPF Configuration and Output on Callisto (Continued)*

```
N IA 192.168.13.0/29      [16] area: 0.0.0.0
                          via 192.168.14.254, eth0
N    192.168.14.0/24      [10] area: 0.0.0.5
                          directly attached to eth0
N IA 192.168.16.0/23      [16] area: 0.0.0.0
                          via 192.168.14.254, eth0
N    192.168.19.0/24      [20] area: 0.0.0.5
                          via 192.168.14.2, eth0
N    192.168.80.0/24      [20] area: 0.0.0.0
                          via 192.168.1.254, eth1
N    192.168.201.1/32     [11] area: 0.0.0.5
                          via 192.168.14.2, eth0
N    192.168.201.2/32     [11] area: 0.0.0.0
                          via 192.168.14.254, eth0
N IA 192.168.201.3/32     [17] area: 0.0.0.0
                          via 192.168.14.254, eth0
N IA 192.168.201.4/32     [21] area: 0.0.0.0
                          via 192.168.14.2, eth0


============ OSPF router routing table =============
R    192.168.1.1      IA [40] area: 0.0.0.0, ASBR
                          via 192.168.1.254, eth1
                          via 192.168.14.254, eth0
                          via 192.168.14.2, eth0
R    192.168.1.254       [10] area: 0.0.0.0, ASBR
                          via 192.168.1.254, eth1
R    192.168.2.7         [20] area: 0.0.0.0, ASBR
                          via 192.168.1.254, eth1
                          via 192.168.14.254, eth0
R    192.168.201.1       [10] area: 0.0.0.5, ASBR
                          via 192.168.14.2, eth0
R    192.168.201.2       [30] area: 0.0.0.0, ABR, ASBR
                          via 192.168.1.254, eth1
                          [10] area: 0.0.0.5, ABR, ASBR
                          via 192.168.14.254, eth0
R    192.168.201.4       [20] area: 0.0.0.5, ABR
                          via 192.168.14.2, eth0


============ OSPF external routing table ===========
N E2 172.16.7.0/24        [20/20] tag: 0
                          via 192.168.1.254, eth1
                          via 192.168.14.254, eth0
N E2 192.168.44.0/24      [10/20] tag: 0
                          via 192.168.1.254, eth1
N E2 111.11.117.0/24      [10/20] tag: 0
                          via 192.168.1.254, eth1


[root@callisto:~#] telnet localhost 2601
Trying 127.0.0.1...
Connected to localhost (127.0.0.1).
Escape character is '^]'.
```

continues

Example 9-19 *Zebra OSPF Configuration and Output on Callisto (Continued)*

```
Hello, this is zebra (version 0.94).
Copyright 1996-2002 Kunihiro Ishiguro.
User Access Verification
Password:

callisto-zebra# show running-config

Current configuration:
!
hostname callisto-zebra
password 8 UUXADe4FP7VQU
enable password 8 6SyP71b.8BZnk
log file /var/log/zebra.log
service advanced-vty
service password-encryption
!
interface lo
!
interface eth0
 multicast
!
interface eth1
 multicast
!
interface ipsec0
!
interface ipsec1
!
interface ipsec2
!
interface ipsec3
!
interface eth1:1
 multicast
!
access-list 1 remark vty-protection
access-list 1 permit 127.0.0.1
access-list 1 permit 192.168.1.0 0.0.0.255
!
!
line vty
 access-class 1
 exec-timeout 15 0
!
end

callisto-zebra# show ip route
Codes: K - kernel route, C - connected, S - static, R - RIP, O - OSPF,
       B - BGP, > - selected route, * - FIB route

K>* 0.0.0.0/0 via 192.168.1.254, eth1
K * 127.0.0.0/8 is directly connected, lo
```

Example 9-19 *Zebra OSPF Configuration and Output on Callisto (Continued)*

```
C>* 127.0.0.0/8 is directly connected, lo
O>* 172.16.7.0/24 [110/20] via 192.168.1.254, eth1, 01:07:00
 *                        via 192.168.14.254, eth0, 01:07:00
O   192.168.1.0/24 [110/10] is directly connected, eth1, 01:14:03
K * 192.168.1.0/24 is directly connected, eth1
C * 192.168.1.0/24 is directly connected, ipsec0
C>* 192.168.1.0/24 is directly connected, eth1
O>* 192.168.2.0/24 [110/20] via 192.168.1.254, eth1, 01:13:53
O>* 192.168.7.0/24 [110/20] via 192.168.14.254, eth0, 01:07:01
O>* 192.168.13.0/29 [110/16] via 192.168.14.254, eth0, 01:07:01
O   192.168.14.0/24 [110/10] is directly connected, eth0, 01:14:03
K * 192.168.14.0/24 is directly connected, eth0
C>* 192.168.14.0/24 is directly connected, eth0
O>* 192.168.16.0/23 [110/16] via 192.168.14.254, eth0, 01:07:01
O>* 192.168.19.0/24 [110/20] via 192.168.14.2, eth0, 01:07:11
O>* 192.168.44.0/24 [110/20] via 192.168.1.254, eth1, 01:13:52
O>* 192.168.80.0/24 [110/20] via 192.168.1.254, eth1, 01:09:05
O>* 192.168.201.1/32 [110/11] via 192.168.14.2, eth0, 01:07:11
O>* 192.168.201.2/32 [110/11] via 192.168.14.254, eth0, 01:07:01
O>* 192.168.201.3/32 [110/17] via 192.168.14.254, eth0, 01:07:01
O>* 192.168.201.4/32 [110/21] via 192.168.14.2, eth0, 01:06:51
O>* 111.11.117.0/24 [110/20] via 192.168.1.254, eth1, 01:13:52

[root@callisto:~#] ip route
192.168.201.2 via 192.168.14.254 dev eth0  proto zebra  metric 11 equalize
192.168.201.3 via 192.168.14.254 dev eth0  proto zebra  metric 17 equalize
192.168.201.1 via 192.168.14.2 dev eth0  proto zebra  metric 11 equalize
192.168.201.4 via 192.168.14.2 dev eth0  proto zebra  metric 21 equalize
192.168.13.0/29 via 192.168.14.254 dev eth0  proto zebra  metric 16 equalize
192.168.7.0/24 via 192.168.14.254 dev eth0  proto zebra  metric 20 equalize
172.16.7.0/24  proto zebra  metric 20 equalize
        nexthop via 192.168.1.254  dev eth1 weight 1
        nexthop via 192.168.14.254  dev eth0 weight 1
111.11.117.0/24 via 192.168.1.254 dev eth1  proto zebra  metric 20 equalize
192.168.19.0/24 via 192.168.14.2 dev eth0  proto zebra  metric 20 equalize
192.168.2.0/24 via 192.168.1.254 dev eth1  proto zebra  metric 20 equalize
192.168.80.0/24 via 192.168.1.254 dev eth1  proto zebra  metric 20 equalize
192.168.1.0/24 dev eth1  scope link
192.168.1.0/24 dev ipsec0  proto kernel  scope link  src 192.168.1.1
192.168.14.0/24 dev eth0  scope link
192.168.44.0/24 via 192.168.1.254 dev eth1  proto zebra  metric 20 equalize
192.168.16.0/23 via 192.168.14.254 dev eth0  proto zebra  metric 16 equalize
127.0.0.0/8 dev lo  scope link
default via 192.168.1.254 dev eth1

[root@callisto:~#] netstat -rne
Kernel IP routing table
Destination     Gateway         Genmask         Flags Metric Ref    Use Iface
192.168.201.2   192.168.14.254  255.255.255.255 UGH   11     0        0 eth0
192.168.201.3   192.168.14.254  255.255.255.255 UGH   17     0        0 eth0
192.168.201.1   192.168.14.2    255.255.255.255 UGH   11     0        0 eth0
192.168.201.4   192.168.14.2    255.255.255.255 UGH   21     0        0 eth0
```

continues

Example 9-19 *Zebra OSPF Configuration and Output on Callisto (Continued)*

```
192.168.13.0     192.168.14.254   255.255.255.248 UG   16    0         0 eth0
192.168.7.0      192.168.14.254   255.255.255.0   UG   20    0         0 eth0
172.16.7.0       192.168.1.254    255.255.255.0   UG   20    0         0 eth1
111.11.117.0     192.168.1.254    255.255.255.0   UG   20    0         0 eth1
192.168.19.0     192.168.14.2     255.255.255.0   UG   20    0         0 eth0
192.168.2.0      192.168.1.254    255.255.255.0   UG   20    0         0 eth1
192.168.80.0     192.168.1.254    255.255.255.0   UG   20    0         0 eth1
192.168.1.0      0.0.0.0          255.255.255.0   U    0     0         0 eth1
192.168.1.0      0.0.0.0          255.255.255.0   U    0     0         0 ipsec0
192.168.14.0     0.0.0.0          255.255.255.0   U    0     0         0 eth0
192.168.44.0     192.168.1.254    255.255.255.0   UG   20    0         0 eth1
192.168.16.0     192.168.14.254   255.255.254.0   UG   16    0         0 eth0
127.0.0.0        0.0.0.0          255.0.0.0       U    0     0         0 lo
0.0.0.0          192.168.1.254    0.0.0.0         UG   0     0         0 eth1
```

Note that one static route, 172.16.7.0/24, has been added to demonstrate administrative distance assignment to a route in Example 9-20.

Example 9-20 *Zebra OSPF Configuration and Output on Castor*

```
[root@castor:~#] netstat -rn -f inet
Routing tables

Internet:
Destination      Gateway          Flags   Refs      Use  Netif Expire
default          192.168.2.254    UGSc     2         0   xl0
127.0.0.1        127.0.0.1        UH       0      4154   lo0
172.16.7/24      link#1           UC1      0         0   xl0
192.168.1        192.168.2.254    UG1c     1        99   xl0
192.168.2        link#1           UC       1         0   xl0
192.168.2.254    52:54:05:e3:e4:2f UHLW    7        96   xl0    1162
192.168.7        link#2           UC       1         0   ed0
192.168.7.254    00:00:0c:1a:a9:a8 UHLW   10       219   ed0     522
192.168.13/29    192.168.7.254    UG1c     0         3   ed0
192.168.14       192.168.7.254    UG1c     0         0   ed0
192.168.16/23    192.168.7.254    UG1c     0         0   ed0
192.168.19       192.168.7.254    UG1c     0         0   ed0
192.168.44       192.168.2.254    UG1c     0         0   xl0
192.168.80       link#14          UC       1         0   vlan8
192.168.80.254   52.54.5.e3.e4.2f UHLW     0         0   vlan8   264
192.168.201.1    192.168.7.254    UGH1     0         0   ed0
192.168.201.2    192.168.7.254    UGH1     0         0   ed0
192.168.201.3    192.168.7.254    UGH1     0        80   ed0
192.168.201.4    192.168.7.254    UGH1     0         0   ed0
111.11.117       192.168.2.254    UG1c     0         0   xl0

[root@castor:~#] telnet localhost 2601
Trying 127.0.0.1...
Connected to localhost.nerdzone.org.
Escape character is '^]'.
Hello, this is zebra (version 0.93a).
```

Example 9-20 *Zebra OSPF Configuration and Output on Castor (Continued)*

```
Copyright 1996-2002 Kunihiro Ishiguro.
User Access Verification
Password:

castor-zebra# show running-config

Current configuration:
!
hostname castor-zebra
password 8 bJFoEOB0obLL6
enable password 8 4DwwIFdKLWvU.
log file /var/log/zebra.log
service advanced-vty
service password-encryption
!
interface xl0
 ip address 192.168.2.7/24
 multicast
 ipv6 nd suppress-ra
!
interface ed0
 ip address 192.168.7.7/24
 multicast
 ipv6 nd suppress-ra
!
interface lp0
 ipv6 nd suppress-ra
!
interface ppp0
 ipv6 nd suppress-ra
!
interface ppp1
 ipv6 nd suppress-ra
!
interface sl0
 ipv6 nd suppress-ra
!
interface sl1
 ipv6 nd suppress-ra
!
interface ds0
!
interface stf0
 ipv6 nd suppress-ra
!
interface faith0
 ipv6 nd suppress-ra
!
interface vlan0
 ipv6 nd suppress-ra
!
```

continues

Example 9-20 *Zebra OSPF Configuration and Output on Castor (Continued)*

```
interface vlan1
 ipv6 nd suppress-ra
!
interface lo0
!
interface vlan8
 multicast
 ipv6 nd suppress-ra
!
interface gif0
 ipv6 nd suppress-ra
!
ip route 172.16.7.0/24 xl0 22
!
access-list 1 remark vty-protection
access-list 1 permit 127.0.0.1
access-list 1 permit 192.168.1.0 0.0.0.255
!
!
line vty
 access-class 1
 exec-timeout 15 0
!
end

castor-zebra# show ip route
Codes: K - kernel route, C - connected, S - static, R - RIP, O - OSPF,
 I - IS-IS,
       B - BGP, > - selected route, * - FIB route

K>* 0.0.0.0/0 via 192.168.2.254, xl0
C>* 127.0.0.0/8 is directly connected, lo0
S>* 172.16.7.0/24 [22/0] is directly connected, xl0
O>* 192.168.1.0/24 [110/20] via 192.168.2.254, xl0, 01:28:22
  *                       via 192.168.80.254, vlan8, 01:28:22
O   192.168.2.0/24 [110/10] is directly connected, xl0, 01:28:22
C>* 192.168.2.0/24 is directly connected, xl0
O   192.168.7.0/24 [110/10] is directly connected, ed0, 01:28:32
C>* 192.168.7.0/24 is directly connected, ed0
O>* 192.168.13.0/29 [110/16] via 192.168.7.254, ed0, 01:27:31
O>* 192.168.14.0/24 [110/20] via 192.168.7.254, ed0, 01:27:41
O>* 192.168.16.0/23 [110/16] via 192.168.7.254, ed0, 01:27:21
O>* 192.168.19.0/24 [110/30] via 192.168.7.254, ed0, 01:26:27
O>* 192.168.44.0/24 [110/20] via 192.168.2.254, xl0, 01:28:21
  *                       via 192.168.80.254, vlan8, 01:28:21
O   192.168.80.0/24 [110/10] is directly connected, vlan8, 01:28:22
C>* 192.168.80.0/24 is directly connected, vlan8
O>* 192.168.201.1/32 [110/21] via 192.168.7.254, ed0, 01:26:27
O>* 192.168.201.2/32 [110/11] via 192.168.7.254, ed0, 01:27:41
O>* 192.168.201.3/32 [110/17] via 192.168.7.254, ed0, 01:27:31
O>* 192.168.201.4/32 [110/31] via 192.168.7.254, ed0, 01:26:07
```

Example 9-20 *Zebra OSPF Configuration and Output on Castor (Continued)*

```
O>* 111.11.117.0/24 [110/20] via 192.168.2.254, xl0, 01:28:21
   *                        via 192.168.80.254, vlan8, 01:28:21

[root@castor:~#] telnet localhost 2604
Trying 127.0.0.1...
Connected to localhost.nerdzone.org.
Escape character is '^]'.
Hello, this is zebra (version 0.93a).
Copyright 1996-2002 Kunihiro Ishiguro.
User Access Verification
Password:

castor-ospfd# show running-config

Current configuration:
!
hostname castor-ospfd
password 8 4DwwIFdKLWvU.
enable password 8 dV8x4MhxDAuaw
log file /var/log/ospfd.log
service advanced-vty
service password-encryption
!
interface xl0
!
interface ed0
!
interface lp0
 ip ospf network point-to-point
!
interface sl0
 ip ospf network point-to-point
!
interface sl1
 ip ospf network point-to-point
!
interface ds0
!
interface stf0
!
interface faith0
!
interface vlan0
!
interface vlan1
!
interface lo0
!
interface ppp0
 ip ospf network point-to-point
!
```

continues

Example 9-20 *Zebra OSPF Configuration and Output on Castor (Continued)*

```
interface ppp1
 ip ospf network point-to-point
!
interface vlan8
!
interface lo1
!
router ospf
 ospf router-id 192.168.2.7
 compatible rfc1583
 redistribute connected
 redistribute static
 network 192.168.2.0/24 area 0
 network 192.168.7.0/24 area 0
 network 192.168.80.0/24 area 0
 capability opaque
!
access-list 1 remark vty-protection
access-list 1 permit 127.0.0.1
access-list 1 permit 192.168.1.0 0.0.0.255
!
line vty
 access-class 1
 exec-timeout 15 0
!
end

castor-ospfd# show ip ospf neighbor

Neighbor ID      Pri   State         Dead Time    Address          Interface
RXmtL RqstL DBsmL
192.168.1.254     1   Full/DR        00:00:40     192.168.2.254    xl0:192.168.2.7
  0     0     0
192.168.201.2     1   Full/Backup    00:00:36     192.168.7.254    ed0:192.168.7.7
  0     0     0
192.168.1.254     1   Full/DR        00:00:40     192.168.80.254   vlan8:192.168.80.1
  0     0     0

castor-ospfd# show ip ospf border-routers
============ OSPF router routing table =============
R    192.168.1.1          [20] area: 0.0.0.0, ABR, ASBR
                          via 192.168.2.254, xl0
                          via 192.168.80.254, vlan8
R    192.168.1.254        [10] area: 0.0.0.0, ASBR
                          via 192.168.2.254, xl0
                          via 192.168.80.254, vlan8
R    192.168.201.1     IA [20] area: 0.0.0.0, ASBR
                          via 192.168.7.254, ed0
R    192.168.201.2        [10] area: 0.0.0.0, ABR, ASBR
                          via 192.168.7.254, ed0
R    192.168.201.4        [30] area: 0.0.0.0, ABR
                          via 192.168.7.254, ed0
```

Example 9-20 *Zebra OSPF Configuration and Output on Castor (Continued)*

```
castor-ospfd# show ip ospf route
============ OSPF network routing table ============
N     192.168.1.0/24        [20] area: 0.0.0.0
                            via 192.168.2.254, xl0
                            via 192.168.80.254, vlan8
N     192.168.2.0/24        [10] area: 0.0.0.0
                            directly attached to xl0
N     192.168.7.0/24        [10] area: 0.0.0.0
                            directly attached to ed0
N IA 192.168.13.0/29        [16] area: 0.0.0.0
                            via 192.168.7.254, ed0
N IA 192.168.14.0/24        [20] area: 0.0.0.0
                            via 192.168.7.254, ed0
N IA 192.168.16.0/23        [16] area: 0.0.0.0
                            via 192.168.7.254, ed0
N IA 192.168.19.0/24        [30] area: 0.0.0.0
                            via 192.168.7.254, ed0
N     192.168.80.0/24       [10] area: 0.0.0.0
                            directly attached to vlan8
N IA 192.168.201.1/32       [21] area: 0.0.0.0
                            via 192.168.7.254, ed0
N     192.168.201.2/32      [11] area: 0.0.0.0
                            via 192.168.7.254, ed0
N IA 192.168.201.3/32       [17] area: 0.0.0.0
                            via 192.168.7.254, ed0
N IA 192.168.201.4/32       [31] area: 0.0.0.0
                            via 192.168.7.254, ed0


============ OSPF router routing table ============
R     192.168.1.1           [20] area: 0.0.0.0, ABR, ASBR
                            via 192.168.2.254, xl0
                            via 192.168.80.254, vlan8
R     192.168.1.254         [10] area: 0.0.0.0, ASBR
                            via 192.168.2.254, xl0
                            via 192.168.80.254, vlan8
R     192.168.201.1      IA [20] area: 0.0.0.0, ASBR
                            via 192.168.7.254, ed0
R     192.168.201.2         [10] area: 0.0.0.0, ABR, ASBR
                            via 192.168.7.254, ed0
R     192.168.201.4         [30] area: 0.0.0.0, ABR
                            via 192.168.7.254, ed0


============ OSPF external routing table ===========
N E2 192.168.44.0/24        [10/20] tag: 0
                            via 192.168.2.254, xl0
                            via 192.168.80.254, vlan8
N E2 111.11.117.0/24        [10/20] tag: 0
                            via 192.168.2.254, xl0
                            via 192.168.80.254, vlan8
```

Example 9-21 *Zebra OSPF Configuration and Output on Ganymed*

```
ganymed-ospfd# show running-config
...
router ospf
 ospf router-id 192.168.1.254
 compatible rfc1583
 redistribute connected
 redistribute static
 network 192.168.1.0/24 area 0
 network 192.168.2.0/24 area 0
 network 192.168.45.0/24 area 0
 network 192.168.80.0/24 area 0
 capability opaque
...

[root@ganymed:~#] netstat -rn -f inet
Routing tables

Internet:
Destination      Gateway            Flags    Refs    Use    Mtu   Interface
default          111.11.117.1       UGS       1     8314   1500   ne5
127/8            127.0.0.1          UGRS      0        0  33224   lo0
127.0.0.1        127.0.0.1          UH        4      714  33224   lo0
172.16.7/24      192.168.2.7        UG1       0        0   1500   ne4
192.168.1/24     link#1             UC        0        0   1500   ne3
192.168.1.1      52:54:5:e3:51:87   UHL       5     2806   1500   ne3
192.168.1.2      8:0:46:64:74:1b    UHL       1    11211   1500   ne3
192.168.1.254    127.0.0.1          UGHS      0        0  33224   lo0
192.168.2/24     link#2             UC        0        0   1500   ne4
192.168.2.7      0:10:5a:c4:2c:4    UHL       6     6466   1500   ne4
192.168.7/24     192.168.2.7        UG1       1      130   1500   ne4
192.168.13.0/29  192.168.2.7        UG1       0        3   1500   ne4
192.168.14/24    192.168.1.1        UG1       0        0   1500   ne3
192.168.16/23    192.168.2.7        UG1       0        0   1500   ne4
192.168.19/24    192.168.1.1        UG1       0        0   1500   ne3
192.168.44.1     192.168.44.1       UH        0        0  33224   lo1
192.168.80/24    link#16            UC        0        0   1496   vlan0
192.168.80.1     0:10:5a:c4:2c:4    UHL       0        0   1496   vlan0
192.168.201.1    192.168.1.1        UGH1      0        0   1500   ne3
192.168.201.2    192.168.2.7        UGH1      0        0   1500   ne4
192.168.201.3    192.168.2.7        UGH1      1       87   1500   ne4
192.168.201.4    192.168.1.1        UGH1      0        1   1500   ne3
111.11.117/24    link#3             UC        0        0   1500   ne5
111.11.117.1     0:5:9a:5b:23:fc    UHL       1        0   1500   ne5

ganymed-zebra# sh ip route
Codes: K - kernel route, C - connected, S - static, R - RIP, O - OSPF,
       B - BGP, > - selected route, * - FIB route

K>* 0.0.0.0/0 via 111.11.117.1, ne5
K * 127.0.0.0/8 via 127.0.0.1 inactive
C>* 127.0.0.0/8 is directly connected, lo0
```

Example 9-21 *Zebra OSPF Configuration and Output on Ganymed (Continued)*

```
O>* 172.16.7.0/24 [110/20] via 192.168.2.7, ne4, 01:35:14
   *                        via 192.168.80.1, vlan0, 01:35:14
O   192.168.1.0/24 [110/10] is directly connected, ne3, 01:50:01
C>* 192.168.1.0/24 is directly connected, ne3
O   192.168.2.0/24 [110/10] is directly connected, ne4, 01:50:00
C>* 192.168.2.0/24 is directly connected, ne4
O>* 192.168.7.0/24 [110/20] via 192.168.2.7, ne4, 01:35:15
   *                        via 192.168.80.1, vlan0, 01:35:15
O>* 192.168.13.0/29 [110/26] via 192.168.2.7, ne4, 01:34:25
   *                         via 192.168.80.1, vlan0, 01:34:25
O>* 192.168.14.0/24 [110/20] via 192.168.1.1, ne3, 01:40:11
O>* 192.168.16.0/23 [110/26] via 192.168.2.7, ne4, 01:34:15
   *                         via 192.168.80.1, vlan0, 01:34:15
O>* 192.168.19.0/24 [110/30] via 192.168.1.1, ne3, 01:33:11
C>* 192.168.44.0/24 is directly connected, lo1
O   192.168.80.0/24 [110/10] is directly connected, vlan0, 01:35:15
C>* 192.168.80.0/24 is directly connected, vlan0
O>* 192.168.201.1/32 [110/21] via 192.168.1.1, ne3, 01:33:11
O>* 192.168.201.2/32 [110/21] via 192.168.2.7, ne4, 01:34:35
   *                          via 192.168.80.1, vlan0, 01:34:35
O>* 192.168.201.3/32 [110/27] via 192.168.2.7, ne4, 01:34:25
   *                          via 192.168.80.1, vlan0, 01:34:25
O>* 192.168.201.4/32 [110/31] via 192.168.1.1, ne3, 01:33:01
C>* 111.11.117.0/24 is directly connected, ne5

ganymed-ospfd# show ip ospf
 OSPF Routing Process, Router ID: 192.168.1.254
 Supports only single TOS (TOS0) routes
 This implementation conforms to RFC2328
 RFC1583Compatibility flag is enabled
 OpaqueCapability flag is enabled
 SPF schedule delay 5 secs, Hold time between two SPFs 10 secs
 Refresh timer 10 secs
 This router is an ASBR (injecting external routing information)
 Number of external LSA 3
 Number of areas attached to this router: 1

 Area ID: 0.0.0.0 (Backbone)
   Number of interfaces in this area: Total: 3, Active: 6
   Number of fully adjacent neighbors in this area: 3
   Area has no authentication
   SPF algorithm executed 15 times
   Number of LSA 29

ganymed-ospfd# show ip ospf neighbor

Neighbor ID    Pri   State         Dead Time   Address       Interface
RXmtL RqstL DBsmL
192.168.1.1     1   Full/Backup   00:00:33   192.168.1.1    ne3:192.168.1.254
 0     0     0
```

continues

Example 9-21 *Zebra OSPF Configuration and Output on Ganymed (Continued)*

```
192.168.2.7    1  Full/Backup    00:00:31    192.168.2.7    ne4:192.168.2.254
0    0    0
192.168.2.7    1  Full/Backup    00:00:31    192.168.80.1   vlan0:192.168.80.254
0    0    0

ganymed-ospfd# show ip ospf border-routers
============ OSPF router routing table =============
R    192.168.1.1       [10] area: 0.0.0.0, ABR, ASBR
                       via 192.168.1.1, ne3
R    192.168.2.7       [10] area: 0.0.0.0, ASBR
                       via 192.168.2.7, ne4
                       via 192.168.80.1, vlan0
R    192.168.201.1  IA [20] area: 0.0.0.0, ASBR
                       via 192.168.1.1, ne3
R    192.168.201.2     [20] area: 0.0.0.0, ABR, ASBR
                       via 192.168.2.7, ne4
                       via 192.168.80.1, vlan0
R    192.168.201.4     [30] area: 0.0.0.0, ABR
                       via 192.168.1.1, ne3


ganymed-ospfd# show ip ospf route
============ OSPF network routing table ============
N    192.168.1.0/24    [10] area: 0.0.0.0
                       directly attached to ne3
N    192.168.2.0/24    [10] area: 0.0.0.0
                       directly attached to ne4
N    192.168.7.0/24    [20] area: 0.0.0.0
                       via 192.168.2.7, ne4
                       via 192.168.80.1, vlan0
N IA 192.168.13.0/29   [26] area: 0.0.0.0
                       via 192.168.2.7, ne4
                       via 192.168.80.1, vlan0
N IA 192.168.14.0/24   [20] area: 0.0.0.0
                       via 192.168.1.1, ne3
N IA 192.168.16.0/23   [26] area: 0.0.0.0
                       via 192.168.2.7, ne4
                       via 192.168.80.1, vlan0
N IA 192.168.19.0/24   [30] area: 0.0.0.0
                       via 192.168.1.1, ne3
N    192.168.80.0/24   [10] area: 0.0.0.0
                       directly attached to vlan0
N IA 192.168.201.1/32  [21] area: 0.0.0.0
                       via 192.168.1.1, ne3
N    192.168.201.2/32  [21] area: 0.0.0.0
                       via 192.168.2.7, ne4
                       via 192.168.80.1, vlan0
N IA 192.168.201.3/32  [27] area: 0.0.0.0
                       via 192.168.2.7, ne4
                       via 192.168.80.1, vlan0
N IA 192.168.201.4/32  [31] area: 0.0.0.0
                       via 192.168.1.1, ne3
```

Example 9-21 *Zebra OSPF Configuration and Output on Ganymed (Continued)*

```
============ OSPF router routing table =============
R    192.168.1.1           [10] area: 0.0.0.0, ABR, ASBR
                           via 192.168.1.1, ne3
R    192.168.2.7           [10] area: 0.0.0.0, ASBR
                           via 192.168.2.7, ne4
                           via 192.168.80.1, vlan0
R    192.168.201.1      IA [20] area: 0.0.0.0, ASBR
                           via 192.168.1.1, ne3
R    192.168.201.2         [20] area: 0.0.0.0, ABR, ASBR
                           via 192.168.2.7, ne4
                           via 192.168.80.1, vlan0
R    192.168.201.4         [30] area: 0.0.0.0, ABR
                           via 192.168.1.1, ne3


============ OSPF external routing table ===========
N E2 172.16.7.0/24         [10/20] tag: 0
                           via 192.168.2.7, ne4
                           via 192.168.80.1, vlan0
```

ECMP—Manipulating Metric and Distance

ECMP is a capability of the underlying operating system. It can be achieved via equal-cost static routes independently of dynamic routing protocols. Still, the question arises whether the resulting load-sharing behavior is packet-based or flow-based.

NOTE   The only ECMP-capable operating system I have tested is Linux (enable ECMP when compiling), which does per-flow balancing, unless forced to alter its behavior by the **equalize** flag of the IP utility.

Link-state protocols such as OSPF and IS-IS were designed to support ECMP, depending on the implementation. GateD is capable of ECMP; however, you must alter the MULTIPATH definition in the sources to enable this feature (see Example 9-22). In my GateD lab, ECMP is disabled.

Example 9-22 *GateD ECMP Configuration*

```
./gated-public-3_6/src/gated/rt_table.h:

/*
 * The number of multipath routes supported by the forwarding engine.
 */
#ifndef RT_N_MULTIPATH
#define RT_N_MULTIPATH  6
#endif  /* RT_N_MULTIPATH */
```

Zebra ospfd is capable of ECMP as well; isisd is not yet capable of ECMP. Including ECMP support has to be decided at compile time (**configure --enable-multipath=6**). It is highly recommended that you read the ECMP RFCs (RFC 2991 and RFC 2992) for a better grasp of this delicate matter.

Keep in mind that load balancing is done only on outbound traffic; be aware of what really resembles a flow when testing your setup, so as not to misjudge the behavior of a correct configuration! Example 9-23 shows an example combination of the ECMP-capable Linux kernel and the Zebra ospfd.

Example 9-23 *Linux ECMP in Action*

```
[root@callisto:~#] ip route
192.168.201.2 via 192.168.14.254 dev eth0  proto zebra  metric 11 equalize
192.168.17.0/29 via 192.168.14.254 dev eth0  proto zebra  metric 16 equalize
192.168.13.0/29 via 192.168.14.254 dev eth0  proto zebra  metric 16 equalize
192.168.7.0/24 via 192.168.14.254 dev eth0  proto zebra  metric 20 equalize
111.11.117.0/24 via 192.168.1.254 dev eth1  proto zebra  metric 20 equalize
192.168.2.0/24 via 192.168.1.254 dev eth1  proto zebra  metric 20 equalize
192.168.80.0/24 via 192.168.1.254 dev eth1  proto zebra  metric 20 equalize
192.168.1.0/24 dev eth1  scope link
192.168.201.0/24  proto zebra  metric 20 equalize
        nexthop via 192.168.14.254  dev eth0 weight 1
        nexthop via 192.168.1.254  dev eth1 weight 1
192.168.14.0/24 dev eth0  scope link
192.168.44.0/24 via 192.168.1.254 dev eth1  proto zebra  metric 20 equalize
192.168.45.0/24 via 192.168.1.254 dev eth1  proto zebra  metric 20 equalize
127.0.0.0/8 dev lo  scope link
default via 192.168.1.254 dev eth1
```

The Art of Redistribution

Redistribution is the art of injecting routes learned from various sources into a dynamic routing protocol. In that respect, UNIX offers one additional hook compared to Cisco IOS Software: the injection of kernel routes. Therefore, the full variety offered is redistribution of kernel, connected/direct, static, and dynamic routes into other routing protocols. The resulting behavior is exactly as expected from the Cisco world. Because the different sources represent different administrative distances/preferences, metrics can be adjusted and redistribution controlled with distribute lists, offset lists, prefix lists, access lists, OSPF export/import/filter lists, and route maps.

Lab 9-6: Route Filtering and Redistribution

Example 9-24 shows an example for the Zebra redistribution commands. They pretty much work as under Cisco IOS Software. Consult Cisco.com for further information. Note that GateD provides similar route-filter facilities.

Example 9-24 *Zebra Redistribution Example*

```
callisto-ospfd# show running-config

Current configuration:
!
hostname callisto-ospfd
password 8 m6eyKycFMHniQ
enable password 8 bjYlnA9YLBWyM
log file /var/log/ospfd.log
service advanced-vty
service password-encryption
!
!
!
interface lo
!
interface eth0
!
interface eth1
 ip ospf message-digest-key 1 md5 zebra
!
interface ipsec0
!
interface ipsec1
!
interface ipsec2
!
interface ipsec3
!
interface eth1:1
 ip ospf message-digest-key 1 md5 zebra
!
interface lo1
!
interface wp1chdlc
 ip ospf network point-to-point
!
router ospf
 ospf router-id 192.168.1.1
 compatible rfc1583
 redistribute connected
 redistribute static
 redistribute rip route-map REDIMAP
 network 192.168.1.0/24 area 0
 network 192.168.14.0/24 area 5
 network 192.168.45.0/24 area 0
 network 192.168.99.0/30 area 0
 area 0.0.0.0 authentication message-digest
 area 5 virtual-link 192.168.201.4
 distribute-list DISTRIMAP out static
 capability opaque
!
```

continues

Example 9-24 *Zebra Redistribution Example (Continued)*

```
access-list 1 remark vty-protection
access-list 1 permit 127.0.0.1
access-list 1 permit 192.168.1.0 0.0.0.255
!
route-map DISTRIMAP permit 1
 match ip address 1
 set metric 10
!
route-map REDIMAP permit 1
 match ip address 1
 set metric-type type-1
!
line vty
 access-class 1
 exec-timeout 0 0
!
end
```

Lab 9-7: OSPF Authentication

Configuring authentication for OSPF or RIP is pretty straightforward under Zebra. You have the choice between clear-text passwords and MD5 hashes (Example 9-25). However, consider that this contributes to CPU load.

Example 9-25 *Configuring MD5 Authentication for Zebra OSPF*

```
castor-ospfd# show running-config

Current configuration:
!
hostname castor-ospfd
password 8 4DwwIFdKLWvU.
enable password 8 dV8x4MhxDAuaw
log file /var/log/ospfd.log
service advanced-vty
service password-encryption
!
!
!
interface xl0
 ip ospf message-digest-key 1 md5 zebra
!
interface ed0
 ip ospf message-digest-key 1 md5 zebra
!
interface lp0
 ip ospf network point-to-point
!
```

Example 9-25 *Configuring MD5 Authentication for Zebra OSPF (Continued)*

```
interface sl0
 ip ospf network point-to-point
!
interface sl1
 ip ospf network point-to-point
!
interface ds0
!
interface stf0
!
interface faith0
!
interface vlan0
!
interface vlan1
!
interface lo0
!
interface ppp0
 ip ospf network point-to-point
!
interface ppp1
 ip ospf network point-to-point
!
interface vlan8
 ip ospf message-digest-key 1 md5 zebra
!
interface lo1
!
router ospf
 ospf router-id 192.168.2.7
 compatible rfc1583
 redistribute connected
 redistribute static
 network 192.168.2.0/24 area 0
 network 192.168.7.0/24 area 0
 network 192.168.80.0/24 area 0
 area 0 authentication message-digest
 capability opaque
!
access-list 1 remark vty-protection
access-list 1 permit 127.0.0.1
access-list 1 permit 192.168.1.0 0.0.0.255
!
line vty
 access-class 1
 exec-timeout 15 0
!
end
```

Route Tagging and Multiple OSPF Processes/Instances

Cisco IOS Software currently allows several OSPF processes. This is not possible with Zebra or GateD. Route tagging is only possible for the entire OSPF domain in GateD, whereas Cisco IOS Software supports tagging in context with redistribution and the **domain-tag** OSPF command.

IS-IS (Intermediate System-to-Intermediate System)

I have included this section to raise more appreciation for the IS-IS routing protocol. In Open System Interconnection (OSI) CLNS environments, CLNP provides a network layer service to peer CLNS entities. CLNP can be seen as the ISO equivalent of (connectionless) IP datagram delivery.

The following dynamic routing approaches can be used to route CLNP:

- IS-IS (Intermediate System-to-Intermediate System)
- ES-IS (End System-to-Intermediate System)
- Cisco proprietary ISO IGRP (Interior Gateway Routing Protocol), capable of routing between CLNP domains

Static CLNS routes can be configured as well. All of these protocols travel via native Layer 2; they do not travel on top of IP, in contrast to OSPF.

An *intermediate system* represents a router in OSI lingo, and an *end-system* represents a workstation. IS-IS is a dynamic classless OSI link-state routing protocol based on the Dijkstra SPF algorithm. It essentially originated from DECnet Phase V routing. It supports a two-level area hierarchy, similar to OSPF, resembling a backbone (Level 2) and leaf areas (Level 1) to support large routing domains. IS-IS does not have a backbone area like the OSPF area 0. A contiguous collection of Level 2 routers resembles the backbone. In contrast to OSPF, the border between areas is on the link that connects two routers that are located in different areas.

IS-IS is popular among Tier-1/2 carriers and some ISPs. Originally, it was designed for CLNS, but it was later extended to support IP as a network layer protocol as well. IS-IS with IP support is referred to as *integrated* or *dual* IS-IS.

Disadvantages of IS-IS

The point that makes IS-IS difficult to grasp is the issue of the network service access point (NSAP) addresses required for node identification in combination with CLNP as an additional network layer protocol. In contrast to IP, one intermediate system in general has only one NSAP address. For more detailed information about addressing and IS-IS operation, see the "Recommended Reading" section at the end of this chapter.

Advantages of IS-IS

One of the big advantages of IS-IS is its exceptional convergence behavior in combination with its scalability to support large areas of several hundred intermediate systems without considerable SPF performance degradation. One can argue whether IS-IS TLVs (Type-Length-Values) or OSPF LSAs (link-state advertisements) are more complicated to understand. IS-IS appears simpler in that respect because the area concept is more straightforward. IS-IS does not implement virtual links. Cisco IOS Software provides some additional features such as route leaking, overload bit, and multi-area routing.

IS-IS is an elegant protocol and in some aspects easier to grasp and easier to manage than OSPF. I consider the only reason for its lack of popularity among noncarrier staff the "strange" NSAP addresses it depends on, its relationship with CLNS/CLNP, and the fact that it uses Layer 2 for transport. Cisco offers an excellent implementation of IS-IS. IS-IS can be deployed or additionally used for "IP out-of-band" management of network nodes, because of the integrated/dual character of IS-IS and its independence of a Layer 3 network protocol for transport.

Relevant IS-IS Standards

To raise more appreciation for IS-IS design and benefits, I have included an exhaustive collection of relevant standards:

- ISO 7498, "Open System Interconnection Model"
- ISO 10589, "ISO IS-IS"
- RFC 1142, "OSI IS-IS Intra-Domain Routing Protocol"
- RFC 2763, "Dynamic Hostname Exchange Mechanisms for IS-IS"
- RFC 2966, "Domain-Wide Prefix Distribution with Two-Level IS-IS"
- RFC 2973, "IS-IS Mesh Groups"
- RFC 1195, "Use of OSI IS-IS for Routing in TCP/IP and Dual Environments (Integrated IS-IS)"
- ISO 9542/RFC 995, "ISO ES-IS"
- ISO 8473/RFC 994/RFC 1069, "ISO CLNS/CLNP"
- ISO 8348-Ad2/RFC 1629, "NSAP Address Formats"
- RFC 3559, "Reserved Type, Length and Value (TLV) Codepoints in Intermediate System to Intermediate System"
- draft-ietf-isis-traffic-04.txt, "TE Extensions to IS-IS" (new TLVs and sub-TLVs)

Current IS-IS Developments

After a quiet period, IS-IS development is quite active again. The following list introduces aspects of current IS-IS evolution:

- Management Information Bases (MIBs)
- IPv6
- Cryptographic authentication
- TE extensions
- Mesh groups

Lab 9-8: IS-IS Flat Backbone Area

IS-IS is currently available only at an early stage as an extension to the Zebra/Quagga package, not as production-grade yet. The configurations in Example 9-26 are provided without the usual accompanying routing table output because of the early development stage of the Zebra isisd. Redistribution is not yet implemented, and neither is passive interfaces or autosummary.

In contrast to Cisco IOS Zebra, isisd does not support ECMP. The **clns routing** statement on Cisco routers is automatically added by Cisco IOS Software and can be safely removed for plain IP operation (**no clns routing**).

Note that three static alias names were added to the Cisco IOS configuration for demonstration purposes only. The router tagging DEAD is optional under Cisco IOS Software, but it is mandatory under Zebra isisd right now. The Cisco IOS **maximum-paths 6** statement configures ECMP for up to six equal-cost paths.

Example 9-26 *Configuring an IS-IS Backbone Area*

```
castor-isisd# sh running-config

Current configuration:
!
hostname castor-isisd
password zebra
enable password zebra
log file /var/log/isisd.log
!
interface ed0
 ip router isis DEAD
 ip address 192.168.7.7/24

interface xl0
interface lp0
interface sl0
interface sl1
```

Example 9-26 *Configuring an IS-IS Backbone Area (Continued)*

```
interface ds0
interface stf0
interface faith0
interface vlan0
interface vlan1
interface lo0
interface ppp0
interface ppp1
interface vlan8
!
router isis DEAD
 net 49.0001.1921.6800.7007.00
 metric-style wide
!
line vty
!
end

callisto-isisd# sh running-config

Current configuration:
!
hostname callisto-isisd
password zebra
enable password zebra
log file /var/log/isisd.log
!
interface eth0
 ip router isis DEAD
 ip address 192.168.14.1/24
interface lo
interface eth1
interface ipsec0
interface ipsec1
interface ipsec2
interface ipsec3
interface eth1:1
!
router isis DEAD
 net 49.0001.1921.6801.4001.00
 metric-style wide
!
line vty
!
end

scar# sh running-config
...
clns routing
!
```

continues

Example 9-26 *Configuring an IS-IS Backbone Area (Continued)*

```
interface Loopback0
 ip address 192.168.201.2 255.255.255.255
!
interface Ethernet0
 ip address 192.168.14.254 255.255.255.0
 ip router isis DEAD
 ip load-sharing per-packet
 no ip mroute-cache
!
interface Ethernet1
 ip address 192.168.7.254 255.255.255.0
 ip router isis DEAD
 ip load-sharing per-packet
 no ip mroute-cache
!
router isis DEAD
 redistribute connected
 redistribute static ip
 passive-interface Serial0
 passive-interface Serial1
 maximum-paths 6
 default-information originate
 net 49.0001.1921.6820.1002.00
 metric-style wide
 log-adjacency-changes
!
clns host castor 49.0001.1921.6800.7007.00
clns host callisto 49.0001.1921.6801.4001.00
clns host laurel 49.0001.1921.6820.1002.00
!
...
```

Lab 9-9: IS-IS Backbone and Leaf Area

As mentioned, IS-IS directly uses Layer 2, not IP, for protocol communication. The sniffer trace in Example 9-27 verifies this statement.

Example 9-27 *Sniffing IS-IS Traffic*

```
[root@callisto:~#] tethereal -V -i eth0

Frame 2 (1514 bytes on wire, 1514 bytes captured)
    Arrival Time: Feb  4, 2003 14:31:44.653860000
    Time delta from previous packet: 0.005838000 seconds
    Time relative to first packet: 0.005838000 seconds
    Frame Number: 2
    Packet Length: 1514 bytes
    Capture Length: 1514 bytes
IEEE 802.3 Ethernet
```

Example 9-27 *Sniffing IS-IS Traffic (Continued)*

```
         Destination: 01:80:c2:00:00:15 (ISIS-all-level-2-IS's)
         Source: 00:e0:b0:6a:69:7e (Cisco_6a:69:7e)
         Length: 1500
Logical-Link Control
    DSAP: ISO Network Layer (0xfe)
    IG Bit: Individual
    SSAP: ISO Network Layer (0xfe)
    CR Bit: Command
    Control field: U, func = UI (0x03)
        000. 00.. = Unnumbered Information
        .... ..11 = Unnumbered frame
ISO 10589 ISIS InTRA Domain Routeing Information Exchange Protocol
    Intra Domain Routing Protocol Discriminator: ISIS (0x83)
    PDU Header Length  : 27
    Version (==1)      : 1
    System ID Length   : 0
    PDU Type           : L2 HELLO (R:000)
    Version2 (==1)     : 1
    Reserved (==0)     : 0
    Max.AREAs: (0==3)  : 0
    ISIS HELLO
        Circuit type            : Level 1 and 2, reserved(0x00 == 0)
        System-ID {Sender of PDU} : 1921.6820.1002
        Holding timer           : 10
        PDU length              : 1497
        Priority                : 64, reserved(0x00 == 0)
        System-ID {Designated IS} : 1921.6820.1002.01
        Protocols Supported (1)
            NLPID(s): IP (0xcc)
        Area address(es) (4)
            Area address (3): 49.0001
        IP Interface address(es) (4)
            IPv4 interface address    : 192.168.14.254 (192.168.14.254)
        Padding (255)
        Padding (255)
        Padding (255)
        Padding (255)
        Padding (255)
        Padding (168)
```

Now we will put callisto in a different area. The only change necessary to assign callisto to area 2 as well is demonstrated in Example 9-28. Remember that the only factor that constitutes a backbone is a contiguous assembly of Layer 2 intermediate systems.

Example 9-28 *IS-IS Area Configuration*

```
callisto-isisd# configure terminal
callisto-isisd(config)# router isis DEAD
callisto-isisd(config)# net 49.0002.1921.6801.4001.00
```

Lab 9-10: OSPF Point-to-Point Lab

For this special setup, we combine the topologies of Figure 9-3 and Figure 4-1 (see Chapter 4, "Gateway WAN/Metro Interfaces") to include a point-to-point link between callisto and castor featuring Cisco HDLC as a Layer 2 line protocol. This point-to-point link is assigned to the backbone OSPF area.

The configuration and output of Examples 9-29 and 9-30 focus on callisto and castor. The highlighted configuration emphasizes the point-to-point configuration aspect and the /30 link network added to the OSPF router configuration.

Example 9-29 *Castor OSPF Configuration with Point-to-Point Link*

```
castor-ospfd# show running-config

Current configuration:
!
hostname castor-ospfd
password 8 4DwwIFdKLWvU.
enable password 8 dV8x4MhxDAuaw
log file /var/log/ospfd.log
service advanced-vty
service password-encryption
!
interface xl0
 ip ospf message-digest-key 1 md5 zebra
!
interface ed0
 ip ospf message-digest-key 1 md5 zebra
!
interface lp0
 ip ospf network point-to-point
!
interface sl0
 ip ospf network point-to-point
!
interface sl1
 ip ospf network point-to-point
!
interface ds0
!
interface stf0
!
interface faith0
!
interface vlan0
!
interface vlan1
!
interface lo0
```

Example 9-29 *Castor OSPF Configuration with Point-to-Point Link (Continued)*

```
!
interface ppp0
 ip ospf network point-to-point
!
interface ppp1
 ip ospf network point-to-point
!
interface vlan8
 ip ospf message-digest-key 1 md5 zebra
!
interface lo1
!
interface wpachdlc0
 ip ospf network point-to-point
!
router ospf
 ospf router-id 192.168.2.7
 compatible rfc1583
 redistribute connected
 redistribute static
 network 192.168.2.0/24 area 0
 network 192.168.7.0/24 area 0
 network 192.168.80.0/24 area 0
 network 192.168.99.0/30 area 0
 area 0 authentication message-digest
 capability opaque
!
access-list 1 remark vty-protection
access-list 1 permit 127.0.0.1
access-list 1 permit 192.168.1.0 0.0.0.255
!
line vty
 access-class 1
 exec-timeout 15 0
!
end
```

Example 9-30 *Callisto OSPF Configuration with Point-to-Point Link*

```
callisto-ospfd# show running-config

Current configuration:
!
hostname callisto-ospfd
password 8 m6eyKycFMHniQ
enable password 8 bjYlnA9YLBWyM
log file /var/log/ospfd.log
service advanced-vty
```

continues

Example 9-30 *Callisto OSPF Configuration with Point-to-Point Link (Continued)*

```
service password-encryption
!
interface lo
!
interface eth0
!
interface eth1
 ip ospf message-digest-key 1 md5 zebra
!
interface ipsec0
!
interface ipsec1
!
interface ipsec2
!
interface ipsec3
!
interface eth1:1
 ip ospf message-digest-key 1 md5 zebra
!
interface lo1
!
interface wp1chdlc
 ip ospf network point-to-point
!
router ospf
 ospf router-id 192.168.1.1
 compatible rfc1583
 redistribute connected
 redistribute static
 network 192.168.1.0/24 area 0
 network 192.168.14.0/24 area 5
 network 192.168.45.0/24 area 0
 network 192.168.99.0/30 area 0
 area 0.0.0.0 authentication message-digest
 area 5 virtual-link 192.168.201.4
 capability opaque
!
access-list 1 remark vty-protection
access-list 1 permit 127.0.0.1
access-list 1 permit 192.168.1.0 0.0.0.255
!
line vty
 access-class 1
 exec-timeout 0 0
!
end
```

Exercise 9-4: Dynamic Routing in Point-to-Multipoint Scenarios

Connect several WAN NICs to a router with Frame Relay switching enabled. Configure a point-to-multipoint (hub-and-spoke) topology with the hub injecting a default route into the Frame Relay network.

Advanced OSPF Features

This section introduces traffic-engineering (TE) extensions to OSPF, opaque LSA types, and a specialty of the Quagga OSPF implementation: the OSPF application programming interface (API).

Traffic-Engineering Extensions

The issue of TE extensions to link-state routing protocols has largely been driven by enthusiastic adoption of the MPLS paradigm. Nowadays, TE extensions are strongly related to MPLS-TE.

To be able to set up LSPs (MPLS label-switched paths) to forward similar traffic belonging to forwarding equivalence classes (FECs), traditional link information stored in an LSDB has proven inadequate and insufficient. Therefore, TE extensions were developed for OSPF and IS-IS, which led to the notion of OSPF-TE and IS-IS (TE). The extended TE topology (link bandwidth and administrative constraints) results in the population of a separate TE-LSDB and the deployment of the extended CSPF (constrained SPF) algorithm for computation. TE introduces additional issues and difficulties at area boundaries as well as increased computation burden on OSPF nodes.

Opaque LSAs

The vehicles used to accommodate the new sets of information discussed in the previous section are opaque LSAs (LSA Type 9,10,11) for OSPF (RFC 2370) and sub-TLVs for IS-IS, which serve the same purpose. This topological knowledge forms the basis for two signaling alternatives, CR-LDP and RSVP-TE, to establish end-to-end unidirectional TE circuits (LSPs in MPLS notation).

The preceding explanation of opaque LSAs is extremely high level, but it is enough to put things into perspective and to sufficiently understand why there exists an MPLS-TE feature for the Zebra ospfd. Early versions of RSVP-TE, CR-LDP, and LDP exist for Linux and some other open-source operating systems. There exist similarities as well as fundamental differences to policy routing approaches.

Opaque LSAs per se are a flexible and generic vehicle to disseminate arbitrary information by flooding mechanisms, because the payload information contained in these LSA types is completely transparent for the OSPF routing process. According to RFC 2370, "The link-state type field of the opaque LSA identifies the LSA's range of topological distribution. This range is referred to as the flooding scope." These LSAs can be picked up and processed by other modules such as MPLS-TE or dedicated applications such as SRRD (Service Routing Redundancy daemon).

Quagga's Implementation

Quagga's OSPF implementation is flexible and supports both opaque LSAs and OSPF-TE. The **capability opaque** configuration statement in the **ospfd** router configuration section indicates this. In addition, the OSPF LSDB of the OSPF daemon can be accessed via a generic interface, the OSPF API.

Besides LSDB access, the API allows origination and dissemination of opaque LSAs and hence provides an interface to arbitrary payload information contained within opaque LSAs. Figure 9-4 demonstrates the architecture (courtesy of Dr. Ralph Keller of the Swiss Federal Institute of Technology). The OSPF API itself consists of a client and server module and is capable of dealing with concurrent client requests. It can retrieve and originate opaque LSAs.

Figure 9-4 *Quagga OSPF Architecture*

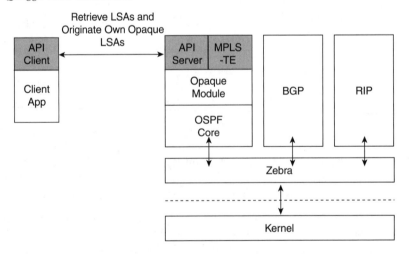

The SRRD uses the opaque LSAs to manage cluster resources based on proven OSPF signaling concepts and timers in contrast to conventional unicast or multicast heartbeat approaches or proprietary cluster management. This results in failover times of less than 30 seconds and significantly improves availability of multi-interface nodes, because a cluster constituent is available as long as one of its interfaces is reachable, thanks to OSPF.

According to my correspondence with SRRD's author, Amir Guindehi, "SRRD uses opaque LSAs for service discovery (member service), service selection, as well as service state and configuration flooding. It then creates service routes by conventional means (interface aliases plus OSPF host routes) using these for service routing to the active node."[3] Therefore, the cluster nodes can be distributed over an entire OSPF domain and even span WANs, which greatly improves redundancy in terms of single-site disasters. This is an especially intriguing concept if OSPF is your choice of IGP anyway; just enable opaque LSAs in Quagga at compile time. Cisco IOS Software supports opaque LSAs as well.

Summary

This chapter and the following about BGP constitute the heart of this book. Based on the discussion of kernel and static routes in the previous chapters, this chapter introduced the features and flexibility of dynamic routing protocols. Intrinsic characteristics of link-state and distance-vector protocols were discussed, and complex lab scenarios were developed to demonstrate RIPv2, OSPF, and IS-IS behavior and their interaction with the UNIX kernel table, static routes, and connected interface routes. The following chapter covers BGPv4, a path-vector routing protocol specialized in interdomain signaling that relies on IGPs for forwarding paths.

Recommended Reading

- The Zebra isisd website, http://isisd.sourceforge.net/
- The OSPF API website, http://www.tik.ee.ethz.ch/%7Ekeller/ospfapi/
- SRRD (Service Routing Redundancy Daemon), http://www.srrd.net
- The Active Network Control Software (ANCS) website, http://www.tik.ee.ethz.ch/%7Ekeller/ancs/
- The Linux MPLS-VRF and LDP Project website, http://sourceforge.net/projects/linux-vrf/, http://sourceforge.net/projects/mpls-linux/
- MPLS Sources from Nortel Networks website, http://www.nortelnetworks.com/products/announcements/mpls/source/index.html
- The Ayame BSD MPLS Project website, http://www.ayame.org/
- Arguably the best MPLS resource, http://www.mplsrc.com/
- RFC 2370, "The OSPF Opaque LSA Option," ftp://ftp.rfc-editor.org/in-notes/rfc2370.txt

- The IETF MPLS charter, http://www.ietf.org/html.charters/mpls-charter.html
- Sam Halabi, "OSPF Design Guide," Cisco Systems, http://www.cisco.com/warp/public/104/1.html
- *OSPF—Anatomy of an Internet Routing Protocol*, by John T. Moy (Addison Wesley, 1998).
- *OSPF—Complete Implementation*, by John T. Moy (Addison Wesley, 2001).
- *OSPF Network Design Solutions*, by Thomas M. Mann II (Cisco Press, 1998).
- The NIST-Switch website, http://is2.antd.nist.gov/itg/nistswitch/
- RSVP-TE daemon for DiffServ over MPLS under Linux, http://ds_mpls.atlantis.rug.ac.be/
- A German RSVP engine, http://www.kom.e-technik.tu-darmstadt.de/rsvp/
- Fujitsu MPLS research, http://www.labs.fujitsu.com/free/te-on-linux/
- MPLS Research Group IIT India, http://www.ee.iitb.ac.in/uma/~mpls/
- RSVP-TE daemon for DiffServ over MPLS under Linux, http://www.linux-kongress.org/2002/papers/lk2002-heuven.html
- Deploying Tight-SLA Services on an IP Backbone, http://www.nanog.org/mtg-0206/ppt/filsfils/sld001.htm
- IGP Fast Convergence IS-IS case study, http://www.ripe.net/ripe/meetings/archive/ripe-41/presentations/eof-isis/sld001.html
- Cisco.com: Cisco IOS Software Release 12.2 Mainline – "Configuring ISO CLNS"
- Cisco.com: CISCO IOS Software Release 12.2 Mainline – "ISO CLNS Commands"
- Cisco.com: OSI Routing – "Intermediate System-to-Intermediate System Protocol"
- Cisco.com: Intermediate System-to-Intermediate System (IS-IS) TLVs
- *IS-IS Network Design Solutions*, by Abe Martey (Cisco Press, 2002).
- *IS-IS: Deployment in IP Networks,* by Russ White and Alvaro Retana (Addison Wesley Professional, 2003).
- *The Complete IS-IS Routing Protocol,* by Hannes Gredler and Walter Goralski (Springer, 2004).
- IS-IS IETF Working Group website, http://www.ietf.org/html.chapters/isis-charter.html
- "Introduction to IS-IS," by Abe Martey, NANOG Presentation http://www.nanog.org/mtg-0010/ppt/martey/
- *Routing TCP/IP Vols. I and II*, by Jeff Doyle (Cisco Press; 1998 and 2001, respectively).

Endnotes

1 *Routing TCP/IP Vol. 1*, by Jeff Doyle (Cisco Press, 1998).

2 *Routing TCP/IP Vol. 1*, by Jeff Doyle (Cisco Press, 1998).

3 Personal correspondence with Amir Guindehi, 2004.

## CHAPTER 10

ISP Connectivity with BGPv4—An Exterior Gateway Path-Vector Routing Protocol for Interdomain Routing

The previous chapters covered signaling and forwarding issues tackled with interior (intra-domain) gateway routing protocols (interior gateway protocols, IGPs). These protocols are used for distribution of reachability information *within* the boundaries of a single administrative realm under a unified administration, also referred to as an *autonomous system* (AS). In practice, this constitutes a set of routers adhering to a set of (hopefully) coherent policies. Thousands of autonomous systems resemble what we know as today's global Internet, populating the global routing table with approximately 130,000 network announcements (prefixes/aggregates). The Internet is a best-effort nondeterministic architecture of hundreds of thousands of nodes (routers) with a connectionless datagram protocol (IP) at its network layer. Border Gateway Protocol (BGP) provides signaling (not forwarding) intelligence to this network.

This chapter focuses on UNIX aspects of BGP and topics not covered in the standard authoritative guides, such as Sam Halabi's *Internet Routing Architectures* or John Stewart's *BGP4 Inter-Domain Routing in the Internet*. My intention is to create a qualitative understanding and awareness of today's Internet operation and challenges and to discuss routing databases, routing registries, and route servers (topics missing from the classical textbooks in the field).

This chapter includes a thorough introduction to interdomain routing and the two BGPv4 flavors: Interior Border Gateway Protocol (IBGP) and Exterior Border Gateway Protocol (EBGP). This chapter also discusses tools and approaches for exchange points, such as route server setups, BGP views, looking glasses, the Internet Routing Registry, and the interface language (Routing Policy Specification Language, RPSL) used to query and update these databases. The load-balancing aspect of BGP scenarios is briefly mentioned as well. BGP filtering and route maps as well as state-of-the-art features of multiprotocol BGP conclude the chapter. BGP is one of the most complex and powerful concepts that networking has to offer. I strongly advise you to make full use of the additional resources listed at the end of this chapter.

Exterior Gateway Protocols: EGP and BGPv4

Between autonomous systems, exterior gateway protocols (EGPs) distribute interdomain routing information, or (to be more precise) *network layer reachability information* (NLRI). The purpose of this approach is to create a loop-free view of the Internet in terms of AS paths and related path attributes. The term *EGP* refers to both the generic family of exterior routing protocols as well as a particular archaic protocol also called EGP, the ancestor of today's predominant signaling protocol, the Border Gateway Protocol version 4 (BGPv4).

The following subsections introduce general aspects of interdomain EGP routing and gradually concentrate on BGPv4 signaling and operation.

BGPv4: Introductory Thoughts

BGP prefix routes carry multiple attributes, in particular one AS_Path itself, for both loop prevention and administrative granularity. Because of this rich set of attributes, BGP offers extended capabilities for policy-based routing, which is of paramount importance to represent complex policies of interprovider communication. Therefore, BGP is the glue that holds the Internet together. The Internet itself essentially consists of transit autonomous systems and stub autonomous systems (as shown in Figure 10-1).

Carriers form the heart of the Internet and are classified into tier 1 (no further upstream) and tier 2 carriers that usually interconnnect at commercial exchange points (MAEs, or metropolitan-area exchanges), IXs (Internet exchanges), or NAPs (network access points). Today, these interconnection points are switched Ethernet colocation centers with frequent deployments of route servers, looking-glass access, and connectivity to the Internet Route Registry (IRR).

Neighboring Relations

Peering, upstream, and subscriber agreements govern neighborship relations. A tier 1 carrier is a telco or Internet service provider (ISP) that is at the top of the Internet telecommunication hierarchy and owns its own network cable infrastructure. These are global players such as Cable & Wireless, AT&T, Sprint, and British Telecom, just to mention a few. Tier 1s do not pay anyone for transit; they are paid to provide transit and peer with other tier 1s. Tier 2s typically buy transit from at least one tier 1, while peering with as many tier 2s as they can technically realize and afford. Tier 2s also own their network infrastructure, but they are not big enough to peer with all tier 1s.

In contrast to the IGPs we investigated, which use unicast, multicast, broadcast, and even data-link addresses (Intermediate System-to-Intermediate System, IS-IS) for communication, BGP facilitates the transport protocol TCP port 179 for reliable sessions between neighbors or peers. It is established practice to secure these TCP-connections with MD5 hashes. On UNIX systems, providing MD5 capabilities for TCP connections is a responsibility of the kernel, but such provision is still missing or in experimental stages with regard to the BGP implementations used in this book. Other approaches are the use of firewall chains on Linux or divert sockets/netgraph hooks on BSD operating systems. This communication is intrinsically connection-oriented and monitored via keepalive packets. Two BGP peers run through several steps of a finite state engine until a neighborship becomes established and messages or notifications can be passed back and forth. Then NLRI can be exchanged and ultimately a BGP table (Routing Information Base, RIB) derived.

Figure 10-1 *The Architecture of the Internet*

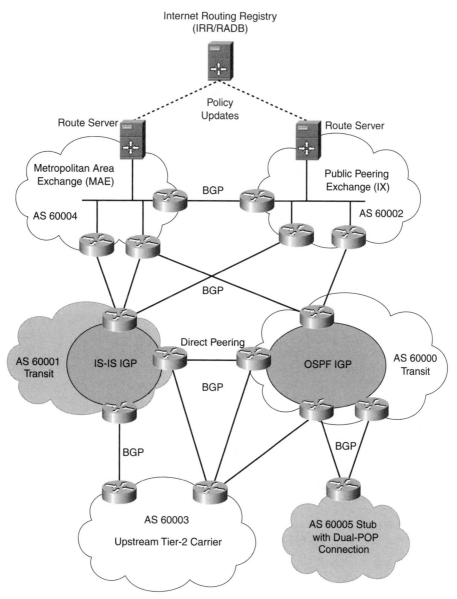

BGP always places a single best path in the actual routing (forwarding) table. Initially, after peering establishment, the two peering routers exchange their full BGP table (flash update). Later on, only incremental updates are sent, and the related BGP table version number is incremented. The table number is an indicator of topological stability or volatility.

Limitations of IGPs

Why can't we use IGPs throughout the Internet? EGPs serve entirely different purposes than IGPs, both technically and from an administrative point of view (policy enforcement). The global routing table is approaching 130,000 prefixes and consists of myriad nodes (network elements). The increase rate of new prefixes appears to have slowed down, however, most likely due to aggregation improvements, stricter policies, Network Address Translation (NAT) deployments, and improved management. This number cannot be handled with the specialized approaches of IGPs.

IGP strengths turn into limits and weaknesses in the case of managing the vast Internet "playground"; just imagine the Shortest Path First (SPF) flooding, database maintenance and calculation burden, and complicated area topologies with Open Shortest Path First (OSPF); the Routing Information Protocol (RIP) hop-count limit would not get us very far either. However, RIP and BGP share a common approach: They are both distance-vector protocols. BGP is referred to as a *path-vector routing protocol* because it transports a sequence of AS numbers (ASNs) that identifies the path that the network prefix has traversed, sometimes referred to as an AS tree or path.

The essential idea of the BGP designers was that it is practically impossible to coordinate interconnected realms without a protocol that has rich capabilities to reflect and transport policies and control *ingress* and *egress* flows in terms of transit. This is the reason why BGP strongly depends on regular expressions and powerful filtering and tagging capabilities. BGP explicitly does not propagate information about the internal structure of autonomous systems. Remember that the primary design goal of the Internet and its predecessors NFSNET, ARPANET, and MILNET was dynamic recovery from link or node failure. BGP has hooks to accommodate this requirement.

BGP itself intrinsically does not load balance. However, one can tune the egress and ingress behavior to some extent to achieve what is referred to as "pseudo" load/flow balancing later in this chapter. This usually includes cooperation of your peering AS, upstream or downstream provider, or carrier. This is the art of attracting certain traffic at a certain ingress point and directing traffic to certain egress gateways.

Flavors of BGPv4

BGPv4 supports two different types of peering sessions: IBGP (Internal BGP) is used within one and the same AS, and EBGP (External BGP) is used between neighboring autonomous systems.

IBGP is used widely to configure transit autonomous systems and BGP-based Multiprotocol Label Switching (MPLS) virtual private network (VPN) architectures. In the MPLS VPN context, IBGP is referred to as *Multiprotocol BGP*. BGP is entirely a signaling protocol, even more than OSPF or IS-IS are; in a strict sense, it is incapable of delivering traffic within an AS solely by its own means. For this purpose, it relies on an underlying IGP and static or connected routes to actually forward traffic and resolve next hops.

EBGP is just the formal protocol used between neighboring (directly connected) autonomous systems to exchange aggregated routing information and to reflect macroscopic routing policies on an AS scale.

BGPv4 is a powerful and feature-rich protocol, but not necessarily complicated. To use it fully, you must understand regular expressions, classless interdomain routing (CIDR), and aggregation. Therefore, a complete discussion goes beyond the scope of almost any book. For this reason, the lab section of this chapter predominantly uses Zebra/Quagga and occasionally GateD for demonstration purposes. The BGP configuration of MRTd is almost equivalent, similar to the Cisco IOS architecture, and supports multiple BGP views; it also has the added benefit of being multithreaded. You will read more about BGP later in this chapter.

BGP Message Types

BGP systems use four different types of messages (see Table 10-1). During normal operation, only UPDATE and KEEPALIVE messages are exchanged. OPEN messages govern connection establishment with optional capabilities negotiation. NOTIFICATIONs gracefully terminate the BGP/TCP session in case of malformed information, errors, or manual-session resets.

Table 10-1 *BGP Message Types*

Message	Explanation
OPEN	Exchange connection parameters, session establishment, optional capabilities negotiation
UPDATE	Routing updates/withdrawals/replacement routes
NOTIFICATION	Handling error conditions and closing the BGP/TCP session
KEEPALIVE	BGP speaker monitoring/heartbeat

Capabilities Negotiation

As described in RFC 3392, "Capabilities Advertisement with BGP-4," capability negotiation was added to the BGPv4 protocol behavior to enable peers to negotiate certain additional capabilities, especially with the success of Multiprotocol BGP extensions. This is done via OPEN/NOTIFICATION messages, as demonstrated in Example 10-1 (highlighted text). When a BGP speaker that supports capability negotiation does not support a particular capability, it should respond with a notification error and a corresponding error subcode. This scheme was introduced to leave the UPDATE message mechanism untouched.

Example 10-1 *Packet Capture to Demonstrate Capabilities Negotiation*

```
[root@callisto:~#] tethereal -i eth0 -V

Frame 5 (111 bytes on wire, 111 bytes captured)
    Arrival Time: May 17, 2003 10:37:28.533785000
    Time delta from previous packet: 0.000059000 seconds
    Time relative to first packet: 0.000442000 seconds
```

continues

Example 10-1 *Packet Capture to Demonstrate Capabilities Negotiation (Continued)*

```
        Frame Number: 5
        Packet Length: 111 bytes
        Capture Length: 111 bytes
Ethernet II, Src: 00:60:08:6a:18:45, Dst: 00:10:5a:d7:93:60
        Destination: 00:10:5a:d7:93:60 (3com_d7:93:60)
        Source: 00:60:08:6a:18:45 (3Com_6a:18:45)
        Type: IP (0x0800)
Internet Protocol, Src Addr: 192.168.14.3 (192.168.14.3), Dst Addr: 192.168.14.1
(192.168.14.1)
        Version: 4
        Header length: 20 bytes
        Differentiated Services Field: 0x00 (DSCP 0x00: Default; ECN: 0x00)
                0000 00.. = Differentiated Services Codepoint: Default (0x00)
                .... ..0. = ECN-Capable Transport (ECT): 0
                .... ...0 = ECN-CE: 0
        Total Length: 97
        Identification: 0x064f
        Flags: 0x04
                .1.. = Don't fragment: Set
                ..0. = More fragments: Not set
        Fragment offset: 0
        Time to live: 1
        Protocol: TCP (0x06)
        Header checksum: 0xd5f3 (correct)
        Source: 192.168.14.3 (192.168.14.3)
        Destination: 192.168.14.1 (192.168.14.1)
Transmission Control Protocol, Src Port: 34665 (34665), Dst Port: bgp (179), Seq:
4182591391, Ack: 439239108, Len: 45
        Source port: 34665 (34665)
        Destination port: bgp (179)
        Sequence number: 4182591391
        Next sequence number: 4182591436
        Acknowledgement number: 439239108
        Header length: 32 bytes
        Flags: 0x0018 (PSH, ACK)
                0... .... = Congestion Window Reduced (CWR): Not set
                .0.. .... = ECN-Echo: Not set
                ..0. .... = Urgent: Not set
                ...1 .... = Acknowledgment: Set
                .... 1... = Push: Set
                .... .0.. = Reset: Not set
                .... ..0. = Syn: Not set
                .... ...0 = Fin: Not set
        Window size: 17376
        Checksum: 0x9b03 (correct)
        Options: (12 bytes)
                NOP
                NOP
                Time stamp: tsval 858918346, tsecr 369997
Border Gateway Protocol
        OPEN Message
                Marker: 16 bytes
                Length: 45 bytes
```

Example 10-1 *Packet Capture to Demonstrate Capabilities Negotiation (Continued)*

```
Type: OPEN Message (1)
Version: 4
My AS: 65002
Hold time: 180
BGP identifier: 192.168.14.3
Optional parameters length: 16 bytes
Optional parameters
    Capabilities Advertisement (8 bytes)
        Parameter type: Capabilities (2)
        Parameter length: 6 bytes
        Multiprotocol extensions capability (6 bytes)
            Capability code: Multiprotocol extensions capability (1)
            Capability length: 4 bytes
            Capability value
                Address family identifier: IPv4 (1)
                Reserved: 1 byte
                Subsequent address family identifier: Unicast (1)
    Capabilities Advertisement (4 bytes)
        Parameter type: Capabilities (2)
        Parameter length: 2 bytes
        Route refresh capability (2 bytes)
            Capability code: Route refresh capability (128)
            Capability length: 0 bytes
    Capabilities Advertisement (4 bytes)
        Parameter type: Capabilities (2)
        Parameter length: 2 bytes
        Route refresh capability (2 bytes)
            Capability code: Route refresh capability (2)
            Capability length: 0 bytes
```

BGP Finite State Machine

A finite state machine (FSM) governs the session establishment between two BGP speakers (see Table 10-2). Because of the bidirectional character of the establishment procedure, several steps (states) are involved between IDLE and ESTABLISHED. An ESTABLISHED BGP session is a mandatory requirement for UPDATE message exchange.

Table 10-2 *BGP Neighbor Negotiation Finite State Engine*

State	Explanation
IDLE	BGP is waiting for a start event (config/reset).
CONNECT	Essentially a TCP three-way handshake.
ACTIVE	BGP connection setup.
OPEN-SENT	One-end identification message transmitted, waiting for neighbor confirm, start sending KEEPALIVES, EBGP/IBGP decision.
OPEN-CONFIRM	Other-end identification message received, waiting for KEEPALIVES.
ESTABLISHED	Bidirectional connection setup complete, the systems start to exchange UPDATE messages.

BGP Path Attributes

BGP path attributes are sets of parameters that are associated with a specific prefix. BGP metrics (path attributes) can be classified as follows:

- Well-known
  - Mandatory
  - Discretionary
- Optional
  - Transitive
  - Nontransitive

BGP attributes have varying significance for or influence on the BGP route-selection process, or, in other words, offer a rich set of tiebreakers to decide on otherwise identically attractive candidate routes. The following is a list of the most important attributes. (For further discussion, consult sources in the "Recommended Reading" section.)

- ORIGIN (IGP/EGP/INCOMPLETE)   (Type Code 1)
- AS_PATH   (Type Code 2)
- NEXT_HOP   (Type Code 3)
- MULTI_EXIT_DISC (MED)   (Type Code 4)
- LOCAL_PREF   (Type Code 5)
- ATOMIC_AGGREGATE   (Type Code 6)
- AGGREGATOR   (Type Code 7)
- COMMUNITY   (Type Code 8)

BGP Active Path-Selection Criteria

With the information contained in neighbor UPDATE messages, BGP builds a BGP table with all available routes. Based on several criteria (path attributes and prefix length) associated with a certain prefix, one single best (active) path is selected by the routing process, placed in the RIB, and propagated to its neighbors. Then the forwarding table (Forwarding Information Base, FIB) or cache are constructed based on the routing table (RIB). The algorithm to determine the active route is governed by the following ranking/tiebreaker system. (Prefix length is the strongest/most significant attribute; two prefixes of equal length are compared via the next attribute in the list, and so forth.)

- Best match (prefix length)
- Drop routes with inaccessible next hop
- Prefer largest WEIGHT
- Prefer largest LOCAL-PREFERENCE

- Prefer shortest AS_PATH
- Prefer lowest origin code (IGP < EGP < Incomplete/Unknown)
- Prefer lowest MED
- Prefer external path over internal (EBGP over IBGP)
- If only internal paths remain, prefer IGP paths through the closest neighbor
- Prefer routes originated from router with lowest IP address for BGP Router_ID (tiebreaker)

NOTE   BGP multipath support depends on which of the least significant BGP attributes are bypassed. Cisco IOS architecture bypasses the last three attributes mentioned. In a nutshell, this means that "roughly" identical prefixes, regardless of "insignificant" tiebreakers, are considered equivalent and worthy candidates for BGP multipath.

BGP Loop Detection

External BGP loop prevention is based on the AS_PATH. Whenever a BGP AS boundary router announces a prefix, it appends its own ASN to the path. When receiving updates, prefixes with their own ASN in the AS_PATH are rejected and discarded. This also explains the loop protection of IBGP (no re-advertisements of IBGP-learned routes except to EBGP speakers).

Because the AS_PATH is appended only to prefix announcements that cross AS boundaries, the EBGP loop-prevention mechanism would not help internally. This is the reason why full-mesh IBGP connections are a necessity for a functioning advertisement scheme within an autonomous system.

Provider-Independent Addresses (PI Prefixes, Provider Aggregates)

Providers get an address block assigned (delegated) by large registries (Réseaux IP Européennes, RIPE; American Registry for Internet Numbers, ARIN; Latin American and Caribbean Internet Address Registry, LACNIC; African Network Information Center, AfriNIC; or Asia Pacific Network Information Center, APNIC). Most of the time, downstream customers or subscribers are part of this provider aggregate. With special requirements (usually dual homing), a customer can request assignment of a PI block (provider independent) in combination with a customer ASN. In fact, dual homing in context with an AS is pretty much the only way to get assigned a PI block. The advantage is that the customer is independent from his upstream providers and can switch easily to alternatives without renumbering his addressing architecture or tampering with NAT settings. The provider he leaves just stops announcing this prefix, and the new ISP takes over this obligation.

With dual homing, both upstreams announce the PI block and, depending on the selection criteria of EBGP, the Internet uses one of the choices to deliver traffic toward the stub enterprise AS. Load balancing of these two ingress/egress points requires coordination with both upstream providers and manual BGP tuning with measures such as path prepending or MED.

Note that the smallest PI block assigned today is a /24 prefix. This can cause trouble with providers that filter announcements based on prefix length such as /22 to unclutter their routing tables. The terms *ingress* and *egress* are rather generic terms to illustrate traffic flows entering or leaving an AS. They are commonly used in context with ingress/egress points or ingress/egress filters.

Internet Exchange Points

The purpose of exchange points is to constitute a regional Internet network segment where ISPs can gather (peer) to exchange local traffic. This measure essentially reduces the number of AS hops that traffic is required to traverse to reach a particular destination prefix. In the old days, this resulted in suboptimal routing to the nearest international network access point (NAP). In the worst case, traffic destined for the same metropolitan network was routed via another continent. Today, with a network of IXs in almost every metropolis of the world, local traffic can be kept local.

The number of AS hops and presence at major exchanges has become a metric often brought up by customers to rate the interconnection quality of carrier services. Modern exchange points provide route servers (and their own AS) to avoid scalability problems with any-to-any peerings. You will read more about this instrument in the section "Route Server and Routing Registries." Therefore, an IX participant only has to set up a peering with the route server.

Historically, exchange points have been known by different names, including the following:

- Metropolitan area exchanges (MAEs) (for example, MAE West)
- Network access points (NAPs)
- Commercial Internet exchanges (CIXs)
- Internet exchanges (IXs) (for example, LINX = London Internet Exchange)

In the United States, these exchange points are usually referred to as MAEs/CIXs; in Europe, IX is used more commonly. NAP (network access/attachment point) is a generic term for a location where one can hook up a BGP speaker to other Internet routers. Participants usually acquire dedicated point-to-point circuits to this exchange point (resembling simple network segments; in general, redundant Ethernet switches).

In general, there are two kinds of Internet exchange points: commercial and noncommercial. ISPs can use exchange points to exchange traffic at a national or international level. At the largest exchange points (usually U.S. MAEs), tier 1 and tier 2 carriers gather. These exchange points offer ATM or switched Ethernet ports up to 1 Gbps as an exchange medium.

In the beginning, Fiber Distributed Data Interface (FDDI) rings were the exchange medium of choice.

An exchange point (network segment) often constitutes an AS by itself but does not necessarily have to. In 2001, the Euro-IX was founded, an organization that includes almost all IXs in Europe. Internet exchanges usually provide looking glasses and traffic statistics via web interfaces and unprivileged Telnet access to route servers.

Figure 10-2 shows an example of the Vienna Internet Exchange (VIX) web-based looking-glass interface; Figure 10-3 shows the result of this query. The corresponding traffic statistics of this exchange are shown in Figure 10-4. As an alternative, Telnet access to route servers is a convenient way of grasping the way the world sees your prefixes. This is demonstrated in Example 10-2.

Figure 10-2 *VIX Looking-Glass Mask*

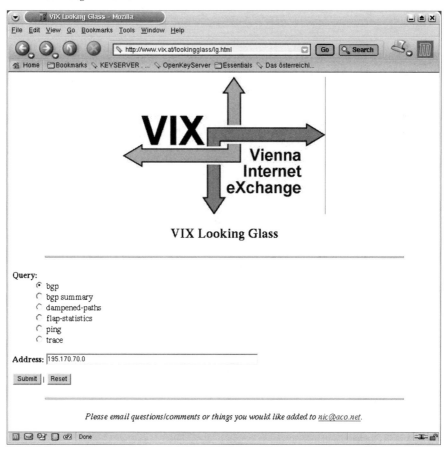

Figure 10-3 *VIX Looking-Glass Query Result*

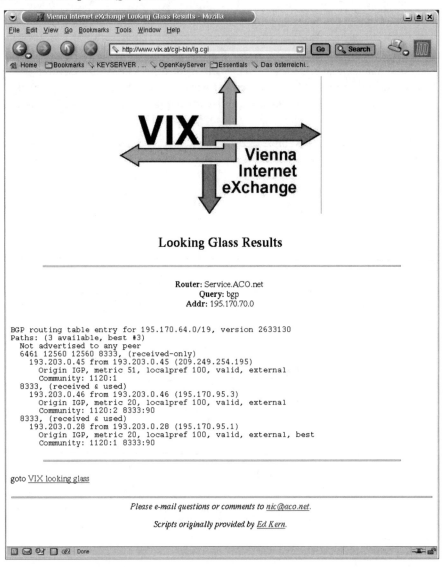

Figure 10-4 *VIX Traffic Statistics*

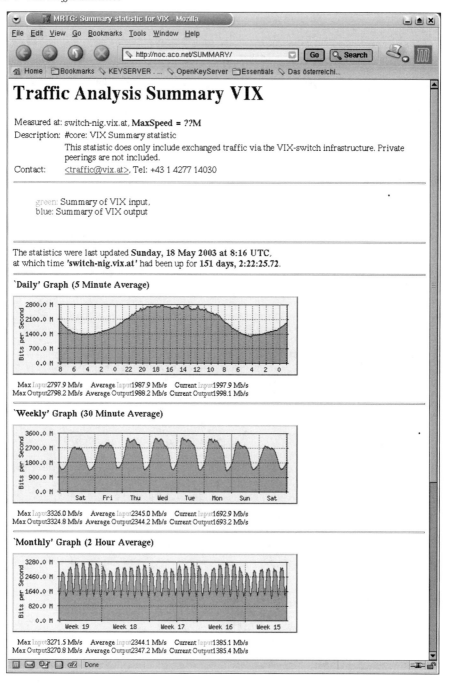

Example 10-2 *Exodus Route Server Telnet Access*

```
[root@callisto~#] telnet route-server-eu.exodus.net

##################### route-server-eu.cw.net #####################
################## European Backbone Route Monitor ##################

166.63.210.40    London          166.63.210.41    London

This is the European view of the routes.

For a North American view, telnet to route-server.cw.net
For an Asian view, telnet to route-server-ap.cw.net

This router should be used to see if a route is in CW routing tables.
This router sets local-preference, MED, etc. for all routes equally.
This router should also be used to verify reachability from CW to other
networks.

This router should _not_ be used to verify CW backbone routing policy.
The best path shown is the current best path _from this router_.

For questions about this route server, send email to hno@cw.net

##################### route-server-eu.cw.net #####################

route-server-eu> show ip bgp summary
BGP router identifier 212.62.0.13, local AS number 3561
BGP table version is 54207646, main routing table version 54207646
132963 network entries and 265900 paths using 21937959 bytes of memory
48287 BGP path attribute entries using 2317776 bytes of memory
759 BGP rrinfo entries using 28664 bytes of memory
20064 BGP AS-PATH entries using 488332 bytes of memory
663 BGP community entries using 25760 bytes of memory
Dampening enabled. 0 history paths, 0 dampened paths
BGP activity 987579/854616 prefixes, 3181892/2915992 paths

Neighbor        V    AS MsgRcvd MsgSent   TblVer  InQ OutQ Up/Down   State/PfxRcd
166.63.210.40   4  3561 12854997  121162 54207588    0    0 12w0d         132937
166.63.210.41   4  3561 12851384  121158 54207595    0    0 12w0d         132963

route-server-eu> show ip bgp

BGP table version is 54206927, local router ID is 212.62.0.13
Status codes: s suppressed, d damped, h history, * valid, > best, i - internal
Origin codes: i - IGP, e - EGP, ? - incomplete

   Network          Next Hop          Metric LocPrf Weight Path
*>i3.0.0.0         166.63.210.40            100      0 7018 80 i
*  i               166.63.210.41            100      0 7018 80 i
*>i4.0.0.0         166.63.210.40            100      0 3356 i
*  i               166.63.210.41            100      0 3356 i
*  i6.1.0.0/16     166.63.210.41            100      0 701 668 7170 1455 i
*>i                166.63.210.40            100      0 701 668 7170 1455 i
```

Example 10-2 *Exodus Route Server Telnet Access (Continued)*

```
* i6.2.0.0/22       166.63.210.41           100     0 701 668 7170 1455 i
*>i                 166.63.210.40           100     0 701 668 7170 1455 i
* i6.3.0.0/18       166.63.210.41           100     0 701 668 7170 1455 i
*>i                 166.63.210.40           100     0 701 668 7170 1455 i
* i6.4.0.0/16       166.63.210.41           100     0 701 668 7170 1455 i
*>i                 166.63.210.40           100     0 701 668 7170 1455 i
* i6.5.0.0/19       166.63.210.41           100     0 701 668 7170 1455 i
*>i                 166.63.210.40           100     0 701 668 7170 1455 i
* i6.8.0.0/20       166.63.210.41           100     0 701 668 7170 1455 i
*>i                 166.63.210.40           100     0 701 668 7170 1455 i
* i6.9.0.0/20       166.63.210.41           100     0 701 668 7170 1455 i
*>i                 166.63.210.40           100     0 701 668 7170 1455 i
* i6.10.0.0/15      166.63.210.41           100     0 701 668 7170 1455 i
*>i                 166.63.210.40           100     0 701 668 7170 1455 i
* i6.14.0.0/15      166.63.210.41           100     0 701 668 7170 1455 i
*>i                 166.63.210.40           100     0 701 668 7170 1455 i
*>i12.0.0.0         166.63.210.40           100     0 7018 i
* i                 166.63.210.41           100     0 7018 i
* i12.0.19.0/24     166.63.210.41           100     0 27487 i
*>i                 166.63.210.40           100     0 27487 i
*>i12.0.48.0/20     166.63.210.40           100     0 209 1742 1742 i
* i                 166.63.210.41           100     0 209 1742 1742 i
...
```

For further information on registries, look at the following websites:

- http://www.ep.net
- http://www.euro-ix.net
- http://www.apnic.net
- http://www.arin.net
- http://www.ripe.net
- http://www.lacnic.net
- http://www.afrinic.com
- http://www.icann.org
- http://www.iana.org
- http://www.ietf.org
- http://www.irtf.org
- http://www.internic.org

EBGP and EBGP Multihop

EBGP exchanges routing information between adjacent autonomous systems, whether they are peers (equal standing), upstreams (providers/carriers), or downstreams (customers/subscribers). This exchange occurs via network announcements, and the corresponding routes are referred to as *prefixes* or *aggregates*.

The routing software decides based on the ASN following the **remote-as** statement whether it is a remote AS (EBGP) or a local (IBGP) connection. EBGP neighbors need to be adjacent (directly connected); for IBGP, this is left to the underlying IGP. If the EBGP neighbor is several hops away, the **ebgp-multihop** neighbor command can satisfy this requirement. This is rather common because EBGP peering sessions are often configured loopback to loopback (recommended), which often results in at least a three-hop distance and improved availability. The **ebgp-multihop** statement is required on both neighbors.

As you will see, this setup is well suited for load balancing over two EBGP links; in fact, the underlying IGP or static routes perform the load balancing as long as Equal-Cost Multi-Path (ECMP) is supported by the network operating system. (See Figure 10-5 and Example 10-3 highlighted text.) Keep in mind that BGP "pseudo" load balancing at geographically distant egress/ingress points is a completely different and tricky matter (even an "art"). Example 10-3 also demonstrates the use of address aggregation for the example aggregate 192.168.0.0/22.

Figure 10-5 *EBGP Load-Sharing and EBGP Multihop Setup*

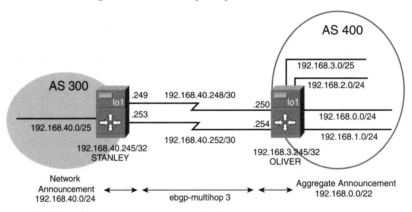

Example 10-3 *EBGP Load-Sharing and EBGP-Multihop Setup*

```
stanley-bgpd# show running-config
...
!
router bgp 300
 bgp router-id 192.168.40.245
 bgp dampening
 no synchronization
 network 192.168.40.0/24
 neighbor 192.168.3.245 remote-as 400
 neighbor 192.168.3.245 description AS-400
 neighbor 192.168.3.245 ebgp-multihop 3
 neighbor 192.168.3.245 update-source lo1
 neighbor 192.168.3.245 soft-reconfiguration inbound
 neighbor 192.168.3.245 next-hop-self
 !
```

Example 10-3 *EBGP Load-Sharing and EBGP-Multihop Setup (Continued)*

```
ip route 192.168.0.0/22 192.168.40.250
ip route 192.168.0.0/22 192.168.40.254
...

oliver-bgpd# show running-config
...
!
router bgp 400
 bgp router-id 192.168.3.245
 bgp dampening
 no synchronization
 network 192.168.0.0/22
 neighbor 192.168.40.245 remote-as 300
 neighbor 192.168.40.245 description AS-300
 neighbor 192.168.40.245 ebgp-multihop 3
 neighbor 192.168.40.245 update-source lo1
 neighbor 192.168.40.245 soft-reconfiguration inbound
 neighbor 192.168.40.245 next-hop-self
!
ip route 192.168.40.0/24 192.168.40.249
ip route 192.168.40.0/24 192.168.40.253
...
```

Weighted Route Dampening

The **bgp dampening** statement enables weighted dampening to compensate for network instabilities in the vicinity of the BGP gateway and "penalizes" autonomous systems with network instabilities (flapping links, for example) to preserve overall BGP stability. BGP is not particularly well suited to cope with the propagation of network instabilities. This limitation proves especially challenging when the instabilities originate from small prefixes and the provider aggregates cannot compensate for the negative effects of such. No penalty is applied to a BGP neighbor reset, however.

The next-hop-self Command

The **next-hop-self** command enables you to force BGP to use a specified IP address as the next hop rather than letting the protocol choose the next hop. This is particularly relevant in context with nonbroadcast multiaccess (NBMA) networks and was used in Example 10-3.

IGP Synchronization

The BGP command **no synchronization** disables synchronization with the underlying IGP. Synchronization is enabled per default on Cisco routers and Zebra bgpd. This is advised only when you are either not forwarding transit traffic or all routers within the AS are running BGP, resulting in faster BGP convergence. In general, it is a good idea to turn off synchronization, but consider the consequences.

The soft-reconfiguration Command

The **soft-reconfiguration inbound** neighbor command allows route policy changes to be applied without a hard reset of the BGP session. It triggers a dynamic soft reconfiguration of new incoming updates only (**clear ip bgp 1.1.1.1 soft in**).

Multiple BGP Instances and Views and the Route Server Context

In general, a BGP router can run only one BGP process at a time. However, some BGP implementations provide the possibility to run multiple BGP pseudo instances featuring multiple BGP tables. These are referred to as *views*. With views, the result of the route selection is not placed in the kernel routing table.

The most popular application of BGP views is a route server for a shared network segment. These were FDDI-rings in the old days and today are switched Ethernet networks. The Zebra/Quagga bgpd can operate as a normal BGP router or route server or both at the same time.

Unlike a normal BGP router, a route server must have several routing tables for managing different routing policies for each BGP speaker. Route servers do not forward traffic; they provide hub-and-spoke signaling information at exchange/interconnect points (NAPs).

Example 10-4 demonstrates multiview configuration and corresponding **show** commands. You must enable this feature with the **bgp multiple-instance** command.

Example 10-4 *Zebra Route Server with BGP View Configuration*

```
callisto-bgpd(config)# bgp multiple-instance
callisto-bgpd(config)# router bgp 65003 view AS65000
callisto-bgpd(config-router)# neighbor 192.168.14.1 remote-as 65000
callisto-bgpd(config-router)# neighbor 192.168.14.1 route-server-client
callisto-bgpd(config)# router bgp 65003 view AS65001
callisto-bgpd(config-router)# neighbor 192.168.14.2 remote-as 65001
callisto-bgpd(config-router)# neighbor 192.168.14.2 route-server-client
callisto-bgpd(config)# router bgp 65003 view AS65002
callisto-bgpd(config-router)# neighbor 192.168.14.254 remote-as 65002
callisto-bgpd(config-router)# neighbor 192.168.14.254 route-server-client

callisto-bgpd# show ip bgp view AS65001 summary
callisto-bgpd# show ip bgp view AS65002 neighbors
```

IBGP Full Mesh, Route Reflectors, and Confederation

In contrast to most fellow authors, I would like to start the BGP discussion with Internal BGP (IBGP). This and all subsequent labs use OSPF as the underlying IGP to provide the necessary connectivity that BGP requires for both session establishment and proper signaling operation. We will start with a manually configured full-mesh IBGP setup and gradually move to a more elegant configuration with the use of peer groups and route reflectors. Confederation as an alternative approach to overcome the scalability limits of full-meshed IBGP is demonstrated as well. In the course of the discussion, we will look at the finite state engine (FSM) and examples of the OPEN and UPDATE messages passed between BGP speakers.

The BGP specifications dictate (for loop-prevention purposes) that a BGP speaker must not advertise prefixes heard from another IBGP speaker to a third IBGP speaker. Because of this convention, you must configure a full-mesh between all IBGP speakers within an AS. Obviously, this approach does not scale. Fortunately, BGPv4 provides two ways to approach this problem—*route reflectors* and *confederation*—in various possible setups and combinations:

- Single route reflector (not recommended, single point of failure)
- Clustered route reflectors
- Redundant route reflectors
- Confederation ("EIBGP")
- Hybrid architectures (route reflector cluster and confederation)

Lab 10-1: Route Reflection

A route reflector setup consists of at least one route reflector and one or several route reflector clients that can also be assigned to a logical cluster via a 4-octet cluster ID. When only one route reflector exists, the implicit cluster ID is the loopback address of the router. The basic idea of the designers was that no changes are necessary on the client.

A connection to a single route reflector does suffice to receive and advertise prefixes. For the purpose of redundancy, it is common practice to connect route reflector clients to at least two redundant route reflectors. In addition, large architectures introduce clustering to create multiple logical groups (BGP CLUSTER-LIST attribute).

The cluster ID has to be consistent throughout a cluster. Of course, all route reflectors require full IBGP connectivity among themselves. Figure 10-6 (part a) demonstrates a single-cluster architecture featuring three fully meshed IBGP route reflectors. In this example, two route reflector clients are connected to multiple route reflectors for redundancy. Figure 10-6 (part b) presents a similar topology featuring multiple clusters.

Figure 10-6 *Route Reflector Approaches*

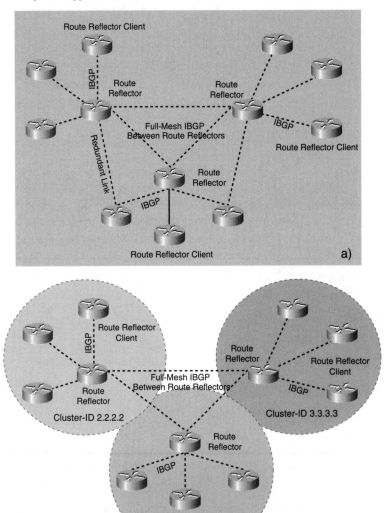

We start with Example 10-5 featuring a conservative full IBGP mesh among the three UNIX servers running Zebra bgpd and scar running Cisco IOS architecture (which was the topology from Chapter 9, "Dynamic Routing Protocols—Interior Gateway Protocols"). The **maximum-paths 6** statement in the scar configuration (highlighted) allows for up to six qualified BGP multipath candidate routes to the same destination to be placed in the routing table for load sharing.

Example 10-5 *Zebra IBGP Configurations*

```
ganymed-bgpd# show running-config

Current configuration:
!
hostname ganymed-bgpd
password 8 bJFoEOB0obLL6
enable password 8 bJFoEOB0obLL6
log file /var/log/bgpd.log
service advanced-vty
service password-encryption
!
router bgp 65000
 bgp router-id 192.168.44.1
 bgp cluster-id 1.1.1.1
 redistribute connected
 neighbor 192.168.1.1 remote-as 65000
 neighbor 192.168.1.1 update-source lo1
 neighbor 192.168.1.1 soft-reconfiguration inbound
 neighbor 192.168.2.7 remote-as 65000
 neighbor 192.168.2.7 update-source lo1
 neighbor 192.168.2.7 soft-reconfiguration inbound
 neighbor 192.168.201.2 remote-as 65000
 neighbor 192.168.201.2 update-source lo1
 neighbor 192.168.201.2 soft-reconfiguration inbound
!
access-list 1 remark vty-protection
access-list 1 permit 127.0.0.1
access-list 1 permit 192.168.1.0 0.0.0.255
!
line vty
 access-class 1
 exec-timeout 15 0
!
end

castor-bgpd# show running-config

Current configuration:
!
hostname castor-bgpd
password 8 4DwwIFdKLWvU.
enable password 8 dV8x4MhxDAuaw
log file /var/log/bgpd.log
service advanced-vty
service password-encryption
!
router bgp 65000
 bgp router-id 192.168.2.7
 bgp cluster-id 1.1.1.1
 redistribute connected
 neighbor 192.168.1.1 remote-as 65000
 neighbor 192.168.1.1 soft-reconfiguration inbound
```

continues

Example 10-5 *Zebra IBGP Configurations (Continued)*

```
 neighbor 192.168.44.1 remote-as 65000
 neighbor 192.168.44.1 soft-reconfiguration inbound
 neighbor 192.168.201.2 remote-as 65000
 neighbor 192.168.201.2 soft-reconfiguration inbound
!
access-list 1 remark vty-protection
access-list 1 permit 127.0.0.1
access-list 1 permit 192.168.1.0 0.0.0.255
!
line vty
 access-class 1
 exec-timeout 15 0
!
end

callisto-bgpd# show running-config

Current configuration:
!
hostname callisto-bgpd
password 8 m6eyKycFMHniQ
enable password 8 bjYlnA9YLBWyM
log file /var/log/bgpd.log
service advanced-vty
service password-encryption
!
router bgp 65000
 bgp router-id 192.168.1.1
 bgp cluster-id 1.1.1.1
 redistribute connected
 neighbor 192.168.2.7 remote-as 65000
 neighbor 192.168.2.7 soft-reconfiguration inbound
 neighbor 192.168.44.1 remote-as 65000
 neighbor 192.168.44.1 soft-reconfiguration inbound
 neighbor 192.168.201.2 remote-as 65000
 neighbor 192.168.201.2 soft-reconfiguration inbound
!
access-list 1 remark vty-protection
access-list 1 permit 127.0.0.1
access-list 1 permit 192.168.1.0 0.0.0.255
!
line vty
 access-class 1
 exec-timeout 0 0
!
end

scar# show running-config
 ...
!
router bgp 65000
 bgp router-id 192.168.201.2
 bgp cluster-id 1.1.1.1
```

Example 10-5 *Zebra IBGP Configurations (Continued)*

```
bgp log-neighbor-changes
redistribute connected
neighbor 192.168.7.7 remote-as 65000
neighbor 192.168.7.7 update-source Loopback0
neighbor 192.168.7.7 soft-reconfiguration inbound
neighbor 192.168.14.1 remote-as 65000
neighbor 192.168.14.1 update-source Loopback0
neighbor 192.168.14.1 soft-reconfiguration inbound
neighbor 192.168.44.1 remote-as 65000
neighbor 192.168.44.1 update-source Loopback0
neighbor 192.168.44.1 soft-reconfiguration inbound
maximum-paths 6
!
...
```

Examples 10-6 and 10-7 demonstrate BGP-related Zebra **show** commands and Zebra and Cisco IOS architecture **debug** choices to gain more insight into the "under-the-hood" operation of BGP. In particular, Example 10-6 highlights a BGP example prefix of *incomplete* origin (highlighted text) due to the redistribution of connected routes. The lab culminates in detailed packet traces in Example 10-8, where we view OPEN and UPDATE messages. Similar analyzer traces regarding KEEPALIVE and NOTIFICATION messages are left as an exercise.

Example 10-6 *Zebra BGP Example Output on Ganymed*

```
ganymed-bgpd# show ip bgp
BGP table version is 0, local router ID is 192.168.44.1
Status codes: s suppressed, d damped, h history, * valid, > best, i - internal
Origin codes: i - IGP, e - EGP, ? - incomplete

   Network          Next Hop          Metric LocPrf Weight Path
* i192.168.1.0      192.168.1.1            0    100      0 ?
*>                  0.0.0.0                0           32768 ?
* i192.168.2.0      192.168.2.7            0    100      0 ?
*>                  0.0.0.0                0           32768 ?
* i192.168.7.0      192.168.201.2          0    100      0 ?
*>i                 192.168.2.7            0    100      0 ?
*>i192.168.13.0     192.168.201.2          0    100      0 ?
* i192.168.14.0     192.168.201.2          0    100      0 ?
*>i                 192.168.1.1            0    100      0 ?
*>i192.168.17.0     192.168.201.2          0    100      0 ?
*> 192.168.44.0     0.0.0.0                0           32768 ?
* i192.168.45.0     192.168.1.1            0    100      0 ?
*>                  0.0.0.0                0           32768 ?
* i192.168.80.0     192.168.2.7            0    100      0 ?
*>                  0.0.0.0                0           32768 ?
*>i192.168.99.0/30  192.168.1.1            0    100      0 ?
*>i192.168.99.2/32  192.168.2.7            0    100      0 ?
*>i192.168.201.0    192.168.201.2          0    100      0 ?
*> 211.11.117.0     0.0.0.0                0           32768 ?
```

continues

Example 10-6 *Zebra BGP Example Output on Ganymed (Continued)*

```
Total number of prefixes 13

ganymed-bgpd# show ip bgp 192.168.80.0
BGP routing table entry for 192.168.80.0/24
Paths: (2 available, best #2, table Default-IP-Routing-Table)
  Advertised to non peer-group peers:
  192.168.1.1 192.168.2.7 192.168.201.2
  Local
    192.168.2.7 from 192.168.2.7 (192.168.2.7)
      Origin incomplete, metric 0, localpref 100, valid, internal
      Last update: Mon Apr 21 11:05:30 2003

  Local
    0.0.0.0 from 0.0.0.0 (192.168.44.1)
      Origin incomplete, metric 0, localpref 100, weight 32768, valid, sourced, best
      Last update: Mon Apr 21 10:12:32 2003

ganymed-bgpd# show ip bgp summary
BGP router identifier 192.168.44.1, local AS number 65000
1 BGP AS-PATH entries
0 BGP community entries

Neighbor        V    AS MsgRcvd MsgSent   TblVer  InQ OutQ Up/Down  State/PfxRcd
192.168.1.1     4 65000     395     417        0    0    0 05:20:58        4
192.168.2.7     4 65000     400     417        0    0    0 05:21:05        4
192.168.201.2   4 65000     229     233        0    0    0 00:41:24        5

Total number of neighbors 3

ganymed-bgpd# show ip bgp neighbors
BGP neighbor is 192.168.1.1, remote AS 65000, local AS 65000, internal link
  BGP version 4, remote router ID 192.168.1.1
  BGP state = Established, up for 05:21:08
  Last read 00:00:08, hold time is 180, keepalive interval is 60 seconds
  Neighbor capabilities:
    Route refresh: advertised and received (old and new)
    Address family IPv4 Unicast: advertised and received
  Received 394 messages, 2 notifications, 0 in queue
  Sent 413 messages, 5 notifications, 0 in queue
  Route refresh request: received 1, sent 1
  Minimum time between advertisement runs is 5 seconds
  Update source is lo1

 For address family: IPv4 Unicast
  Inbound soft reconfiguration allowed
  Community attribute sent to this neighbor (both)
  4 accepted prefixes

  Connections established 10; dropped 9
Local host: 192.168.44.1, Local port: 34695
Foreign host: 192.168.1.1, Foreign port: 179
Nexthop: 192.168.44.1
```

Example 10-6 *Zebra BGP Example Output on Ganymed (Continued)*

```
Nexthop global: ::1
Nexthop local: fe80::1
BGP connection: non shared network
Read thread: on  Write thread: off

BGP neighbor is 192.168.2.7, remote AS 65000, local AS 65000, internal link
  BGP version 4, remote router ID 192.168.2.7
  BGP state = Established, up for 05:21:15
  Last read 00:00:15, hold time is 180, keepalive interval is 60 seconds
  Neighbor capabilities:
    Route refresh: advertised and received (old and new)
    Address family IPv4 Unicast: advertised and received
  Received 396 messages, 4 notifications, 0 in queue
  Sent 414 messages, 3 notifications, 0 in queue
  Route refresh request: received 1, sent 1
  Minimum time between advertisement runs is 5 seconds
  Update source is lo1

 For address family: IPv4 Unicast
  Inbound soft reconfiguration allowed
  Community attribute sent to this neighbor (both)
  4 accepted prefixes

  Connections established 10; dropped 9
Local host: 192.168.44.1, Local port: 179
Foreign host: 192.168.2.7, Foreign port: 1062
Nexthop: 192.168.44.1
Nexthop global: ::1
Nexthop local: fe80::1
BGP connection: non shared network
Read thread: on  Write thread: off

BGP neighbor is 192.168.201.2, remote AS 65000, local AS 65000, internal link
  BGP version 4, remote router ID 192.168.201.2
  BGP state = Established, up for 00:41:34
  Last read 00:00:33, hold time is 180, keepalive interval is 60 seconds
  Neighbor capabilities:
    Route refresh: advertised and received (old and new)
    Address family IPv4 Unicast: advertised and received
  Received 229 messages, 0 notifications, 0 in queue
  Sent 232 messages, 1 notifications, 0 in queue
  Route refresh request: received 0, sent 0
  Minimum time between advertisement runs is 5 seconds
  Update source is lo1

 For address family: IPv4 Unicast
  Inbound soft reconfiguration allowed
  Community attribute sent to this neighbor (both)
  5 accepted prefixes

  Connections established 5; dropped 4
Local host: 192.168.44.1, Local port: 7928
```

continues

Example 10-6 *Zebra BGP Example Output on Ganymed (Continued)*

```
Foreign host: 192.168.201.2, Foreign port: 179
Nexthop: 192.168.44.1
Nexthop global: ::1
Nexthop local: fe80::1
BGP connection: non shared network
Read thread: on  Write thread: off


ganymed-bgpd# show ip bgp neighbors 192.168.1.1 advertised-routes
BGP table version is 0, local router ID is 192.168.44.1
Status codes: s suppressed, d damped, h history, * valid, > best, i - internal
Origin codes: i - IGP, e - EGP, ? - incomplete

   Network          Next Hop        Metric LocPrf Weight Path
*> 192.168.1.0      192.168.44.1         0    100  32768 ?
*> 192.168.2.0      192.168.44.1         0    100  32768 ?
*> 192.168.44.0     192.168.44.1         0    100  32768 ?
*> 192.168.45.0     192.168.44.1         0    100  32768 ?
*> 192.168.80.0     192.168.44.1         0    100  32768 ?
*> 211.11.117.0     192.168.44.1         0    100  32768 ?

Total number of prefixes 6
```

Example 10-7 *Cisco IOS Architecture and Zebra BGP Debug Choices*

```
scar# debug ip bgp ?
  A.B.C.D      BGP neighbor address
  dampening    BGP dampening
  events       BGP events
  in           BGP Inbound information
  keepalives   BGP keepalives
  out          BGP Outbound information
  updates      BGP updates
  vpnv4        VPNv4 NLRI information

scar# debug ip bgp
BGP debugging is on

scar# clear ip bgp 192.168.14.1

00:30:33: BGP: 192.168.14.1 went from Established to Idle
*Mar  1 00:30:36: %BGP-5-ADJCHANGE: neighbor 192.168.14.1 Down User reset
00:30:33: BGP: 192.168.14.1 closing
00:30:33: BGP: 192.168.14.1 went from Idle to Active
00:30:33: BGP: 192.168.14.1 open active, delay 7016ms
00:30:40: BGP: 192.168.14.1 open active, local address 192.168.201.2
00:30:40: BGP: 192.168.14.1 went from Active to OpenSent
00:30:40: BGP: 192.168.14.1 sending OPEN, version 4, my as: 65000
00:30:40: BGP: 192.168.14.1 send message type 1, length (incl. header) 45
00:30:40: BGP: 192.168.14.1 rcv message type 1, length (excl. header) 26
00:30:40: BGP: 192.168.14.1 rcv OPEN, version 4
00:30:40: BGP: 192.168.14.1 rcv OPEN w/ OPTION parameter len: 16
00:30:40: BGP: 192.168.14.1 rcvd OPEN w/ optional parameter type 2 (Capability) len 6
```

Example 10-7 *Cisco IOS Architecture and Zebra BGP Debug Choices (Continued)*

```
00:30:40: BGP: 192.168.14.1 OPEN has CAPABILITY code: 1, length 4
00:30:40: BGP: 192.168.14.1 OPEN has MP_EXT CAP for afi/safi: 1/1
00:30:40: BGP: 192.168.14.1 rcvd OPEN w/ optional parameter type 2 (Capability) len 2
00:30:40: BGP: 192.168.14.1 OPEN has CAPABILITY code: 128, length 0
00:30:40: BGP: 192.168.14.1 OPEN has ROUTE-REFRESH capability(old) for all address-
families
00:30:40: BGP: 192.168.14.1 rcvd OPEN w/ optional parameter type 2 (Capability) len 2
00:30:40: BGP: 192.168.14.1 OPEN has CAPABILITY code: 2, length 0
00:30:40: BGP: 192.168.14.1 OPEN has ROUTE-REFRESH capability(new) for all address-
families
00:30:40: BGP: 192.168.14.1 went from OpenSent to OpenConfirm
00:30:40: BGP: 192.168.14.1 send message type 4, length (incl. header) 19
00:30:40: BGP: 192.168.14.1 rcv message type 4, length (excl. header) 0
00:30:40: BGP: 192.168.14.1 went from OpenConfirm to Established
*Mar  1 00:30:43: %BGP-5-ADJCHANGE: neighbor 192.168.14.1 Up
00:30:41: BGP: 192.168.14.1 send message type 4, length (incl. header) 19
00:30:41: BGP: 192.168.14.1 send message type 4, length (incl. header) 19
00:30:41: BGP: 192.168.14.1 rcv message type 4, length (excl. header) 0
00:30:54: BGP: 192.168.7.7 send message type 4, length (incl. header) 19
00:30:54: BGP: 192.168.7.7 rcv message type 4, length (excl. header) 0
00:30:57: BGP: 192.168.44.1 send message type 4, length (incl. header) 19
00:30:57: BGP: 192.168.44.1 rcv message type 4, length (excl. header) 0
00:31:22: BGP: Applying map to find origin for 192.168.13.0/29
00:31:22: BGP: Applying map to find origin for 192.168.14.0/24
00:31:22: BGP: Applying map to find origin for 192.168.201.0/32
00:31:22: BGP: Applying map to find origin for 192.168.7.0/24
00:31:22: BGP: Applying map to find origin for 192.168.17.0/29
00:31:40: BGP: 192.168.14.1 send message type 4, length (incl. header) 19
00:31:40: BGP: 192.168.14.1 rcv message type 4, length (excl. header) 0
00:31:54: BGP: 192.168.7.7 send message type 4, length (incl. header) 19
00:31:54: BGP: 192.168.7.7 rcv message type 4, length (excl. header) 0
00:31:57: BGP: 192.168.44.1 send message type 4, length (incl. header) 19
00:31:57: BGP: 192.168.44.1 rcv message type 4, length (excl. header) 0

scar# show ip bgp summary
BGP router identifier 192.168.201.2, local AS number 65000
BGP table version is 11, main routing table version 11
13 network entries and 19 paths using 1945 bytes of memory
2 BGP path attribute entries using 120 bytes of memory
0 BGP route-map cache entries using 0 bytes of memory
0 BGP filter-list cache entries using 0 bytes of memory
BGP activity 26/13 prefixes, 38/19 paths, scan interval 60 secs

Neighbor        V    AS MsgRcvd MsgSent   TblVer  InQ OutQ Up/Down  State/PfxRcd
192.168.7.7     4 65000      21      23       11    0    0 00:00:59        4
192.168.14.1    4 65000      21      24       11    0    0 00:00:39        4
192.168.44.1    4 65000      22      24       11    0    0 00:01:02        6

#
# The effect on callisto (the peer router):
#
```

continues

Example 10-7 *Cisco IOS Architecture and Zebra BGP Debug Choices (Continued)*

```
callisto-bgpd# debug bgp ?
  events      BGP events
  filters     BGP filters
  fsm         BGP Finite State Machine
  keepalives  BGP keepalives
  updates     BGP updates

callisto-bgpd# debug bgp
BGP debugging is on
callisto-bgpd# BGP: 192.168.201.2 went from Established to Idle
BGP: 192.168.201.2 went from Idle to Connect
BGP: 192.168.201.2 went from Connect to Active
BGP: Performing BGP general scanning
BGP: 192.168.2.7 send message type 4, length (incl. header) 19
BGP: 192.168.2.7 rcv message type 4, length (excl. header) 0
BGP: 192.168.201.2 went from Active to OpenSent
BGP: 192.168.201.2 rcv message type 1, length (excl. header) 26
BGP: 192.168.201.2 rcv OPEN, version 4, remote-as 65000, holdtime 180,
id 192.168.201.2
BGP: 192.168.201.2 sending OPEN, version 4, my as 65000, holdtime 180, id 192.168.1.1
BGP: 192.168.201.2 send message type 1, length (incl. header) 45
BGP: 192.168.201.2 rcv OPEN w/ OPTION parameter len: 16
BGP: 192.168.201.2 rcvd OPEN w/ optional parameter type 2 (Capability) len 6
BGP: 192.168.201.2 OPEN has CAPABILITY code: 1, length 4
BGP: 192.168.201.2 OPEN has MP_EXT CAP for afi/safi: 1/1
BGP: 192.168.201.2 rcvd OPEN w/ optional parameter type 2 (Capability) len 2
BGP: 192.168.201.2 OPEN has CAPABILITY code: 128, length 0
BGP: 192.168.201.2 OPEN has ROUTE-REFRESH capability(old) for all address-families
BGP: 192.168.201.2 rcvd OPEN w/ optional parameter type 2 (Capability) len 2
BGP: 192.168.201.2 OPEN has CAPABILITY code: 2, length 0
BGP: 192.168.201.2 OPEN has ROUTE-REFRESH capability(new) for all address-families
BGP: 192.168.201.2 went from OpenSent to OpenConfirm
BGP: 192.168.201.2 send message type 4, length (incl. header) 19
BGP: 192.168.201.2 rcv message type 4, length (excl. header) 0
BGP: 192.168.201.2 went from OpenConfirm to Established
BGP: 192.168.201.2 send message type 4, length (incl. header) 19
BGP: 192.168.201.2 rcv message type 4, length (excl. header) 0
BGP: 192.168.201.2 rcv message type 4, length (excl. header) 0
BGP: 192.168.44.1 send message type 4, length (incl. header) 19
BGP: 192.168.44.1 rcv message type 4, length (excl. header) 0
BGP: Performing BGP general scanning
BGP: 192.168.2.7 send message type 4, length (incl. header) 19
BGP: 192.168.2.7 rcv message type 4, length (excl. header) 0
BGP: 192.168.201.2 send message type 4, length (incl. header) 19
BGP: 192.168.201.2 rcv message type 4, length (excl. header) 0
BGP: 192.168.44.1 send message type 4, length (incl. header) 19
BGP: 192.168.44.1 rcv message type 4, length (excl. header) 0

callisto-bgpd# show ip bgp summary
BGP router identifier 192.168.1.1, local AS number 65000
1 BGP AS-PATH entries
0 BGP community entries
```

Example 10-7 *Cisco IOS Architecture and Zebra BGP Debug Choices (Continued)*

```
Neighbor        V    AS MsgRcvd MsgSent  TblVer  InQ OutQ Up/Down  State/PfxRcd
192.168.2.7     4 65000     347     356       0    0    0 04:44:50           4
192.168.44.1    4 65000     350     359       0    0    0 04:44:42           6
192.168.201.2   4 65000     188     197       0    0    0 00:04:45           5

Total number of neighbors 3
```

Example 10-8 *BGP Peer Negotiation Sniffer Traces on Callisto*

```
#
# The big picture:
#

[root@callisto:#] tethereal -i eth0
  0.248208 192.168.201.2 -> 192.168.14.1 TCP 11008 > bgp [FIN, PSH, ACK]
Seq=2941710864 Ack=2857752019 Win=16176 Len=0
  0.266164 192.168.201.2 -> 192.168.14.1 TCP 11008 > bgp [ACK] Seq=2941710865
Ack=2857752020 Win=16176 Len=0
 10.166053 192.168.201.2 -> 192.168.14.1 TCP 11009 > bgp [SYN] Seq=1316263762 Ack=0
Win=16384 Len=0
 10.168416 192.168.201.2 -> 192.168.14.1 TCP 11009 > bgp [ACK] Seq=1316263763
Ack=3128246379 Win=16384 Len=0
 10.173305 192.168.201.2 -> 192.168.14.1 BGP OPEN Message
 10.181018 192.168.201.2 -> 192.168.14.1 BGP KEEPALIVE Message
 10.306394 192.168.201.2 -> 192.168.14.1 BGP UPDATE Message
 10.309838 192.168.201.2 -> 192.168.14.1 BGP KEEPALIVE Message


#
# Frame dissector for BGP OPEN and UPDATE messages:
#

[root@callisto:#] tethereal -i eth0 -V
Frame 14 (99 bytes on wire, 99 bytes captured)
    Arrival Time: Apr 21, 2003 16:11:54.071528000
    Time delta from previous packet: 0.004929000 seconds
    Time relative to first packet: 8.687585000 seconds
    Frame Number: 14
    Packet Length: 99 bytes
    Capture Length: 99 bytes
Ethernet II, Src: 00:00:0c:1a:a9:ab, Dst: 00:10:5a:d7:93:60
    Destination: 00:10:5a:d7:93:60 (3com_d7:93:60)
    Source: 00:00:0c:1a:a9:ab (Cisco_1a:a9:ab)
    Type: IP (0x0800)
Internet Protocol, Src Addr: 192.168.201.2 (192.168.201.2), Dst Addr: 192.168.14.1
(192.168.14.1)
    Version: 4
    Header length: 20 bytes
    Differentiated Services Field: 0xc0 (DSCP 0x30: Class Selector 6; ECN: 0x00)
        1100 00.. = Differentiated Services Codepoint: Class Selector 6 (0x30)
        .... ..0. = ECN-Capable Transport (ECT): 0
        .... ...0 = ECN-CE: 0
```

continues

Example 10-8 *BGP Peer Negotiation Sniffer Traces on Callisto (Continued)*

```
        Total Length: 85
        Identification: 0x0002
        Flags: 0x00
            .0.. = Don't fragment: Not set
            ..0. = More fragments: Not set
        Fragment offset: 0
        Time to live: 255
        Protocol: TCP (0x06)
        Header checksum: 0x628c (correct)
        Source: 192.168.201.2 (192.168.201.2)
        Destination: 192.168.14.1 (192.168.14.1)
Transmission Control Protocol, Src Port: 11010 (11010), Dst Port: bgp (179),
Seq: 1279472448, Ack: 3236382097, Len: 45
        Source port: 11010 (11010)
        Destination port: bgp (179)
        Sequence number: 1279472448
        Next sequence number: 1279472493
        Acknowledgement number: 3236382097
        Header length: 20 bytes
        Flags: 0x0018 (PSH, ACK)
            0... .... = Congestion Window Reduced (CWR): Not set
            .0.. .... = ECN-Echo: Not set
            ..0. .... = Urgent: Not set
            ...1 .... = Acknowledgment: Set
            .... 1... = Push: Set
            .... .0.. = Reset: Not set
            .... ..0. = Syn: Not set
            .... ...0 = Fin: Not set
        Window size: 16384
        Checksum: 0xbb96 (correct)
Border Gateway Protocol
    OPEN Message
        Marker: 16 bytes
        Length: 45 bytes
        Type: OPEN Message (1)
        Version: 4
        My AS: 65000
        Hold time: 180
        BGP identifier: 192.168.201.2
        Optional parameters length: 16 bytes
        Optional parameters
            Capabilities Advertisement (8 bytes)
                Parameter type: Capabilities (2)
                Parameter length: 6 bytes
                Multiprotocol extensions capability (6 bytes)
                    Capability code: Multiprotocol extensions capability (1)
                    Capability length: 4 bytes
                    Capability value
                        Address family identifier: IPv4 (1)
                        Reserved: 1 byte
                        Subsequent address family identifier: Unicast (1)
```

Example 10-8 *BGP Peer Negotiation Sniffer Traces on Callisto (Continued)*

```
                      Capabilities Advertisement (4 bytes)
                          Parameter type: Capabilities (2)
                          Parameter length: 2 bytes
                          Route refresh capability (2 bytes)
                              Capability code: Route refresh capability (128)
                              Capability length: 0 bytes
                      Capabilities Advertisement (4 bytes)
                          Parameter type: Capabilities (2)
                          Parameter length: 2 bytes
                          Route refresh capability (2 bytes)
                              Capability code: Route refresh capability (2)
                              Capability length: 0 bytes

Frame 16 (125 bytes on wire, 125 bytes captured)
    Arrival Time: Apr 21, 2003 16:11:54.204807000
    Time delta from previous packet: 0.126977000 seconds
    Time relative to first packet: 8.820864000 seconds
    Frame Number: 16
    Packet Length: 125 bytes
    Capture Length: 125 bytes
Ethernet II, Src: 00:00:0c:1a:a9:ab, Dst: 00:10:5a:d7:93:60
    Destination: 00:10:5a:d7:93:60 (3com_d7:93:60)
    Source: 00:00:0c:1a:a9:ab (Cisco_1a:a9:ab)
    Type: IP (0x0800)
Internet Protocol, Src Addr: 192.168.201.2 (192.168.201.2), Dst Addr: 192.168.14.1
(192.168.14.1)
    Version: 4
    Header length: 20 bytes
    Differentiated Services Field: 0xc0 (DSCP 0x30: Class Selector 6; ECN: 0x00)
        1100 00.. = Differentiated Services Codepoint: Class Selector 6 (0x30)
        .... ..0. = ECN-Capable Transport (ECT): 0
        .... ...0 = ECN-CE: 0
    Total Length: 111
    Identification: 0x0004
    Flags: 0x00
        .0.. = Don't fragment: Not set
        ..0. = More fragments: Not set
    Fragment offset: 0
    Time to live: 255
    Protocol: TCP (0x06)
    Header checksum: 0x6270 (correct)
    Source: 192.168.201.2 (192.168.201.2)
    Destination: 192.168.14.1 (192.168.14.1)
Transmission Control Protocol, Src Port: 11010 (11010), Dst Port: bgp (179),
Seq: 1279472512, Ack: 3236382161, Len: 71
    Source port: 11010 (11010)
    Destination port: bgp (179)
    Sequence number: 1279472512
    Next sequence number: 1279472583
    Acknowledgement number: 3236382161
    Header length: 20 bytes
    Flags: 0x0018 (PSH, ACK)
        0... .... = Congestion Window Reduced (CWR): Not set
```

continues

Example 10-8 *BGP Peer Negotiation Sniffer Traces on Callisto (Continued)*

```
                    .0.. .... = ECN-Echo: Not set
                    ..0. .... = Urgent: Not set
                    ...1 .... = Acknowledgment: Set
                    .... 1... = Push: Set
                    .... .0.. = Reset: Not set
                    .... ..0. = Syn: Not set
                    .... ...0 = Fin: Not set
          Window size: 16320
          Checksum: 0xe59b (correct)
    Border Gateway Protocol
        UPDATE Message
            Marker: 16 bytes
            Length: 71 bytes
            Type: UPDATE Message (2)
            Unfeasible routes length: 0 bytes
            Total path attribute length: 28 bytes
            Path attributes
                ORIGIN: INCOMPLETE (4 bytes)
                    Flags: 0x40 (Well-known, Transitive, Complete)
                        0... .... = Well-known
                        .1.. .... = Transitive
                        ..0. .... = Complete
                        ...0 .... = Regular length
                    Type code: ORIGIN (1)
                    Length: 1 byte
                    Origin: INCOMPLETE (2)
                AS_PATH: empty (3 bytes)
                    Flags: 0x40 (Well-known, Transitive, Complete)
                        0... .... = Well-known
                        .1.. .... = Transitive
                        ..0. .... = Complete
                        ...0 .... = Regular length
                    Type code: AS_PATH (2)
                    Length: 0 bytes
                NEXT_HOP: 192.168.201.2 (7 bytes)
                    Flags: 0x40 (Well-known, Transitive, Complete)
                        0... .... = Well-known
                        .1.. .... = Transitive
                        ..0. .... = Complete
                        ...0 .... = Regular length
                    Type code: NEXT_HOP (3)
                    Length: 4 bytes
                    Next hop: 192.168.201.2
                MULTI_EXIT_DISC: 0 (7 bytes)
                    Flags: 0x80 (Optional, Non-transitive, Complete)
                        1... .... = Optional
                        .0.. .... = Non-transitive
                        ..0. .... = Complete
                        ...0 .... = Regular length
                    Type code: MULTI_EXIT_DISC (4)
                    Length: 4 bytes
                    Multiple exit discriminator: 0
```

Example 10-8 *BGP Peer Negotiation Sniffer Traces on Callisto (Continued)*

```
              LOCAL_PREF: 100 (7 bytes)
                 Flags: 0x40 (Well-known, Transitive, Complete)
                    0... .... = Well-known
                    .1.. .... = Transitive
                    ..0. .... = Complete
                    ...0 .... = Regular length
                 Type code: LOCAL_PREF (5)
                 Length: 4 bytes
                 Local preference: 100
        Network layer reachability information: 20 bytes
           192.168.7.0/24
           192.168.13.0/24
           192.168.14.0/24
           192.168.17.0/24
           192.168.201.0/24
```

Obviously, configuring full-meshed IBGP networks does not scale. To remedy this shortcoming, ganymed was configured as a route reflector for scar, castor, and callisto. All routers inhabit the same cluster with the BGP cluster ID 1.1.1.1. Therefore, the configuration of a cluster ID is redundant, although it is a good idea in large architectures. Example 10-9 demonstrates this setup in combination with peer groups, including statements valid for all peer-group members.

Example 10-9 *IBGP Lab Improvement (Cluster ID, Ganymed as Route Reflector Server, Peer Group)*

```
ganymed-bgpd# show running-config

Current configuration:
!
hostname ganymed-bgpd
password 8 bJFoEOB0obLL6
enable password 8 bJFoEOB0obLL6
log file /var/log/bgpd.log
service advanced-vty
service password-encryption
!
router bgp 65000
 bgp router-id 192.168.44.1
 bgp cluster-id 1.1.1.1
 redistribute connected
 neighbor INTERNAL peer-group
 neighbor INTERNAL remote-as 65000
 neighbor INTERNAL update-source lo1
 neighbor INTERNAL route-reflector-client
 neighbor INTERNAL soft-reconfiguration inbound
 neighbor 192.168.1.1 peer-group INTERNAL
 neighbor 192.168.2.7 peer-group INTERNAL
 neighbor 192.168.201.2 peer-group INTERNAL
 !
```

continues

Example 10-9 *IBGP Lab Improvement (Cluster ID, Ganymed as Route Reflector Server, Peer Group) (Continued)*

```
access-list 1 remark vty-protection
access-list 1 permit 127.0.0.1
access-list 1 permit 192.168.1.0 0.0.0.255
!
line vty
 access-class 1
 exec-timeout 15 0
!
end

scar# show running-config
...
!
router bgp 65000
 bgp router-id 192.168.201.2
 bgp cluster-id 1.1.1.1
 bgp log-neighbor-changes
 redistribute connected
 neighbor 192.168.44.1 remote-as 65000
 neighbor 192.168.44.1 update-source Loopback0
 neighbor 192.168.44.1 soft-reconfiguration inbound
 maximum-paths 6
!
...

scar# show ip bgp neighbors
BGP neighbor is 192.168.44.1, remote AS 65000, internal link
  BGP version 4, remote router ID 192.168.44.1
  BGP state = Established, up for 00:02:42
  Last read 00:00:42, hold time is 180, keepalive interval is 60 seconds
  Neighbor capabilities:
    Route refresh: advertised and received(new)
    Address family IPv4 Unicast: advertised and received
  Received 150 messages, 5 notifications, 0 in queue
  Sent 143 messages, 0 notifications, 0 in queue
  Route refresh request: received 1, sent 0
  Default minimum time between advertisement runs is 5 seconds

 For address family: IPv4 Unicast
  BGP table version 6, neighbor version 6
  Index 3, Offset 0, Mask 0x8
  Inbound soft reconfiguration allowed
  6 accepted prefixes consume 216 bytes
  Prefix advertised 55, suppressed 0, withdrawn 0
  Number of NLRIs in the update sent: max 5, min 0

  Connections established 10; dropped 9
  Last reset 00:02:57, due to BGP Notification received, cease
Connection state is ESTAB, I/O status: 1, unread input bytes: 0
Local host: 192.168.201.2, Local port: 179
Foreign host: 192.168.44.1, Foreign port: 11513
```

Example 10-9 *IBGP Lab Improvement (Cluster ID, Ganymed as Route Reflector Server, Peer Group) (Continued)*

```
Enqueued packets for retransmit: 0, input: 0  mis-ordered: 0 (0 bytes)

Event Timers (current time is 0x5C4870):
Timer          Starts    Wakeups         Next
Retrans            8          0          0x0
TimeWait           0          0          0x0
AckHold            8          2          0x0
SendWnd            0          0          0x0
KeepAlive          0          0          0x0
GiveUp             0          0          0x0
PmtuAger           0          0          0x0
DeadWait           0          0          0x0

iss:  465643069  snduna:  465643281  sndnxt:  465643281     sndwnd:  16616
irs: 3432198257  rcvnxt: 3432198602  rcvwnd:        16040 delrcvwnd:    344

SRTT: 197 ms, RTTO: 984 ms, RTV: 787 ms, KRTT: 0 ms
minRTT: 4 ms, maxRTT: 300 ms, ACK hold: 200 ms
Flags: passive open, nagle, gen tcbs

Datagrams (max data segment is 536 bytes):
Rcvd: 14 (out of order: 0), with data: 8, total data bytes: 344
Sent: 10 (retransmit: 0), with data: 7, total data bytes: 211

scar# show ip bgp summary
BGP router identifier 192.168.201.2, local AS number 65000
BGP table version is 6, main routing table version 6
11 network entries and 11 paths using 1463 bytes of memory
2 BGP path attribute entries using 120 bytes of memory
0 BGP route-map cache entries using 0 bytes of memory
0 BGP filter-list cache entries using 0 bytes of memory
BGP activity 65/76 prefixes, 137/126 paths, scan interval 60 secs

Neighbor        V    AS MsgRcvd MsgSent    TblVer   InQ OutQ Up/Down  State/PfxRcd
192.168.44.1    4 65000     151     144         6     0    0 00:03:31            6

scar# show ip bgp
BGP table version is 6, local router ID is 192.168.201.2
Status codes: s suppressed, d damped, h history, * valid, > best, i - internal
Origin codes: i - IGP, e - EGP, ? - incomplete

   Network          Next Hop         Metric LocPrf Weight Path
* i192.168.1.0      192.168.44.1          0    100      0 ?
* i192.168.2.0      192.168.44.1          0    100      0 ?
*> 192.168.7.0      0.0.0.0               0           32768 ?
*> 192.168.13.0     0.0.0.0               0           32768 ?
*> 192.168.14.0     0.0.0.0               0           32768 ?
*> 192.168.17.0     0.0.0.0               0           32768 ?
* i192.168.44.0     192.168.44.1          0    100      0 ?
* i192.168.45.0     192.168.44.1          0    100      0 ?
* i192.168.80.0     192.168.44.1          0    100      0 ?
*> 192.168.201.0    0.0.0.0               0           32768 ?
* i211.11.117.0     192.168.44.1          0    100      0 ?
```

Exercise 10-1: BGP and IGP Interaction

For demonstration purposes, stop the underlying OSPF Zebra daemon ospfd. This will
result in some IBGP sessions remaining in *ACTIVE state* because of the loss of IGP
connectivity to some interfaces (especially the loopbacks).

Exercise 10-2: BGP Synchronization

Turn off IGP synchronization and experiment with the behavior within a transit AS. Develop
a good understanding of potential AS traversal problems.

Lab 10-2: Confederation

Confederation takes a different approach to the full-mesh IBGP scalability problem
(see Figure 10-7). A confederation AS is defined and the IBGP mesh divided into smaller sub-
autonomous systems that connect via EBGP to the confederation AS. Some people refer to
this as an "EIBGP" (External IBGP) session. Example 10-10 presents a confederation setup
for the topology in Figure 10-7 featuring Zebra bgpd.

Figure 10-7 *BGP Confederation*

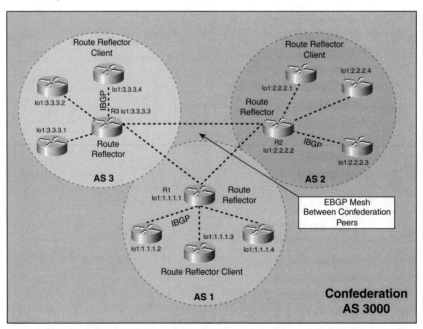

Example 10-10 *BGP Confederation Example with Zebra*

```
R3-bgpd# show running-config
...
!
router bgp 3
 bgp router-id 3.3.3.3
 bgp cluster-id 3.3.3.3
 bgp confederation identifier 3000
 bgp confederation peers 1 2
 neighbor 1.1.1.1 remote-as 1
 neighbor 1.1.1.1 ebgp-multihop 3
 neighbor 1.1.1.1 soft-reconfiguration inbound
 neighbor 1.1.1.1 update-source lo1
 neighbor 2.2.2.2 remote-as 2
 neighbor 2.2.2.2 ebgp-multihop 3
 neighbor 2.2.2.2 soft-reconfiguration inbound
 neighbor 2.2.2.2 update-source lo1
 neighbor INTERNAL peer-group
 neighbor INTERNAL remote-as 3
 neighbor INTERNAL update-source lo1
 neighbor INTERNAL route-reflector-client
 neighbor INTERNAL soft-reconfiguration inbound
 neighbor 3.3.3.1 peer-group INTERNAL
 neighbor 3.3.3.2 peer-group INTERNAL
 neighbor 3.3.3.4 peer-group INTERNAL
!
...

R2-bgpd# show running-config
...
!
router bgp 2
 bgp router-id 2.2.2.2
 bgp cluster-id 2.2.2.2
 bgp confederation identifier 3000
 bgp confederation peers 1 3
 neighbor 1.1.1.1 remote-as 1
 neighbor 1.1.1.1 ebgp-multihop 3
 neighbor 1.1.1.1 soft-reconfiguration inbound
 neighbor 1.1.1.1 update-source lo1
 neighbor 3.3.3.3 remote-as 3
 neighbor 3.3.3.3 ebgp-multihop 3
 neighbor 3.3.3.3 soft-reconfiguration inbound
 neighbor 3.3.3.3 update-source lo1
 neighbor INTERNAL peer-group
 neighbor INTERNAL remote-as 2
 neighbor INTERNAL update-source lo1
 neighbor INTERNAL route-reflector-client
 neighbor INTERNAL soft-reconfiguration inbound
 neighbor 2.2.2.1 peer-group INTERNAL
 neighbor 2.2.2.3 peer-group INTERNAL
 neighbor 2.2.2.4 peer-group INTERNAL
```

continues

Example 10-10 *BGP Confederation Example with Zebra (Continued)*

```
!
...

R1-bgpd# show running-config
...
!
router bgp 1
 bgp router-id 1.1.1.1
 bgp cluster-id 1.1.1.1
 bgp confederation identifier 3000
 bgp confederation peers 2 3
 neighbor 3.3.3.3 remote-as 3
 neighbor 3.3.3.3 ebgp-multihop 3
 neighbor 3.3.3.3 soft-reconfiguration inbound
 neighbor 3.3.3.3 update-source lo1
 neighbor 2.2.2.2 remote-as 2
 neighbor 2.2.2.2 ebgp-multihop 3
 neighbor 2.2.2.2 soft-reconfiguration inbound
 neighbor 2.2.2.2 update-source lo1
 neighbor INTERNAL peer-group
 neighbor INTERNAL remote-as 1
 neighbor INTERNAL update-source lo1
 neighbor INTERNAL route-reflector-client
 neighbor INTERNAL soft-reconfiguration inbound
 neighbor 1.1.1.2 peer-group INTERNAL
 neighbor 1.1.1.3 peer-group INTERNAL
 neighbor 1.1.1.4 peer-group INTERNAL

!
...
```

Lab 10-3: Multi-AS BGP Topology

This BGP lab demonstrates several aspects of IBGP and EBGP in combination with a route reflector, peer groups, and a route server. It essentially consists of two different EBGP topologies and simulates stub, transit, and multi-exit autonomous systems using OSPF as underlying IGP as well as an exchange segment. The IGP fulfills the connectivity requirements of IBGP. The examples of this lab include the following:

- EBGP mesh without a route server

- EBGP at an exchange point featuring a Zebra route server

- EBGP at an exchange point featuring Merrit's RSng (RSd, IRRd)

- Looking-glass access to route servers

The lab also demonstrates redistribution of OSPF into BGP (**redistribute ospf**) in contrast to **network** statements for prefix announcements to EBGP neighbors. This is not always advisable, but it really depends on your individual situation.

Zebra does not support EBGP multipath (**maximum-paths**), but Cisco IOS architecture does. Keep in mind, however, that **bgp-multipath** only takes care of storing more than one path to a given prefix in the BGP table (which is a necessary condition for load balancing, but not a sufficient one). In fact, it is the FIB, not BGP, that really sees that those are two ECMP-eligible routes and uses them appropriately per-flow or per-packet.

With EBGP, directly connected peers (exchange network segment) or **ebgp-multihop** configuration with IGP resolution of loopbacks is required. Figure 10-8 shows the topology and address concept used throughout this part of the lab. Note that the networks 192.168.7.0/ 24 and 192.168.14.0/24 are considered "neutral" networks and are not announced by any EBGP participant. Figure 10-9 shows the logical BGP setup.

Figure 10-8 *Multi-AS BGP Topology*

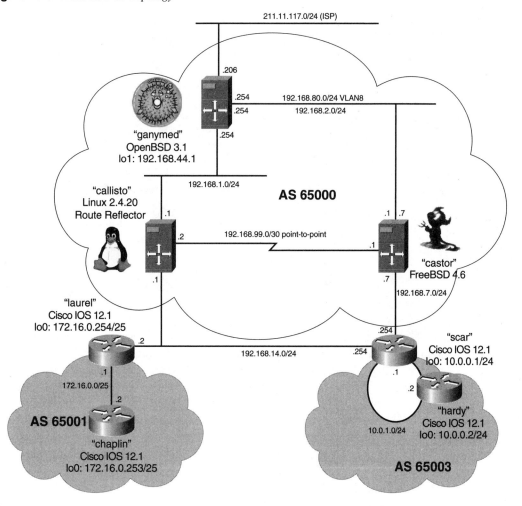

Figure 10-9 *Logical BGP Topology with Shared EBGP Segment*

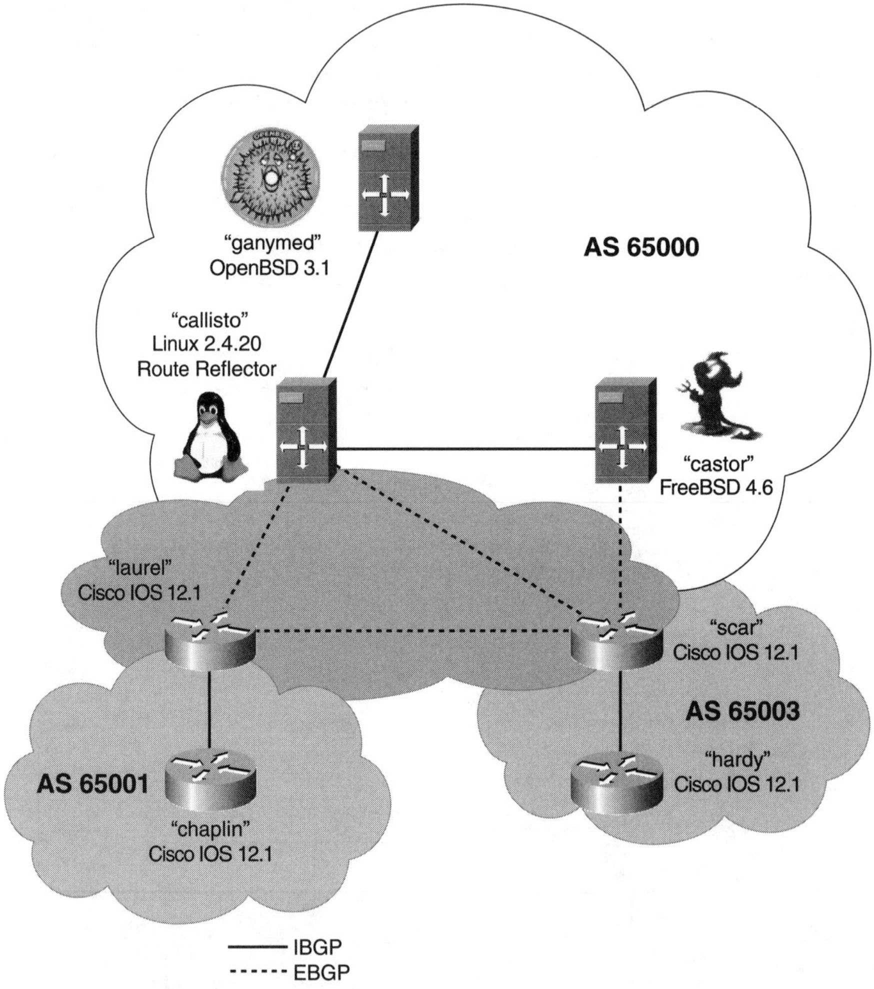

Examples 10-11 through 10-17 present the relevant parts of the router OSPF and BGP configurations, nothing really fancy. To demonstrate two variants of origin, OSPF redistribution into BGP is used on callisto and castor, whereas laurel and scar use network statements to announce their prefixes to the exchange segment in contrast to the redistribution of connected routes you have seen in the previous lab. Callisto acts as a route reflector for the AS 65000 IBGP speakers.

Example 10-11 *Castor OSPF and BGP Configuration*

```
castor-ospfd# show running-config

Current configuration:
!
```

Example 10-11 *Castor OSPF and BGP Configuration (Continued)*

```
hostname castor-ospfd
password 8 4DwwIFdKLWvU.
enable password 8 dV8x4MhxDAuaw
log file /var/log/ospfd.log
service advanced-vty
service password-encryption
!
!
!
interface xl0
 ip ospf message-digest-key 1 md5 zebra
!
interface ed0
 ip ospf message-digest-key 1 md5 zebra
!
interface lp0
 ip ospf network point-to-point
!
interface sl0
 ip ospf network point-to-point
!
interface sl1
 ip ospf network point-to-point
!
interface ds0
!
interface stf0
!
interface faith0
!
interface vlan0
!
interface vlan1
!
interface lo0
!
interface ppp0
 ip ospf network point-to-point
!
interface ppp1
 ip ospf network point-to-point
!
interface vlan8
 ip ospf message-digest-key 1 md5 zebra
!
interface lo1
!
interface wpachdlc0
 ip ospf network point-to-point
!
router ospf
 ospf router-id 192.168.2.7
```

continues

Example 10-11 *Castor OSPF and BGP Configuration (Continued)*

```
 compatible rfc1583
 redistribute connected
 redistribute static
 passive-interface ed0
 network 192.168.2.0/24 area 0
 network 192.168.80.0/24 area 0
 network 192.168.99.0/30 area 0
 area 0 authentication message-digest
 capability opaque
!
access-list 1 remark vty-protection
access-list 1 permit 127.0.0.1
access-list 1 permit 192.168.1.0 0.0.0.255
!
line vty
 access-class 1
 exec-timeout 15 0
!
end

castor-bgpd# show running-config

Current configuration:
!
hostname castor-bgpd
password 8 4DwwIFdKLWvU.
enable password 8 dV8x4MhxDAuaw
log file /var/log/bgpd.log
service advanced-vty
service password-encryption
!
router bgp 65000
 bgp router-id 192.168.2.7
 bgp cluster-id 1.1.1.1
 bgp dampening
 redistribute ospf
 neighbor 192.168.1.1 remote-as 65000
 neighbor 192.168.1.1 soft-reconfiguration inbound
 neighbor 192.168.7.254 remote-as 65003
 neighbor 192.168.7.254 soft-reconfiguration inbound
!
access-list 1 remark vty-protection
access-list 1 permit 127.0.0.1
access-list 1 permit 192.168.1.0 0.0.0.255
!
line vty
 access-class 1
 exec-timeout 15 0
!
end
```

Example 10-12 *Ganymed OSPF and BGP Configuration*

```
ganymed-ospfd# show running-config

Current configuration:
!
hostname ganymed-ospfd
password 8 bJFoEOB0obLL6
enable password 8 nVitURFKR/y3M
log file /var/log/ospfd.log
service advanced-vty
service password-encryption
!
!
!
interface lo0
!
interface lo1
!
interface ne3
 ip ospf message-digest-key 1 md5 zebra
!
interface ne4
 ip ospf message-digest-key 1 md5 zebra
!
interface ne5
!
interface ppp0
 ip ospf network point-to-point
!
interface ppp1
 ip ospf network point-to-point
!
interface tun0
 ip ospf network point-to-point
!
interface tun1
 ip ospf network point-to-point
!
interface enc0
!
interface vlan0
 ip ospf message-digest-key 1 md5 zebra
!
interface vlan1
!
interface gre0
 ip ospf network point-to-point
!
interface gif0
 ip ospf network point-to-point
!
interface gif1
 ip ospf network point-to-point
```

continues

Example 10-12 *Ganymed OSPF and BGP Configuration (Continued)*

```
!
interface gif2
 ip ospf network point-to-point
!
interface gif3
 ip ospf network point-to-point
!
interface faith0
!
interface pflog0
!
interface sl0
 ip ospf network point-to-point
!
interface sl1
 ip ospf network point-to-point
!
interface bridge0
!
interface bridge1
!
router ospf
 ospf router-id 192.168.1.254
 compatible rfc1583
 redistribute connected
 redistribute static
 network 192.168.1.0/24 area 0
 network 192.168.2.0/24 area 0
 network 192.168.45.0/24 area 0
 network 192.168.80.0/24 area 0
 area 0 authentication message-digest
 capability opaque
!
access-list 1 remark vty-protection
access-list 1 permit 127.0.0.1
access-list 1 permit 192.168.1.0 0.0.0.255
!
line vty
 access-class 1
 exec-timeout 15 0
!
end

ganymed-bgpd# show running-config

Current configuration:
!
hostname ganymed-bgpd
password 8 bJFoEOB0obLL6
enable password 8 bJFoEOB0obLL6
log file /var/log/bgpd.log
service advanced-vty
```

Example 10-12 *Ganymed OSPF and BGP Configuration (Continued)*

```
service password-encryption
!
router bgp 65000
 bgp router-id 192.168.44.1
 bgp cluster-id 1.1.1.1
 bgp dampening
 neighbor 192.168.1.1 remote-as 65000
 neighbor 192.168.1.1 update-source lo1
 neighbor 192.168.1.1 soft-reconfiguration inbound
!
access-list 1 remark vty-protection
access-list 1 permit 127.0.0.1
access-list 1 permit 192.168.1.0 0.0.0.255
!
line vty
 access-class 1
 exec-timeout 15 0
!
end
```

Example 10-13 *Callisto OSPF and BGP Configuration*

```
callisto-ospfd# show running-config

Current configuration:
!
hostname callisto-ospfd
password 8 m6eyKycFMHniQ
enable password 8 bjYlnA9YLBWyM
log file /var/log/ospfd.log
service advanced-vty
service password-encryption
!
!
!
interface lo
!
interface eth0
!
interface eth1
 ip ospf message-digest-key 1 md5 zebra
!
interface ipsec0
!
interface ipsec1
!
interface ipsec2
!
interface ipsec3
!
```

continues

Example 10-13 *Callisto OSPF and BGP Configuration (Continued)*

```
interface eth1:1
 ip ospf message-digest-key 1 md5 zebra
!
interface lo1
!
interface wp1chdlc
 ip ospf network point-to-point
!
router ospf
 ospf router-id 192.168.1.1
 compatible rfc1583
 redistribute connected
 redistribute static
 passive-interface eth0
 network 192.168.1.0/24 area 0
 network 192.168.45.0/24 area 0
 network 192.168.99.0/30 area 0
 area 0.0.0.0 authentication message-digest
 capability opaque
!
access-list 1 remark vty-protection
access-list 1 permit 127.0.0.1
access-list 1 permit 192.168.1.0 0.0.0.255
!
line vty
 access-class 1
 exec-timeout 0 0
!
end

callisto-bgpd# show running-config

Current configuration:
!
hostname callisto-bgpd
password 8 m6eyKycFMHniQ
enable password 8 bjYlnA9YLBWyM
log file /var/log/bgpd.log
service advanced-vty
service password-encryption
!
router bgp 65000
 bgp router-id 192.168.1.1
 bgp cluster-id 1.1.1.1
 bgp dampening
 redistribute ospf
 neighbor INTERNAL peer-group
 neighbor INTERNAL remote-as 65000
 neighbor INTERNAL route-reflector-client
 neighbor INTERNAL soft-reconfiguration inbound
 neighbor 192.168.2.7 peer-group INTERNAL
 neighbor 192.168.14.2 remote-as 65001
```

Example 10-13 *Callisto OSPF and BGP Configuration (Continued)*

```
 neighbor 192.168.14.2 soft-reconfiguration inbound
 neighbor 192.168.14.254 remote-as 65003
 neighbor 192.168.14.254 soft-reconfiguration inbound
 neighbor 192.168.44.1 peer-group INTERNAL
!
access-list 1 remark vty-protection
access-list 1 permit 127.0.0.1
access-list 1 permit 192.168.1.0 0.0.0.255
!
line vty
 access-class 1
 exec-timeout 0 0
!
end
```

Example 10-14 *Scar OSPF and BGP Configuration*

```
scar# show running-config
...
!
ip subnet-zero
!
interface Loopback0
 ip address 10.0.0.1 255.255.255.0
!
interface Ethernet0
 ip address 192.168.7.254 255.255.255.0
 no ip proxy-arp
!
interface Ethernet1
 ip address 192.168.14.254 255.255.255.0
!
interface TokenRing0
 ip address 10.0.1.1 255.255.255.0
 early-token-release
 ring-speed 16
!
router ospf 1
 router-id 10.0.0.1
 log-adjacency-changes
 area 0 authentication message-digest
 redistribute connected subnets
 redistribute static subnets
 passive-interface Ethernet0
 passive-interface Ethernet1
 passive-interface Serial0
 passive-interface Serial1
 passive-interface Serial2
 passive-interface Serial3
 passive-interface TokenRing1
 network 10.0.0.0 0.0.0.255 area 0
 network 10.0.1.0 0.0.0.255 area 0
```

continues

Example 10-14 *Scar OSPF and BGP Configuration (Continued)*

```
 default-information originate
 !
 router bgp 65003
  no synchronization
  bgp router-id 10.0.0.1
  bgp cluster-id 1.1.1.1
  bgp log-neighbor-changes
  bgp dampening
  network 10.0.0.0 mask 255.255.255.0
  network 10.0.1.0 mask 255.255.255.0
  neighbor 10.0.1.2 remote-as 65003
  neighbor 10.0.1.2 update-source Loopback0
  neighbor 10.0.1.2 soft-reconfiguration inbound
  neighbor 192.168.7.7 remote-as 65000
  neighbor 192.168.7.7 soft-reconfiguration inbound
  neighbor 192.168.14.1 remote-as 65000
  neighbor 192.168.14.1 soft-reconfiguration inbound
  neighbor 192.168.14.2 remote-as 65001
  neighbor 192.168.14.2 soft-reconfiguration inbound
  maximum-paths 2
 !
 ip classless
 ip route 0.0.0.0 0.0.0.0 192.168.14.1
 ip route 0.0.0.0 0.0.0.0 192.168.7.7 2
 ...
```

Example 10-15 *Laurel OSPF and BGP Configuration*

```
laurel# show running-config
 ...
 ip subnet-zero
 !
 interface Loopback0
  ip address 172.16.0.254 255.255.255.128
 !
 interface Ethernet0
  ip address 192.168.14.2 255.255.255.0
 !
 interface Ethernet1
  ip address 172.16.0.1 255.255.255.128
  ip ospf message-digest-key 1 md5 7 061C0A235E4F
 !
 router ospf 1
  router-id 172.16.0.254
  log-adjacency-changes
  area 0 authentication message-digest
  redistribute connected subnets
  redistribute static subnets
  passive-interface Ethernet0
  passive-interface Serial0
  passive-interface Serial1
  network 172.16.0.0 0.0.0.127 area 0
```

Example 10-15 *Laurel OSPF and BGP Configuration (Continued)*

```
 network 172.16.0.128 0.0.0.127 area 0
 default-information originate
!
router bgp 65001
 no synchronization
 bgp router-id 172.16.0.254
 bgp cluster-id 1.1.1.1
 bgp log-neighbor-changes
 bgp dampening
 network 172.16.0.0 mask 255.255.255.128
 network 172.16.0.128 mask 255.255.255.128
 neighbor 172.16.0.253 remote-as 65001
 neighbor 172.16.0.253 soft-reconfiguration inbound
 neighbor 192.168.14.1 remote-as 65000
 neighbor 192.168.14.1 soft-reconfiguration inbound
 neighbor 192.168.14.254 remote-as 65003
 neighbor 192.168.14.254 soft-reconfiguration inbound
 maximum-paths 2
!
ip classless
ip route 0.0.0.0 0.0.0.0 192.168.14.1
ip route 0.0.0.0 0.0.0.0 192.168.7.7 2
```

Example 10-16 *Chaplin OSPF and BGP Configuration*

```
chaplin# show running-config
...
!
ip subnet-zero
!
interface Loopback0
 ip address 172.16.0.253 255.255.255.128
!
interface Ethernet0
 ip address 172.16.0.2 255.255.255.128
 ip ospf message-digest-key 1 md5 7 01090306490A
!
router ospf 1
 router-id 172.16.0.253
 log-adjacency-changes
 area 0 authentication message-digest
 redistribute connected subnets
 redistribute static subnets
 passive-interface Serial0
 passive-interface Serial1
 network 172.16.0.0 0.0.0.127 area 0
 network 172.16.0.128 0.0.0.127 area 0
!
router bgp 65001
 no synchronization
 bgp router-id 172.16.0.253
 bgp cluster-id 1.1.1.1
```

continues

Example 10-16 *Chaplin OSPF and BGP Configuration (Continued)*

```
 bgp log-neighbor-changes
 bgp dampening
 neighbor 172.16.0.254 remote-as 65001
 neighbor 172.16.0.254 soft-reconfiguration inbound
 !
 ip classless
 ...
```

Example 10-17 *Hardy OSPF and BGP Configuration*

```
hardy# show running-config
...
!
ip subnet-zero
!
interface Loopback0
 ip address 10.0.0.2 255.255.255.0
!
interface TokenRing0
 ip address 10.0.1.2 255.255.255.0
 ip ospf network broadcast
 early-token-release
 ring-speed 16
!
router ospf 1
 router-id 10.0.0.2
 log-adjacency-changes
 area 0 authentication message-digest
 redistribute connected subnets
 redistribute static subnets
 network 10.0.0.0 0.0.0.255 area 0
 network 10.0.1.0 0.0.0.255 area 0
!
router bgp 65003
 no synchronization
 bgp router-id 10.0.0.2
 bgp cluster-id 1.1.1.1
 bgp log-neighbor-changes
 bgp dampening
 neighbor 10.0.0.1 remote-as 65003
 neighbor 10.0.0.1 update-source Loopback0
 neighbor 10.0.0.1 soft-reconfiguration inbound
!
ip classless
...
```

Example 10-18 demonstrates the result of this setup with several **show** commands. The last traceroute shows the effect of the BGP-multipath capability of Cisco IOS architecture using two equal-cost paths.

Example 10-18 *Results of This EBGP Setup*

```
[root@ganymed:~#] netstat -rn -f inet
Routing tables

Internet:
Destination        Gateway             Flags    Refs     Use    Mtu   Interface
default            211.11.117.1        UGS      4      10366   1500   ne5
10.0.0/24          192.168.1.1         UG1      0          0   1500   ne3
10.0.1/24          192.168.1.1         UG1      0          0   1500   ne3
127/8              127.0.0.1           UGRS     0          0  33224   lo0
127.0.0.1          127.0.0.1           UH       2          0  33224   lo0
172.16.0.0/25      192.168.1.1         UG1      0          0   1500   ne3
172.16.0.128/25    192.168.1.1         UG1      0          0   1500   ne3
192.168.1/24       link#1              UC       0          0   1500   ne3
192.168.1.1        52:54:5:e3:51:87    UHL      7       6620   1500   ne3
192.168.1.2        8:0:46:64:74:1b     UHL      1       2213   1500   ne3
192.168.1.254      127.0.0.1           UGHS     0          0  33224   lo0
192.168.2/24       link#2              UC       0          0   1500   ne4
192.168.2.7        0:10:5a:c4:2c:4     UHL      3        977   1500   ne4
192.168.7/24       192.168.2.7         UG1      0         33   1500   ne4
192.168.14/24      192.168.1.1         UG1      0          0   1500   ne3
192.168.44.1       192.168.44.1        UH       0          0  33224   lo1
192.168.45/24      link#1              UC       0          0   1500   ne3
192.168.45.253     52:54:5:e3:51:87    UHL      0          0   1500   ne3
192.168.80/24      link#16             UC       0          0   1496   vlan0
192.168.80.1       0:10:5a:c4:2c:4     UHL      0          0   1496   vlan0
192.168.99.1       192.168.1.1         UGH1     0          0   1500   ne3
192.168.99.2       192.168.2.7         UGH1     0          0   1500   ne4
211.11.117/24      link#3              UC       0          0   1500   ne5
211.11.117.1       0:0:c:7:ac:12       UHL      1          0   1500   ne5

[root@castor:~#] netstat -rn -f inet
Routing tables

Internet:
Destination        Gateway             Flags    Refs     Use  Netif Expire
default            192.168.2.254       UGSc     3         12   xl0
10/24              192.168.7.254       UG1c     0          0   ed0
10.0.1/24          192.168.7.254       UG1c     0          0   ed0
127.0.0.1          127.0.0.1           UH       0          0   lo0
172.16/25          192.168.2.254       UG1c     0          0   xl0
172.16.0.128/25    192.168.2.254       UG1c     0          0   xl0
192.168.1          192.168.2.254       UG1c     2          0   xl0
192.168.2          link#1              UC       1          0   xl0
192.168.2.254      52:54:05:e3:e4:2f   UHLW     14        33   xl0    679
192.168.7          link#2              UC       1          0   ed0
192.168.7.254      00:00:0c:1a:a9:a8   UHLW     4        516   ed0    583
192.168.44         192.168.2.254       UG1c     0          0   xl0
192.168.45         192.168.2.254       UG1c     0          0   xl0
192.168.80         link#15             UC       1          0   vlan8
192.168.80.254     52.54.5.e3.e4.2f    UHLW     0          0   vlan8  777
192.168.99.1       192.168.2.254       UGH1     0          0   xl0
192.168.99.2       192.168.99.1        UH       0          6 wpachd =>
```

continues

Example 10-18 *Results of This EBGP Setup (Continued)*

```
192.168.99.2/32    wpachdlc0        U1c       0        0 wpachd
211.11.117         192.168.2.254    UG1c      0        0    x10

castor-bgpd# show ip bgp summary
BGP router identifier 192.168.2.7, local AS number 65000
5 BGP AS-PATH entries
0 BGP community entries
Dampening enabled.

Neighbor         V    AS MsgRcvd MsgSent  TblVer  InQ OutQ Up/Down  State/PfxRcd
192.168.1.1      4 65000     51      54       0    0    0 00:46:07            9
192.168.7.254    4 65003     55      54       0    0    0 00:46:43            4

Total number of neighbors 2

castor-bgpd# show ip bgp neighbors 192.168.1.1 received-routes
BGP table version is 0, local router ID is 192.168.2.7
Status codes: s suppressed, d damped, h history, * valid, > best, i - internal
Origin codes: i - IGP, e - EGP, ? - incomplete

   Network          Next Hop          Metric LocPrf Weight Path
*> 10.0.0.0/24      192.168.14.254         0    100      0 65003 i
*> 10.0.1.0/24      192.168.14.254         0    100      0 65003 i
*> 172.16.0.0/25    192.168.14.2           0    100      0 65001 i
*> 172.16.0.128/25  192.168.14.2           0    100      0 65001 i
*> 192.168.2.0      192.168.1.254         20    100      0 ?
*> 192.168.44.0     192.168.1.254         20    100      0 ?
*> 192.168.80.0     192.168.1.254         20    100      0 ?
*> 192.168.99.1/32  192.168.1.1           10    100      0 ?
*> 211.11.117.0     192.168.1.254         20    100      0 ?

Total number of prefixes 9

castor-bgpd# show ip bgp
BGP table version is 0, local router ID is 192.168.2.7
Status codes: s suppressed, d damped, h history, * valid, > best, i - internal
Origin codes: i - IGP, e - EGP, ? - incomplete

    Network          Next Hop          Metric LocPrf Weight Path
*  i10.0.0.0/24      192.168.14.254         0    100      0 65003 i
*>                   192.168.7.254          0             0 65003 i
*  i10.0.1.0/24      192.168.14.254         0    100      0 65003 i
*>                   192.168.7.254          0             0 65003 i
*>i172.16.0.0/25     192.168.14.2           0    100      0 65001 i
*                    192.168.7.254                        0 65003 65001 i
*>i172.16.0.128/25   192.168.14.2           0    100      0 65001 i
*                    192.168.7.254                        0 65003 65001 i
*> 192.168.1.0       192.168.2.254         20         32768 ?
*>i192.168.2.0       192.168.1.254         20    100      0 ?
*  i192.168.44.0     192.168.1.254         20    100      0 ?
*>                   192.168.2.254         20         32768 ?
*> 192.168.45.0      192.168.2.254         20         32768 ?
```

Example 10-18 *Results of This EBGP Setup (Continued)*

```
*>i192.168.80.0     192.168.1.254      20    100     0 ?
*>i192.168.99.1/32  192.168.1.1        10    100     0 ?
*> 192.168.99.2/32  0.0.0.0            10          32768 ?
* i211.11.117.0     192.168.1.254      20    100     0 ?
*>                  192.168.2.254      20          32768 ?


Total number of prefixes 12

[root@callisto:~#] netstat -rn
Kernel IP routing table
Destination    Gateway        Genmask          Flags  MSS Window  irtt Iface
192.168.99.1   0.0.0.0        255.255.255.255  UH      40 0          0 wp1chdlc
192.168.99.2   192.168.1.254  255.255.255.255  UGH     40 0          0 eth1
192.168.99.0   0.0.0.0        255.255.255.252  U       40 0          0 wp1chdlc
172.16.0.128   192.168.14.2   255.255.255.128  UG      40 0          0 eth0
172.16.0.0     192.168.14.2   255.255.255.128  UG      40 0          0 eth0
211.11.117.0   192.168.1.254  255.255.255.0    UG      40 0          0 eth1
10.0.0.0       192.168.14.254 255.255.255.0    UG      40 0          0 eth0
10.0.1.0       192.168.14.254 255.255.255.0    UG      40 0          0 eth0
192.168.2.0    192.168.1.254  255.255.255.0    UG      40 0          0 eth1
192.168.80.0   192.168.1.254  255.255.255.0    UG      40 0          0 eth1
192.168.1.0    0.0.0.0        255.255.255.0    U       40 0          0 eth1
192.168.1.0    0.0.0.0        255.255.255.0    U       40 0          0 ipsec0
192.168.14.0   0.0.0.0        255.255.255.0    U       40 0          0 eth0
192.168.44.0   192.168.1.254  255.255.255.0    UG      40 0          0 eth1
192.168.45.0   0.0.0.0        255.255.255.0    U       40 0          0 eth1
127.0.0.0      0.0.0.0        255.0.0.0        U       40 0          0 lo
0.0.0.0        192.168.1.254  0.0.0.0          UG      40 0          0 eth1


callisto-bgpd# show ip bgp summary
BGP router identifier 192.168.1.1, local AS number 65000
6 BGP AS-PATH entries
0 BGP community entries
Dampening enabled.


Neighbor         V    AS MsgRcvd MsgSent  TblVer  InQ OutQ Up/Down  State/PfxRcd
192.168.2.7      4 65000      46      46       0    0    0 00:39:42            7
192.168.14.2     4 65001      48      47       0    0    0 00:39:38            4
192.168.14.254   4 65003      50      47       0    0    0 00:39:38            4
192.168.44.1     4 65000      39      48       0    0    0 00:38:05            0


Total number of neighbors 4

callisto-bgpd# show ip bgp neighbors 192.168.2.7
BGP neighbor is 192.168.2.7, remote AS 65000, local AS 65000, internal link
 Member of peer-group INTERNAL for session parameters
  BGP version 4, remote router ID 192.168.2.7
  BGP state = Established, up for 00:40:44
  Last read 00:00:44, hold time is 180, keepalive interval is 60 seconds
  Neighbor capabilities:
    Route refresh: advertised and received (old and new)
    Address family IPv4 Unicast: advertised and received
```

continues

Example 10-18 *Results of This EBGP Setup (Continued)*

```
           Received 47 messages, 0 notifications, 0 in queue
           Sent 47 messages, 0 notifications, 0 in queue
           Route refresh request: received 0, sent 0
           Minimum time between advertisement runs is 5 seconds

  For address family: IPv4 Unicast
   INTERNAL peer-group member
   Route-Reflector Client
   Inbound soft reconfiguration allowed
   Community attribute sent to this neighbor (both)
   7 accepted prefixes

 Connections established 1; dropped 0
 Local host: 192.168.1.1, Local port: 32923
 Foreign host: 192.168.2.7, Foreign port: 179
 Nexthop: 192.168.1.1
 Read thread: on  Write thread: off

callisto-bgpd# show ip bgp neighbors 192.168.2.7 advertised-routes
BGP table version is 0, local router ID is 192.168.1.1
Status codes: s suppressed, d damped, h history, * valid, > best, i - internal
Origin codes: i - IGP, e - EGP, ? - incomplete

     Network          Next Hop         Metric LocPrf Weight Path
  *> 10.0.0.0/24      192.168.14.254        0    100      0 65003 i
  *> 10.0.1.0/24      192.168.14.254        0    100      0 65003 i
  *> 172.16.0.0/25    192.168.14.2          0    100      0 65001 i
  *> 172.16.0.128/25  192.168.14.2          0    100      0 65001 i
  *> 192.168.2.0      192.168.1.254        20    100  32768 ?
  *> 192.168.44.0     192.168.1.254        20    100  32768 ?
  *> 192.168.80.0     192.168.1.254        20    100  32768 ?
  *> 192.168.99.1/32  192.168.1.1          10    100  32768 ?
  *> 211.11.117.0     192.168.1.254        20    100  32768 ?

Total number of prefixes 9

callisto-bgpd# show ip bgp
BGP table version is 0, local router ID is 192.168.1.1
Status codes: s suppressed, d damped, h history, * valid, > best, i - internal
Origin codes: i - IGP, e - EGP, ? - incomplete

     Network          Next Hop         Metric LocPrf Weight Path
  *> 10.0.0.0/24      192.168.14.254        0             0 65003 i
  *                   192.168.14.254                      0 65001 65003 i
  * i                 192.168.7.254         0    100      0 65003 i
  *> 10.0.1.0/24      192.168.14.254        0             0 65003 i
  *                   192.168.14.254                      0 65001 65003 i
  * i                 192.168.7.254         0    100      0 65003 i
  *  172.16.0.0/25    192.168.14.2                        0 65003 65001 i
  *>                  192.168.14.2          0             0 65001 i
  *  172.16.0.128/25  192.168.14.2                        0 65003 65001 i
  *>                  192.168.14.2          0             0 65001 i
```

Example 10-18 *Results of This EBGP Setup (Continued)*

```
*>i192.168.1.0      192.168.2.254      20   100    0 ?
*> 192.168.2.0      192.168.1.254      20         32768 ?
*  i192.168.44.0    192.168.2.254      20   100    0 ?
*>                  192.168.1.254      20         32768 ?
*>i192.168.45.0     192.168.2.254      20   100    0 ?
*> 192.168.80.0     192.168.1.254      20         32768 ?
*> 192.168.99.1/32  0.0.0.0            10         32768 ?
*>i192.168.99.2/32  192.168.2.7        10   100    0 ?
*  i211.11.117.0    192.168.2.254      20   100    0 ?
*>                  192.168.1.254      20         32768 ?

Total number of prefixes 12

callisto-bgpd# show ip bgp 172.16.0.0/25
BGP routing table entry for 172.16.0.0/25
Paths: (2 available, best #2, table Default-IP-Routing-Table)
  Advertised to non peer-group peers:
  192.168.2.7 192.168.14.254 192.168.44.1
  65003 65001
    192.168.14.2 from 192.168.14.254 (10.0.0.1)
      Origin IGP, localpref 100, valid, external
      Last update: Fri May  2 12:54:37 2003

  65001
    192.168.14.2 from 192.168.14.2 (172.16.0.254)
      Origin IGP, metric 0, localpref 100, valid, external, best
      Last update: Fri May  2 12:54:37 2003

scar# show ip bgp summary
BGP router identifier 10.0.0.1, local AS number 65003
BGP table version is 19, main routing table version 19
12 network entries and 32 paths using 2316 bytes of memory
7 BGP path attribute entries using 420 bytes of memory
4 BGP AS-PATH entries using 96 bytes of memory
0 BGP route-map cache entries using 0 bytes of memory
0 BGP filter-list cache entries using 0 bytes of memory
Dampening enabled. 0 history paths, 0 dampened paths
BGP activity 12/49 prefixes, 32/0 paths, scan interval 60 secs

Neighbor        V    AS MsgRcvd MsgSent   TblVer  InQ OutQ Up/Down  State/PfxRcd
10.0.1.2        4 65003     298     308       19    0    0 04:54:26        0
192.168.7.7     4 65000      66      69       19    0    0 00:58:15       10
192.168.14.1    4 65000      65      70       19    0    0 00:57:36       10
192.168.14.2    4 65001     303     307       19    0    0 04:54:24       10

scar# show ip bgp neighbors 192.168.7.7
BGP neighbor is 192.168.7.7,  remote AS 65000, external link
  BGP version 4, remote router ID 192.168.2.7
  BGP state = Established, up for 00:59:07
  Last read 00:00:07, hold time is 180, keepalive interval is 60 seconds
```

continues

Example 10-18 *Results of This EBGP Setup (Continued)*

```
 Neighbor capabilities:
   Route refresh: advertised and received(new)
   Address family IPv4 Unicast: advertised and received
 Received 67 messages, 0 notifications, 0 in queue
 Sent 70 messages, 0 notifications, 0 in queue
 Route refresh request: received 0, sent 0
 Default minimum time between advertisement runs is 30 seconds

 For address family: IPv4 Unicast
 BGP table version 19, neighbor version 19
 Index 2, Offset 0, Mask 0x4
 Inbound soft reconfiguration allowed
 10 accepted prefixes consume 360 bytes
 Prefix advertised 10, suppressed 0, withdrawn 1
 Number of NLRIs in the update sent: max 2, min 0

 Connections established 1; dropped 0
 Last reset never
Connection state is ESTAB, I/O status: 1, unread input bytes: 0
Local host: 192.168.7.254, Local port: 179
Foreign host: 192.168.7.7, Foreign port: 1024

Enqueued packets for retransmit: 0, input: 0  mis-ordered: 0 (0 bytes)

Event Timers (current time is 0x10FB800):
Timer        Starts    Wakeups         Next
Retrans         70          0          0x0
TimeWait         0          0          0x0
AckHold         67         37          0x0
SendWnd          0          0          0x0
KeepAlive        0          0          0x0
GiveUp           0          0          0x0
PmtuAger         0          0          0x0
DeadWait         0          0          0x0

iss:  939562101  snduna:  939563660  sndnxt:  939563660     sndwnd:   33580
irs: 2226264130  rcvnxt: 2226265600  rcvwnd:      16384 delrcvwnd:       0

SRTT: 300 ms, RTTO: 303 ms, RTV: 3 ms, KRTT: 0 ms
minRTT: 4 ms, maxRTT: 300 ms, ACK hold: 200 ms
Flags: passive open, nagle, gen tcbs

Datagrams (max data segment is 1460 bytes):
Rcvd: 135 (out of order: 0), with data: 67, total data bytes: 1469
Sent: 108 (retransmit: 0), with data: 69, total data bytes: 1558

scar# show ip bgp neighbors 192.168.7.7 received-routes
BGP table version is 19, local router ID is 10.0.0.1
Status codes: s suppressed, d damped, h history, * valid, > best, i - internal
Origin codes: i - IGP, e - EGP, ? - incomplete
```

Example 10-18 *Results of This EBGP Setup (Continued)*

```
     Network          Next Hop          Metric LocPrf Weight Path
   *  172.16.0.0/25    192.168.7.7                        0 65000 65001 i
   *  172.16.0.128/25  192.168.7.7                        0 65000 65001 i
   *  192.168.1.0      192.168.7.7         20             0 65000 ?
   *> 192.168.2.0      192.168.7.7                        0 65000 ?
   *  192.168.44.0     192.168.7.7         20             0 65000 ?
   *  192.168.45.0     192.168.7.7         20             0 65000 ?
   *> 192.168.80.0     192.168.7.7                        0 65000 ?
   *> 192.168.99.1/32  192.168.7.7                        0 65000 ?
   *  192.168.99.2/32  192.168.7.7         10             0 65000 ?
   *  211.11.117.0     192.168.7.7         20             0 65000 ?

Total number of prefixes 10

scar# show ip route
Codes: C - connected, S - static, I - IGRP, R - RIP, M - mobile, B - BGP
       D - EIGRP, EX - EIGRP external, O - OSPF, IA - OSPF inter area
       N1 - OSPF NSSA external type 1, N2 - OSPF NSSA external type 2
       E1 - OSPF external type 1, E2 - OSPF external type 2, E - EGP
       i - IS-IS, L1 - IS-IS level-1, L2 - IS-IS level-2, ia - IS-IS inter area
       * - candidate default, U - per-user static route, o - ODR
       P - periodic downloaded static route

Gateway of last resort is 192.168.14.1 to network 0.0.0.0

C    192.168.14.0/24 is directly connected, Ethernet1
B    192.168.44.0/24 [20/20] via 192.168.7.7, 00:50:56
B    192.168.45.0/24 [20/0] via 192.168.14.1, 00:50:46
     172.16.0.0/25 is subnetted, 2 subnets
B       172.16.0.128 [20/0] via 192.168.14.2, 04:48:45
B       172.16.0.0 [20/0] via 192.168.14.2, 04:48:45
     192.168.99.0/32 is subnetted, 2 subnets
B       192.168.99.2 [20/0] via 192.168.14.1, 00:52:46
B       192.168.99.1 [20/0] via 192.168.7.7, 00:52:26
B    192.168.80.0/24 [20/0] via 192.168.7.7, 00:50:56
B    211.11.117.0/24 [20/20] via 192.168.7.7, 00:50:56
     10.0.0.0/8 is variably subnetted, 3 subnets, 2 masks
O       10.0.0.2/32 [110/7] via 10.0.1.2, 04:49:47, TokenRing0
C       10.0.0.0/24 is directly connected, Loopback0
C       10.0.1.0/24 is directly connected, TokenRing0
C    192.168.7.0/24 is directly connected, Ethernet0
B    192.168.1.0/24 [20/0] via 192.168.14.1, 00:50:46
B    192.168.2.0/24 [20/0] via 192.168.7.7, 00:50:56
S*   0.0.0.0/0 [1/0] via 192.168.14.1

scar# show ip bgp
BGP table version is 17, local router ID is 10.0.0.1
Status codes: s suppressed, d damped, h history, * valid, > best, i - internal
Origin codes: i - IGP, e - EGP, ? - incomplete

     Network          Next Hop          Metric LocPrf Weight Path
   *> 10.0.0.0/24      0.0.0.0               0          32768 i
```

continues

Example 10-18 *Results of This EBGP Setup (Continued)*

```
*> 10.0.1.0/24      0.0.0.0              0       32768 i
*  172.16.0.0/25    192.168.7.7                  0 65000 65001 i
*                   192.168.14.2                 0 65000 65001 i
*>                  192.168.14.2         0       0 65001 i
*  172.16.0.128/25  192.168.7.7                  0 65000 65001 i
*                   192.168.14.2                 0 65000 65001 i
*>                  192.168.14.2         0       0 65001 i
*  192.168.1.0      192.168.14.1                 0 65001 65000 ?
*>                  192.168.14.1                 0 65000 ?
*                   192.168.7.7          20      0 65000 ?
*  192.168.2.0      192.168.14.1                 0 65001 65000 ?
*                   192.168.14.1         20      0 65000 ?
*>                  192.168.7.7                  0 65000 ?
*  192.168.44.0     192.168.14.1                 0 65001 65000 ?
*                   192.168.14.1         20      0 65000 ?
*>                  192.168.7.7          20      0 65000 ?
*  192.168.45.0     192.168.14.1                 0 65001 65000 ?
*>                  192.168.14.1                 0 65000 ?
*                   192.168.7.7          20      0 65000 ?
*  192.168.80.0     192.168.14.1                 0 65001 65000 ?
*                   192.168.14.1         20      0 65000 ?
*>                  192.168.7.7                  0 65000 ?
*> 192.168.99.1/32  192.168.7.7                  0 65000 ?
*                   192.168.14.1                 0 65001 65000 ?
*                   192.168.14.1         10      0 65000 ?
*  192.168.99.2/32  192.168.14.1                 0 65001 65000 ?
*>                  192.168.14.1                 0 65000 ?
*                   192.168.7.7          10      0 65000 ?
*  211.11.117.0     192.168.14.1                 0 65001 65000 ?
*                   192.168.14.1         20      0 65000 ?
*>                  192.168.7.7          20      0 65000 ?

scar# show ip bgp 192.168.44.1
BGP routing table entry for 192.168.44.0/24, version 18
Paths: (3 available, best #2, table Default-IP-Routing-Table)
  Advertised to non peer-group peers:
  10.0.1.2 192.168.7.7 192.168.14.2
  65001 65000, (received & used)
    192.168.14.1 from 192.168.14.2 (172.16.0.254)
      Origin incomplete, localpref 100, valid, external
  65000, (received & used)
    192.168.14.1 from 192.168.14.1 (192.168.1.1)
      Origin incomplete, metric 20, localpref 100, valid, external, multipath, best
  65000, (received & used)
    192.168.7.7 from 192.168.7.7 (192.168.2.7)
      Origin incomplete, metric 20, localpref 100, valid, external, multipath

scar# traceroute 192.168.44.1

Type escape sequence to abort.
Tracing the route to 192.168.44.1
```

Example 10-18 *Results of This EBGP Setup (Continued)*

```
1 192.168.14.1 0 msec
  192.168.7.7 4 msec
  192.168.14.1 4 msec
2 192.168.44.1 [AS 65000] 4 msec 0 msec 0 msec
```

Lab 10-4: BGP with GateD

Now we replace the Zebra daemons on callisto and castor with GateD (see Examples 10-19 and 10-20). The secondary interface connecting callisto and ganymed is disabled, and OSPF authentication is turned off to accommodate GateD restrictions.

Although GateD lacks some of the features of Zebra, the configuration tries to mimic the Zebra configurations (Examples 10-11 to 10-13) as closely as possible. GateD uses different **group <type> peeras** types to configure peerings (**<type>=external, IGP, internal, routing**) that can be used to configure IBGP and EBGP scenarios. For a more detailed explanation, refer to the V3.6 documentation.

NOTE   Note that the highlighted export statement in Example 10-19 is used to accomplish IBGP route reflector behavior.

Example 10-19 *Castor GateD Route Reflector Setup*

```
[root@castor:~#] cat /etc/gated.cfg
routerid 192.168.2.7;
autonomoussystem 65000;

rip off;

ospf yes{
        backbone{
                networks{
                        192.168.2.0  mask 255.255.255.0;
                        192.168.80.0 mask 255.255.255.0;
                        192.168.99.0  mask 255.255.255.252;
                };
                interface x10 vlan8 wpachdlc0;
        };
};

bgp yes{
        group type routing peeras 65000 proto ospf
        {
                peer 192.168.1.1;
        };
```

continues

Example 10-19 *Castor GateD Route Reflector Setup (Continued)*

```
            group type external peeras 65003
            {
                    peer 192.168.7.254;
            };
};

static{
        default gateway 192.168.2.254;
};

#exporting to OSPF
export proto ospfase{
        proto static{all; };
        proto direct{all; };
};

export proto bgp as 65000 {
        proto bgp as 65000 {all;}; # for reflection
        proto ospf{all;};
};

export proto bgp as 65003 {
        proto ospf{all;};
};

GateD-castor> show bgp sum
100 Neighbor        V    AS MsgRcvd MsgSent State
100 192.168.1.1    4 65000      3      4 Established
100 192.168.7.254  4 65003      5      4 Established
100 BGP summary, 2 groups, 2 peers.

GateD-castor> show bgp routes 0/0
100 Proto       Route/Mask NextHop       MED    ASPath
100 BGP              10/24 192.168.7.254 0      (65000) 65003 IGP (Id 5)
100 BGP            10.0.1/24 192.168.7.254 0      (65000) 65003 IGP (Id 5)
100 BGP           172.16/25 192.168.7.254 -1     (65000) 65003 65001 IGP (Id 4)
100 BGP    172.16.0.128/25 192.168.7.254 -1     (65000) 65003 65001 IGP (Id 4)

GateD-castor> show ip walkdown 0/0
100 Ker         0.0.0.0/0  192.168.2.254 IGP (Id 1)
100 BGP              10/24 192.168.7.254 (65000) 65003 IGP (Id 5)
100 BGP            10.0.1/24 192.168.7.254 (65000) 65003 IGP (Id 5)
100 Sta            127/8  127.0.0.1     IGP (Id 1)
100 Dir      127.0.0.1/32 127.0.0.1     IGP (Id 1)
100 BGP           172.16/25 192.168.7.254 (65000) 65003 65001 IGP (Id 4)
100 BGP    172.16.0.128/25 192.168.7.254 (65000) 65003 65001 IGP (Id 4)
100 OSP      192.168.1/24 192.168.2.254 (65000) IGP (Id 2)
100 Ker   192.168.1.1/32 192.168.2.254 IGP (Id 1)
100 Ker   192.168.1.2/32 192.168.2.254 IGP (Id 1)
```

Example 10-19 *Castor GateD Route Reflector Setup (Continued)*

```
100 Dir       192.168.2/24 192.168.2.7     IGP (Id 1)
100 Dir       192.168.7/24 192.168.7.7     IGP (Id 1)
100 OSP      192.168.14/24 192.168.2.254   (65000) Incomplete (Id 3)
100 OSP      192.168.44/24 192.168.2.254   (65000) Incomplete (Id 3)
100 Dir      192.168.80/24 192.168.80.1    IGP (Id 1)
100 Dir    192.168.99.1/32 127.0.0.1       IGP (Id 1)
100 Dir    192.168.99.2/32 192.168.99.1    IGP (Id 1)
100 OSP      211.11.117/24 192.168.2.254   (65000) Incomplete (Id 3)

GateD-castor> show bgp peeras 65003
100 group type External AS 65003 local 65000 flags <>
100   peer 192.168.7.254 version 4 lcladdr (null) gateway (null)
100     flags 0x0
100     state 0x6 <Established>
100     options 0x0 <>
100     metric_out -1
100     preference 170
100     preference2 0
100     recv buffer size 0
100     send buffer size 0
100     messages in 24 (updates 3, not updates 21) 559 octets
messages out 23 (updates 1, not updates 22) 473 octets

[root@castor:~#] netstat -rn -f inet
Routing tables

Internet:
Destination        Gateway            Flags    Refs      Use   Netif Expire
default            192.168.2.254      UGSc       1        62    xl0
10/24              192.168.7.254      UGc        0         0    ed0
10.0.1/24          192.168.7.254      UGc        0         0    ed0
127                127.0.0.1          URc        0         0    lo0
127.0.0.1          127.0.0.1          UH         2       186    lo0
172.16/25          192.168.7.254      UGc        0         0    ed0
172.16.0.128/25    192.168.7.254      UGc        0         0    ed0
192.168.1          192.168.2.254      UGc        2         2    xl0
192.168.2          link#1             UC         1         0    xl0
192.168.2.254      52:54:05:e3:e4:2f  UHLW       7         0    xl0      337
192.168.7          link#2             UC         1         0    ed0
192.168.7.254      00:00:0c:1a:a9:a8  UHLW       7        67    ed0      347
192.168.14         192.168.2.254      UGc        0         0    xl0
192.168.44         192.168.2.254      UGc        0         3    xl0
192.168.80         link#15            UC         0         0    vlan8
192.168.99.1       127.0.0.1          UGH        0         0    lo0
192.168.99.2       192.168.99.1       UH         0         3    wpachd
211.11.117         192.168.2.254      UGc        0         0    xl0
224.0.0.5          127.0.0.1          UH         0         0    lo0
224.0.0.6          127.0.0.1          UH         0         0    lo0
```

Example 10-20 *Callisto GateD Setup*

```
[root@callisto:~#] cat /etc/gated.conf
routerid 192.168.1.1;
autonomoussystem 65000;

rip off;

ospf yes{
        backbone{
                networks{
                        192.168.1.0  mask 255.255.255.0;
                        192.168.99.0  mask 255.255.255.252;
                        192.168.45.0 mask 255.255.255.0;
                };
                interface eth1 wp1chdlc;
        };
};

bgp yes{
        group type routing peeras 65000 proto ospf
        {
                peer 192.168.44.1;
                peer 192.168.2.7;
        };
        group type external peeras 65001
        {
                peer 192.168.14.2;
        };
        group type external peeras 65003
        {
                peer 192.168.14.254;
        };
};

static{
        default gateway 192.168.1.254;
};

#exporting to OSPF
export proto ospfase{
        #restrict;
        proto static{all; };
        proto direct{all; };
        #proto kernel{all; };
};

export proto bgp as 65000 {
        proto bgp as 65000 {all;}; # for reflection
        proto ospf{all;};
};

export proto bgp as 65001 {
        proto ospf{all;};
```

Example 10-20 *Callisto GateD Setup (Continued)*

```
};

export proto bgp as 65003 {
        proto ospf{all;};
};

GateD-callisto> show bgp sum
100 Neighbor        V   AS MsgRcvd MsgSent State
100 192.168.44.1    4 65000     90      96 Established
100 192.168.2.7     4 65000     27      29 Established
100 192.168.14.2    4 65001    103      98 Established
100 192.168.14.254  4 65003    108      98 Established
100 BGP summary, 3 groups, 4 peers.

GateD-callisto> show bgp routes 0/0
100 Proto         Route/Mask NextHop       MED   ASPath
100 BGP                10/24 192.168.14.254 0     (65000) 65003 IGP (Id 7)
100 BGP              10.0.1/24 192.168.14.254 0   (65000) 65003 IGP (Id 7)
100 BGP              172.16/25 192.168.14.2 0     (65000) 65001 IGP (Id 5)
100 BGP       172.16.0.128/25 192.168.14.2 0     (65000) 65001 IGP (Id 5)

GateD-callisto> show ip walkdown 0/0
100 Sta         0.0.0.0/0 192.168.1.254   IGP (Id 1)
100 BGP             10/24 192.168.14.254  (65000) 65003 IGP (Id 7)
100 BGP           10.0.1/24 192.168.14.254  (65000) 65003 IGP (Id 7)
100 Sta             127/8 127.0.0.1       IGP (Id 1)
100 Dir       127.0.0.1/32 127.0.0.1      IGP (Id 1)
100 BGP           172.16/25 192.168.14.2    (65000) 65001 IGP (Id 5)
100 BGP    172.16.0.128/25 192.168.14.2    (65000) 65001 IGP (Id 5)
100 Dir      192.168.1/24 192.168.1.1     IGP (Id 1)
100 OSP      192.168.2/24 192.168.1.254   (65000) IGP (Id 8)
100 OSP      192.168.7/24 192.168.1.254   (65000) IGP (Id 8)
100 Dir     192.168.14/24 192.168.14.1    IGP (Id 1)
100 OSP     192.168.44/24 192.168.1.254   (65000) Incomplete (Id 3)
100 OSP     192.168.80/24 192.168.1.254   (65000) IGP (Id 8)
100 Dir    192.168.99/32 192.168.99.2     IGP (Id 1)
100 Dir   192.168.99.2/32 127.0.0.1       IGP (Id 1)
100 OSP    211.11.117/24 192.168.1.254    (65000) Incomplete (Id 3)

[root@callisto:~#] netstat -rn
Kernel IP routing table
Destination     Gateway         Genmask         Flags   MSS Window  irtt Iface
224.0.0.6       127.0.0.1       255.255.255.255 UGH      40 0          0 lo
224.0.0.5       127.0.0.1       255.255.255.255 UGH      40 0          0 lo
192.168.99.0    0.0.0.0         255.255.255.255 UH       40 0          0 wp1chdlc
192.168.99.2    127.0.0.1       255.255.255.255 UGH      40 0          0 lo
127.0.0.1       0.0.0.0         255.255.255.255 UH       40 0          0 lo
192.168.99.0    0.0.0.0         255.255.255.252 U        40 0          0 wp1chdlc
172.16.0.128    192.168.14.2    255.255.255.128 UG       40 0          0 eth0
172.16.0.0      192.168.14.2    255.255.255.128 UG       40 0          0 eth0
192.168.7.0     192.168.1.254   255.255.255.0   UG       40 0          0 eth1
```

continues

Example 10-20 *Callisto GateD Setup (Continued)*

```
211.11.117.0    192.168.1.254    255.255.255.0    UG    40 0    0 eth1
10.0.0.0        192.168.14.254   255.255.255.0    UG    40 0    0 eth0
10.0.1.0        192.168.14.254   255.255.255.0    UG    40 0    0 eth0
192.168.2.0     192.168.1.254    255.255.255.0    UG    40 0    0 eth1
192.168.80.0    192.168.1.254    255.255.255.0    UG    40 0    0 eth1
192.168.1.0     0.0.0.0          255.255.255.0    U     40 0    0 eth1
192.168.14.0    0.0.0.0          255.255.255.0    U     40 0    0 eth0
192.168.44.0    192.168.1.254    255.255.255.0    UG    40 0    0 eth1
127.0.0.0       -                255.0.0.0        !     - -     - -
0.0.0.0         192.168.1.254    0.0.0.0          UG    40 0    0 eth1
```

Avoiding Single Points of Failure

The introduction of links to multiple points of presence (POPs) of one or several ISPs can eliminate single points of failure. Such autonomous systems can provide transit services or not. The following subsections discuss several popular BGP scenarios.

Single-Homed Nontransit (Stub) Scenario with a Private AS

In a nutshell, stub and single-homed autonomous systems do not justify the assignment of a regular ASN in the eyes of Internet Assigned Numbers Authority (IANA) and company. In case of special requirements, upstream providers do assign a private ASN (64512–65534, RFC 1930); and in case of a PI block assigned to the downstream customer, upstream providers announce this network to the Internet while stripping the private AS. The first level of redundancy would be to attach this customer to two different POP of the same ISP and provide traffic granularity via BGP measures. BGP offers a clean demarcation point. I strongly advise against ISDN dial-on-demand backups in BGP scenarios.

Multi-Homed Nontransit (Stub) Scenario

Entities that require the added redundancy of two independent upstreams usually register an ASN and a PI block. Upstream ISPs/carriers announce the PI prefix, which frequently results in suboptimal utilization of one upstream link. Remember, BGP was not designed for load balancing. This situation can be improved with the cooperation of both upstreams to tune BGP's advanced capabilities, such as path prepending, MED, and community attributes, to achieve at least a better distribution of traffic. To say the least, this is a tedious task that requires strong BGP knowledge and needs to be taken care of incoming and outgoing. In general, providing transit services *through* a public exchange violates the policy established by the exchange managers.

Transit Services

Transit traffic usually serves topological and commercial purposes. As long as the corresponding ingress and egress traffic of two transit partners is roughly equivalent, transit AS owners tend to agree to mutually beneficial no-charge peering/transit agreements. If this is not the case, transit traffic might be subject to charge.

In fact, providing transit traffic (be it for free or not) through a public IX is a violation of policy of almost any IX in the world (of which I am aware of). What has changed over the past few years, however, is the perception of what is considered "transit traffic" by the IX operators: Because carriers and ISPs have become multinational, IXs have to deal with peering entities (in a commercial sense) that cover numerous autonomous systems (combined administratively to an AS set, or macro), so IX operators usually allow such providers to announce their entire AS set at a given (national) IX instead of only their (national) AS. So a certain AS providing transit (in the strict BGP meaning) has nothing to do with public peering in the first place, but merely with the combination of some autonomous systems under common (international) administration, or is simply necessary because a provider has customers with their own autonomous systems (which, of course, have always been permitted on the IXs).

The question of traffic symmetry is a different one that does not really touch the transit/nontransit topic. As mentioned earlier, providers were picky about this symmetry when peering privately, and some kept enforcing this policy on the public IXs. Today, however, most of them realize that the advantages of public peering easily compensate for the possible drawbacks, so most do not care about symmetry anymore, and many just do not want to go through the added accounting hassle involved.

Route Server and Routing Registries

Over time, it became increasingly difficult to manage routing policies without a central database service. Starting from early approaches such as the NFSNET databases, today the Internet policies are stored in the Internet Routing Registry (IRR), which is a set of distributed databases. The Routing Assets Database (RADB) is the most prominent among them. Route servers are the regional entities that enforce parts of these policies on behalf of their EBGP route server clients. However, not all ISPs use them.

Requesting ASNs and IP Addresses

Suppose you work out your design and decide to request an ASN and a PI address block based on legitimate administrative requirements (for example, dual homing). Internet customers and subscribers are assigned IPv4/IPv6 addresses by ISPs and cannot directly approach registries. ISPs themselves obtain allocations from one of the following:

- Local Internet registries (LIRs)
- National Internet registries (NIRs)
- Regional Internet registries (RIRs)

Internet Assigned Numbers Authority/Internet Corporation for Assigned Names and Numbers (IANA/ICANN) and its supporting organizations and delegates are in charge of domain name services, IP address services (including ASNs), and protocol number assignment services (http://www.icann.org, http://www.iana.net).

Five RIRs form the Address Supporting Organization (ASO) and have ICANN-delegated responsibility to ASNs and IP addresses:

- http://www.ripe.net
- http://www.arin.net
- http://www.apnic.net
- http://www.lacnic.net
- http://www.afrinic.net

NOTE AfriNIC (http://www.afrinic.net) is the emerging organization that will be in charge of administering Internet number resources for the continent of Africa in the near future. At the time of this writing, they are finalizing their set of policies and expect to reach operational status soon.

Zebra Route Server with Multiple Views

A route server is commonly placed on a shared segment that resembles an exchange point. The purpose of the route server is to provide a single point of BGP signaling connectivity for all participants of the exchange to remove the need of any-to-any BGP peering setup. Thus, the route server and the exchange segment usually resemble a unique AS. The route server (europa) solely runs BGP for signaling purposes and does not get involved with forwarding real traffic and will never participate as a next hop. It just reflects EBGP announcements and acts as a central information repository.

Route servers are used to centralize routing and configuration functions and to collect Internet statistics. Zebra's bgpd does provide the capability to act as a route server via the neighbor **route-server-client** command. Together with its capability to use multiple views, it is a flexible engine for route server deployments.

Europa just runs bgpd, no zebra master daemon and no ospfd. It does not even require kernel IP forwarding to be turned on, or a default route (except for some minimal management access). A route server computes a collection of routes (a *view*) on behalf of each of its route server clients. A view is that part of a client's routing table that contains routes heard from other ISP routers at a NAP through a route server.

Most route server maintainers provide unprivileged Telnet or looking-glass access to their Zebra/Cisco nodes. Figure 10-10 simplifies the EBGP setup with the introduction of a route server (europa) running on OpenBSD 3.3. Figure 10-11 represents the physical layout.

Figure 10-10 *Logical BGP Topology with Exchange Point and Route Server*

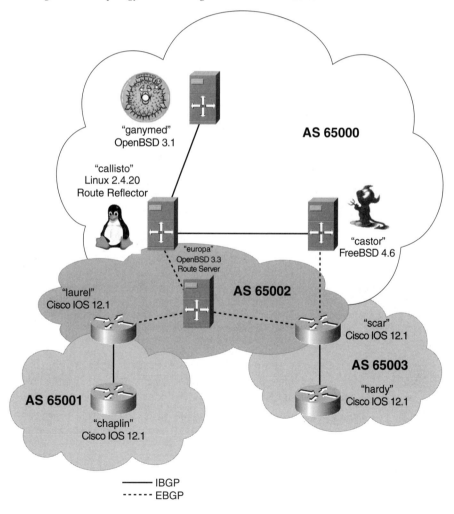

Figure 10-11 *Physical BGP Topology with Exchange Point and Route Server*

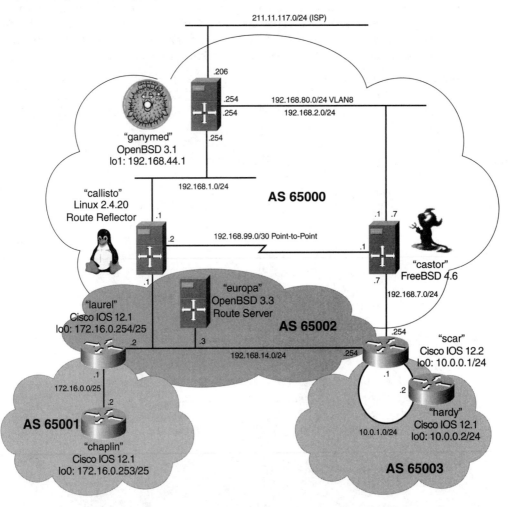

Example 10-21 reflects the configuration of the route server and the changed and simplified configurations for the route server EBGP clients. At the time of this writing, the route server feature of Quagga is evolving rapidly and might include features and extensions not covered here. Consult the Quagga mailing lists or source code for new features.

Example 10-21 *Route Server/Route Server Client Configurations*

```
europa-bgpd# show running-config

Current configuration:
!
hostname europa-bgpd
password 8 m6eyKycFMHniQ
```

Example 10-21 *Route Server/Route Server Client Configurations (Continued)*

```
enable password 8 bjYlnA9YLBWyM
log file /var/log/bgpd.log
service advanced-vty
service password-encryption
!
router bgp 65002
 bgp router-id 192.168.14.3
 bgp dampening
 neighbor RSERVER peer-group
 neighbor RSERVER soft-reconfiguration inbound
 neighbor RSERVER maximum-prefix 50 warning-only
 neighbor RSERVER route-server-client
 neighbor 192.168.14.1 remote-as 65000
 neighbor 192.168.14.1 peer-group RSERVER
 neighbor 192.168.14.2 remote-as 65001
 neighbor 192.168.14.2 peer-group RSERVER
 neighbor 192.168.14.254 remote-as 65003
 neighbor 192.168.14.254 peer-group RSERVER
!
access-list 1 remark vty-protection
access-list 1 permit 127.0.0.1
access-list 1 permit 192.168.1.0 0.0.0.255
!
line vty
 access-class 1
 exec-timeout 0 0
!
end

callisto-bgpd# show running-config

Current configuration:
!
hostname callisto-bgpd
password 8 m6eyKycFMHniQ
enable password 8 bjYlnA9YLBWyM
log file /var/log/bgpd.log
service advanced-vty
service password-encryption
!
router bgp 65000
 bgp router-id 192.168.1.1
 bgp cluster-id 1.1.1.1
 bgp dampening
 redistribute ospf
 neighbor INTERNAL peer-group
 neighbor INTERNAL remote-as 65000
 neighbor INTERNAL route-reflector-client
 neighbor INTERNAL soft-reconfiguration inbound
 neighbor 192.168.2.7 peer-group INTERNAL
```

continues

Example 10-21 *Route Server/Route Server Client Configurations (Continued)*

```
 neighbor 192.168.14.3 remote-as 65002
 neighbor 192.168.14.3 soft-reconfiguration inbound
 neighbor 192.168.44.1 peer-group INTERNAL
!
access-list 1 remark vty-protection
access-list 1 permit 127.0.0.1
access-list 1 permit 192.168.1.0 0.0.0.255
!
line vty
 access-class 1
 exec-timeout 0 0
!
end

laurel# show running-config
...
!
router bgp 65001
 no synchronization
 bgp router-id 172.16.0.254
 bgp cluster-id 1.1.1.1
 bgp log-neighbor-changes
 bgp dampening
 network 172.16.0.0 mask 255.255.255.128
 network 172.16.0.128 mask 255.255.255.128
 neighbor 172.16.0.253 remote-as 65001
 neighbor 172.16.0.253 soft-reconfiguration inbound
 neighbor 192.168.14.3 remote-as 65002
 neighbor 192.168.14.3 soft-reconfiguration inbound
 maximum-paths 2
!
...

scar# show running-config
...
!
router bgp 65003
 no synchronization
 bgp router-id 10.0.0.1
 bgp cluster-id 1.1.1.1
 bgp log-neighbor-changes
 bgp dampening
 network 10.0.0.0 mask 255.255.255.0
 network 10.0.1.0 mask 255.255.255.0
 neighbor 10.0.1.2 remote-as 65003
 neighbor 10.0.1.2 update-source Loopback0
 neighbor 10.0.1.2 soft-reconfiguration inbound
 neighbor 192.168.7.7 remote-as 65000
 neighbor 192.168.7.7 soft-reconfiguration inbound
```

Example 10-21 *Route Server/Route Server Client Configurations (Continued)*

```
 neighbor 192.168.14.3 remote-as 65002
 neighbor 192.168.14.3 soft-reconfiguration inbound
 maximum-paths 2
!
...

callisto-bgpd# show ip bgp
BGP table version is 0, local router ID is 192.168.1.1
Status codes: s suppressed, d damped, h history, * valid, > best, i - internal
Origin codes: i - IGP, e - EGP, ? - incomplete

   Network          Next Hop          Metric LocPrf Weight Path
*> 10.0.0.0/24      192.168.14.254        0             0 65003 i
* i                 192.168.7.254         0     100     0 65003 i
*> 10.0.1.0/24      192.168.14.254        0             0 65003 i
* i                 192.168.7.254         0     100     0 65003 i
*> 172.16.0.0/25    192.168.14.2          0             0 65001 i
*> 172.16.0.128/25  192.168.14.2          0             0 65001 i
*>i192.168.1.0      192.168.2.254        20     100     0 ?
*> 192.168.2.0      192.168.1.254        20         32768 ?
* i192.168.44.0     192.168.2.254        20     100     0 ?
*>                  192.168.1.254        20         32768 ?
*>i192.168.45.0     192.168.2.254        20     100     0 ?
*> 192.168.80.0     192.168.1.254        20         32768 ?
*> 192.168.99.1/32  0.0.0.0              10         32768 ?
*>i192.168.99.2/32  192.168.2.7          10     100     0 ?
* i211.11.117.0     192.168.2.254        20     100     0 ?
*>                  192.168.1.254        20         32768 ?

Total number of prefixes 12

europa-bgpd# show ip bgp
BGP table version is 0, local router ID is 192.168.14.3
Status codes: s suppressed, d damped, h history, * valid, > best, i - internal
Origin codes: i - IGP, e - EGP, ? - incomplete

   Network          Next Hop          Metric LocPrf Weight Path
*> 10.0.0.0/24      192.168.14.254        0             0 65003 i
*                   192.168.14.1                        0 65000 65003 i
*> 10.0.1.0/24      192.168.14.254        0             0 65003 i
*                   192.168.14.1                        0 65000 65003 i
*> 172.16.0.0/25    192.168.14.2          0             0 65001 i
*> 172.16.0.128/25  192.168.14.2          0             0 65001 i
*  192.168.1.0      192.168.14.254                      0 65003 65000 ?
*>                  192.168.14.1                        0 65000 ?
*  192.168.2.0      192.168.14.254                      0 65003 65000 ?
*>                  192.168.14.1         20             0 65000 ?
*  192.168.44.0     192.168.14.254                      0 65003 65000 ?
*>                  192.168.14.1         20             0 65000 ?
```

continues

Example 10-21 *Route Server/Route Server Client Configurations (Continued)*

```
*   192.168.45.0      192.168.14.254                  0 65003 65000 ?
*>                    192.168.14.1                    0 65000 ?
*   192.168.80.0      192.168.14.254                  0 65003 65000 ?
*>                    192.168.14.1           20       0 65000 ?
*   192.168.99.1/32   192.168.14.254                  0 65003 65000 ?
*>                    192.168.14.1           10       0 65000 ?
*   192.168.99.2/32   192.168.14.254                  0 65003 65000 ?
*>                    192.168.14.1                    0 65000 ?
*   211.11.117.0      192.168.14.254                  0 65003 65000 ?
*>                    192.168.14.1           20       0 65000 ?

Total number of prefixes 12

europa-bgpd# show ip bgp summary
BGP router identifier 192.168.14.3, local AS number 65002
6 BGP AS-PATH entries
0 BGP community entries
Dampening enabled.

Neighbor          V    AS MsgRcvd MsgSent   TblVer  InQ OutQ Up/Down   State/PfxRcd
192.168.14.1      4 65000      74      66        0    0    0 00:00:38         8
192.168.14.2      4 65001      45      53        0    0    0 00:00:37         2
192.168.14.254    4 65003      49      47        0    0    0 00:00:35         5

Total number of neighbors 3
```

The Route Server Next Generation Project (RSng)

The Route Server Next Generation software (RSd, Route Server Daemon, http://www.isi.edu/ra/RSd/) was developed by the University of Southern California Information Sciences Institute (ISI) as their contribution to the Routing Arbiter Project, and later to RSng carried out together with Merit Network Inc. Merit Network provides the Routing Arbiter Database (RADB) as part of a distributed set of databases that form the IRR.

NOTE   The community still uses both expressions, Routing Arbiter Database and Routing Asset Database, when talking about the RADB.

IRRd is the routing database engine for RSng. Since the decommissioning of the NFSNET, these route servers have provided routing services to noncommercial NAPs (IXPs). The RSng service is by Merit Network Inc.

The RSd was derived from Merit GateD and designed to support BGP and provide SNMP support via the ISODE SMUX interface. The newest release of RSd does not install routes to the kernel forwarding tables per default. The configuration in Example 10-22 tries to mimic the Zebra route server setup in the previous example.

Example 10-22 *RSd Configuration for Europa*

```
autonomoussystem 65002;
routerid 192.168.14.3;

bgp yes {

        # We do not want the RS to prepend its ASN in AS paths
        # advertised to AS 65000, so we include the "transparent" clause.

        group type external peeras 65000 {
                peer 192.168.14.1 holdtime 180 transparent;
        };

        # We do not want the RS to prepend its ASN in AS paths
        # advertised to AS 65001 and heard from AS 65000, so we include
        # the "transparent 192.168.14.1" clause.

        group type external peeras 65001 {
                peer 192.168.14.2 holdtime 180 transparent 192.168.14.1;
        };
        group type external peeras 65003 {
                peer 192.168.14.254 holdtime 180;
        };
};

dampen-flap {};

#    Following this, you would configure the views for different
#    clients and the local view. The view descriptions are not
#    required to be in any particular order. However, the import
#    statements within a view are sensitive to order of specification:
#    Routes are matched against import statements in the order specified.

# Note that we do not specify a view for AS 65000. This means
# that no routes are ever propagated by the RS to AS 65000.

# View for client AS 65001. # In this view, we install any route that matches
# the "import" statement shown.

view {

        # This client has asked that the RS dampen route flaps on its behalf.

        peer 192.168.14.2 preference 60 dampen;

        # Import all routes heard from AS 65003 into this view.
        #
```

continues

Example 10-22 *RSd Configuration for Europa (Continued)*

```
            import proto bgp as 65003 {
                    all;
            };
    };

    # View for client AS 65003.

    view {

            # Never include any route advertised by AS 65003 in this view.

            peer 192.168.14.254 preference 180;

            import proto bgp as 65003 {
                    all restrict;
            };

            # Include those non-AS65003 routes that contain AS 32000
            # in their AS path in this view.

            import proto bgp as 65000 {
                    all;
            };
    };
```

Internet Routing Registries

The IRR is a collection of Internet routing policy databases that exchange or mirror routing information. These databases run Merit Network's IRRd as a database server and are populated with objects via the Routing Policy Specification Language (RPSL, RFC 2622), an evolution of the original RIPE design (RFC 1786/RIPE 181). Right now the first testbeds (for example, RIPE) for RPLSng (next generation) are emerging. RPSLng addresses the need for including routing policies for IPv6 and multicast address families and is currently based on two draft documents:

- draft-damas-rpslng-00.txt
- draft-blunk-rpslng-00.txt

The most prominent and oldest of these IRR databases is the Merit RADB. RADB mirrors the data of more than 30 other IRR object repositories. RADB objects are managed via e-mail or web form updates that support three types of authentication:

- Pretty Good Privacy/GNU Privacy Guard (PGP/GPG) keys
- Crypto-passwords
- Mail-From (mail header check)

IRRd originally was designed for the Routing Arbiter Project. It offers a Telnet Cisco-like command-line interface (CLI) and can be used as an integral part of the distributed IRR or as an independent local database server. IRRd can digest both RIPE 181 and RPSL routing registry syntax and perform conversion between these two representations.

A set of tools was designed to interface with IRRd and to provide policy analysis: the IRRToolSet, which is based on the RAToolSet (Routing Arbiter Toolset) developed by the USC Information Sciences Institute. The content of these databases can be used to create automated configurations and filter and access lists for route servers or peering routers (see Figure 10-12). Almost all Network Information Centers (NICs) offer sophisticated web interfaces as an alternative to traditional e-mail updates.

Figure 10-12 *Schematic of the IRR*

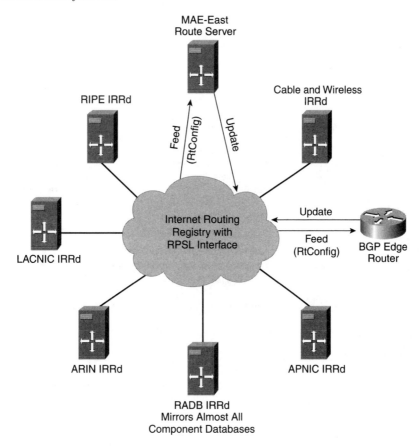

The Whois/Rwhois Interface

The whois protocol is used widely to query IRR databases and other Internet whois/nicname servers (see Example 10-23). Several tools exist that provide basic or enhanced whois client functionality:

- Traditional whois (RFC 954, "NICNAME/WHOIS"; comes with almost any system)

- Enhanced whois (http://www.linux.it/~md/software/)

- rwhois (supports the "referral" whois RFC 2167 v1.5 protocol, http://www.rwhois.net)

- GNU jwhois (http://www.gnu.org/software/jwhois/)

Example 10-23 *Querying the IRR via the Whois Interface*

```
[root@callisto:~#] whois -h whois.ripe.net help
% This is the RIPE Whois server.
% The objects are in RPSL format.
%
% Rights restricted by copyright.
% See http://www.ripe.net/ripencc/pub-services/db/copyright.html

% -l <ip-lookup>    Returns first level less specific inetnum,
%                   inet6num or route objects, excluding exact matches.
% -L <ip-lookup>    Returns all level less specific inetnum,
%                   inet6num or route objects, including exact matches.
% -m <ip-lookup>    Returns first level more specific inetnum,
%                   inet6num or route objects, excluding exact matches.
% -M <ip-lookup>    Returns all level more specific inetnum,
%                   inet6num or route objects, excluding exact matches.
% -x <ip-lookup>    Requests that only an exact match on a prefix be
%                   performed. If no exact match is found, no objects are
%                   returned.
% -c <ip-lookup>    Requests first level less specific inetnum or inet6num
%                   objects with the "mnt-irt:" attribute.
% -d <ip-lookup>    Enables use of the -m, -M, -l, and -L flags for lookups on
%                   reverse delegation domains.
%
% -i <attribute-name> <inverse-key> Perform an inverse query.
%
% -F                Produce output using short hand notation for attribute
%                   names.
% -K                Requests that only the primary keys of an object be
%                   returned. The exceptions are set objects, where the
%                   members attributes will also be returned. This flag does
%                   not apply to person and role objects.
% -k (optional normal query) Requests a persistent connection. After
%                   returning the result, the connection will not be closed by
%                   the server, and a client may issue multiple queries on the
%                   same connection.
%                   Note that server implements 'stop-and-wait' protocol,
```

Example 10-23 *Querying the IRR via the Whois Interface (Continued)*

```
%                       when no next query can be sent before receiving a reply
%                       for the previous one. Use RIPE whois3 client to be able
%                       to send queries in batch mode.
%                       Except the first -k query, -k without an argument closes
%                       the persistent connection.
% -g (mirroring request) Request a NRTM stream from the server.
%                       See [REF], section 4. "Mirroring the RIPE Database" for
%                       more information."
%
% -R                    Switches off use referral mechanism for domain lookups,
%                       so that the database returns an object in the RIPE
%                       database with the exact match with the lookup argument,
%                       rather than doing a referral lookup.
% -r                    Switches off recursion for contact information after
%                       retrieving the objects that match the lookup key.
% -T (comma separated list of object types, no white space is allowed)
%                       Restricts the types of objects to look up in the query.
% -a                    Specifies that the server should perform look ups in all
%                       available sources. See also -q sources" query.
% -s (comma separated list of sources, no white space is allowed) Specifies
%                       which sources and in which order are to be looked up when
%                       performing a query.
%
% -q sources            Returns the current set of sources along with the
%                       information required for mirroring. See [REF], section
%                       2.9 "Other Server Features" for more information.
% -q version            Displays the current version of the server.
% -t <object-type>      Requests a template for the specified object type.
% -V<client-tag>        Sends information about the client to the server.
% -v <object-type>      Requests a verbose template for the specified object
%                       type.
%
% [REF] RIPE Database Reference Manual.
%        http://www.ripe.net/ripe/docs/databaseref-manual.html

[root@callisto:~#] whois -h whois.radb.net 193.154.180.0
route:          193.154.0.0/16
descr:          Provider Local Registry Block
descr:          EUnet EDV und Internet Dienstleistungs AG
descr:          former KPNQwest Austria GmbH
descr:          former EUnet EDV-Dienstleistungs GmbH
origin:         AS1901
remarks:        ----------------------------------------
remarks:        Please report abuse incidents like spam
remarks:        origination, network scanning etc to
remarks:        Abuse@EUnet-AG.at or +43 1 899 33 222
remarks:        ----------------------------------------
mnt-by:         AS1901-MNT
changed:        chytil@Austria.EU.net 19960401
```

continues

Example 10-23 *Querying the IRR via the Whois Interface (Continued)*

```
changed:        Waldner@KPNQwest.at 20001204
changed:        Rene.Avi@EUnet-AG.at 20030307
changed:        Rene.Avi@EUnet-AG.at 20030606
changed:        Rene.Avi@EUnet-AG.at 20031020
source:         RIPE

[root@callisto:~#] whois -h whois.radb.net AS1233
[whois.radb.net]
aut-num:        AS1233
as-name:        ERX-NASDA-ASN
descr:          National Space Development Agency
descr:          Shiba-Ryoshin Building
descr:          2-5-6, Shiba, Minato-ku
descr:          Tokyo 105
country:        JP
admin-c:        JO71-AP
tech-c:         JO71-AP
remarks:        This aut-num object created as part of the ER-Transfer from ARIN
mnt-by:         MAINT-JP-NASDA
changed:        hostmaster@apnic.net 20020803
source:         APNIC

[root@callisto:~#] whois -h whois.radb.net AS1901-MNT
mntner:         AS1901-MNT
descr:          EUnet EDV Dienstleistungs AG
descr:          formerly KPNQwest Austria GmbH
descr:          formerly EUnet EDV DienstleistungsgmbH
admin-c:        OL122
tech-c:         MD13304-RIPE
tech-c:         RA773-RIPE
tech-c:         TF5295-RIPE
tech-c:         AST2
tech-c:         JH15046-RIPE
tech-c:         MM28666-RIPE
tech-c:         DK5882-RIPE
upd-to:         hostmaster@eunet-ag.at
mnt-nfy:        hostmaster@eunet-ag.at
auth:           CRYPT-PW bocEHQ0niH52I
notify:         hostmaster@eunet-ag.at
mnt-by:         AS1901-MNT
referral-by:    RIPE-DBM-MNT
changed:        Hostmaster@Austria.EU.net 19981104
changed:        Waldner@KPNQwest.at 20010103
changed:        Hostmaster@KPNQwest.at 20010510
changed:        Rene.Avi@KPNQwest.com 20010607
changed:        M.Mohler@KPNQwest.at 20010824
changed:        Hostmaster@KPNQwest.at 20011106
changed:        a.staunig@eunet-ag.at 20020808
source:         RIPE
```

Example 10-23 *Querying the IRR via the Whois Interface (Continued)*

```
[root@callisto:~#] whois -h whois.radb.net AS1901
aut-num:      AS1901
as-name:      EUNETAT-AS
descr:        EUnet Austria
descr:        former KPNQwest Austria
descr:        former EUnet Austria
remarks:      ----------------------------------------------------------
remarks:      Upstreams
remarks:      ----------------------------------------------------------
import:       from AS1273
              action pref=80;
              accept ANY
export:       to AS1273
              announce AS-EUNETAT
import:       from AS6461
              action pref=100;
              accept ANY
export:       to AS6461
              announce AS-EUNETAT
import:       from AS3561
              action pref=100;
              accept ANY
export:       to AS3561
              announce AS-EUNETAT
import:       from AS3257
              action pref=100;
              accept ANY
export:       to AS3257
              announce AS-EUNETAT
remarks:      ----------------------------------------------------------
remarks:      Customers
remarks:      ----------------------------------------------------------
import:       from AS5424
              action pref=200;
              accept AS-VBSAT
....
export:       to AS21478
              announce AS-EUNETAT
import:       from AS28685
              action pref=100;
              accept AS-ROUTIT
export:       to AS28685
              announce AS-EUNETAT
import:       from AS28788
              action pref=100;
              accept AS-UNILOGICNET
export:       to AS-UNILOGICNET
              announce AS-EUNETAT
```

continues

Example 10-23 *Querying the IRR via the Whois Interface (Continued)*

```
import:         from AS28836
                action pref=100;
                accept AS-ICSNL
export:         to AS28836
                announce AS-EUNETAT
import:         from AS28841
                action pref=100;
                accept AS-MEGABIT
export:         to AS28841
                announce AS-EUNETAT
import:         from AS29081
                action pref=100;
                accept AS-WVNET
export:         to AS29081
                announce AS-EUNETAT
remarks:        ---------------------------------------------------------
admin-c:        RA773-RIPE
tech-c:         IPEA1-RIPE
remarks:        ---------------------------------------------------------
remarks:        Communities for traffic engineering
remarks:        ---------------------------------------------------------
remarks:        1901:11 Prepend (1x) to VIX
remarks:        1901:12 Prepend (2x) to VIX
remarks:        1901:13 Prepend (3x) to VIX
remarks:        1901:15 Do not announce to VIX
remarks:        1901:16 Prepend (1x) to AMS-IX
remarks:        1901:17 Prepend (2x) to AMS-IX
remarks:        1901:18 Prepend (3x) to AMS-IX
remarks:        1901:20 Do not announce to AMS-IX
remarks:        1901:21 Prepend (1x) to DE-CIX
remarks:        1901:22 Prepend (2x) to DE-CIX
remarks:        1901:23 Prepend (3x) to DE-CIX
remarks:        1901:25 Do not announce to DE-CIX
remarks:        1901:26 Prepend (1x) to LINX
remarks:        1901:27 Prepend (2x) to LINX
remarks:        1901:28 Prepend (3x) to LINX
remarks:        1901:30 Do not announce to LINX
remarks:        1901:81 Prepend (1x) to TINET-AS3257
remarks:        1901:82 Prepend (2x) to TINET-AS3257
remarks:        1901:83 Prepend (3x) to TINET-AS3257
remarks:        1901:85 Do not announce to TINET-AS3257
remarks:        1901:86 Prepend (1x) to C&W-AS1273
remarks:        1901:87 Prepend (2x) to C&W-AS1273
remarks:        1901:88 Prepend (3x) to C&W-AS1273
remarks:        1901:90 Do not announce to C&W-AS1273
remarks:        1901:91 Prepend (1x) to C&W-AS3561
remarks:        1901:92 Prepend (2x) to C&W-AS3561
remarks:        1901:93 Prepend (3x) to C&W-AS3561
remarks:        1901:95 Do not announce to C&W-AS3561
```

Example 10-23 *Querying the IRR via the Whois Interface (Continued)*

```
remarks:        1901:96 Prepend (1x) to Abovenet-MFNX-AS6461
remarks:        1901:97 Prepend (2x) to Abovenet-MFNX-AS6461
remarks:        1901:98 Prepend (3x) to Abovenet-MFNX-AS6461
remarks:        1901:100 Do not announce to Abovenet-MFNX-AS6461
remarks:        ------------------------------------------------------
remarks:        Communities for traffic origination
remarks:        ------------------------------------------------------
remarks:        1901:1 AS1901 originating routes
remarks:        1901:2 AS1901 customers as in AS-EUNETAT
remarks:        1901:3 AS1901 peers
remarks:        1901:9 AS1901 upstreams
remarks:        1901:996 received at LINX
remarks:        1901:997 received at AMS-IX
remarks:        1901:998 received at DE-CIX
remarks:        1901:999 received at VIX
remarks:        1901:3xxxx origin city w/ xxxx being the postal address
remarks:        ------------------------------------------------------
remarks:        send peering requests to peering@eunet-ag.at
remarks:        ------------------------------------------------------
notify:         Hostmaster@eunet-ag.at
mnt-by:         AS1901-MNT
changed:        Alexander.Staunig@eunet-ag.at 20021029
changed:        Rene.Avi@EUnet-AG.at 20030224
changed:        Rene.Avi@EUnet-AG.at 20030311
changed:        Rene.Avi@EUnet-AG.at 20030317
changed:        Rene.Avi@EUnet-AG.at 20030327
changed:        Rene.Avi@EUnet-AG.at 20030402
changed:        Rene.Avi@EUnet-AG.at 20030409
changed:        Rene.Avi@EUnet-AG.at 20030414
changed:        Rene.Avi@EUnet-AG.at 20030519
changed:        Alexander.Staunig@eunet-ag.at 20030523
changed:        Rene.Avi@EUnet-AG.at 20030523
changed:        Rene.Avi@EUnet-AG.at 20030526
changed:        Rene.Avi@EUnet-AG.at 20030526
changed:        Rene.Avi@EUnet-AG.at 20030527
changed:        Rene.Avi@EUnet-AG.at 20030527
changed:        Rene.Avi@EUnet-AG.at 20030528
changed:        Alexander.Staunig@eunet-ag.at 20030528
changed:        Alexander.Staunig@eunet-ag.at 20030603
changed:        Alexander.Staunig@eunet-ag.at 20030623
changed:        Alexander.Staunig@eunet-ag.at 20030626
changed:        Rene.Avi@EUnet-AG.at 20030710
changed:        Rene.Avi@EUnet-AG.at 20030710
changed:        Rene.Avi@EUnet-AG.at 20030721
changed:        Rene.Avi@EUnet-AG.at 20030818
changed:        Alexander.Staunig@eunet-ag.at 20030822
changed:        martin.dirnhofer@eunet-ag.at 20030822
changed:        martin.dirnhofer@eunet-ag.at 20040105
changed:        martin.dirnhofer@eunet-ag.at 20040326
source:         RIPE
```

Figures 10-13 and 10-14 provide examples for the modern RADB and RIPE web interfaces to IRR management. In addition, the traditional e-mail-based submission system can be used.

Figure 10-13 *RADB Web Interface*

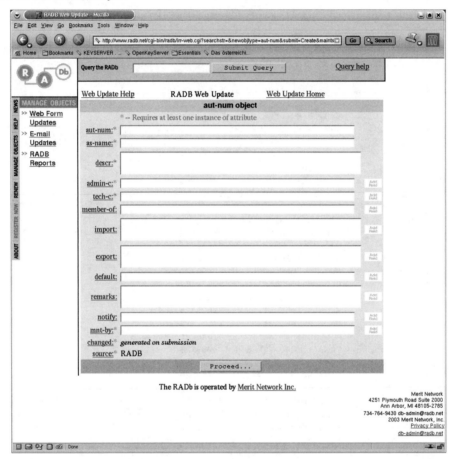

Figure 10-14 *RIPE Web Interface*

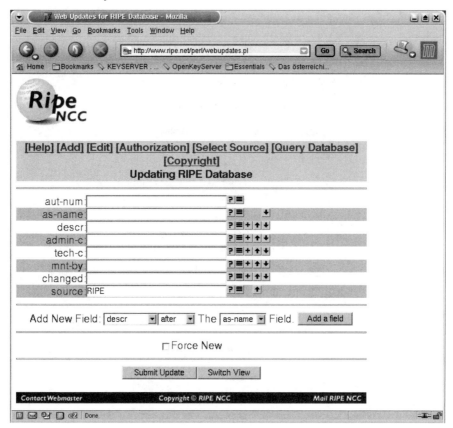

IRRd

IRRd is set up easily. For compilation and installation details, consult http://www.irr.net. The parameters of the irrd daemon itself and the important tools irrdcacher and irr_rpsl_submit are demonstrated in Example 10-24. irrdcacher is used to retrieve a copy of a IRR database. After successful retrieval, the database is kept current via a mirroring mechanism. The tool can convert between RIPE 181 and RPSL format. irr_rpsl_submit can submit RPSL-style data to IRRd servers.

Example 10-24 irrd.conf *and* irrdcacher *Retrieval with RPSL Conversion*

```
[root@callisto:~#] irrd -?
irrd: invalid option -- ?
Usage: irrd
   [-a turn on atomic transaction mode]
   [-d <irr_directory>]
   [-f <irrd.conf file>]
```

continues

Example 10-24 irrd.conf *and* irrdcacher *Retrieval with RPSL Conversion (Continued)*

```
        [-g <groupname>]
        [-l <username>]
        [-n do not daemonize]
        [-s <password>]
        [-u don't allow privileged commands]
        [-v verbose mode]
        [-w <irr_port>]
        [-x cancel bootstrap missing DB auto-fetch]

IRRd 2.1.5 [17Oct2002] compiled on May  3 2003

[root@callisto:~#] irrdcacher -?
Unknown option: ?
irrdcacher: unknown command-line option or missing flag parm!
usage: /usr/local/sbin/irrdcacher [options] files...

options: -p irrd port (default 43)
         -s ftp server and remote directory URL
            (default 'ftp://ftp.radb.net/routing.arbiter/radb/dbase')
         -w add component to your default search path
         -f full path name of the irrd.conf file (default /etc/irrd.conf)
         -S suppress the cache refresh signal to irrd
         -C do RPSL conversion

example: /usr/local/sbin/irrdcacher -p 5555 radb mci RADB.CURRENTSERIAL

special note: If you are running via cron be sure to use the '-w' flag

[root@callisto:~#] irr_rpsl_submit -?
irr_rpsl_submit: invalid option -- ?
Usage: irr_rpsl_submit [options] [filename]
  -v verbose logging, turn on debugging
  -c <crypted password> (default 'foo')
  -E DB admin address for new maintainer requests
  -f <IRRd config file location> (default '/etc/irrd.conf')
  -h <IRRd host> (default 'localhost')
  -l <log directory> (default 'irrd_directory')
  -p <IRRd port> (default 43)
  -r <pgp directory>  (default is ~/.pgp)
  -s <DB source> source is authoritative
  The file is chosen by irr_submit
  -R RPS Dist mode
  -D Inetd mode, read/write to STDIN/STDOUT
  -x do not send notifications
  The '-x' flag will cause updates to be sent to IRRd only.
  The default is to send all notifications.

  Command line options will override irrd.conf options.
  -F " enclosed response footer string.
  -O " enclosed host/IP web origin string.

irr_submit compiled on May  3 2003
```

The daemon from Example 10-24 uses the default configuration file /etc/irrd.conf, as shown in Example 10-25.

Example 10-25 irrd.conf *and* irrdcacher *Retrieval with RPSL Conversion*

```
[root@callisto:~#] cat /etc/irrd.conf
######################################################################
# MRTd -- MRT version 2.1.5 [17Oct2002]
######################################################################
#
debug all /var/log/irrd.log 0
irr_directory /var/spool/irr_database
#irr_mirror_interval 1800
#irr_database radb mirror whois.radb.net 43
irr_database radb mirror_host 198.108.0.18 43
irr_database radb clean 172800
line vty
  login
  password cisco
!
tmp directory /var/tmp
db_admin gernot.schmied@iktech.net
irr_mirror_interval 1800
irr_database iktech authoritative
irr_database iktech clean 172800
irr_server localhost
irr_max_connections 10
debug submission file-name /var/log/irr-submission.log
override_cryptpw rTTLizvPtcv8Q

[root@callisto:~#] irrdcacher -C radb RADB.CURRENTSERIAL
Successful operation

callisto IRRd# show database
Listening on port 43 (fd=13)
Memory-only indexing
RPSL Syntax

Default Database Query Order: radb iktech

  Database       Size (kb)    Rt Obj    AutNum Obj    Serial #    Last Export #
  -----------    ---------    ------    ----------    --------    -------------
  iktech              1.2         0             5           0
  radb            22686.9     68378          2480      183568
  TOTAL           22688.0     68378          2485

iktech  AUTHORITATIVE
    Last email/tcp update Never
    Last loaded 00:13:33 05/17/2003
    Next dbclean in 37:19:01
radb
    Mirroring 198.108.0.18:43 (Next in 131 seconds)
    Last mirrored 00:33:23 05/17/2003
    52 bytes, 0 change(s)
    Next dbclean in 60:02:02
```

continues

Example 10-25 irrd.conf *and* irrdcacher *Retrieval with RPSL Conversion (Continued)*

```
callisto IRRd# show mirror-status radb
radb (Mirror)

Local Information:
  Oldest journal serial number: 181769
  Current serial number: 183568

Remote Information:
  Mirror host: 198.108.0.18:43
  Mirrorable.
  Oldest journal serial number: 177225.
  Current serial number: 183568.
  Last exported at serial number: 155408.

[root@callisto:~#] ls -al /var/spool/irr_database/
total 27752
drwxr-xr-x    2 root      root         4096 May 17 00:33 ./
drwxr-xr-x   24 root      root         4096 May 11 18:34 ../
-rw-------    1 root      root         5062 May 17 00:02 ack.log
-rw-------    1 root      root            0 May 16 23:38 ack.log.LOCK
-rw-r--r--    1 root      root         1175 May 17 00:13 iktech.db
-rw-r--r--    1 root      root            0 May 17 00:12 iktech.db~
-rw-r--r--    1 root      root            0 May 17 00:13 iktech.JOURNAL
-rw-r--r--    1 root      root           29 May 17 00:33 IRRD_STATUS
-rw-rw-rw-    1 root      root            6 May 17 00:33 RADB.CURRENTSERIAL
-rw-rw-rw-    1 root      root     25187193 May 17 00:33 radb.db
-rw-r--r--    1 root      root      3155326 May 17 00:33 radb.JOURNAL
-rw-r--r--    1 root      root           52 May 17 00:53 .radb.mirror
-rw-------    1 root      root         2131 May 17 00:02 trans.log
-rw-------    1 root      root            0 May 16 23:16 trans.log.LOCK
```

Use irrdcacher to fetch an initial copy of the IRR databases. This might take a couple of minutes; don't interrupt the download. The RPSL version of the RADB is 23 MB long. From now on, mirroring updates the local database. After establishing a local authoritative server and database, you can query the local server via whois clients (see Example 10-26).

Example 10-26 *Local IRRd Whois Query*

```
[root@callisto:~#] whois -h whois.radb.net 193.154.180.0
route:      193.154.0.0/16
descr:      Provider Local Registry Block
descr:      EUnet EDV und Internet Dienstleistungs AG
descr:      former KPNQwest Austria GmbH
descr:      former EUnet EDV-Dienstleistungs GmbH
origin:     AS1901
remarks:    ----------------------------------------
remarks:    Please report abuse incidents like spam
remarks:    origination, network scanning etc to
remarks:    Abuse@EUnet-AG.at or +43 1 899 33 222
remarks:    ----------------------------------------
mnt-by:     AS1901-MNT
```

Example 10-26 *Local IRRd Whois Query (Continued)*

```
changed:        chytil@Austria.EU.net 19960401
changed:        Waldner@KPNQwest.at 20001204
changed:        Rene.Avi@EUnet-AG.at 20030307
changed:        Rene.Avi@EUnet-AG.at 20030606
changed:        Rene.Avi@EUnet-AG.at 20031020
source:         RIPE
```

Figure 10-15 presents an architectural suggestion for a modern provisioning system in sync with the IRR.

Figure 10-15 *Relationship Between the IRR and Provisioning Systems*

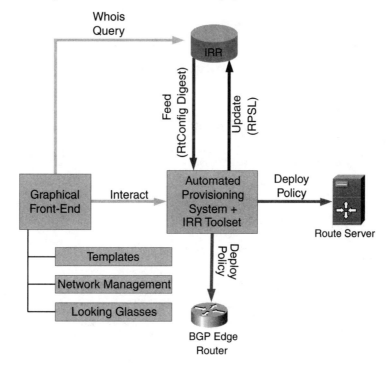

The IRRToolSet

The IRRToolSet is a collection of RPSL-aware policy-analysis tools to improve the utilization of the information stored in the IRR. This toolbox contains the following useful tools:

- roe (Route Object Editor)
- aoe (Autonomous System Object Editor)
- CIDRAdvisor (suggests safe CIDR aggregates)
- prtraceroute (extended version of traceroute; displays autonomous systems)

- Prpath (full path between two autonomous systems)
- RtConfig (generates router configuration files)
- Peval (low-level policy-evaluation tool)
- Rpslcheck (RPSL syntax check for the aut-num object)

As a prominent example of these tools, look at the RtConfig tool via the RIPE web interface at http://www.ripe.net/cgi-bin/RtConfig.cgi to produce a Cisco configuration file (see Figure 10-16). You can deploy this configuration on BGP edge routers or route servers.

Figure 10-16 *RtConfig Cisco Configuration via RIPE Web Interface and IRR Access*

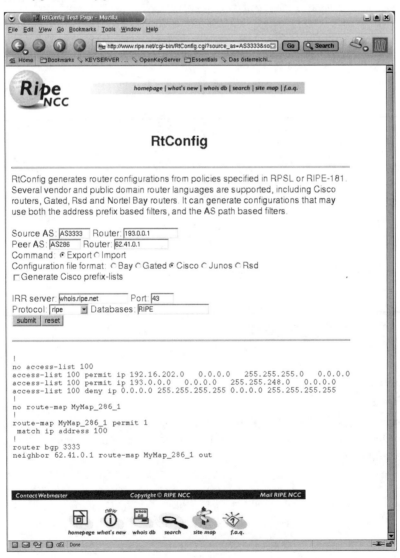

Example 10-27 demonstrates the enhanced AS_Path capabilities of the prtraceroute utility. Figures 10-17 and 10-18 offer a quick impression of the aoe and roe graphical object editor approach of the IRRToolSet.

Example 10-27 *prtraceroute Extensions to Regular Traceroute*

```
prtraceroute to whois.arin.net (192.149.252.21), 30 hops max, 12 byte packets
 1   [AS3333] ve01.homer.ripe.net (193.0.1.126)  5.718 ms  5.297 ms  3.931 ms
 2   [AS3333] e11.pampus.ripe.net (193.0.6.9)  58.872 ms  8.394 ms  6.442 ms
 3   [AS3333] fe20.marken.ripe.net (193.0.0.244)  6.897 ms  5.747 ms  5.123 ms
 4   [AS1200] GigabitEthernet0-0-0.amsix1.ams1.level3.net (193.148.15.110) 3.756 ms
62.783 ms  5.724 ms
 5   [AS9057] ge-4-3-0.mp2.Amsterdam1.Level3.net (213.244.165.2)  5.74 ms  138.052 ms
4.119 ms
 6   [AS9057] so-3-0-0.mp2.London1.Level3.net (212.187.128.57)  42.934 ms  19.489 ms
9.607 ms
 7   [AS9057] so-1-0-0.mp2.NewYork1.level3.net (212.187.128.153)  85.252 ms  124.122 ms
79.839 ms
 8   [AS3356] so-2-0-0.mp1.Washington1.level3.net (209.247.9.94)  85.334 ms
84.541 ms  96.936 ms
 9   [AS3356] pos8-0.core1.Washington1.Level3.net (209.247.10.66)  113.381 ms
125.655 ms  88.541 ms
10   [AS3356] unknown.Level3.net (209.244.219.146)  178.945 ms  155.78 ms  106.295 ms
11   [AS2548] dca6-cpe3-pos1-0.atlas.icix.net (165.117.59.214)  123.884 ms
146.101 ms  148.038 ms
12   [AS2548] 206.181.39.162 (206.181.39.162)  147.257 ms  195.018 ms  200.805 ms
13   [AS0] rs1.arin.net (192.149.252.21)  271.957 ms  135.78 ms  *

Path taken:
AS3333 AS1200 AS9057 AS3356 AS2548 (???)

   13  AS0 rs1.arin.net                          destination -> !registered
   12  AS2548 206.181.39.162                        import: 2 -> internal
   11  AS2548 dca6-cpe3-pos1-0.atlas.icix.net       internal -> !export
   10  AS3356 unknown.Level3.net                  !registered -> internal
    9  AS3356 pos8-0.core1.Washington1.Level3.net   internal -> internal
    8  AS3356 so-2-0-0.mp1.Washington1.level3.net   internal -> !registered
    7  AS9057 so-1-0-0.mp2.NewYork1.level3.net     import: 2 -> internal
    6  AS9057 so-3-0-0.mp2.London1.Level3.net       internal -> internal
    5  AS9057 ge-4-3-0.mp2.Amsterdam1.Level3.net    internal -> !export
    4  AS1200 GigabitEthernet0-0-0.amsix1.ams1.level3.net  import: 2 -> export
    3  AS3333 fe20.marken.ripe.net                 import: 2 -> internal
    2  AS3333 e11.pampus.ripe.net                   internal -> internal
    1  AS3333 ve01.homer.ripe.net                   internal -> internal
    0  AS3333 x9.ripe.net                           internal -> source
```

Figure 10-17 *aoe GUI*

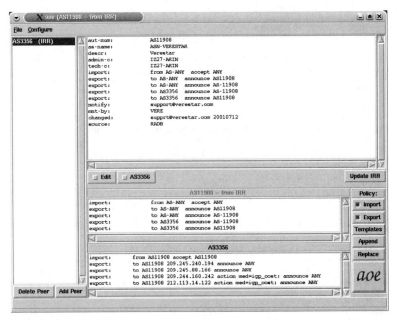

Figure 10-18 *roe GUI*

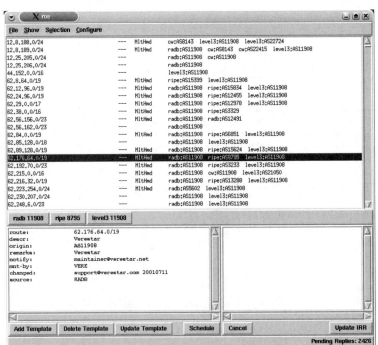

Looking Glasses

Public looking glasses are web interfaces to the world of BGP route server and peering routers at NAPs. They consist of a web front end and query router interfaces via remote shell (rsh), Telnet, secure shell (ssh), or Simple Network Management Protocol (SNMP) embedded in PHP or Perl scripts. Relevant Perl modules are as listed in http://www.cpan.org:

- Net-Telnet
- Net-Telnet-Cisco
- Cisco-Conf
- Cisco-CopyConfig
- Cisco-Reconfig

Looking-glass scripts present the output of CLI commands that are relayed to these nodes. Looking glasses historically were used for BGP queries; however, they can be used for every command a CLI provides. They are useful tools for operations and engineering departments and integrate well into web-based network management tools.

The following subsections present looking-glass setups for Cisco IOS devices and Zebra. It is strongly recommended to train operations staff on the use of looking glasses for debugging and troubleshooting BGP problems.

Cisco IOS Configuration

This configuration requires that the user wwwdata exists on the host 192.168.1.1 and restricts access to the Cisco IOS CLI via rsh to this particular host/user combination (see Example 10-28). For additional security, you could kerberize rsh access. Strong security is recommended on 192.168.1.1. For the Cisco IOS rsh configuration to work, the user wwwdata has to execute the query.

Example 10-28 *Cisco IOS rsh Configuration*

```
...
username wwwdata access-class 9 nopassword
ip rcmd rsh-enable
ip rcmd remote-host wwwdata 192.168.1.1 wwwdata
access-list 99 permit 192.168.1.1
...
```

The Looking Glass CGI Script and HTML Code

You need to place the script, Example 10-29, in an executable script directory of your web server, and place the code in Example 10-30 in the document tree. Figure 10-19 presents the web interface of this looking glass.

Example 10-29 *Looking-Glass Source Code (Based on DIGEX Script)*

```perl
#!/usr/local/bin/perl

#####################################################
#
# Looking Glass Based on DIGEX Code
#
#####################################################

## The script will now cache the results as simple files in the $cache_dir,
## named after the type of query (queries must, of course, be one word no
## spaces).  Modify $max_time_diff to set the lifetime for each cache.
## Currently, cache lifetime is the same for all queries.

###### Set these appropriately: #####################

  # for most web servers, cache_dir must be writable by uid nobody
  #
  $cache_dir = "/var/www/lglass/cache" ;
  #
  # when to display cache?  max time difference (in seconds)
  #
  $max_time_diff = "600" ;
  $max_time_diff = "60" ;

###### Should be okay from here on ##################

# grab CGI data
&cgi_receive ;
&cgi_decode ;

$ROUTER = $FORM{router};

#
# first, make sure they typed in something,
# for bgp make sure addr is specified
#

if (!$FORM{query} || ($FORM{query} eq "bgp" && !$FORM{addr}))
{ $results[0] = "A full BGP table dump would cause too much stress on the router and
this machine. <p>Please step back and input an address.\n" ; &print_results ; }
#{ $results[0] = "You did not supply all of the requested information. \n<p>Please
step back and try again.\n" ; &print_results ; }


#
# handle ip addr
#

#if (($FORM{query} eq "ping" || $FORM{query} eq "trace")
#       && ($FORM{addr} !~ /^\d+\.\d+\.\d+\.\d+$/) )
#{ $results[0] = "The IP address \"$FORM{addr}\" is not valid.\n
#<p>
#Please step back and try again.\n" ; &print_results ; }
```

Example 10-29 *Looking-Glass Source Code (Based on DIGEX Script) (Continued)*

```
if ($FORM{query} eq "bgp flap-statistics") {

  if (!$FORM{addr}) {  # cache requests with no addr

        $file = "$cache_dir/$FORM{query}" ;

        if (-e $file)
        { # see if cache exists
              @stat = stat($file);
              $ftime = $stat[9] ;
              $dtime = time - $stat[9] ;

              if ($dtime <= $max_time_diff)
              { # see if we are within cache time
                    open(CACHE,"$file") ;
                    while (<CACHE>) { $results[$#results + 1] = $_ ; }
                    close CACHE ;
                    $seconds = $dtime ;
                    &print_results ;
              }
        }

        # else, execute command

        @results = &DoRsh($ROUTER,"sh ip $FORM{query}");

        open(CACHE,">$file") || die "couldn't create file $file" ;
        foreach $n (0 .. $#results)
          {
            print CACHE $results[$n] ;
          }
        close CACHE ;
        &print_results ;
  }

  else { # if addr, execute command
        @results = &DoRsh($ROUTER,"sh ip $FORM{query} $FORM{addr}");
        &print_results ;
  }

} # end flap-statistics

elsif ($FORM{query} eq "bgp dampened-paths")  {
        @results = &DoRsh($ROUTER,"sh ip bgp dampened-paths");
        &print_results ;
}

elsif ($FORM{query} eq "trace")  {
        @results = &DoRsh($ROUTER,"trace $FORM{addr}");
        &print_results ;
}
```

continues

Example 10-29 *Looking-Glass Source Code (Based on DIGEX Script) (Continued)*

```
    elsif ($FORM{query} eq "ping")  {
            @results = &DoRsh($ROUTER,"ping $FORM{addr}");
            &print_results ;
    }

    elsif ($FORM{query} eq "environmental all")  {
            @results = &DoRsh($ROUTER,"sh enviro all");
            &print_results ;
    }

    elsif ($FORM{query} eq "environmental table")  {
            @results = &DoRsh($ROUTER,"sh enviro table");
            &print_results ;
    }

    elsif ($FORM{query} eq "proc mem")  {
            @results = &DoRsh($ROUTER,"sh proc mem");
            &print_results ;
    }

    elsif ($FORM{query} eq "proc cpu")  {
            @results = &DoRsh($ROUTER,"sh proc cpu");
            &print_results ;
    }

    elsif ($FORM{query} eq "buffers")  {
            @results = &DoRsh($ROUTER,"sh buffers");
            &print_results ;
    }

    elsif ($FORM{query} eq "version")  {
            @results = &DoRsh($ROUTER,"sh version");
            &print_results ;
    }

    elsif ($FORM{query} eq "hardware")  {
            @results = &DoRsh($ROUTER,"sh hard");
            &print_results ;
    }

    elsif ($FORM{query} eq "bgp community") {
            if ($FORM{commu})
            { @results = &DoRsh($ROUTER,"sh ip bgp community $FORM{commu}"); }
            # don't let them execute without a community identifier.
            # This should be taken care of above, but this is a double-check.
            else { $results[0] = "Please specify a community identifier." ; }
            &print_results ;
    }

    elsif ($FORM{query} eq "bgp regexpr")  {
            @results = &DoRsh($ROUTER,"sh ip bgp regexpr");
```

Example 10-29 *Looking-Glass Source Code (Based on DIGEX Script) (Continued)*

```
        &print_results ;
}

elsif ($FORM{query} eq "bgp") {
        if ($FORM{addr})
         { @results = &DoRsh($ROUTER,"sh ip bgp $FORM{addr}"); }
        # don't let them execute without a host name.
        # This should be taken care of above, but this is a double-check.
        else { $results[0] = "Please specify a host." ; }
         &print_results ;
}

elsif ($FORM{query} eq "bgp regexp") {
        if ($FORM{addr})
        { @results = &DoRsh($ROUTER,"sh ip bgp regexp $FORM{addr}"); }
        # don't let them execute without a host name or regexp.
        # This should be taken care of above, but this is a double-check.
        else { $results[0] = "Please specify a host or regexp." ; }
        &print_results ;
}

elsif ($FORM{query} eq "summary") {
        @results = &DoRsh($ROUTER,"sh ip bgp summary");
        $FORM{addr} = "" ;
         &print_results ;
}

exit ;



sub print_results {

#if ($ENV{'SERVER_NAME'}) { #i.e. if we're in CGI land

print <<END ;
Content-type: text/html

<html>
<HEAD>
<title>IKTech Looking Glass Results</title>
</HEAD>

<BODY>
<center>
<img src="http://192.168.1.1/lglass/iktech.jpg" align="center">
</center>
<center>
<h2>IKTech Looking Glass Results</h2>
</center>
```

continues

Example 10-29 *Looking-Glass Source Code (Based on DIGEX Script) (Continued)*

```
<p>
<hr size=2 width=85%>
<p>

<!--- start page content --->

<center>
<b>Query:</b> $FORM{query}
<br>
END

if ($FORM{addr}) { print "<b>Addr:</b> $FORM{addr}\n"; }
print <<END ;
<!--$cached-->
</center>
<p>

<pre>

END

if ($seconds) { print "<b>From cache (number of seconds old (max 600)):</b>
    $seconds\n" ; }

foreach $n (0 .. $#results)
 { print $results[$n] ; }

print <<END ;
</pre>

<!--- end page content --->

</body>

<p>
<hr size=2 width=85%>
<p>


</body>

<tail>
<center>
<i>
  Please e-mail questions or comments to Gernot Schmied,
 <a href=mailto:gernot.schmied\@iktech.net>gernot.schmied\@iktech.net</a>
</i>
</center>
</tail>
</html DIGEX_LAST_MODIFIED="">
END
```

Example 10-29 *Looking-Glass Source Code (Based on DIGEX Script) (Continued)*

```
#}
#else { print "$results\n"; }

#  date, host name, query, addr

$date = `/bin/date` ;
chop $date ;
open(LOG,">>$cache_dir/log") ;
($ENV{REMOTE_HOST}) && ( print LOG "$ENV{'REMOTE_HOST'} ") ;
($ENV{REMOTE_ADDR}) && ( print LOG "$ENV{'REMOTE_ADDR'} ")  ;
print LOG "- - [$date] $FORM{query} $FORM{addr}\n"  ;
close LOG ;

exit;

}  #end sub print_results


######## The rest is borrowed from NCSA WebMonitor "mail" code

sub cgi_receive {
    if ($ENV{'REQUEST_METHOD'} eq "POST") {
        read(STDIN, $incoming, $ENV{'CONTENT_LENGTH'});
    }
    else {
        $incoming = $ENV{'QUERY_STRING'};
    }
}


sub cgi_decode {
    @pairs = split(/&/, $incoming);

    foreach (@pairs) {
        ($name, $value) = split(/=/, $_);

        $name  =~ tr/+/ /;
        $value =~ tr/+/ /;
        $name  =~ s/%([A-F0-9][A-F0-9])/pack("C", hex($1))/gie;
        $value =~ s/%([A-F0-9][A-F0-9])/pack("C", hex($1))/gie;

        #### Strip out semicolons unless for special character
        $value =~ s/;/$$/g;
        $value =~ s/&(\S{1,6})$$/&\1;/g;
        $value =~ s/$$/ /g;

        $value =~ s/\|/ /g;
        $value =~ s/^!/ /g; ## Allow exclamation points in sentences

        #### Skip blank text entry fields
        next if ($value eq "");
```

continues

Example 10-29 *Looking-Glass Source Code (Based on DIGEX Script) (Continued)*

```
        #### Check for "assign-dynamic" field names
        #### Mainly for on-the-fly input names, especially check boxes
        if ($name =~ /^assign-dynamic/) {
            $name = $value;
            $value = "on";
        }

        #### Allow for multiple values of a single name
        $FORM{$name} .= ", " if ($FORM{$name});

        $FORM{$name} .= $value;
        push (@fields, $name) unless ($name eq $fields[$#fields]);
    }
}

sub DoRsh
{
        local ($router,$cmd)=@_;
        return &DoCmd("/usr/bin/rsh","$router $cmd");
}

sub DoCmd
{
        local ($program,$cmd)=@_;

        local (@cmd)=($program);
        push(@cmd,split(/\s+/,$cmd));
        local (@results);

        return @results;
}# add error processing as above
        local($sleep_count) = (0);
        local ($pid);
        do {
                $pid = open(KID_TO_READ, "-I");
                unless (defined $pid) {
                        warn "cannot fork: $!";
                        die "bailing out" if $sleep_count++ > 6;
                        sleep 10;
                }
          until defined $pid;

        if ($pid) {   # parent
                while (<KID_TO_READ>) {
                        # do something interesting
                        push(@results,$_);
                }
                close(KID_TO_READ) || warn "kid exited $?";
        } else {      # child
                ($EUID, $EGID) = ($UID, $GID); # suid only
                exec(@cmd) || die "can't exec program '$cmd[0]': $!";
                # NOTREACHED
        }
```

Example 10-30 *Looking-Glass HTML Code*

```html
<html>
<HEAD>
<title>IKTech Looking Glass</title>
</HEAD>

<BODY>

<center>
<img src="IKTech.gif" width="210" height="209">
<h2>IKTech Looking Glass</h2>
</center>

<p>
<hr size=2 width=85%>
<p>

<!--- start page content --->

<form method="POST" action="http://192.168.1.1/lglass/lg.cgi">

<b>Router </b>
<select name="router" size="1">
<option selected>ganymed</option>
<option>callisto</option>
<option>castor</option>
<option>pollux</option>
<option>europa</option>
<option>scar</option>
<option>laurel</option>
<option>hardy</option>
<option>chaplin</option>
</select>

<dl>
<dt> <b>Query</b>
   <dd>
   <input type="radio" name="query" value="bgp"> bgp
   <dd>
   <input type="radio" name="query" value="bgp community"> bgp community
   <dd>
   <input type="radio" name="query" value="summary"> bgp summary
   <dd>
   <input type="radio" name="query" value="bgp dampened-paths"> bgp dampened-paths
   <dd>
  <input type="radio" name="query" value="bgp flap-statistics"> bgp flap-statistics
   <dd>
   <input type="radio" name="query" value="bgp regexp"> bgp regexp
   <dd>
   <input type="radio" name="query" value="ping"> ping
   <dd>
   <input type="radio" name="query" value="trace"> trace
   <dd>
```

continues

Example 10-30 *Looking-Glass HTML Code (Continued)*

```
        <input type="radio" name="query" value="version"> sh version
        <dd>
        <input type="radio" name="query" value="hardware"> sh hardware
        <dd>
        <input type="radio" name="query" value="proc mem"> sh processes memory
        <dd>
        <input type="radio" name="query" value="buffers"> sh buffers
        <dd>
        <input type="radio" name="query" value="proc cpu"> sh processes cpu
        <dd>
        <input type="radio" name="query" value="environmental all"> sh environmental all
        <dd>
        <input type="radio" name="query" value="environmental table"> sh environmental
          table
        <dd>
   </dd>

   <p>
   <dt> <b>Address or regular expression </b>  <input name="addr" value="_65000$"
   size=40>
   <a href=http://www.cisco.com/en/US/products/hw/switches/ps718/
   products_command_reference_chapter09186a008009166c.html></br> CISCO Regexp
   Reference </a>
   </dl>

   <b>BGP community identifier </b>
   <select name="commu" size="1">
   <option selected>65000:090</option>
   <option>65000:100</option>
   <option>65000:110</option>
   <option>65000:120</option>
   </select>
   <a href=http://192.168.1.1/community.html> IKTech Community Overview </a>
   <p>

   <input type="submit" value="Submit">
   <input type="reset" value="Reset">

   </form>

   <!--- end page content --->

   <p>
   <hr size=2 width=85%>
   <p>


   <p>
   <center>
   <i>
     Please email questions/comments or things you would like added to
    <a href="mailto:gernot.schmied@iktech.net">gernot.schmied@iktech.net</a>
   </i>
```

Example 10-30 *Looking-Glass HTML Code (Continued)*

```
</center>
</tail>

</body>

<tail>
</html IKTech_LAST_MODIFIED="16-05-2003">
```

Figure 10-19 *Web Interface to This Script*

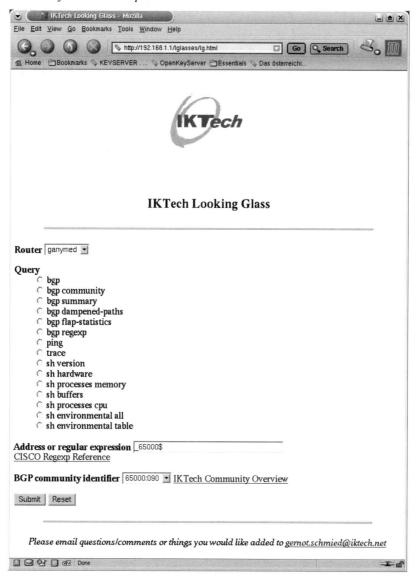

Zebra Looking Glasses

Besides the mother of all looking glasses from DIGEX, other useful approaches have evolved. The DIGEX code supports only rsh approaches. This section covers two newer-generation looking glasses: Data Telekom LG and MRLG.

Data Telecom LG (http://www.version6.net/) provides a Perl Common Gateway Interface (CGI) script capable of ssh, Telnet, and rsh access to Zebra, Cisco, and Juniper routers. It supports both IPv4 and IPv6 commands, almost all BGP-related commands, ping, traceroute, and the relaying of these queries to other looking glasses. Figure 10-20 shows a screenshot of the Data Telecom LG.

Figure 10-20 *Data Telecom Looking Glass*

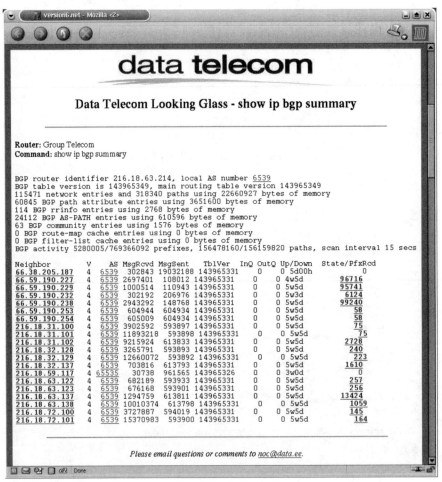

As a second example, I want to introduce Denis Ovsienko's MRLG (Multi-Router Looking Glass), which is a PHP script capable of querying Zebra and Cisco routers (see Figure 10-21). You can retrieve MRLG from http://pilot.org.ua/mrlg/.

Figure 10-21 *Web Interface to the MRLG*

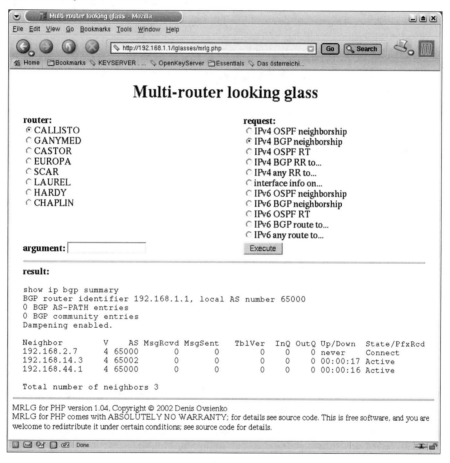

NOTE   A few words on looking-glass security: Whenever possible, at least protect your Cisco routers via the methods presented in the rsh example (unpriviledged dedicated user, kerberized rsh access, access lists). In addition, protect the UNIX workstation that the looking glass is running on (web server security, rsh user ID, ssh, firewalls).

Routing Policies

The power of BGP unfolds when filtering comes into play. Consider a BGP edge device and the ingress and egress traffic traversing it (both signaling and forwarding traffic). Naturally, AS policies are enforced at the network edge or perimeter, thus at the contact points to other autonomous systems. As a rule of thumb, transit autonomous systems tend to have more elaborate policies than stub autonomous systems. The same statement is valid for multihomed autonomous systems.

Policies and configurations that are implemented to enforce such policies act on BGP path attributes. Remember that BGP is purely a signaling protocol that relies on an underlying IGP for next-hop resolution and forwarding. Nevertheless, no signaling equals no forwarding.

An important aspect of BGP mastery is a thorough understanding of regular expressions used extensively in BGP filter configuration statements (usually route maps with **set** and **match** clauses). Regular expressions essentially are an extended view of wildcard approaches used in a broad context in information sciences.

NOTE   For an in-depth discussion of regular expressions, consult the book *Mastering Regular Expressions* (O'Reilly and Associates, 2002) mentioned in the "Recommended Reading" section of this chapter. Cisco.com also contains several documents about regular expressions, especially with regard to BGP.

Defining an AS Policy

What actually constitutes a policy for an AS? It is a set of rules that govern ingress and egress behavior at the network perimeter to neighboring BGP speakers and foreign autonomous systems. It is concerned with traffic attracted as well as traffic leaving the AS at one or several attachment points to the world. Participation at public peering points or commercial exchanges and transit scenarios extend this set of rules.

How can we learn about other people's policies? We can do this easily by consulting the RADB or other databases of the IRR, such as the major databases of the RIPE, APNIC, ARIN, AfriNIC, and LACNIC. This can be either a simple whois query or a complete mirror of the IRR distributed database. These policies often form the foundation of automatically created router and route server configurations deployed at consecutive provisioning intervals. The vehicles of choice to represent policies are route maps, as discussed in the following section.

BGP Route Maps and Filters

Zebra/Quagga BGP provides extensive capabilities to filter incoming and outgoing announcements and set certain attributes or tags via route maps (see Figure 10-22).

Figure 10-22 *BGP Filtering Context*

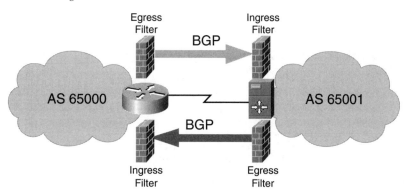

You can choose from a rich set of filter mechanisms:

- Filter lists (filter ASNs based on AS path lists)
- Prefix lists (filter prefixes)
- AS path lists
- Distribute lists
- Community lists
- Extcommunity lists
- Route maps (**set**, **match**, and **on-match goto/next** clauses)

The topic of BGP route maps and filters alone would cover hundreds of pages. The syntax is compatible with the Cisco IOS architecture, and their capabilities are too vast to be discussed in detail here. Therefore, the following introduction to route maps is not even close to exhaustive and is only a qualitative overview. For example, several (not necessarily meaningful) filters are deployed on the route server europa, whose configuration was rewritten to demonstrate views. The highlighted markers demonstrate the results of path prepending and community tagging via route maps (see Examples 10-31 and 10-32).

Example 10-31 *Demonstration of Various BGP Filters on Europa*

```
europa-bgpd# show running-config

Current configuration:
!
hostname europa-bgpd
password 8 m6eyKycFMHniQ
enable password 8 bjYlnA9YLBWyM
log file /var/log/bgpd.log
service advanced-vty
service password-encryption
!
bgp multiple-instance
!
```

continues

Example 10-31 *Demonstration of Various BGP Filters on Europa (Continued)*

```
router bgp 65002 view ROUTESERVER
 bgp router-id 192.168.14.3
 bgp dampening
 neighbor 192.168.14.1 remote-as 65000
 neighbor 192.168.14.1 soft-reconfiguration inbound
 neighbor 192.168.14.1 maximum-prefix 50 warning-only
 neighbor 192.168.14.1 route-server-client
 neighbor 192.168.14.1 prefix-list callisto-out in
 neighbor 192.168.14.1 attribute-unchanged as-path next-hop
 neighbor 192.168.14.2 remote-as 65001
 neighbor 192.168.14.2 soft-reconfiguration inbound
 neighbor 192.168.14.2 maximum-prefix 50 warning-only
 neighbor 192.168.14.2 route-server-client
 neighbor 192.168.14.2 route-map prepend in
 neighbor 192.168.14.2 route-map restrict out
 neighbor 192.168.14.2 attribute-unchanged as-path next-hop
 neighbor 192.168.14.254 remote-as 65003
 neighbor 192.168.14.254 soft-reconfiguration inbound
 neighbor 192.168.14.254 maximum-prefix 50 warning-only
 neighbor 192.168.14.254 route-server-client
 neighbor 192.168.14.254 route-map comm in
 neighbor 192.168.14.254 filter-list aspath in
 neighbor 192.168.14.254 attribute-unchanged as-path next-hop
!
access-list 1 remark vty-protection
access-list 1 permit 127.0.0.1
access-list 1 permit 192.168.1.0 0.0.0.255
access-list prepend remark path-prepend-filter
access-list prepend permit 172.16.0.0/16
access-list prepend deny any
!
ip prefix-list callisto-out seq 5 deny 211.11.117.0/24
ip prefix-list callisto-out seq 10 permit any
!
ip as-path access-list aspath deny _65000_
ip as-path access-list aspath permit _65003$
!
ip community-list 1 permit 65003:100
!
route-map prepend permit 10
 match ip address prepend
 set as-path prepend 65001 65001
!
route-map comm permit 10
 match as-path aspath
 set community 65003:100
!
route-map restrict permit 10
 match community 1
 set weight 400
!
```

Example 10-31 *Demonstration of Various BGP Filters on Europa (Continued)*

```
line vty
 access-class 1
 exec-timeout 0 0
!
end

europa-bgpd# show ip access-list
Standard IP access list 1
    permit 127.0.0.1
    permit 192.168.1.0, wildcard bits 0.0.0.255
Zebra IP access list prepend
    permit 172.16.0.0/16
    deny   any

europa-bgpd# show ip prefix-list detail
Prefix-list with the last deletion/insertion: callisto-out
ip prefix-list callisto-out:
    count: 2, range entries: 0, sequences: 5 - 10
    seq 5 deny 211.11.117.0/24 (hit count: 5, refcount: 52)
    seq 10 permit any (hit count: 47, refcount: 47)

europa-bgpd# show ip community-list
Community standard list 1
    permit 65003:100

europa-bgpd# show ip bgp 172.16.0.0/25
BGP routing table entry for 172.16.0.0/25
Paths: (1 available, best #1, table Default-IP-Routing-Table)
  Advertised to non peer-group peers:
  192.168.14.1 192.168.14.254
  65001 65001 65001, (Received from an RS-client)
    192.168.14.2 from 192.168.14.2 (172.16.0.254)
      Origin IGP, metric 0, localpref 100, valid, external, best
      Last update: Fri May 16 10:46:59 2003

europa-bgpd# show ip bgp 10.0.0.0/24
BGP routing table entry for 10.0.0.0/24
Paths: (2 available, best #2, table Default-IP-Routing-Table)
  Advertised to non peer-group peers:
  192.168.14.1 192.168.14.2
  65000 65003, (Received from a RS-client) (history entry)
    192.168.14.1 from 192.168.14.1 (192.168.1.1)
      Origin IGP, localpref 100, external
      Dampinfo: penalty 601, flapped 1 times in 00:10:51
      Last update: Fri May 16 10:47:02 2003

  65003, (Received from a RS-client)
    192.168.14.254 from 192.168.14.254 (10.0.0.1)
      Origin IGP, metric 0, localpref 100, valid, external, best
      Community: 65003:100
      Last update: Fri May 16 10:47:01 2003
```

continues

Example 10-31 *Demonstration of Various BGP Filters on Europa (Continued)*

```
europa-bgpd# show ip bgp filter-list aspath
BGP table version is 0, local router ID is 192.168.14.3
Status codes: s suppressed, d damped, h history, * valid, > best, i - internal
Origin codes: i - IGP, e - EGP, ? - incomplete

   Network          Next Hop          Metric LocPrf Weight Path
*> 10.0.0.0/24      192.168.14.254         0            0 65003 i
*> 10.0.1.0/24      192.168.14.254         0            0 65003 i

Total number of prefixes 2

europa-bgpd# show ip bgp route-map comm
BGP table version is 0, local router ID is 192.168.14.3
Status codes: s suppressed, d damped, h history, * valid, > best, i - internal
Origin codes: i - IGP, e - EGP, ? - incomplete

   Network          Next Hop          Metric LocPrf Weight Path
*> 10.0.0.0/24      192.168.14.254         0            0 65003 i
*> 10.0.1.0/24      192.168.14.254         0            0 65003 i

Total number of prefixes 2

europa-bgpd# show ip bgp community 65003:100
BGP table version is 0, local router ID is 192.168.14.3
Status codes: s suppressed, d damped, h history, * valid, > best, i - internal
Origin codes: i - IGP, e - EGP, ? - incomplete

   Network          Next Hop          Metric LocPrf Weight Path
*> 10.0.0.0/24      192.168.14.254         0            0 65003 i
*> 10.0.1.0/24      192.168.14.254         0            0 65003 i

Total number of prefixes 2

europa-bgpd# show ip bgp neighbors 192.168.14.1 advertised-routes
BGP table version is 0, local router ID is 192.168.14.3
Status codes: s suppressed, d damped, h history, * valid, > best, i - internal
Origin codes: i - IGP, e - EGP, ? - incomplete

   Network          Next Hop          Metric LocPrf Weight Path
*> 10.0.0.0/24      192.168.14.254         0            0 65003 i
*> 10.0.1.0/24      192.168.14.254         0            0 65003 i
*> 172.16.0.0/25    192.168.14.2           0            0 65001 65001 65001 i
*> 172.16.0.128/25  192.168.14.2           0            0 65001 65001 65001 i

Total number of prefixes 4

europa-bgpd# show ip bgp neighbors 192.168.14.254 received-routes
BGP table version is 0, local router ID is 192.168.14.3
Status codes: s suppressed, d damped, h history, * valid, > best, i - internal
Origin codes: i - IGP, e - EGP, ? - incomplete
```

Example 10-31 *Demonstration of Various BGP Filters on Europa (Continued)*

```
      Network          Next Hop           Metric LocPrf Weight Path
 *> 10.0.0.0/24        192.168.14.254        0              0 65003 i
 *> 10.0.1.0/24        192.168.14.254        0              0 65003 i
 *> 192.168.2.0        192.168.14.254                       0 65003 65000 ?
 *> 192.168.80.0       192.168.14.254                       0 65003 65000 ?
 *> 192.168.99.1/32    192.168.14.254                       0 65003 65000 ?
 *> 211.11.117.0       192.168.14.254                       0 65003 65000 ?

Total number of prefixes 6

europa-bgpd# show ip bgp
BGP table version is 0, local router ID is 192.168.14.3
Status codes: s suppressed, d damped, h history, * valid, > best, i - internal
Origin codes: i - IGP, e - EGP, ? - incomplete

      Network          Next Hop           Metric LocPrf Weight Path
 h 10.0.0.0/24         192.168.14.1                         0 65000 65003 i
 *>                    192.168.14.254        0              0 65003 i
 h 10.0.1.0/24         192.168.14.1                         0 65000 65003 i
 *>                    192.168.14.254        0              0 65003 i
 *> 172.16.0.0/25      192.168.14.2          0              0 65001 65001 65001 i
 *> 172.16.0.128/25    192.168.14.2          0              0 65001 65001 65001 i
 *> 192.168.1.0        192.168.14.1                         0 65000 ?
 *> 192.168.2.0        192.168.14.1         20              0 65000 ?
 *> 192.168.44.0       192.168.14.1         20              0 65000 ?
 *> 192.168.45.0       192.168.14.1                         0 65000 ?
 *> 192.168.80.0       192.168.14.1         20              0 65000 ?
 *> 192.168.99.1/32    192.168.14.1         10              0 65000 ?
 *> 192.168.99.2/32    192.168.14.1                         0 65000 ?

Total number of prefixes 11
```

Example 10-32 *Effects on Laurel (AS 65001)*

```
laurel(config)# ip bgp-community new-format

laurel# show ip bgp 10.0.0.0/24
BGP routing table entry for 10.0.0.0/24, version 82
Paths: (1 available, best #1, table Default-IP-Routing-Table)
  Not advertised to any peer
  65003, (received & used)
    192.168.14.254 from 192.168.14.3 (192.168.14.3)
      Origin IGP, metric 0, localpref 100, valid, external, best
      Community: 65003:100
```

BGP Communities and Extended Communities

You can set the community attributes (RFC 1997) via route maps. They are a flexible and popular vehicle to tag destinations, implement policy routing, and apply routing decisions such as preference, acceptance, and redistribution of destination prefixes. The BGP community attribute is used most commonly to control transit scenarios and multihoming subscribers.

Extended communities play an important role in BGP-based MPLS VPN architectures. In a way, communities are used to categorize routes on a large scale similar to traditional class of service (CoS) and MPLS forwarding equivalent class (FEC) labeling approaches. All three approaches share the concept of treating similar traffic in the same way with regard to classes of service or, in the case of communities, being subject to manipulation by the same policy.

A few well-known communities have been predefined and associated with standard behavior. Zebra provides alias names for well-known community numbers, as demonstrated in Example 10-33. For instance, *rt* stands for route target, *soo* for site of origin. Well-known communities of global significance are as follows (quoted from RFC 1997):

NO_EXPORT (0xFFFFFF01)

All routes received carrying a communities attribute containing this value *must not* be advertised outside a BGP confederation boundary (a stand-alone autonomous system that is not part of a confederation should be considered a confederation itself).

NO_ADVERTISE (0xFFFFFF02)

All routes received carrying a communities attribute containing this value *must not* be advertised to other BGP peers.

NO_EXPORT_SUBCONFED (0xFFFFFF03)

All routes received carrying a communities attribute containing this value *must not* be advertised to external BGP peers (this includes peers in other members autonomous systems inside a BGP confederation).

Sending of communities (standard/extended) has to be enabled explicitly. Communities are 4 octets long and can replace existing tags (default) or can be used additive via the **additive** keyword in route map **set** statements. By convention, uniqueness requirements, and additive treatment requirements, the first 2 octets are representing the AS, the remaining 2 AS-related values. All state-of-the-art implementations support community values formatted as 65000:450, using the colon to separate the ASN part and the 2 low-order octets. By default, all prefixes belong to the general and global Internet community.

Example 10-33 *Two Special Zebra Community List Examples*

```
callisto-bgpd(config)# ip community-list 1 deny ?
  AA:NN  Community number in aa:nn format or internet|local-AS|no-advertise|no-export
  <cr>

callisto-bgpd# show running-config
...
!
ip community-list 1 deny no-export
ip community-list 1 permit 65003:333
ip community-list 1 deny 65003:444
ip extcommunity-list 1 deny rt 65001:1234333
ip extcommunity-list 1 deny soo 1.1.1.1:222222222
...
```

Extended communities are 8 octets long (the 2 higher-order octets are used for the ASN) and were introduced with the advent of MPLS VPN technology. Zebra provides community-lists and extcommunity-lists to match and manipulate BGP (extended) communities in prefix updates. The relevant RFC draft is draft-ietf-idr-bgp-ext-communities-05.txt.

Special BGP Topics

To conclude the BGP coverage, several modern features of BGP are discussed in the remaining sections.

BGP "Pseudo" Load Balancing

As already mentioned, BGP intrinsically was not designed to carry out load balancing; it is a protocol optimized for reflecting highly granular routing policies and picks a single best path based on prefix length and shortest AS path. However, certain levels of equal ingress or egress traffic distribution can be achieved via manual measures such as weight, local preference, or MED, AS path prepending and route deaggregation of provider aggregates.

Several measures naturally have negative side effects; they are circumventing what the protocol was designed for after all. Just because the underlying IGP is capable of load balancing does not mean that BGP behaves similarly. For example, MED and community concepts especially require acceptance of your peering partners to take effect.

The real challenge of load balancing is to equalize flows over geographically distant edge nodes for both attracted and exiting traffic for at least EBGP and preferably for IBGP, too. The Cisco IOS BGP multipath load-sharing feature in combination with the **maximum-paths** command installs up to six most recently received paths in the IP routing and CEF tables. This works per packet or per flow, but only for EBGP and multiple paths to the same EBGP neighbor AS. Zebra/Quagga and GateD lack this feature. For more sophisticated BGP load-sharing approaches, Cisco IOS Software Release 12.2 has introduced several EBGP and IBGP unequal-cost features based on MPLS VPN technology.

BGP Security Considerations

As should be obvious by now, BGP represents the "blood" that keeps the organism (Internet) alive and its "organs" (the autonomous systems) connected and cooperating. Disruption or a state of nonequilibrium of this critical resource can, in the worst case, affect large regions, continents, or even the entire worldwide Internet. These effects occur regardless of the nature of the cause, which, among others, can include any of the following:

- Distributed denial-of-service (DDoS) attacks
- Human configuration error

- Aggregate decomposition
- Scripting and database errors
- Malicious update injection
- TCP session hijacking attempts
- Spoofing
- Secondary effects caused by triggering route flaps
- Blackholing
- Suboptimal routing

TCP itself and the BGP protocol provide certain mechanisms that can be used proactively to prevent or counteract these incidents, accelerate recovery, or reduce the magnitude/range of these negative effects. A common problem (human error) is the announcement of prefixes that do not belong to your administrative realm or, even worse, announcing a default route 0.0.0.0/0 to the Internet and blackholing all traffic. In addition, folks are often leaking private autonomous systems, martian networks, or bogon routes, which are often used as the source for (D) DoS attacks (resource-saturation attacks), such as SYN flooding. Martian networks are essentially RFC 1918 aggregates, and bogon routes are a superset of these—routes that never should appear in the global Internet routing table (see Example 10-34). The obvious countermeasure of choice is thorough filters. For further information, look at RFC 3330, "Special-Use IPv4 Addresses."

Example 10-34 *RADB Martian Filter-Set Entries*

```
[root@callisto:~#] whois -h whois.radb.net fltr-martian
[whois.radb.net]
filter-set: fltr-martian
filter:      {
             0.0.0.0/8^+ ,
             10.0.0.0/8^+ ,
             127.0.0.0/8^+ ,
             169.254.0.0/16^+ ,
             172.16.0.0/12^+ ,
             192.0.2.0/24^+ ,
             192.168.0.0/16^+ ,
             198.18.0.0/15^+ ,
             224.0.0.0/3^+
             }
descr:       Special use and reserved IPv4 prefixes.
remarks:     For the complete set of bogons, please see:
             fltr-unallocated - unallocated prefixes.
             fltr-bogons - fltr-unallocated + fltr-martian.
             http://www.cymru.com/Documents/bogon-list.html
admin-c:     Rob Thomas RT624
tech-c:      Rob Thomas RT624
notify:      radb@cymru.com
mnt-by:      MAINT-BOGON-FILTERS
changed:     radb@cymru.com 20021229
changed:     radb@cymru.com 20021230
```

Example 10-34 *RADB Martian Filter-Set Entries (Continued)*

```
changed:      radb@cymru.com 20021230
source:       RADB

[root@callisto:~#] whois -h whois.radb.net RS-MARTIAN
[whois.radb.net]
route-set:        rs-martian
descr:            Routes non desirables
members:          0.0.0.0/0,
                  0.0.0.0/0^32,
                  127.0.0.0/8^9-32,
                  10.0.0.0/8^+,
                  172.16.0.0/12^+,
                  192.168.0.0/16^+,
                  192.0.2.0/24^+,
                  128.0.0.0/16^+,
                  191.255.0.0/16^+,
                  192.0.0.0/24^+,
                  223.255.255.0/24^+,
                  224.0.0.0/3^+,
                  169.254.0.0/16^+
remarks:          NONE
admin-c:          YB4
tech-c:           YB4
notify:           routing@risq.qc.ca
mnt-by:           MAINT-AS376
changed:          boudreau@risq.qc.ca 20010814
source:           RISQ
```

Modern BGP implementations provide the MD5 signature option to secure the BGP TCP connection (RFC 2385) via MD5 digests. Keep in mind that enabling this feature might increase the CPU load on a BGP speaker. In addition, there exists a transparent wrapper approach for Linux (Secure BGP for Linux), which you can retrieve from http://shell.webchat.org/~jk/securebgp/. You can retrieve another Perl script facilitating netfilter QUEUE targets from http://www.pilotsoft.com/bgpmd5/bgpmd5.pl. MD5 digest capabilities are not yet included in Zebra bgpd and are completely missing from GateD-public v3.6. In addition, a kernel IPSec approach exists via the TCP_SIGNATURE, and a FAST_IPSEC configuration option exists for 4.10 FreeBSD.

There was a discussion thread going on recently on the Zebra list as to whether the proposed Internet Engineering Task Force (IETF) MD5 password option (RFC 2385) or external IP Security (IPSec) should be implemented to secure peerings.

The 3.5 release of OpenBSD includes a standalone bgpd that is not part of this discussion yet. This implementation of BGP uses OpenBSD's TCP MD5 signature capabilities for added security. For an excellent discussion of BGP exploits and countermeasures, I highly recommend http://www.cymru.com/Documents/barry2.pdf. This website also operates a bogon route server via private AS EBGP multihop peerings (a helpful gesture worth supporting).

In summary, the following approaches/countermeasures to BGP security have emerged:

- IETF TCP MD5 signature option (RFC 2385)
- The BBN Secure BGP Project (S-BGP)
- Secure Origin BGP by Cisco Systems according to draft-ng-sobgp-bgp-extensions-00.txt and draft-white-sobgp-bgp-extensions-00.txt
- Route flap damping
- MAX Prefix Filter
- Ingress/Egress filtering
- BGP over IPSec
- The BGP TTL Security Hack (draft-gill-btsh-01.txt)

Also look at draft-ietf-rpsec-routing-threats-01.txt (RPSEC), draft-murphy-bgp-vuln-02.txt, and draft-turk-bgp-dos-04.txt. I also highly recommend that you investigate and deploy Rob Thomas's Secure BGP Configuration Template available at http://www.cymru.com/Documents/secure-bgp-template.html and the bogon list at http://www.cymru.com/Documents/bogon-list.html.

Remember that a clear policy and sound community concept will save you from a lot of headache, result in more readable configurations, and help define different service classes for transit and downstream customers. Religiously maintaining these policies in RADB can save a lot of administrative work if you do as most professional providers and run your router config scripts once or twice per day. I would even say that maintaining strict and coherent routing policies is *the* key to professional and successful international/intercarrier service provisioning of any kind. And it will earn you a good reputation with registries and your fellow providers.

Multiprotocol BGP Extensions

Multiprotocol BGP is a generic term for several extensions of BGP, also referred to as BGP4+ and optionally negotiated via BGP capabilities during session setup. The framework is covered in RFC 2858, "Multiprotocol Extensions for BGP-4." It includes the ability to carry NLRI for IPv6, IPX, BGP MPLS VPNs, interdomain Multicast BGP (MBGP), and any non-IPv4 network layer protocol (in principle).

To identify individual network layer protocols, *address families* and *subaddress families* were introduced. RFC 1700, "Assigned Numbers," is quoted often in the literature. (However, it is not authoritative anymore, because its status was changed to "historic" and replaced by the IANA online database.)

Zebra provides the necessary hooks to deal with multicast, IPv6, and IPv4 NLRI. For example, when a BGP router enables interdomain Multicast BGP, it manages two separate RIBs for unicast and multicast prefixes (or for two address families, so to speak).

Table 10-3   *16-Bit Address Family Number Assignments Quoted from RFC 1700 (Historic Information)*

Number	Description
0	Reserved
1	IP (IP version 4)
2	IP6 (IP version 6)
3	NSAP
4	HDLC (8-bit multidrop)
5	BBN 1822
6	802 (includes all 802 media plus Ethernet "canonical format")
7	E.163
8	E.164 (SMDS, Frame Relay, ATM)
9	F.69 (Telex)
10	X.121 (X.25, Frame Relay)
11	IPX
12	AppleTalk
13	DECnet IV
14	Banyan Vines
65535	Reserved

Note the following quote from RFC 2858, "Multiprotocol Extensions for BGP-4":

To provide backward compatibility, as well as to simplify introduction of the multiprotocol capabilities into BGP-4, this document uses two new attributes: Multiprotocol Reachable NLRI (MP_REACH_NLRI), and Multiprotocol Unreachable NLRI (MP_UNREACH_NLRI). The first one (MP_REACH_NLRI) is used to carry the set of reachable destinations together with the next hop information to be used for forwarding to these destinations. The second one (MP_UNREACH_NLRI) is used to carry the set of unreachable destinations. Both of these attributes are optional and nontransitive. This way a BGP speaker that doesn't support the multiprotocol capabilities will just ignore the information carried in these attributes, and will not pass it to other BGP speakers.

MPLS work in progress specific to Linux can be found at http://linux-vrf.sourceforge.net, and http://mpls-linux.sourceforge.net. You can find an MPLS implementation for NetBSD with Zebra integration at http://www.ayame.org.

UNIX MPLS implementations are at an early stage and require coexistence, hooks, and interfaces with several tools for beneficial operation:

- The kernel (multiple routing tables)
- iproute2

- iptables/netfilter
- mplsadm2
- Zebra/Quagga
- RSVP-TE (http://dsmpls.atlantis.rug.ac.be)
- Diffserv (http://diffserv.sourceforge.net)

NOTE   By the way, the ethereal packet analyzer is capable of decoding MPLS LDP (Label Distribution Protocol).

Summary

This chapter provided an overview of the BGP4 path vector routing protocol that forms the glue that holds together today's Internet consisting of tens of thousands of autonomous systems and BGP nodes. BGP can appear as either IBGP or EBGP.

A detailed description of full-mesh IBGP, route reflectors, and confederation was provided. In contrast, EBGP and EBGP multihop provides signaling connectivity to neighbor autonomous systems. A significant portion of this chapter dealt with components such as route servers, looking glasses, and the IRR.

This chapter concluded the discussion of dynamic routing protocols as such. A discussion of BGP security and Multiprotocol BGP ended the chapter and thus the routing part of this book. The following chapters deal with traffic shaping, queuing, and tunnel issues.

Recommended Reading

- *BGP4—Inter-Domain Routing in the Internet, by John W. Stewart III.* (Addison-Wesley Professional, 1998).
- *BGP4 Case Studies/Tutorial*, by Sam Halabi. Cisco Systems, http://www.ittc.ku.edu/EECS/EECS_800.ira/bgp_tutorial/
- *Internet Routing Architectures, Second Edition*, by Sam Halabi. (Cisco Press, 2001).
- *Routing TCP/IP, Volume II*, by Jeff Doyle and Jennifer DeHaven Carroll. (Cisco Press, 2001).
- *Cisco BGP-4 Command & Configuration Handbook*, by William R. Parkhurst. (Cisco Press, 2001).
- *Mastering Regular Expressions, Second Edition*, by Jeffrey E. F. Friedl. (O'Reilly and Associates, 2002).
- *BGP—Building Reliable Networks with the Border Gateway Protocol*, by Iljitsch van Beijnum.

- "BGP Multipath Load Sharing for Both eBGP and iBGP in an MPLS-VPN" at Cisco.com
- "Configuring BGP" at Cisco.com
- http://www.traceroute.org
- http://joe.lindsay.net/bgp.html
- http://www.bgp4.as/
- http://www.stonesoft.com/products/StoneGate/Features_and_Benefits/Multi-Link_Technology/?from_google=5
- http://www.radware.com/content/products/lp/default.asp
- "Route Server Daemon," at http://www.isi.edu/ra/RSd/
- http://www.nanog.org
- http://www.ietf.org
- http://www.isoc.org
- http://www.caida.org
- http://www.radb.net
- http://www.rsng.net
- http://www.bgpexpert.com
- RFC 1771, "A Border Gateway Protocol 4 (BGP-4)"
- RFC 1772, "Application of the Border Gateway Protocol in the Internet"
- RFC 1966, "BGP Route Reflection: An Alternative to Full-Mesh IBGP"
- RFC 1997, "BGP Communities Attribute"
- RFC 2270, "Using a Dedicated AS for Sites Homed to a Single Provider"
- RFC 2283, "Multiprotocol Extensions for BGP-4"
- RFC 2385, "Protection of BGP Sessions via the TCP MD5 Signature Option"
- RFC 2439, "BGP Route Flap Damping"
- RFC 2545, "Use of BGP-4 Multiprotocol Extensions for IPv6 Inter-Domain Routing"
- RFC 2796, "BGP Route Reflection"
- RFC 3065, "Autonomous System Confederations for BGP"
- RFC 2858, "Multiprotocol Extensions for BGP-4"
- "Capabilities Negotiation with BGP4," IETF draft draft-ietf-idr-cap-neg-01
- "BGP Extended Communities Attribute," IETF draft-ramachandra-bgp-ext-communities-04.txt
- "BGP4+ Peering Using IPv6 Link-Local Address," draft-kato-bgp-ipv6-link-local-00.txt

## CHAPTER 11

VPN Technologies, Tunnel Interfaces, and Architectures

This chapter discusses various tunnel approaches as building blocks of virtual private networks (VPNs) and special-purpose routing architectures. Some tunnel approaches result in dedicated virtual interfaces at the UNIX level; others that usually reside outside the kernel space do not. In addition, this chapter concisely reviews today's predominant tunnel approaches for gateways and PPP sessions and discusses factors to consider when choosing the appropriate technology to accomplish specific design goals.

NOTE Although IP Security (IPSec) is discussed thoroughly, neither this chapter nor the entire book elaborates on security aspects and issues per se. Security is too vast a field and justifies an entire publication. If I receive a lot of requests, a second volume (perhaps *Integrated Cisco and UNIX Security Architectures*) might follow. In addition, please understand that Microsoft PPTP/L2TP implementation issues go beyond both the scope and focus of this book.

This chapter concludes with examples that combine the dynamic routing approaches of the previous chapters with tunnel approaches to add a powerful feature to our toolbox. A significant resource quoted quite frequently in this chapter is the Virtual Private Network Consortium (VPNC, http://www.vpnc.org). VPNC is an association of VPN product manufacturers. It is active in the area of interoperability and compliance testing with regard to VPN Standards established by the Internet Engineering Task Force (IETF, http://www.ietf.org).

The Rationale for Tunnels in Routing Environments

Some tunnels are authenticated, some are compressed, and some are even encrypted; some lack all these capabilities and primarily support signaling, transport, and connectivity. The primary goal of the IPSec framework or suite of protocols is the provisioning and setup of authenticated and encrypted tunnels. It is a complex suite because it has to deal with complex tasks.

IPSec is an extension of IPv4 and intrinsically included in IPv6. Tunnels are virtual point-to-point overlay links that consist of only two endpoints; there is nothing in between, just plain nondeterministic best-effort IP delivery. Two endpoints need to be configured. With the exception of Multiprotocol Label Switching (MPLS), tunnels form the foundation of most VPNs.

Virtual private dial-up networks (VPDNs) have different requirements to transport PPP connections securely over Digital Subscriber Line (DSL), Integrated Services Digital Network (ISDN), or Public Switched Telephone Network (PSTN) architectures. Figure 11-1 offers an overview of common tunnel scenarios.

Figure 11-1 *Tunnel Applications*

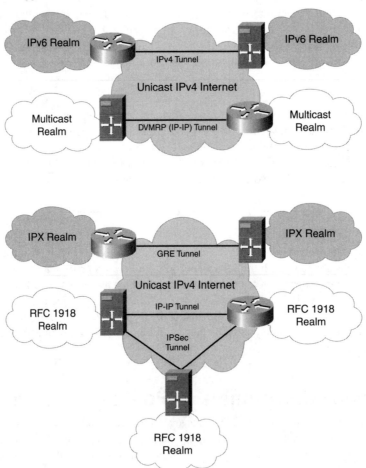

The VPNC Concept of VPNs

To grasp the concept of virtual privacy, you have to understand the character of conventional private networks. The opposite of VPNs are good, old circuit-switched *dedicated* private networks based on a number of dedicated leased lines (DLLs). VPNs commonly are deployed on a shared public infrastructure across "untrusted territory" beyond Open System Inteconnection (OSI) Layer 1 and use point-to-point or point-to-multipoint concepts such as virtual circuits, either switched or permanent, or "cloudlike" any-to-any connectivity, as with MPLS network edge architectures and MPLS Border Gateway Protocol (BGP) VPNs. Several virtual links constitute a virtual network that accomplishes privacy at arbitrary layers of the OSI stack. Although a common misperception, VPNs do not necessarily require encryption and authentication to achieve some level of privacy.

Note that a network of virtual links constitutes a VPN and that a tunnel carries out three basic tasks:[1]

1   It provides a virtual link.
2   It provides data encryption; that is, it transmits the data in a secret code.
3   It provides remote-end authentication; that is, it guarantees who is doing the sending and receiving.

The OSI Stack Perspective

In principle, the position of a tunnel or VPN technology relative to the OSI stack defines its degree of transparency, exposure to attacks, probability for compromise, and method for accomplishing secrecy or privacy (see Table 11-1).

Table 11-1   *VPN Approaches in the OSI Layer Context*

OSI Layer	Example Technology
Layer 1	Dedicated physical circuits (copper, dark/lit fiber), (D)WDM*, multiplexing (TDM)**, SDH/SONET*** circuits
Layer 2	ATM/Frame Relay/VLANs/L2TP/Layer 2 over MPLS (pseudo-wires), BGP/MPLS VPNs
Layer 3	IPSec crypto tunnel, BGP/MPLS VPNs
Layer 4	TCP/UDP user-space tunnel
> Layer 4	Application tunnels

*(D)WDM = (dense) wavelength-division multiplexing

**TDM = Time-Division Multiplexing

***SDH/SONET = Synchronous Digital Hierarchy/Synchronous Optical Network

The data transmission technology has consequences such as in wireless networks. In this particular case, anybody can eavesdrop on a conversation over wireless realms. Fiber or high-security ducts (waveguides) cannot easily be compromised without notice. Sniffing becomes more difficult when large bandwidths are involved. Beyond Layer 3, the degree of hostility considerably increases because of internationally routed and thus reachable official IP addresses and transport layer ports. Below Layer 3, physical access to ATM, Frame Relay, MPLS edge routers, or Ethernet switch access ports is necessary to constitute real threats. Essentially, attacks against telco equipment can target either a link or a network element (SDH, ATM, Frame Relay) and are rarely heard of.

It is highly recommended that you read draft-behringer-mpls-security-06.txt, "Analysis of the Security of the MPLS Architecture" (http://www.ietf.org/internet-drafts/draft-behringer-mpls-security-06.txt), to get an idea about how MPLS VPN security compares to trusted Layer 2 VPNs such as ATM or Frame Relay.

Reasons for considering or deploying tunnels include the following:

- Broadcast and multicast relay requirements
- IPv6 over IPv4 transport (connecting isolated IPv6 realms)
- Transport of private addresses (RFC 1918)
- Transport of non-IP network layer protocols (Internetwork Packet Exchange, IPX)
- Authentication requirements
- Dynamic routing protocols
- Traffic shaping
- Encryption
- Mobile IP applications
- DSL architectures
- VPN/VPDN deployments

Internet, Intranet, and Extranet Terminology

Intranet and extranet concepts are understood differently by different people—for example, product manager, analysts, sales people, and engineers—in much the same way that VPNs are understood. For purposes of this discussion, however, an intranet is a trusted realm within a corporate organization that also can be geographically disperse and tied in via a VPN architecture.

Hub-and-spoke or partial-mesh physical or virtual topologies (architectures resulting from administrative considerations) are common, with the majority of the computing power and services located at the hub site (corporate headquarters). Any-to-any connectivity is rarely used in context with tunnel-based topologies because of administrative burden, difficulty of policy enforcement, and lack of scalability. MPLS VPNs are a different story because their design is not based on point-to-point tunnel links but a "point-to-cloud" paradigm. With all these choices, network administrators and architects have flexible and scalable measures to realize routing policies within a VPN, including topological measures, default-route injection, or route filters. Withholding routing information constitutes an excellent security mechanism.

An extranet usually refers to a lower trust level commonly separated via security measures such as firewalls, demilitarized network segments, and proxies from the actual intranet (as well as the Internet).

Extranets are deployed to support the requirements for limited and controlled connectivity to commercial partners, organizations, and other third parties.

IP-IP Tunnel

Tunneling is a somewhat misleading term; there is nothing to actually "dig" through. Network tunnels consist only of two endpoints (an encapsulator and a decapsulator), gateways, a passenger, and a transport protocol. Granted, these are point-to-point links. In between, ordinary destination prefix-based routing and best-effort delivery over IP infrastructures occurs.

In the case of IP-IP tunneling (RFC 1853, RFC 2003), an IP datagram (passenger) travels encapsulated in another IP datagram (transport). The inner IP header is not changed by the encapsulator, except to decrement the Time To Live (TTL) by 1 if the tunneling is carried out as part of forwarding the datagram. The decapsulator does not alter the TTL value, though. An encapsulator must not encapsulate an inner datagram with TTL=0; and vice versa, if after decapsulation the inner TTL equals 0, the decapsulator must discard the datagram.

There is no tunnel management besides the usual Internet Control Message Protocol (ICMP) mechanisms. Obvious applications are policy routing, multicasting and tunneling of RFC 1918 address space, connecting discontinuous subnetworks, providing multiprotocol transport, and overcoming hop-count limits of certain protocols. However, IP-IP tunnels don't work from behind Network Address Translation (NAT) gateways. RFC 2003 does not specify an authentication mechanism; however, header authentication could be used in between the original inner and transport outer header.

IP-IP tunneling is supported by Linux and all BSD operating systems. They are not necessarily compatible with the Cisco IP-IP tunnel implementation. Cisco has introduced an authentication option. Take a look at the article "Configuring Logical Interfaces" (http://www.cisco.com/en/US/products/sw/iosswrel/ps1835/products_configuration_guide_chapter09186a0080087093.html).

Lab 11-1: IP-IP Tunnel Linux-to-FreeBSD

FreeBSD Tunnel setup for either IP-IP or generic routing encapsulation (GRE) involves three steps. Step one involves establishing the tunnel endpoints; in essence, this means two addresses that can reach and ping each other. These addresses constitute the outer transport header. In a Cisco tunnel setup, the tunnel source could also be a directly connected routable interface and the tunnel endpoint an unnumbered interface.

Step two consists of adding IP addresses to the tunnel itself, usually a /30 RFC 1918 address pair. This is optional, but it is beneficial for debugging and routing purposes. Note that route utilities that cannot route a network toward a tunnel device such as Linux require these addresses for forwarding purposes.

The third step involves adding routing entries for prefixes that are reachable via the tunnel. Whether you use the near or far end as a next hop depends on the pickiness of your underlying operating system (trial and failure). As a rule of thumb, use the near end on UNIX. Figure 11-2 shows the lab topology for this and the following labs in this chapter.

Figure 11-2 *Lab Setup for Tunnel Demonstrations*

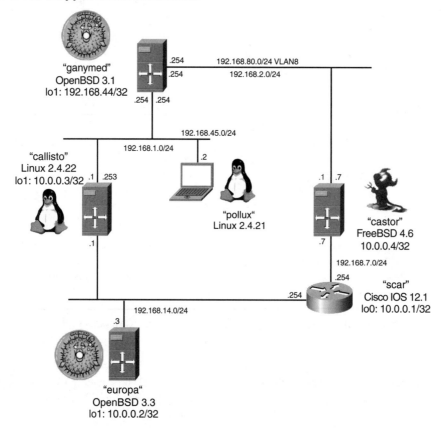

The Linux **ip tunnel** command sequence (Example 11-1) offers several other options such as tunnel keys, TTL/TOS manipulation, and other features. I do not recommend using keys or TOS options for tunnel setup with non-Linux/Cisco gateways for compatibility reasons. The Linux IP-IP tunnel supports tunnel checksum, sequence datagrams, and path maximum transmission unit (MTU) discovery compatible with Cisco IOS IP-IP tunnels. Example 11-1 demonstrates inheritance of TTL from the payload datagrams; this is not always desirable. If you encounter problems, add the **ttl 255** statement to the **ip tunnel** setup line to alter this inheritance behavior.

Example 11-1 *Linux IP-IP Tunnels (**iptunnel** Is Equivalent to **ip tunnel**)*

```
### Establish Tunnel:

[root@callisto:~#] iptunnel -?
Usage: iptunnel { add | change | del | show } [ NAME ]
          [ mode { ipip | gre | sit } ] [ remote ADDR ] [ local ADDR ]
          [ [i|o]seq ] [ [i|o]key KEY ] [ [i|o]csum ]
          [ ttl TTL ] [ tos TOS ] [ nopmtudisc ] [ dev PHYS_DEV ]
        iptunnel -V | --version

Where: NAME := STRING
       ADDR := { IP_ADDRESS | any }
       TOS  := { NUMBER | inherit }
       TTL  := { 1..255 | inherit }
       KEY  := { DOTTED_QUAD | NUMBER }

[root@callisto:~#] modprobe ipip
[root@callisto:~#] iptunnel add TUNNEL mode ipip remote 192.168.2.7 local 192.168.1.1
[root@callisto:~#] ifconfig TUNNEL 10.1.1.1 netmask 255.255.255.252 pointopoint 10.1.1.2
[root@callisto:~#] route add -net 192.168.7.0/24 gw 192.168.1.254 dev TUNNEL

[root@callisto:~#] ifconfig -a
TUNNEL    Link encap:IPIP Tunnel  HWaddr
          inet addr:10.1.1.1  P-t-P:10.1.1.2  Mask:255.255.255.252
          UP POINTOPOINT RUNNING NOARP  MTU:1480  Metric:1
          RX packets:48 errors:0 dropped:0 overruns:0 frame:0
          TX packets:102 errors:0 dropped:0 overruns:0 carrier:0
          collisions:0 txqueuelen:0
          RX bytes:3948 (3.8 Kb)  TX bytes:12996 (12.6 Kb)

tunl0     Link encap:IPIP Tunnel  HWaddr
          NOARP  MTU:1480  Metric:1
          RX packets:0 errors:0 dropped:0 overruns:0 frame:0
          TX packets:0 errors:0 dropped:0 overruns:0 carrier:0
          collisions:0 txqueuelen:0
          RX bytes:0 (0.0 b)  TX bytes:0 (0.0 b)

[root@callisto:~#] iptunnel show
tunl0:  ip/ip  remote any          local any          ttl inherit nopmtudisc
TUNNEL: ip/ip  remote 192.168.2.7  local 192.168.1.254  ttl inherit

#### Test Tunnel Itself:

[root@callisto:~#] ping 10.1.1.2
PING 10.1.1.2 (10.1.1.2) from 10.1.1.1 : 56(84) bytes of data.
64 bytes from 10.1.1.2: icmp_seq=1 ttl=64 time=1.15 ms
64 bytes from 10.1.1.2: icmp_seq=2 ttl=64 time=1.15 ms
64 bytes from 10.1.1.2: icmp_seq=3 ttl=64 time=1.15 ms
--- 10.1.1.2 ping statistics ---
3 packets transmitted, 3 received, 0% loss, time 2019ms
rtt min/avg/max/mdev = 1.154/1.156/1.159/0.039 ms
```

continues

Example 11-1 *Linux IP-IP Tunnels (**iptunnel** Is Equivalent to **ip tunnel**) (Continued)*

```
### Tear Down Tunnel:

[root@callisto:~#] iptunnel del TUNNEL
[root@callisto:~#] modprobe -r ipip
```

The FreeBSD implementation facilitates the generic tunnel interface gif(4), a pseudo-device that supports all possible combinations of IPv4 and IPv6 as the transport and payload protocol. By default, gif tunnels might not be nested, and parallel tunnels are not permitted. To change this behavior, consult the gif(4) man page. Example 11-2 demonstrates the IP-IP tunnel setup. Alternatively, you can use ip-tun(8) via the tun pseudo-device on FreeBSD. Consult the manual page for further details. The highlighted text in Examples 11-2 through 11-4 emphasizes the representation of the prefix routed via the tunnel.

Example 11-2 *FreeBSD IP-IP Tunnels*

```
[root@castor:~#] ifconfig gif0 tunnel 192.168.2.7 192.168.1.1
[root@castor:~#] ifconfig gif0 inet 10.1.1.2 10.1.1.1 netmask 255.255.255.252
[root@castor:~#] route add -net 192.168.14.0/24 10.1.1.2

[root@castor:~#] ifconfig -a
gif0: flags=8051<UP,POINTOPOINT,RUNNING,MULTICAST> mtu 1280
        tunnel inet 192.168.2.7 --> 192.168.1.1
        inet6 fe80::210:5aff:fec4:2c04%gif0 prefixlen 64 scopeid 0xf
        inet 10.1.1.2 --> 10.1.1.1 netmask 0xfffffffc

[root@castor:~#] gifconfig -a
gif0: flags=8051<UP,POINTOPOINT,RUNNING,MULTICAST> mtu 1280
        inet6 fe80::210:5aff:fec4:2c04%gif0  prefixlen 64
        inet 10.1.1.2 --> 10.1.1.1 netmask 0xfffffffc
        physical address inet 192.168.2.7 --> 192.168.1.1

[root@castor:~#] netstat -rn -f inet
Routing tables

Internet:
Destination       Gateway            Flags   Refs     Use   Netif Expire
default           192.168.2.254      UGSc      8      14     xl0
10.1.1.1          10.1.1.2           UH        0       0     gif0
127.0.0.1         127.0.0.1          UH        0       0     lo0
192.168.2         link#1             UC        1       0     xl0
192.168.2.254     52:54:05:e3:e4:2f  UHLW      7       0     xl0     933
192.168.7         link#2             UC        1       0     ed0
192.168.7.7       52:54:05:e3:e4:88  UHLW      0       4     lo0
192.168.14        10.1.1.2           UGSc      0       7     xl0
192.168.80        link#14            UC        0       0     vlan8

[root@castor:~#] netstat -rn -f inet -i
Name  Mtu    Network    Address          Ipkts Ierrs   Opkts Oerrs  Coll
xl0   1500   192.168.2  192.168.2.7       992    -      1433    -     -
ed0   1500   192.168.7  192.168.7.7       128    -       613    -     -
lo0   16384  127        127.0.0.1           0    -         0    -     -
```

Example 11-2 *FreeBSD IP-IP Tunnels (Continued)*

```
vlan8 1496  192.168.80     192.168.80.1      0    -    0    -    -
gif0  1280  10.1.1/30      10.1.1.2          0    -    0    -    -

[root@castor:~#] tcpdump
tcpdump: listening on xl0
14:54:48.408903 192.168.1.1 > 192.168.2.7: 10.1.1.1 > 10.1.1.2: icmp: echo request
   (DF) (ipip)
14:54:48.409071 192.168.2.7 > 192.168.1.1: 10.1.1.2 > 10.1.1.1: icmp: echo reply
   (DF) (ipip)
```

Lab 11-2: IP-IP Tunnel OpenBSD-to-Cisco

OpenBSD provides the same gif pseudo-device concept as FreeBSD. The entire configuration is done via ifconfig. Example 11-3 demonstrates the OpenBSD setup, and Example 11-4 shows the Cisco tunnel endpoint.

Example 11-3 *OpenBSD IP-IP Tunnel Setup*

```
[root@ganymed:~#] ifconfig gif0 tunnel 192.168.1.254 192.168.14.254 up
[root@ganymed:~#] ifconfig gif0 10.2.2.1 10.2.2.2 netmask 255.255.255.252 up
[root@ganymed:~#] route add -host 10.0.0.1 10.2.2.1

[root@ganymed:~#] ifconfig -A
gif0: flags=8051<UP,POINTOPOINT,RUNNING,MULTICAST> mtu 1280
        physical address inet 192.168.1.254 --> 192.168.14.254
        inet6 fe80::4a54:e8ff:fe8c:a3f%gif0 -> :: prefixlen 64 scopeid 0x13
        inet 10.2.2.1 --> 10.2.2.2 netmask 0xfffffffc

[root@ganymed:~#] netstat -rn -f inet
Routing tables

Internet:
Destination      Gateway           Flags   Refs     Use    Mtu  Interface
default          213.47.70.1       UGS       3   46134   1500  ne5
10.0.0.1         10.2.2.1          UGHS      0       3   1500  gif0
10.2.2.2         10.2.2.1          UH        0      10   1280  gif0
127/8            127.0.0.1         UGRS      0       0  33224  lo0
127.0.0.1        127.0.0.1         UH        2       0  33224  lo0
192.168.1/24     link#1            UC        0       0   1500  ne3
192.168.1.1      52:54:5:e3:51:87  UHL       2   59207   1500  ne3
192.168.1.2      8:0:46:64:74:1b   UHL       1   11898   1500  ne3
192.168.1.254    127.0.0.1         UGHS      0       0  33224  lo0
192.168.2/24     link#2            UC        0       0   1500  ne4
192.168.2.7      0:10:5a:c4:2c:4   UHL       1   23012   1500  ne4
192.168.7/24     192.168.2.7       UGS       1      55   1500  ne4
192.168.14/24    192.168.1.1       UGS       0      21   1500  ne3
192.168.44.1     192.168.44.1      UH        0       0  33224  lo1
192.168.45/24    link#1            UC        0       0   1500  ne3
192.168.80/24    link#16           UC        0       0   1496  vlan0
213.47.70/24     link#3            UC        0       0   1500  ne5
213.47.70.1      0:5:9a:5a:fb:fc   UHL       1       0   1500  ne5
```

continues

Example 11-3 *OpenBSD IP-IP Tunnel Setup (Continued)*

```
[root@ganymed:~#] traceroute 10.0.0.1
traceroute to 10.0.0.1 (10.0.0.1), 64 hops max, 40 byte packets
 1  10.2.2.2 (10.2.2.2)  3.303 ms *  3.168 ms
```

Example 11-4 *IP-IP Tunnel Setup with Cisco IOS Architecture*

```
scar(config-if)# tunnel ?
  checksum            enable end to end checksumming of packets
  destination         destination of tunnel
  key                 security or selector key
  mode                tunnel encapsulation method
  path-mtu-discovery  Enable Path MTU Discovery on tunnel
  sequence-datagrams  drop datagrams arriving out of order
  source              source of tunnel packets
  udlr                associate tunnel with unidirectional interface

scar(config-if)# tunnel mode ?
  aurp    AURP TunnelTalk AppleTalk encapsulation
  cayman  Cayman TunnelTalk AppleTalk encapsulation
  dvmrp   DVMRP multicast tunnel
  eon     EON compatible CLNS tunnel
  gre     generic route encapsulation protocol
  ipip    IP over IP encapsulation
  iptalk  Apple IPTalk encapsulation
  nos     IP over IP encapsulation (KA9Q/NOS compatible)

scar# show running-config
...
!
interface Loopback0
 ip address 10.0.0.1 255.255.255.0
!
interface Tunnel0
 ip address 10.2.2.2 255.255.255.252
 tunnel source Ethernet1
 tunnel destination 192.168.1.254
 tunnel mode ipip
!
interface Ethernet0
 bandwidth 10000
 ip address 192.168.7.254 255.255.255.0
 no ip proxy-arp
 ip load-sharing per-packet
 no ip route-cache
 no ip mroute-cache
 media-type 10BaseT
 random-detect
!
interface Ethernet1
 bandwidth 10000
 ip address 192.168.14.254 255.255.255.0
```

Example 11-4 *IP-IP Tunnel Setup with Cisco IOS Architecture (Continued)*

```
 no ip proxy-arp
 ip load-sharing per-packet
 no ip route-cache
 ip ospf network broadcast
 no ip mroute-cache
 media-type 10BaseT
 random-detect
!
ip route 0.0.0.0 0.0.0.0 192.168.14.1
ip route 0.0.0.0 0.0.0.0 192.168.7.7 2
ip route 192.168.44.1 255.255.255.255 Tunnel0
...

scar# show interface tunnel 0
Tunnel0 is up, line protocol is up
  Hardware is Tunnel
  Internet address is 10.2.2.2/30
  MTU 1514 bytes, BW 9 Kbit, DLY 500000 usec,
     reliability 255/255, txload 28/255, rxload 1/255
  Encapsulation TUNNEL, loopback not set
  Keepalive not set
  Tunnel source 192.168.14.254 (Ethernet1), destination 192.168.1.254
  Tunnel protocol/transport IP/IP, key disabled, sequencing disabled
  Checksumming of packets disabled,  fast tunneling enabled
  Last input 00:00:00, output 00:00:00, output hang never
  Last clearing of "show interface" counters never
  Input queue: 0/75/0/0 (size/max/drops/flushes); Total output drops: 0
  Queueing strategy: fifo
  Output queue :0/0 (size/max)
  5 minute input rate 0 bits/sec, 1 packets/sec
  5 minute output rate 1000 bits/sec, 1 packets/sec
     140 packets input, 6615 bytes, 0 no buffer
     Received 0 broadcasts, 0 runts, 0 giants, 0 throttles
     0 input errors, 0 CRC, 0 frame, 0 overrun, 0 ignored, 0 abort
     118 packets output, 15128 bytes, 0 underruns
     0 output errors, 0 collisions, 0 interface resets
     0 output buffer failures, 0 output buffers swapped out

scar# show ip route
Codes: C - connected, S - static, I - IGRP, R - RIP, M - mobile, B - BGP
       D - EIGRP, EX - EIGRP external, O - OSPF, IA - OSPF inter area
       N1 - OSPF NSSA external type 1, N2 - OSPF NSSA external type 2
       E1 - OSPF external type 1, E2 - OSPF external type 2, E - EGP
       i - IS-IS, L1 - IS-IS level-1, L2 - IS-IS level-2, ia - IS-IS inter area
       * - candidate default, U - per-user static route, o - ODR
       P - periodic downloaded static route

Gateway of last resort is 192.168.14.1 to network 0.0.0.0

C    192.168.14.0/24 is directly connected, Ethernet1
     192.168.44.0/32 is subnetted, 1 subnets
```

continues

Example 11-4 *IP-IP Tunnel Setup with Cisco IOS Architecture (Continued)*

```
S        192.168.44.1 is directly connected, Tunnel0
         10.0.0.0/8 is variably subnetted, 3 subnets, 2 masks
C        10.2.2.0/30 is directly connected, Tunnel0
C        10.0.0.0/24 is directly connected, Loopback0
C        10.0.1.0/24 is directly connected, TokenRing0
C        192.168.7.0/24 is directly connected, Ethernet0
S*       0.0.0.0/0 [1/0] via 192.168.14.1

scar# traceroute 192.168.44.1

Type escape sequence to abort.
Tracing the route to 192.168.44.1

  1 192.168.44.1 4 msec 24 msec 0 msec
```

Generic Router Encapsulation (GRE) Tunnel

The word *generic* has significant consequences; the relevant and ancillary RFCs are RFC 2784, RFC 1701, RFC 1702, RFC 2890, and RFC 3147. According to the RFC 2784, *generic* specifies "a protocol for encapsulation of an arbitrary network layer protocol over another arbitrary network layer protocol." In a general case, the actual payload packet is first encapsulated in a GRE packet, which can be encapsulated further in an arbitrary forwarding network layer protocol for regular delivery. Cisco IOS architecture provides a tunnel identification key that provides some weak security against malicious packet injection. GRE uses protocol number 47. Configure your filters/firewalls accordingly. Table 11-2 lists an overview of the special tunnel-related interfaces on BSD platforms. As you will see, this works differently on Linux (tunl0/TUNNEL, gre0/GRE).

Table 11-2 *Open- and FreeBSD Special Interfaces*

Interface	OpenBSD	FreeBSD	Description
tun	X	X	Tunnel network interface (also used by gre-tun)
enc	X		IPSec encapsulating interface
gre	X		GRE/Mobile-IP encapsulation interface
gif	X	X	Generic IPv4/IPv6 tunnel interface
faith	X	X	IPv6 and IPv4 translation
stf		X	6to4 over IPv4 encapsulation

Lab 11-3: GRE Tunnel OpenBSD-to-Cisco

Example 11-5 demonstrates the GRE tunnel setup without special features. Remember, **tunnel mode gre ip** is the default setting of Cisco IOS architecture.

Example 11-5 *GRE Tunnel OpenBSD-to-Cisco IOS Architecture*

```
[root@europa:~#] ifconfig gre0 tunnel 192.168.14.3 192.168.14.254 up
[root@europa:~#] ifconfig gre0 10.2.2.1 10.2.2.2 netmask 255.255.255.252 up
[root@europa:~#] route add -host 10.0.0.1 10.2.2.2

scar# show running-config
...
interface Tunnel0
 ip address 10.2.2.2 255.255.255.252
 tunnel source Ethernet1
 tunnel destination 192.168.14.3
!
ip route 10.0.0.2 255.255.255.255 Tunnel0
...
```

Lab 11-4: GRE Tunnel Linux-to-FreeBSD (Featuring gre-tun)

This lab uses the gre-tun package from http://mike.spottydogs.org/projects/gre-tun/ to show an alternative GRE setup for FreeBSD. Example 11-6 presents the Linux tunnel endpoint, and Example 11-7 shows the gre-tun configuration at the FreeBSD endpoint. The highlighted text in Example 11-6 emphasizes the default Linux MTU setting for GRE tunnels.

Example 11-6 *Linux GRE Configuration*

```
[root@callisto:~#] insmod ip_gre
[root@callisto:~#] iptunnel add GRE mode gre remote 192.168.2.7 local 192.168.1.1 ttl 255
[root@callisto:~#] ifconfig GRE 10.1.1.1 netmask 255.255.255.252 pointopoint 10.1.1.2
[root@callisto:~#] route add -net 192.168.7.0/24 gw 192.168.1.254 dev GRE

[root@callisto:~#] ifconfig -a
GRE       Link encap:UNSPEC  HWaddr C0-A8-01-01-00-00-00-00-00-00-00-00-00-00-00-00
          inet addr:10.1.1.1  P-t-P:10.1.1.2  Mask:255.255.255.252
          UP POINTOPOINT RUNNING NOARP  MTU:1476 Metric:1
          RX packets:0 errors:0 dropped:0 overruns:0 frame:0
          TX packets:0 errors:0 dropped:0 overruns:0 carrier:0
          collisions:0 txqueuelen:0
          RX bytes:0 (0.0 b)  TX bytes:0 (0.0 b)

gre0      Link encap:UNSPEC  HWaddr 00-00-00-00-00-00-00-00-00-00-00-00-00-00-00-00
          NOARP  MTU:1476 Metric:1
          RX packets:0 errors:0 dropped:0 overruns:0 frame:0
          TX packets:0 errors:0 dropped:0 overruns:0 carrier:0
          collisions:0 txqueuelen:0
          RX bytes:0 (0.0 b)  TX bytes:0 (0.0 b)
```

Example 11-7 *FreeBSD gre-tun Configuration*

```
[root@castor:~#] gre-tun -tunnel /dev/tun0 -local 192.168.2.7 -remote 192.168.1.1
-source 10.1.1.2 -destination 10.1.1.1 -netmask 255.255.255.252
[root@castor:~#] route add -net 192.168.14.0/24 10.1.1.1
```

Lab 11-5: Linux-to-Cisco GRE Tunnel

Finally, look at a Linux-to-Cisco combination (Example 11-8). Linux GRE defaults to inherit the carrier GRE packet TTL from the payload packet. Cisco IOS architecture is picky about it, and hence the **ttl 255** parameter added (highlighted text).

Example 11-8 *Linux-to-Cisco GRE Tunnel Setup*

```
[root@callisto:~#] insmod ip_gre
[root@callisto:~#] iptunnel add GRE mode gre remote 192.168.2.254 local 192.168.14.1
ttl 255
[root@callisto:~#] ifconfig GRE 10.2.2.1 netmask 255.255.255.252 pointopoint 10.2.2.2
[root@callisto:~#] route add -host 10.0.0.1 dev GRE

[root@callisto:~#] ifconfig -a
GRE       Link encap:UNSPEC  HWaddr C0-A8-0E-01-00-00-00-00-00-00-00-00-00-00-00-00
          inet addr:10.2.2.1  P-t-P:10.2.2.2  Mask:255.255.255.252
          UP POINTOPOINT RUNNING NOARP  MTU:1476  Metric:1
          RX packets:49 errors:0 dropped:0 overruns:0 frame:0
          TX packets:106 errors:0 dropped:0 overruns:0 carrier:0
          collisions:0 txqueuelen:0
          RX bytes:4836 (4.7 Kb)  TX bytes:16229 (15.8 Kb)

eth0      Link encap:Ethernet  HWaddr 00:10:5A:D7:93:60
          inet addr:192.168.14.1  Bcast:192.168.14.255  Mask:255.255.255.0
          UP BROADCAST RUNNING MULTICAST  MTU:1500  Metric:1
          RX packets:2639 errors:0 dropped:0 overruns:0 frame:0
          TX packets:2614 errors:0 dropped:0 overruns:0 carrier:0
          collisions:0 txqueuelen:100
          RX bytes:257278 (251.2 Kb)  TX bytes:185819 (181.4 Kb)
          Interrupt:5 Base address:0xd800

eth1      Link encap:Ethernet  HWaddr 52:54:05:E3:51:87
          inet addr:192.168.1.1  Bcast:192.168.1.255  Mask:255.255.255.0
          UP BROADCAST RUNNING MULTICAST  MTU:1500  Metric:1
          RX packets:10419 errors:0 dropped:0 overruns:0 frame:0
          TX packets:6349 errors:0 dropped:0 overruns:0 carrier:0
          collisions:137 txqueuelen:100
          RX bytes:2674761 (2.5 Mb)  TX bytes:612601 (598.2 Kb)
          Interrupt:9 Base address:0xd400

eth1:1    Link encap:Ethernet  HWaddr 52:54:05:E3:51:87
          inet addr:192.168.45.253  Bcast:192.168.45.255  Mask:255.255.255.0
          UP BROADCAST RUNNING MULTICAST  MTU:1500  Metric:1
          Interrupt:9 Base address:0xd400

gre0      Link encap:UNSPEC  HWaddr 00-00-00-00-00-00-00-00-00-00-00-00-00-00-00-00
          NOARP  MTU:1476  Metric:1
          RX packets:0 errors:0 dropped:0 overruns:0 frame:0
          TX packets:0 errors:0 dropped:0 overruns:0 carrier:0
          collisions:0 txqueuelen:0
          RX bytes:0 (0.0 b)  TX bytes:0 (0.0 b)

lo        Link encap:Local Loopback
          inet addr:127.0.0.1  Mask:255.0.0.0
```

Example 11-8 *Linux-to-Cisco GRE Tunnel Setup (Continued)*

```
                  UP LOOPBACK RUNNING  MTU:16436  Metric:1
                  RX packets:72 errors:0 dropped:0 overruns:0 frame:0
                  TX packets:72 errors:0 dropped:0 overruns:0 carrier:0
                  collisions:0 txqueuelen:0
                  RX bytes:5416 (5.2 Kb)  TX bytes:5416 (5.2 Kb)

[root@callisto:~#] iptunnel show
gre0: gre/ip  remote any  local any  ttl inherit  nopmtudisc
GRE: gre/ip  remote 192.168.14.254  local 192.168.14.1  ttl 255

[root@callisto:~#] netstat -i
Kernel Interface table
Iface   MTU Met   RX-OK RX-ERR RX-DRP RX-OVR   TX-OK TX-ERR TX-DRP TX-OVR Flg
GRE    1476 0        56      0      0      0     113      0      0      0 OPRU
eth0   1500 0      2717      0      0      0    2652      0      0      0 BMRU
eth1   1500 0     10856      0      0      0    6767      0      0      0 BMRU
eth1:  1500 0       - no statistics available -                          BMRU
lo    16436 0        72      0      0      0      72      0      0      0 LRU

[root@callisto:~#] ip -s tunnel
gre0: gre/ip  remote any  local any  ttl 255
RX: Packets     Bytes         Errors CsumErrs OutOfSeq Mcasts
    0           0             0       0        0        0
TX: Packets     Bytes         Errors DeadLoop NoRoute  NoBufs
    0           0             0       0        0        0
GRE: gre/ip  remote 192.168.14.254  local 192.168.14.1  ttl 255
RX: Packets     Bytes         Errors CsumErrs OutOfSeq Mcasts
    56          5424          0       0        0        0
TX: Packets     Bytes         Errors DeadLoop NoRoute  NoBufs
    115         17511         0       0        0        0

[root@callisto:~#] netstat -rne
Kernel IP routing table
Destination     Gateway         Genmask         Flags Metric Ref    Use Iface
10.0.0.1        0.0.0.0         255.255.255.255 UH    0      0        0 GRE
10.2.2.0        0.0.0.0         255.255.255.252 U     0      0        0 GRE
192.168.1.0     0.0.0.0         255.255.255.0   U     0      0        0 eth1
192.168.14.0    0.0.0.0         255.255.255.0   U     0      0        0 eth0
192.168.45.0    0.0.0.0         255.255.255.0   U     0      0        0 eth1
127.0.0.0       0.0.0.0         255.0.0.0       U     0      0        0 lo
0.0.0.0         192.168.1.254   0.0.0.0         UG    0      0        0 eth1

scar# show running-config
...
interface Tunnel0
 ip address 10.2.2.2 255.255.255.252
 tunnel source Ethernet1
 tunnel destination 192.168.14.1
!
ip route 192.168.45.0 255.255.255.0 Tunnel0
...
```

continues

Example 11-8 *Linux-to-Cisco GRE Tunnel Setup (Continued)*

```
scar# show interfaces tunnel 0
Tunnel0 is up, line protocol is up
  Hardware is Tunnel
  Internet address is 10.2.2.2/30
  MTU 1514 bytes, BW 9 Kbit, DLY 500000 usec,
      reliability 255/255, txload 1/255, rxload 1/255
  Encapsulation TUNNEL, loopback not set
  Keepalive not set
  Tunnel source 192.168.14.254 (Ethernet1), destination 192.168.14.1
  Tunnel protocol/transport GRE/IP, key disabled, sequencing disabled
  Checksumming of packets disabled,  fast tunneling enabled
  Last input 00:01:35, output 00:37:36, output hang never
  Last clearing of "show interface" counters never
  Input queue: 0/75/0/0 (size/max/drops/flushes); Total output drops: 3
  Queueing strategy: fifo
  Output queue :0/0 (size/max)
  5 minute input rate 0 bits/sec, 0 packets/sec
  5 minute output rate 0 bits/sec, 0 packets/sec
     101 packets input, 13185 bytes, 0 no buffer
     Received 0 broadcasts, 0 runts, 0 giants, 0 throttles
     0 input errors, 0 CRC, 0 frame, 0 overrun, 0 ignored, 0 abort
     47 packets output, 7204 bytes, 0 underruns
     0 output errors, 0 collisions, 0 interface resets
     0 output buffer failures, 0 output buffers swapped out

scar# show ip route
Codes: C - connected, S - static, I - IGRP, R - RIP, M - mobile, B - BGP
       D - EIGRP, EX - EIGRP external, O - OSPF, IA - OSPF inter area
       N1 - OSPF NSSA external type 1, N2 - OSPF NSSA external type 2
       E1 - OSPF external type 1, E2 - OSPF external type 2, E - EGP
       i - IS-IS, L1 - IS-IS level-1, L2 - IS-IS level-2, ia - IS-IS inter area
       * - candidate default, U - per-user static route, o - ODR
       P - periodic downloaded static route

Gateway of last resort is 192.168.14.1 to network 0.0.0.0

C    192.168.14.0/24 is directly connected, Ethernet1
S    192.168.45.0/24 is directly connected, Tunnel0
     10.0.0.0/8 is variably subnetted, 4 subnets, 3 masks
S       10.0.0.2/32 is directly connected, Tunnel0
C       10.2.2.0/30 is directly connected, Tunnel0
C       10.0.1.0/24 is directly connected, TokenRing0
C       10.0.0.1/32 is directly connected, Loopback0
S*   0.0.0.0/0 [1/0] via 192.168.14.1

scar# debug tunnel
Tunnel Interface debugging is on

scar# terminal monitor
scar# ping 192.168.45.253

Type escape sequence to abort.
```

Example 11-8 *Linux-to-Cisco GRE Tunnel Setup (Continued)*

```
Sending 5, 100-byte ICMP Echos to 192.168.45.253, timeout is 2 seconds:
!!!!!
Success rate is 100 percent (5/5), round-trip min/avg/max = 4/5/8 ms
scar#
01:09:52: Tunnel0: GRE/IP encapsulated 192.168.14.254->192.168.14.1 (linktype=7,
len=124)
01:09:52: Tunnel0: GRE/IP encapsulated 192.168.14.254->192.168.14.1 (linktype=7,
len=124)
01:09:52: Tunnel0: GRE/IP encapsulated 192.168.14.254->192.168.14.1 (linktype=7,
len=124)
01:09:52: Tunnel0: GRE/IP encapsulated 192.168.14.254->192.168.14.1 (linktype=7,
len=124)
01:09:52: Tunnel0: GRE/IP encapsulated 192.168.14.254->192.168.14.1 (linktype=7,
len=124)
```

Exercise 11-1: GRE Advanced Features

I suggest that you experiment with advanced GRE parameters such as sequencing and keys. Be aware, however, that this might introduce incompatibilities between the implementations.

Special Multicast and IPv6 Tunneling (RFC 2473, RFC 3053)

IPv6 over IPv4 tunneling is done via the command sequence **iptunnel mode sit** under Linux. gif devices under Open/FreeBSD can handle arbitrary IPv4/IPv6 transport and carrier combinations. DVMRP erects IP-IP tunnel for multicast transport over the unicast Internet. Distance-Vector Multicast Routing Protocol (DVMRP) operation and termination affects manually configured IP-IP tunnels. For a more detailed discussion of multicasting concepts and DVMRP tunnels, see Chapter 14, "Multicast Architectures."

Cisco L2F (Layer 2 Forwarding)

L2F was designed by Cisco Systems (RFC 2341) to support the creation of secure VPDNs via tunnels over public infrastructure. The primary goal was (quoted from RFC 2341) "to divorce the location of the initial dial-up server from the location at which the dial-up protocol connection is terminated and access to the network provided."

This is primarily of interest for carriers and service providers with regard to VPDN design, aggregation, and so on. L2F has been superseded by L2TP, does not provide encryption, and is rarely used anymore. It was one of the first scalable approaches to VPDNs. L2F uses port 1701/udp and supports PPP/SLIP as encapsulated payload protocols. For an overview discussion, see the Cisco.com white papers "L2F Case Study Overview" (http://www.cisco.com/en/US/tech/tk801/tk703/technologies_design_guide_chapter09186a00800de9d6.html) and "Understanding VPDN" (http://www.cisco.com/en/US/tech/tk801/tk703/technologies_tech_note09186a0080094586.shtml).

PPTP (Point-to-Point Tunnel Protocol)

PPTP (RFC 2637) has received quite some attention—both praise and flames—because of its integration into the Windows operating system in combination with Microsoft Point-to-Point Encryption (MPPE) to realize on-demand VPN client access. MPPE works as a subfeature of Microsoft Point-to-Point Compression (MPPC) and provides encryption for PPP links.

PPTP itself does not provide encryption. It is used in client/server setups with enterprise remote-access servers (RASs) and was not designed with support for gateway-to-gateway tunnels in mind. MPPE is multiprotocol-capable, uses MS Challenge Handshake Authentication Protocol version 2 (CHAPv2) for authentication, and supports 40-bit and 128-bit encryption based on the RSA RC4 algorithm to provide data confidentiality. PPTP is based on an enhanced GRE approach. It is documented widely, and tons of example setups for Microsoft and UNIX are available. For further information, look at the RFCs relevant to MPPC (RFC 2118) and MPPE (RFC 3078/3079).

PPTP uses TCP/1723 to set up its control channel and IP protocol 47 (GRE) to move data. Enabling PPTP traffic to flow through a firewall requires you to establish bidirectional rules for both sets of traffic.[2]

This book does not provide a thorough discussion of PPTP in practice for several reasons:

- It is not that relevant in non-Microsoft environments. There are far better choices for tunnel setup for UNIX and Cisco integrated architectures.

- PPTP is deprecated, and Microsoft has moved on to L2TP/IPSec as a strategic technology.

- Many documents, recipes, and configurations are available with regard to PPTP setups involving Microsoft clients and RAS servers (and for PPTP configurations in context with DSL setups, which are common in some European countries).

The following list identifies the most mature PPTP implementations for Linux and BSD operating systems:

- **UNIX PPTP Client Package**—This is the recommended client package for Linux and BSD and integrates well with the PoPToP server. (http://pptpclient.sourceforge.net/)

- **PoPToP**—An OpenSource PPTP server for Linux and BSD that works perfectly with the PPTP client package. (http://www.poptop.org/)

- **MPD**—A multilink PPP daemon for FreeBSD. It is a robust and mature implementation based on the FreeBSD Netgraph facility. (http://www.dellroad.org/mpd/index)

- **PPTP-Proxy**—A useful daemon that forwards a PPTP VPN connection through a Linux firewall. (http://www.mgix.com/pptpproxy/)

- **The MPPE/MPPC kernel module for Linux**—This is an alternative to user-space approaches. It requires patching **pppd** and the kernel sources. It works with the current 2.4 Linux kernel. (http://www.polbox.com/h/hs001)

Exercise 11-2: PPTP on UNIX

Use PPTP Client and PoPToP to familiarize yourself with the UNIX implementation. For example, you can set up DSL access or provide RAS services to Microsoft roaming users.

L2TP (Layer 2 Tunnel Protocol)

L2TP (RFC 2661, RFC 2888) unites the best features and approaches of L2F and PPTP. This reflects the name, too. L2TP is the preferred choice to realize state-of-the-art protocol-independent VPDNs and is a replacement for PPTP and L2F. L2TP uses port 1701/udp and protocol number 115; adjust possible security filters accordingly.

Securing L2TP Using IPSec (RFC 3193)

Although L2TP supports tunnel endpoint authentication, it lacks a tunnel-protection mechanism. However, because it encapsulates PPP, it inherits PPP authentication and the PPP Encryption/Compression Control Protocol (ECP/CCP). The IPSec protocol suite provides features such as tunnel authentication, privacy protection, integrity checking, and replay protection at the network layer for IP networks.

L2TP Operation

L2TP offers the capability to separate the actual call termination of Layer 2 connections such as plain old telephone service (POTS), Integrated Services Digital Network (ISDN), or Digital Subscriber Line (DSL) from the transport of the associated PPP session. This means that the terminating device (modem line card, DSLAM) can reside geographically and logically separated from the network access server (NAS). The PPP sessions are tunneled from the concentrator/aggregator device to the NAS architecture, and the PPP call is terminated there. Therefore, L2TP is a logical extension of PPP over a packet-switched (IP) infrastructure.

Modern DSL metro architectures consisting of DSLAMs, aggregator devices, and service-selection gateways facilitating L2TP tunnels to transport large quantities of PPP sessions represent good examples of L2TP deployment. L2TP is downward compatible with L2F and works with NAT. The latest-and-greatest gadgets and gizmos are included in the L2TPv3 standards.

L2TP also offers a potential solution to the multilink-multichassis hunt-group problem: The strict requirement that all channels composing a multilink bundle must reside on the same NAS can be circumvented.

L2TPv3 and Related "Work in Progress"

L2TP's evolution is determined largely by its usefulness for Internet service providers (ISPs), with occasional features finding their way into enterprise networking (such as IPSec). To sum it up, L2TPv3 offers the following:

- A clearer separation from PPP
- Extended address-value pairs (AVPs)
- 32-bit session ID and control connection ID
- Pseudo wire extensions for High-Level Data Link Control (HDLC) and Frame Relay transport
- Transport of Ethernet and VLAN frames over L2TP pseudo wires
- Header compression
- Multicast extensions

L2TPd for UNIX: A Project in Transition

This package (http://www.l2tpd.org) is not considered production grade, but it is reported to work with Cisco L2TP setups, the Microsoft implementation, and L2TP/IPSec combinations. It is the only implementation for UNIX I am aware of. If you encounter problems, try the previous package at http://sourceforge.net/projects/rp-l2tp.

Form your own opinion as to whether L2TPd for UNIX is stable enough for your purposes. If you have questions, consult the mailing list at http://www.l2tpd.org and be sure you have a good foundation in PPP debugging. The terms *LNS* and *LAC* are IETF lingo and mean L2TP network server and L2TP access concentrator, respectively.

Figure 11-3 presents a standard L2TP architecture useful for most applications.

Figure 11-3 *L2TP Architecture*

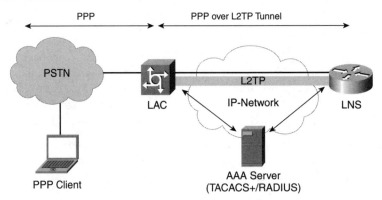

In Example 11-9, a Linux gateway can act as an LAC or LNS. See the configuration in Example 11-9 as a start for your own tests.

Example 11-9 *L2TPd Configuration Example and Secrets File*

```
[root@callisto:~#] cat /etc/l2tp/l2tpd.conf
;
; Sample l2tpd configuration file
;
;
; [global]                                    ; Global parameters:
; port = 1701                                 ; * Bind to port 1701
; auth file = /etc/l2tp/l2tp-secrets          ; * Where our challenge secrets are
; access control = yes                        ; * Refuse connections without IP match
; rand source = dev                           ; Source for entropy for random
;                                             ; numbers, options are:
;                                             ; dev - reads of /dev/urandom
;                                             ; sys - uses rand()
;                                             ; egd - reads from egd socket
;                                             ; egd is not yet implemented
;
; [lns default]                               ; Our fallthrough LNS definition
; exclusive = no                              ; * Only permit one tunnel per host
; ip range = 192.168.0.1-192.168.0.20         ; * Allocate from this IP range
; no ip range = 192.168.0.3-192.168.0.9       ; * Except these hosts
; ip range = 192.168.0.5                      ; * But this one is okay
; ip range = lac1-lac2                        ; * And anything from lac1 to lac2's IP
; lac = 192.168.1.4 - 192.168.1.8             ; * These can connect as LACs
; no lac = untrusted.marko.net                ; * This guy can't connect
; hidden bit = no                             ; * Use hidden AVPs?
; local ip = 192.168.1.2                      ; * Our local IP to use
; length bit = yes                            ; * Use length bit in payload?
; require chap = yes                          ; * Require CHAP auth. by peer
; refuse pap = yes                            ; * Refuse PAP authentication
; refuse chap = no                            ; * Refuse CHAP authentication
; refuse authentication = no                  ; * Refuse authentication altogether
; require authentication = yes                ; * Require peer to authenticate
; unix authentication = no                    ; * Use /etc/passwd for auth.
; name = myhostname                           ; * Report this as our host name
; ppp debug = no                              ; * Turn on PPP debugging
; pppoptfile = /etc/ppp/options.l2tpd.lns        ; * ppp options file
; call rws = 10                               ; * RWS for call (-1 is valid)
; tunnel rws = 4                              ; * RWS for tunnel (must be > 0)
; flow bit = yes                              ; * Include sequence numbers
; challenge = yes                             ; * Challenge authenticate peer ;
;
; [lac cisco]                                 ; Example VPN LAC definition
; lns = lns.marko.net                         ; * Who is our LNS?
; lns = lns2.marko.net                        ; * A backup LNS (not yet used)
; redial = yes                                ; * Redial if disconnected?
; redial timeout = 15                         ; * Wait n seconds between redials
; max redials = 5                             ; * Give up after n consecutive failures
; hidden bit = yes                            ; * User hidden AVPs?
```

continues

Example 11-9 *L2TPd Configuration Example and Secrets File (Continued)*

```
; local ip = 192.168.1.1                     ; * Force peer to use this IP for us
; remote ip = 192.168.1.2                    ; * Force peer to use this as their IP
; length bit = no                            ; * Use length bit in payload?
; require pap = no                           ; * Require PAP auth. by peer
; require chap = yes                         ; * Require CHAP auth. by peer
; refuse pap = yes                           ; * Refuse PAP authentication
; refuse chap = no                           ; * Refuse CHAP authentication
; refuse authentication = no                 ; * Refuse authentication altogether
; require authentication = yes               ; * Require peer to authenticate
; name = marko                               ; * Report this as our host name
; ppp debug = no                             ; * Turn on PPP debugging
; pppoptfile = /etc/ppp/options.l2tpd.marko  ; * ppp options file for this lac
; call rws = 10                              ; * RWS for call (-1 is valid)
; tunnel rws = 4                             ; * RWS for tunnel (must be > 0)
; flow bit = yes                             ; * Include sequence numbers
; challenge = yes                            ; * Challenge authenticate peer


[root@callisto:~#] cat /etc/l2tp/l2tp-secrets
# Secrets for authenticating l2tp tunnels
# us      them     secret
# *                marko blah2
# zeus             marko    blah
# *       *        interop
```

Exercise 11-3: L2TP

Configure a Linux/BSD LAC and LNS in combination with a Cisco LNS and figure out the degree of interoperability. Then analyze the Microsoft IPSec/L2TP implementation in combination with this architecture.

Mobile IP

Mobile IP is both part of IPv4 and IPv6 (RFC 3344, RFC 2004) and enables a host device to roam different networks regardless of the access technology identified by a single fixed IP address, without the need for user intervention. Mobile IP uses protocol number 55, which is supported by the gre pseudo-device on OpenBSD. The implications are vast and the applications obvious—from cell phones over PDAs or handhelds to notebooks accessing the Internet via 802.11 Wi-Fi, GPRS, UMTS, Bluetooth, or other emerging access technologies. The challenge essentially is to provide routing reachability for roaming users/devices in combination with adequate security measures.

RFC 2002 introduces the concept of "mobile nodes" identified by care-of address, home agents, and foreign agents. The connection between a foreign and a home agent occurs via a virtual secure point-to-point tunnel of some sort (IP-IP or GRE). The mobile IP connection setup includes agent discovery (foreign and home) by the mobile user device, registration (with the foreign and the home agent), and the actual reverse tunneling from the home agent to the foreign agent. Both agents advertise their service via an extended version of the Internet Router Discovery Protocol (IRDP) to potential roaming customers. As in plain IRDP operation, the mobile node can send out agent solicitations and trigger agent advertisements. RFC 3519, "Mobile IP Traversal of Network Address Translation (NAT) Devices," covers this subject in detail.

User-Space Tunneling

User-space tunnels are not an integral part of the operating system. They carry out their duty on top of TCP and UDP. This section discusses several representative examples, but a much larger variety exists. Several approaches are designed to circumvent corporate security by creating transparent tunnels (tcp80/tcp443) over HTTP(S) proxies or SOCKS5 relays.

Note that I do not discuss these approaches; they are potentially dangerous for corporate security. In addition, to a large extent, they are responsible for deployments of expensive and performance-impaired application layer gateways. Security compromises from the inside are difficult to tackle, time-consuming, and considerably increase administrative and logging burden. Proxies are there for good reasons and add security to corporate Internet architectures. Transparent proxies are one building block of modern security architectures; their caching purpose is of diminishing importance. Olaf Titz, from the CIPE Project,[3] says it best:

There are several different places where encryption can be built in to an existing network infrastructure, corresponding to the different protocol layers:

1 **On the network level**—Packets traveling between hosts on the network are encrypted. The encryption engine is placed near the driver, which sends and receives packets. An implementation is found in CIPE.

2 **On the socket level**—A logical connection between programs running on different hosts (TCP connection; transport or session layer in OSI) is encrypted. The encryption engine intercepts or proxies connections. SSH and SSL work this way.

3 **On the application level**—Applications contain their own encryption engine and encrypt data themselves. The best-known example is PGP for encrypting mail.

CIPE (Crypto IP Encapsulation)

CIPE is an established tunnel approach in the Linux community, based on tunneling IP datagrams over encrypted UDP carrier datagrams. This procedure offers transparency in contrast to TCP-tied approaches such as secure shell (SSH) or Secure Sockets Layer (SSL). CIPE creates point-to-point tunnels differentiated by port number. Because of its lightweight and elegant design, its performance characteristics are impressive. It behaves well in NAT and SOCKS5 relay environments, can to some extent handle dynamic IP addresses, and is based on Blowfish/IDEA cryptographic algorithms with a 128-bit key length.

CIPE also was ported to the Windows 2000 Server platform. The CIPE protocol performs two main tasks: encryption and checksumming of the payload packets, and dynamic key exchange. The CIPE suite consists of a kernel module, which resembles a pseudo network device, the ciped driver, and the pkcipe utility for key management. pkcipe introduced Diffie-Hellman key exchange and RSA signatures to tackle the security problem of long-lived static keys and administrative burden with many tunnels. As we know from partial or full-meshed IPSec architectures, point-to-point tunnels scale horribly (one issue successfully addressed by MPLS VPNs). For installation and operational details, consult the CIPE page at http://sites.inka.de/sites/bigred/devel/cipe.html. The next version of CIPE will take advantage of the Linux CryptoAPI, thus marking another major step toward a homogeneous architecture on Linux.

CIPE links can be qualified as belonging to different classes of carriers. Those classes are based on how they are able to reach the Internet:[4]

- Direct connection on a static IP address
- Direct connection on a dynamic IP address
- Indirect connection through a SOCKS server
- Indirect connection through a NAT (masquerading) router

Example 11-10 demonstrates a static CIPE setup between two Linux gateways and a configuration with pkcipe.

Example 11-10 *Linux CIPE Tunnel Setup*

```
[root@callisto:~#] modprobe cipcb cipe_debug=0

[root@callisto:/etc/cipe#] ls -al
total 36
drwx------    3 root     root         4096 Aug 15 16:27 ./
drwxr-xr-x   86 root     root         8192 Aug 15 10:15 ../
-rw-r-----    1 root     root          272 Aug 15 12:37 identity
-r--------    1 root     root          887 Aug 15 12:37 identity.priv
-rwxr-x---    1 root     root          620 Feb 22  2002 ip-down*
-rwxr-x---    1 root     root         1632 Feb 22  2002 ip-up*
-rw-------    1 root     root          679 Aug 15 12:40 options
drwx------    2 root     root         4096 Aug 15 12:37 pk/

[root@callisto:/etc/cipe#] cat options
# This is probably the minimal set of options that has to be set
# Without a "device" line, the device is picked dynamically

# the peer's IP address
ptpaddr         10.1.1.2
mask            255.255.255.252
# our CIPE device's IP address
ipaddr          10.1.1.1
# my UDP address. Note: if you set port 0 here, the system will pick
# one and tell it to you via the ip-up script. Same holds for IP 0.0.0.0.
me              192.168.1.1:6789
```

Example 11-10 *Linux CIPE Tunnel Setup (Continued)*

```
# ...and the UDP address we connect to. Of course no wildcards here.
peer            192.168.1.2:6543
# The static key. Keep this file secret!
# The key is 128 bits in hexadecimal notation.
key             3248fd20adf9c00ccf9ecc2393bbb3e4

[root@callisto:/etc/cipe/pk#] cat pollux
-----BEGIN PUBLIC KEY-----
MIGfMA0GCSqGSIb3DQEBAQUAA4GNADCBiQKBgQDl3o1MUEQN8IjZ9g74Ow01i8Cn
+nveaW0rqsH8qDmgwe2ofQH2RdHADhd+OgbWDzODxlKp/iSTPAExeDo2gvfy+V3f
cFn04T+Zsng5uDl6YZ/h35r937l9ve/XoxDGzIyg1RSnl6xvIsO9BFu6J7dc5JES
+bzICr4T58q6kauTlwIDAQAB
-----END PUBLIC KEY-------
ipaddr  10.1.1.1
ptpaddr 10.1.1.2
mask    255.255.255.252

[root@callisto:~#] modprobe cipcb cipe_debug=1 cipe_maxdev=10

[root@callisto:~#] ciped-cb -o /etc/cipe/options

[root@callisto:~#] ifconfig -a
cipcb0     Link encap:IPIP Tunnel  HWaddr
           inet addr:10.1.1.1  P-t-P:10.1.1.2  Mask:255.255.255.252
           UP POINTOPOINT RUNNING NOARP  MTU:1442  Metric:1
           RX packets:0 errors:0 dropped:0 overruns:0 frame:0
           TX packets:42 errors:0 dropped:0 overruns:0 carrier:0
           collisions:0 txqueuelen:100
           RX bytes:0 (0.0 b)  TX bytes:7104 (6.9 Kb)

[root@callisto:/etc/xinetd.d#] cat pkcipe
service pkcipe
{
        socket_type     = stream
        protocol        = tcp
        wait            = no
        user            = root
        server          = /usr/local/sbin/pkcipe
        server_args     = -s 963
        disable         = no
}

[root@pollux:~#] pkcipe -c 192.168.1.1:pkcipe
```

V-TUN (Virtual Tunnel)

V-TUN (http://vtun.sourceforge.net/) runs on Linux, BSD, and Solaris platforms. I consider it the most flexible and feature-rich package for VPN deployments outside kernel space. It supports encryption, traffic shaping, and compression for TCP-/UDP-based tunnels for point-to-point VPN or mobile IP architectures via IP, PPP, SLIP, Ethernet, and other tunnel types. V-TUN requires the universal TUN/TAP driver, which resembles a virtual point-to-point network device or virtual Ethernet network device respectively and can be found at http://vtun.sourceforge.net/tun/index.html.

The good news is that on all tested current operating systems (Linux 2.4, OpenBSD 3.3, FreeBSD 4.6, NetBSD 1.6.1), the TUN/TAP driver is an integral part or module of the kernel. It requires recompiling of the kernels but no additional software besides V-TUN. For additional information, consult the man pages vtund(8) and vtund.conf(5).

Examples 11-11 and 11-12 demonstrate a V-TUN setup between Linux and OpenBSD.

Example 11-11 *V-TUN Tunnel Setup on Linux*

```
[root@callisto:~#] modprobe tun
[root@callisto:/etc#] cat vtund.myconfig
options {
  port 5000;            # Listen on this port.

  # Syslog facility
  syslog daemon;

  # Path to various programs
  ppp            /usr/sbin/pppd;
  ifconfig       /sbin/ifconfig;
  route          /sbin/route;
  firewall       /sbin/iptables;
  ip             /sbin/ip;
}

default {
  compress no;          # Compression is off by default
  speed 0;              # By default maximum speed, No shaping
  keepalive yes;        # Keepalives
  stat yes;
  encrypt yes;
}

pollux {
  passwd cisco;         # Password
  type  tun;            # IP tunnel
  proto udp;            # UDP protocol
  compress  lzo:9;      # LZO compression level 9
  device tun0;
  encrypt  yes;         # Encryption
  keepalive yes;        # Keep connection alive
  stat yes;
  speed 128:64;         # Tunnel shaping Kbps IN:OUT

  up {
        ifconfig "%% 10.2.2.1 pointopoint 10.2.2.2 mtu 1450";
  };

  down {
```

Example 11-11 *V-TUN Tunnel Setup on Linux (Continued)*

```
    };
  }

  castor {
    passwd cisco;        # Password
    type  tun;           # IP tunnel
    proto udp;           # UDP protocol
    compress lzo:9;      # LZO compression level 9
    device tun1;
    encrypt  yes;        # Encryption
    keepalive yes;       # Keep connection alive
    stat yes;

    up {
        ifconfig "%% 10.3.3.1 pointopoint 10.3.3.2 mtu 1450";
    };
  }

  europa {
    passwd cisco;        # Password
    type  tun;           # IP tunnel
    proto udp;           # UDP protocol
    compress lzo:9;      # LZO compression level 9
    device tun2;
    encrypt  yes;        # Encryption
    keepalive yes;       # Keep connection alive
    stat yes;

    up {
        ifconfig "%% 10.4.4.1 pointopoint 10.4.4.2 mtu 1450";
    };
  }

  *** Start the vtund in server mode ***

  [root@callisto:~#] vtund -s -f /etc/vtund.myconfig

  [root@callisto:~#] ifconfig -a
  ...
  tun2     Link encap:Point-to-Point Protocol
           inet addr:10.4.4.1  P-t-P:10.4.4.2  Mask:255.255.255.255
           UP POINTOPOINT RUNNING NOARP MULTICAST  MTU:1450  Metric:1
           RX packets:7 errors:0 dropped:0 overruns:0 frame:0
           TX packets:10 errors:0 dropped:0 overruns:0 carrier:0
           collisions:0 txqueuelen:10
           RX bytes:588 (588.0 b)  TX bytes:840 (840.0 b)
  ...

  [root@callisto:~#] ps ax | grep vtun
   2404 ?       S<    0:00 vtund[s]: europa tun tun2
   6103 pts/4   S     0:00 grep vtun
```

Example 11-12 *V-TUN Tunnel Setup on OpenBSD*

```
[root@europa:~#] modprobe tun

[root@europa:/etc#] cat vtund.myconfig
options {
  port 5000;            # Connect to this port.
  timeout 60;           # General timeout

  # Path to various programs
  ppp           /usr/sbin/pppd;
  ifconfig      /sbin/ifconfig;
  route         /sbin/route;
  firewall      /sbin/ipf;
}

default {
  keepalive yes;        # Keepalives
}

europa {
  passwd cisco;         # Password
  device tun1;          # Device tun1
 #persist yes;          # Persist mode
  up {
        ifconfig "%% 10.4.4.2 10.4.4.1 mtu 1450";
        ifconfig "%% up";
        #route "add -net 192.168.45.0/24 gw 10.4.4.1";
  };
}

*** Start the vtund in client mode ***

[root@europa:~#] vtund -f /etc/vtund.myconfig europa 192.168.1.1

[root@europa:~#] ifconfig -A
...
tun1: flags=51<UP,POINTOPOINT,RUNNING> mtu 1450
        inet 10.4.4.2 --> 10.4.4.1 netmask 0xff000000
...

[root@europa:~#] ping 10.4.4.1
PING 10.4.4.1 (10.4.4.1): 56 data bytes
64 bytes from 10.4.4.1: icmp_seq=0 ttl=64 time=1.350 ms
64 bytes from 10.4.4.1: icmp_seq=1 ttl=64 time=1.288 ms
64 bytes from 10.4.4.1: icmp_seq=2 ttl=64 time=1.227 ms
--- 10.4.4.1 ping statistics ---
3 packets transmitted, 3 packets received, 0% packet loss
round-trip min/avg/max/std-dev = 1.227/1.288/1.350/0.058 ms

[root@callisto:~#] tcpdump -i tun2
tcpdump: listening on tun2
18:32:32.081336 10.4.4.2 > 10.4.4.1: icmp: echo request
18:32:32.081351 10.4.4.1 > 10.4.4.2: icmp: echo reply
```

Example 11-12 *V-TUN Tunnel Setup on OpenBSD (Continued)*

```
18:32:33.091594 10.4.4.2 > 10.4.4.1: icmp: echo request
18:32:33.091611 10.4.4.1 > 10.4.4.2: icmp: echo reply
18:32:34.101714 10.4.4.2 > 10.4.4.1: icmp: echo request
18:32:34.101730 10.4.4.1 > 10.4.4.2: icmp: echo reply
```

WARNING   Be aware of the fact that user-space tunneling solutions interfere with each other when run simultaneously. This might cause problems with binding to sockets or several programs controlling one and the same tun device. This is most certainly the case with V-TUN and OpenVPN. Never run these tools at the same time on the same gateway!

OpenVPN

OpenVPN (http://openvpn.sourceforge.net/) and V-TUN are somewhat related approaches, because both rely on the universal TUN/TAP driver to tunnel an IP subnet or virtual Ethernet adapter. OpenVPN is the most portable solution I came across in my evaluation. It can connect MAC OS X, Linux, BSD, Solaris, and Microsoft Windows via a VPN user-space daemon over TCP/UDP ports and a highly evolved SSL/TLS protocol integration (OpenSSL) with PKI support. It can handle dynamic IP addresses and operate in NAT environments. It offers tunnel bandwidth shaping, compression, encryption, and authentication featuring preshared key conventional encryption or certificate-based public key encryption. Example 11-13 demonstrates an example setup between Linux and OpenBSD.

Example 11-13 *Callisto-to-Europa (OpenVPN Tunnel with Static-Key Security (Preshared Secret)*

```
[root@europa:~#] openvpn --remote 192.168.14.1 --dev tun3 --ifconfig 10.5.5.2 10.5.5.1
                         --verb 5 --secret /etc/openvpn.key &

[root@europa:~#] ifconfig -A
...
tun3: flags=51<UP,POINTOPOINT,RUNNING> mtu 1256
        inet 10.5.5.2 --> 10.5.5.1 netmask 0xffffffff
...

[root@callisto:~#] openvpn --remote 192.168.14.3 --dev tun3 --ifconfig 10.5.5.1 10.5.5.2
                           --verb 5 --secret /etc/openvpn.key &

[root@callisto:~#] ifconfig -a
...
tun3      Link encap:Point-to-Point Protocol
          inet addr:10.5.5.1  P-t-P:10.5.5.2  Mask:255.255.255.255
          UP POINTOPOINT RUNNING NOARP MULTICAST  MTU:1256  Metric:1
          RX packets:4 errors:0 dropped:0 overruns:0 frame:0
          TX packets:30 errors:0 dropped:0 overruns:0 carrier:0
          collisions:0 txqueuelen:10
```

continues

Example 11-13 *Callisto-to-Europa (OpenVPN Tunnel with Static-Key Security (Preshared Secret) (Continued)*

```
          RX bytes:336 (336.0 b)   TX bytes:2520 (2.4 Kb)
...

[root@callisto:~#] ping 10.5.5.2
PING 10.5.5.2 (10.5.5.2) from 10.5.5.1 : 56(84) bytes of data.
WR64 bytes from 10.5.5.2: icmp_seq=1 ttl=255 time=1.36 ms
WR64 bytes from 10.5.5.2: icmp_seq=2 ttl=255 time=1.40 ms
WR64 bytes from 10.5.5.2: icmp_seq=3 ttl=255 time=1.12 ms

--- 10.5.5.2 ping statistics ---
3 packets transmitted, 3 received, 0% loss, time 2016ms
rtt min/avg/max/mdev = 1.129/1.298/1.403/0.124 ms
```

Stunnel/SSLwrap—SSL/TLS-Based "Wrapped" Tunnels and SSL Proxying/Relaying

SSL-based wrapper approaches work only for the TCP transport protocol. For example, Stunnel can encrypt TCP connections via SSL transport encryption acting as a multiplatform SSL tunneling proxy. Almost all open-source implementations are based on the OpenSSL (http://www.openssl.org) library. As mentioned at http://www.stunnel.org, "Stunnel can allow you to secure non-SSL aware daemons and protocols (like POP, IMAP, LDAP, etc) by having Stunnel provide the encryption, requiring no changes to the daemon's code."[5] SSLwrap takes a similar approach.

Secure Shell (SSH)

Although there is probably no need to introduce secure shell, I want to put it in context with our tunnel discussion. SSH uses port 21/tcp, sftp port 115/tcp, and its home base is at http://www.openssh.org. It evolved from an initial replacement for Telnet, rlogin, FTP, and rexec into a versatile and highly secure transport tunnel/relay solution with integrated strong authentication and single-sign-on capabilities. Although encrypted, the scp/sftp transfer performs extremely well. Many of OpenSSH's cryptography features rely on the OpenSSL library.

The following is a list of OpenSSH features:[6]

- Open-source project
- Free licensing
- Strong encryption (3DES, Blowfish)
- X11 forwarding (encrypt X Window System traffic)
- Port forwarding (encrypted channels for legacy protocols)
- Strong authentication (public key, one-time password, and Kerberos authentication)

- Agent forwarding (single sign-on)
- Interoperability (compliance with SSH 1.3, 1.5, and 2.0 protocol standards)
- sftp client and server support in both SSH1 and SSH2 protocols
- Kerberos and AFS ticket passing
- Data compression

At the time of this writing, Cisco devices support only SSHv1, and there are no plans to support SSHv2 in the foreseeable future because of a focus on the IPSec architectures as a strategic platform. Cisco implements SSH server and client features and SSH terminal-line access. To figure out which Cisco IOS releases support SSH, consult Cisco.com. For example configurations, look at the Cisco.com document "Configuring Secure Shell on Routers and Switches Running Cisco IOS." SSH is straightforward to set up, but only as an integral part of authentication, authorization, and accounting (AAA).

IPSec Foundation

IPSec is a suite of protocols operating at the network layer to secure communication between IPSec peers, either client to gateway, host to host, or gateway to gateway. IPSec tunnel connections can originate from gateways (routers, firewalls), hosts, or IPSec hardware/software clients and can terminate at VPN concentrators, hosts, or gateways (routers, firewalls).

IPSec provides both authentication and encryption services. Encryption renders intercepted payload over intrinsically hostile or untrusted infrastructures useless, and authentication ensures that packets are from a legitimate peer and have not been altered in transit or maliciously injected (man-in-the-middle attacks).

Figure 11-4 demonstrates the most popular applications for IPSec. Although IPSec introduces some caveats with regard to NAT and MTU issues, it is still the approach of choice to secure IP datagram transport transparently over hostile or untrusted (shared) environments, such as the Internet per se or wireless or powerline infrastructures. A lot of work is going on right now to make IPSec more "NAT-friendly" (NAT-Traversal). For further details about current work in the IPSec area, visit the IPSec Charter of the IETF (http://www.ietf.org/html.charters/ipsec-charter.html).

NOTE   IPSec is an extension of IPv4 and a mandatory part of IPv6.

The protocol suite consists of the following major building blocks:

- The IPSec security architecture for the Internet (RFC 2401)
- IKE key management (RFC 2409)
- ESP (RFC 2406) and AH (RFC 2402) to protect IP traffic

- ISAKMP security association (SA) management (RFC 2408)
- IPSec DOI for ISAKMP (RFC 2407)
- The OAKLEY key determination protocol (RFC 2412)
- PKI X.509v3 certificate management protocol (RFC 2510, RFC 2527)

Figure 11-4 *IPSec Applications*

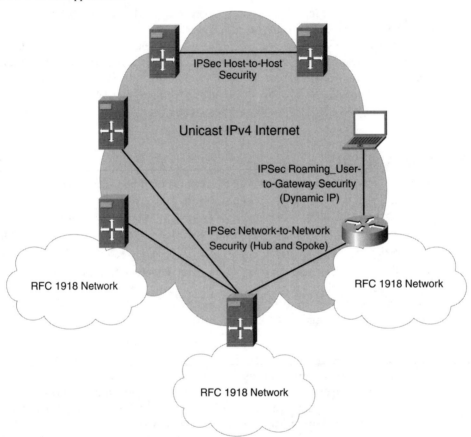

IPSec is a complex architecture because it has to handle complex tasks. This makes the concepts difficult to grasp. It would require hundreds of pages to cover IPSec appropriately, and even more for an introduction to cryptography and PKI (Public Key Infrastructure); therefore, you are referred to the standard documents and Internet resources.

IPSec ESP/AH and Tunnel and Transport Mode

IPSec offers two services: authentication and encryption. These can be used separately, but they often are used in combination. The protocols Encapsulating Security Payload (ESP) and Authenticated Header (AH) form the heart of the IPSec architecture. They provide authenticity, integrity, and replay protection and, in the case of ESP, confidentiality (based on payload encryption). Central to the ESP and AH concept is an abstraction referred to as security association (SA), which is explained later. ESP/AH protocol information is inserted between the IP header and the payload portion of the IP datagram. This example is referred to as IPSec transport mode, protection of payload, and transport of self-originated IP datagrams. In the case of a VPN setup, IPSec tunnel mode is used. This means that IPSec gateways deliver IP datagrams on behalf of other hosts/secure network segments. In this case, the gateway adds a completely new outer transport header, and the entire original IP datagram is encrypted. ESP most often is the approach of choice because it supports authentication *and* encryption and has a better chance of working with NAT gateways.

Manual/Automatic Keying, Preshared Secrets, and Certificates

Manual key management is tedious, less secure (no rekeying), more error prone, and (even worse) does not scale at all. It requires pregenerated keys to be distributed securely. If no key management daemon (such as racoon or isakmpd) is running (with the added benefit of automatic rekeying), manual keys have to suffice. This also means that SA setup has to be handled manually. The following scenarios are deployed commonly:

- IPSec with manual key. (IPSec secret key will not change over time.)
- IPSec with IKE with preshared secret. (IPSec secret key changes over time.)
- IPSec with IKE with X.509v3 certificates. (IPSec secret key changes over time, requires a PKI.)

IKE Phase 1 and 2: Main Mode and Aggressive Mode

IKE uses a two-phase process for establishing IPSec parameters between two IPSec peering nodes that would otherwise have to be configured manually (for instance, by OpenBSD ipsecadm(8)). IKE phase 1 deals with initially establishing a secure and authenticated channel (a security association = SA) between IPSec peers with either preshared keys or X.509v3 certificates to ensure that the other side is who it claims to be. This can work either in main mode or aggressive mode and forms the foundation for phase 2. That is, "main mode sends the various authentication information in a certain sequence, providing identity protection. Aggressive mode does not provide identity protection because all of the authentication information is sent at the same time."[7]

In phase 2, unidirectional endpoint SAs are negotiated on behalf of IPSec and deal with the actual key exchange necessary for data encryption. Because phase 1 has already established and verified the credentials of the peers, Quick mode suffices in phase 2.

Resolving the IKE, PKI, SA, ISAKMP, and Oakley Confusion

Internet Key Exchange (IKE) is a somewhat generic hybrid protocol that approaches the issue of negotiation and provisioning of keying material for security associations in a protected manner. It does not per se claim to be compatible with Oakley or SKEME. IKE takes into consideration client mode negotiation (negotiation proxies) independent of the actual endpoints of SAs. An SA qualitatively is a logical point-to-point security channel between two security entities (peer IP addresses).

Security associations are by their nature connection-oriented and unidirectional. From the view of IKE, an SA is nothing more than "a set of policies and key(s) used to protect information. The ISAKMP SA is the shared policy and key(s) used by the negotiating peers in this protocol to protect their communication" (quoted from RFC 2409). IKE negotiations have two phases: UDP/500 (phase 1 and phase 2).

ISAKMP provides a framework for authentication, SA management, and cryptographic key exchange, but it was designed to be intrinsically key exchange independent and thus not defining a specific key exchange. Oakley specifically describes a series of key exchanges. SKEME describes a specific, versatile key exchange technique. Oakley and SKEME are designed to be compatible with the ISAKMP framework; however, they do not form a hierarchy.

A key exchange specification essentially defines a protocol by which two already authenticated parties or peers can agree on secure and secret keying material. Public Key Infrastructure (PKI) essentially brings into play X.509v3 certificates (digital signatures), frameworks, and architectures to deal with certificates (certificate authorities [CAs], dissemination and revocation of certificates, tokens, and so on). Certificates identify organizations, sites, entities, accounts, services, and individuals. LDAP interfaces to PKI are the most common way of interfacing with other systems.

What Is Opportunistic Encryption (OE)?

You can find the basic principles of OE in context with IPSec, IKE, and DNSsec in draft-richardson-ipsec-opportunistic-12.txt (available from the http://www.ietf.org drafts archive). Linux FreeS/WAN was among the first strong supporters and contributors to this idea. The general idea is to provide a method for ad-hoc encryption for secure communication without a lot of effort for prearrangements involving the end systems/parties. The approach relies on DNS (DNS TXT resource records [RRs] in the case of FreeS/WAN) for public key distribution and can be secured via DNSsec. This requires intervention from system administrators to add ancillary DNS records for opportunistic encryption support. This approach certainly has architectural drawbacks. For further information, consult the work of the IETF IPSec and ISAKMP/Oakley Work Group and the IETF DNSEXT Work Group, where DNSsec work is done.

What Is NAT-Traversal (NAT-T)?

NAT in context with IPSec is almost always a source for trouble. Try to avoid this combination, or at least perform NAT and IPSec tunnel termination on the same box and always use ESP. See draft-ietf-ipsec-nat-reqts-04.txt for an excellent introduction as to why and in what way

NAT breaks IPSec in most cases. STUN (RFC 3489) offers another solution to the NAT problem. On the plus side, tunnels in general can be the solution for NAT-ignorant protocols such as H.323 (for example, Microsoft NetMeeting).

You will find that draft-ietf-ipsec-nat-t-ike-06.txt "describes how to detect one or more Network Address Translation devices (NATs) between IPSec hosts, and how to negotiate the use of UDP encapsulation of the IPSec packets through the NAT boxes in Internet Key Exchange (IKE)." The NAT-T capability negotiation with remote gateways is done in IKE phase 1 and allows safe IPSec traversal through firewalls performing NAT. In addition, the path between the two gateways is checked for NAT presence. The negotiation of UDP-encapsulated IPSec packets is performed in IKE Quick mode.

DHCP Provisioning over IPSec Tunnel Mode

RFC 3456, "Dynamic Host Configuration Protocol (DHCPv4) Configuration of IPSec Tunnel Mode," describes a mechanism that allows remote hosts to be assigned addresses of a corporate address space. Therefore, the host would appear to be part of the intranet it securely connects to via IPSec.

IPSec Implementations

The VPNC IPSec/IKE conformance test suite uses KAME/racoon and OpenBSD's isakmpd as reference code. This should demonstrate the maturity, interoperability, and reliability of the open-source code base. It works extremely well with Cisco IPSec implementations and IPSec client software. Nevertheless, it took the IPSec vendors a long time to work out interoperability issues. Occasionally I get the impression that some vendors, for awkward commercial reasons, deliberately break what took them years to fix. This is an especially big problem with IPSec intervendor client-to-gateway interoperability. (You are invited to draw your own conclusion.)

Linux IPSec

Until recently, Linux FreeS/WAN (http://www.freeswan.org) was the most popular implementation of IPSec and IKE for the Linux 2.2/2.4 kernel (IPv4 only). A related project called Super FreeS/WAN (http://www.freeswan.ca) included all the latest-and-greatest patches and early development features (NAT-Traversal, AES, X.509, ALG [all ciphers/hashes as modules], Dead Peer Detection IETF Draft, and so on). Because of disagreements about the evolution of FreeS/WAN and some peculiar points of view (removal of AH, focus on opportunistic encryption, and lack of interest in IPSec standard compliance and interoperability), the project has been discontinued and is no longer actively maintained.

The OpenSWAN Project (http://www.openswan.org) has started as a code fork of FreeS/WAN and will continue the work. The FreeS/WAN maintainer had a strategic interest in pushing a new approach to IPSec tunnel/VPN provisioning referred to as "opportunistic encryption" involving advanced DNS features, plug-and-play friendliness at the cost of IPSec generic compliance, and reduced security. It escaped the attention of some people that FreeS/WAN gateways do not necessarily talk only to FreeS/WAN gateways. This led to a misjudgment of the community support of that strategic direction.

OpenSWAN is a huge kernel patch and module with accompanying user-space tools that never made it into the mainstream kernel. KLIPS is the kernel IPSec module, and pluto is the IKE daemon. The new 2.6 Linux kernel drastically changed this picture. The current state of affairs is this: "As of Linux 2.5.47, there is a native IPSec implementation in the kernel. It was written by Alexey Kuznetsov and Dave Miller, inspired by the work of the USAGI IPv6 group. With its merge, James Morris' CrypoAPI also became part of the kernel—it does the actual crypting. As of 2.5.49, IPSec works without further patches."[8]

Linux native IPSec for the new 2.6 Linux kernel is based on the KAME Project's IKE daemon racoon, which is a big leap forward for consistent IPSec interoperability between BSD platforms and Linux. OpenBSD's isakmpd also has been ported to Linux, and OpenSWAN is completing 2.6 integration support of their own implementation. OpenSWAN is easy to install; just follow the ReadMe that comes with the sources. IPSec-Tools is a port of KAME's IPSec utilities to the Linux 2.6 including racoon/setkey. isakmpd and racoon/setkey can be retrieved from the following resources:

- http://bender.thinknerd.de/~thomas/IPsec/isakmpd-linux.html
- http://ipsec-tools.sourceforge.net/

KAME

The KAME Project is a software kit that provides reference implementations of IPv6 and IPSec (both IPv4/IPv6) for BSD operating systems as well as the alternate queuing framework (ALTQ) discussed in Chapter 13, "Policy Routing, Bandwidth Management, and QoS." KAME's IKE daemon is called racoon.

During IPSec setup, the kernel needs to know what traffic to encrypt or secure and how. This is referred to as establishing an *IPSec security policy*. On BSD systems, this information is stored in a table in the kernel known as the *security policy database (SPD)*.

The setkey(8) utility is the tool to manipulate the SPD. Another table (the *security association database [SAD]*) stores the various encryption keys needed to secure communications between hosts, clients, and gateways. In case of manual keying, the setkey(8) program also is used to configure the manual keys in the SAD. With an IKE approach, racoon will handle the adding and deleting of entries from the SAD automatically.

FreeBSD

To add IPSec support to your FreeBSD kernel, add the code in Example 11-14 to your kernel config file, and then recompile and install the new kernel. You essentially need the two utilities setkey and the IKE daemon racoon.

Example 11-14 *FreeBSD IPSec Kernel Configuration Options*

```
options       IPSEC              #IP security
options       IPSEC_ESP          #IP security
options       IPSEC_DEBUG        #debug for IP security
device        gif 4              #For IPSec Tunnel Mode
```

FreeBSD IPSec configuration includes the following steps:

1 Retrieve and install the racoon daemon from ports by using **cd /usr/ports/security/racoon** followed by **make all, make install, make clean**.

2 Define the IPSec security policy via **setkey -DFP** (for manual policy management) and **setkey -f /etc/ipsec.conf**.

3 You also can do that dynamically via the IKE daemon racoon. It requires two configuration files: **/usr/local/etc/racoon/psk.txt** (for preshared keys) and **/usr/local/etc/racoon/racoon.conf**.

4 Then start racoon via **racoon -l /var/log/racoon -f usr/local/etc/racoon/racoon.conf**.

NOTE   IPSec tunnel connections between two FreeBSD gateways require the configuration of the gif pseudo-interface for proper routing between the protected private (RFC 1918) networks behind these gateways (Example 11-15).

Example 11-15 *Castor gif Pseudo-Interface Setup*

```
[root@castor:~#] gifconfig gif0 192.168.2.7 192.168.2.254
[root@castor:~#] ifconfig gif0 inet 192.168.7.7 netmask 255.255.255.0 192.168.45.254
  netmask 255.255.255.0

[root@castor:~#] gifconfig gif0
[gif0: flags=8051<UP,POINTOPOINT,RUNNING,MULTICAST> mtu 1280
        inet6 fe80::210:5aff:fec4:2c04%gif0  prefixlen 64
        inet 192.168.7.7 --> 192.168.45.254 netmask 0xffffff00
        physical address inet 192.168.2.7 --> 192.168.2.254

[root@castor:~#] netstat -rn -f inet
Routing tables

Internet:
Destination       Gateway          Flags    Refs      Use  Netif Expire
default           192.168.2.254    UGSc        3      121   xl0
```

continues

Example 11-15 *Castor gif Pseudo-Interface Setup (Continued)*

```
10.0.0.4          10.0.0.4           UH    0      0    lo0
127.0.0.1         127.0.0.1          UH    1     32    lo0
192.168.2         link#1             UC    2      0    xl0
192.168.2.7       00:10:5a:c4:2c:04  UHLW  3      4    lo0
192.168.2.254     52:54:05:e3:e4:2f  UHLW  5    446    xl0    402
192.168.7         link#2             UC    0      0    ed0
192.168.45.254    192.168.7.7        UH    0      0    gif0
192.168.80        link#15            UC    0      0    vlan8
```

NOTE   Consult http://www.freebsd.org/doc/en_US.ISO8859-1/books/handbook/ipsec.html for
further details.

OpenBSD

isakmpd is the OpenBSD ISAKMP/Oakley (a.k.a. IKE) key management daemon. The
isakmpd daemon is responsible for the establishment of management of security associations
for encrypted or authenticated network traffic. It is the only scalable alternative to manual
keying with tedious and error-prone manual SA setups and ESP/AH flows on top. isakmpd
is also available for NetBSD. There you have the luxury to choose between isakmpd and
racoon. Example 11-16 shows the kernel configuration options required by OpenBSD
and related sysctl parameters.

Example 11-16 *OpenBSD IPSec Kernel Configuration Options*

```
### kernel config:

option    CRYPTO         # Cryptographic Framework
option    IPSEC          # IPSec VPN
#option   KEY            # KEY implied by IPSec
pseudo-device enc 4      # Encapsulation device used by IPSec

### sysctl:

[root@ganymed:~#] sysctl -w net.inet.esp.enable=1
[root@ganymed:~#] sysctl -w net.inet.ah.enable=1
[root@ganymed:~#] sysctl -w net.inet.ip.forwarding=1
[root@ganymed:~#] sysctl -w net.inet6.ip6.forwarding=1
[root@ganymed:~#] sysctl -w net.inet.ipcomp.enable = 1
```

An OpenBSD IPSec setup consists of these components:

- /etc/rc.vpn (for manual keying only, manual SAs, and IPSec flows)
- /etc/isamkmpd/isakmpd.conf
- /etc/isamkmpd/isakmpd.policy
- isakmpd (not required for manual keying)

- The keynote utility (optional, man pages 1, 3, 4, 5; RFC 2704), public/private key generation, and trust management
- ipsecadm (generic admin interface for manual setup)
- The enc(4) pseudo-interface for encryption (adjust your firewall filters accordingly)

<table>
<tr><td>**NOTE**</td><td>photurisd is an alternative key management daemon for OpenBSD. It is based on RFC 2522 and RFC 2523. A word of wisdom: Stay away from the OpenBSD photurisd. It has major limitations, and the whole community is using ISAKMP anyway. photurisd was removed from the OpenBSD tree with version 3.3 for good reason and can be considered deprecated.</td></tr>
</table>

General Tunnel and Specific IPSec Caveats

Tunnels introduce several issues unknown to regular networking connections. The following brief discussion sheds some light on these issues.

Tunnels and Firewalls

Depending on the layer on which certain tunnel solutions reside, it is necessary to configure firewalls and packet filters to pass certain IP protocol numbers or UDP/TCP ports (see Table 11-3). The lower in the stack the tunnel sits, the more transparent it usually is. The higher it sits, the more application-specific it is (for example, SSH).

Table 11-3   *Tunnel Protocol and Port Numbers Overview*

Tunnel Approach	Protocol Number	TCP/UDP Port Number
IPencap IP encapsulated in IP (officially "IP")	4	—
IP-IP	94	—
ENCAP	98	—
GRE	47	—
IP mobile	55	—
IPCOMP (IP Payload Compression Protocol)	108	—
IPSec AH	51	—
IPSec ESP	50	—
IKE/ISAKMP	—	500tcp/udp
L2F/L2TP	—	1701tcp/udp
PPTP	—	1723tcp/udp
HTTP/HTTPS/proxy ports	—	80/443/8080/tcp
SSH	—	22tcp/udp

NOTE	When deploying IPSec in context with ipfilter, enable the ipfilter IPSec proxy in the configuration.

Tunnels Do Not Like NAT

Most traditional tunnel approaches such as GRE and IPSec do not like NAT. This is a dislike they share with some protocols that cannot cope with NAT without help such as proxies (for example, MS NetMeeting facilitating H.323). Doing NAT and tunnel termination on an integrated gateway usually works. With IPSec, tunnel mode via ESP is the best approach to avoid NAT hassle. As already mentioned, the NAT-Traversal IETF draft deals exactly with this challenge.

Tunnels Cause MTU Issues

Tunnels add protocol overhead and reduce the effective MTU a frame can have. It is pretty much the same with VLAN tagging (giants or jumbo frames) and MPLS Layer 2 overhead that needs to be accounted for on switches. A workaround for legacy switches that are incapable of dealing with jumbo frames is VLAN trunking. If you encounter strange problems with large packets such as FTP and smaller ones such as ICMP work, it is most likely an MTU problem.

Some operating systems adjust the MTU of tunnel or pseudo-interfaces by default; others leave it to the educated system administrator. With some protocols, such as GRE or 802.1q, it is easy to derive the increment value from the protocol design; with others, such as ESP/AH, it is guesswork because of padding and variable-length headers.

There exist several misperceptions of MTU and TCP maximum segment size. Just because the standards define an MTU of 1500 for Ethernet, it does not mean that it does not work beyond that limit. Tunnels also add a new chapter to the entire issue of fragmentation. MTU symptoms are often not diagnosed correctly. Classic symptoms include web pages not displaying properly (without images) even though the host is pingable, or directory listings not displaying even though the primary connection is established.

Tunnels Add Protocol Overhead

The efficiency and attractiveness of a tunnel solution also is determined by its protocol overhead. This is the reason why user-space UDP tunneling is efficient and it is not a good idea to encapsulate tunnels within tunnels without a good reason (for instance, GRE, IPSec, and SSH in combination). Therefore, you should account for the protocol overhead when designing gateways and links.

Unnumbered Links and Tunnel Routing

Some dynamic routing protocols are somewhat sensible with regard to point-to-point links (such as tunnels), unnumbered interfaces, and NBMA issues. Keep this in mind if you encounter problems with Open Shortest Path First (OSPF) and switch to the latest Quagga sources where a lot of point-to-point fixes have been added.

Multicast Transit via Point-to-Point Tunnels

GRE is capable of transporting multicast traffic. This is useful when a multicast-incapable network cloud separates the multicast sender and receiver. It usually is configured featuring Protocol Independent Multicast (PIM). One alternative is DVMRP, which facilitates underlying IP-IP tunnels. For more detailed configuration instructions, see Chapter 14.

Crypto Performance

CPU processing of hashes (SHA, MD5) and cryptographic transforms (AES, 3DES) is considerable and starts affecting design choices starting with a few megabits-per-second tunnel performance. Whenever possible, choose AES, which considerably reduces the strain compared to 3DES. DES and 3DES originally were designed to run in hardware and poorly perform in software, whereas the AES Rijndael algorithm was chosen for its performance characteristics. In addition, for tunnel throughput beyond 10 Mbps, a hardware crypto accelerator is certainly a good idea. It relieves the CPU from the computation of transforms and even hashes. These crypto devices/cards are well supported on BSD and Linux operating systems and often are referred to as *Fast IPSec*.

High Availability

With the introduction of tunnels, the design and operation of high-availability gateway architectures is becoming far more challenging.

This involves clustering, virtual instances, dynamic routing protocols, heartbeat approaches, VRRP, and other measures. The biggest challenge for firewalls is to resume gigabit forwarding and crypto operation without breaking stateful inspection, existing tunnels, and NAT. Here it really becomes an art to operate two parallel firewalls that constantly mirror NAT tables and stateful inspection pseudo-caches. Takeover of authenticated tunnels bound to a particular IP address without breaking the SA or client TCP sessions is difficult, too. In this scenario, commercial approaches are ahead of the open-source community, but even they struggle to deliver on their promises.

VPN Deployment and Scalability

When you are deploying large VPN installations or a huge road-warrior (roaming user) base, consider a sound design that includes PKI, VPN concentrators, and a unified approach toward VPN clients with a clear set of policies. Also keep in mind that DHCP over IPSec is "not yet there."

Point-to-point tunnels do not scale; however, hub-and-spoke topologies remedy the problem to at least some extent. A sound IP addressing concept and routing architecture is of crucial importance, too. Keep in mind that tunnels per se do not provide security to the involved clients, hosts, or gateways, and because of their transparent nature, tunnels do nothing for malicious code defense. Therefore, it is recommended to secure tunnel termination devices with packet filters, stateful-inspection firewalls, or personal firewalls.

NOTE Some VPN client software implementations such as Cisco's offer the feature of a simple integrated firewall that blocks all traffic that does not traverse legitimate tunnels. This is far easier to deploy and manage than complicated policies pushed down to complex client firewall engines. Be warned also that personal firewalls do not always happily coexist with VPN client software and can cause unrecoverable system screwups. Finally, do not ruin a sound architecture to accommodate IPSec clients behind a NAT gateway.

Advice About IPSec Lab Scenarios

Host-to-host security hardly is used anymore today, and the same is true for manual IPSec keying and manual SA setup. IKE dominates the picture with rapid acceptance of X.509v3 certificate integration. The most widespread deployments of IPSec feature gateway-to-gateway and road-warrior-to-gateway configurations. VPN client software is required on the road warrior (PDA, notebook).

Because OpenSWAN and native kernel IPSec for 2.6 kernels is rapidly approaching its final stage of consolidation, we will wait until the dust settles and focus on FreeBSD and OpenBSD IKE here. Dynamically negotiated IPSec requires configuration of the IKE daemons and a policy that defines qualified traffic that triggers SA establishment (for example, network to network via tunnel mode).

Lab 11-8: An IPSec with IKE (racoon/isakmpd) Scenario (Gateway-to-Gateway Tunnel Mode)

In this lab, we require the discussed gif tunnel setup on the FreeBSD side. Example 11-17 demonstrates the setup and output of the IPSec gateway ganymed (OpenBSD), and Example 11-18 shows the configuration of the IPSec peer castor (FreeBSD). FreeBSD has a dedicated configuration file for the IPSec policy, and OpenBSD isakmpd contains everything in a single configuration file. The tunnel operation is verified via extended pings from castor and callisto in combination with sniffer traces. The highlighted text emphasizes successful SA establishment.

Example 11-17 *OpenBSD IPSec with ISAKMPD and Preshared Key*

```
[root@ganymed:/etc/isakmpd#] cat isakmpd.policy
KeyNote-Version: 2
Authorizer: "POLICY"
Licensees: "passphrase:cisco"
Conditions: app_domain == "IPsec policy" &&
            esp_present == "yes" &&
            esp_enc_alg == "3des" &&
            esp_auth_alg == "hmac-md5" -> "true";

[root@ganymed:/etc/isakmpd#] cat isakmpd.conf
#
# A configuration sample VPN for the isakmpd ISAKMP/Oakley (a.k.a. IKE) daemon.
# "ganymed" and "castor" are the respective security gateways (a.k.a. VPN nodes).
#

[General]
Retransmits=            5
Exchange-max-time=      120
Listen-on=              192.168.2.254

[Phase 1]
192.168.2.7=            ISAKMP-peer-castor

[Phase 2]
Connections=            IPsec-ganymed-castor

[ISAKMP-peer-castor]
Phase=                  1
Transport=              udp
Local-address=          192.168.2.254
Address=                192.168.2.7
Authentication=         cisco
Configuration=          Default-main-mode

[IPsec-ganymed-castor]
Phase=                  2
ISAKMP-peer=            ISAKMP-peer-castor
Configuration=          Default-quick-mode
Local-ID=               Net-ganymed
Remote-ID=              Net-castor

[Net-ganymed]
ID-type=                IPV4_ADDR_SUBNET
Network=                192.168.45.0
Netmask=                255.255.255.0

[Net-castor]
ID-type=                IPV4_ADDR_SUBNET
Network=                192.168.7.0
Netmask=                255.255.255.0
```

continues

Example 11-17 *OpenBSD IPSec with ISAKMPD and Preshared Key (Continued)*

```
[Default-main-mode]
EXCHANGE_TYPE=          ID_PROT
Transforms=             3DES-MD5-GRP2

[Default-quick-mode]
DOI=                    IPSEC
EXCHANGE_TYPE=          QUICK_MODE
Suites=                 QM-ESP-3DES-MD5-PFS-GRP2-SUITE

### Proof of the two uni-directional SAs ###

[root@ganymed:~#] cat /kern/ipsec
Hashmask: 31, policy entries: 2
SPI = 0ea713d5, Destination = 192.168.2.7, Sproto = 50
        Established 416 seconds ago
        Source = 192.168.2.254
        Flags (00011082) = <tunneling,usedtunnel>
        Crypto ID: 1
        xform = <IPsec ESP>
                Encryption = <3DES>
                Authentication = <HMAC-MD5>
        3528 bytes processed by this SA
        Last used 378 seconds ago
        Expirations:
                Hard expiration(1) in 784 seconds
                Soft expiration(1) in 664 seconds

SPI = b6297e4e, Destination = 192.168.2.254, Sproto = 50
        Established 416 seconds ago
        Source = 192.168.2.7
        Flags (00001082) = <tunneling>
        Crypto ID: 2
        xform = <IPsec ESP>
                Encryption = <3DES>
                Authentication = <HMAC-MD5>
        3696 bytes processed by this SA
        Last used 378 seconds ago
        Expirations:
                Hard expiration(1) in 784 seconds
                Soft expiration(1) in 664 seconds

### The encap routing situation as derived from the VPN policy setup
   (isakmpd.policy) ###

[root@ganymed:~#] netstat -f encap -rn
Routing tables

Encap:
Source          Port  Destination    Port  Proto SA(Address/Proto/Type/Direction)
192.168.7/24    0     192.168.45/24  0     0     192.168.2.7/50/use/in
192.168.45/24   0     192.168.7/24   0     0     192.168.2.7/50/require/out
```

Example 11-17 *OpenBSD IPSec with ISAKMPD and Preshared Key (Continued)*

```
### Detailed Protocol Statistics for ESP/AH ###

[root@ganymed:~#] netstat -p esp
esp:
        42 input ESP packets
        42 output ESP packets
        0 packets from unsupported protocol families
        0 packets shorter than header shows
        0 packets dropped due to policy
        0 packets for which no TDB was found
        0 input packets that failed to be processed
        0 packets with bad encryption received
        0 packets that failed verification received
        0 packets for which no XFORM was set in TDB received
        0 packets were dropped due to full output queue
        0 packets where counter wrapping was detected
        0 possibly replayed packets received
        0 packets with bad payload size or padding received
        0 packets attempted to use an invalid tdb
        0 packets got larger than max IP packet size
        0 packets that failed crypto processing
        3696 input bytes
        3528 output bytes

[root@ganymed:~#] netstat -p ah
ah:
        0 input AH packets
        0 output AH packets
        0 packets from unsupported protocol families
        0 packets shorter than header shows
        0 packets dropped due to policy
        0 packets for which no TDB was found
        0 input packets that failed to be processed
        0 packets that failed verification received
        0 packets for which no XFORM was set in TDB received
        0 packets were dropped due to full output queue
        0 packets where counter wrapping was detected
        0 possibly replayed packets received
        0 packets with bad authenticator length received
        0 packets attempted to use an invalid tdb
        0 packets got larger than max IP packet size
        0 packets that failed crypto processing
        0 input bytes
        0 output bytes

### And the sniffer traces to prove that we are really encrypting ###

[root@castor:~#] ping -S 192.168.7.7 192.168.45.1
PING 192.168.45.1 (192.168.45.1) from 192.168.7.7: 56 data bytes
64 bytes from 192.168.45.1: icmp_seq=0 ttl=63 time=2.412 ms
64 bytes from 192.168.45.1: icmp_seq=1 ttl=63 time=2.382 ms
64 bytes from 192.168.45.1: icmp_seq=2 ttl=63 time=2.320 ms
```

continues

Example 11-17 *OpenBSD IPSec with ISAKMPD and Preshared Key (Continued)*

```
^C
--- 192.168.45.1 ping statistics ---
3 packets transmitted, 3 packets received, 0% packet loss
round-trip min/avg/max/stddev = 2.320/2.371/2.412/0.038 ms

[root@callisto:~#] ping -I 192.168.45.1 192.168.7.7
PING 192.168.7.7 (192.168.7.7) from 192.168.45.1 : 56(84) bytes of data.
64 bytes from 192.168.7.7: icmp_seq=1 ttl=63 time=3.84 ms
64 bytes from 192.168.7.7: icmp_seq=2 ttl=63 time=2.64 ms
64 bytes from 192.168.7.7: icmp_seq=3 ttl=63 time=2.51 ms

--- 192.168.7.7 ping statistics ---
3 packets transmitted, 3 received, 0% packet loss, time 2018ms
rtt min/avg/max/mdev = 2.515/3.002/3.846/0.600 ms

[root@ganymed:~#] tethereal -i ne4
Capturing on ne4
  0.000000 castor.nerdzone.org -> 192.168.2.254 ESP ESP (SPI=0x2b76d234)
  0.001213 192.168.2.254 -> castor.nerdzone.org ESP ESP (SPI=0x01a960cc)
  0.272924 192.168.2.254 -> castor.nerdzone.org ESP ESP (SPI=0x01a960cc)
  0.273586 castor.nerdzone.org -> 192.168.2.254 ESP ESP (SPI=0x2b76d234)
  1.001848 castor.nerdzone.org -> 192.168.2.254 ESP ESP (SPI=0x2b76d234)
  1.003015 192.168.2.254 -> castor.nerdzone.org ESP ESP (SPI=0x01a960cc)
  1.282909 192.168.2.254 -> castor.nerdzone.org ESP ESP (SPI=0x01a960cc)
  1.283591 castor.nerdzone.org -> 192.168.2.254 ESP ESP (SPI=0x2b76d234)

[root@ganymed:~#] tethereal -i enc0
Capturing on enc0
  0.000000           ->            UNKNOWN WTAP_ENCAP = 0
  0.001566           ->            UNKNOWN WTAP_ENCAP = 0
  0.668721           ->            UNKNOWN WTAP_ENCAP = 0
  0.669053           ->            UNKNOWN WTAP_ENCAP = 0
  1.009968           ->            UNKNOWN WTAP_ENCAP = 0
  1.011561           ->            UNKNOWN WTAP_ENCAP = 0
  1.670448           ->            UNKNOWN WTAP_ENCAP = 0
  1.670744           ->            UNKNOWN WTAP_ENCAP = 0
```

Example 11-18 *FreeBSD IPSec with racoon and Preshared Key*

```
### gif tunnel setup for routing ###

[root@castor:~#] gifconfig gif0 192.168.2.7 192.168.2.254

[root@castor:~#] ifconfig gif0 inet 192.168.7.7 netmask 255.255.255.0
192.168.45.254 netmask 255.255.255.0

[root@castor:~#] gifconfig gif0
[gif0: flags=8051<UP,POINTOPOINT,RUNNING,MULTICAST> mtu 1280
        inet6 fe80::210:5aff:fec4:2c04%gif0  prefixlen 64
        inet 192.168.7.7 --> 192.168.45.254 netmask 0xffffff00
        physical address inet 192.168.2.7 --> 192.168.2.254
```

Example 11-18 *FreeBSD IPSec with racoon and Preshared Key (Continued)*

```
[root@castor:~#] netstat -rn -f inet
Routing tables

Internet:
Destination        Gateway            Flags   Refs     Use  Netif Expire
default            192.168.2.254      UGSc       3     121   xl0
10.0.0.4           10.0.0.4           UH         0       0   lo0
127.0.0.1          127.0.0.1          UH         1      32   lo0
192.168.2          link#1             UC         2       0   xl0
192.168.2.7        00:10:5a:c4:2c:04  UHLW       3       4   lo0
192.168.2.254      52:54:05:e3:e4:2f  UHLW       5     446   xl0    402
192.168.7          link#2             UC         0       0   ed0
192.168.45.254     192.168.7.7        UH         0       0   gif0
192.168.80         link#15            UC         0       0   vlan8


### IPsec configurations ###

[root@castor:~#] cat /etc/ipsec.conf
spdadd 192.168.7.0/24 192.168.45.0/24 any -P out ipsec
esp/tunnel/192.168.2.7-192.168.2.254/require;
spdadd 192.168.45.0/24 192.168.7.0/24 any -P in ipsec
esp/tunnel/192.168.2.254-192.168.2.7/require;

[root@castor:~#] cat /usr/local/etc/racoon/psk.txt
# IPv4/v6 addresses
192.168.2.254    cisco

[root@castor:~#] cat /usr/local/etc/racoon/racoon.conf

path include "/usr/local/etc/racoon" ;

# search this file for pre_shared_key with various ID key.
path pre_shared_key "/usr/local/etc/racoon/psk.txt" ;

# racoon will look for certificate file in the directory,
# if the certificate/certificate request payload is received.
path certificate "/usr/local/etc/cert" ;

# "log" specifies logging level.  It is followed by either "notify," "debug,"
# or "debug2."
#log debug;

# "padding" defines some parameter of padding.  You should not touch these.
padding
{
        maximum_length 20;      # maximum padding length.
        randomize off;          # enable randomize length.
        strict_check off;       # enable strict check.
        exclusive_tail off;     # extract last one octet.
}
```

continues

Example 11-18 *FreeBSD IPSec with racoon and Preshared Key (Continued)*

```
# if no listen directive is specified, racoon will listen to all
# available interface addresses.
listen
{
        isakmp 192.168.2.7 [500];
        #admin [7002];            # administrative port by kmpstat.
        strict_address;          # all addresses must be bound.
}

# Specification of various default timers.
timer
{
        # These value can be changed per remote node.
        counter 5;               # maximum trying count to send.
        interval 20 sec;         # maximum interval to resend.
        persend 1;               # the number of packets per a send.

        # timer for waiting to complete each phase.
        phase1 30 sec;
        phase2 15 sec;
}

### gateway-to-gateway ###

remote 192.168.2.254
{
        exchange_mode main,aggressive;
        doi ipsec_doi;
        situation identity_only;

        my_identifier address 192.168.2.7;
        peers_identifier address 192.168.2.254;

        nonce_size 16;
        lifetime time 1 min;     # sec,min,hour

        proposal {
                encryption_algorithm 3des;
                hash_algorithm md5;
                authentication_method pre_shared_key ;
                dh_group 2 ;
        }
}

sainfo address 192.168.2.7 any address 192.168.2.254 any
{
        pfs_group 2 ;
        lifetime time 30 sec;
        encryption_algorithm 3des ;
        authentication_algorithm hmac_md5;
        compression_algorithm deflate ;
}
```

Example 11-18 *FreeBSD IPSec with racoon and Preshared Key (Continued)*

```
[root@castor:~#] cat /var/log/racoon
2004-04-04 13:44:36: INFO: main.c:174:main(): @(#)internal version 20001216
sakane@kame.net
2004-04-04 13:44:36: INFO: main.c:175:main(): @(#)This product linked OpenSSL 0.9.7c
30 Sep 2003 (http://www.openssl.org/)
2004-04-04 13:44:36: INFO: isakmp.c:1358:isakmp_open(): 192.168.2.7[500] used as
isakmp port (fd=5)
2004-04-04 13:44:51: INFO: isakmp.c:894:isakmp_ph1begin_r(): respond new phase 1
negotiation: 192.168.2.7[500]<=>192.168.2.254[500]
2004-04-04 13:44:51: INFO: isakmp.c:899:isakmp_ph1begin_r(): begin Identity
Protection mode.
2004-04-04 13:44:51: WARNING: isakmp_inf.c:1281:isakmp_check_notify(): ignore
INITIAL-CONTACT notification, because it is only accepted after phase1.
2004-04-04 13:44:51: WARNING: ipsec_doi.c:3099:ipsecdoi_checkid1(): ID value
mismatched.
2004-04-04 13:44:51: INFO: isakmp.c:2412:log_ph1established(): ISAKMP-SA
established 192.168.2.7[500]-192.168.2.254[500] spi:1340537a78e1b7d8
:d25809b27e1f5e75
2004-04-04 13:44:52: INFO: isakmp.c:1049:isakmp_ph2begin_r(): respond new phase 2
negotiation: 192.168.2.7[0]<=>192.168.2.254[0]
2004-04-04 13:44:52: INFO: pfkey.c:1134:pk_recvupdate(): IPsec-SA established: ESP/
Tunnel 192.168.2.254->192.168.2.7 spi=245830613(0xea713d5)
2004-04-04 13:44:52: INFO: pfkey.c:1357:pk_recvadd(): IPsec-SA established: ESP/
Tunnel 192.168.2.7->192.168.2.254 spi=3056172622(0xb6297e4e)
2004-04-04 13:45:51: INFO: isakmp.c:1516:isakmp_ph1expire(): ISAKMP-SA expired
192.168.2.7[500]-192.168.2.254[500] spi:1340537a78e1b7d8:d2580
9b27e1f5e75
2004-04-04 13:45:52: INFO: isakmp.c:1564:isakmp_ph1delete(): ISAKMP-SA deleted
192.168.2.7[500]-192.168.2.254[500] spi:1340537a78e1b7d8:d2580
9b27e1f5e75
```

Road-Warrior Scenarios (Road Warrior-to-OpenBSD/ FreeBSD Gateway with IKE)

Road warriors (multiuser configurations) are roaming user clients with dynamically assigned IP addresses unknown to the home IPSec gateway or VPN concentrator. Hence the configuration has to rely on other means of authentication such as deployment of signatures or certificates. This requires a PKI.

Deployment of preshared secrets does not scale and often compromises entire architectures that rely on only one key. Because of an architectural change in the Cisco IPSec client for group authentication, interoperability with UNIX IPSec implementations has severely suffered (although arguably added benefit to Cisco-to-Cisco connections).

OpenBSD, FreeBSD, and Linux IPSec clients offer excellent granularity to adjust to interoperability requirements. As a rule of thumb, the same IPSec implementation on the client and the gateway saves lots of headaches and debugging effort. For sample road-warrior setups, see http://www.ipsec-howto.org, http://www.linuxsecurity.com/resource_files/ cryptography/ipsec-howto/HOWTO.html, and http://www.allard.nu/openbsd/index.html. This last website covers certificate handling in depth.

Example 11-19 provides a certificate-based racoon example for road-warrior access.

Example 11-19 *FreeBSD Gateway racoon Configuration for Road-Warrior Access*

```
### Road Warrior to Gateway ####


path include "/usr/local/etc/racoon" ;

# search this file for pre_shared_key with various ID key.
path pre_shared_key "/usr/local/etc/racoon/psk.txt" ;

# racoon will look for certificate file in the directory,
# if the certificate/certificate request payload is received.
path certificate "/usr/local/etc/cert" ;

# "log" specifies logging level.  It is followed by either "notify," "debug,"
# or "debug2."
#log debug;

remote anonymous {
        exchange_mode main;
        generate_policy on;
        passive on;
        certificate_type x509 "my_certificate.pem" "my_private_key.pem";
        my_identifier cisco;
        peers_identifier cisco;
        proposal {
                encryption_algorithm 3des;
                hash_algorithm md5;
                authentication_method rsasig;
                dh_group modp1024;
        }
}

sainfo anonymous {
        pfs_group modp1024;
        encryption_algorithm 3des;
        authentication_algorithm hmac_md5;
        compression_algorithm deflate;
}
```

Dynamic Routing Protocols over Point-to-Point Tunnels—Transparent Infrastructure VPN

In general, IPSec tunnel setups cannot transfer routing protocols such as OSPF. IPSec does not always support the notion of an interface on which a routing engine (such as ospfd) can rely. (Remember, IPSec deals with SAs.) This can be accomplished by deploying OSPF over IP-IP/GRE tunnels over IPSec or out-of-band routing signaling not taking the crypto path.

Given the caveat mentioned with regard to TTL (TTL=1 breaks tunnel and multicasting) and MTUs, dynamic routing protocols work over tunnels pretty much the same way as over regular point-to-point links, as long as the routing engine can recognize the special interfaces associated with tunnels. Zebra/Quagga can deal with most implementations thanks to sound interface abstraction. For example setups of GRE over IPSec, see http://www.freeswan.ca/docs/HA/HA_VPNS_With_FreeSWAN.html.

IPSec Development and Evolution

The current efforts focus on specification of IKEv2, NAT-Traversal and firewall traversal, opportunistic encryption, DHCP over IKE, tight AES integration, and IPSec domains of interpretation (DOIs) for secure group communication and final touches to the IPv6 architecture. Currently, there is a significant trend toward hardware crypto-accelerator cards and chipsets that relieve the CPU from performing 3DES/AES encryption (and, most recently, that perform hashing calculations in hardware).

AES has improved crypto efficiency greatly; however, sustainable gigabit crypto throughput is still a domain of expensive commercial firewalls. An interesting addition to IPSec is the keynote trust management system that remedies some of the disadvantages of PKIs (introduced in RFC 2704 and RFC 2796). Also visit http://www1.cs.columbia.edu/~angelos/keynote.html.

Summary

This chapter focused on traditional and modern VPN architectures. Traditional private networks are based on DLLs, Frame Relay, or ATM PVCs. Today, corporate customers can rent dark or lit fiber in addition to SDH circuits or single DWDM wavelengths. With the widespread introduction of IPSec and MPLS, various VPN offerings considerably changed.

This chapter also discussed tunnel solutions such as IP-IP, GRE, and user-space approaches in terms of transparency and application areas. Tunnels also play prominent roles connecting multicast or IPv6 islands over unicast and IPv4 transport networks. A thorough discussion of PPTP, L2F, and L2TP concluded the first part of this chapter. The second part was dedicated to user-space tunnels such as CIPE, V-TUN, and OpenVPN. The chapter concluded with a discussion of IPSec and general tunnel caveats.

Recommended Reading

- The VPN Consortium, http://www.vpnc.org
- The IETF, http://www.ietf.org
- RFC-Editor's IETF RFCs, http://www.rfc-editor.org

- The Linux Advanced Routing and Traffic Control HOWTO, http://lartc.org/howto/lartc.ipsec.html
- Linux CryptoAPI, http://www.kerneli.org
- Another IPSec tunnel implementation for Linux 2.4 from Tobias Ringström at http://ringstrom.mine.nu/ipsec_tunnel/
- The IETF IPSec Charter, http://www.ietf.org/html.charters/ipsec-charter.html
- Stunnel, http://www.stunnel.org
- CIPE, http://sites.inka.de/sites/bigred/devel/cipe.html
- IBM Redbook about VPNs, http://www.redbooks.ibm.com/redbooks/SG245234/nn4/SG245234_1.html
- Linux 2.6 IPSec, http://www.ipsec-howto.org/
- Internet IPSec Overlay Architecture X-Bone, http://www.isi.edu/xbone/
- DHCPv4 Configuration of IPSec Tunnel Mode HOWTO, http://www.strongsec.com/freeswan/dhcprelay/ipsec-dhcp-howto.html
- ftp://ftp.rfc-editor.org/in-notes/rfc3456.txt
- The FreeBSD IPSec Mini-HOWTO, http://www.x-itec.de/projects/tuts/ipsec-howto.txt
- The FreeBSD Handbook IPSec, http://www.freebsd.org/doc/en_US.ISO8859-1/books/handbook/ipsec.html
- The KAME Project, http://www.kame.net/
- USAGI, http://www.linux-ipv6.org/
- OpenBSD IPSec HOWTO, http://www.se.openbsd.org/faq/faq13.html
- VPNLabs, http://www.vpnlabs.com/
- Useful VPN Resources, http://vpn.shmoo.com/
- The Keynote Trust Management Concept, http://www1.cs.columbia.edu/~angelos/keynote.html
- IPSec road-warrior configuration, http://www.allard.nu/openbsd/index.html
- Using IPSec on OpenBSD, http://www.se.openbsd.org/faq/faq13.html#

Endnotes

1 http://www.netheaven.com/TunnelTypes.html

2 http://vpn.shmoo.com/vpn/vpn-pptp.html

3 Olaf Titz from the CIPE

4 CIPE web page

5 http://www.quiltaholic.com/rickk/sslwrap/

6 OpenSSH web page

7 http://www.se.openbsd.org/faq/faq13.html#SeeAlso

8 http://lartc.org/howto/lartc.ipsec.html

CHAPTER 12

Designing for High Availability

High-availability architectures represent a wide-ranging subject of interlocked complexity stretching over all layers of the OSI (Open System Interconnection) stack.

Keep in mind that the end-user's perception of service availability is the ultimate and most relevant criterion; perception will be favorable if you did your job right. Toward that end, high-availability architectures satisfy the following needs:

- **Redundancy**—This includes equipment (node) and topology (link) redundancy precautions and redundant services available for a user base.

- **Load balancing**—Naturally, load balancing primarily serves the purpose of distributing load among candidates of a pool or farm of devices. Next-hop redundancy considerations and load balancing are important aspects of such an overall design. Dynamic DNS can accomplish this also with different means.

- **Clustering**—This involves logical grouping of constituents to a service. Clustering groups might include performance clusters, load-balancing clusters, or fault-tolerance clusters. It is another generic approach to presenting one highly robust virtual service to the outside world with a group of real servers behind the scene. Dedicated cluster management software maintains the overall picture of cluster controllers and component servers, thus increasing overall availability, robustness, and performance.

- **Heartbeat/keepalives**—Heartbeat/keepalive protocols and agents monitor the availability and operational parameters of network elements and services.

- **(D)DoS defenses**—Robust high-availability architectures can more likely withstand or mitigate the effects of (D)DoS attacks or are an attribute of a sound design.

- **Network failover strategies**—These approaches in general include VRRP/HSRP mechanisms in combination with gratuitous ARP for the purpose of providing a gateway failover mechanism.

- **Reliable failure detection and fast recovery/restoration of service**—This is the domain of routing protocols. The general goal of modern routing designs is subsecond convergence. This is a mandatory requirement for real-time traffic such as voice or video.

This chapter discusses support for such services from a networker's point of view (OSI Layers 1 through 4). The application layers (Layers 5 through 7) are intentionally underrepresented in this chapter because they use other mechanisms beyond the scope of a network/transport layer discussion.

Increasing Availability

The essential questions for high-availability (HA) designers have always been (and will continue to be) "How can I increase the overall availability of a special service or application, and what do I have to do to eliminate weak links in the chain or single points of failure? Tackling these challenges involves thorough planning across all OSI layers and the removal of *all* single points of failure wherever possible. A chain is as strong as its weakest link. Therefore, it is highly advisable to have at least one backup system, link, or resource available at all times.

Of course, the efforts and costs associated with such an endeavor can get out of hand easily and should, therefore, be governed by common sense and commercial feasibility. This is a particularly interesting topic in times of "best effort" services. Best effort is always a commercial dictate. The particular task of network engineers is to provide highly robust IP infrastructures to support higher-layer redundancy approaches, and the task of systems engineers is to accomplish OS resilience with concepts such as clustering or distributed architectures. This is the foundation for high-availability applications (services); a good implementation should result in robust and stable services from the point of view of the end user. How this is accomplished means little to the customer.

Withstanding a (D)DoS Attack

In light of recent Internet attacks, whether a sound HA architecture should withstand a massive (distributed) denial-of-service ([D]DoS) attack or be able to mitigate its effects has become a legitimate question. From my point of view, a state-of-the-art HA architecture should have some inherent self-healing capabilities; HA architects should also add another line of defense to assist in at least crippling or weakening (D)DoS attacks and their progeny. Several, sometimes complementary and orthogonal, lines of defense are crucial to prevent (D)DoS attacks, as they are to overall security architectures.

HA in terms of almost 100 percent service availability within strict service level agreements (SLAs) and monitored key performance indicators (KPIs) represents a significant challenge for today's finest engineers and designers. The problem with any (D)DoS defense is that every system's strength defines its weaknesses, too. For example, handing over control of a firewall ruleset to a network intrusion detection system (NIDS) means that any successful trigger of this defense mechanism (spoofing) effectively locks out legitimate networks from crucial services. Therefore, a system designed to protect or prevent might become the perfect DoS trap.

NOTE   Recent hostile activities on the Internet have proven to me that, in general, operational staff are overwhelmed by and overburdened with reactive actions because of weak underlying network design and planning.

Network HA Approaches

The fundamental principle, and the foundation of network HA, is network link redundancy and redundant hardware (network elements).

Redundant Paths

The underlying design principle is that, for a critical service, at least two equivalent systems should be provided and topologies chosen in a way that there always exist, at the least, two redundant paths to the next device. This is why for so many years many robust and scalable photonic network approaches have been based successfully on protected ring topologies (for example, Synchronous Digital Hierarchy/Synchronous Optical Network [SDH/SONET]) and Resilient Packet Ring (RPR). Just because a lot of folks disliked Token Ring technology for no apparent reason does not mean that ring topologies per se are inferior to bus architectures or star topologies; on the contrary. With a small number of network elements, point-to-point links will suffice. Usually a collapsed network core consists of three or four network elements (as shown in Figure 12-1).

Figure 12-1 *Typical Network Core Topologies*

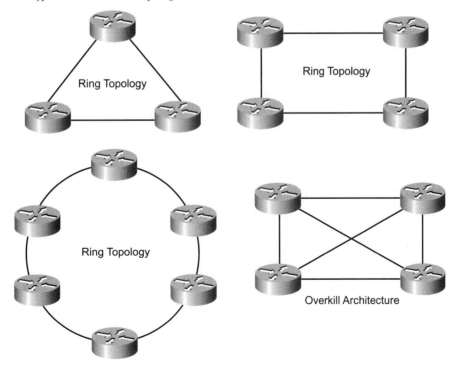

My approach to network redundancy is that more than one alternative link is unnecessary and unjustifiable commercially.

Standby Equipment

Another concept is the provisioning of cold- and hot-standby equipment, meaning components that need power up and hardware configuration (versus up-and-running failover candidates). Occasionally, engineers or management throw hardware resources at a simple design problem. However, HA concepts that are too exhaustive add considerable complexity to networks, occasionally defeating the purpose (and at unjustifiable expense).

As an introduction to the challenge of HA, Figure 12-2 presents a typical corporate Internet connectivity example in two variants.

Figure 12-2 *Example Corporate HA Architecture*

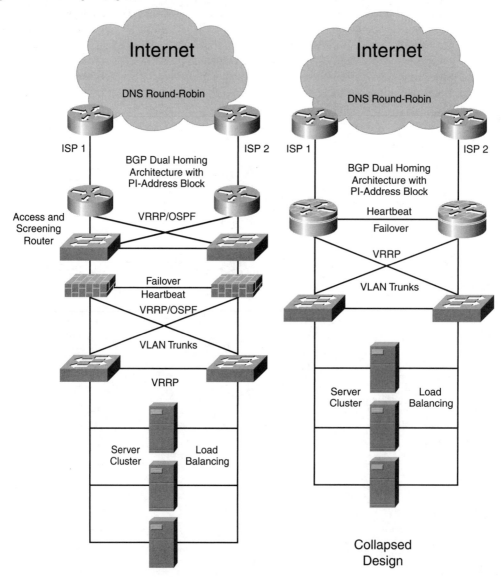

Simple but Effective Approaches to Server HA

Let us consider the network vicinity of a server in the context of its connected network interface cards (NICs), its LAN switch environment, VLAN membership, and exit gateways. Note that two or more NICs attached to redundant switch access ports provide sufficient redundancy, and channel bonding or interface teaming provides another useful combination of link aggregation (with an added redundancy benefit).

Route equalizing per destination or per packet can be configured to exit the two VLAN broadcast domains to which a server is usually hooked up. Beyond VLANs, dynamic routing protocols provide sufficiently fast rerouting around failures. It is fairly straightforward to provide redundant VLAN trunks and trunk termination (redundant routers on a stick) via Virtual Router Redundancy Protocol (VRRP) or Hot Standby Router Protocol (HSRP). This can be combined with equalized default routes (Linux) or floating static route concepts. Manual load distribution can be manipulated via manually tuned more-specific prefix routes. Return-packet load balancing originating from distant sites is an entirely different story; Domain Name System round-robin (DNS RR), Border Gateway Protocol (BGP) approaches (MED or path prepending), or dedicated load-balancing devices represent possible solutions.

When experimenting with special load-distribution approaches, keep in mind that Internet Control Message Protocol (ICMP) redirects might affect what you try to accomplish. sysctl provides a hook to disable dissemination of ICMP redirect messages (as shown in Example 12-1).

Example 12-1 *Disabling ICMP Redirects for Special Cases*

```
[root@ganymed:~#] sysctl -a | grep redirect
net.inet.ip.redirect = 1
net.inet6.ip6.redirect = 1
```

Address Resolution Protocol (ARP) cache latency is another issue that considerably affects certain setups. How long an ARP entry remains in a cache until it is removed is implementation-specific and might require manual intervention. To compensate for long timeouts, failover concepts such as VRRP/HSRP use gratuitous ARP featuring unsolicited updates.

Split-view DNS setups are popular, especially in enterprise networks where Network Address Translation (NAT) is used. Split-view DNS essentially means that an internal name server responds to queries for names associated with corporate RFC 1918 addresses and consults the external name server if it fails to resolve global records. Therefore, for true redundancy, two internal and two external DNS servers are advisable.

DNS Shuffle Records and Round-Robin (DNS RR)

DNS round-robin (DNS RR), as shown in Example 12-2, is the concept of entering multiple IP addresses for one fully qualified domain name (FQDN). It is qualitatively described in RFC 1794, "DNS Support for Load Balancing." When a DNS resolver (client) request reaches the server, it answers in an unweighted round-robin fashion. Although the server answers with the complete round-robin set, most clients consider only the first entry, which works as long as the server cycles the entries. This results in almost equal but crude and inefficient (unweighted) load distribution to resources of equal content or services. Nevertheless, this approach has several drawbacks, such as DNS caching problems and a considerable percentage of the requests directed lost when just one constituent of the DNS RR group becomes unavailable.

DNS RR essentially is deployed for migration scenarios, load balancing, and in poor-man redundancy architectures. For the Internet Systems Consortium's (ISC) point of view regarding the implications on Berkeley Internet Name Domain (BIND), read the excellent BIND load-balancing comment at http://www.isc.org/products/BIND/docs/bind-load-bal.html. For BIND-specific configuration options, consult the documentation that comes with your version of BIND.

Example 12-2 *DNS RR Server Setup*

```
www.iktech.net    300    IN   A    192.168.1.1
www.iktech.net    300    IN   A    192.168.2.1
www.iktech.net    300    IN   A    192.168.3.1
```

To my knowledge, DNS servers support the following approaches to round-robin-like regimes:[1]

- **Shuffle**—Only one address at any given time from a list of address candidates is presented to the resolver (not possible in BIND, but with commercial load balancers).

- **SRV records**—An added weight integer specifically describes the ordering (weighted DNS RR). This requires application support, however.

- **Sortlists** (Example 12-3)—This refers to sorting of all address pools according to the source address of the querying resolver. For a detailed discussion, consult the BIND documentation at http://www.isc.org/products/BIND/.

Example 12-3 *BIND Sortlist*

```
sortlist {
          { localhost;
            { localnets;
              192.168.1/24;
              { 192,168.2/24; 192.168.3/24; }; }; };
          { 192.168.1/24;
            { 192.168.1/24;
              { 192.168.2/24; 192.168.3/24; }; }; };
};
```

- **Rrset order** (Example 12-4)—When a DNS response contains multiple records, it might be useful to configure the order in which the records are placed into the response (shuffle, cyclic round-robin, user-defined).

Example 12-4 *BIND Rrset Order*

```
rrset-order {
        class IN type A name "www.iktech.net" order random;
          order cyclic;
      };
```

An alternative to these server-side approaches is to put the intelligence into the resolver/ client application. However, this is difficult to predict and to deploy because resolvers are often part of an application.

If you want to manipulate the amount of traffic a specific round-robin participant receives, you can add alias addresses to the server and add additional entries to the DNS configuration. That's pretty much all you can do to alter the unweighted behavior. Be aware of possible caching issues and nondeterministic behavior and have a client-side sniffer ready to debug the queries and responses.

In closing, note that going one step further to ensure that the receiving server is up and available requires commercial-grade load-balancing solutions such as the Cisco server load balancing (SLB) IOS feature or the Cisco Local Director. Consult Cisco.com for a feature overview.

NOTE   For a flexible load-balancing name server written in Perl, by Roland Schemers, see the resources at http://www.stanford.edu/~riepel/lbnamed/.

Dynamic Routing Protocols

Dynamic routing is the most flexible and effective approach to provide redundancy for alternative paths and the only way to detect network node, port, or link failures reliably. Routing and standby protocols rely on the simple principle that if a speaker hasn't heard from a neighbor in a certain time, something must be wrong. Load balancing over multiple links can be accomplished in several ways: BGP "pseudo" load balancing can be achieved in dual-homed Internet service provider (ISP) architectures, Multilink PPP, and link-state Equal-Cost Multi-Path (ECMP) for interior gateway protocol (IGP) paths. It is a good idea to fine-tune protocol parameters for fast-converging resilient architectures or deploy incremental SPF (iSPF). Routing provides the signaling protocols to detect and route around failures within highly meshed nondeterministic IP networks.

Firewall Failover

Firewall failover is the art of exchanging state information for stateful inspection gateways and NAT tables, at the least, for the purpose of taking over for an equivalent resource. Such a takeover also involves stateful IP Security (IPSec) failover concepts for IPSec tunnel termination and security associations. This usually requires a heartbeat protocol between the master and slave firewall(s) on a dedicated crossover link. Most of the failover devices run in hot-standby mode or in expensive commercial (per-flow) load-balancing clusters.

The OpenBSD packet filter team is already working on a stateful failover concept using the newly introduced pfsync pseudo-device and a crude multicast pfsyncd in context with the OpenBSD firewall (pf) and the shiny new redundancy protocol Common Address Redundancy Protocol (CARP). The first integrated release of OpenBSD with all these features available is 3.5. I am sorry that the discussion did not make it into this first edition.

Clustering and Distributed Architectures

The basic idea behind redundant systems and services is to provide at least a second resource that can either take over the duty in a hot-standby fashion or, even better, is a member of a server/service farm that constantly contributes via load-balancing schemes. One step further would distribute such architecture geographically, and that would pretty much define the boundaries (not limits) of such an architecture.

One big advantage of a loosely coupled load-sharing cluster approach is that it is independent of the failure of one component. This approach affects overall cluster performance only to a certain extent, depending on the capacity planning of the cluster architect. One major reason for such deployments is the possibility to schedule maintenance for a cluster constituent without affecting normal operation in high-availability networks.

Historically, clustering is a domain of the (Open)VMS world. OpenVMS is a product of HP after HP bought Compaq and Compaq bought Digital. If you are interested in OpenVMS, look at http://www.openvms.org and Hewlett Packard's web page.

The apex of clustering is a tight integration (virtual supercomputer) of an almost arbitrary number of multiprocessor systems to form a modern cluster under the control of redundant cluster controllers with distributed storage, memory, sockets, and I/O. Examples of such an approach are high-performance clusters (HPC). In contrast, GRID architectures (computing grids) for scientific number crunching such as the well-known SET@Home project (http://setiathome.ssl.berkeley.edu) have evolved, where every home or office workstation contributes to a calculation when idle. A thorough discussion of cluster concepts, such as MOSIX and Beowulf, goes beyond the scope of this book. Nevertheless, the following sections cover three prominent examples of Linux HA approaches.

Linux Virtual Server Project (LVSP)

The LVSP is a scalable and transparent load-balancing architecture based on the Linux operating system. It requires a kernel patch and a user-space administration tool, ipvsadm. The constituent servers of a load-balancing group can be dispersed geographically and still can be Layer 4 controlled by the LVS architecture.

Detection of node or daemon failures and the appropriate reconfiguring of the system lead to high availability. IP-level load balancing offers performance and transparency advantages over application-level solutions such as caches and proxies. The virtual server uses three different load-balancing techniques and a repertoire of scheduling algorithms. The load-balancing techniques are as follows:

- **Virtual server via NAT**—Based on Port Address Translation and port forwarding.

- **Virtual server via IP tunneling**—The virtual server sends requests to physical servers via IP-IP tunnels.

- **Virtual server via direct routing**—The return packets to client requests are routed directly from the real servers without involving the load balancer.

The scheduling algorithms are as follows

- Least connection
- Weighted least-connection
- Round-robin (allocates connections evenly to all real servers)
- Weighted round-robin
- Locality-based least connection
- Locality-based least connection with replication
- Destination hashing
- Source hashing

For further configuration details and ancillary tools, consult http://www.linuxvirtualserver.org/.

Connection Integrity Issues

Modern director approaches such as LVS support connection-integrity maintenance. Connection integrity refers to the capability of the director to maintain a connection in a way that it never changes the real server after the first scheduling decision has been made based on the initial packets. This is necessary for certain protocols such as Secure Sockets Layer (SSL) and File Transfer Protocol (FTP). This is sometimes referred to as *stateful load balancing*. Optionally, the connection behavior of a service can be marked *persistent*. Persistency can be accomplished via manual configuration, whereas connection-integrity tracking works on a per-connection basis with finer granularity.

LVS—Virtual Services

You can configure Linux Director virtual service definition in these ways:

- **IP address**—The virtual IP address of a global service.
- **TCP/UDP port**—The port of a service.
- **Protocol**—For example, HTTPS of FTP.
- **Linux netfilter/iptables firewall marks**—A firewall mark can be matched to virtual services. This adds another level of flexibility and granularity (for example, for persistency setups).

Linux Ultra Monkey

Ultra Monkey is a project to create load-balanced and highly available services on a LAN using open-source components on the Linux operating system. Figure 12-3 describes the entire architecture.

Figure 12-3 *Linux Ultra Monkey (LVS) Architecture*

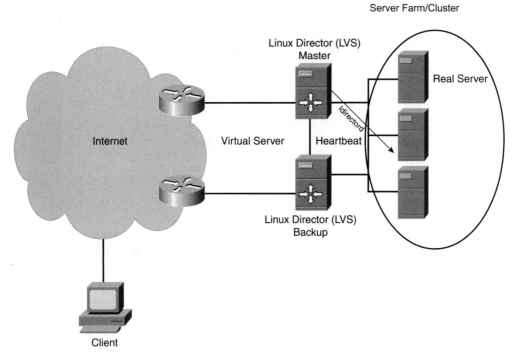

Ultra Monkey includes the following key features/components:

- Layer 4 switching using the Linux Virtual Server (LVS)
- High availability provided by Heartbeat protocol
- Service-level monitoring using ldirectord
- Supports highly available or load-balanced topologies
- Integrates with Super Sparrow
- Supports monitoring of HTTP, HTTPS, FTP, IMAP, POP, SMTP, LDAP, and NNTP

IP Address Takeover with Heartbeat

The takeover approach chosen largely depends on topology and effective switchover timer requirements. As a rule of thumb, MAC address takeover works fastest, IP address takeover is a little bit slower, and dynamic DNS reconfiguration takes its time. Heartbeat is an integral part of the Ultra Monkey architecture, based on ARP spoofing/gratuitous ARP for takeover with the help of an additional physical interface or an IP alias.

All Heartbeat protocols are based on the assumption that keepalive messages (hence the name *heartbeat*) are exchanged between systems. If a message is not received in due time, a failure is assumed and takeover or master node re-election activities are triggered. The useful thing about the heartbeat protocol is that it works over serial links, PPP links, and Ethernet and incorporates aspects of VRRP such as virtual addresses. It is much more cost-effective to use RS232 interfaces instead of committing dedicated, although almost idle, Ethernet NIC resources.

The Service Routing Redundancy Daemon (SRRD)

You have already learned a fair bit about SRRD in Chapter 9, "Dynamic Routing Protocols— Interior Gateway Protocols." For purposes of this discussion, just be aware that SRRD can do without an external heartbeat mechanism and instead just requires Quagga Open Shortest Path First (OSPF) for signaling based on opaque link-state advertisements (LSAs). Undeservedly, this elegant concept is underrepresented in HA architectures. According to http://www.srrd.org, "SRRD is fully configurable over the web and supports SSL and PKI client and server authentication. It implements cluster server features like Service Groups, Service Dependencies, as well as Critical Services."[2]

IPv4/IPv6 Anycast

Originally I intended to introduce you to anycast in Chapter 14, "Multicast Architectures." However, I am introducing it here instead because I consider its most important purpose is to add redundancy and load balancing to connectionless client/server services and improve availability and possibly latency.

Anycast is a communication model (network service) for IPv4 and IPv6. As originally described in RFC 1546, "Host Anycast Service," the purpose of anycast is to assign an identical anycast address to a group of geographically distributed nodes. IP datagrams approach the nearest destination node in the set of available destination nodes, based on the unicast routing measure of distance transparent to the clients. The network (routing system) decides where to guide the client request. An IPv4 anycast address is distinguishable from a unicast address because they are allocated from a special reserved range. This is different in IPv6.

The real-world applications of anycast I am aware of are limited to DNS root server concepts and Protocol Independent Multicast (PIM) rendezvous points, stateless protocols in general. For further details about anycast and the problems of protocols that maintain state, visit the excellent Carnegie Mellon resources at http://www.net.cmu.edu/pres/anycast/.

A Few Words About Content Caches and Proxies

Content-caching architectures and engines such as in the Cisco product palette deal with the challenge to deliver content reliably, efficiently, and effectively to the network edge and access layer where customers subscribe to certain content. Vice versa, they are necessary to provide sufficiently clustered server farms to feed these requests.

NOTE Historically, caching was the initial purpose of proxies and proxy chaining. Protection of expensive and rare WAN bandwidth was their prime directive. Today, with cheap bandwidth in abundance, the focus has shifted toward intelligent security, content screening, and load-balancing content and cache-engine architectures. However, these are Layer 4 through 7 issues and not the focus of this chapter. For a background on caching strategies, look at the Internet's most popular open-source proxy, squid, at http://www.squid-cache.org/, and the proxy capabilities of the Apache web server, at http://www.apache.org.

Modern proxies fall in different categories:

- Transparent caching proxies
- Security (intercepting) proxies
- Load-balancing proxies
- Mangling proxies (packet rewrites)
- Reverse proxies

Load Balancing

A load-balancing system or device is a device that can redirect incoming traffic to one or more real servers. In the case of one destination, it resembles a simple relay of the forwarder. The commercial solutions, such as Cisco Local Director, offer advanced features and a choice of algorithms that enable you to choose a suitable server, including surveillance of candidate availability via polling or agents/clients (see Figure 12-4). Because of their implementation, they are often referred to as *reverse-NAT engines* or *reverse proxies*.

Various approaches to load balancing/distribution exist:

- Round-robin
- Weighted round-robin
- Static weight
- Least load
- Measured response time
- (Weighted) Least connections/users/sessions
- Least network traffic
- NAT/PAT-based commercial approaches
- Server agents (probes)

Figure 12-4 *Integrated Load-Balancing Architecture*

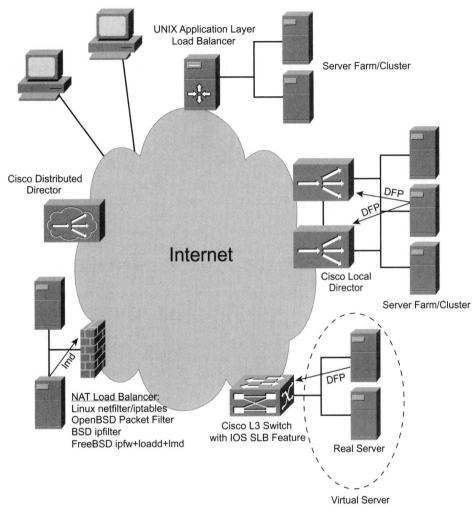

Most Layer 3/4 load balancers use reverse NAT/PAT in combination with dynamic algorithms to determine load and probe candidate operational status to make forwarding decisions. Load balancing directs traffic to the most available (feedback control via agents/polling) server farm (through intelligent DNS/distributed traffic direction) or the optimal server (through local traffic redirection). Availability systems monitor the health and responsiveness of websites or shared services and direct traffic accordingly.

According to Cisco.com, server clustering and traffic load balancing offer the following major advantages:

- Scalability
- Nondisruptive growth

- Load distribution
- Continuous availability

Scalability and nondisruptive growth are somewhat related in that they refer to the cluster's property, that a particular user's session remains bound to a particular cluster constituent. This allows addition of new cluster members or maintenance of existing ones without service interruption. Load distribution refers to equally spread load without underutilizing or overwhelming physical cluster resources. Finally, continuous availability is ensured by instant switchover to other systems if failure of a cluster constituent occurs.

Firewall Load-Balancing Approaches

Linux iptables, BSD ipfilter, FreeBSD ipfw, and OpenBSD packet filter pf provide features for load balancing incoming requests (see Examples 12-5 and 12-6).

Example 12-5 *OpenBSD pf Load Balancer*

```
web_servers = "{ 192.168.2.4, 192.168.2.5, 192.168.2.6 }"
rdr on ne5_if proto tcp from any to any port 80 -> $web_servers round-robin
```

Example 12-6 *FreeBSD ipfilter Load Balancer*

```
### Single-Port Redirects (one_port-to-one_port) ###

rdr ne5 111.11.117.206/32 port 23 -> 192.168.2.3 port 23 tcp
### NAT Load Balancer (round-robin) ###

rdr ne5 111.11.117.206/32 port 80 -> 192.168.2.3 port 8000 tcp round-robin
red ne5 111.11.117.206/32 port 80 -> 192.168.2.4 port 8000 top round-robin
rdr ne5 111.11.117.206/32 port 80 -> 192.168.2.5 port 8000 tcp round-robin
```

Note that pf address pools and load balancing are explained at http://www.openbsd.org/faq/ pf/pools.html. Also note that OpenBSD pf provides four methods for using an address pool:

- Bitmask
- Random
- Source hash
- Round-robin

HighUpTime Project loadd Daemon

loadd is a load-balancing daemon of the HighUpTime (HUT) Project (http://www.bsdshell. net/hut_loadd.html) that depends on the FreeBSD ipfw firewall and works via the generic DIVERT socket. (Recompile your kernel with DIVERT and IPFIREWALL options). You can configure a divert rule easily with ipfw and redirect packets into the loadd system (see Example 12-7).

The loadd daemon checks the destination service and does reverse NAT on matching traffic according to a choice of two algorithms: round-robin algorithm and intelligence load sharing (balancing according to real-time load as reported via the lmd client on real servers). The daemon communicates with server agents (lmd) and needs to be compiled on the real server platforms.

According to the author of loadd, it currently includes the following capabilities:

- Support of TCP (no UDP yet)
- Support of multiple IP services (except FTP and SSL for the moment)
- Choice of IP aliasing
- Choice of port number to load balance
- Support of multiple daemons on the same host without conflict
- Support of lmd client modules (HTTP module testing service is provided with this package)

Example 12-7 *FreeBSD ipfw+loadd Example*

```
[root@castor:~#] ipfw add divert 8670 tcp from any to any

[root@castor:~#] /usr/local/libexec/loadd -h
LOADD - Load Balancing Daemon for FreeBSD and ipfw
Choose one of the following:
-f : specify a path to a configuration file
-p : specify a port number for loadd
-b : specify a method for load balancing (roundrobbin, loadsharing, intlloadsharing)
     !! Caution !! Due to active development load sharing may be
     broken at this time. The best load-balancing method is intlloadsharing.
-d : run loadd in daemon mode, this is not the default at this time
-v : run loadd in verbose mode
-t : transparent proxy support (default is on and off doesn't work yet)
-h : this screen ;)

[root@castor:~#] /usr/local/libexec/loadd -p 8670 -f /usr/local/etc/loadd.conf

[root@castor:~#] cat loadd.conf
servers = 192.168.7.10, 192.168.7.11, 192.168.7.12
ipaliasing = 10.10.10.10
ports = 80
verbosemode = yes
balancingmode = intlloadsharing
daemon = yes
transparent_proxy = yes

[root@castor:~#] cat lmd.conf
loaddservers = 192.168.7.7

# Just set loaddservers to the IP of your loadd server. You can specify multiple
# loadd servers with the ',' separator.
```

Pure Load Balancer

Pure Load Balancer (PLB, http://plb.sunsite.dk/) is a performance-optimized user-space plain round-robin load balancer for the HTTP and SMTP protocols only. It provides failover abilities while operating as a reverse HTTP proxy. When a back-end server goes down, it automatically removes it from the server pool and tries to bring it back to life later.

PLB has full IPv6 support and works on OpenBSD, NetBSD, FreeBSD, Mac OS X, and Linux. As an added performance benefit, PLB accepts client sessions and buffers their initial request. And only after the full request has been received does it establish a connection to a back-end web server.

PLB can be started via **/usr/local/bin/plb –daemonize --config /etc/plb.conf &**. Example 12-8 shows a configuration derived from the one presented at http://plb.sunsite.dk/.

Example 12-8 *Pure Load Balancer Example Configuration*

```
# This is the IP address and port that the load balancer answers on.
# To listen to all interfaces, just use 0.0.0.0 for the IP address.

listen_ip                   0.0.0.0
listen_port                 80

# Bind family. 0 for IPv4, 1 for IPv6.

bind_ipv6                   0

# Protocol to balance : HTTP (SMTP is not implemented yet)

protocol                    HTTP

# IP addresses of the real web servers. Use space as a separator.
# IPv4 and IPv6 addresses are allowed.

servers_ip                  192.168.7.10 192.168.7.11 192.168.7.12
servers_port                80

# After binding ports, the load balancer chroots to an empty (recommended)
# directory and drops privileges.

user                        nobody
group                       nobody
chroot_dir                  /var/empty

# Timeouts to avoid clients use unneeded slots on your servers
# with idle connections. Values are in seconds.

timeout_header_client_read   30
timeout_header_client_write  30
timeout_header_server_read   30
timeout_header_server_write  30
timeout_forward_client_read  30
```

Example 12-8 *Pure Load Balancer Example Configuration (Continued)*

```
timeout_forward_client_write 30
timeout_forward_server_read  30
timeout_forward_server_write 30

# When a server goes down, the load balancer will try to probe it at regular
# intervals to bring it back to life.
# This is the delay, in seconds, between probes.

timeout_cleanup             15

# Really mark a server down after this many consecutive failures.

server_retry                5

# The total maximum number of clients to allow

max_clients                 1000

# The backlog. Try something like (max_clients / 10) for extreme cases.

backlog                     100

# The log file verbosity.
# 0 => everything, including debugging info (not recommended)
# 1 => all errors, all warnings, all common notifications
# 2 => all errors, all warnings
# 3 => quiet mode, fatal errors only
# Default is 2. Leave this commented if you want to override it with
# the -d command-line switch.

# log_level                 2
# log_file                  /var/log/plb.log
```

The PEN Load Balancer

PEN (http://siag.nu/pen/) is another load balancer for "simple" TCP-based protocols such as HTTP. It implements a stateful connection-integrity regime that maintains correlation of a client session to the initially chosen real server behind a virtual service.

Super Sparrow

Super Sparrow (http://www.supersparrow.org/) handles geographically weighted load balancing and direction by means of accessing BGP routing information (for instance, from a route server), which is a major advantage over DNS-based approaches. This enables the tool to reliably and effectively identify the site closest to the requesting client. The concept is intriguing; I am not sure how actively maintained the project is, so form your own opinion if you want to deploy it. It's definitely worth looking at the architecture.

Cisco Gateway Load Balancing Protocol (GLBP)

GLBP works similarly to HSRP/VRRP approaches for servers. It protects a network from failing gateway nodes and circuits with the added capability of load sharing among a group of redundant routers. GLBP implements a weighted round-robin approach to load sharing for a group of gateways. This feature was introduced in Cisco IOS 12.2 (S/T) releases.

A requirement for GLBP is the support of multiple MAC addresses on physical router interfaces. The notable difference to HSRP/VRRP is the capability of the protocol to actively load share featuring a virtual first-hop IP router. Hence, only one default route needs to be configured on the client workstations.

NOTE	In a lot of features, the protocol has inherited proven approaches from HSRP/VRRP. For configuration details, consult the Cisco.com document "GLBP—Gateway Load Balancing Protocol."

Cisco HA and Load-Balancing Approaches

Cisco offers several architectural approaches to high availability, ranging from lower-layer concepts such as resilient packet ring and Multiprotocol Label Switching (MPLS) node protection up to protocol-intrinsic or application layer approaches.

The lower-layer concepts (Layers 1 through 3) are summarized under the Cisco Global Resilient IP Framework (GRIP). This framework consists of the following building blocks:

- Stateful NAT (SNAT) for translation groups
- IPSec stateful failover (VPN HA in combination with HSRP)
- Multicast subsecond convergence
- GLBP
- Nonstop forwarding with stateful switchover
- MPLS fast reroute

Approaches that are relevant to the transport and application layers are discussed briefly in the following two subsections.

Cisco IOS Server Load Balancing (SLB) Feature

The Cisco IOS SLB feature is available for certain Cisco IOS routers and catalyst switches. It provides two load-balancing algorithms: weighted round-robin and weighted least connections. With SLB enabled, a virtual server (VIP) represents a cluster of real servers. Clients are configured to connect to the IP address of the virtual server (directed or dispatched redirection mode). DNS records usually point to the virtual IP address.

The Cisco IOS SLB intelligence picks a real server to satisfy the requesting client based on one of the load-balancing algorithms mentioned earlier. It can perform NAT, provide added security by hiding real servers, and provide rudimentary DoS protection such as maximum connection limits and SYNGuard (SYN flooding protection).

IOS SLB for Layer 3 switches works with HSRP to prevent single points of failure for virtual IP addresses. In contrast to crude round-robin approaches, the cluster constituents provide input into the IP load-balancing device by means of the Dynamic Feedback Protocol (DFP), indicating the level of CPU utilization, application, and user identity. DFP is implemented with workload agents (Windows, UNIX) that reside on IP server platforms. For further configuration information, consult the Cisco.com document "Configuring Server Load Balancing."

Cisco Content Networking Devices and Software

These devices, software and hardware, operate at Layers 4 through 7 and consist of the following products:

*   Local Director (local traffic distribution)
*   Network Director
*   Distributed Director (geographically disperse traffic distribution)
*   Content engines
*   Content routers (redirect the user to the most suitable site on a network based on a set of metrics such as delay topology, server load, and a set of policies such as location of content)
*   Content networking software (carries out the same duty without a dedicated appliance)

The main features of these approaches are caching, intelligent content delivery, traffic distribution, intelligent DNS services, and load balancing.

VRRP

Gateway redundancy protocols solve the problem of eliminating single points of failure in a LAN environment for clients that require a reliable HA default path and next hop. Provisioning of a default route/multiple routes can, in general, be achieved in various ways:

*   Dynamic Host Configuration Protocol (DHCP) with default gateway provisioning
*   Manual default route entry/entries plus load balancing (optional Linux feature)

- Dynamic routing protocols on the client workstation
- Internet Router Discovery Protocol (IRDP) clients
- Virtual Router Redundancy Protocol/Hot Standby Router/Protocol/Gateway Load Balancing Protocol (VRRP/HSRP/GLBP)

The concept of a secondary default route (floating static route) does not work on multi-access networks. The affected workstation has no standardized and reliable way of telling that a particular gateway just went down, and an incomplete ARP entry does not trigger a route removal from the forwarding table. This is implementation-specific and different on point-to-point links with line protocols.

VRRP (RFC 2338) is essentially an election protocol that elects a master from a pool of candidate routers and takes care of associated Layer 3 and Layer 2 virtual and real addresses for resilient LAN forwarding responsibility. The virtual router that is associated with each alternate path under VRRP uses the same IP address and MAC address as the routers for other paths. As a result, the host's gateway information does not change, no matter which path is used. This applies to both the IP and MAC address used for the actual frame delivery.

VRRP is related to the Cisco proprietary and highly successful HSRP and supplemented by GLBP. Look at the Cisco.com document "Virtual Router Redundancy Protocol" for more information. The Cisco implementation requires Cisco IOS Release 12.2(T)or 12.0ST.

CAUTION   HSRP is not compatible with VRRP.

The following sections discuss two implementations of VRRP for UNIX.

VRRPd

VRRPd is a Linux implementation of the Virtual Router Redundancy Protocol originally developed by ImageStream and released to the public as a GNU project.

VRRP's primary design goal is eliminating a single point of failure represented by a next-hop gateway for static LAN routes, often routes of last resort. Figure 12-5 presents the lab layout used for the following configurations. The specification of VRRP was influenced considerably by the Cisco HSRP protocol. In addition to this primary function (next-hop redundancy), RFC 2338 also states that the protocol should

- Minimize the duration of black holes.
- Minimize the steady-state bandwidth overhead and processing complexity.

- Function over a variety of multiaccess LAN technologies that support IP traffic.
- Provide for election of multiple virtual routers on a network for load balancing.
- Support multiple logical IP subnets on a single LAN segment.

Figure 12-5 *VRRP Lab Architecture*

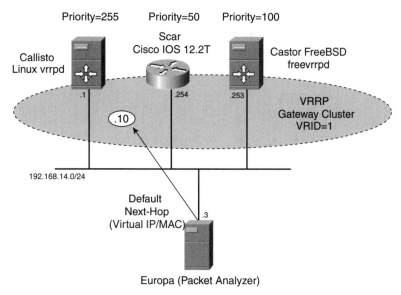

Freevrrpd

Freevrrpd is part of the HUT Project. A feature overview according to the HUT Project includes the following:

- Provides an RFC 2338-compliant daemon
- Implements virtual addresses
- Supports multiple virtual router IDs (VRIDs)
- Enables master state announcement (by sending multicast packets via BPF)
- Changes routes and IP in 3 seconds
- Performs gratuitous ARP requests to clean the cache of all hosts
- Elects from among different slave servers
- Allows the same host to be slave and master simultaneously
- Automatically downgrades to slave if a master is up again
- Provides anti-address-conflict system
- Provides multithreaded vrrp daemon

- Supports plain-text passwords
- Supports netmask for virtual IP address(es)
- Simple version of "monitored circuits"
- Supports executing master/backup scripts during transition state

Comparison of the VRRP Implementations

Example 12-9 provides a comparison of different VRRP implementations.

Example 12-9 *VRRP Lab (Linux VRRPd, CISCO IOS Architecture, and FreeBSD freevrrpd)*

```
scar# show running-config
...
interface ethernet 1/0
 ip address 192.168.14.254 255.255.255.0
 vrrp 1 priority 50
 vrrp 1 ip 192.168.14.10
...

[root@castor:~#] cat /usr/local/etc/freevrrpd.conf

# Each VRID section must begin with [VRID] keyword
[VRID]
# serverid is needed to specify the number of the VRID, here VRID = 1
serverid = 1

# you must set the interface with a real interface name of your system
interface = ed0

# priority = 255 is a MASTER of the VRID
# priority < 255 is a BACKUP with a priority 0 to 254
# 254 is a higher BACKUP priority
priority = 100

# addr option is needed to specify ip address(es) associated with the VRID
# you can specify multiple addresses separated by ','
# netmask is specified with CIDR notation, so numbers after '/' represent the
# number of bits set to 1 for the netmask.
# eg: /24 is 11111111 11111111 11111111 00000000 = 255.255.255.0
addr = 192.168.14.10/24

[root@castor:~#] freevrrpd -f /usr/local/etc/freevrrpd.conf

[root@callisto~#] vrrpd i eth0 -p 255 -v 1 192.168.14.10
```

OpenBSD CARP

Because of patent issues with VRRP and the Internet Engineering Task Force's (IETF) point of view about patented technology in standards (that is, RAND [reasonable and nondiscriminatory]), the OpenBSD community developed their own redundancy protocol,

Common Address Redundancy Protocol (CARP), which was introduced in the OpenBSD 3.5 release. One positive aspect of that architecture is the tight integration with the pf firewall and pf's clustering capabilities via pfsync.

For more information about OpenBSD CARP, look at the CARP man page at http://www.openbsd.org/cgi-bin/man.cgi?query=carp&sektion=4. Notable features are ARP-based Layer 2 load-balancing capabilities, support for both IPv4 and IPv6, and hash protection for enhanced protocol security. Example setups are provided at http://www.countersiege.com/doc/pfsync-carp/.

IRDP

The Internet Router Discovery Protocol (IRDP, RFC 1256), sometimes also referred to as the ICMP Router Discovery Protocol, is the ancestor of redundancy concepts such as VRRP or HSRP. It is a timelessly elegant concept that recently has attracted renewed attention because of its essential role in mobile IP deployments (RFC 3344). Extensions to the original protocol were necessary to provide for the requirements of mobile node-to-agent communication.

The IRDP is a protocol based on multicast route discovery ICMP messages. It eliminates the need for manual configuration of router addresses and is independent of any specific routing protocol. Therefore, it supplements a statically configured default router.

The ICMP router discovery messages are called router advertisements and router solicitations. By default, neither router discovery advertisements nor solicitations are sent over point-to-point links (for example, PPP). As the advertisement address, the router defaults to 224.0.0.1 if the router supports IP multicast on the interface; otherwise, 255.255.255.255 is used. Router solicitations are sent to 224.0.0.2. For further information, consult the RFC and the BSD manual page routed(8).

Example 12-10 demonstrates the IRDP featuring advertisements and client solicitations. In the gated example, IRDP server (advertiser) is running on ganymed, the Cisco IOS IRDP server on scar, callisto is listening via rdisc client, and castor is running **routed -q** "quiet mode" to demonstrate routed's IRDP client behavior; no dynamic routing protocols are running.

The **preference** statements (as highlighted in Example 12-10) allow weighting of the two available gateways. (This also works with two gateways on the same network.) The server side of the ICMP router discovery protocol is supported by Cisco IOS architecture, routed, and gated and can be tuned with **preference** statements. The command **ip irdp multicast** turns off the Cisco default broadcast behavior (also highlighted in Example 12-10).

Note that MRTd and Zebra do not support IRDP currently. Experimental code was added recently to Quagga's Zebra daemon, though. GateD and routed can run in either server or client mode. Linux provides a client implementation with the rdisc(8) tool. As you can see from the configurations and output, ganymed and scar are acting as IRDP advertisers (servers), whereas castor and callisto act as IRDP clients sending IRDP solicitations to trigger responses from candidate IRDP routers on directly connected networks.

Example 12-10 *IRDP Server and Client Operation*

```
[root@ganymed:~#] cat /etc/gated.cfg
### IRDP section ###
routerdiscovery server yes{
        traceoptions state;
        address 192.168.1.254 preference 100 multicast;
};
#routerdiscovery client yes{
#       traceoptions state;
#       interface ne3 multicast solicit;
#};
icmp{
    traceoptions routerdiscovery;
};

[root@castor:~#]routed -q -T /var/log/routed.log

scar# show running-config
...
interface Ethernet1
 ip address 192.168.14.254 255.255.255.0
 no ip proxy-arp
 ip irdp
 ip irdp preference 10
 ip irdp multicast
 no ip route-cache
 no ip mroute-cache
 media-type 10BaseT
!
interface Ethernet0
 ip address 192.168.7.254 255.255.255.0
 no ip proxy-arp
 ip irdp
 ip irdp multicast
 ip irdp preference 20
 no ip route-cache
 no ip mroute-cache
 media-type 10BaseT
...

scar(config-if)# ip irdp ?
  <cr>
  address             addresses to proxy-advertise
  holdtime            how long a receiver should believe the information
  maxadvertinterval   maximum time between advertisements
```

Example 12-10 *IRDP Server and Client Operation (Continued)*

```
      minadvertinterval  minimum time between advertisements
      multicast          advertisements are sent with multicasts
      preference         preference level for this interface

scar# show ip irdp ethernet 1
Ethernet1 has router discovery enabled
Advertisements will occur between every 450 and 600 seconds.
Advertisements are sent with multicasts.
Advertisements are valid for 1800 seconds.
Default preference will be 10.

[root@callisto:~#] rdisc -vst
Sending solicitation to ALL-ROUTERS.MCAST.NET (224.0.0.2)
ICMP Router Advertise from 192.168.14.254, lifetime 1800
        address 192.168.14.254, preference 0xa
ICMP Router Advertise from ganymed (192.168.1.254), lifetime 1800
        address ganymed (192.168.1.254), preference 0x64
        address 192.168.45.254, preference 0x0
ICMP Router Advertise from 192.168.45.254, lifetime 1800
        address ganymed (192.168.1.254), preference 0x64
        address 192.168.45.254, preference 0x0

[root@castor:~#]cat /var/log/routed.log
...
turn on Router Discovery client using 192.168.7.254 via ed0
Add     0.0.0.0         -->192.168.7.254    metric=15 ed0 <RDISC>
...

[root@callisto:~#] tethereal -i eth0
Capturing on eth0
  0.000000 192.168.14.1 -> 224.0.0.2         ICMP Router solicitation
  0.001527 192.168.14.254 -> 192.168.14.1    ICMP Router advertisement
...
167.026360 192.168.14.254 -> 224.0.0.1       ICMP Router advertisement

[root@callisto:~#] tethereal -i eth1
  0.343388 192.168.1.1 -> 224.0.0.2          ICMP Router solicitation
  0.344884 192.168.45.253 -> 224.0.0.2       ICMP Router solicitation
  2.360836 192.168.1.254 -> 192.168.1.1      ICMP Router advertisement
  2.361085 192.168.45.254 -> 192.168.45.253  ICMP Router advertisement

[root@callisto:~#] netstat -rne
Kernel IP routing table
Destination     Gateway         Genmask         Flags Metric Ref    Use Iface
192.168.1.0     0.0.0.0         255.255.255.0   U     0      0        0 eth1
192.168.1.0     0.0.0.0         255.255.255.0   U     0      0        0 ipsec0
192.168.14.0    0.0.0.0         255.255.255.0   U     0      0        0 eth0
192.168.45.0    0.0.0.0         255.255.255.0   U     0      0        0 eth1
127.0.0.0       0.0.0.0         255.0.0.0       U     0      0        0 lo
0.0.0.0         192.168.1.254   0.0.0.0         UG    0      0        0 eth1
```

Summary

This chapter presented an overview of building blocks for modern high-availability architectures for network resources and services. As discussed in this chapter, HA is an endeavor that involves thorough architectural planning; planning for network elements, links, and server resources; and a thorough consideration of both hardware and software. Issues such as load balancing, failover concepts, redundancy protocols, and heartbeat were discussed. Toward the end of this chapter, the art of clustering was introduced and address takeover approaches were explained. An introduction to IRDP focusing on gateway discovery and redundancy concluded the chapter.

Recommended Reading

- *Server Load Balancing*, by Tony Bourke (O'Reilly, 2001).
- *Load Balancing Servers, Firewalls, and Caches*, by Chandra Kopparapu (Wiley, 2002).
- *High Availability Network Fundamentals*, by Chris Oggerino (Cisco Press 2001).
- *High Availability Networking with Cisco*, by Vincent C. Jones (Addison-Wesley, 2001).
- *VRRP*, by A. Srikanth and A. A. Onart (Addison-Wesley, 2003).
- *Blueprints for High Availability*, by E. Marcus and H. Stern (Wiley, 2000).
- RFC 1256, "Internet Router Discovery Protocol (IRDP)"
- routed manual page, routed(8)
- The CARP manual page, http://www.openbsd.org/cgi-bin/man.cgi?query=carp&sektion=4
- http://www.supersparrow.org/
- http://www.linuxvirtualserver.org/
- http://www.ultramonkey.org/
- http://www.linux-ha.org/
- The squid proxy, http://www.squid-cache.org/
- The VRRP Protocol for UNIX, http://www.imagestream.com/VRRP.html
- The HighUpTime Project, http://www.bsdshell.net/
- The PEN load balancer, http://siag.nu/pen/
- Pure Load Balancer, http://plb.sunsite.dk/

- CARP architecture and examples, http://www.countersiege.com/doc/pfsync-carp/
- Carnegie Mellon University anycast resources, http://www.net.cmu.edu/pres/anycast/

Endnotes

1   http://www.isc.org/products/BIND/docs/config/options.html

2   http://www.srrd.org

## CHAPTER 13

Policy Routing, Bandwidth Management, and QoS

IP networks, in general, and the Internet, as a particularly prominent example, are inherently nondeterministic in their predictability regarding operational parameters such as latency, delay, round-trip time (RTT), jitter (delay variation), and packet loss. The default service offering associated with the Internet is characterized as a best-effort variable-service response (RFC 2990, "Next Steps for the IP QoS Architecture").

To improve the situation for certain traffic classes, policy routing and quality of service (QoS) measures were introduced. Prioritizing one class of service always works at the cost of regular best-effort traffic. There is no free lunch, and statistical overbooking is the foundation of affordable Internet service provider (ISP) offerings. One strong driving force for QoS is expedited transport of real-time delay-sensitive traffic such as voice, video, and delicate data (such as storage traffic or dedicated business applications).

Note that queuing and scheduling on UNIX systems is often an integral part of packet filtering and Network Address Translation (NAT) implementations. This chapter covers neither firewall features nor NAT. (See Chapter 15, "Network Address Translation.") However, this chapter does cover packet-filtering architectures as they relate to queuing and scheduling.

Policy Routing

Policy routing is the art of deviating from destination-based shortest-path routing decisions of dynamic routing protocols. Policy routing considers aspects such as source/destination address, ports, protocol, type of service (ToS), and entry interfaces; do not confuse it with a *routing policy* or *traffic policing*. Traffic policing and shaping are sometimes summarized as traffic conditioning. Linux offers by far the most evolved policy routing approach of all Unices via multiple routing tables, the Routing Policy Database (RPDB), and the iproute2 (ip and tc) package for administration. Most other UNIX implementations implement policy routing via firewall marks and packet-mangling hooks.

Policy Routing on BSD

Policy-routing setup on BSD platforms is pretty straightforward, limited, and essentially integrated into firewall architectures. Examples 13-1 and 13-2 demonstrate its use by forwarding certain traffic based on source address or incoming interface (highlighted text).

Firewalling, NAT, and policy enforcement are done by basically the same "packet-mangling" structures.

Example 13-1 *Policy-Routing Example with FreeBSD ipfilter*

```
pass out quick on fxp0 to fxp1:192.168.2.1 from 192.168.2.200 to any
```

Example 13-2 *Policy-Routing Example with OpenBSD Packet Filter (pf)*

```
pass out log quick on xl0 route-to tl0:192.168.1.1 proto icmp from tl0 to any
pass out log quick on xl0 proto icmp from any to any
```

Linux iproute2 Policy Routing

The Linux OS can place routes within multiple routing tables that are identified by an 8-bit numeric ID or by a pseudo-name that is mapped in the file /etc/iproute2/rt_tables. By default, three tables exist: the default, the local, and the main (ID 254), as follows:

- The default table can be discarded safely. It is reserved for last-resort postprocessing for the unlikely case that previous rules/routing tables did not process the packet.

- The important local table (ID 255) consists of routes for local and broadcast addresses (as directly connected interfaces in Cisco lingo). The kernel maintains this table automatically. As a rule of thumb, it should not be tampered with.

- By default, all route manipulations act on the main routing table (forwarding table). The RPDB supervises the different routing tables. Policy routing is configured via the **ip rule** and **ip route** commands.

Multiple routing tables come into play when policy routing is used, for traffic control and in the context of Multiprotocol Label Switching (MPLS) multiple routing instances (VRFs, or virtual routing and forwarding instances). In policy routing, the routing table identifier becomes one additional criterion capable of handling otherwise-identical prefix routes in different tables that will not conflict because of this tiebreaker mechanism. Example 13-3 illustrates the capabilities of the Linux policy-routing toolbox. Example 13-4 offers an example of a custom policy-routing table.

Example 13-3 *Policy-Routing iproute2 Commands*

```
[root@callisto:~#] ip rule help
Usage: ip rule [ list | add | del ] SELECTOR ACTION
SELECTOR := [ from PREFIX ] [ to PREFIX ] [ tos TOS ] [ fwmark FWMARK ]
            [ dev STRING ] [ pref NUMBER ]
ACTION := [ table TABLE_ID ] [ nat ADDRESS ]
          [ prohibit | reject | unreachable ]
          [ realms [SRCREALM/]DSTREALM ]
TABLE_ID := [ local | main | default | NUMBER ]

[root@callisto:~#] ip rule list
0:      from all lookup local
32766:  from all lookup main
32767:  from all lookup default
```

Example 13-3 *Policy-Routing iproute2 Commands (Continued)*

```
[root@callisto:~#] ls -al /etc/iproute2/
total 36
drwxr-xr-x    2 root     root         4096 Aug 28 08:10 ./
drwxr-xr-x   86 root     root         8192 Aug 28 08:03 ../
-rw-r--r--    1 root     root          299 Mar 15  2002 rt_dsfield
-rw-r--r--    1 root     root          296 Mar 15  2002 rt_protos
-rw-r--r--    1 root     root          114 Mar 15  2002 rt_realms
-rw-r--r--    1 root     root           98 Mar 15  2002 rt_scopes
-rw-r--r--    1 root     root           81 Aug 28 08:10 rt_tables

[root@callisto:~#] cat /etc/iproute2/rt_tables
#
# reserved values
#
255     local
254     main
253     default
0       unspec


#
# local values
#
1       lab

[root@callisto:~#] cat /etc/iproute2/rt_scopes
#
# reserved values
#
#0      global
#255    nowhere
#254    host
#253    link


#
# pseudo-reserved
#
#200    site

[root@callisto:~#] ip route help
Usage: ip route { list | flush } SELECTOR
       ip route get ADDRESS [ from ADDRESS iif STRING ]
                           [ oif STRING ] [ tos TOS ]
       ip route { add | del | change | append | replace | monitor } ROUTE
SELECTOR := [ root PREFIX ] [ match PREFIX ] [ exact PREFIX ]
            [ table TABLE_ID ] [ proto RTPROTO ]
            [ type TYPE ] [ scope SCOPE ]
ROUTE := NODE_SPEC [ INFO_SPEC ]
NODE_SPEC := [ TYPE ] PREFIX [ tos TOS ]
             [ table TABLE_ID ] [ proto RTPROTO ]
             [ scope SCOPE ] [ metric METRIC ]
INFO_SPEC := NH OPTIONS FLAGS [ nexthop NH ]...
```

continues

Example 13-3 *Policy-Routing iproute2 Commands (Continued)*

```
NH := [ via ADDRESS ] [ dev STRING ] [ weight NUMBER ] NHFLAGS
OPTIONS := FLAGS [ mtu NUMBER ] [ advmss NUMBER ]
           [ rtt NUMBER ] [ rttvar NUMBER ]
           [ window NUMBER] [ cwnd NUMBER ] [ ssthresh REALM ]
           [ realms REALM ]
TYPE := [ unicast | local | broadcast | multicast | throw |
         unreachable | prohibit | blackhole | nat ]
TABLE_ID := [ local | main | default | all | NUMBER ]
SCOPE := [ host | link | global | NUMBER ]
FLAGS := [ equalize ]
NHFLAGS := [ onlink | pervasive ]
RTPROTO := [ kernel | boot | static | NUMBER ]

[root@callisto:~#] ip route list table local
local 192.168.1.1 dev eth1  proto kernel  scope host  src 192.168.1.1
local 192.168.45.253 dev eth1  proto kernel  scope host  src 192.168.45.253
broadcast 192.168.1.0 dev eth1  proto kernel  scope link  src 192.168.1.1
broadcast 127.255.255.255 dev lo  proto kernel  scope link  src 127.0.0.1
broadcast 192.168.14.255 dev eth0  proto kernel  scope link  src 192.168.14.1
broadcast 192.168.45.255 dev eth1  proto kernel  scope link  src 192.168.45.253
broadcast 192.168.1.255 dev eth1  proto kernel  scope link  src 192.168.1.1
broadcast 192.168.14.0 dev eth0  proto kernel  scope link  src 192.168.14.1
broadcast 192.168.45.0 dev eth1  proto kernel  scope link  src 192.168.45.253
local 192.168.14.1 dev eth0  proto kernel  scope host  src 192.168.14.1
broadcast 127.0.0.0 dev lo  proto kernel  scope link  src 127.0.0.1
local 127.0.0.1 dev lo  proto kernel  scope host  src 127.0.0.1
local 127.0.0.0/8 dev lo  proto kernel  scope host  src 127.0.0.1

[root@callisto:~#] ip route list table main
192.168.1.0/24 dev eth1  scope link
192.168.14.0/24 dev eth0  scope link
192.168.45.0/24 dev eth1  proto kernel  scope link  src 192.168.45.253
127.0.0.0/8 dev lo  scope link
default via 192.168.1.254 dev eth1

[root@callisto:~#] ip route list table main scope link
192.168.1.0/24 dev eth1
192.168.14.0/24 dev eth0
192.168.45.0/24 dev eth1  proto kernel  src 192.168.45.253
127.0.0.0/8 dev lo
```

Example 13-4 *Creating and Populating a Custom Routing Table*

```
[root@callisto:~#] echo 1 lab >> /etc/iproute2/rt_tables
[root@callisto:~#] echo 1 lab >> /etc/iproute2/rt_realms
[root@callisto:~#] ip rule del pref 32767
[root@callisto:~#] ip rule add from 192.168.14.0/24 to 192.168.7.0/24 table lab pref
                   32765 realms lab/lab

[root@callisto:~#] ip rule list
0:      from all lookup local
32765:  from 192.168.14.0/24 to 192.168.7.0/24 lookup lab realms lab/lab
32766:  from all lookup main
```

Example 13-4 *Creating and Populating a Custom Routing Table (Continued)*

```
[root@callisto:~#] ip route add default via 192.168.14.254 table lab

[root@callisto:~#] ip route flush cache

[root@callisto:~#] ip route list table lab
default via 192.168.14.254 dev eth0

[root@callisto:~#] rtacct lab
Realm    BytesTo     PktsTo     BytesFrom  PktsFrom
lab      0           0          0          0
```

Linux routing also incorporates the concept of *realms*. A routing realm essentially can be compared to a route aggregate in Border Gateway Protocol (BGP) lingo; however, it is a grouping based on human logic and not necessarily on bitmasks. Realms often are used for tracking, traffic control, and packet path-accounting purposes that can be inspected via the rtacct utility. Realms are demonstrated in Example 13-4, too. Each route can be assigned to a realm either dynamically by a routing daemon or statically via the **REALM** option of the **ip route** command. I am aware of a patched version of GateD with patches from Alexej Kuznetsov that can classify prefixes to realms and can handle multiple Linux routing table IDs. For a concise discussion of realms and scope, check out the original writings of Alexej Kuznetsov, the creator of the iproute2 toolbox, at http://www.policyrouting.org/.

Cisco IOS Policy-Routing Example

Policy-based routing (PBR) enables you to classify traffic based on extended access list criteria or assign the traffic to different service classes via an IP precedence setting. Consult the Cisco.com article "Configuring Policy-Based Routing" for further information. Example 13-5 demonstrates the use of policy route maps to achieve this goal.

Example 13-5 *Cisco IOS Policy Route Map for Different Next Hops and Priority*

```
...
!
access-list 1 permit ip 192.168.1.1
access-list 2 permit ip 192.168.2.1
!
interface ethernet 1
 ip policy route-map LAB
!
route-map LAB permit 10
 match ip address 1
 set ip precedence priority
 set ip next-hop 192.168.3.1
!
route-map LAB permit 20
 match ip address 2
```

continues

Example 13-5 *Cisco IOS Policy Route Map for Different Next Hops and Priority (Continued)*

```
  set ip precedence critical
  set ip next-hop 192.168.3.2
!
...
```

Traffic Shaping, Queuing, Reservation, and Scheduling

Queuing works only for packets in the *outbound* (egress) direction. The only viable way to improve this situation is to enable bidirectional queuing on adjacent routers—for example, by configuring committed access rate (CAR)/rate limits on Cisco IOS architecture. Adjacency essentially means connected via point-to-point links or Ethernet crossover links. When no other queuing regimes are activated, almost all stack implementations resort to default first-in/first-out (FIFO) behavior.

The actual tasks involved in traffic shaping and implementing QoS include reserving resources, buffering, and scheduling behind the scenes. The choice of a *queuing discipline* is tricky, depending on the load on a link, and requires a thorough understanding of the internal workings of the queuing mechanism.

Queuing disciplines are a classical area of academic and applied research and go beyond the scope of this book. They are essentially procedures or measures that influence the way data is sent, delayed, and queued. You will find excellent resources for further information about queuing in the "Recommended Reading" section at the end of this chapter.

Queuing disciplines essentially come in two flavors: classless queuing disciplines (no subdivision granularity; reschedule, delay, or drop on a flat scale) and classful (class-context) queuing disciplines. The most popular queuing regimes are as follows:

- **CBQ**—Class-based queuing
- **RED**—Random early detection
- **WFQ**—Weighted fair queuing
- **PRIQ**—Priority queuing

Permanently saturated links require other strategies than bursty traffic patterns. Nothing really prevents permanently overburdened queues and interface buffers from dropping datagrams/frames. Proactively dealing with that problem is the art of congestion avoidance/management. Queuing is an integral part of the IP stack and forwarding engine and, therefore, the responsibility of the kernel. User-space utilities for administration complement the implementations. Shaping serves two purposes: limiting available bandwidth, and smoothing the use of virtual pipes.

Traffic conditioning is the art of dealing with *incoming* (ingress) traffic via a policer or shaper. A policer just enforces a rate limit, whereas a shaper smoothes the traffic flow to a specified rate by the use of buffers. Standard mechanisms of the Cisco IOS architecture are CAR, generic traffic shaping (GTS), and Frame Relay traffic shaping (FRTS).

Linux QoS

Linux provides a powerful and feature-rich subsystem for traffic control (traffic shaping, queuing disciplines, classification, prioritizing, sharing, filter chains), of both ingress and egress traffic. You configure such by having multiple sets of routing tables (iproute2) and by using the tc tool.

The main application of realms is in conjunction with the tc route classifier, where they help assign packets to traffic classes for accounting, policing, and scheduling. The tc tool handles these tasks:

- Setup of queuing disciplines (QDISC) such as CBQ, RED, and SFQ
- Setup of parent and child classes for classful queuing
- Flexible filtering of classful queuing disciplines
- Combinations of all these features

You also can shape inbound via the ingress option of the tc utility. It is up to you to decide whether inbound policing makes sense. Examples 13-6 through 13-10 demonstrate classless QDISCs.

Note that Example 13-6 facilitates a simple token-bucket filter (TBF) applied to interface eth0 (highlighted text), with certain parameters that influence shaping and allow short bursts while reacting with delays and drops to lasting overload conditions. In the current implementation, tokens correspond to bytes, not packets. A similar effect is achieved via a shaper device attached to eth0 in Example 13-7.

NOTE   For more details on TBF and an in-depth discussion of classful and classless queuing disciplines, see the "Linux Advanced Routing & Traffic Control HOWTO," especially for generic RED, weighted RED, and weighted round-robin (WRR).

Example 13-6 *Interface Shaping with a TBF*

```
[root@callisto:~#] tc qdisc add dev eth0 root tbf rate 220kbit latency 50ms burst 1540

[root@callisto:~#] tc -d qdisc
qdisc tbf 8001: dev eth0 rate 220Kbit burst 1539b/8 mpu 0b lat 61.0ms

[root@callisto:~#] tc -s qdisc
qdisc tbf 8001: dev eth0 rate 220Kbit burst 1539b lat 61.0ms
 Sent 425 bytes 5 pkts (dropped 0, overlimits 0)
```

Example 13-7 *Alternative Interface Shaping with the Shaper Device*

```
[root@callisto:~#] insmod shaper
Using /lib/modules/2.4.21/kernel/drivers/net/shaper.o

[root@callisto:~#] shapecfg -?
shapecfg attach <device> <device>
shapecfg speed <device> <speed>

[root@callisto:~#] shapecfg attach shaper0 eth0

[root@callisto:~#] shapecfg speed shaper0 2000000

[root@callisto:~#] ifconfig shaper0 192.168.80.1 netmask 255.255.255.0 up

[root@callisto:~#] ifconfig -a
eth0      Link encap:Ethernet  HWaddr 00:10:5A:D7:93:60
          inet addr:192.168.14.1  Bcast:192.168.14.255  Mask:255.255.255.0
          UP BROADCAST RUNNING MULTICAST  MTU:1500  Metric:1
          RX packets:0 errors:0 dropped:0 overruns:0 frame:0
          TX packets:476 errors:0 dropped:0 overruns:0 carrier:0
          collisions:0 txqueuelen:100
          RX bytes:0 (0.0 b)  TX bytes:53487 (52.2 Kb)
          Interrupt:5 Base address:0xd800

eth1      Link encap:Ethernet  HWaddr 52:54:05:E3:51:87
          inet addr:192.168.1.1  Bcast:192.168.1.255  Mask:255.255.255.0
          UP BROADCAST RUNNING MULTICAST  MTU:1500  Metric:1
          RX packets:19895 errors:0 dropped:0 overruns:0 frame:0
          TX packets:14777 errors:0 dropped:0 overruns:0 carrier:0
          collisions:43 txqueuelen:100
          RX bytes:5879639 (5.6 Mb)  TX bytes:1302730 (1.2 Mb)
          Interrupt:9 Base address:0xd400

eth1:1    Link encap:Ethernet  HWaddr 52:54:05:E3:51:87
          inet addr:192.168.45.253  Bcast:192.168.45.255  Mask:255.255.255.0
          UP BROADCAST RUNNING MULTICAST  MTU:1500  Metric:1
          Interrupt:9 Base address:0xd400

lo        Link encap:Local Loopback
          inet addr:127.0.0.1  Mask:255.0.0.0
          UP LOOPBACK RUNNING  MTU:16436  Metric:1
          RX packets:72 errors:0 dropped:0 overruns:0 frame:0
          TX packets:72 errors:0 dropped:0 overruns:0 carrier:0
          collisions:0 txqueuelen:0
          RX bytes:5416 (5.2 Kb)  TX bytes:5416 (5.2 Kb)

shaper0   Link encap:Ethernet  HWaddr 00:00:00:00:00:00
          inet addr:192.168.80.1  Mask:255.255.255.0
          UP RUNNING  MTU:1500  Metric:1
          RX packets:0 errors:0 dropped:0 overruns:0 frame:0
          TX packets:0 errors:0 dropped:0 overruns:0 carrier:0
          collisions:0 txqueuelen:10
          RX bytes:0 (0.0 b)  TX bytes:0 (0.0 b)
```

Stochastic fair queuing (SFQ), as shown in Example 13-8, represents an "almost" fair queuing mechanism with reduced calculation burden. It helps on saturated links to distribute utilization in a fair way among sessions.

Example 13-8 *Stochastic Fair Queuing*

```
[root@callisto:~#] tc qdisc add dev eth0 root sfq perturb 10 quantum 2

[root@callisto:~#] tc -s -d qdisc list
qdisc sfq 8003: dev eth0 quantum 2b limit 128p flows 128/1024 perturb 10sec
 Sent 0 bytes 0 pkts (dropped 0, overlimits 0)
```

Example 13-9 *pFIFO-Fast*

```
[root@callisto:~#] tc qdisc add dev eth0 root pfifo limit 200k

[root@callisto:~#] tc -s -d qdisc list
qdisc pfifo 8004: dev eth0 limit 204800p
 Sent 0 bytes 0 pkts (dropped 0, overlimits 0)
```

Example 13-10 *Random Early Detect/Discard with Explicit Congestion Notification*

```
[root@callisto:~#] tc qdisc add dev eth0 root red limit 100 min 80 max 90 avpkt
10 burst 10 probability 1 bandwidth 200 ecn

[root@callisto:~#] tc -s -d qdisc list
qdisc red 8006: dev eth0 limit 100b min 80b max 90b ecn ewma 2 Plog 4 Scell_log 17
 Sent 0 bytes 0 pkts (dropped 0, overlimits 0)
   marked 0 early 0 pdrop 0 other 0
```

In contrast to the previous examples, Example 13-11 offers a variant of *classful* queuing (priority queuing) in combination with filter chains. Class-based queuing (CBQ) is a huge field that is covered exhaustively in the HOWTO.

Example 13-11 *Priority Queuing (PRIQ)*

```
[root@callisto:~#] tc qdisc add dev eth0 root handle 1: prio

[root@callisto:~#] tc -s -d qdisc
qdisc prio 1: dev eth0 bands 3 priomap  1 2 2 2 1 2 0 0 1 1 1 1 1 1 1 1
 Sent 1097 bytes 5 pkts (dropped 0, overlimits 0)

[root@callisto:~#] tc qdisc add dev eth0 parent 1:1 handle 10: sfq

[root@callisto:~#] tc qdisc add dev eth0 parent 1:2 handle 20: tbf rate 20kbit buffer
1600 limit 3000

[root@callisto:~#] tc qdisc add dev eth0 parent 1:3 handle 30: sfq

[root@callisto:~#] tc -s -d qdisc
qdisc sfq 30: dev eth0 quantum 1514b limit 128p flows 128/1024
 Sent 0 bytes 0 pkts (dropped 0, overlimits 0)
```

continues

Example 13-11 *Priority Queuing (PRIQ) (Continued)*

```
qdisc tbf 20: dev eth0 rate 20Kbit burst 1599b/8 mpu 0b lat 667.6ms
Sent 85 bytes 1 pkts (dropped 0, overlimits 0)

qdisc sfq 10: dev eth0 quantum 1514b limit 128p flows 128/1024
Sent 0 bytes 0 pkts (dropped 0, overlimits 0)

qdisc prio 1: dev eth0 bands 3 priomap  1 2 2 2 1 2 0 0 1 1 1 1 1 1 1 1
Sent 1182 bytes 6 pkts (dropped 0, overlimits 0)

[root@callisto:~#] tc -s -d qdisc list dev eth0
qdisc sfq 30: quantum 1514b limit 128p flows 128/1024
Sent 0 bytes 0 pkts (dropped 0, overlimits 0)

qdisc tbf 20: rate 20Kbit burst 1599b/8 mpu 0b lat 667.6ms
Sent 85 bytes 1 pkts (dropped 0, overlimits 0)

qdisc sfq 10: quantum 1514b limit 128p flows 128/1024
Sent 0 bytes 0 pkts (dropped 0, overlimits 0)

qdisc prio 1: bands 3 priomap  1 2 2 2 1 2 0 0 1 1 1 1 1 1 1 1
Sent 1182 bytes 6 pkts (dropped 0, overlimits 0)

[root@callisto:~#] tc filter add dev eth0 protocol ip parent 1: prio 1 u32 match ip
dport 22 0xffff flowid 1:1

[root@callisto:~#] tc filter add dev eth0 protocol ip parent 1: prio 1 u32 match ip
sport 80 0xffff flowid 1:1

[root@callisto:~#] tc -s -d filter list dev eth0
filter parent 1: protocol ip pref 1 u32
filter parent 1: protocol ip pref 1 u32 fh 800: ht divisor 1
filter parent 1: protocol ip pref 1 u32 fh 800::800 order 2048 key ht 800 bkt 0
  flowid 1:1 match 00000016/0000ffff at 20
filter parent 1: protocol ip pref 1 u32 fh 800::801 order 2049 key ht 800 bkt 0
  flowid 1:1 match 00500000/ffff0000 at 20
```

Layer 3 QoS: IP ToS, Precedence, CoS, IntServ, and DiffServ Codepoints

QoS definitions vary by service and approach chosen. For data communication networks, typical QoS characteristics and metrics include bandwidth, delay (latency), delay variation (jitter), and reliability, as follows:

- **Bandwidth**—Peak data rate (PDR), sustained data rate (SDR), minimum data rate (MDR).

- **Delay/latency**—End-to-end or round-trip delay, delay variation (jitter), node-processing delay.

- **Reliability**—Availability (as percent of uptime), mean time between failures/mean time to repair (MTBF/MTTR), errors, and packet loss.

The IP header contains a Type of Service (ToS) field (see Example 13-12). Applications can set the three precedence bits of this ToS field at the network interface card (NIC) level according to their requirements.

Example 13-12 *IPv4 Header with ToS Field*

```
 0 1 2 3 4 5 6 7 8 9 0 1 2 3 4 5 6 7 8 9 0 1 2 3 4 5 6 7 8 9 0 1
+-+-+-+-+-+-+-+-+-+-+-+-+-+-+-+-+-+-+-+-+-+-+-+-+-+-+-+-+-+-+-+-+
|Version|  IHL  |Type of Service|          Total Length         |
+-+-+-+-+-+-+-+-+-+-+-+-+-+-+-+-+-+-+-+-+-+-+-+-+-+-+-+-+-+-+-+-+
|         Identification        |Flags|      Fragment Offset    |
+-+-+-+-+-+-+-+-+-+-+-+-+-+-+-+-+-+-+-+-+-+-+-+-+-+-+-+-+-+-+-+-+
| Time to Live |    Protocol    |        Header Checksum         |
+-+-+-+-+-+-+-+-+-+-+-+-+-+-+-+-+-+-+-+-+-+-+-+-+-+-+-+-+-+-+-+-+
|                        Source Address                         |
+-+-+-+-+-+-+-+-+-+-+-+-+-+-+-+-+-+-+-+-+-+-+-+-+-+-+-+-+-+-+-+-+
|                      Destination Address                      |
+-+-+-+-+-+-+-+-+-+-+-+-+-+-+-+-+-+-+-+-+-+-+-+-+-+-+-+-+-+-+-+-+
|                  Options                 |      Padding        |
+-+-+-+-+-+-+-+-+-+-+-+-+-+-+-+-+-+-+-+-+-+-+-+-+-+-+-+-+-+-+-+-+
```

In the context of IP QoS considerations, a 3-bit field in the ToS byte of the IP header is referred to as *precedence* (see Example 13-13). Using IP precedence, a network administrator can assign values from 0 (the default) to 7 to classify and prioritize types of traffic.

Example 13-13 *ToS and Precedence*

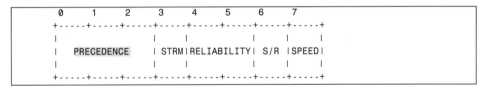

Many applications and routers support IP precedence. The ToS and differentiated services (DiffServ) approach directly tag the traffic itself, which therefore contains in-band QoS markings. An out-band approach is the Resource Reservation Protocol (RSVP). An integrated services (IntServ) approach provides end-to-end QoS in IP networks and relies on per-flow state information and integration with RSVP as a signaling protocol at every involved hop. (IntServ is considered to have some weaknesses.)

DiffServ takes a simpler approach with less signaling overhead and no QoS-aware intermediate network nodes for the entire path. Packets are classified and marked to receive a particular per-hop forwarding behavior on nodes along their path (RFC 2475). The DiffServ (DS) field is supposed to succeed the IPv4 ToS field in the IPv4 header, which is deprecated and in IPv6 context "rejuvenated" as the traffic-class octet (see Example 13-14).

NOTE   For DiffServ internals, see RFC 2474, "Definition of Differentiated Services Field (DS Field) in the IPv4 and IPv6 Headers."

Example 13-14 *DiffServ Codepoints*

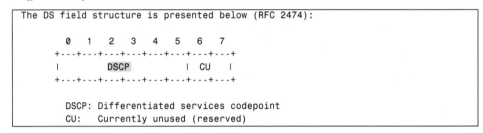

```
The DS field structure is presented below (RFC 2474):

        0   1   2   3   4   5   6   7
      +---+---+---+---+---+---+---+---+
      |         DSCP          | CU    |
      +---+---+---+---+---+---+---+---+

      DSCP: Differentiated services codepoint
      CU:   Currently unused (reserved)
```

Note that when you are dealing with DiffServ, two expressions are used frequently: *PHB* (per-hop behavior) and *DSCP* (DiffServ codepoint). In current architectures, IP precedence values are mapped into DSCPs.

802.1P/Q Tagging/Priority—QoS at the Data-Link/MAC Sublayer

802.1P provides for eight traffic classes drawn from priority fields in 802.1Q VLAN tags. The IEEE 802.1P standard describes important methods for providing QoS at the MAC level and defines traffic-class expediting (3 bits) and dynamic-multicast filtering to ensure traffic does not traverse the boundaries of Layer 2-switched networks.

NOTE   Both 802.1P and 802.1Q are part of 802.1D.

Most vendors support 802.1P/Q in their Layer 2/3 equipment and modern NICs. This means that QoS tagging is pushed out to the network edge down to the NIC level. However, privileged treatment of these frames still is best effort in Layer 2-switched networks and does not involve reservation setup. The 3 priority bits can be mapped easily into the Layer 3 IP precedence bits or a subset of DSCPs. Therefore, we have coherent tagging, which is easy to implement. The remaining question—and there exists no uniform approach—is how to implement queuing for these priority flows at Layer 2 and Layer 3.

There is no 802.1P without 802.1Q VLAN tagging. The VLAN tag carries VLAN information—the VLAN ID (12 bits) and prioritization (3 bits). The Prioritization field was never defined in the VLAN standard, so 802.1P steps in and actually brings it to life. This effort defines a 32-bit tag header that is inserted after a frame's normal destination and source address header info. Switches, routers, servers, and even desktop systems can set these priority bits.

802.1Q priority is supported only rudimentary on UNIX. Linux vconfig can set these bits (see Example 13-15). Whether this works depends on the 802.1Q VLAN implementation of the OS.

Example 13-15 *802.1Q Priority Setting on Linux*

```
[root@callisto:~#] vconfig add eth0 1
[root@callisto:~#] vconfig set_egress_map eth0.1 8
[root@callisto:~#] ifconfig -a
...
eth0.1    Link encap:Ethernet  HWaddr 00:10:5A:D7:93:60
          BROADCAST MULTICAST  MTU:1500  Metric:1
          RX packets:0 errors:0 dropped:0 overruns:0 frame:0
          TX packets:0 errors:0 dropped:0 overruns:0 carrier:0
          collisions:0 txqueuelen:0
          RX bytes:0 (0.0 b)  TX bytes:0 (0.0 b)
...
[root@callisto:~#] cat /proc/net/vlan/eth0.1
eth0.1  VID: 1   REORDER_HDR: 1  dev->priv_flags: 1
total frames received:           0
total bytes received:            0
Broadcast/Multicast Rcvd:        0
total frames transmitted:        0
total bytes transmitted:         0
total headroom inc:              0
total encap on xmit:             0
Device: eth0
INGRESS priority mappings: 0:0  1:0  2:0  3:0  4:0  5:0  6:0 7:0
EGRESSS priority Mappings: 8:0
```

MPLS Exp Field and MPLS Traffic Engineering

The 3-bit MPLS Exp field (see Example 13-16) of the MPLS shim header (Layer 2 label-insertion header) can support eight different service classes (CoS, or class of service); thus DiffServ edge marking can be carried over.

Example 13-16 *MPLS Label Stack Entry*

```
The label stack is represented as a sequence of "label stack entries." Each label
stack entry is represented by 4 octets. The label stack entries appear after the
data link layer headers, but before any network layer headers. The top of the label
stack appears earliest in the packet, and the bottom appears latest. The network
layer packet immediately follows the label stack entry, which has the S bit set.
(RFC 3032, "MPLS Label Stack Encoding")
```

continues

Example 13-16 *MPLS Label Stack Entry (Continued)*

```
0                   1                   2                   3
0 1 2 3 4 5 6 7 8 9 0 1 2 3 4 5 6 7 8 9 0 1 2 3 4 5 6 7 8 9 0 1
+-+-+-+-+-+-+-+-+-+-+-+-+-+-+-+-+-+-+-+-+-+-+-+-+-+-+-+-+-+-+-+-+ Label
|                Label                  | Exp |S|       TTL      | Stack
+-+-+-+-+-+-+-+-+-+-+-+-+-+-+-+-+-+-+-+-+-+-+-+-+-+-+-+-+-+-+-+-+ Entry

                   Label:   Label Value, 20 bits
                   Exp:     Experimental Use, 3 bits
                   S:       Bottom of Stack, 1 bit
                   TTL:     Time To Live, 8 bits
```

This mechanism adds QoS to MPLS label-switched paths (LSPs). Integrated MPLS and DiffServ architectures are state-of-the art and the subject of active research and standard development. In addition, from a phenomenological point of view, CoS maps nicely into the MPLS concept of forwarding equivalence classes (FECs). FECs are a concept of treating equivalent traffic the same generic way.

MPLS uses RSVP-TE (traffic engineering) and Constraint-based Label-Distribution Protocol (CR-LDP) for special-purpose signaling. According to the recent Internet Engineering Task Force (IETF) activities, it looks as if RSVP-TE has won the race. There is a lot of work going on in the DiffServ/MPLS-TE integration area, too. This appears to be the only viable approach to the scalability problem that ISPs and carriers face when dealing with flows and service classes.

NOTE   For further information, consult the "Quality of Service" white paper at Cisco.com.

You can find more information about UNIX MPLS activities at the following website:

* http://www.ayame.org/
* http://www.nortelnetworks.com/products/announcements/mpls/index.html
* http://mpls-linux.sourceforge.net/
* http://linux-vrf.sourceforge.net/
* http://www.cs.virginia.edu/~mngroup/projects/mpls/software.html
* http://www.tel.fer.hr/zec/BSD/vimage/index.html

DiffServ and RSVP/RSVP-TE Implementations for UNIX

It appears that the most active work in this area is done in the context of integrating DiffServ, RSVP-TE, Open Shortest Path First traffic engineering (OSPF-TE), and MPLS/LDP implementations, mostly on Linux platforms. The main Linux DiffServ resource is http://diffserv.sourceforge.net/. I am aware of two RSVP packages available at http://www.isi.edu/div7/rsvp/rsvp.html and http://www.kom.e-technik.tu-darmstadt.de/rsvp/.

Cisco IOS QoS and Queuing Architectures

The Cisco QoS architecture has evolved quite significantly over time with a strong foundation in (distributed [D]) CAR, (CB) WFQ, PRIQ, custom queuing, WRED, and the new D-WRED. It has evolved into a complete architecture that incorporates the capabilities of Frame Relay (discard eligibility [DE]) and ATM (cell loss priority [CLP]); IP to ATM CoS; in addition to 802.1P/Q marking, IntServ/RSVP and DiffServ, and a strong focus on MPLS-TE and MPLS QoS.

As in most IP stacks, FIFO queuing is the default behavior. Because of lab constraints, I am unable to present labs with 802.1P/Q, DiffServ, and advanced features here.

Recently, AutoQoS was added to the Cisco portfolio, which essentially covers the following in a more proactive way:

- QoS classification and marking
- QoS configuration and monitoring
- QoS congestion avoidance
- QoS congestion management
- QoS link-efficiency mechanisms
- QoS policing and shaping
- QoS signaling
- ATM/Frame Relay QoS
- LAN switching QoS

UNIX Firewalling Engines and Queuing

In the UNIX world, traffic conditioning, policy routing, and shaping are tied closely to the packet filters available for the different platforms, forming conceptual pairs such as packet filter/ALTQ (Alternate Queuing), ipfirewall/dummynet, or iptables/tc. The reason for this design is simple: Packet filters already provide the necessary hooks within the forwarding engine of the IP network stack.

On Linux, the relationship between netfilter/iptables and the iproute2 package (ip/tc/rtmon) constitutes a firewall-marking and packet-mangling symbiosis to build sophisticated QoS routers. Packet mangling (manipulation) is the altering of certain bits of the IP header—for example, the ToS field or DSCP.

Table 13-1 shows an overview of the platform availability of these components. Figure 13-1 shows the lab layout for the following subsections.

Table 13-1 *Packet Filtering and Traffic Control on UNIX Platforms*

Packet Filter	Linux	OpenBSD	NetBSD	FreeBSD
netfilter/iptables	x			
packet filter (pf)		x	x	x
ipfilter (ipf)		x	x	x
ipfirewall (ipfw)				x
Traffic Control				
iproute2 (ip & tc)	x			
dummynet				x
ALTQ		x	x	x

Figure 13-1 *Packet Filter and Traffic-Conditioning Lab*

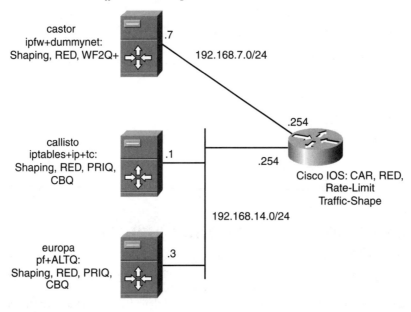

OpenBSD ALTQ+pf

Packet filter (pf) is OpenBSD's stateful-inspection firewall system, packet filter, and NAT engine. It has been ported to NetBSD and FreeBSD recently. pf also is capable of normalizing and conditioning TCP/IP traffic and providing bandwidth control and packet prioritization via ALTQ. The ALTQ system is a framework to manage queuing disciplines on network interfaces.

Starting with OpenBSD 3.3, ALTQ has been integrated into pf (http://www.benzedrine.cx/ pf.html). OpenBSD's ALTQ implementation supports CBQ and PRIQ schedulers (see Examples 13-17 and 13-18). It also supports RED and explicit congestion notification (ECN). The /etc/pf.conf file is the only relevant configuration file (pf.conf(5), pf(4), pfctl(8), pflogd(8), ftp-proxy(8)).

Example 13-17 *OpenBSD pf/ALTQ PRIQ Example*

```
[root@europa:~#] cat /etc/pf.conf
#
# Queuing: rule-based bandwidth control
#
# PRIQ Example
altq on xl0 bandwidth 2Mb priq queue {dflt engineering testlab}
queue dflt priority 7 qlimit 50 priq(default red ecn)
queue engineering priority 6 qlimit 50 priq(red ecn)
queue testlab priority 5 qlimit 50 priq(rio ecn)

# Filtering:
pass in log all
pass out on xl0 proto tcp from any to any port 22 queue dflt
pass out on xl0 proto icmp from any to any queue testlab
pass out on xl0 from 172.16.0.0/16 to any queue engineering
pass out log all


[root@europa:~#] pfctl -s queue -v
queue dflt priority 7 priq( red ecn default )
[ pkts:        468 bytes:      47560 dropped pkts:      0 bytes:      0 ]
[ qlength:   0/ 50 ]
queue engineering priority 6 priq( red ecn )
[ pkts:          0 bytes:          0 dropped pkts:      0 bytes:      0 ]
[ qlength:   0/ 50 ]
queue testlab priority 5 priq( red ecn rio )
[ pkts:          0 bytes:          0 dropped pkts:      0 bytes:      0 ]
[ qlength:   0/ 50 ]


[root@europa:~#] pfctl -s queue -v -v
queue dflt priority 7 priq( red ecn default )
[ pkts:        495 bytes:      50376 dropped pkts:      0 bytes:      0 ]
[ qlength:   0/ 50 ]
queue engineering priority 6 priq( red ecn )
[ pkts:          0 bytes:          0 dropped pkts:      0 bytes:      0 ]
[ qlength:   0/ 50 ]
queue testlab priority 5 priq( red ecn rio )
[ pkts:          0 bytes:          0 dropped pkts:      0 bytes:      0 ]
[ qlength:   0/ 50 ]

queue dflt priority 7 priq( red ecn default )
[ pkts:        511 bytes:      52212 dropped pkts:      0 bytes:      0 ]
```

continues

Example 13-17 *OpenBSD pf/ALTQ PRIQ Example (Continued)*

```
[ qlength:    0/ 50 ]
[ measured:     3.2 packets/s, 2.93Kb/s ]
queue engineering priority 6 priq( red ecn )
[ pkts:          0  bytes:          0  dropped pkts:      0 bytes:      0 ]
[ qlength:    0/ 50 ]
[ measured:     0.0 packets/s, 0 b/s ]
queue testlab priority 5 priq( red ecn rio )
[ pkts:          0  bytes:          0  dropped pkts:      0 bytes:      0 ]
[ qlength:    0/ 50 ]
[ measured:     0.0 packets/s, 0 b/s ]

queue dflt priority 7 priq( red ecn default )
[ pkts:        532  bytes:      54538  dropped pkts:      0 bytes:      0 ]
[ qlength:    0/ 50 ]
[ measured:     4.2 packets/s, 3.71Kb/s ]
queue engineering priority 6 priq( red ecn )
[ pkts:          0  bytes:          0  dropped pkts:      0 bytes:      0 ]
[ qlength:    0/ 50 ]
[ measured:     0.0 packets/s, 0 b/s ]
queue testlab priority 5 priq( red ecn rio )
[ pkts:          0  bytes:          0  dropped pkts:      0 bytes:      0 ]
[ qlength:    0/ 50 ]
[ measured:     0.0 packets/s, 0 b/s ]

[root@europa:~#] pfctl -s rules -v
scrub in all random-id fragment reassemble
[ Evaluations: 2979      Packets: 1482      Bytes: 0          States: 0      ]

pass in log all
[ Evaluations: 1536      Packets: 759       Bytes: 64806      States: 0      ]

pass out on xl0 proto tcp from any to any port = ssh queue dflt
[ Evaluations: 1539      Packets: 0         Bytes: 0          States: 0      ]

pass out on xl0 proto icmp all queue testlab
[ Evaluations: 783       Packets: 0         Bytes: 0          States: 0      ]

pass out on xl0 inet from 172.16.0.0/16 to any queue engineering
[ Evaluations: 786       Packets: 0         Bytes: 0          States: 0      ]

pass out log all
[ Evaluations: 789       Packets: 789       Bytes: 73176      States: 0      ]
```

Example 13-18 *OpenBSD pf/ALTQ CBQ Example*

```
[root@europa:~#] cat /etc/pf.conf
#
# Queuing: rule-based bandwidth control
#
```

Example 13-18 *OpenBSD pf/ALTQ CBQ Example (Continued)*

```
# CBQ Example
altq on xl0 bandwidth 2Mb cbq queue {dflt engineering testlab}
queue dflt bandwidth 50% priority 7 qlimit 50 cbq(default red ecn)
queue engineering priority 6 bandwidth 30% qlimit 50 cbq(red ecn borrow)
queue testlab priority 5 bandwidth 20% qlimit 50 cbq(red ecn)

# Filtering
pass in log all
pass out on xl0 proto tcp from any to any port 22 queue dflt
pass out on xl0 proto icmp from any to any queue testlab
pass out on xl0 from 172.16.0.0/16 to any queue engineering
pass out log all

[root@europa:~#] pfctl -s queue -v
queue root_xl0 bandwidth 2Mb priority 0 cbq( wrr root ) {dflt, engineering, testlab}
[ pkts:        25  bytes:       2256  dropped pkts:      0 bytes:      0 ]
[ qlength:   0/ 50  borrows:      0  suspends:       0 ]
queue  dflt bandwidth 1Mb priority 7 cbq( red ecn default )
[ pkts:        25  bytes:       2256  dropped pkts:      0 bytes:      0 ]
[ qlength:   0/ 50  borrows:      0  suspends:       0 ]
queue  engineering bandwidth 600Kb priority 6 cbq( red ecn borrow )
[ pkts:         0  bytes:          0  dropped pkts:      0 bytes:      0 ]
[ qlength:   0/ 50  borrows:      0  suspends:       0 ]
queue  testlab bandwidth 400Kb priority 5 cbq( red ecn )
[ pkts:         0  bytes:          0  dropped pkts:      0 bytes:      0 ]
[ qlength:   0/ 50  borrows:      0  suspends:       0 ]

[root@europa:~#] pfctl -s queue -v -v
queue root_xl0 bandwidth 2Mb priority 0 cbq( wrr root ) {dflt, engineering, testlab}
[ pkts:        60  bytes:       6010  dropped pkts:      0 bytes:      0 ]
[ qlength:   0/ 50  borrows:      0  suspends:       0 ]
queue  dflt bandwidth 1Mb priority 7 cbq( red ecn default )
[ pkts:        60  bytes:       6010  dropped pkts:      0 bytes:      0 ]
[ qlength:   0/ 50  borrows:      0  suspends:       0 ]
queue  engineering bandwidth 600Kb priority 6 cbq( red ecn borrow )
[ pkts:         0  bytes:          0  dropped pkts:      0 bytes:      0 ]
[ qlength:   0/ 50  borrows:      0  suspends:       0 ]
queue  testlab bandwidth 400Kb priority 5 cbq( red ecn )
[ pkts:         0  bytes:          0  dropped pkts:      0 bytes:      0 ]
[ qlength:   0/ 50  borrows:      0  suspends:       0 ]

queue root_xl0 bandwidth 2Mb priority 0 cbq( wrr root ) {dflt, engineering, testlab}
[ pkts:        80  bytes:       8454  dropped pkts:      0 bytes:      0 ]
[ qlength:   0/ 50  borrows:      0  suspends:       0 ]
[ measured:    4.0 packets/s, 3.90Kb/s ]
queue  dflt bandwidth 1Mb priority 7 cbq( red ecn default )
[ pkts:        80  bytes:       8454  dropped pkts:      0 bytes:      0 ]
[ qlength:   0/ 50  borrows:      0  suspends:       0 ]
[ measured:    4.0 packets/s, 3.90Kb/s ]
```

continues

Example 13-18 *OpenBSD pf/ALTQ CBQ Example (Continued)*

```
queue  engineering bandwidth 600Kb priority 6 cbq( red ecn borrow )
[ pkts:            0  bytes:           0  dropped pkts:       0 bytes:       0 ]
[ qlength:   0/ 50  borrows:        0  suspends:       0 ]
[ measured:        0.0 packets/s, 0 b/s ]
queue  testlab bandwidth 400Kb priority 5 cbq( red ecn )
[ pkts:            0  bytes:           0  dropped pkts:       0 bytes:       0 ]
[ qlength:   0/ 50  borrows:        0  suspends:       0 ]
[ measured:        0.0 packets/s, 0 b/s ]

[root@europa:~#] pfctl -s rules -v
scrub in all random-id fragment reassemble
[ Evaluations: 584        Packets: 287      Bytes: 0         States: 0       ]

pass in log all
[ Evaluations: 10         Packets: 5        Bytes: 380       States: 0       ]

pass out on xl0 proto tcp from any to any port = ssh queue dflt
[ Evaluations: 10         Packets: 0        Bytes: 0         States: 0       ]

pass out on xl0 proto icmp all queue testlab
[ Evaluations: 5          Packets: 0        Bytes: 0         States: 0       ]

pass out on xl0 inet from 172.16.0.0/16 to any queue engineering
[ Evaluations: 5          Packets: 0        Bytes: 0         States: 0       ]

pass out log all
[ Evaluations: 5          Packets: 5        Bytes: 380       States: 0       ]
```

FreeBSD ipfilter+ALTQ

In contrast to OpenBSD pf, ipfilter and ALTQ do not form an integrated architecture. ALTQ does not natively ship with FreeBSD; it is now part of the KAME Project (http://www.kame.net/). The original web page is located at http://www.csl.sony.co.jp/~kjc/software.html#ALTQ.

ALTQ is concerned with queuing disciplines and resource-sharing QoS approaches. Remember, a queuing discipline controls outgoing traffic only. It provides stubs for RSVP and DiffServ support and enforces the following queuing regimes:

- **CBQ**—Class-based queuing
- **HFSC**—The hierarchical fair service curve algorithm for Link sharing, real-time, and priority service
- **JoBS**—Joint buffer management and scheduling algorithm

- **RED**—Random early detection
- **RIO**—RED with in/out
- **Blue**—A queue-management algorithm focusing on eliminating packet loss in congestion situations (an alternative to RED)
- **WFQ**—Weighted fair queuing
- **PRIQ**—Priority queuing

CBQ, HFSC, and RED are the most mature and recommended approaches. Relevant management tools and man pages are as follows:

- **tbrconfig(8)**—Configure a token-bucket regulator for an output queue
- **altq(9)**—Kernel interfaces for manipulating output queues on network interfaces
- **altq.conf(5)**—ALTQ configuration file for altqd(8)
- **altqd(8)**—The ALTQ daemon
- **altqstat(1)**—Show ALTQ status
- **pf.conf(5)**—Packet filter configuration file
- **pfctl(8)**—Control the packet filter (PF) and NAT device

You can use the ALTQ token-bucket regulator to rate-limit an interface (see Example 13-19).

Example 13-19 *Interface Rate-Limiting Without Queuing Discipline*

```
[root@castor:~#] tbrconfig ed0 30M auto
        ed00: tokenrate 30.00M(bps)  bucketsize 36.62K(bytes)

[root@castor:~#] tbrconfig -d ed0
        deleted token bucket regulator on ed0
```

FreeBSD IP Firewall(ipfw) + dummynet

FreeBSD's ipfw(4) is the utility that is responsible for controlling the ipfirewall(4) and dummynet(4) system facilities. ipfirewall is used for filtering, redirection, accounting, and NAT, whereas dummynet is a flexible bandwidth manager and delay emulator for traffic shaping and networking protocol testing on the FreeBSD operating system. dummynet supports a variant of WFQ and can be used on any type of workstation or gateway acting as either a router or bridge (see Example 13-20). For a detailed introduction, check out the following excellent man pages: divert(4), ipfirewall(4), ipfw(4), ipfw-graph(8), ipfw-al(1).

Example 13-20 *Traffic Shaping on a Crossover-Link FreeBSD with RED and WF2Q+ <--> Cisco IOS Architecture with CAR/GTS and RED on the Cisco Side*

```
[root@castor:~#] ipfw add pipe 1 icmp from any to any out xmit ed0
[root@castor:~#] ipfw pipe 1 config bw 8Kbit/s queue 10 delay 10ms red
[root@castor:~#] ipfw queue 1 config pipe 1 weight 1 red

[root@castor:~#] ping 192.168.7.254
PING 192.168.7.254 (192.168.7.254): 56 data bytes
64 bytes from 192.168.7.254: icmp_seq=0 ttl=255 time=94.281 ms
64 bytes from 192.168.7.254: icmp_seq=1 ttl=255 time=95.006 ms
64 bytes from 192.168.7.254: icmp_seq=2 ttl=255 time=95.030 ms
64 bytes from 192.168.7.254: icmp_seq=3 ttl=255 time=95.002 ms

scar# show running-config
...
!
interface Ethernet0
 bandwidth 10000
 ip address 192.168.14.254 255.255.255.0
 media-type 10BaseT
 random-detect
 traffic-shape rate 8000 8000 8000 1000
!
interface Ethernet1
 ip address 192.168.7.254 255.255.255.0
 rate-limit output 8000 1500 2000 conform-action transmit exceed-action drop
 media-type 10BaseT
 random-detect
!...

scar# show traffic-shape ethernet 0

Interface   Et0
      Access Target  Byte   Sustain  Excess   Interval  Increment Adapt
VC    List   Rate    Limit  bits/int bits/int (ms)      (bytes)   Active
-            8000    2000   8000     8000     1000      1000      -

scar# show traffic-shape statistics ethernet 0
            Access Queue   Packets  Bytes    Packets  Bytes    Shaping
I/F         List   Depth                     Delayed  Delayed  Active
Et0                0       351      32902     0        0        no

scar# show int ethernet 1 rate-limit
Ethernet1
  Output
    matches: all traffic
      params:  8000 bps, 1500 limit, 2000 extended limit
      conformed 340 packets, 33320 bytes; action: transmit
      exceeded 0 packets, 0 bytes; action: drop
```

Example 13-20 *Traffic Shaping on a Crossover-Link FreeBSD with RED and WF2Q+ <--> Cisco IOS Architecture with CAR/GTS and RED on the Cisco Side (Continued)*

```
        last packet: 940ms ago, current burst: 0 bytes
        last cleared 00:12:30 ago, conformed 0 bps, exceeded 0 bps

scar# ping 192.168.7.7

Type escape sequence to abort.
Sending 5, 100-byte ICMP Echos to 192.168.7.7, timeout is 2 seconds:
!!!!!
Success rate is 100 percent (5/5), round-trip min/avg/max = 108/112/116 ms
```

dummynet works in symbiosis with ipfw by "intercepting packets and passing them through one or more objects called *queues* and *pipes*, which simulate the effects of bandwidth limitations, propagation delays, bounded-size queues, packet losses, and multipath."[1]

Pipes represent fixed-bandwidth channels that can contain one or multiple queues. Think of a pipe as analogous to ATM virtual paths (VPs) and virtual channels (VCs). You can control the utilization and, as a consequence, the proportional bandwidth share of a pipe by associating queues with a weight.

Linux Firewall Marking and iproute2 (ip/tc)

netfilter and iptables are elements of the firewalling, NAT/NAPT, policy router, and packet-mangling architecture for the 2.4.x and 2.6.x Linux kernels. netfilter and iptables(8) allow marking and tagging of a packet with a number via the **--set-mark** facility. This is a mark of local significance only (packet metadata) and does not alter the IP header after forwarding. This mark can assign a different routing table (routing policy), as demonstrated in Example 13-21.

Example 13-21 *Policy Routing Based on iptables Markings*

```
[root@callisto:~#] iptables -A PREROUTING -i eth0 -t mangle -p tcp --dport 25 -j
MARK --set-mark 1

[root@callisto:~#] echo 1 lab >> /etc/iproute2/rt_tables
[root@callisto:~#] ip rule add fwmark 1 table lab
[root@callisto:~#] ip rule list
0:      from all lookup local
32764: from all fwmark        1 lookup lab
32766: from all lookup main
32767: from all lookup default

[root@callisto:~#] ip route add default via 192.168.14.254 table lab
```

Bell Labs' Eclipse—An Operating System with QoS Support

The Eclipse operating system (http://www.bell-labs.com/project/eclipse/release/) is a QoS test platform from Lucent Technologies. It is an independent OS approach that is compatible with FreeBSD and provides a simple application-programming interface (API) for fine-grained QoS support.

Summary

This chapter covered the important issues of policy routing, bandwidth management, and QoS architectures at Layer 2 (802.1P/Q, MPLS) and Layer 3(IP ToS, precedence, CoS, IntServ/RSVP, and DiffServ) of the Open System Interconnection (OSI) stack. The UNIX approaches were compared to Cisco QoS architecture, and the entanglement of QoS and packet filtering on the UNIX side was discussed.

Recommended Reading

- ALTQ: Alternate Queuing for BSD UNIX, http://www.csl.sony.co.jp/~kjc/software.html#ALTQ
- http://www.kame.net/
- http://www.iptables.org
- http://www.ipfilter.org
- http://www.netfilter.org
- http://www.benzedrine.cx/pf.html
- http://www.openbsd.org/faq/pf/index.html
- http://www.bsdnews.org/0101/policy_routing.php
- http://lartc.org/
- http://www.policyrouting.org/
- http://www.bell-labs.com/project/eclipse/release
- http://info.iet.unipi.it/~luigi/ip_dummynet/
- RFC 2474, RFC 2475, RFC 3260 (DiffServ)
- RFC 2430, "A Provider Architecture for Differentiated Services and Traffic Engineering (PASTE)" (MPLS+RSVP)
- *IP Quality of Service*, by Srinivas Vegesna (Cisco Press, 2001)

- *Administering Cisco QOS in IP Networks*, by Mike Flannagan (Syngress Publishing, 2001)
- The Blue queue-management algorithm, http://www.thefengs.com/wuchang/work/blue/

Endnote

1 http://info.iet.unipi.it/~luigi/ip_dummynet/

## CHAPTER 14

Multicast Architectures

In contrast to my original intention, I have decided not to just offer some hints about multicast architecture, but also to offer a quick qualitative introduction to UNIX multicast issues, routing, MBONE tunneling, and multicast-monitoring and -debugging techniques. I hope this provides just enough of a teaser to put things into perspective and to encourage you to play with intradomain multicast issues and eventually create enough interest that you seek out additional interdomain details. Three example applications are used to demonstrate multicasting:

- nte (a network text editor)
- ntpd (Network Time Protocol) in multicast mode
- mtest (send and receive)

Multicast Deployments

Multicast is one-to-many (1:n) or many-to-many (n:m) source-to-sink data delivery for multicast applications over multicast-enabled transport networks and data link layers. The most obvious reason for multicast deployments is bandwidth and server resource conservation with regard to efficient content distribution. That can be summarized as efficient and scalable multicasting, instead of costly unicast services, by simultaneously delivering a single stream of information to thousands of subscribers or recipients.

This potential is especially interesting as an additional mechanism in modern converged networks with regard to videoconferencing, video on demand, Internet audio, interactive gaming, multimedia events, e-learning software distribution, newscasts, and content delivery. Converged networks transport voice, video, data, and storage traffic over multipurpose IP networks. This variety of applications spans multimedia and data-only uses with or without real-time (latency, jitter) and high-availability requirements. The following discussion separates multicasting into data link layer, network layer, and application layer multicasting. Because of its intrinsically connectionless mode of operation, multicast uses User Datagram Protocol (UDP) as its transport protocol. Occasionally, raw IP sockets are used. These are exceptions to the common UDP rule.

Multicasting essentially can be seen from both intradomain and interdomain points of view, similar to intra- and interdomain traditional unicast routing. An in-depth discussion of multiprotocol (multicast) BGP used for interdomain signaling goes beyond the scope of this book. Note that we have to abandon a client/server perception when discussing multicasting and think instead in terms of content sources, transport networks, and sinks. Another important aspect is the distribution of multicast sinks (group subscribers), which can be either *dense* or *sparse*. Some algorithms have proven more suitable for the former, and some others for the latter. As a rule of thumb, dense distributions correlate with LANs or small campus networks, whereas metropolitan networks or the global Internet show a sparse distribution of multicast participants. The purpose of multicast signaling protocols is to build efficient *multicast distribution trees* for each multicast group of subscribers and not to burden routers and links with group traffic when no associated recipients exist. The process of adding and removing branches to this tree is referred to as *grafting and pruning*.

Multicasting is easy to configure, but its foundation is quite complex, especially the interface between intra and interdomain multicasting. Therefore, I recommend extensive research before deploying multicast architectures.

NOTE Currently we face a "hen and egg" problem: Internet service providers (ISPs) complain about the lack of multicast applications to make multicast service offerings commercially feasible, and application developers counter with the lack of multicast-enabled autonomous systems and interdomain multicast deployments. However, one thing is certain: Conventional unicast streams cause a horrible waste of network and server resources.

Multicast Addresses and Scope

On a single LAN segment, you need to map multicast groups to special MAC addresses for proper delivery to a network interface card (NIC). You accomplish this by mapping the least significant 23 bits of the multicast IP address into the least significant 23 bits of the Ethernet MAC address. In addition, all multicast MAC addresses start with the leading sequence 01:00:5E. For example, the multicast MAC address for RIPv2 routers (224.0.0.9) is represented as 01:00:5E:00:00:09.

Every address in the 224.0.0.0/4 Class D aggregate is referred to as multicast group. This is similar to FF:FF:FF:FF:FF:FF representing a subnet broadcast. This Class D address space is organized as presented in Table 14-1. However, from a modern classless point of view, you should avoid referring to "Class D" addresses.

Table 14-1 *Important Multicast Address Ranges*

Class	Range
Reserved link-local addresses	224.0.0.0/24
Globally scoped addresses	224.0.1.0–238.255.255.255
Source-specific multicast (SSM)	232.0.0.0/8
GLOP addresses	233.0.0.0/8
Limited-scope addresses	239.0.0.0/8

GLOP integrates the autonomous system number (ASN) of a domain into the second and third octet of the 233.x.x.0/8 prefix to accomplish uniqueness for interdomain multicast routing. Relevant additional resources include the following:

- RFC 3180/RFC 3138, "GLOP"
- RFC 2365, "Administrative Scoped Multicast"
- RFC 3171, "IANA Guidelines for IPv4 Multicast Address Assignments"
- "Source-Specific Protocol Independent Multicast in 232/8," draft-ietf-mboned-ssm232-06.txt
- "IPv4 Multicast Unusable Group And Source Addresses," draft-ietf-mboned-ipv4-mcast-unusable-01.txt

It is particularly interesting to ping the group address 224.0.0.1 (all multicast hosts on this subnet) and 224.0.0.2 (all multicast routers on this subnet) to figure out which hosts are multicast enabled on your LAN or act as multicast routers. For a complete list, see the Internet Assigned Numbers Authority (IANA) Internet multicast address summary at http://www.iana.org/assignments/multicast-addresses.

Some important multicast group addresses of the reserved local control block are printed in Table 14-2. Most likely, you will find a couple of familiar addresses. No multicast router—regardless of its Time To Live (TTL)—should *ever* forward IP datagrams with these destination addresses. Hence the name *local scope*.

Table 14-2   *Important Reserved Local Multicast Group Addresses (Local Network Control Block, Local Scope Only)*

Address	Multicast Group Assignment
224.0.0.0	Base address (reserved)
224.0.0.1	All systems on this subnet
224.0.0.2	All routers on this subnet
224.0.0.3	*Unassigned*
224.0.0.4	DVMRP routers
224.0.0.5	All OSPF routers
224.0.0.6	All OSPF designated routers
224.0.0.7	Internet Stream Protocol V2+ (ST2+) routers
224.0.0.8	Internet Stream Protocol V2+ (ST2+) hosts/agents
224.0.0.9	RIPv2 routers
224.0.0.10	IGRP routers
224.0.0.11	Mobile agents
224.0.0.12	DHCP server/relay agent
224.0.0.13	All PIM routers
224.0.0.18	VRRP
224.0.0.102	HSRP

NOTE	It is necessary to set net.inet.icmp.bmcastecho to 1 on BSD systems for pings to multicast groups to succeed. Either add this entry to /etc/sysctl.conf or set it manually by typing **sysctl -w net.inet.icmp.bmcastecho=1.**

Administratively Scoped IP Multicast

Scoping is the art of limiting multicast traffic distribution to certain administrative boundaries defined by boundary routers capable of per-interface scoped IP multicast configurations and filters (RFC 2365). Historically, TTL scoping (topological scoping) has been used to control the distribution of multicast traffic, especially within the multicast backbone (MBONE). However, TTL scoping negatively impacts Distance Vector Multicast Routing Protocol (DVMRP) pruning efficiency.

The administratively scoped IPv4 multicast address space is defined as 239.0.0.0/8. Scoped addresses are required to be unique only within administrative boundaries. According to RFC 2365, "The basic forwarding rule for interfaces with configured TTL thresholds is that a packet is not forwarded across the interface unless its remaining TTL is greater than the threshold."

Cisco boundary filters can be configured with the **ip multicast boundary {ACL}** interface command. mrouted scope examples are provided with the manual page and default configuration file; the setup is straightforward.

The Multicast Protocol Cocktail

An entire zoo of protocols is related to multicast and can be divided into intra- and interdomain multicast protocols.

The intradomain multicast protocols are as follows:

- **DVMRP**—Distance Vector Multicast Routing Protocol, RFC 1075
- **PIM-SM/PIM-DM**—Protocol Independent Multicast Sparse/Dense Mode, RFC 2362
- **IGMPv1/v2/v3**—Internet Group Management Protocol, RFCs 2236 and 3376
- **CGMP**—Cisco (proprietary) Group Management Protocol
- **MOSPF**—Multicast OSPF, RFCs 1584 and 1585
- **CBTv2/v3**—Core-Based Tree Multicast Protocol, RFC 2189
- **RGMP**—Router-Port Group Management Protocol (IETF draft)
- **SDP**—Session Directory Protocol
- **PGM**—Pragmatic General Multicast, RFC 3208
- **MLD**—Multicast Listener Discovery Protocol, RFC 3590

The interdomain multicast protocols are as follows:

- **MBGP**—Multiprotocol BGP, a.k.a. "Multicast" BGP

- **MSDP**—Multicast Source Discovery Protocol, RFC 3618
- **BGMP**—Border Gateway Multicast Protocol, draft-ietf-bgmp-spec-05.txt

Although these really are a lot of standards and protocols, do not be intimidated. Although they all serve specific and structured purposes, this chapter deals only with IGMP, DVMRP, and PIM-DM/PIM-SM. These protocols are presented in a LAN context in Figure 14-1.

Figure 14-1 *Important Multicast LAN Protocols*

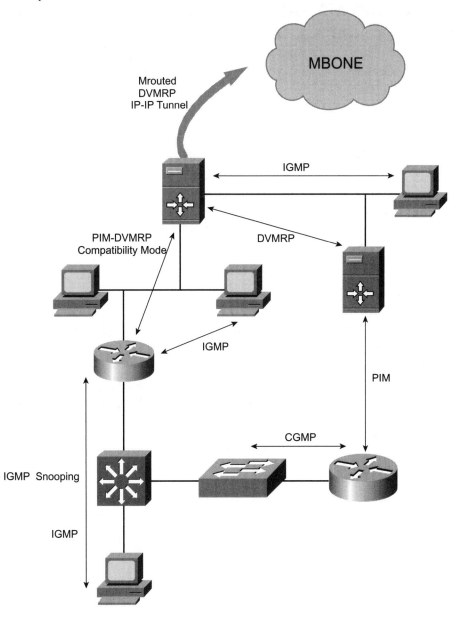

There exists a clear differentiation between multicast signaling information and actual data forwarding (reverse-path forwarding to be precise). Some approaches rely on their own signaling (mrouted), whereas others require additional unicast routing information (for example, PIM). For an excellent introduction to these protocols, consult the Cisco.com article "Configuring IP Multicast Routing."

Internet Group Management Protocol (IGMP) and Cisco Group Management Protocol (CGMP)

By design, a conventional Layer 2 LAN switch is supposed to flood multicast and broadcast traffic within the broadcast domain (VLAN). This results in wasted resources when no recipients of multicast traffic are present on its physical ports, uplinks, or VLAN trunks.

In a switched network, you can restrain multicast traffic in two ways:

- **IGMP snooping**—This is a feature of modern Layer 2/3 switches.
- **CGMP**—CGMP is used on Cisco Layer 2 switches.

Availability depends greatly on the model and OS version of your Cisco equipment. I am not aware of any noncommercial UNIX implementations that implement IGMP snooping. (It only makes sense on switches.) Cisco IOS architecture defaults to IGMPv2, whereas Linux and BSD operating systems implement IGMPv1/v2 (with early IGMPv3 packages available).

IGMPv1 Operation

The purpose of IGMP is to report end-system application group memberships to multicast routers in its vicinity, which easily can be identified via 224.0.0.2. The protocol has evolved from v1 up to v3.

IGMPv1 works as follows: When a host joins a particular group for the first time, it sends an unsolicited group membership report to the relevant group address. In addition, multicast routers periodically submit IGMP query messages to 224.0.0.1 that trigger IGMP group membership reports from all multicast-enabled hosts. IGMP protocol packets are always sent with a TTL of 1 and are not supposed to be forwarded. If a router does not hear from a registered host for a while, it assumes the host has left the group. If the requesting router receives no reports, the group is removed ("pruned") from the distribution tree. Therefore, this concept is referred to as *flood and prune*.

NOTE   On Linux systems, you can alter the default IGMP group membership limit of 20 via the **net.ipv4.igmp_max_memberships** sysctl parameter.

IGMPv2 Operation

IGMPv2 offers an important improvement over IGMPv1: explicit leave_group_messages that reduce the timeout-based leave group latency of IGMPv1 from several minutes to a few seconds, which dramatically reduces traffic on busy network segments. Join latencies are of no concern in this picture. Hosts send explicit leave_group_messages to 224.0.0.2 when they want to leave a subscribed group immediately. Examples 14-1 and 14-2 demonstrate IGMP-relevant commands and their output for Linux and BSD. The highlighted text emphasizes the mapping between multicast IP and MAC addresses.

Example 14-1 *Linux IGMP Status Information*

```
[root@callisto:~#] netstat -g
IPv6/IPv4 Group Memberships
Interface       RefCnt Group
--------------- ------ --------------------
lo              1      ALL-SYSTEMS.MCAST.NET
eth0            1      ALL-ROUTERS.MCAST.NET
eth0            1      DVMRP.MCAST.NET
eth0            1      ALL-SYSTEMS.MCAST.NET
eth1            1      224.2.2.2
eth1            1      ALL-ROUTERS.MCAST.NET
eth1            1      DVMRP.MCAST.NET
eth1            1      NTP.MCAST.NET
eth1            1      ALL-SYSTEMS.MCAST.NET

[root@callisto:~#] netstat -gn
IPv6/IPv4 Group Memberships
Interface       RefCnt Group
--------------- ------ --------------------
lo              1      224.0.0.1
eth0            1      224.0.0.2
eth0            1      224.0.0.4
eth0            1      224.0.0.1
eth1            1      224.2.2.2
eth1            1      224.0.0.2
eth1            1      224.0.0.4
eth1            1      224.0.1.1
eth1            1      224.0.0.1

[root@callisto:~#] ip mroute
(192.168.2.7, 224.2.2.2)        Iif: eth1      Oifs: eth0
(192.168.1.2, 224.2.2.2)        Iif: eth1      Oifs: eth0
(192.168.1.1, 224.2.2.2)        Iif: eth1      Oifs: eth0
(192.168.1.1, 224.0.1.1)        Iif: eth1

[root@callisto:~#] ip maddr
1:      lo

        inet  224.0.0.1
2:      eth0
        link  01:00:5e:00:00:02
        link  01:00:5e:00:00:04
```

continues

Example 14-1 *Linux IGMP Status Information (Continued)*

```
        link  01:00:5e:00:00:01
        inet  224.0.0.2
        inet  224.0.0.4
        inet  224.0.0.1
3:      eth1
        link  01:00:5e:02:02:02
        link  01:00:5e:00:00:02
        link  01:00:5e:00:00:04
        link  01:00:5e:00:01:01
        link  01:00:5e:00:00:01
        inet  224.2.2.2
        inet  224.0.0.2
        inet  224.0.0.4
        inet  224.0.1.1
        inet  224.0.0.1
```

Example 14-2 *BSD IGMP Status Information*

```
[root@castor:~#]  netstat -g -f inet

Virtual Interface Table
 Vif    Thresh   Rate   Local-Address   Remote-Address    Pkts-In   Pkts-Out
  0        1       0     192.168.2.7                         1373      5237
  1        1       0     192.168.7.7                         1007      5174
  2        1       0     192.168.80.1                           0         0

IPv4 Multicast Forwarding Cache
 Origin           Group           Packets  In-Vif  Out-Vifs:Ttls
 192.168.2.7      224.2.2.2         4230      0      1:1
 192.168.1.1      224.2.2.2         2347      0      1:1

[root@castor:~#]  netstat -gs -f inet
IPv4 multicast forwarding:
        7898 multicast forwarding cache lookups
        3 multicast forwarding cache misses
        3 upcalls to mrouted
        0 upcall queue overflows
        0 upcalls dropped due to full socket buffer
        0 cache cleanups
        3 datagrams with no route for origin
        0 datagrams arrived with bad tunneling
        0 datagrams could not be tunneled
        1006 datagrams arrived on wrong interface
        0 datagrams selectively dropped
        0 datagrams dropped due to queue overflow
        0 datagrams dropped for being too large
```

IGMPv3 Implementations

IGMPv3 allows joining a specific group with the addition of source-specific granularity, via source-specific include/exclude reports (S,G). This is the reason why it is often mentioned in an SSM context (single-source multicast). When a multicast router receives an IGMPv3

(S,G) join report, it must be able to build the source-specific tree with a source-aware multicast routing protocol such as PIM-SM. The IGMPv2 leave group message was extended to support source-specific operation.

If you want to play with it on Linux, try the Cisco implementation at http://www.multicasttech. com/igmpv3/ or http://www-sop.inria.fr/planete/Hitoshi.Asaeda/igmpv3/ for NetBSD, or http://www.kloosterhof.com/~wilbert/igmpv3.html for FreeBSD.

Cisco IOS Multicast Router Configuration and IGMP/CGMP Operation

Example 14-3 shows the Cisco IOS configuration that enables scar to communicate with mrouted DVMRP gateways via the PIM-DVMRP compatibility mechanism. In addition, the configuration includes an example DVMRP tunnel setup to communicate with ganymed regardless of possible non-multicast-capable gateways in its topological path. The **ip igmp join-group 224.2.2.2** statement is just an example of manual IGMP configuration. IGMP-relevant **show** and **debug** sequences conclude Example 14.3.

Example 14-3 *Cisco IOS General Multicast Setup and IGMP Configuration*

```
scar# show running-config
...
!
ip multicast-routing
ip multicast route-limit 100
!
interface Loopback0
 ip address 10.0.0.1 255.255.255.255
!
interface Tunnel0
 ip unnumbered Loopback0
 ip pim sparse-dense-mode
 ip igmp join-group 224.2.2.2
 tunnel source 192.168.14.254
 tunnel destination 192.168.1.254
 tunnel mode dvmrp
!
interface Ethernet0
 bandwidth 10000
 ip address 192.168.7.254 255.255.255.0
 no ip proxy-arp
 ip pim sparse-dense-mode
 ip load-sharing per-packet
 no ip route-cache
 ip igmp join-group 224.2.2.2
 ip cgmp
 no ip mroute-cache
 media-type 10BaseT
 random-detect
!
interface Ethernet1
 bandwidth 10000
```

continues

Example 14-3 *Cisco IOS General Multicast Setup and IGMP Configuration (Continued)*

```
 ip address 192.168.14.254 255.255.255.0
 no ip proxy-arp
 ip pim sparse-dense-mode
 ip load-sharing per-packet
 no ip route-cache
 ip ospf network broadcast
 ip igmp join-group 224.2.2.2
 ip cgmp
 no ip mroute-cache
 media-type 10BaseT
 random-detect
 !
 ...

scar# show ip igmp groups
IGMP Connected Group Membership
Group Address    Interface          Uptime    Expires   Last Reporter
224.0.1.111      Ethernet0          00:16:51  00:01:09  192.168.7.254
224.0.1.40       Ethernet0          00:16:49  00:01:05  192.168.7.254
224.2.2.2        Ethernet1          00:16:51  00:02:02  192.168.14.254
224.2.2.2        Ethernet0          00:16:51  00:01:02  192.168.7.254
224.2.2.2        Tunnel0            00:16:51  stopped   0.0.0.0

scar# debug ip igmp
IGMP debugging is on
01:11:01: IGMP: Send v2 general Query on Ethernet1
01:11:01: IGMP: Set report delay time to 5.6 seconds for 224.0.1.40 on Ethernet1
01:11:07: IGMP: Send v2 Report for 224.0.1.40 on Ethernet1
01:11:07: IGMP: Received v2 Report on Ethernet1 from 192.168.14.254 for 224.0.1.40
01:11:07: IGMP: Received Group record for group 224.0.1.40, mode 2 from
192.168.14.254 for 0 sources
01:11:07: IGMP: Updating EXCLUDE group timer for 224.0.1.40
01:11:30: IGMP: Previous querier for Ethernet0 has timed out.
01:11:30: IGMP: v2 querier for Ethernet0 is this system.
01:11:30: IGMP: Send v2 init Query on Ethernet0

scar# show ip igmp interface tunnel 0
Tunnel0 is up, line protocol is up
  Interface is unnumbered. Using address of Loopback0 (10.0.0.1)
  IGMP is enabled on interface
  Current IGMP host version is 2
  Current IGMP router version is 2
  IGMP query interval is 60 seconds
  IGMP querier timeout is 120 seconds
  IGMP max query response time is 10 seconds
  Last member query count is 2
  Last member query response interval is 1000 ms
  Inbound IGMP access group is not set
  IGMP activity: 1 joins, 0 leaves
  Multicast routing is enabled on interface
  Multicast TTL threshold is 0
  IGMP querying router is 0.0.0.0 (this system)
```

Example 14-3 *Cisco IOS General Multicast Setup and IGMP Configuration (Continued)*

```
     DVMRP/mrouted neighbors present for 00:27:02
        [version mrouted 3.255] [flags: GPM]
     2 DVMRP neighbor up transitions since system restart
     6 DVMRP routes + 0 poison-reverse routes received in last 00:01:00
     2/4 Unicast/DVMRP routes last advertised by DVMRP
     DVMRP output report delay is 100 ms, with burst size of 2
     Multicast groups joined by this system (number of users):
        224.2.2.2(1)

scar# show ip igmp interface ethernet 0
Ethernet0 is up, line protocol is up
  Internet address is 192.168.7.254/24
  IGMP is enabled on interface
  Current IGMP host version is 2
  Current IGMP router version is 2
  CGMP is enabled on interface
  IGMP query interval is 60 seconds
  IGMP querier timeout is 120 seconds
  IGMP max query response time is 10 seconds
  Last member query count is 2
  Last member query response interval is 1000 ms
  Inbound IGMP access group is not set
  IGMP activity: 2 joins, 0 leaves
  Multicast routing is enabled on interface
  Multicast TTL threshold is 0
  Multicast designated router (DR) is 192.168.7.254 (this system)
  IGMP querying router is 192.168.7.7
  DVMRP/mrouted neighbors present for 02:27:24
  DVMRP interface ordinal mask: FFFFFFFD
  DVMRP neighbors:
     192.168.7.7, ordinal: 1, [version mrouted 3.255] [flags: GPM]
  1 DVMRP neighbor up transitions since system restart
  0 DVMRP routes + 0 poison-reverse routes received in last 00:00:02
  2/4 Unicast/DVMRP routes last advertised by DVMRP
  DVMRP output report delay is 100 ms, with burst size of 2
  Multicast groups joined by this system (number of users):
     224.0.1.40(1)  224.2.2.2(1)

scar# show ip interface ethernet 0
Ethernet0 is up, line protocol is up
  Internet address is 192.168.7.254/24
  Broadcast address is 255.255.255.255
  Address determined by non-volatile memory
  MTU is 1500 bytes
  Helper address is not set
  Directed broadcast forwarding is disabled
  Multicast reserved groups joined: 224.0.0.1 224.0.0.2 224.0.0.22 224.0.0.13
  Outgoing access list is not set
  Inbound  access list is not set
  Proxy ARP is disabled
  Security level is default
```

continues

Example 14-3 *Cisco IOS General Multicast Setup and IGMP Configuration (Continued)*

```
Split horizon is enabled
ICMP redirects are always sent
ICMP unreachables are always sent
ICMP mask replies are never sent
IP fast switching is disabled
IP fast switching on the same interface is disabled
IP Flow switching is disabled
IP CEF switching is disabled
IP Fast switching turbo vector
IP multicast fast switching is disabled
IP multicast distributed fast switching is disabled
IP route-cache flags are No CEF
Router Discovery is enabled
IP output packet accounting is disabled
IP access violation accounting is disabled
TCP/IP header compression is disabled
RTP/IP header compression is disabled
Probe proxy name replies are disabled
Policy routing is disabled
Network address translation is disabled
WCCP Redirect outbound is disabled
WCCP Redirect inbound is disabled
WCCP Redirect exclude is disabled
BGP Policy Mapping is disabled
IP multicast multilayer switching is disabled
```

Cisco Group Management Protocol (CGMP)

Cisco CGMP runs between Cisco switches and Cisco routers and limits the forwarding of IP multicast packets to only those switch ports that serve IP multicast recipients. These hosts automatically join and leave groups that receive IP multicast traffic, and the switch dynamically changes its forwarding behavior according to these requests after consulting the subnet's/VLAN's router via CGMP. In contrast to IGMP snooping, the switch does not need to provide its own intelligence to intercept IGMP, but instead relies on the intelligence of Cisco multicast routers. CGMP can be configured per router interface with the **ip cgmp** command. There are no router **show** commands available for CGMP; however, **debug ip cgmp** provides sufficient details. CGMP leave processing is a new feature of this protocol that uses the leave group message extension of IGMPv2.

The Cisco IOS Multicast Routing Monitor (MRM)

The MRM feature is a Cisco IOS component that is useful for multicast deployments and surveillance. MRM consists of three components, which usually reside on three different routers:

- Manager
- Test sender
- Test receiver

A detailed discussion of this versatile tool goes beyond the scope of this chapter. Consult the Cisco.com article "Using IP Multicast Tools" (IOS 12.2) for a detailed discussion.

mrouted and DVMRP

For direct communication of two multicast participants on the same subnet, no multicast routing protocols are necessary; IGMP completely suffices. As soon as the multicast traffic traverses intermediate routers, multicast routing (signaling) becomes mandatory to forward this traffic successfully. Static multicast routing entries do not scale at all. mrouted is the dominant UNIX multicast routing daemon, currently version 3.9-beta3, and was developed by Steve Deering and Bill Fenner. This tool compiles well on all platforms; however, it requires a patch on Linux gateways and a change to the Makefile of older OpenBSD versions (as described later in this chapter).

mrouted is based on DVMRP and consists of three binaries: mrouted, map-mbone, and mrinfo (which is an ancillary tool). In contrast, DVMRP is a protocol for densely distributed multicast subscribers in high-bandwidth LAN environments and uses the flood-and-prune or implicit join method. For a detailed explanation of the protocol, consult RFC 1075.

mrouted and the MBONE

Although Cisco does not natively support DVMRP, mrouted cooperates with the Cisco IOS DVMRP interoperability implementation of PIM. That is why PIM is configured in all the following labs involving Cisco routers.

MBONE is the former multicast testbed of the Internet research community. It is based on DVMRP and has more or less been replaced by PIM-based modern architectures such as the European research network GEANT, the M6BONE, or the Internet2 "Abilene" Project.

MBONE tunneling was an approach analogous to IPv6 tunnel connections to the 6BONE (IPv6 backbone). An Internet (isolated multicast islands) not yet or only partially capable of native multicast routing delivers unicast tunnel traffic between multicast realms. The same is true for IPv6. Not all Internet routers can deal with IPv6 yet; therefore, the traffic is encapsulated into IPv4 headers and delivered that way. Essentially, these are either IP-IP or Generic Routing Encapsulation (GRE) tunnels. mrouted provides its own tunnel setup (IP-IP) and facilitates DVMRP. DVMRP is plagued by the usual scalability and convergence problems of all distance-vector routing protocols. Figure 14-2 illustrates the traditional MBONE architecture.

Although MBONE is outdated and not maintained anymore, mrouted and DVMRP still are a viable solution for smaller networks based on UNIX gateways. mrouted includes native IP-IP tunnel support (as long as it is supported by the underlying operating system).

NOTE   mtrace and mstat are additional useful tools that are available on some systems to debug multicast problems. The mrouted default configuration file is /etc/mrouted.conf. Consult the excellent manual page and command-line help for further information, especially how to send UNIX signals to the daemon to dump status information (SIGUSR1, SIGUSR2).

Figure 14-2 *Traditional MBONE Architecture*

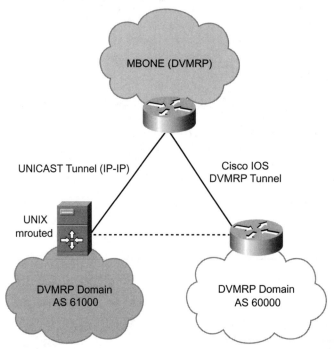

Cisco IOS architecture supports DVMRP only for backward compatibility for mrouted gateways and MBONE tunnel connections. If you want to hook up to the MBONE, contact your Internet service provider (ISP) or research networks in your vicinity to provide you with a DVMRP tunnel neighbor address.

Lab 14-1: DVMRP via mrouted

This lab facilitates the topology in Figure 14-3, in which we observe the DVMRP dialogue between all four multicast gateways and one redundant DVMRP tunnel between ganymed and scar (Example 14-4). The threshold in Example 14-4 is DVMRP's way of implementing TTL scoping, as described earlier in this chapter. The scar configuration, as shown in Example 14-3, has not changed.

Note that some operating systems require a default routing entry for multicast prefixes, such as **route add -net 224.0.0.0 netmask 240.0.0.0 eth0**, to deal with multicast groups properly when not using a multicast routing daemon such as mrouted or pimd.

NOTE   To be able to compile mrouted from sources on older OpenBSD versions, you must add **-DRAW_OUTPUT_IS_RAW** to the **CFLAGS** line in the Makefile, as follows: **CFLAGS= -O ${MCAST_INCLUDE} ${SNMPDEF} ${RSRRDEF} -DRAW_OUTPUT_IS_RAW**. Thanks to Bill Fenner for pointing this out.

Figure 14-3 *mrouted Lab Topology*

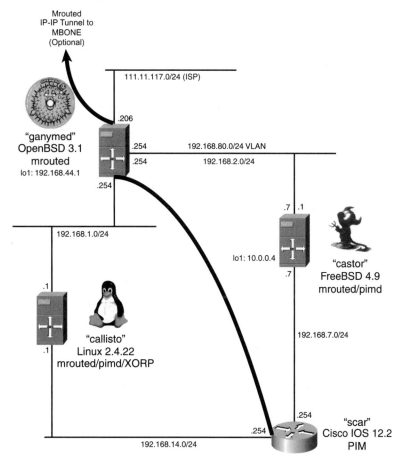

CAUTION   When configuring mrouted tunnels on Linux, do not forget to load the tunnel kernel module
(**insmod ipip**).

Example 14-4 *mrouted Tunnel Setup on Ganymed*

```
[root@ganymed:~#] cat /etc/mrouted.conf
#
# DVMRP IP-IP tunnel ganymed <--> scar with a multicast rate_limit of 500 kbps
tunnel 192.168.1.254 192.168.14.254 metric 1 threshold 64 rate_limit 500
```

If you require DVMRP tunnels from a Linux gateway, mrouted creates DVMRP
interfaces automatically at runtime (Example 14-5). Examples 14-6 through 14-9 show

various multicast and DVMRP-related commands, debugging of, and output for the UNIX multicast gateways. Finally, Example 14-10 shows sniffer output of the DVMRP protocol operation.

Example 14-5 *Automatic Linux DVMRP Tunnel Interface Creation*

```
[root@callisto:~#] ifconfig
...
dvmrp2    Link encap:IPIP Tunnel  HWaddr
          UP POINTOPOINT RUNNING NOARP MULTICAST  MTU:1480  Metric:1
          RX packets:1 errors:0 dropped:0 overruns:0 frame:0
          TX packets:0 errors:0 dropped:0 overruns:0 carrier:0
          collisions:0 txqueuelen:0
          RX bytes:76 (76.0 b)  TX bytes:0 (0.0 b)
...
```

Example 14-6 *Scar DVMRP Operation*

```
scar# show ip mroute summary
IP Multicast Routing Table
Flags: D - Dense, S - Sparse, B - Bidir Group, s - SSM Group, C - Connected,
       L - Local, P - Pruned, R - RP-bit set, F - Register flag,
       T - SPT-bit set, J - Join SPT, M - MSDP created entry,
       X - Proxy Join Timer Running, A - Candidate for MSDP Advertisement,
       U - URD, I - Received Source Specific Host Report
Outgoing interface flags: H - Hardware switched
Timers: Uptime/Expires
Interface state: Interface, Next-Hop or VCD, State/Mode

(*, 224.0.1.111), 00:19:03/00:00:00, RP 0.0.0.0, OIF count: 3, flags: DCL
(*, 224.0.1.40), 00:19:03/00:00:00, RP 0.0.0.0, OIF count: 3, flags: DCL
(*, 224.2.2.2), 00:19:03/00:00:00, RP 0.0.0.0, OIF count: 3, flags: DCL
  (192.168.1.1, 224.2.2.2), 00:00:25/00:02:34, OIF count: 1, flags: CL
  (192.168.2.7, 224.2.2.2), 00:01:43/00:01:16, OIF count: 2, flags: CL

scar# show ip mroute
IP Multicast Routing Table
Flags: D - Dense, S - Sparse, B - Bidir Group, s - SSM Group, C - Connected,
       L - Local, P - Pruned, R - RP-bit set, F - Register flag,
       T - SPT-bit set, J - Join SPT, M - MSDP created entry,
       X - Proxy Join Timer Running, A - Candidate for MSDP Advertisement,
       U - URD, I - Received Source Specific Host Report
Outgoing interface flags: H - Hardware switched
Timers: Uptime/Expires
Interface state: Interface, Next-Hop or VCD, State/Mode

(*, 224.0.1.111), 00:18:16/00:00:00, RP 0.0.0.0, flags: DCL
  Incoming interface: Null, RPF nbr 0.0.0.0
  Outgoing interface list:
    Tunnel0, Forward/Dvmrp, 00:17:20/00:00:00
    Ethernet0, Forward/Sparse-Dense, 00:18:16/00:00:00
    Ethernet1, Forward/Sparse-Dense, 00:17:51/00:00:00
```

Example 14-6 *Scar DVMRP Operation (Continued)*

```
(*, 224.0.1.40), 00:18:16/00:00:00, RP 0.0.0.0, flags: DCL
  Incoming interface: Null, RPF nbr 0.0.0.0
  Outgoing interface list:
    Tunnel0, Forward/Dvmrp, 00:17:20/00:00:00
    Ethernet0, Forward/Sparse-Dense, 00:18:16/00:00:00
    Ethernet1, Forward/Sparse-Dense, 00:17:51/00:00:00

(*, 224.2.2.2), 00:18:16/00:00:00, RP 0.0.0.0, flags: DCL
  Incoming interface: Null, RPF nbr 0.0.0.0
  Outgoing interface list:
    Tunnel0, Forward/Dvmrp, 00:17:27/00:00:00
    Ethernet0, Forward/Sparse-Dense, 00:18:16/00:00:00
    Ethernet1, Forward/Sparse-Dense, 00:18:10/00:00:00

(192.168.1.1, 224.2.2.2), 00:02:40/00:00:19, flags: CL
  Incoming interface: Tunnel0, RPF nbr 192.168.1.254, Dvmrp
  Outgoing interface list:
    Ethernet1, Forward/Sparse-Dense, 00:02:32/00:00:00
    Ethernet0, Forward/Sparse-Dense, 00:01:23/00:00:00

(192.168.2.7, 224.2.2.2), 00:00:55/00:02:04, flags: CL
  Incoming interface: Tunnel0, RPF nbr 192.168.1.254, Dvmrp
  Outgoing interface list:
    Ethernet1, Forward/Sparse-Dense, 00:00:28/00:00:00

scar# show ip dvmrp route
DVMRP Routing Table - 6 entries
192.168.1.0/24 [0/2] uptime 00:09:41, expires 00:02:43, poison 0x00000000
    via 192.168.1.254, Tunnel0, [version mrouted 3.255] [flags: GPM]
192.168.2.0/24 [0/2] uptime 00:09:38, expires 00:02:43
    via 192.168.1.254, Tunnel0, [version mrouted 3.255] [flags: GPM]
192.168.7.0/24 [0/3] uptime 00:09:41, expires 00:02:43, poison 0x00020000
    via 192.168.1.254, Tunnel0, [version mrouted 3.255] [flags: GPM]
192.168.14.0/24 [0/3] uptime 00:09:38, expires 00:02:43, poison 0x00010000
    via 192.168.1.254, Tunnel0, [version mrouted 3.255] [flags: GPM]
192.168.80.0/24 [0/2] uptime 00:09:21, expires 00:02:43
    via 192.168.1.254, Tunnel0, [version mrouted 3.255] [flags: GPM]
211.11.117.0/24 [0/2] uptime 00:09:21, expires 00:02:43
    via 192.168.1.254, Tunnel0, [version mrouted 3.255] [flags: GPM]

scar# mrinfo 192.168.1.254
192.168.1.254 [version mrouted 3.255] [flags: GPM]:
  192.168.1.254 -> 192.168.1.1 [1/1]
  192.168.2.254 -> 192.168.2.7 [1/1]
  211.11.117.206 -> 0.0.0.0 [1/1/querier/leaf]
  192.168.80.254 -> 192.168.80.1 [1/1]
  192.168.1.254 -> 192.168.14.254 [1/64/tunnel]
  211.11.117.206 -> 62.178.158.124 [1/64/tunnel/down/leaf]

scar# mstat 192.168.14.254
Type escape sequence to abort.
Mtrace from 192.168.14.254 to 192.168.14.254 via RPF
```

continues

Example 14-6 *Scar DVMRP Operation (Continued)*

```
From source (?) to destination (?)
Waiting to accumulate statistics......
Results after 10 seconds:

   Source           Response Dest    Packet Statistics For      Only For Traffic
192.168.14.254     192.168.14.254    All Multicast Traffic     From 192.168.14.254
    |        __/  rtt 0    ms   Lost/Sent = Pct  Rate     To 0.0.0.0
    v        /    hop 0    ms   --------------------      --------------------
192.168.14.254  ?
    |        \__  ttl   0
    v        \  hop 0    ms        0          0 pps          0     0 pps
192.168.14.254  192.168.14.254
  Receiver       Query Source


scar# mtrace
Source address or name: 192.168.14.254
Destination address or name: 192.168.1.254
Group address or name:
Multicast request TTL [64]:
Response address for mtrace:
Type escape sequence to abort.
Mtrace from 192.168.14.254 to 192.168.1.254 via RPF
From source (?) to destination (?)
Querying full reverse path...
  0   192.168.1.254
 -1   192.168.1.254 DVMRP Wrong interface [192.168.14.0/24]
 -2   192.168.1.1 DVMRP  [192.168.14.0/24]
```

Example 14-7 *Callisto mrouted Operation (DVMRP)*

```
[root@callisto~-#] ps ax | grep mrouted
 4307 pts/0    S     0:00 mrouted
 5617 pts/2    R     0:00 grep mrouted

[root@callisto:~#] kill -SIGUSR1 4307
[root@callisto:~#] kill -SIGUSR2 4307

[root@callisto:~#] cat /var/tmp/mrouted.cache
mrouted version 3.9-beta3 up  5:54:15 Tue Dec 30 00:42:43 2003

Multicast Routing Cache Table (4 entries)
 Origin            Mcast-group          CTmr      Age       Ptmr Rx IVif Forwvifs
<(prunesrc:vif[idx]/tmr) prunebitmap
>Source            Lifetime SavPkt        Pkts     Bytes RPFf
 192.168.1/24      224.0.1.1          0:03:30  5:53:45     - -  1
>192.168.1.1       5:53:45     0          175      5600     0
 192.168.1/24      224.2.2.2          0:03:40  1:07:51     - -  1   0
>192.168.1.1       1:07:51     0         2306    449866     0
>192.168.1.2       1:07:34     0         3816    577632     0
 192.168.2/24      224.2.2.2          0:03:32  0:47:45     - -  1   0
>192.168.2.7       0:47:45     0         2344    404059     0

[root@callisto:~#] cat /var/tmp/mrouted.dump
mrouted version 3.9-beta3 up  5:54:11 Tue Dec 30 00:42:39 2003
```

Example 14-7 *Callisto mrouted Operation (DVMRP) (Continued)*

```
vifs_with_neighbors = 2

Virtual Interface Table
Vif  Name  Local-Address                          M  Thr  Rate   Flags
0    eth0  192.168.14.1    subnet: 192.168.14/24   1   1    0    querier
                           peers: 192.168.14.254 (12.2) [0] up  2:58:36
             group host (time left): 224.2.2.2      192.168.14.254 ( 0:03:52)
                                     224.0.0.4      192.168.14.1   ( 0:03:52)
                                     224.0.0.2      192.168.14.1   ( 0:03:49)
                         IGMP querier: 192.168.14.1     (this system)
                         Nbr bitmaps: 0x0000000000000001
                         pkts/bytes in : 0/0
                         pkts/bytes out: 3413/619795

1    eth1  192.168.1.1     subnet: 192.168.1/24    1   1    0    querier
                           peers: 192.168.1.254 (3.255) [1] have-genid up  0:47:54
             group host (time left): 224.2.2.2      192.168.1.1    ( 0:03:43)
                                     239.255.255.250 192.168.1.2   ( 0:03:52)
                                     224.0.1.1      192.168.1.1    ( 0:03:44)
                                     224.0.0.4      192.168.1.1    ( 0:03:49)
                                     224.0.0.2      192.168.1.1    ( 0:03:43)
                         IGMP querier: 192.168.1.1      (this system)
                         Nbr bitmaps: 0x0000000000000002
                         pkts/bytes in : 8820/1461369
                         pkts/bytes out: 0/0


Multicast Routing Table (6 entries)
  Origin-Subnet       From-Gateway      Metric Tmr Fl In-Vif  Out-Vifs
  211.11.117/24       192.168.1.254       2    45  ..   1    0*
  192.168.80/24       192.168.1.254       2    45  ..   1    0*
  192.168.14/24                           1    90  ..   0    1[1]
  192.168.7/24        192.168.14.254      2    45  ..   0    1*
  192.168.2/24        192.168.1.254       2    45  ..   1    0*
  192.168.1/24                            1    90  ..   1    0*
```

Example 14-8 *Castor mrouted Operation (DVMRP)*

```
[root@castor:~#] netstat -g -f inet

Virtual Interface Table
  Vif    Thresh   Rate   Local-Address   Remote-Address   Pkts-In   Pkts-Out
  0        1       0     192.168.2.7                        1373      5237
  1        1       0     192.168.7.7                        1007      5174
  2        1       0     192.168.80.1                          0         0

IPv4 Multicast Forwarding Cache
  Origin         Group           Packets  In-Vif  Out-Vifs:Ttls
  192.168.2.7    224.2.2.2        4230      0      1:1
  192.168.1.1    224.2.2.2        2347      0      1:1
```

continues

Example 14-8 *Castor mrouted Operation (DVMRP) (Continued)*

```
[root@castor:~#] netstat -gs -f inet
IPv4 multicast forwarding:
        7898 multicast forwarding cache lookups
        3 multicast forwarding cache misses
        3 upcalls to mrouted
        0 upcall queue overflows
        0 upcalls dropped due to full socket buffer
        0 cache cleanups
        3 datagrams with no route for origin
        0 datagrams arrived with bad tunneling
        0 datagrams could not be tunneled
        1006 datagrams arrived on wrong interface
        0 datagrams selectively dropped
        0 datagrams dropped due to queue overflow
        0 datagrams dropped for being too large

[root@castor:~#] map-mbone 192.168.14.254

192.168.7.254 (scar.nerdzone.org): alias for 192.168.14.254

192.168.14.254: <v12.2>
    192.168.14.254:  192.168.1.254 [1/0/tunnel]
                     192.168.14.254 [1/0/querier]
    192.168.7.254:   192.168.7.254 (scar.nerdzone.org) [1/0/querier]

[root@castor:~#] mtrace 192.168.14.254
mtrace: WARNING: no multicast group specified, so no statistics printed
Mtrace from 192.168.14.254 to 192.168.2.7 via group 0.0.0.0
Querying full reverse path...
  0  castor.nerdzone.org (192.168.2.7)
 -1  castor.nerdzone.org (192.168.2.7)   DVMRP  thresh^ 1
 -2  scar.nerdzone.org (192.168.7.254)   PIM  thresh^ 0
 -3  ? (192.168.14.254)
Round trip time 2 ms; total ttl of 1 required.

[root@castor:~#] mrinfo 192.168.14.254
192.168.14.254 (192.168.14.254) [version 12.2]:
  192.168.7.254 -> 0.0.0.0 (local) [1/0/pim/querier]
  192.168.14.254 -> 0.0.0.0 (local) [1/0/pim/querier]
  192.168.14.254 -> 192.168.1.254 (192.168.1.254) [1/0/tunnel]
```

Example 14-9 *Ganymed mrouted Operation (DVMRP)*

```
[root@ganymed:~#] netstat -g -f inet

Virtual Interface Table
 Vif  Thresh  Limit  Local-Address   Remote-Address   Pkt_in  Pkt_out
   0      1      0  192.168.1.254                       1814    2966
   1      1      0  192.168.2.254                       3010    1814
   2      1      0  211.11.117.206                         0       0
```

Example 14-9 *Ganymed mrouted Operation (DVMRP) (Continued)*

```
   3      1      0   192.168.80.254                          0        0
   4     64    500   192.168.1.254   192.168.14.254          0        0
   5     64    500   211.11.117.206  62.178.158.124          0        0

Multicast Forwarding Cache
  Hash  Origin          Mcastgroup       Traffic  In-Vif  Out-Vifs/Forw-ttl
    90  192.168.2.7     224.2.2.2           2k       1    0/1 4/64
   250  192.168.1.1     224.2.2.2           1k       0    1/1 4/64

Total no. of entries in cache: 2

[root@ganymed:~#] netstat -gs
multicast routing:
        5 datagrams with no route for origin
        5 upcalls made to mrouted
        0 datagrams with malformed tunnel options
        0 datagrams with no room for tunnel options
        5 datagrams arrived on wrong interface
        0 datagrams dropped due to upcall Q overflow
        0 datagrams dropped due to upcall socket overflow
        0 datagrams cleaned up by the cache
        0 datagrams dropped selectively by ratelimiter
        0 datagrams dropped - bucket Q overflow
        0 datagrams dropped - larger than bkt size
multicast forwarding:
        0 multicast forwarding cache lookups
        0 multicast forwarding cache misses
        0 upcalls to mrouted
        0 upcall queue overflows
        0 upcalls dropped due to full socket buffer
        0 cache cleanups
        0 datagrams with no route for origin
        0 datagrams arrived with bad tunneling
        0 datagrams could not be tunneled
        0 datagrams arrived on wrong interface
        0 datagrams selectively dropped
        0 datagrams dropped due to queue overflow
        0 datagrams dropped for being too large

[root@ganymed:~#] cat /var/tmp/mrouted.cache
mrouted version 3.9-beta3+IOS12 up  1:00:43 Tue Dec 30 00:55:39 2003

Multicast Routing Cache Table (2 entries)
  Origin           Mcast-group        CTmr     Age      Ptmr Rx IVif Forwvifs
 <(prunesrc:vif[idx]/tmr) prunebitmap
 >Source            Lifetime SavPkt        Pkts     Bytes RPFf
   192.168.7/24     224.0.1.32      0:01:10  0:03:51  0:56:10  0  1P
   192.168.1/24     224.2.2.2       0:01:20  1:00:42     -  -  0   1  4
 >192.168.1.1       1:00:42       0          1869     371617  1
   192.168.2/24     224.2.2.2       0:02:30  1:00:42     -  -  1   0  4
 >192.168.2.7       1:00:42       0          3065     520226  1
```

continues

Example 14-9 *Ganymed mrouted Operation (DVMRP) (Continued)*

```
[root@ganymed:~#] cat /var/tmp/mrouted.dump
mrouted version 3.9-beta3+IOS12 up  1:00:40 Tue Dec 30 00:55:36 2003


vifs_with_neighbors = 4


Virtual Interface Table
Vif  Name  Local-Address                           M  Thr  Rate   Flags
0    ne3   192.168.1.254   subnet: 192.168.1/24     1   1     0
                           peers: 192.168.1.1 (3.255) [3] have-genid up  1:00:44
          group host (time left): 239.255.255.250 192.168.1.2   ( 0:03:23)
                                   224.0.1.1        192.168.1.1   ( 0:03:19)
                                   224.0.0.9        192.168.1.2   ( 0:03:23)
                                   224.2.2.2        192.168.1.2   ( 0:03:19)
                                   224.0.0.2        192.168.1.1   ( 0:03:25)
                                   224.0.0.4        192.168.1.1   ( 0:03:23)
                  IGMP querier: 192.168.1.1     up 0:59:24 last heard 0:01:05 ago
                    Nbr bitmaps: 0x0000000000000008
                  pkts/bytes in : 1865/370669
                  pkts/bytes out: 3018/512513


1    ne4   192.168.2.254   subnet: 192.168.2/24     1   1     0
                           peers: 192.168.2.7 (3.255) [1] have-genid up  1:00:46
          group host (time left): 224.2.2.2       192.168.2.7   ( 0:04:04)
                                   224.0.0.4       192.168.2.7   ( 0:04:05)
                                   224.0.0.2       192.168.2.7   ( 0:04:02)
                  IGMP querier: 192.168.2.7     up 1:00:46 last heard 0:00:25 ago
                    Nbr bitmaps: 0x0000000000000002
                  pkts/bytes in : 3062/519723
                  pkts/bytes out: 1865/370669


2    ne5   211.11.117.206   subnet: 211.11.117/24     1   1     0   querier leaf
                  IGMP querier: 211.11.117.206     (this system)
                    Nbr bitmaps: 0x0000000000000000
                  pkts/bytes in : 0/0
                  pkts/bytes out: 0/0


3    vlan0  192.168.80.254  subnet: 192.168.80/24     1   1     0
                           peers: 192.168.80.1 (3.255) [2] have-genid up  1:00:46
          group host (time left): 224.0.0.2       192.168.80.1   ( 0:04:02)
                                   224.0.0.4       192.168.80.1   ( 0:04:01)
                  IGMP querier: 192.168.80.1     up 1:00:46 last heard 0:00:20 ago
                    Nbr bitmaps: 0x0000000000000004
                  pkts/bytes in : 0/0
                  pkts/bytes out: 0/0


4    ne3   192.168.1.254   tunnel: 192.168.14.254     1   64    500   rexmit_prunes
old-tunnel
                           peers: 192.168.14.254 (12.2) [0] up  1:00:51
                    Nbr bitmaps: 0x0000000000000001
                  pkts/bytes in : 0/0
                  pkts/bytes out: 0/0
```

Example 14-9 *Ganymed mrouted Operation (DVMRP) (Continued)*

```
5   ne5  211.11.117.206   tunnel: 62.178.158.124    1  64   500   leaf
rexmit_prunes old-tunnel
                      Nbr bitmaps: 0x0000000000000000
                  pkts/bytes in : 0/0
                  pkts/bytes out: 0/0


Multicast Routing Table (6 entries)
  Origin-Subnet      From-Gateway    Metric Tmr Fl In-Vif  Out-Vifs
  211.11.117/24                        1    50 ..   2    0[3] 1[1] 3* 4[0]
  192.168.80/24                        1    50 ..   3    0[3] 2* 4[0]
  192.168.14/24      192.168.1.1       2    40 ..   0    2*
  192.168.7/24       192.168.2.7       2    35 ..   1    2*
  192.168.2/24                         1    50 ..   1    0[3] 2* 4[0]
  192.168.1/24                         1    50 ..   0    1[1] 2* 3* 4[0]
```

Example 14-10 *What Is Happening on the Multicast LAN (tcpdump Sniffer Output on Castor)*

```
...
23:21:14.363044 192.168.2.254 > DVMRP.MCAST.NET: igmp dvmrp Probe [tos 0xc0]
[ttl 1]
23:21:18.366233 192.168.2.7 > DVMRP.MCAST.NET: igmp dvmrp Probe [tos 0xc0]  [ttl 1]
23:21:24.421728 192.168.2.254 > DVMRP.MCAST.NET: igmp dvmrp Probe [tos 0xc0]
[ttl 1]
23:21:28.424732 192.168.2.7 > DVMRP.MCAST.NET: igmp dvmrp Probe [tos 0xc0]  [ttl 1]
23:21:28.424881 192.168.2.7 > DVMRP.MCAST.NET: igmp dvmrp Report [tos 0xc0]  [ttl 1]
23:21:34.480417 192.168.2.254 > DVMRP.MCAST.NET: igmp dvmrp Probe [tos 0xc0]
[ttl 1]
23:21:38.483146 192.168.2.7 > DVMRP.MCAST.NET: igmp dvmrp Probe [tos 0xc0]  [ttl 1]
23:21:44.153874 192.168.2.254 > DVMRP.MCAST.NET: igmp dvmrp Probe [tos 0xc0]
[ttl 1]
23:21:48.156638 192.168.2.7 > DVMRP.MCAST.NET: igmp dvmrp Probe [tos 0xc0]  [ttl 1]
23:21:54.207863 192.168.2.254 > DVMRP.MCAST.NET: igmp dvmrp Probe [tos 0xc0]
[ttl 1]
23:21:58.211078 192.168.2.7 > DVMRP.MCAST.NET: igmp dvmrp Probe [tos 0xc0]  [ttl 1]
23:22:04.266496 192.168.2.254 > DVMRP.MCAST.NET: igmp dvmrp Probe [tos 0xc0]
[ttl 1]
23:22:04.266958 192.168.2.254 > DVMRP.MCAST.NET: igmp dvmrp Report [tos 0xc0]
[ttl 1]
...
23:57:18.303887 192.168.2.254 > 192.168.2.7: igmp dvmrp Ask-neighbors2 [tos 0xc0]
23:57:18.304018 192.168.2.7 > 192.168.2.254: igmp dvmrp Neighbors2 (v 3.255):
[192.168.2.7 -> 192.168.2.254 (1/1/querier)] [192.168.7.7 -> 0.0.0.0 (1/1/querier)]
[tos 0xc0]
...
```

NOTE Besides the DVMRP probes and reports in Example 14-10, you also see ASK_NEIGHBORS IGMP messages used by the mrinfo and map-mbone tools.

Native-Multicast Test Applications

As examples of real-world multicast applications, the well-known ntpd (Network Time Protocol daemon) and nte (a multicast whiteboard) were chosen. ntpd was configured to run in multicast mode (224.0.1.1), and nte was configured to utilize 224.2.2.2 and UDP port 34000. This is just for testing purposes. Choose more appropriate addresses according to the IANA assignments discussed at the beginning of this chapter for your deployments. Example 14-11 shows the setup and operation of these tools.

Example 14-11 *Setup and Operation of Multicast Test Applications ntp and nte*

```
[root@castor:~#] nte 224.2.2.2/34000 &

[root@callisto:~#] nte 224.2.2.2/34000 &

[root@castor:~#] cat /etc/ntp.conf
manycastclient 224.0.1.1
multicastclient 224.0.1.1
logfile /var/log/ntp.log
driftfile /etc/ntp.drift
authenticate no

[root@castor:~#] ntpd -A -c /etc/ntp.conf

[root@callisto:~#] cat /etc/ntp.conf
manycastserver 224.0.1.1
server ntp2.curie.fr prefer minpoll 10
server ntp.obspm.fr
logfile /var/log/ntp.log
driftfile /etc/ntp.drift
authenticate no

[root@callisto:~#] ntpd -A -c /etc/ntp.conf

[root@castor:~#] netstat -g -f inet

Virtual Interface Table
 Vif    Thresh    Rate    Local-Address    Remote-Address    Pkts-In    Pkts-Out
  0        1        0     192.168.2.7                            73        5387
  1        1        0     192.168.7.7                             0          16
  2        1        0     192.168.80.1                            0           0

IPv4 Multicast Forwarding Cache
 Origin            Group           Packets  In-Vif   Out-Vifs:Ttls
 192.168.2.7       224.2.2.2         1997      0      1:1
 192.168.1.1       224.2.2.2           73      0      1:1

[root@castor:~#] netstat -gs -f inet
IPv4 multicast forwarding:
        6064 multicast forwarding cache lookups
        4 multicast forwarding cache misses
        4 upcalls to mrouted
        0 upcall queue overflows
```

Example 14-11 *Setup and Operation of Multicast Test Applications ntp and nte (Continued)*

```
                0 upcalls dropped due to full socket buffer
                0 cache cleanups
                4 datagrams with no route for origin
                0 datagrams arrived with bad tunneling
                0 datagrams could not be tunneled
                0 datagrams arrived on wrong interface
                0 datagrams selectively dropped
                0 datagrams dropped due to queue overflow
                0 datagrams dropped for being too large

[root@callisto:~#] netstat -g
IPv6/IPv4 Group Memberships
Interface       RefCnt Group
--------------- ------ --------------------
lo              1      ALL-SYSTEMS.MCAST.NET
eth0            1      ALL-ROUTERS.MCAST.NET
eth0            1      DVMRP.MCAST.NET
eth0            1      ALL-SYSTEMS.MCAST.NET
eth1            1      224.2.2.2
eth1            1      NTP.MCAST.NET
eth1            1      ALL-ROUTERS.MCAST.NET
eth1            1      DVMRP.MCAST.NET
eth1            1      ALL-SYSTEMS.MCAST.NET

[root@callisto:~#] tcpdump -i eth1 host 224.0.1.1
tcpdump: listening on eth1
14:14:48.005140 callisto > NTP.MCAST.NET: igmp v2 report NTP.MCAST.NET (DF) [tos
0xc0]  [ttl 1]

[root@castor:~#] tcpdump -i xl0 host 224.0.1.1
tcpdump: listening on xl0
14:14:01.031783 castor.nerdzone.org.ntp > NTP.MCAST.NET.ntp:  v4 client strat 0 poll
6 prec -28 [tos 0x10]  [ttl 1]
14:15:01.575187 castor.nerdzone.org > NTP.MCAST.NET: igmp v2 report NTP.MCAST.NET
[ttl 1]
```

NOTE   When you run into problems with multicast applications, pay close attention to what interface(s) the application actually binds. The mtest package is a great tool to debug such issues.

The ip and smcroute Multicast Utilities

Linux multicast setup is performed via the ip utility. smcroute(8) is an alternative to ip and to mrouted/pimd, which manipulates Linux kernel multicast routes statically. You can find this utility at http://www.cschill.de/smcroute; it might come in handy in the absence of mrouted/pimd or if you lack IGMP signaling. This utility essentially adds/removes multicast routes and joins/leaves multicast groups. You can start smcroute as a daemon by typing **smcroute -d,** whereas ip is just a powerful vehicle to manipulate the kernel multicast settings. Example 14-12 offers an example of joining a multicast group via smcroute as well as adding a static multicast routing entry. Example 14-13 summarizes the multicast command section of the Linux ip utility.

Example 14-12 *smcroute Utility*

```
[root@callisto:~#] smcroute -h
usage: smcroute [-v] [-d]
               [-a <InputIntf> <OriginIpAdr> <McGroupAdr> <OutputIntf> [<OutputIntf>]
               ...]
                [-r <InputIntf> <OriginIpAdr> <McGroupAdr>]
                [-j <InputIntf> <McGroupAdr>]
                [-l <InputIntf> <McGroupAdr>]

[root@callisto:~#] smcroute -d

[root@callisto:~#] smcroute  -j eth1 224.7.7.7

[root@callisto:~#] smcroute  -a eth1 182.168.2.254 224.4.4.4 eth0

[root@callisto:~#] netstat -g
IPv6/IPv4 Group Memberships
Interface        RefCnt Group
--------------- ------ --------------------
lo               1      ALL-SYSTEMS.MCAST.NET
eth0             1      ALL-SYSTEMS.MCAST.NET
eth1             1      224.7.7.7
eth1             1      224.2.2.2
eth1             1      NTP.MCAST.NET
eth1             1      ALL-SYSTEMS.MCAST.NET

[root@callisto:~#] ip mroute show
(182.168.2.254, 224.4.4.4)      Iif: eth1      Oifs: eth0
(192.168.1.1, 224.2.2.2)        Iif: unresolved
(192.168.2.7, 224.2.2.2)        Iif: unresolved
```

NOTE   Only one multicast router daemon can be active at any time. It is impossible to run smcroute and mrouted or pimd simultaneously.

Example 14-13 *Multicast Commands of the ip Utility*

```
[root@callisto:~#] ip mroute help
Usage: ip mroute show [ PREFIX ] [ from PREFIX ] [ iif DEVICE ]

[root@callisto:~#] ip maddr help
Usage: ip maddr [ add | del ] MULTIADDR dev STRING
       ip maddr show [ dev STRING ]
```

Example 14-13 *Multicast Commands of the ip Utility (Continued)*

```
[root@callisto:~#] ip -s mroute
(192.168.2.7, 224.2.2.2)        Iif: eth1
  4169 packets, 621166 bytes
(192.168.1.1, 224.2.2.2)        Iif: eth1
  6302 packets, 2012324 bytes
(192.168.1.1, 224.0.1.1)        Iif: eth1
  315 packets, 10184 bytes

[root@callisto:~#] ip -s maddr
1:      lo
        inet  224.0.0.1
2:      eth0
        link  01:00:5e:00:00:02
        link  01:00:5e:00:00:04
        link  01:00:5e:00:00:01
        inet  224.0.0.2
        inet  224.0.0.4
        inet  224.0.0.1
3:      eth1
        link  01:00:5e:02:02:02
        link  01:00:5e:00:01:01
        link  01:00:5e:00:00:02
        link  01:00:5e:00:00:04
        link  01:00:5e:00:00:01
        inet  224.2.2.2
        inet  224.0.1.1
        inet  224.0.0.2
        inet  224.0.0.4
        inet  224.0.0.1
```

PIM Operation and Daemons

Both Linux and FreeBSD support PIM-SMv2 and PIM-DM natively, with the requirement of additional user-space PIM daemons (either USC pimd or XORP). PIM-SM is a sparse-mode shared-tree multicast routing protocol, whereas PIM-DM is a dense-mode distance-vector protocol. PIM is a complex protocol, and its discussion goes far beyond this quick introductory chapter. For more information, consult RFC 2362.

Lab 14-2: Native Linux and FreeBSD Multicast (PIM-SMv2) in Combination with Cisco PIM-SM-DM

For this lab, you must enable PIM-SMv2 in the Linux and FreeBSD kernel (see the configurations in Appendix A, "UNIX Kernel Configuration Files") and install the USC pimd. The pimd configuration file is /etc/pimd.conf. Just start pimd with the sequence **pimd -c /etc/pimd.conf** or use **pimd -c /etc/pimd.conf -d all** for extensive debugging output.

For this lab, pimd is running on callisto and castor; the Cisco configuration of scar is shown in Example 14-14. Note that ganymed still runs mrouted and remains connected to scar via the DVMRP tunnel. Therefore, scar acts as a DVMRP-PIM gateway, which is quite common when connecting legacy DVMRP domains to PIM domains. In this lab, you will learn about essential PIM operation, rendezvous points (RPs), and the PIM bootstrap mechanism router (BSR) for propagating RP sets.

CAUTION   An empty pimd.conf results in pimd not being available as a candidate RP (rendezvous point) and candidate BSR (bootstrap router).

NOTE   pimd can define scope zones that are similar to mrouted. This enables you to prevent certain multicast prefixes to be forwarded beyond a certain network boundary. (For example, add **phyint eth0 scoped 239.0.0.0 masklen 8** to your pimd.conf file.)

Example 14-14 *Scar IOS Multicast Configuration Featuring PIM and DVMRP*

```
scar# show running-config
...
!
ip multicast-routing
ip multicast route-limit 100
!
interface Loopback0
 ip address 10.0.0.1 255.255.255.255
!
interface Tunnel0
 ip unnumbered Loopback0
 ip pim sparse-dense-mode
 ip igmp join-group 224.2.2.2
 tunnel source 192.168.14.254
 tunnel destination 192.168.1.254
 tunnel mode dvmrp
!
interface Ethernet0
 bandwidth 10000
 ip address 192.168.7.254 255.255.255.0
 no ip proxy-arp
 ip pim sparse-dense-mode
 ip load-sharing per-packet
 no ip route-cache
 ip igmp join-group 224.2.2.2
 ip cgmp
 no ip mroute-cache
 media-type 10BaseT
 random-detect
!
interface Ethernet1
```

Example 14-14 *Scar IOS Multicast Configuration Featuring PIM and DVMRP (Continued)*

```
 bandwidth 10000
 ip address 192.168.14.254 255.255.255.0
 no ip proxy-arp
 ip pim sparse-dense-mode
 ip load-sharing per-packet
 no ip route-cache
 ip ospf network broadcast
 ip igmp join-group 224.2.2.2
 ip cgmp
 no ip mroute-cache
 media-type 10BaseT
 random-detect
 !
ip pim bsr-candidate Ethernet1 30 4
ip pim rp-candidate Ethernet1 group-list 11
 !
access-list 11 permit 224.0.0.0 15.255.255.255
...
```

Examples 14-15, 14-16, and 14-17 demonstrate PIM output, debugging, and operation on Linux, Cisco IOS, and FreeBSD. It is worth mentioning that pimd operation creates its own interface (pimreg) on Linux systems (as shown in Example 14-15).

Example 14-15 *pimd Results and Operation on Callisto*

```
[root@callisto:~#] ifconfig
eth0      Link encap:Ethernet  HWaddr 00:10:5A:D7:93:60
          inet addr:192.168.14.1  Bcast:192.168.14.255  Mask:255.255.255.0
          UP BROADCAST RUNNING MULTICAST  MTU:1500  Metric:1
          RX packets:2211 errors:0 dropped:0 overruns:0 frame:0
          TX packets:2826 errors:0 dropped:0 overruns:0 carrier:0
          collisions:0 txqueuelen:100
          RX bytes:252609 (246.6 Kb)  TX bytes:314945 (307.5 Kb)
          Interrupt:5 Base address:0xd800

eth1      Link encap:Ethernet  HWaddr 52:54:05:E3:51:87
          inet addr:192.168.1.1  Bcast:192.168.1.255  Mask:255.255.255.0
          UP BROADCAST RUNNING MULTICAST  MTU:1500  Metric:1
          RX packets:27746 errors:0 dropped:0 overruns:0 frame:0
          TX packets:32340 errors:0 dropped:0 overruns:0 carrier:0
          collisions:490 txqueuelen:100
          RX bytes:14612252 (13.9 Mb)  TX bytes:4162570 (3.9 Mb)
          Interrupt:9 Base address:0xd400

lo        Link encap:Local Loopback
          inet addr:127.0.0.1  Mask:255.0.0.0
          UP LOOPBACK RUNNING  MTU:16436  Metric:1
          RX packets:717 errors:0 dropped:0 overruns:0 frame:0
          TX packets:717 errors:0 dropped:0 overruns:0 carrier:0
          collisions:0 txqueuelen:0
          RX bytes:337307 (329.4 Kb)  TX bytes:337307 (329.4 Kb)
```

continues

Example 14-15 *pimd Results and Operation on Callisto (Continued)*

```
pimreg     Link encap:UNSPEC  HWaddr 00-00-00-00-00-00-00-00-00-00-00-00-00-00-00-00
           UP RUNNING NOARP  MTU:1472  Metric:1
           RX packets:3 errors:0 dropped:0 overruns:0 frame:0
           TX packets:0 errors:0 dropped:0 overruns:0 carrier:0
           collisions:0 txqueuelen:0
           RX bytes:356 (356.0 b)  TX bytes:0 (0.0 b)

[root@callisto:~#] netstat -g
IPv6/IPv4 Group Memberships
Interface       RefCnt Group
--------------- ------ --------------------
lo              1      ALL-SYSTEMS.MCAST.NET
eth0            1      ALL-ROUTERS.MCAST.NET
eth0            1      PIM-ROUTERS.MCAST.NET
eth0            1      ALL-SYSTEMS.MCAST.NET
eth1            1      ALL-ROUTERS.MCAST.NET
eth1            1      PIM-ROUTERS.MCAST.NET
eth1            1      NTP.MCAST.NET
eth1            1      ALL-SYSTEMS.MCAST.NET
eth1            1      224.2.2.2
pimreg          1      ALL-SYSTEMS.MCAST.NET

[root@callisto:~#] mtrace 192.168.7.7 192.168.14.1 224.2.2.2
Mtrace from 192.168.7.7 to 192.168.14.1 via group 224.2.2.2
Querying full reverse path...
  0   ? (192.168.14.1)
 -1   scar (192.168.14.254)  PIM  thresh^ 0  Reached RP/Core
Round trip time 2 ms; total ttl of 1 required.

Waiting to accumulate statistics...Results after 10 seconds:

    Source          Response Dest   Overall      Packet Statistics For Traffic From
    * * *           224.0.1.32      Packet       192.168.7.7 To 224.2.2.2
      v           __/  rtt    1 ms  Rate         Lost/Sent = Pct   Rate
192.168.14.254  scar              Reached RP/Core
      v           \__  ttl    2      0 pps         ?/0               0 pps
192.168.14.1    192.168.14.1
    Receiver        Query Source

[root@callisto:~#] pimd -c /etc/pimd.conf -d all
debug level 0xffffffff
(dvmrp_detail,dvmrp_prunes,dvmrp_mrt,dvmrp_neighbors,dvmrp_timers,igmp_proto,
igmp_timers,igmp_members,trace,timeout,pkt,interfaces,kernel,cache,rsrr,pim_detail,
pim_hello,pim_register,pim_join_prune,pim_bootstrap,pim_asserts,pim_cand_rp,
pim_routes,pim_timers,pim_rpf)
16:17:17.768 pimd version 2.1.0-alpha29.18 starting
16:17:17.768 Got 262144 byte send buffer size in 0 iterations
16:17:17.768 Got 262144 byte recv buffer size in 0 iterations
16:17:17.768 Got 262144 byte send buffer size in 0 iterations
16:17:17.768 Got 262144 byte recv buffer size in 0 iterations
16:17:17.769 Getting vifs from kernel
16:17:17.769 installing eth0 (192.168.14.1 on subnet 192.168.14) as vif #0-2 - rate=0
16:17:17.769 installing eth1 (192.168.1.1 on subnet 192.168.1) as vif #1-3 - rate=0
```

Example 14-15 *pimd Results and Operation on Callisto (Continued)*

```
16:17:17.769 installing gre1 (10.10.10.1 -> 10.10.10.2) as vif #2-12 - rate=0
16:17:17.769 Getting vifs from /etc/pimd.conf
16:17:17.769 Local Cand-RP address is 192.168.14.1
16:17:17.769 Local Cand-RP priority is 30
16:17:17.769 Local Cand-RP advertisement period is 30 sec.
16:17:17.769 Local Cand-BSR address is 192.168.14.1
16:17:17.769 Local Cand-BSR priority is 3
16:17:17.770 Adding prefix 224.0.0.0/4
16:17:17.770 data_rate_limit is 50000 (bits/s)
16:17:17.770 data_rate_interval is 20 (seconds)
16:17:17.770 reg_rate_limit is 50000 (bits/s)
16:17:17.770 reg_rate_interval is 20 (seconds)
16:17:17.770 eth0 comes up; vif #0 now in service
16:17:17.770 SENT IGMP Membership Query     from 192.168.14.1   to 224.0.0.1
16:17:17.770 SENT PIM v2 Hello              from 192.168.14.1   to 224.0.0.13
16:17:17.770 eth1 comes up; vif #1 now in service
16:17:17.770 warning - sendto to 224.0.0.1 on 192.168.1.1: Invalid argument
16:17:17.771 warning - sendto from 192.168.1.1 to 224.0.0.13: Invalid argument
16:17:17.771 gre1 is DOWN; vif #2 out of service
16:17:17.771 register_vif0 comes up; vif #3 now in service


Virtual Interface Table
  Vif  Local-Address    Subnet              Thresh  Flags      Neighbors
    0  192.168.14.1     192.168.14          1       DR NO-NBR
    1  192.168.1.1      192.168.1           1       DR NO-NBR
    2  10.10.10.1       10.10.10/30         1       DOWN
    3  192.168.14.1     register_vif0       1

Multicast Routing Table
  Source         Group          RP-addr       Flags
------------------------(*,*,RP)------------------------
Number of Groups: 0
Number of Cache MIRRORs: 0


16:17:17.772 PIM HELLO holdtime from 192.168.14.254 is 105
16:17:17.772 SENT PIM v2 Hello              from 192.168.14.1   to 224.0.0.13
16:17:17.773 sending PIM v2 Bootstrap       from 192.168.14.1   to 192.168.14.254

Virtual Interface Table
  Vif  Local-Address    Subnet              Thresh  Flags      Neighbors
    0  192.168.14.1     192.168.14          1       PIM        192.168.14.254
    1  192.168.1.1      192.168.1           1       DR NO-NBR
    2  10.10.10.1       10.10.10/30         1       DOWN
    3  192.168.14.1     register_vif0       1


Virtual Interface Table
  Vif  Local-Address    Subnet              Thresh  Flags      Neighbors
    0  192.168.14.1     192.168.14          1       PIM        192.168.14.254
    1  192.168.1.1      192.168.1           1       DR NO-NBR
    2  10.10.10.1       10.10.10/30         1       DOWN
    3  192.168.14.1     register_vif0       1
```

Example 14-16 *Cisco IOS PIM Statistics, Output and Debug*

```
scar# show ip pim neighbor
PIM Neighbor Table
Neighbor          Interface          Uptime/Expires    Ver   DR
Address                                                      Prio/Mode
192.168.7.7       Ethernet0          00:03:53/00:01:22 v2    N /
192.168.14.1      Ethernet1          00:03:22/00:01:22 v2    N /

scar# show ip pim interface

Address           Interface          Ver/  Nbr   Query  DR    DR
                                     Mode  Count Intvl  Prior
192.168.7.254     Ethernet0          v2/SD 1     30     1     192.168.7.254
192.168.14.254    Ethernet1          v2/SD 1     30     1     192.168.14.254
10.0.0.1          Tunnel0            v2/DV 1     30     1     0.0.0.0

scar# show ip mroute
IP Multicast Routing Table
Flags: D - Dense, S - Sparse, B - Bidir Group, s - SSM Group, C - Connected,
       L - Local, P - Pruned, R - RP-bit set, F - Register flag,
       T - SPT-bit set, J - Join SPT, M - MSDP created entry,
       X - Proxy Join Timer Running, A - Candidate for MSDP Advertisement,
       U - URD, I - Received Source Specific Host Report
Outgoing interface flags: H - Hardware switched
Timers: Uptime/Expires
Interface state: Interface, Next-Hop or VCD, State/Mode

(*, 224.0.1.111), 05:05:18/00:00:00, RP 192.168.14.254, flags: SJCL
  Incoming interface: Null, RPF nbr 0.0.0.0
  Outgoing interface list:
    Tunnel0, Forward/Dvmrp, 04:49:28/00:00:00
    Ethernet1, Forward/Sparse-Dense, 05:05:18/00:01:31
    Ethernet0, Forward/Sparse-Dense, 05:05:18/00:02:11

(*, 224.0.1.40), 05:05:17/00:00:00, RP 0.0.0.0, flags: DCL
  Incoming interface: Null, RPF nbr 0.0.0.0
  Outgoing interface list:
    Tunnel0, Forward/Dvmrp, 04:49:28/00:00:00
    Ethernet0, Forward/Sparse-Dense, 05:05:17/00:00:00
    Ethernet1, Forward/Sparse-Dense, 05:05:17/00:00:00

(*, 224.2.2.2), 05:05:18/00:00:00, RP 192.168.14.254, flags: SJCL
  Incoming interface: Null, RPF nbr 0.0.0.0
  Outgoing interface list:
    Tunnel0, Forward/Dvmrp, 04:53:28/now
    Ethernet1, Forward/Sparse-Dense, 05:05:18/00:01:33
    Ethernet0, Forward/Sparse-Dense, 05:05:18/00:02:17

(192.168.2.7, 224.2.2.2), 00:00:06/00:02:53, flags: CLJ
  Incoming interface: Tunnel0, RPF nbr 192.168.1.254, Dvmrp
  Outgoing interface list:
    Ethernet1, Forward/Sparse-Dense, 00:00:06/00:02:53
    Ethernet0, Forward/Sparse-Dense, 00:00:06/00:02:53
```

Example 14-16 *Cisco IOS PIM Statistics, Output and Debug (Continued)*

```
scar# show ip pim bsr-router
PIMv2 Bootstrap information
This system is the Bootstrap Router (BSR)
  BSR address: 192.168.14.254 (?)
  Uptime:      04:49:04, BSR Priority: 4, Hash mask length: 30
  Next bootstrap message in 00:00:59
  Candidate RP: 192.168.14.254(Ethernet1)
    Advertisement interval 60 seconds
    Next advertisement in 00:00:55
    Group acl: 11

scar# show ip pim rp
Group: 224.0.1.111, RP: 192.168.14.254, v2, next RP-reachable in 00:00:32
Group: 224.2.2.2, RP: 192.168.14.254, v2, next RP-reachable in 00:00:32

scar# show ip pim rp mapping
PIM Group-to-RP Mappings
This system is a candidate RP (v2)
This system is the Bootstrap Router (v2)
Group(s) 224.0.0.0/4
  RP 192.168.14.254 (?), v2
    Info source: 192.168.14.254 (?), via bootstrap
         Uptime: 04:50:32, expires: 00:02:56

scar# show ip pim interface detail
Ethernet0 is up, line protocol is up
  Internet address is 192.168.7.254/24
  Multicast switching: process
  Multicast packets in/out: 6474/0
  Multicast boundary: not set
  Multicast TTL threshold: 0
  PIM: enabled
    PIM version: 2, mode: sparse-dense
    PIM DR: 192.168.7.254 (this system)
    PIM neighbor count: 1
    PIM Hello/Query interval: 30 seconds
    PIM State-Refresh processing: enabled
    PIM State-Refresh origination: disabled
    PIM State-Refresh: 1 non-capable neighbor
    PIM NBMA mode: disabled
    PIM ATM multipoint signaling: disabled
    PIM domain border: disabled
  Multicast Tagswitching: disabled
Ethernet1 is up, line protocol is up
  Internet address is 192.168.14.254/24
  Multicast switching: process
  Multicast packets in/out: 0/0
  Multicast boundary: not set
  Multicast TTL threshold: 0
  PIM: enabled
    PIM version: 2, mode: sparse-dense
    PIM DR: 192.168.14.254 (this system)
```

continues

Example 14-16 *Cisco IOS PIM Statistics, Output and Debug (Continued)*

```
        PIM neighbor count: 1
        PIM Hello/Query interval: 30 seconds
        PIM State-Refresh processing: enabled
        PIM State-Refresh origination: disabled
        PIM State-Refresh: 1 non-capable neighbor
        PIM NBMA mode: disabled
        PIM ATM multipoint signaling: disabled
        PIM domain border: disabled
      Multicast Tagswitching: disabled
  Tunnel0 is up, line protocol is up
    Interface is unnumbered. Using address of Loopback0 (10.0.0.1)
    Multicast switching: fast
    Multicast packets in/out: 0/0
    Multicast boundary: not set
    Multicast TTL threshold: 0
    PIM: enabled
      PIM version: 2, mode: sparse-dense
      PIM DR: 0.0.0.0 (this system)
      PIM neighbor count: 0
      PIM Hello/Query interval: 30 seconds
      PIM State-Refresh processing: enabled
      PIM State-Refresh origination: disabled
      PIM NBMA mode: disabled
      PIM ATM multipoint signaling: disabled
      PIM domain border: disabled
    Multicast Tagswitching: disabled

  scar# debug ip pim
  PIM debugging is on

  scar# terminal monitor
  05:01:34: PIM: Building Join/Prune message for 224.0.1.32
  05:01:36: PIM: Received v2 Hello on Ethernet1 from 192.168.14.1
  05:01:41: PIM: Received v2 Bootstrap on Ethernet1 from 192.168.14.1
  05:01:42: PIM: Send periodic v2 Hello on Ethernet1
  05:01:42: PIM: Send RP-reachability for 224.0.1.111 on Ethernet1
  05:01:42: PIM: Send RP-reachability for 224.0.1.111 on Ethernet0
  05:01:42: PIM: Send RP-reachability for 224.2.2.2 on Ethernet1
  05:01:42: PIM: Send RP-reachability for 224.2.2.2 on Ethernet0
  05:01:48: PIM: Send periodic v2 Hello on Ethernet0
  05:01:48: PIM: Received v2 Hello on Ethernet0 from 192.168.7.7
  05:01:53: PIM: Received v2 Bootstrap on Ethernet0 from 192.168.7.7
  05:02:06: PIM: Received v2 Hello on Ethernet1 from 192.168.14.1
  05:02:08: PIM: Received v2 Candidate-RP-Advertisement on Ethernet1 from
  192.168.14.254
  05:02:08: PIM: Update (224.0.0.0/4, RP:192.168.14.254), PIMv2
  05:02:11: PIM: Received v2 Bootstrap on Ethernet1 from 192.168.14.1
  05:02:12: PIM: Send periodic v2 Hello on Ethernet1
  05:02:14: PIM: Building Join/Prune message for 224.2.2.2
  05:02:16: PIM: Building Join/Prune message for 224.0.1.111
  05:02:18: PIM: Received v2 Hello on Ethernet0 from 192.168.7.7
  05:02:18: PIM: Send periodic v2 Hello on Ethernet0
```

Example 14-16 *Cisco IOS PIM Statistics, Output and Debug (Continued)*

```
05:02:23: PIM: Received v2 Bootstrap on Ethernet0 from 192.168.7.7
05:02:34: PIM: Building Join/Prune message for 224.0.1.32
05:02:36: PIM: Received v2 Hello on Ethernet1 from 192.168.14.1
05:02:41: PIM: Received v2 Bootstrap on Ethernet1 from 192.168.14.1
05:02:42: PIM: Send periodic v2 Hello on Ethernet1
05:02:48: PIM: Received v2 Hello on Ethernet0 from 192.168.7.7
05:02:48: PIM: Send periodic v2 Hello on Ethernet0
05:02:53: PIM: Received v2 Bootstrap on Ethernet0 from 192.168.7.7
05:03:06: PIM: Received v2 Hello on Ethernet1 from 192.168.14.1
05:03:08: PIM: Received v2 Candidate-RP-Advertisement on Ethernet1 from
192.168.14.254
05:03:08: PIM: Update (224.0.0.0/4, RP:192.168.14.254), PIMv2
05:03:11: PIM: Received v2 Bootstrap on Ethernet1 from 192.168.14.1
05:03:12: PIM: Send periodic v2 Hello on Ethernet1
05:03:12: PIM: Send RP-reachability for 224.0.1.111 on Ethernet1
05:03:12: PIM: Send RP-reachability for 224.0.1.111 on Ethernet0
05:03:13: PIM: Send RP-reachability for 224.2.2.2 on Ethernet1
05:03:13: PIM: Send RP-reachability for 224.2.2.2 on Ethernet0
05:03:14: PIM: Building Join/Prune message for 224.2.2.2
05:03:16: PIM: Building Join/Prune message for 224.0.1.111
```

Example 14-17 *Castor pimd Operation and Debug Output*

```
[root@castor:~#] netstat -g -f inet

Virtual Interface Table
 Vif  Thresh  Rate  Local-Address  Remote-Address  Pkts-In  Pkts-Out
  0      1      0    192.168.2.7                         0      1040
  1      1      0    192.168.7.7                         0       990
  2      1      0    192.168.80.1                        0         0
  4      1      0    192.168.2.7                         0         0

IPv4 Multicast Forwarding Cache
 Origin          Group          Packets  In-Vif  Out-Vifs:Ttls
 192.168.2.7     224.2.2.2          48      0     1:1

[root@castor:~#] netstat -gs -f inet
IPv4 multicast forwarding:
        3875 multicast forwarding cache lookups
        1462 multicast forwarding cache misses
        961 upcalls to mrouted
        50 upcall queue overflows
        0 upcalls dropped due to full socket buffer
        952 cache cleanups
        1462 datagrams with no route for origin
        0 datagrams arrived with bad tunneling
        0 datagrams could not be tunneled
        18 datagrams arrived on wrong interface
        0 datagrams selectively dropped
        0 datagrams dropped due to queue overflow
        0 datagrams dropped for being too large
```

continues

Example 14-17 *Castor pimd Operation and Debug Output (Continued)*

```
[root@castor:~#] pimd -c /etc/pimd.conf -d all
debug level 0xffffffff
(dvmrp_detail,dvmrp_prunes,dvmrp_mrt,dvmrp_neighbors,dvmrp_timers,igmp_proto,
igmp_timers,igmp_members,trace,timeout,pkt,interfaces,kernel,cache,rsrr,pim_detail,
pim_hello,pim_register,pim_join_prune,pim_bootstrap,pim_asserts,pim_cand_rp,
pim_routes,pim_timers,pim_rpf)
16:25:02.309 pimd version 2.1.0-alpha29.18 starting
16:25:02.325 Got 232448 byte send buffer size in 8 iterations
16:25:02.325 Got 232448 byte recv buffer size in 8 iterations
16:25:02.325 Got 232448 byte send buffer size in 8 iterations
16:25:02.326 Got 232448 byte recv buffer size in 8 iterations
16:25:02.326 Getting vifs from kernel
16:25:02.327 installing xl0 (192.168.2.7 on subnet 192.168.2) as vif #0 - rate=0
16:25:02.327 installing ed0 (192.168.7.7 on subnet 192.168.7) as vif #1 - rate=0
16:25:02.327 installing vlan8 (192.168.80.1 on subnet 192.168.80) as vif #2 - rate=0
16:25:02.328 installing tun0 (10.10.10.2 -> 10.10.10.1) as vif #3 - rate=0
16:25:02.328 Getting vifs from /etc/pimd.conf
16:25:02.328 Local Cand-RP address is 192.168.80.1
16:25:02.328 Local Cand-RP priority is 20
16:25:02.329 Local Cand-RP advertisement period is 30 sec.
16:25:02.329 Local Cand-BSR address is 192.168.80.1
16:25:02.329 Local Cand-BSR priority is 5
16:25:02.329 Adding prefix 224.0.0.0/4
16:25:02.329 data_rate_limit is 50000 (bits/s)
16:25:02.329 data_rate_interval is 20 (seconds)
16:25:02.329 reg_rate_limit is 50000 (bits/s)
16:25:02.329 reg_rate_interval is 20 (seconds)
16:25:02.344 xl0 comes up; vif #0 now in service
16:25:02.344 SENT IGMP Membership Query     from 192.168.2.7    to 224.0.0.1
16:25:02.345 SENT PIM v2 Hello              from 192.168.2.7    to 224.0.0.13
16:25:02.345 ed0 comes up; vif #1 now in service
16:25:02.346 SENT IGMP Membership Query     from 192.168.7.7    to 224.0.0.1
16:25:02.347 SENT PIM v2 Hello              from 192.168.7.7    to 224.0.0.13
16:25:02.347 vlan8 comes up; vif #2 now in service
16:25:02.348 SENT IGMP Membership Query     from 192.168.80.1   to 224.0.0.1
16:25:02.348 SENT PIM v2 Hello              from 192.168.80.1   to 224.0.0.13
16:25:02.349 tun0 is DOWN; vif #3 out of service
16:25:02.349 register_vif0 comes up; vif #4 now in service


Virtual Interface Table
 Vif  Local-Address     Subnet            Thresh   Flags        Neighbors
   0  192.168.2.7       192.168.2           1      DR NO-NBR
   1  192.168.7.7       192.168.7           1      DR NO-NBR
   2  192.168.80.1      192.168.80          1      DR NO-NBR
   3  10.10.10.2        10.10.10/29         1      DOWN
   4  192.168.2.7       register_vif0       1

Multicast Routing Table
 Source         Group         RP-addr        Flags
------------------------------(*,*,RP)---------------------------
Number of Groups: 0
Number of Cache MIRRORs: 0
```

Example 14-17 *Castor pimd Operation and Debug Output (Continued)*

```
16:25:02.354 PIM HELLO holdtime from 192.168.7.254 is 105
16:25:02.355 SENT PIM v2 Hello           from 192.168.7.7    to 224.0.0.13
16:25:02.355 sending PIM v2 Bootstrap    from 192.168.7.7    to 192.168.7.254

Virtual Interface Table
Vif  Local-Address    Subnet           Thresh  Flags        Neighbors
  0  192.168.2.7      192.168.2          1     DR NO-NBR
  1  192.168.7.7      192.168.7          1     PIM          192.168.7.254
  2  192.168.80.1     192.168.80         1     DR NO-NBR
  3  10.10.10.2       10.10.10/29        1     DOWN
  4  192.168.2.7      register_vif0      1

16:25:02.953 Cache miss, src 192.168.1.1, dst 224.2.2.2, iif 0
16:25:02.964 Cache miss, src 192.168.2.7, dst 224.2.2.2, iif 0
16:25:02.964 create group entry, group 224.2.2.2
16:25:04.823 Cache miss, src 192.168.1.1, dst 224.2.2.2, iif 0
16:25:05.094 Cache miss, src 192.168.2.7, dst 224.2.2.2, iif 0
16:25:05.095 create group entry, group 224.2.2.2
16:25:06.433 Cache miss, src 192.168.1.1, dst 224.2.2.2, iif 0
16:25:06.703 Cache miss, src 192.168.2.7, dst 224.2.2.2, iif 0
16:25:06.704 create group entry, group 224.2.2.2
16:25:06.991 create group entry, group 224.0.1.1
```

Example 14-18 demonstrates bidirectional operation of the mtest utility package, which is available at the same place as mrouted. It consists of two tools: a sender part (msend) and a receiver part (mrcv). mtest is useful to test multicast operation between two distinguished hosts and interfaces. Often it is not quite clear to what interface multicast applications bind, which often results in problems. Finally, if all other diagnosis fails and all friends abandon you, a sniffer is always your last (or first) best hope.

Example 14-18 *mtest Utilities (msend/mrcv)*

```
[root@castor:~#] msend
multicast sending test program; enter ? for list of commands
?
 i i.i.i.i                   - set the multicast interface
 t ttl_value                 - set the ttl_value for multicast
 z min-max                   - set packet size range in byte
 v min-max                   - set inter-packet interval range in second
                               ex. v 0.5-2 or v 1-1 for fixed interval
 a rate                      - set packet sending rate
 d type #pkts_or_#sec        - set communication duration
                               type=1 set #pkt ex. d 1 20
                               type=2 set #sec ex. d 0 25
 s g.g.g.g port#             - send to IP  multicast group
 q                           - quit

i 192.168.7.7
interface set
t 5
ttl set to 5
s 224.2.2.2 34000
```

continues

Example 14-18 *mtest Utilities (msend/mrcv) (Continued)*

```
Sending... for 10 packets
Sent pkt # 0, for mgroup 224.2.2.2 port -31536, length=1006, interval=982421
microseconds
Sent pkt # 1, for mgroup 224.2.2.2 port -31536, length=1006, interval=982421
microseconds
Sent pkt # 2, for mgroup 224.2.2.2 port -31536, length=1006, interval=982421
microseconds
Sent pkt # 3, for mgroup 224.2.2.2 port -31536, length=1006, interval=982421
microseconds

[root@callisto:~#] mrcv
multicast receiving test program; enter ? for list of commands
?
 j g.g.g.g i.i.i.i           - join IP multicast group
 l g.g.g.g i.i.i.i           - leave IP multicast group
 r g.g.g.g port#             - receive from multicast interface
 q                           - quit

j 224.2.2.2 192.168.14.1
group joined
r 224.2.2.2 34000
Bind socket
Receive pkt # 0, for mgroup 224.2.2.2 port 34000, length=1006, t_sec=134744073,
t_usec=133744072
Receive pkt # 1, for mgroup 224.2.2.2 port 34000, length=1006, t_sec=134744073,
t_usec=133744072
Receive pkt # 2, for mgroup 224.2.2.2 port 34000, length=1006, t_sec=134744073,
t_usec=133744072
Receive pkt # 3, for mgroup 224.2.2.2 port 34000, length=1006, t_sec=134744073,
t_usec=133744072
```

Example 14-19 offers a configuration scenario for enabling multicast on a Linux GRE tunnel interface in case this is required for some topological reason.

Example 14-19 *Callisto GRE Multicast Tunnel Configuration*

```
[root@callisto:~#] modprobe ip_gre
[root@callisto:~#] ip tunnel add gre1 mode gre remote 192.168.2.7 local 192.168.1.1
ttl 127 dev eth0
[root@callisto:~#] ip addr add 10.10.10.1/30 peer 10.10.10.2/30 dev gre1
[root@callisto:~#] ip link set gre1 up multicast on
```

Lab 14-3: XORP PIM Operation

The XORP multicast architecture currently consists of the MLD6/IGMP and the PIM-SM elements. They are not yet integrated in the router manager (rtrmgr), but you can use them in a standalone way as demonstrated in this lab. At the time of this writing, the milestone release 1.0 was not yet available. That should simplify and consolidate things. This lab features the same lab as shown previously with the exception of callisto running XORP

PIM-SM instead of the USC pimd. XORP PIM-SM works with Linux 2.4.x and FreeBSD > 4.8 because of the availability of PIM hooks in the kernel.

To start PIM-SM (standalone mode), follow these steps:

1 cd to the pim subdirectory of your XORP source distribution.

2 Edit **./configure_pim**

3 Execute **./test_pim &**

4 Execute **./configure_pim**

5 Access the PIM-SM CLI by typing **telnet localhost 12000**

Example 14-20 introduces the XORP PIM-SM command-line interface and IGMP and PIM-SM relevant output.

Example 14-20 *XORP PIM-SM Command-Line Interface*

```
[root@callisto:~#] telnet localhost 12000
Trying 127.0.0.1...
Connected to localhost (127.0.0.1).
Escape character is '^]'.
Welcome, and may the Xorp be with you!

Xorp> show ?
Possible completions:
  igmp          Display information about IGMP
  log           Display information about log files and users
  mfea          Display information about MFEA
  pim           Display information about PIM

Xorp> show igmp ?
Possible completions:
  group         Display information about IGMP group membership
  interface     Display information about IGMP configured interfaces

Xorp> show igmp group
Interface     Group         Source        Last Reported     Timeout
eth0          224.0.0.2     0.0.0.0       192.168.14.1         244
eth0          224.0.0.13    0.0.0.0       192.168.14.1         242
eth0          224.0.1.111   0.0.0.0       192.168.14.254       247
eth0          224.2.2.2     0.0.0.0       192.168.14.254       244
eth1          224.0.0.2     0.0.0.0       192.168.1.1          244
eth1          224.0.0.13    0.0.0.0       192.168.1.1          241

Xorp> show igmp interface
Interface     State     Querier        Timeout Version  Groups
eth0          UP        192.168.14.1      None    2        4
eth1          UP        192.168.1.1       None    2        2
ipsec0        DISABLED 0.0.0.0            None    2        0
ipsec1        DISABLED 0.0.0.0            None    2        0
ipsec2        DISABLED 0.0.0.0            None    2        0
ipsec3        DISABLED 0.0.0.0            None    2        0
```

continues

Example 14-20 *XORP PIM-SM Command-Line Interface (Continued)*

```
lo               DISABLED 0.0.0.0              None      2       0
register_vif     DISABLED 0.0.0.0              None      2       0
pimreg           DISABLED 0.0.0.0              None      2       0

Xorp> show mfea ?
Possible completions:
  dataflow         Display information about MFEA dataflow filters
  interface        Display information about MFEA interfaces
  mrib             Display MRIB information inside MFEA

Xorp> show mfea interface
Interface        State      Vif/PifIndex  Addr          Flags
eth0             UP                   0/2  192.168.14.1  MULTICAST BROADCAST KERN_UP
eth1             UP                   1/3  192.168.1.1   MULTICAST BROADCAST KERN_UP
ipsec0           DISABLED            2/4  192.168.1.1
ipsec1           DISABLED            3/5
ipsec2           DISABLED            4/6
ipsec3           DISABLED            5/7
lo               DISABLED            6/1  127.0.0.1     LOOPBACK KERN_UP
register_vif     UP                  7/2  192.168.14.1  PIM_REGISTER KERN_UP
pimreg           DISABLED            8/9                KERN_UP

Xorp> show mfea mrib
DestPrefix          NextHopRouter   VifName VifIndex  MetricPreference Metric
0.0.0.0/0           192.168.1.254   eth1    1                      100    100
10.0.0.1/32         192.168.1.254   eth1    1                      100    100
127.0.0.0/8         0.0.0.0         lo      6                      100    100
192.168.1.0/24      0.0.0.0         eth1    1                      100    100
192.168.2.0/24      192.168.1.254   eth1    1                      100    100
192.168.7.0/24      192.168.1.254   eth1    1                      100    100
192.168.14.0/24     0.0.0.0         eth0    0                      100    100
192.168.45.0/24     0.0.0.0         eth1    1                      100    100
192.168.80.0/24     192.168.1.254   eth1    1                      100    100
211.11.117.0/24     192.168.1.254   eth1    1                      100    100

Xorp> show pim mrib
DestPrefix          NextHopRouter   VifName VifIndex  MetricPreference Metric
0.0.0.0/0           192.168.1.254   eth1    1                      100    100
10.0.0.1/32         192.168.1.254   eth1    1                      100    100
127.0.0.0/8         0.0.0.0         lo      6                      100    100
192.168.1.0/24      0.0.0.0         eth1    1                      100    100
192.168.2.0/24      192.168.1.254   eth1    1                      100    100
192.168.7.0/24      192.168.1.254   eth1    1                      100    100
192.168.14.0/24     0.0.0.0         eth0    0                      100    100
192.168.45.0/24     0.0.0.0         eth1    1                      100    100
192.168.80.0/24     192.168.1.254   eth1    1                      100    100
211.11.117.0/24     192.168.1.254   eth1    1                      100    100

Xorp> show pim neighbors
Interface        DRpriority NeighborAddr     V Mode     Holdtime Timeout
eth0                      1 192.168.14.254   2 Sparse        105      102
Xorp> show pim rps
```

Example 14-20 *XORP PIM-SM Command-Line Interface (Continued)*

```
RP              Type     Pri Holdtime Timeout ActiveGroups GroupPrefix
192.168.14.254  bootstrap  0    208     182             2 224.0.0.0/4

Xorp> show pim ?
Possible completions:
  bootstrap     Display information about PIM bootstrap routers
  interface     Display information about PIM configured interfaces
  join          Display information about PIM groups
  mfc           Display information about PIM Multicast Forwarding Cache
  mrib          Display MRIB information inside PIM
  neighbors     Display information about PIM neighbors
  rps           Display information about PIM RPs
  scope         Display information about PIM scope zones

Xorp> show pim bootstrap
Active zones:
BSR             Pri LocalAddress    Pri State        Timeout SZTimeout
192.168.14.254    4 192.168.1.1       1 Candidate       105        -1
Expiring zones:
BSR             Pri LocalAddress    Pri State        Timeout SZTimeout
Configured zones:
BSR             Pri LocalAddress    Pri State        Timeout SZTimeout
192.168.1.1       1 192.168.1.1       1 Init             -1        -1

Xorp> show pim interface
Interface       State     Mode    V PIMstate  Priority DRaddr         Neighbors
eth0            UP        Sparse  2 NotDR            1 192.168.14.254         1
eth1            UP        Sparse  2 DR               1 192.168.1.1            0
ipsec0          DISABLED  Sparse  2 NotDR            1 0.0.0.0                0
ipsec1          DISABLED  Sparse  2 NotDR            1 0.0.0.0                0
ipsec2          DISABLED  Sparse  2 NotDR            1 0.0.0.0                0
ipsec3          DISABLED  Sparse  2 NotDR            1 0.0.0.0                0
lo              DISABLED  Sparse  2 NotDR            1 0.0.0.0                0
register_vif    UP        Sparse  2 NotDR            1 0.0.0.0                0
pimreg          DISABLED  Sparse  2 NotDR            1 0.0.0.0                0

Xorp> show pim join
Group           Source       RP              Flags
224.0.1.111     0.0.0.0      192.168.14.254  WC
    Upstream interface (RP):   eth0
    Upstream MRIB next hop (RP): 192.168.14.254
    Upstream RPF'(*,G):        192.168.14.254
    Upstream state:            NotJoined
    Join timer:                -1
    Local receiver include WC: O........
    Joins RP:                  ........
    Joins WC:                  ........
    Join state:                ........
    Prune state:               ........
    Prune pending state:       ........
    I am assert winner state:  ........
```

continues

Example 14-20 *XORP PIM-SM Command-Line Interface (Continued)*

```
          I am assert loser state:   .........
          Assert winner WC:          .........
          Assert lost WC:            .........
          Assert tracking WC:        .........
          Could assert WC:           .........
          I am DR:                   .O......
          Immediate olist RP:        .........
          Immediate olist WC:        .........
          Inherited olist SG:        .........
          Inherited olist SG_RPT:    .........
          PIM include WC:            .........
224.2.2.2       0.0.0.0          192.168.14.254  WC
          Upstream interface (RP):   eth0
          Upstream MRIB next hop (RP): 192.168.14.254
          Upstream RPF'(*,G):        192.168.14.254
          Upstream state:            NotJoined
          Join timer:                -1
          Local receiver include WC: O.......
          Joins RP:                  .........
          Joins WC:                  .........
          Join state:                .........
          Prune state:               .........
          Prune pending state:       .........
          I am assert winner state:  .........
          I am assert loser state:   .........
          Assert winner WC:          .........
          Assert lost WC:            .........
          Assert tracking WC:        .........
          Could assert WC:           .........
          I am DR:                   .O......
          Immediate olist RP:        .........
          Immediate olist WC:        .........
          Inherited olist SG:        .........
          Inherited olist SG_RPT:    .........
          PIM include WC:            .........
```

Multicast Open Shortest Path First (MOSPF)

MOSPF is another dense-mode intradomain multicast routing protocol used in some scientific research networks, including the MBONE. One of the first testbed implementations was MOSPF for Proteon Routers by John Moy.

MOSPF introduces a new link-state advertisement (LSA)—the group-membership LSA, which is flooded through the entire area—and identifies MOSPF-enabled routers via a special flag in their router LSAs. MOSPF does not deviate from regular OSPF in its fundamental operation, though. Therefore, you can easily integrate it in a stepwise manner into existing OSPF networks. MOSPF routers avoid nonmulticast-aware OSPF neighbors in their shortest-path first (SPF) calculation. Interoperability with MBONE DVMRP routers is carried out via border gateway routers running both protocols.

Cisco decided not to implement MOSPF because of inherent scalability problems and a clear commitment to PIM. With the router configuration command **ignore lsa mospf**, syslog messages regarding unsupported LSA type 6 can be suppressed.

Multicast Source Discovery Protocol (MSDP)

MSDP essentially connects PIM-SM domains beyond the borders of autonomous systems. MSDP in combination with MBGP can connect easily multicast-enabled ISP domains at private or public peering points by maintaining their individual RPs. MSDP is also a key enabler for anycast RPs. Anycast RPs add load sharing and redundancy to PIM-SM multicast networks. The MSDP peering connection is implemented in TCP, whereas PIM-SM takes care of the actual forwarding between domains.

BGPv4 Multicast Extensions (Multiprotocol BGP, RFC 2858)

The pragmatic way of interconnecting isolated multicast realms or islands is to use unicast tunnels (GRE or IP-IP) constituting the MBONE. With the advent of multiprotocol features for BGP, it is now possible to let BGP deal with separate sets of unicast and multicast network layer reachability information (NLRI). This is also the evolution we see today— fewer tunnels, more and more MBGP/MSDP-enabled border or peering routers, and MBGP/MSDP and PIM-SM replacing DVMRP for interautonomous system multicast routing, as sketched in Figure 14-4.

Figure 14-4 *Modern MBGP Architecture*

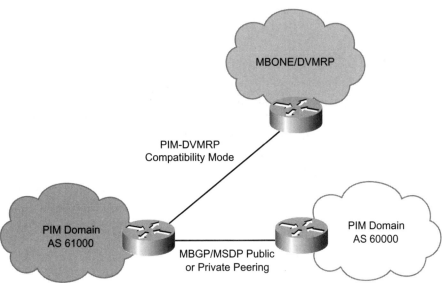

It is the general consensus that this task has to be carried out with a sparse-mode protocol. Zebra/Quagga supports MBGP hooks. I consider BGP peering points and exchanges the best place to exchange interdomain multicast signaling information. Eventually, multicast route server and looking glasses will become as popular as their unicast counterparts.

Multicast Transport Layer Protocols

These research endeavors deal with the issue of adding reliable transport mechanisms to intrinsically unreliable UDP multicasting transport to suit the needs of special multicast application layer requirements. For details, consult the resources at the IETF Reliable Multicast Transport (rmt) Working Group at http://www.ietf.org/html.charters /rmt-charter.html.

Multicast Invitations and Session Announcements

There exists a formal description format for multicast sessions, the Session Description Protocol (SDP, RFC 2327). The most widely adopted manifestation of this protocol is the graphical SDR tool (Session Directory Tool). A user can join an advertisement by clicking the particular entry.

Alternative approaches use web portals or Java applets to display session announcements. For detailed information on these tools and multicast applications in general, visit the excellent repository of the UCL Networked Multimedia Research Group at http:// www-mice.cs.ucl.ac.uk/multimedia/software.

Multicast Security

Discussion of multicast security issues is primarily carried out in the IETF Multicast Security (msec) Working Group. It deals with secure group communication for large groups involving a single trusted entity (authoritative group controller), which establishes and enforces the group's security policy and join/leave procedures to secure groups.

Of course, group key management and distribution involving a mechanism called group security associations (GSAs) is essential to the overall architecture. A GSA represents the multicast equivalent of a unicast security association (SA) that is well known from the IPSec protocol framework.

Another important aspect of multicast security is the delicate issue of (distributed) denial of service ([D]DoS) in multicast environments. For further details, look at the foundation document for multicast security, the IETF draft "The Multicast Security Architecture" (http://www.ietf.org/internet-drafts/draft-ietf-msec-arch-04.txt). This document describes an end-to-end security framework independent of aspects such as NAT, multicast routing, admission control protocols, and reliable multicast mechanisms.

Summary

This chapter offered an introduction to multicast building blocks and protocols. It covered historical developments in addition to modern multicasting approaches, LAN/WAN issues, dense/sparse subscriber distribution, interdomain/intradomain architectures, and a comparison of link/network/application layer issues. Note that essentially all the routing packages discussed in Chapter 2, "User-Space Routing Software," are incapable of dealing with multicast signaling, with the exception of XORP PIM and generic MBGP hooks in Zebra/Quagga. The user-space daemons mrouted and pimd add DVMRP and PIM-SM routing capabilities to the UNIX operating systems.

All discussed UNIX kernels natively support IGMPv1/v2; IGMPv3 packages and patches are available, too. IGMPv3 is closely connected to SSM receiver operation.

A lot of development work focuses on the area of SSM, reliable multicast, multicast security, and DoS issues. SSM is a PIM extension to increase one-to-many communication efficiency without the involvement of RPs. Modern interarea multicast approaches are based on a combination of MSDP, BGMP, and MBGP; eventually, however, one single protocol will prevail.

Note that this chapter really just introduced the concept of interdomain multicasting; a thorough discussion of interdomain multicast signaling protocols goes beyond the scope of this book.

Recommended Reading

- *Developing IP Multicast Networks, Volume I*, by Beau Williamson (Cisco Press, 2000)
- *Interdomain Multicast Solution Guide*, by Brian Adams et al. (Cisco Press, 2002)
- *Interdomain Multicast Routing*, by Brian M. Edwards et al. (Addison-Wesley Professional, 2002)
- The mrouted man page mrouted(8)
- Linux 2.4 Advanced Routing HOWTO

- Linux Advanced Routing & Traffic Control HOWTO
- RFC 1112, "Host Extensions for IP Multicasting"
- pimd, http://netweb.usc.edu/pim
- SMCRoute, http://www.cschill.de/smcroute
- European MBONE website, http://www.mbone.de
- IETF Multicast Working Groups, http://www.ietf.org
- IANA Address Assignments, http://www.iana.org/assignments/multicast-addresses
- Cisco IOS Software – Multicast, http://www.cisco.com/warp/public/732/Tech/multicast/
- "Multicast in a Campus Network: CGMP and IGMP Snooping," Cisco.com, http://www.cisco.com/warp/public/473/22.html
- RFC 1112, "Host Extensions for IP Multicasting" (Steve Deering, August 1989)
- RFC 1584, "Multicast Extensions to OSPF" (John Moy)
- RFC 1585, "MOSPF: Analysis and Experience" (John Moy)
- mrouted & mtest utility, ftp://ftp.research.att.com/dist/fenner/mrouted/
- mrouted Linux patch, ftp://ftp.debian.org/debian/dists/potato/non-free/source/net/mrouted_3.9-beta3-1.diff.gz
- IETF draft, "The Multicast Security Architecture," http://www.ietf.org/internet-drafts/draft-ietf-msec-arch-04.txt
- IETF Multicast & Anycast Group Membership (magma), http://www.ietf.org/html.charters/magma-charter.html
- IETF MBONE Deployment (mboned), http://www.ietf.org/html.charters/mboned-charter.html
- IETF Multicast Security (msec), http://www.ietf.org/html.charters/msec-charter.html
- IETF Border Gateway Multicast Routing Protocol (bgmp), http://www.ietf.org/html.charters/bgmp-charter.html
- IETF Inter-Domain Multicast Routing (idmr), http://www.ietf.org/html.charters/idmr-charter.html
- IETF Multicast Source Discovery Protocol (msdp), http://www.ietf.org/html.charters/msdp-charter.html
- IETF Protocol Independent Multicast (pim), http://www.ietf.org/html.charters/pim-charter.html
- IETF Source-Specific Multicast (ssm), http://www.ietf.org/html.charters/ssm-charter.html

- IETF Reliable Multicast Transport (rmt), http://www.ietf.org/html.charters/rmt-charter.html
- IETF The Secure Multicast Research Group (SmuG), http://www.securemulticast.org/smug-index.htm
- IETF The Reliable Multicast Research Group, http://www.east.isi.edu/rm/UCL Networked Multimedia Research Group at http://www-mice.cs.ucl.ac.uk/multimedia/software.
- GEANT, http://www.geant.net
- DANTE, http://www.dante.net
- TERENA, http://www.terena.nl

## CHAPTER 15

Network Address Translation

The concept of Network Address Translation (NAT) goes back to the origin of the feared IP address shortage. An IP address shortage was a distinct possibility because, historically, huge address blocks were assigned, which were underutilized or were assigned inefficiently, in the early days before the classless interdomain routing (CIDR) and variable-length subnet masking (VLSM) of today's Internet. Today's address-assignment policies are much stricter, and registration authorities now try to free underutilized address aggregates by demanding them back for reassignment. Historically, most addresses were assigned to North America and Europe. NAT improves aggregation and scalability of enterprise routing, too, so it contributes to keeping the global Internet routing table "relatively" small.

From a "workaround" for address exhaustion, NAT has evolved into a flexible vehicle for enterprises and Internet service providers (ISPs). Although NAT per se is not a security vehicle, it arguably improves privacy. An attacker usually does not know which and how many addresses remain hidden (masqueraded) behind corporate NAT gateways. One can attack only the outside addresses of these gateways or the address pools deployed for NAT.

This chapter discusses UNIX NAT approaches, frequently used terminology, and caveats in context with NAT-incapable protocols. The chapter concludes by looking at future developments with regard to IPv4 NAT.

The NAT Foundation—Basic/Traditional NAT

NAT enables hosts with RFC 1918 addresses to access officially routed Internet IPv4 addresses, but it also can be deployed for migration scenarios with overlapping address space. RFC 3022 exhaustively describes the evolution of NAT variants and is highly recommended reading. In the most general case (basic NAT), inside RFC 1918 private address pools are mapped to outside address pools that are transparent to end users. The original approach featured a 1:1 mapping from internal to external addresses, which by itself did not provide address preservation. The introduction of Network Address Port Translation (NAPT or PAT) changed this picture in a way—that is, via TCP/UDP ports, many internal addresses can be mapped into one outside address. This is also referred to as *port multiplexing*.

NAT gateways store information that is relevant for mapping/reverse mapping in state tables. NAT/PAT mappings come in several flavors:

- One-to-one or bidirectional mapping (1:1) (static mappings)
- One-to-many (1:*n*) (single gateway address = NAPT/PAT/masquerading or dynamic NAT)
- Many-to-many (*n:m*) (NAT address pools)

NAT, PAT(NAPT), Masquerading, and Port Mapping/Multiplexing

In the Linux world, the term *IP masquerading* often is used for historical reasons. In pre-iptables times, the masquerading engine was separate from the packet filter and stateful inspection engine. In a way, IP masquerading is a point of view that emphasizes the stealthy character of the procedure. In contrast, PAT describes the mechanism more accurately.

NAT gateways (NAT translators in Internet Engineering Task Force [IETF] parlance) internally operate as TCP/UDP port multiplexing/demultiplexing engines. This procedure also is referred to as *mapping and reverse mapping*. NAPT is IETF parlance for PAT.

You occasionally will find that Cisco differentiates between NAT and PAT. From the Cisco perspective, this is a differentiation of one-to-one and many-to-one/many-to-many mappings.

Static NAT and ARP/Routing Issues

Keep in mind that NAT gateways need to reply to Address Resolution Protocol (ARP) requests for NAT-mapped global addresses under their administrative authority. In the case of such pool addresses, the outside gateway interface and the access router's inside interface share the same broadcast domain, ARP is used, and the NAT gateway is required to reply on behalf of the static address pool. This behavior can be accomplished by adding static ARP entries or, even better, alias interface addresses. Most of the time, the firewall/NAT software takes care of this by itself, though.

In the case of ordinary routing such as in Figure 15-1, remember to add explicit routes for NAT pools on screening/access routers toward the NAT engine. In that case, the pool is routed, and this is no longer an ARP issue. On some implementations, however, it might be necessary to add an explicit route for static mappings from the outside to the inside address; others handle this automatically. Now you know the two showstoppers to look out for in case of problems.

Figure 15-1 *Generic NAT Architecture for Corporate Networks*

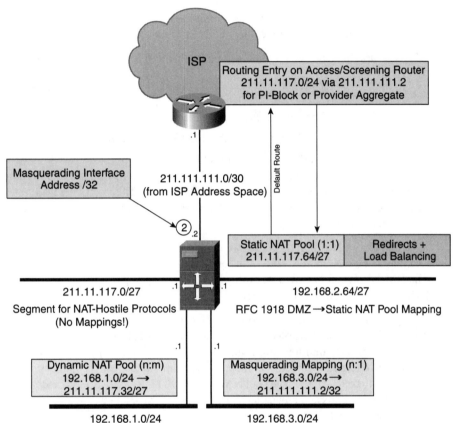

Redirection (Port Forwarding/Relaying or Transparent Proxying)

Port forwarding redirects incoming connection requests to the NAT gateway to an arbitrary address/port. In certain configurations (port rewrite), this is referred to as *transparent proxying*. Also keep in mind that under certain circumstances (in/out on the same interface), it might be necessary to disable Internet Control Message Protocol (ICMP) redirects (**sysctl -w net.inet.ip.redirect=0**); otherwise, it might interfere with what you want to accomplish.

UNIX NAT Approaches

The topology in Figure 15-1 serves as a basis for the labs in this chapter. This is a generic example featuring a five-interface firewall/NAT gateway, as follows:

- The first interface is a special segment inhabited by protocols that cannot coexist with NAT.
- The second interface features an Ethernet crossover link to a screening access router.
- The third interface represents a demilitarized zone (DMZ) with RFC 1918 addresses.
- Finally, two internal interfaces with RFC 1918 address pools complete the picture.

The assumption is that this setup serves a fairly large corporate network. Suppose, for example, we have acquired a /24 address block from our upstream ISP, either a provider aggregate or a PI address block (does not really matter). This prefix is routed toward the firewall. Likewise, the firewall defaults toward the access router, which by itself defaults to the upstream provider.

Note that Figure 15-1 demonstrates two different ways to dynamically map client requests to either an outside address pool (n:m) or a single interface address (n:1 = masquerading). The DMZ design offers great flexibility: 1:1 static mappings, port forwarding, and load balancing can be utilized in a combined fashion.

NAT gateways are an additional hop in an IP packet's path. Therefore, they alter the Time To Live (TTL). Depending on the implementation, NAT gateways always use the same pool of port numbers for multiplexing connections. These are either predetermined at compile time or can be altered via sysctl or user-space configuration such as with ipfilter (ipf). Therefore, if you want to better camouflage your NAT gateway, taking care of a good random distribution of multiplexing ports and an unaltered TTL does not leave an investigator much evidence to detect a NAT gateway.

On the other hand, if you are in the role of an auditor, look for patterns in the high-port range for evidence of NAT conversion. Usually NAT is an integrated function of modern commercial or open-source firewalls, so do not reveal the existence of a firewall by politely rejecting packets by returning ICMP information; instead, just silently discard probes and attacks. The less information you reveal, the more difficult it is for attackers to gather useful information to penetrate defenses. Also keep in mind that the checksum of several headers has to be recomputed by the NAT gateway.

Lab 15-1: OpenBSD ipfilter

This lab (as detailed in Example 15-1) features a masquerading n:1 mapping scenario commonly found in small office/home office (SOHO) broadband and dial-up scenarios, for which a subscriber gets only one address from the service provider. The external addresses of SOHO devices such as broadband routers usually are deployed via Dynamic Host Configuration Protocol (DHCP). DHCP serves internal segments or VLANs, too.

Therefore, it is recommended that you use interface descriptors or shell variables rather than IP addresses in firewall/NAT configuration files wherever possible. You will also find examples for many-to-many configurations (NAT pools), port relaying, application proxies, and load balancing in this configuration (comments inline).

Example 15-1 *OpenBSD ipfilter (ipf) NAT Configuration*

```
[root@ganymed:~#] cat /etc/ipnat.rules
##########################################################################
# NAT/PAT Generic Configuration                                          #
# Gernot Schmied, March 2003                                             #
# This configuration example assumes that the network is 20.20.20.0/24. #
##########################################################################
#                                                                        #
# To get information, try "ipnat -lsv"                                   #
# Manually start via "ipnat -CF -f /etc/ipnat.rules"                     #
# To clear and flush, try  "ipnat -CF"                                   #
#                                                                        #
##########################################################################

#OUTSIDE="ne5"
#INSIDE ="ne3"
#DMZ    ="ne4"
#NONAT  ="ne2"


################################################################
### application proxies (always place before portmap rules!) ###
################################################################
# active ftp #
map ne5 192.168.1.0/24 -> ne5/32 proxy port ftp ftp/tcp
map ne5 192.168.2.0/24 -> ne5/32 proxy port ftp ftp/tcp
# H.323 proxy support #
map ne5 192.168.1.0/24 -> ne5/32 proxy port 1720 h323/tcp
# RealAudio #
map ne5 192.168.1.0/24 -> ne5/32 proxy port 7070 raudio/tcp
# IPsec Proxy #
map ne5 192.168.1.0/24 -> ne5/32 proxy port 500 ipsec/udp


#####################################
### dynamic NAT (many-to-one = n:1) ###
#####################################

map ne5 192.168.1.0/24 -> ne5/32 portmap tcp/udp 60000:65535
map ne5 192.168.1.0/24 -> ne5/32        # for ICMP
map ne5 192.168.2.0/24 -> ne5/32 portmap tcp/udp 60000:65535
map ne5 192.168.2.0/24 -> ne5/32        # for ICMP
map ne5 192.168.14.0/24 -> ne5/32 portmap tcp/udp 60000:65535
map ne5 192.168.14.0/24 -> ne5/32       # for ICMP
# alternative #
#map ne5 192.168.1.0/24 -> ne5/32 portmap tcp/udp auto
#map ne5 192.168.1.0/24 -> ne5/32       # for ICMP
```

continues

Example 15-1 *OpenBSD ipfilter (ipf) NAT Configuration (Continued)*

```
####################################################
### working with NAT pools (many-to-many = n:m) ###
####################################################

#map ne5 192.168.7.0/24 -> 20.20.20.0/24 portmap tcp/udp 60000:65535
#map ne5 192.168.7.0/24 -> 20.20.20.0/24
# exclude from NAT pool #
#map-block ne5 192.168.2.18/32 -> 20.20.20.0/24 ports 64


###############################################
### static NAT entries (one-to-one = bimap) ###
###############################################

# Do not forget to set static routes when necessary
# e.g. "route add 211.11.117.65 192.168.2.65"
# There is no need to manually establish corresponding static ARP entries;
# however, in combination with some ill-behaving access devices,
# this is always a nice workaround.
# e.g. "arp -s 211.11.117.65 00:d0:ba:4c:a5:c0"

#bimap ne5 211.11.117.65/32 -> 192.168.2.65/32
# or alternatively #
# bimap ne5 211.11.117.64/27 -> 192.168.2.64/27


#########################################
### NAT Load Balancer (round-robin) ###
#########################################

#rdr ne5 211.111.111.2/32 port 80 -> 192.168.2.3 port 8000 tcp round-robin
#rdr ne5 211.111.111.2/32 port 80 -> 192.168.2.4 port 8000 tcp round-robin
#rdr ne5 211.111.111.2/32 port 80 -> 192.168.2.5 port 8000 tcp round-robin
```

Example 15-2 presents status information of the NAT configuration of Example 15-1 in action.

Example 15-2 *OpenBSD NAT Operation Output*

```
[root@ganymed:~#] ipnat -l
List of active MAP/Redirect filters:
map ne5 192.168.1.0/24 -> 0.0.0.0/32 portmap tcp/udp 60000:65535
map ne5 192.168.1.0/24 -> 0.0.0.0/32
map ne5 192.168.2.0/24 -> 0.0.0.0/32 portmap tcp/udp 60000:65535
map ne5 192.168.2.0/24 -> 0.0.0.0/32
map ne5 192.168.14.0/24 -> 0.0.0.0/32 portmap tcp/udp 60000:65535
map ne5 192.168.14.0/24 -> 0.0.0.0/32

List of active sessions:
MAP 192.168.1.1      34240 <- -> 211.111.111.2 61761 [195.34.133.149 80]
MAP 192.168.1.1      34239 <- -> 211.111.111.2 61760 [213.229.60.9 80]
MAP 192.168.1.1      34238 <- -> 211.111.111.2 61759 [138.22.167.21 80]
MAP 192.168.1.1      34237 <- -> 211.111.111.2 61758 [205.156.51.200 80]
```

Example 15-2 *OpenBSD NAT Operation Output (Continued)*

```
MAP 192.168.1.1       34236 <- -> 211.111.111.2 61757 [213.229.60.100 110]
MAP 192.168.1.1       34235 <- -> 211.111.111.2 61756 [213.229.60.100 110]
MAP 192.168.1.1       34234 <- -> 211.111.111.2 61755 [213.229.60.100 110]
MAP 192.168.1.1       34233 <- -> 211.111.111.2 61754 [213.229.60.100 110]
MAP 192.168.1.1       34232 <- -> 211.111.111.2 61753 [213.46.255.2 110]
MAP 192.168.1.1       32895 <- -> 211.111.111.2 61752 [195.34.133.10 53]
MAP 192.168.1.1       32894 <- -> 211.111.111.2 61751 [195.34.133.10 53]
MAP 192.168.1.1       32893 <- -> 211.111.111.2 61745 [195.34.133.10 53]
MAP 192.168.1.1       32892 <- -> 211.111.111.2 61744 [195.34.133.10 53]
MAP 192.168.1.1       32890 <- -> 211.111.111.2 61738 [195.34.133.10 53]
MAP 192.168.1.1       32889 <- -> 211.111.111.2 61737 [195.34.133.10 53]
MAP 192.168.1.1       32888 <- -> 211.111.111.2 61731 [195.34.133.10 53]

[root@ganymed:~#] ipnat -lv
List of active MAP/Redirect filters:
map ne5 192.168.1.0/24 -> 0.0.0.0/32 portmap tcp/udp 60000:65535
map ne5 192.168.1.0/24 -> 0.0.0.0/32
map ne5 192.168.2.0/24 -> 0.0.0.0/32 portmap tcp/udp 60000:65535
map ne5 192.168.2.0/24 -> 0.0.0.0/32
map ne5 192.168.14.0/24 -> 0.0.0.0/32 portmap tcp/udp 60000:65535
map ne5 192.168.14.0/24 -> 0.0.0.0/32

List of active sessions:
MAP 192.168.1.1       34240 <- -> 211.111.111.2 61761 [195.34.133.149 80]
        age 299 use 0 sumd 0xc586/0xc586 pr 6 bkt 0/60 flags 1
        ifp ne5 bytes 5157 pkts 19
MAP 192.168.1.1       34239 <- -> 211.111.111.2 61760 [213.229.60.9 80]
        age 299 use 0 sumd 0xc586/0xc586 pr 6 bkt 89/38 flags 1
        ifp ne5 bytes 12208 pkts 27
MAP 192.168.1.1       34238 <- -> 211.111.111.2 61759 [138.22.167.21 80]
        age 254 use 0 sumd 0xc586/0xc586 pr 6 bkt 46/122 flags 1
        ifp ne5 bytes 2129 pkts 11
MAP 192.168.1.1       34237 <- -> 211.111.111.2 61758 [205.156.51.200 80]
        age 255 use 0 sumd 0xc586/0xc586 pr 6 bkt 20/80 flags 1
        ifp ne5 bytes 8635 pkts 33
MAP 192.168.1.1       34236 <- -> 211.111.111.2 61757 [213.229.60.100 110]
        age 227 use 0 sumd 0xc586/0xc586 pr 6 bkt 100/49 flags 1
        ifp ne5 bytes 1515 pkts 24
MAP 192.168.1.1       34235 <- -> 211.111.111.2 61756 [213.229.60.100 110]
        age 226 use 0 sumd 0xc586/0xc586 pr 6 bkt 98/47 flags 1
        ifp ne5 bytes 1264 pkts 20
MAP 192.168.1.1       34234 <- -> 211.111.111.2 61755 [213.229.60.100 110]
        age 226 use 0 sumd 0xc586/0xc586 pr 6 bkt 96/45 flags 1
        ifp ne5 bytes 2481 pkts 30
MAP 192.168.1.1       34233 <- -> 211.111.111.2 61754 [213.229.60.100 110]
        age 226 use 0 sumd 0xc586/0xc586 pr 6 bkt 94/43 flags 1
        ifp ne5 bytes 1280 pkts 20
MAP 192.168.1.1       34232 <- -> 211.111.111.2 61753 [213.46.255.2 110]
        age 220 use 0 sumd 0xc586/0xc586 pr 6 bkt 75/24 flags 1
        ifp ne5 bytes 1539 pkts 22
```

continues

Example 15-2 *OpenBSD NAT Operation Output (Continued)*

```
MAP 192.168.1.1     32895 <- -> 211.111.111.2 61752 [195.34.133.10 53]
        age 992 use 0 sumd 0xcabe/0xcabe pr 17 bkt 93/32 flags 2
        ifp ne5 bytes 1150 pkts 10
MAP 192.168.1.1     32894 <- -> 211.111.111.2 61751 [195.34.133.10 53]
        age 940 use 0 sumd 0xcabe/0xcabe pr 17 bkt 91/30 flags 2
        ifp ne5 bytes 198 pkts 2
MAP 192.168.1.1     32893 <- -> 211.111.111.2 61745 [195.34.133.10 53]
        age 940 use 0 sumd 0xcab9/0xcab9 pr 17 bkt 89/18 flags 2
        ifp ne5 bytes 480 pkts 4
MAP 192.168.1.1     32892 <- -> 211.111.111.2 61744 [195.34.133.10 53]
        age 580 use 0 sumd 0xcab9/0xcab9 pr 17 bkt 87/16 flags 2
        ifp ne5 bytes 198 pkts 2
MAP 192.168.1.1     32890 <- -> 211.111.111.2 61738 [195.34.133.10 53]
        age 580 use 0 sumd 0xcab5/0xcab5 pr 17 bkt 83/4 flags 2
        ifp ne5 bytes 464 pkts 4
MAP 192.168.1.1     32889 <- -> 211.111.111.2 61737 [195.34.133.10 53]
        age 220 use 0 sumd 0xcab5/0xcab5 pr 17 bkt 81/2 flags 2
        ifp ne5 bytes 182 pkts 2
MAP 192.168.1.1     32888 <- -> 211.111.111.2 61731 [195.34.133.10 53]
        age 220 use 0 sumd 0xcab0/0xcab0 pr 17 bkt 79/117 flags 2
        ifp ne5 bytes 464 pkts 4

List of active host mappings:
192.168.1.1 -> 0.0.0.0 (use = 16 hv = 32)

[root@ganymed:~#] ipnat -s
mapped   in      34077   out       34425
added    1763    expired 1746
no memory        0       bad nat 0
inuse    17
rules    6
wilds    0
```

Lab 15-2: FreeBSD ipfw+natd

The user-space FreeBSD application natd(8) requires both the ipfw and the ipdivert sockets in the kernel configuration (options IPFIREWALL, options IPDIVERT). In addition, the following settings must be in /etc/rc.conf, as shown in Example 15-3).

Example 15-3 *FreeBSD natd Requirements*

```
gateway_enable="YES"
firewall_enable="YES"
firewall_type="OPEN"
natd_enable="YES"
natd_interface="en5" # Indicates which interface to forward packets through
                     # (the interface connected to the Internet).
natd_flags=" -l -m  -u -f /etc/natd.conf"
```

The FreeBSD natd supports traditional NAT and port/protocol/address redirection. Consult the man page natd(8) for further operational details. Example 15-4 presents a short example of port relaying.

Example 15-4 *FreeBSD natd Example for Redirects*

```
-redirect_port tcp 192.168.1.2:6667 6667
-redirect_port tcp 192.168.1.3:80 80
-redirect_port tcp 192.168.1.4:2000-3000 2000-3000
-redirect_address 192.168.1.2 128.1.1.2
-redirect_address 192.168.1.3 128.1.1.3
-redirect_proto encap 192.168.1.4
```

Lab 15-3: BSD Packet Filter (pf)

The pf packet filter is OpenBSD's native packet-inspection, stateful firewall, and NAT engine. It recently was ported to other BSD operating systems. Because it was inspired by ipfilter and works similarly, it is not discussed in detail here. For further information, consult the sources (especially the pf FAQ) in the "Recommended Reading" section at the end of this chapter.

Lab 15-4: Linux NAT (iptables)

The firewall/NAT engine for the 2.4 and 2.6 Linux kernels is iptables/netfilter. Because of the large number of features available, only a short example of IP masquerading on PPP links is presented in Example 15-5 (which is quoted from the iptables NAT tutorial).

Example 15-5 *Linux iptables Masquerading Example*

```
# Load the NAT module. (This pulls in all the others.)
modprobe iptable_nat

# In the NAT table (-t nat), append a rule (-A) after routing
# (POSTROUTING) for all packets going out ppp0 (-o ppp0), which says to
# masquerade the connection (-j MASQUERADE).
iptables -t nat -A POSTROUTING -o ppp0 -j MASQUERADE

# Turn on IP forwarding.
echo 1 > /proc/sys/net/ipv4/ip_forward
```

NAT-Hostile Protocols

Because of their intrinsic operation, NAT gateways in the communication path of certain protocols might disturb their inner working. Good examples are H.323/SIP, FTP, end-to-end IPSec, and peer-to-peer applications. Unfortunately, these problems often are caused by inconsiderate application development and easily could have been avoided (RFC 3235, "Network Address Translator (NAT)—Friendly Application Design Guidelines"). In the case of H.323, this can be compensated easily by application level gateway (ALG) mappings of modern firewall engines (for example, Cisco PIX Firewall) or the use of H.323 gatekeepers/proxies.

Keep in mind that stateful NAT and stateful inspection firewall issues are related and often intertwined. Special pains are applications that use random ports.

Future Developments: NAT-T, MPLS+NAT, Load Balancer

Current development focuses on NAT failover solutions, with added functionality of load balancers and transparent proxies. The latter features usually are accomplished via the redirection engine.

Especially interesting for ISP deployments and product offerings is the capability of modern Multiprotocol Label Switching (MPLS) implementations (edge routers) to configure NAT between MPLS virtual private networks (VPNs) with overlapping address space (for example, extranets) and the global routing table.

NAT-T (NAT Traversal) essentially sums up attempts to reduce issues of tunnel deployments and protocol traversal in the context of NAT gateways. For more information, see the IETF draft document "Negotiation of NAT-Traversal in the IKE" (referenced in the "Recommended Reading" section at this end of this chapter), a self-description of which follows:

This document describes how to detect one or more network address translation devices (NATs) between IPSec hosts, and how to negotiate the use of UDP encapsulation of IPSec packets through NAT boxes in Internet Key Exchange (IKE).

With regard to NAT-hostile protocols, the current approach of choice to remedy the problem is described in RFC 3489, "STUN-Simple Traversal of User Datagram Protocol (UDP) Through Network Address Translation." In addition, consult RFC 3519, "Mobile IP Traversal of Network Address Translation (NAT) Devices," for caveats in the context of mobile deployments.

NAT Redundancy—Stateful Failover

Asymmetrical routing in general does not work with NAT gateways and stateful inspection firewalls. (It might even break packet fragmentation/reassembly.) This has to be taken into consideration when designing gateway failover solutions. Dynamic routing protocols might help on occasion, especially with static 1:1 mappings.

This particular potential problem can be overcome if the routers share the same NAT configuration and rapidly and constantly exchange state information to ensure a failsafe backup for each other. Nevertheless, a busy enterprise gateway most likely will still lose some connections or drop packets during a short transitional switch-over phase.

OpenBSD's pf is the first integrated gateway/NAT engine of open-source character that has NAT and stateful inspection table synchronization under development (pfsync). The Cisco PIX Firewall offers a proprietary failover approach, and Cisco IOS routers are capable of dealing with stateful failover translation groups.

Note that stateful NAT (SNAT in Cisco lingo) enables continuous service for dynamically mapped NAT sessions and works with Hot Standby Router Protocol (HSRP). Occasionally, NAT gateways also provide DHCP services to internal network segments. A true redundancy architecture also requires mirroring/synchronizing of DHCP lease tables. This is possible with the ISC dhcpd.

Summary

This chapter introduced Network and Port Address Translation for single-IP SOHO masquerading connections and for many-to-many address pool mappings for corporate networks. The chapter also briefly covered various ISP features. Port forwarding and NAT deployment issues were discussed, and the chapter concluded with a look at NAT evolution and stateful failover concepts.

Recommended Reading

- RFC 3022, "Traditional IP Network Address Translator (Traditional NAT)"
- RFC 3027, "Protocol Complications with the IP Network Address Translator"
- RFC 3235, "Network Address Translator (NAT)-Friendly Application Design Guidelines"
- RFC 2663, "IP Network Address Translator (NAT) Terminology and Considerations"
- RFC 2694, "DNS Extensions to Network Address Translators (DNS_ALG)"
- RFC 2709, "Security Model with Tunnel-Mode IPSec for NAT Domains"
- RFC 2391, "Load Sharing Using IP Network Address Translation (LSNAT)"
- RFC 2993, "Architectural Implications of NAT"
- RFC 3519, "Mobile IP Traversal of Network Address Translation (NAT) Devices"
- RFC 3715, "IPSec-Network Address Translation (NAT) Compatibility Requirements"
- RFC 3489, "STUN—Simple Traversal of User Datagram Protocol (UDP) Through Network Address Translators (NATs)"
- The pf FAQ, ftp://ftp.openbsd.org/pub/OpenBSD/doc/pf-faq.txt
- The ipfilter HOWTO, http://www.obfuscation.org/ipf/ipf-howto.html
- The pf website, http://www.benzedrine.cx/pf.html
- The ipfilter website, http://coombs.anu.edu.au/~avalon/ip-filter.html
- The Linux netfilter website, http://www.netfilter.org/
- IETF draft-ietf-ipsec-nat-t-ike-08.txt, "Negotiation of NAT-Traversal in the IKE," http://www.ietf.org/internet-drafts/draft-ietf-ipsec-nat-t-ike-08.txt
- Cisco.com NAT introduction, http://www.cisco.com/en/US/tech/tk648/tk361/technologies_white_paper09186a0080091cb9.shtml

UNIX Kernel Configuration Files

This appendix presents the network-relevant configuration file portions for Linux, OpenBSD, and FreeBSD. It is assumed that you are familiar with how to configure and compile modular kernels on the respective platform. Relevant remarks are offered as comments within the configuration. Be warned that these are not full configurations, just fragments to be incorporated in the labs for this book, and they might differ slightly within minor revisions of your kernel series. Example A-1 presents a Linux configuration for the 2.4.*x* kernel series, Example A-2 shows an OpenBSD configuration for 3.*x*, and Example A-3 lists a configuration for the 4.*x* FreeBSD kernel series.

Example A-1 *Linux 2.4.22 Network Kernel Options*

```
#
# Code maturity-level options
#
CONFIG_EXPERIMENTAL=y

#
# Loadable module support
#
CONFIG_MODULES=y
CONFIG_MODVERSIONS=y
CONFIG_KMOD=y

#
# Networking options
#
CONFIG_PACKET=y
CONFIG_PACKET_MMAP=y
CONFIG_NETLINK_DEV=y
CONFIG_NETFILTER=y
CONFIG_NETFILTER_DEBUG=y
CONFIG_FILTER=y
CONFIG_UNIX=y
CONFIG_INET=y
CONFIG_IP_MULTICAST=y
CONFIG_IP_ADVANCED_ROUTER=y
CONFIG_IP_MULTIPLE_TABLES=y
CONFIG_IP_ROUTE_FWMARK=y
CONFIG_IP_ROUTE_NAT=y
CONFIG_IP_ROUTE_MULTIPATH=y
CONFIG_IP_ROUTE_TOS=y
```

continues

Example A-1 *Linux 2.4.22 Network Kernel Options (Continued)*

```
CONFIG_IP_ROUTE_VERBOSE=y
# CONFIG_IP_PNP is not set
CONFIG_NET_IPIP=m
CONFIG_NET_IPGRE=m
CONFIG_NET_IPGRE_BROADCAST=y
CONFIG_IP_MROUTE=y
CONFIG_IP_PIMSM_V1=y
CONFIG_IP_PIMSM_V2=y
# CONFIG_ARPD is not set
# CONFIG_INET_ECN is not set
CONFIG_SYN_COOKIES=y

#
#    IP: Netfilter Configuration
#
CONFIG_IP_NF_CONNTRACK=m
CONFIG_IP_NF_FTP=m
# CONFIG_IP_NF_AMANDA is not set
# CONFIG_IP_NF_TFTP is not set
CONFIG_IP_NF_IRC=m
CONFIG_IP_NF_QUEUE=m
CONFIG_IP_NF_IPTABLES=m
CONFIG_IP_NF_MATCH_LIMIT=m
CONFIG_IP_NF_MATCH_MAC=m
CONFIG_IP_NF_MATCH_PKTTYPE=m
CONFIG_IP_NF_MATCH_MARK=m
CONFIG_IP_NF_MATCH_MULTIPORT=m
CONFIG_IP_NF_MATCH_TOS=m
# CONFIG_IP_NF_MATCH_RECENT is not set
CONFIG_IP_NF_MATCH_ECN=m
CONFIG_IP_NF_MATCH_DSCP=m
CONFIG_IP_NF_MATCH_AH_ESP=m
CONFIG_IP_NF_MATCH_LENGTH=m
CONFIG_IP_NF_MATCH_TTL=m
CONFIG_IP_NF_MATCH_TCPMSS=m
CONFIG_IP_NF_MATCH_HELPER=m
CONFIG_IP_NF_MATCH_STATE=m
CONFIG_IP_NF_MATCH_CONNTRACK=m
CONFIG_IP_NF_MATCH_UNCLEAN=m
CONFIG_IP_NF_MATCH_OWNER=m
CONFIG_IP_NF_FILTER=m
CONFIG_IP_NF_TARGET_REJECT=m
CONFIG_IP_NF_TARGET_MIRROR=m
CONFIG_IP_NF_NAT=m
CONFIG_IP_NF_NAT_NEEDED=y
CONFIG_IP_NF_TARGET_MASQUERADE=m
CONFIG_IP_NF_TARGET_REDIRECT=m
# CONFIG_IP_NF_NAT_LOCAL is not set
# CONFIG_IP_NF_NAT_SNMP_BASIC is not set
CONFIG_IP_NF_NAT_IRC=m
CONFIG_IP_NF_NAT_FTP=m
CONFIG_IP_NF_MANGLE=m
CONFIG_IP_NF_TARGET_TOS=m
# CONFIG_IP_NF_TARGET_ECN is not set
```

Example A-1 *Linux 2.4.22 Network Kernel Options (Continued)*

```
# CONFIG_IP_NF_TARGET_DSCP is not set
CONFIG_IP_NF_TARGET_MARK=m
CONFIG_IP_NF_TARGET_LOG=m
CONFIG_IP_NF_TARGET_ULOG=m
CONFIG_IP_NF_TARGET_TCPMSS=m
# CONFIG_IP_NF_ARPTABLES is not set
# CONFIG_IP_NF_COMPAT_IPCHAINS is not set
# CONFIG_IP_NF_COMPAT_IPFWADM is not set
CONFIG_IPV6=m

#
#   IPv6: Netfilter Configuration
#
CONFIG_IP6_NF_QUEUE=m
CONFIG_IP6_NF_IPTABLES=m
CONFIG_IP6_NF_MATCH_LIMIT=m
CONFIG_IP6_NF_MATCH_MAC=m
# CONFIG_IP6_NF_MATCH_RT is not set
# CONFIG_IP6_NF_MATCH_OPTS is not set
# CONFIG_IP6_NF_MATCH_FRAG is not set
# CONFIG_IP6_NF_MATCH_HL is not set
CONFIG_IP6_NF_MATCH_MULTIPORT=m
CONFIG_IP6_NF_MATCH_OWNER=m
CONFIG_IP6_NF_MATCH_MARK=m
# CONFIG_IP6_NF_MATCH_IPV6HEADER is not set
# CONFIG_IP6_NF_MATCH_AHESP is not set
CONFIG_IP6_NF_MATCH_LENGTH=m
CONFIG_IP6_NF_MATCH_EUI64=m
CONFIG_IP6_NF_FILTER=m
CONFIG_IP6_NF_TARGET_LOG=m
CONFIG_IP6_NF_MANGLE=m
CONFIG_IP6_NF_TARGET_MARK=m
# CONFIG_KHTTPD is not set
# CONFIG_ATM is not set
CONFIG_VLAN_8021Q=y

#
#
#
# CONFIG_IPX is not set
# CONFIG_ATALK is not set

#
# AppleTalk devices
#
# CONFIG_DECNET is not set
CONFIG_BRIDGE=y
# CONFIG_X25 is not set
# CONFIG_LAPB is not set
# CONFIG_LLC is not set
# CONFIG_NET_DIVERT is not set
# CONFIG_ECONET is not set
# CONFIG_WAN_ROUTER is not set
# CONFIG_NET_FASTROUTE is not set
```

continues

Example A-1 *Linux 2.4.22 Network Kernel Options (Continued)*

```
# CONFIG_NET_HW_FLOWCONTROL is not set

#
# QoS and/or fair queuing
#
CONFIG_NET_SCHED=y
CONFIG_NET_SCH_CBQ=m
CONFIG_NET_SCH_HTB=m
CONFIG_NET_SCH_CSZ=m
CONFIG_NET_SCH_PRIO=m
CONFIG_NET_SCH_RED=m
CONFIG_NET_SCH_SFQ=m
CONFIG_NET_SCH_TEQL=m
CONFIG_NET_SCH_TBF=m
CONFIG_NET_SCH_GRED=m
CONFIG_NET_SCH_DSMARK=m
CONFIG_NET_SCH_INGRESS=m
CONFIG_NET_QOS=y
CONFIG_NET_ESTIMATOR=y
CONFIG_NET_CLS=y
CONFIG_NET_CLS_TCINDEX=m
CONFIG_NET_CLS_ROUTE4=m
CONFIG_NET_CLS_ROUTE=y
CONFIG_NET_CLS_FW=m
CONFIG_NET_CLS_U32=m
CONFIG_NET_CLS_RSVP=m
CONFIG_NET_CLS_RSVP6=m
CONFIG_NET_CLS_POLICE=y

#
# Network testing
#
CONFIG_NET_PKTGEN=m
CONFIG_IPSEC=y

#
# IPSec options (FreeS/WAN)
#
CONFIG_IPSEC_IPIP=y
CONFIG_IPSEC_AH=y
CONFIG_IPSEC_AUTH_HMAC_MD5=y
CONFIG_IPSEC_AUTH_HMAC_SHA1=y
CONFIG_IPSEC_ESP=y
CONFIG_IPSEC_ENC_3DES=y
CONFIG_IPSEC_IPCOMP=y
CONFIG_IPSEC_DEBUG=y

#
# Network device support
#
CONFIG_NETDEVICES=y

#
# ARCnet devices
```

Example A-1 *Linux 2.4.22 Network Kernel Options (Continued)*

```
#
# CONFIG_ARCNET is not set
CONFIG_DUMMY=m
CONFIG_BONDING=m
CONFIG_EQUALIZER=m
CONFIG_TUN=m
# CONFIG_ETHERTAP is not set
# CONFIG_NET_SB1000 is not set

#
# Ethernet (10 or 100 Mb)
#
CONFIG_NET_ETHERNET=y
# CONFIG_HAPPYMEAL is not set
# CONFIG_SUNGEM is not set
CONFIG_NET_VENDOR_3COM=y
# CONFIG_EL1 is not set
# CONFIG_EL2 is not set
# CONFIG_ELPLUS is not set
# CONFIG_EL16 is not set
# CONFIG_EL3 is not set
# CONFIG_3C515 is not set
CONFIG_VORTEX=y
# CONFIG_TYPHOON is not set
# CONFIG_LANCE is not set
# CONFIG_NET_VENDOR_SMC is not set
# CONFIG_NET_VENDOR_RACAL is not set
# CONFIG_AT1700 is not set
# CONFIG_DEPCA is not set
# CONFIG_HP100 is not set
# CONFIG_NET_ISA is not set
CONFIG_NET_PCI=y
# CONFIG_PCNET32 is not set
# CONFIG_AMD8111_ETH is not set
# CONFIG_ADAPTEC_STARFIRE is not set
# CONFIG_AC3200 is not set
# CONFIG_APRICOT is not set
# CONFIG_B44 is not set
# CONFIG_CS89x0 is not set
# CONFIG_TULIP is not set
# CONFIG_DE4X5 is not set
# CONFIG_DGRS is not set
# CONFIG_DM9102 is not set
# CONFIG_EEPRO100 is not set
# CONFIG_E100 is not set
# CONFIG_FEALNX is not set
# CONFIG_NATSEMI is not set
CONFIG_NE2K_PCI=y
# CONFIG_8139CP is not set
# CONFIG_8139TOO is not set
# CONFIG_SIS900 is not set
# CONFIG_EPIC100 is not set
# CONFIG_SUNDANCE is not set
```

continues

Example A-1 *Linux 2.4.22 Network Kernel Options (Continued)*

```
# CONFIG_TLAN is not set
# CONFIG_VIA_RHINE is not set
# CONFIG_WINBOND_840 is not set
# CONFIG_NET_POCKET is not set


#
# Ethernet (1000 Mb)
#
# CONFIG_ACENIC is not set
# CONFIG_DL2K is not set
# CONFIG_E1000 is not set
# CONFIG_NS83820 is not set
# CONFIG_HAMACHI is not set
# CONFIG_YELLOWFIN is not set
# CONFIG_R8169 is not set
# CONFIG_SK98LIN is not set
# CONFIG_TIGON3 is not set
# CONFIG_FDDI is not set
# CONFIG_HIPPI is not set
CONFIG_PLIP=m
CONFIG_PPP=m
CONFIG_PPP_MULTILINK=y
CONFIG_PPP_FILTER=y
CONFIG_PPP_ASYNC=m
CONFIG_PPP_SYNC_TTY=m
CONFIG_PPP_DEFLATE=m
CONFIG_PPP_BSDCOMP=m
CONFIG_PPPOE=m
# CONFIG_SLIP is not set


#
# Wireless LAN (non ham radio)
#
# CONFIG_NET_RADIO is not set


#
# Token Ring devices
#
CONFIG_TR=y
CONFIG_IBMTR=m
CONFIG_IBMOL=m
CONFIG_IBMLS=m
CONFIG_3C359=m
CONFIG_TMS380TR=m
CONFIG_TMSPCI=m
CONFIG_TMSISA=m
CONFIG_ABYSS=m
CONFIG_SMCTR=m
# CONFIG_NET_FC is not set
# CONFIG_RCPCI is not set
CONFIG_SHAPER=m


#
# Network File Systems
```

Example A-1 *Linux 2.4.22 Network Kernel Options (Continued)*

```
#
CONFIG_CODA_FS=m
# CONFIG_INTERMEZZO_FS is not set
CONFIG_NFS_FS=m
CONFIG_NFS_V3=y
# CONFIG_NFS_DIRECTIO is not set
CONFIG_NFSD=m
CONFIG_NFSD_V3=y
# CONFIG_NFSD_TCP is not set
CONFIG_SUNRPC=m
CONFIG_LOCKD=m
CONFIG_LOCKD_V4=y
CONFIG_SMB_FS=m
# CONFIG_SMB_NLS_DEFAULT is not set
# CONFIG_NCP_FS is not set
# CONFIG_ZISOFS_FS is not set

#
# Cryptographic options
#
CONFIG_CRYPTO=y
CONFIG_CRYPTO_HMAC=y
CONFIG_CRYPTO_NULL=m
CONFIG_CRYPTO_MD4=m
CONFIG_CRYPTO_MD5=m
CONFIG_CRYPTO_SHA1=m
CONFIG_CRYPTO_SHA256=m
CONFIG_CRYPTO_SHA512=m
CONFIG_CRYPTO_DES=m
CONFIG_CRYPTO_BLOWFISH=m
CONFIG_CRYPTO_TWOFISH=m
CONFIG_CRYPTO_SERPENT=m
CONFIG_CRYPTO_AES=m
CONFIG_CRYPTO_DEFLATE=m
CONFIG_CRYPTO_TEST=m
```

Example A-2 *OpenBSD 3.1 Network Kernel Options*

```
#option     INSECURE        # default to secure
option      NTP             # hooks supporting the Network Time Protocol
option      DIAGNOSTIC      # internal consistency checks
option      KTRACE          # system call tracing, via ktrace(1)
option      KMEMSTATS       # collect malloc(9) statistics
option      PTRACE          # ptrace(2) system call
option      CRYPTO          # cryptographic framework
option      SYSVMSG         # System V-like message queues
option      SYSVSEM         # System V-like semaphores
option      SYSVSHM         # System V-like memory sharing
option      UVM_SWAP_ENCRYPT# support encryption of pages going to swap
option      LKM             # loadable kernel modules
option      FFS             # UFS
option      FFS_SOFTUPDATES # Soft updates
```

continues

Example A-2 *OpenBSD 3.1 Network Kernel Options (Continued)*

```
option          QUOTA               # UFS quotas
option          EXT2FS              # Second Extended File System
option          MFS                 # memory file system
option          XFS                 # xfs file system
option          TCP_SACK            # Selective acknowledgements for TCP
option          TCP_FACK            # Forward acknowledgements for TCP
option          TCP_SIGNATURE       # TCP MD5 signatures, for BGP routing sessions
option          NFSCLIENT           # Network File System client
option          NFSSERVER           # Network File System server
option          CD9660              # ISO 9660 + Rock Ridge file system
option          MSDOSFS             # MS-DOS file system
option          FDESC               # /dev/fd
option          FIFO                # FIFOs; Recommended
option          KERNFS              # /kern
option          NULLFS              # loopback file system
option          PORTAL              # dynamically created file system objects
option          PROCFS              # /proc
option          UMAPFS              # NULLFS + uid and gid remapping
option          GATEWAY             # packet forwarding
option          INET                # IP + ICMP + TCP + UDP
option          IPFILTER_DEFAULT_BLOCK
option          ALTQ                # ALTQ base
option          INET6               # IPv6 (needs INET)
option          PULLDOWN_TEST       # use m_pulldown for IPv6 packet parsing
option          IPSEC               # IPSec
option          IPFILTER            # IP packet filter for security
option          IPFILTER_LOG        # use /dev/ipl to log IPF
option          PPP_BSDCOMP         # PPP BSD compression
option          PPP_DEFLATE
option          MROUTING            # Multicast router

pseudo-device   pf       1          # packet filter
pseudo-device   pflog    1          # pf log if
pseudo-device   loop     2          # network loopback
pseudo-device   bpfilter 8          # packet filter
pseudo-device   sl       2          # CSLIP
pseudo-device   ppp      2          # PPP
pseudo-device   sppp     1          # Sync PPP/HDLC
pseudo-device   tun      2          # network tunneling over tty
pseudo-device   enc      1          # option IPSec needs the encapsulation interface
pseudo-device   bridge   2          # network bridging support
pseudo-device   vlan     2          # IEEE 802.1Q VLAN
pseudo-device   gre      1          # GRE encapsulation interface

pseudo-device   pty      64         # pseudo-terminals
pseudo-device   tb       1          # tablet line discipline
pseudo-device   vnd      4          # paging to files
pseudo-device   ksyms    1          # kernel symbols device

# for IPv6
pseudo-device   gif      4          # IPv[46] over IPv[46] tunnel (RFC 1933)
pseudo-device   faith    1          # IPv[46] tcp relay translation i/f

option          BOOT_CONFIG         # add support for boot -c
```

Example A-2 *OpenBSD 3.1 Network Kernel Options (Continued)*

```
options        ALTQ_CBQ         # class-based queuing
options        ALTQ_WFQ         # weighted fair queuing
options        ALTQ_FIFOQ       # FIFO queuing
options        ALTQ_RED         # random early detection
options        ALTQ_FLOWVALVE   # flowvalve for RED (needs RED)
options        ALTQ_RIO         # triple red for diffserv (needs RED)
options        ALTQ_LOCALQ      # local use
options        ALTQ_HFSC        # hierarchical fair service curve
options        ALTQ_JOBS        # joint buffer management and scheduling
options        ALTQ_IPSEC       # check IPSec in IPv4
options        ALTQ_CDNR        # diffserv traffic conditioner
options        ALTQ_BLUE        # blue by wu-chang feng
options        ALTQ_PRIQ        # priority queue
#options       ALTQ_NOPCC       # don't use processor-cycle counter
#options       ALTQ_DEBUG       # for debugging

machine        i386            # architecture, used by config; required

option         I586_CPU
option         I686_CPU
option         GPL_MATH_EMULATE    # floating point emulation.
option         NMBCLUSTERS=8192
option         USER_PCICONF        # user-space PCI configuration
option         XSERVER             # diddle with console driver
option         APERTURE            # in-kernel aperture driver for XFree86
option         DUMMY_NOPS          # speed hack; recommended
option         COMPAT_SVR4         # binary compatibility with SVR4
option         COMPAT_IBCS2        # binary compatibility with SCO and ISC
option         COMPAT_LINUX        # binary compatibility with Linux
option         COMPAT_FREEBSD      # binary compatibility with FreeBSD
option         COMPAT_BSDOS        # binary compatibility with BSD/OS
maxusers       32                  # estimated number of users

# Networking devices
ne0    at isa? port 0x240 irq 9    # NE[12]000 Ethernet
ne1    at isa? port 0x300 irq 10   # NE[12]000 Ethernet
ne2    at isa? port 0x280 irq 9    # NE[12]000 Ethernet
ne*    at isapnp?                  # NE[12]000 PnP Ethernet

# crypto support
#hifn*    at pci? dev ? function ?    # Hi/fn 7751 crypto card
#ubsec*   at pci? dev ? function ?    # Bluesteel Networks 5xxx crypto card
#ises*    at pci? dev ? function ?    # Pijnenburg PCC-ISES

# mouse & keyboard multiplexor pseudo-devices
pseudo-device    wsmux      2
pseudo-device    crypto     1
```

Example A-3 *FreeBSD 4.9 Network Kernel Options*

```
machine        i386
cpu            I686_CPU
ident          GENERIC
maxusers       0
```

continues

Example A-3 *FreeBSD 4.9 Network Kernel Options (Continued)*

```
options         MATH_EMULATE            # Support for x87 emulation
options         INET                    # Internetworking
options         INET6                   # IPv6 communications protocols
options         FFS                     # Berkeley Fast File System
options         FFS_ROOT                # FFS usable as root device (Keep this!)
options         SOFTUPDATES             # Enable FFS soft updates support
options         UFS_DIRHASH             # Improve performance on big directories
options         MFS                     # Memory File System
options         MD_ROOT                 # MD is a potential root device
options         NFS                     # Network File System
options         NFS_ROOT                # NFS usable as root device, NFS required
options         MSDOSFS                 # MS-DOS File System
options         CD9660                  # ISO 9660 File System
options         CD9660_ROOT             # CD-ROM usable as root, CD9660 required
options         PROCFS                  # Process file system
options         COMPAT_43               # Compatible with BSD 4.3 [KEEP THIS!]
options         SCSI_DELAY=15000        # Delay (in ms) before probing SCSI
options         UCONSOLE                # Allow users to grab the console
options         USERCONFIG              # boot -c editor
options         VISUAL_USERCONFIG       # visual boot -c editor
options         KTRACE                  # ktrace(1) support
options         SYSVSHM                 # SYSV-style shared memory
options         SYSVMSG                 # SYSV-style message queues
options         SYSVSEM                 # SYSV-style semaphores
options         P1003_1B                # Posix P1003_1B real-time extensions
options         _KPOSIX_PRIORITY_SCHEDULING
options         ICMP_BANDLIM            # Rate limit bad replies
options         KBD_INSTALL_CDEV        # install a CDEV entry in /dev
options         SMBFS                   # SMB/CIFS file system
options         HZ=1000
options         SOFTUPDATES             # FFS soft Updates

# Directory hashing improves the speed of operations on very large
# directories at the expense of some memory.
options         UFS_DIRHASH

# Allow this to swap many devices.
#
# To manage swap, the system must reserve bitmap space that
# scales with the largest mounted swap device multiplied by NSWAPDEV,
# regardless of whether other swap devices exist.  So it
# is not a good idea to make this value too large.
options         NSWAPDEV=5

# Disk quotas are supported when this option is enabled.
options         QUOTA                           # enable disk quotas

options         IPSEC                   # IP security
options         IPSEC_ESP               # IP security (crypto; define w/IPSEC)
options         IPSEC_DEBUG             # debug for IP security
# Set IPSEC_FILTERGIF to force packets coming through a gif tunnel
# to be processed by any configured packet filtering (ipfw, ipf).
```

Example A-3 *FreeBSD 4.9 Network Kernel Options (Continued)*

```
# The default is that packets coming from a tunnel are not processed;
# they are assumed trusted.
#
# Note that enabling this can be problematic as there are no mechanisms
# in place for distinguishing packets coming out of a tunnel (e.g., no
# encX devices as found on OpenBSD).
#
options         IPSEC_FILTERGIF        # filter IPSec packets from a tunnel
#
# Experimental IPSec implementation that uses the kernel crypto
# framework. This cannot be configured together with IPSec and
# (currently) supports only IPv4. To use this, you must also
# configure the crypto device (see below). Note that with this
# you get all the IPSec protocols (e.g., there is no FAST_IPSEC_ESP).
# IPSEC_DEBUG is used, as above, to configure debugging support
# within the IPSec protocols.
#
# options         FAST_IPSEC            # new IPsec

options         MROUTING               # Multicast routing
options         PIM                    # Protocol Independent Multicast
options         IPFIREWALL             # firewall
options         IPFIREWALL_VERBOSE     # enable logging to syslogd(8)
options         IPFIREWALL_FORWARD     # enable transparent proxy support
options         IPFIREWALL_VERBOSE_LIMIT=100    # limit verbosity
options         IPFIREWALL_DEFAULT_TO_ACCEPT    # allow everything by default
options         IPV6FIREWALL           # firewall for IPv6
options         IPV6FIREWALL_VERBOSE
options         IPV6FIREWALL_VERBOSE_LIMIT=100
options         IPV6FIREWALL_DEFAULT_TO_ACCEPT
options         IPDIVERT               # divert sockets
options         IPFILTER               # ipfilter support
options         IPFILTER_LOG           # ipfilter logging
options         IPFILTER_DEFAULT_BLOCK # block all packets by default
options         IPSTEALTH              # support for stealth forwarding
options         TCPDEBUG               # TCP-related debugging info

# RANDOM_IP_ID causes the ID field in IP packets to be randomized
# instead of incremented by 1 with each packet generated. This
# option closes a minor information leak, which allows remote
# observers to determine the rate of packet generation on the
# machine by watching the counter.
options         RANDOM_IP_ID

#
# TCP_DROP_SYNFIN adds support for ignoring TCP packets with SYN+FIN. This
# prevents nmap et al. from identifying the TCP/IP stack, but it breaks support
# for RFC 1644 extensions and is not recommended for web servers.
#
options         TCP_DROP_SYNFIN        # drop TCP packets with SYN+FIN

# ICMP_BANDLIM enables icmp error response bandwidth limiting. You
# typically want this option because it will help protect the machine from
```

continues

Example A-3 *FreeBSD 4.9 Network Kernel Options (Continued)*

```
# DoS packet attacks.
#
options         ICMP_BANDLIM

# DUMMYNET enables the "dummynet" bandwidth limiter. You need
# IPFIREWALL, too. See the dummynet(4) and ipfw(8) man pages for more info.
# When you run DUMMYNET, it is advisable to also have "options HZ=1000"
# to achieve a smoother scheduling of the traffic.
#
# BRIDGE enables bridging between ethernet cards; see bridge(4).
# You can use IPFIREWALL and DUMMYNET together with bridging.
#
options         DUMMYNET
options         BRIDGE

options         ATM_CORE            # core ATM protocol family
options         ATM_IP              # IP over ATM support
options         ATM_SIGPVC          # SIGPVC signaling manager
options         ATM_SPANS           # SPANS signaling manager
options         ATM_UNI             # UNI signaling manager
device          hea                 # Efficient ENI-155p ATM PCI
device          hfa                 # FORE PCA-200E ATM PCI
device          proatm              # ProSum's ProATM-155
pseudo-device   atm                 # The ATM pseudo-device
device          en                  # Efficient Networks ATM Driver
options         NATM                # native ATM

# SMB/CIFS requester
# NETSMB enables support for SMB protocol; it requires LIBMCHAIN and LIBICONV
# options.
# NETSMBCRYPTO enables support for encrypted passwords.
options         NETSMB              # SMB/CIFS requester
options         NETSMBCRYPTO        # encrypted password support for SMB
# mchain library. It can be either loaded as KLD or compiled into kernel
options         LIBMCHAIN           # mbuf management library
options         LIBICONV
# netgraph(4). Enable the base Netgraph code with the NETGRAPH option.
# Individual node types can be enabled with the corresponding option
# listed below; however, this is not strictly necessary because Netgraph
# will automatically load the corresponding KLD module if the node type
# is not already compiled into the kernel. Each type below has a
# corresponding man page; e.g., ng_async(8).
options         NETGRAPH            # netgraph(4) system
options         NETGRAPH_ASYNC
options         NETGRAPH_BPF
options         NETGRAPH_CISCO
options         NETGRAPH_ECHO
options         NETGRAPH_ETHER
options         NETGRAPH_FRAME_RELAY
options         NETGRAPH_HOLE
options         NETGRAPH_IFACE
options         NETGRAPH_KSOCKET
options         NETGRAPH_L2TP
```

Example A-3 *FreeBSD 4.9 Network Kernel Options (Continued)*

```
options         NETGRAPH_LMI
# MPPC compression requires proprietary files (not included)
#options        NETGRAPH_MPPC_COMPRESSION
options         NETGRAPH_MPPC_ENCRYPTION
options         NETGRAPH_ONE2MANY
options         NETGRAPH_PPP
options         NETGRAPH_PPPOE
options         NETGRAPH_PPTPGRE
options         NETGRAPH_RFC1490
options         NETGRAPH_SOCKET
options         NETGRAPH_TEE
options         NETGRAPH_TTY
options         NETGRAPH_UI
options         NETGRAPH_VJC

# Coda stuff:
options         CODA                    # CODA file system.
pseudo-device   vcoda   4               # coda minicache <-> venus comm.

# PCI Ethernet NICs that use the common MII bus controller code.
# Note: Be sure to keep the 'device miibus' line in order to use these NICs!
device          miibus      # MII bus support
device          xl          # 3Com 3c90x (``Boomerang'', ``Cyclone'')

# ISA Ethernet NICs.
# 'device ed' requires 'device miibus'
device          ed0    at isa? disable port 0x280 irq 10 iomem 0xd8000

# Pseudo devices - the number indicates how many units to allocate.
pseudo-device   loop    3       # Network loopback
pseudo-device   ether           # Ethernet support
pseudo-device   sl      1       # Kernel SLIP
pseudo-device   ppp     1       # Kernel PPP
pseudo-device   tun     3       # Packet tunnel
pseudo-device   pty             # Pseudo-ttys (Telnet etc.)
pseudo-device   md              # Memory "disks"
pseudo-device   vlan    3       # VLAN support
pseudo-device   token           # Generic Token Ring
pseudo-device   sppp            # Generic Synchronous PPP
pseudo-device   bpf             # Berkeley packet filter
pseudo-device   disc            # Discard device (ds0, ds1, etc.)
pseudo-device   sl      2       # Serial Line IP
pseudo-device   gre     3       # IP over IP tunneling
pseudo-device   ppp     2       # Point-to-Point Protocol
options         PPP_BSDCOMP     # PPP BSD-compress support
options         PPP_DEFLATE     # PPP zlib/deflate/gzip support
options         PPP_FILTER      # enable bpf filtering (needs bpf)

# for IPv6
pseudo-device   gif             # IPv6 and IPv4 tunneling
pseudo-device   faith   1       # for IPv6 and IPv4 translation
pseudo-device   stf             # 6to4 IPv6 over IPv4 encapsulation
```

The FreeBSD Netgraph Facility

Netgraph is a kernel-space networking facility (subsystem) with an architecture that consists of nodes (the tools) and edges (connectors) that connect to certain hooks of neighbor nodes and form a "graph." Data packets are passed along following this graph from node to node; out-of-band control messages and reply control messages do not follow the connectors; they are passed back and forth directly between the nodes. Within a node, data packets are processed, modified, or just passed along edges to other nodes. A node also can terminate a flow or act as the originating source for new data. Entire network architectures and stacks could be built upon this foundation.

Reasons for Netgraph

Very well, but why do we need Netgraph, and why should we care? Because some user-space applications rely on the Netgraph facility, such as the mpd tool often used for PPTP connections or the Netgraph ATM implementation. Individual node types form kernel modules and are loaded automatically if they are not compiled into the kernel. Example B-1 presents the Netgraph kernel configuration options for various device-independent node types.

Example B-1 *FreeBSD Netgraph Kernel Configuration Options*

```
# netgraph(4). Enable the base Netgraph code with the NETGRAPH option.
# Individual node types can be enabled with the corresponding option
# listed below; however, this is not strictly necessary because netgraph
# will automatically load the corresponding KLD module if the node type
# is not already compiled into the kernel. Each type below has a
# corresponding man page; e.g., ng_async(8).

options         NETGRAPH                 #netgraph(4) system
options         NETGRAPH_ASYNC
options         NETGRAPH_BPF
options         NETGRAPH_CISCO
options         NETGRAPH_ECHO
options         NETGRAPH_ETHER
options         NETGRAPH_FRAME_RELAY
options         NETGRAPH_HOLE
options         NETGRAPH_IFACE
options         NETGRAPH_KSOCKET
options         NETGRAPH_L2TP
options         NETGRAPH_LMI
```

continues

Example B-1 *FreeBSD Netgraph Kernel Configuration Options (Continued)*

```
# MPPC compression requires proprietary files (not included)
#options        NETGRAPH_MPPC_COMPRESSION
options         NETGRAPH_MPPC_ENCRYPTION
options         NETGRAPH_ONE2MANY
options         NETGRAPH_PPP
options         NETGRAPH_PPPOE
options         NETGRAPH_PPTPGRE
options         NETGRAPH_RFC1490
options         NETGRAPH_SOCKET
options         NETGRAPH_TEE
options         NETGRAPH_TTY
options         NETGRAPH_UI
options         NETGRAPH_VJC
```

Netgraph consists of kernel code and hooks, a user library for using the socket node, and the two command-line utilities—nghook(8) and ngctl(8)—that allow interaction with the kernel Netgraph system. For a thorough discussion of these tools and implementation details, turn to Archie Cobbs's excellent article on DaemonNews (http://www.daemonnews.org/200003/netgraph.html), which forms the authoritative guide to the Netgraph facility; also check the relevant manual pages.

Recommended Reading

- The Netgraph Networking System, http://www.elischer.org/netgraph/
- The Netgraph user library man page, netgraph(3)
- The Netgraph facility man page, netgraph(4)
- The ngctl configuration program man page, ngctl(3)
- The nghook utility program man page, nghook(3)
- DaemonNews Netgraph article, http://www.daemonnews.org/200003/netgraph.html
- Netgraph ATM, http://www.fokus.gmd.de/research/cc/cats/employees/hartmut.brandt/ngatm/

INDEX

Numerics

A

E

F

G

H

I

N

O

DISCUSS
NETWORKING PRODUCTS AND TECHNOLOGIES WITH CISCO EXPERTS AND NETWORKING PROFESSIONALS WORLDWIDE

VISIT NETWORKING PROFESSIONALS
A CISCO ONLINE COMMUNITY
WWW.CISCO.COM/GO/DISCUSS

CISCO SYSTEMS

THIS IS THE POWER OF THE NETWORK. now.

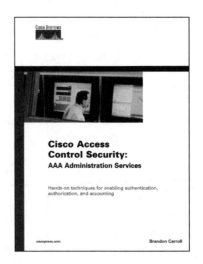

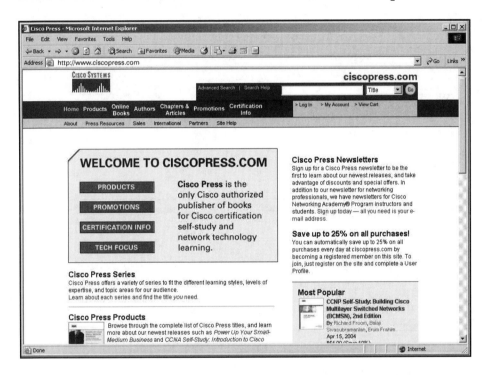
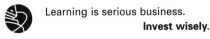

CISCO SYSTEMS

Cisco Press

3 STEPS TO LEARNING

STEP 1

First-Step

STEP 2

Fundamentals

STEP 3

**Networking
Technology Guides**

STEP 1 **First-Step**—Benefit from easy-to-grasp explanations. No experience required!

STEP 2 **Fundamentals**—Understand the purpose, application, and management of technology.

STEP 3 **Networking Technology Guides**—Gain the knowledge to master the challenge of the network.

NETWORK BUSINESS SERIES

The Network Business series helps professionals tackle the business issues surrounding the network. Whether you are a seasoned IT professional or a business manager with minimal technical expertise, this series will help you understand the business case for technologies.

Justify Your Network Investment.

Look for Cisco Press titles at your favorite bookseller today.

Visit **www.ciscopress.com/series** for details on each of these book series.